The Radical Right in Switzerland

THE RADICAL RIGHT IN SWITZERLAND

Continuity and Change, 1945–2000

Damir Skenderovic

Berghahn Books
New York • Oxford

First published in 2009 by

Berghahn Books

www.berghahnbooks.com

©2009 Damir Skenderovic

Published with the support of the
Swiss National Science Foundation
Stiftung Irene Bollag-Herzheimer
Adolf und Mary Mil-Stiftung

All rights reserved. Except for the quotation of short passages
for the purposes of criticism and review, no part of this book
may be reproduced in any form or by any means, electronic or
mechanical, including photocopying, recording, or any information
storage and retrieval system now known or to be invented,
without written permission of the publisher.

Library of Congress Cataloging-in-Publication Data

Skenderovic, Damir.
    The radical right in Switzerland : continuity and change, 1945–2000 /
Damir Skenderovic.
        p. cm.
    Includes bibliographical references and index.
    ISBN 978-1-84545-580-4 (hardback : alk. paper)
    1. Radicalism—Switzerland—History—20th century. 2. Right-wing
extremists—Switzerland—History—20th century. 3. Switzerland—Politics
and government—1945– I. Title.

HN49.R33S54 2008
320.5—dc22

2008032705

British Library Cataloguing in Publication Data
A catalogue record for this book is available from the British Library

Printed in the United States on acid-free paper.

ISBN: 978-1-84545-580-4 (hardback)

For Nada

Contents

List of Figures ix

List of Tables x

List of Abbreviations xii

Introduction 1
Recent Challenges in Swiss Politics and Society 1
The Swiss Radical Right: Underrated in Academic Research 4
An Actor-oriented Approach 5
Main Arguments and Structure of the Book 7
Acknowledgments 10

1. The Concept of the Radical Right 13
Distinctions and Boundaries 13
The Ideology and Politics of Exclusionism 16
A Political Family and a Collective Actor 27

2. Success Conditions and Organisational Variation
in Switzerland 39
National Traditions: The Front Movement in the 1930s 39
Social Changes and the Support for the Radical Right 41
The Openness of the Swiss Political System 45
National Identity, Swiss Exceptionalism and Fears of
    'Overforeignization' 47
The Political Family of the Radical Right in Switzerland 50

3. An Early Precursor: The Movement against
Overforeignization in the 1960s and 1970s 57
A Divided Movement of Fringe Parties 58
The Power of Direct Democracy 65
Populist Strategy and Exclusionist Ideology 71

4. Outsiders in the Party System: Fringe Parties in the 1980s
and 1990s 77
The Swiss Democrats: Survivors of the Movement against
    Overforeignization 78
The Swiss Democratic Union: A Fundamentalist Party and its
    Exclusionist Worldview 92

viii | Contents

    The Car Party/Freedom Party: Rise and Fall of a New Radical
       Right-wing Populist Party 99
    The *Lega dei Ticinesi*: A Regionalist, Anti-establishment Party 114

**5. Entering the Mainstream: The Emergence of
the New SVP in the 1990s**   123
    The Old SVP: The History of a Right-wing, Mainstream Party 124
    Towards the New SVP: The Process of Structural Transformation 129
    The Extraordinary Electoral Rise of the New SVP 145
    Political and Ideological Radicalisation 159
    Reasons for the Success of the New SVP 171

**6. A Supplier of Ideology: The New Right in the
German-speaking Part of Switzerland**   173
    The Neoconservatives: Renewing Conservatism and Approaching
       the New Right 177
    The Ecologists: A Right-wing Version of Environmentalism 206
    The Neo-nationalists: For the Defence of Swiss Exceptionalism 214

**7. An Intellectual Elite: The New Right in the
French-speaking Part of Switzerland**   229
    The Counter-revolutionaries: Contesting Pluralistic and
       Parliamentarian Democracy 231
    The Integrists: Catholicism and Politics 242
    The Nouvelle droite: Importing the French Legacy 252

**8. At the Margins of Society and Politics: The Subculture
of the Extreme Right**   275
    Ideologues and Propagandists: Disseminating Thought
       and Ideas 277
    Combative and Violent Groups: Emergence and
       Consolidation since the Mid 1980s 304
    Between Distance and Proximity: Linkages with
       Political Parties 322

    CONCLUSION   331
    The Process of Normalisation 331
    The Radical Right as a Collective Actor: Linkages and
       Collaborations 333
    The Radical Right as a Political Family: Ideology and Intellectual
       Agenda 336
    The 1990s and Beyond 340

    NOTES   343

    REFERENCES   425

    INDEX   453

Figures

Figure 1.1 The Radical Right as Political Family and
Collective Actor 30

Figure 6.1 Ideological Typology of the German-speaking
New Right 176

Figure 7.1 Ideological Typology of the Francophone
New Right 231

Figure 8.1 Typology of the Extreme Right in Switzerland 277

Tables

Table 3.1	Results of NA and SRB in National Council Elections, 1967–1987	60
Table 3.2	Seats of NA, SRB and Vigilance in the National Council, 1967–1987	60
Table 3.3	Federal Initiatives and Referendums by National Action, 1968–1988	66
Table 3.4	Federal Initiatives and Referendums by the Swiss Republican Movement, 1972–1985	67
Table 4.1	Results of National Action/Swiss Democrats in National Council Elections, 1987–1999	79
Table 4.2	Occupational Profile of Swiss Democrats Supporters, 1995	81
Table 4.3	Priority Issues of Swiss Democrats Supporters, 1995	81
Table 4.4	Federal Initiatives and Referendums by the Swiss Democrats in the 1990s	84
Table 4.5	Results of Car Party/Freedom Party in National Council Elections, 1987–1999	103
Table 4.6	Social Profile of Car Party Supporters, 1991	105
Table 4.7	Priority Issues of Car Party Supporters, 1991	105
Table 4.8	Trust of Car Party Supporters in Federal Council and Parliament, 1991	106
Table 4.9	Self-placement of Car Party Supporters on the Left–Right Continuum, 1991	106
Table 4.10	Federal Initiatives and Referendums by Car Party/Freedom Party in the 1990s	109

Table 4.11	Results of the Lega dei Ticinesi in Great Council and National Council Elections, 1991–1999	115
Table 5.1	Federal Initiatives by the SVP in the 1990s	138
Table 5.2	Results of all Parties in National Council and Council of States Elections, 1987–1999	146
Table 5.3	Results of the SVP in National Council Elections, 1987–1999	148
Table 5.4	Social Profile of SVP Supporters, 1991–1999	155
Table 5.5	Attitudes of SVP Supporters on Political Issues, 1995 and 1999	157
Table 5.6	Self-placement of SVP Supporters on the Left–Right Continuum, 1991–1999	157
Table 5.7	Trust of SVP Supporters in Federal Council and Parliament, 1991–1999	158
Table 8.1	Final Verdicts against Negationist Propaganda under the Anti-racism Law, 1995–2000	291
Table 8.2	Violent Racist Acts, 1992–2002	306
Table 8.3	Non-violent Racist Acts, 1992–2002	306
Table 8.4	Violent Acts against Asylum Seekers' Accommodations, 1990–2000	307

 ABBREVIATIONS

Parties and Organisations

AEZ	Working Group for Breaking the Taboo on Contemporary History (Arbeitsgemeinschaft zur Enttabuisierung der Zeitgeschichte)
AfM	Campaign for Freedom of Speech – Against the Imposition of the UN's Will (Aktion für freie Meinungsäusserung – Gegen UNO-Bevormundung)
AGG	Living History Working Group (Arbeitskreis Gelebte Geschichte)
AN	National Alliance (Alleanza Nazionale)
ANAG	Federal Statute of Abode and Settlement of Foreigners (Bundesgesetz über Aufenthalt und Niederlassung der Ausländer)
APS	Car Party of Switzerland (Auto-Partei Schweiz)
ARB	Association of the Friends of Robert Brasillach (Association des amis de Robert Brasillach)
BDP	Bourgeois Democratic Party (Bürgerlich-Demokratische Partei)
BdS	Federation of Tax Payers (Bund der Steuerzahler)
BFB	Federation of Free Citizens (Bund freier Bürger)
BGB	Farmers, Artisans and Citizens Party (Bauern-, Gewerbe- und Bürgerpartei)
CDU	Christian Democratic Union (Christlich-Demokratische Union)
CERA	European Centre for Research and Action on Racism and Anti-Semitism (Centre européen de recherche et d'action sur le racisme et l'antisémitisme)
CESNUR	Study Centre on New Religions (Centre d'études sur les nouvelles religions)

CINS	Campaign for an Independent and Neutral Switzerland (Aktion für eine unabhängige und neutrale Schweiz)
CVP	Christian-Democratic People's Party (Christlichdemokratische Volkspartei)
EAföP	European Working Group for Ecological Politics (Europäischer Arbeitskreis für ökologische Politik)
EAME	European Working Group 'Courage to Take a Moral Stance' (Europäische Arbeitsgemeinschaft 'Mut zur Ethik')
EC	European Community
ECOPOP	Ecology and Population Association (Vereinigung Umwelt und Bevölkerung/Association Ecologie et Population)
EDU	Swiss Democratic Union (Eidgenössisch-Demokratische Union)
EEA	European Economic Area
EKR	Federal Commission against Racism (Eidgenössische Kommission gegen Rassismus)
ESB	European Social Movement (Mouvement social européen)
EU	European Union
EVP	Protestant People's Party (Evangelische Volkspartei)
FDP	Liberal Democratic Party (Freisinnig-Demokratische Partei)
FN	National Front (Front national)
FPÖ	Freedom Party of Austria (Freiheitliche Partei Österreichs)
FPS	Freedom Party of Switzerland (Freiheits-Partei der Schweiz)
GFPM	Society for Advancing the Psychological Knowledge of Human Nature (Gesellschaft zur Förderung der psychologischen Menschenkenntnis)
GPS	Green Party of Switzerland (Grüne Partei Schweiz)
GRECE	Group for the Research and Study of European Civilisation (Groupement de recherche et d'études pour la civilisation européenne)
ICE	Independent Commission of Experts Switzerland – Second World War
IDA	International Development Association
IG	Interest Group Switzerland – Second World War (Interessengemeinschaft Schweiz – Zweiter Weltkrieg)

IHR	Institute for Historical Review
IMF	International Monetary Fund
IPM	Institute for Advancing the Psychological Knowledge of Human Nature (Institut zur Förderung der psychologischen Menschenkenntnis)
JES	Young European Pupils and Students Initiative of Switzerland (Junge europäische Schüler- und Studenteninitiative der Schweiz)
JHR	The Journal of Historical Review
JNA	Young National Action (Junge Nationale Aktion)
JNR	Nationalist Revolutionary Youths (Jeunesses nationalistes révolutionnaires)
JSVP	Young SVP (Junge SVP)
KCVP	Conservative Christian-Social People's Party (Konservativ-Christlichsoziale Volkspartei)
KFRD	Committee for Freedom of Speech and Thinking (Komitee für Freiheit im Reden und Denken)
KKK	Ku Klux Klan
KVP	Catholic People's Party (Katholische Volkspartei)
LDU	Alliance of Independents (Landesring der Unabhängigen)
LN	Northern League (Lega Nord)
LPS	Liberal Party of Switzerland (Liberale Partei der Schweiz)
MPE	Geneva Patriotic Movement (Mouvement patriotique genevois)
MSI	Italian Social Movement (Movimento Sociale Italiano)
NA	National Action (Nationale Aktion)
NATO	Northern Atlantic Treaty Organisation
NBS	National Basis of Switzerland (Nationale Basis Schweiz)
NDP	National-Democratic Party (Nationaldemokratische Partei)
NIS	National Initiative of Switzerland (Nationale Initiative Schweiz)
NK	National Coordination (Nationale Koordination)
NNF	New National Front (Neue Nationale Front)
NOE	European New Order (Nouvel ordre européen)

NOS	New Social Order (Nouvel ordre social)
NPD	National-Democratic Party of Germany (Nationaldemokratische Partei Deutschlands)
NPS	National Party of Switzerland (Nationale Partei Schweiz)
NR	New Resistance (Nouvelle résistance)
NRP	National-Revolutionary Party of Switzerland (Nationalrevolutionäre Partei der Schweiz)
NSDAP	National-Socialist German Workers' Party (Nationalsozialistische Deutsche Arbeiterpartei)
ÖDP	Ecological Democratic Party (Ökologisch-Demokratische Partei)
ÖFP	Ecological Libertarian Party of Switzerland (Ökologische Freiheitliche Partei der Schweiz)
ON	New Order (Ordre nouveau)
PF	Patriotic Front (Patriotische Front)
PNFE	French and European Nationalist Party (Parti nationaliste français et européen)
PNOS	Party of National Oriented Swiss (Partei National Orientierter Schweizer)
PNSE	Swiss and European Nationalist Party (Parti nationaliste suisse et européen)
PVP	Patriotic People's Party (Patriotische Volkspartei)
SAfB	Swiss Working Group for Population Questions (Schweizerische Arbeitsgemeinschaft für Bevölkerungsfragen)
SAKU	Swiss Campaign Committee Against UN Membership (Schweizerisches Aktionskomitee gegen den UNO-Beitritt)
SBN	Swiss Federation for Nature Conservation (Schweizerischer Bund für Naturschutz)
SD	Swiss Democrats (Schweizer Demokraten)
SGB	Swiss Trade Union Federation (Schweizerischer Gewerkschaftsbund)
SHARP	Skinheads Against Racial Prejudices
SHS	Swiss Hammerskins (Schweizerische Hammerskins)
SHS-AO	Swiss Organisation for the Development of Hammerskins (Schweizerische Hammerskin-Aufbauorganisation)

Sifa	Security for All (Sicherheit für alle)
SKVP	Swiss Conservative People's Party (Schweizerische Konservative Volkspartei)
SLfbL	Swiss League for Biological National Defense (Schweizerische Liga für biologische Landesverteidigung)
SPS	Social-Democratic Party of Switzerland (Sozialdemokratische Partei der Schweiz)
SRB	Swiss Republican Movement (Schweizerische Republikanische Bewegung)
SSPX	Priestly Society of Saint Pius X (Fraternité sacerdotale Saint-Pie X; Priesterbruderschaft St. Pius X)
STAB	Foundation for Occidental Consciousness (Stiftung für Abendländische Besinnung)
SVP	Swiss People's Party (Schweizerische Volkspartei)
TV	Third Way (Troisième voie)
UDL	Union for the Defence of Liberties (Union pour la défense des libertés)
UK	Universal Church (Universale Kirche)
UN	United Nations
UNESCO	United Nations Educational, Scientific and Cultural Organisation
VB	Flemish Block (Vlaams Blok)
VgT	Society Against Animal Factories (Verein gegen Tierfabriken)
VHO	Free Historical Research (Vrij Historisch Onderzoek)
VPM	Society for Advancing the Psychological Knowledge of Human Nature (Verein zur Förderung der psychologischen Menschenkenntnis)
VPS	People's Party of Switzerland (Volkspartei der Schweiz)
VSP	People's Socialist Party of Switzerland (Volkssozialistische Partei der Schweiz)
WACL	World Anti-Communist League
WJS	Viking Youth Switzerland (Wiking-Jugend Schweiz)
WSL	World Federation for the Protection of Life (Weltbund zum Schutze des Lebens)
WTO	World Trade Organisation

Swiss Cantons

AG	Aargau	NW	Nidwald
AI	Appenzell Inner Rhodes	OW	Obwald
AR	Appenzell Outer Rhodes	SG	St. Gallen
BE	Bern	SH	Schaffhausen
BL	Basel Country	SO	Solothurn
BS	Basel City	SZ	Schwyz
FR	Fribourg	TG	Thurgau
GE	Geneva	TI	Ticino
GL	Glarus	UR	Uri
GR	Graubünden	VD	Vaud
JU	Jura	VS	Valais
LU	Lucerne	ZG	Zug
NE	Neuchâtel	ZH	Zurich

Introduction

In a recent book on Swiss politics, Clive Church points out that Switzerland has largely been neglected by English language social science research and that the country is seen as a *'cas à part*, divorced from the European norms domestically, just as it stands outside the EU'.[1] This assessment is even more accurate when it comes to research on the political history of postwar Switzerland. Historians and political scientists have looked into certain distinct institutions of the Swiss political system, such as direct democracy and federalism, and have studied some of the political actors, such as the new social movements, which had a particularly lively history in the 1970s and 1980s. However, the development of Swiss society and politics has received little overall attention from the academic community outside the country and when they have shown an interest, observers from abroad have tended to draw an idealised picture of the country and mainly seen it as an island of peace, democratic tradition, political stability, economic prosperity and a high standard of living in the midst of Europe. As Clive Church correctly notes, therefore, the view from outside Switzerland is still very much marked by the fact that 'the country generates a large number of inaccurate myths about the utter harmony and boring nature' of its society.[2]

Recent Challenges in Swiss Politics and Society

In the last two decades, however, a number of events and developments have left scratches on the surface of this picture of a harmonious and monotonous country that has largely been spared major crises and conflicts. As Jonathan Steinberg has put it, Switzerland's 'complacency has vanished'.[3] To begin with, the social landscape revealed growing fissures in the 1990s, as the Swiss economy, one of the strongest globalised economies in the world, exhibited some degree of vulnerability and instability. The country experienced its highest rates of unemployment since the 1930s and the number of working poor people increased considerably. In addition, disagreements over several particularly contentious issues not only caused tensions among the domestic public in the 1990s, but also stained the image of the country in the eye of the international public. For example, Switzerland's reluctance to fully engage in the process of European unification, the continent's greatest postwar project of integration and stability, and the vigour with which Switzerland has clung to its own self-perception as a special case, have generated deep lines of cleavage inside the country. Switzerland's standing aside from the process of unification was not met with a great deal of understanding from abroad and critics considered reprehensible the self-centeredness of a wealthy and prosperous country whose industry and business had already been fully integrated in the global market.

The reassessment of Switzerland's conduct during the Second World War caused another controversial debate that caught the international eye in the 1990s, in which the notion of Swiss exceptionalism was at stake. While some continued to claim that the well-prepared army, the inhabitants' determination to defend their country, and the long-standing tradition of Swiss neutrality were decisive factors in Switzerland's escaping invasion, others insisted that, as academic research has ascertained since the 1980s, financial and economic ties to the National Socialist regime should be regarded as the main reasons why the country was spared the catastrophe of war. Some also argued that ideologies of exclusion and practices of discrimination, both founded on anti-Semitism and xenophobia, were more common in Swiss politics and far more widely endorsed in Swiss society than many had wanted to believe and that Switzerland was in no way different, therefore, from most other European countries at that time.

Swiss exceptionalism has also come under scrutiny for other reasons. In parallel with the controversies over European integration and the history of the Second World War, Swiss politics has become more conflictual and less consensual as long-standing patterns of negotiated cooperation and consensual politics among the government parties have seemed to fade away. Over the course of a long historical process, Swiss consociationalism had evolved into a way of power-sharing that has had a highly integrative effect in a society that is characterised by internal divisions along social, political, linguistic and religious lines. It has helped to reduce the degree of antagonism between social classes, between the political right and the left, between Protestants and Catholics, and between the four linguistic groups (German, French, Italian and Rhaeto-Romance) that territorially are based in different regions.

As the political and social elite complied with the need to accept rules based on agreement and cooperation and to follow specific negotiational modes and practices, a set of consociational arrangements also shaped the country's political culture and found expression in everyday politics as well as in particular institutional settings.[4] However, in recent years the use of a divisive style in political campaigning and the deepening of cleavages has brought about a significant increase in the polarisation of party competition and begun to undermine the longstanding tradition of Swiss consociationalism. In some ways, this move towards more oppositional politics has brought Switzerland closer to the competitive party systems of most other Western democracies.

A key reason for Swiss politics becoming more antagonistic and contentious has been the role of the Swiss People's Party (*Schweizerische Volkspartei* – SVP), a centre-right party that was transformed in the 1990s into a proponent of radical right-wing populism. By adopting a populist strategy and an exclusionist agenda, the party succeeded in bringing about a remarkable expansion of its constituency in elections. Consequently, the party has been recognised as a prominent example of what some have called the third wave of postwar radical right-wing populism in Western Europe. This led the Council of Europe, in a report from 2000, to list the SVP as part of the same trend as the Flemish Block in Belgium and the Freedom Party in Austria, and thereby to express its concern about the rise of political parties that directly or indirectly foster xenophobia, intolerance and racism.[5]

It would be a mistake to think, however, as many contemporary observers tend to, that the Swiss radical right only started to gain momentum in the early 1990s, and as a consequence to restrict one's perspective to recent developments in Swiss politics. On the contrary, political parties, intellectual circles and propagandists at the far right of the political spectrum show a remarkable continuity that extends throughout the postwar era. As early as the 1960s, for example, the emergence of the so-called Movement against Overforeignization, comprised of political parties advocating a fierce anti-immigration agenda, should be considered a precursor to radical right-wing populism in Western Europe. This is a fact that has consistently been ignored in historical overviews of the postwar radical right in Western Europe. To take another example, propagandists of the Swiss extreme right played an important role in the efforts to establish the 'fascist international' in the immediate aftermath of the Second World War and were among the first who sought to relativize and deny the Shoah and other crimes committed by the National Socialist regime.

The Swiss Radical Right: Underrated in Academic Research

Despite this early manifestation and remarkable pattern of continuity, the Swiss case is very sparsely represented in comparative work concerning the radical right, and international scholarship in the area of the radical right has so far shown little interest in the Swiss case. In contrast to other small European countries such as Austria, Belgium, the Netherlands, Denmark or Norway, there has been no English language study on the postwar history of the radical right in Switzerland. Virtually none of the recognised edited volumes and articles of recent years have taken the Swiss case into consideration. However, domestic research on the Swiss radical right would also appear to still be in its infancy. While there has been some recent improvement, very few historians, political scientists or sociologists show an interest in the topic. Few studies have consistently applied the theoretical and conceptual premises of international scholarship in this field and many lack cross-national comparisons. This stands in striking contrast with general scholarship on the radical right, which has improved significantly since the early 1990s and has produced a massive body of academic literature on various aspects of the postwar radical right.

The fact that many scholars tend to view Switzerland as a special case is perhaps the key reason for the lack of attention that international research on the radical right have paid to the country. As a consequence, most of the literature wrongly characterises the Swiss case and claims that Switzerland represents a case of failure of the radical right. Historical aspects, along with features of the political system and political culture, as well as the economic situation, have all been put forward in arguments suggesting that such factors must be seen as having created contextual conditions in Switzerland that are disadvantageous for the strength of radical-right politics. Assuming this line of argument, scholars have taken a historical perspective contending that Switzerland has no experience of fascism in the way that most other European countries have known it. As a consequence, they have assumed a very low level of acceptance in the Swiss political culture for an anti-democratic right-wing stance, or a revitalisation of radical-right patterns of thought.

It has also been claimed that Swiss consociational democracy exerts a highly unifying effect, which is reflected, for example, in the strong integrative capacity of the party system. According to this viewpoint, the Swiss party system does not accommodate radical parties unless they follow an opposition policy that is loyal to the system. Another argument has stressed that direct democracy serves as an institutionalised safety valve for fringe political parties from the radical right, since they receive relatively little support in parliamentary elections. Taking this perspective, direct democratic opportunities allow small parties and voters to express their disagreement with public policy without requiring a strong parliamentary position. Another set of arguments draws on theses concerning the material grievances and economic causes which are often used in research on the radical right. Following this reasoning, it has been argued that good economic conditions and low rates of unemployment in Switzerland have prevented support for the radical right. Finally, a further argument to explain the supposed lack of potential for a radical right in Switzerland has highlighted the alleged existence of a pronounced notion of respect and tolerance toward minorities and other cultures among large segments of the Swiss population. These values purportedly contrast with the ideas and aims of radical right-wing actors, whose ideology generally draws on resentment and intolerance toward minorities.[6]

As I shall show in this book, however, there is a need to review and ultimately revise most of these arguments. While some scarcely stand up to the findings of a longitudinal examination of the postwar Swiss radical right or in the face of new research approaches to Swiss national identity and multiculturalism, other arguments such as those relating to direct democracy and consociationalism actually appear to indicate the existence of conditions and factors that support, rather than impede, the emergence of a radical right. I shall provide evidence that the tendency to present Switzerland as a special case is for the most part untenable and that, on the contrary, the Swiss radical right is certainly suitable for inclusion in comparative research.

An Actor-oriented Approach

The approach applied in this book is in line with recent trends seen in the literature on the radial right which increasingly devotes attention to actor-oriented research and explanations. As Matthew Goodwin argues in an inspiring review article, the study of the radical right has long been dominated by scholars from political science and political sociology who have explained the rise of the radical right as being mainly a result of socioeconomic change and have therefore primarily focused on demand-side dimensions and especially on the sociodemographic or attitudinal characteristics of voters.[7] This prime interest in dimensions that are external to the actors of the radical right is reflected in approaches which 'typically stress the primacy of demand factors over supply, of structure over agency'.[8] Following this perspective, factors such as new social cleavages, political disaffection, partisan dealignment, protest politics and a low threshold in the electoral system are regarded as structural conditions that facilitate the success of the radical right. Explanations centred on supply-side dimensions, which look at groups and parties of the radical right 'as strategic actors attempting to best respond [to] their political and institutional environments, have, by contrast, received much less attention'.[9] However, looking at the findings so far produced by research on the radical right, demand-side explanations have basically failed to shed light on questions relating to the notable variations seen in the organisational strength and electoral fortunes of the radical right across different countries in Europe. Another question which remains unanswered is why countries that experience similar socioeconomic and sociocultural changes show such large variation in radical right-wing formations and significant spatial and temporal differences in the success and support of the radical right.

Facing this growing criticism of the 'externalist bias' in the study of the radical right, it has been acknowledged that more attention needs to be paid to 'internalist dimensions' and that instead of portraying the parties and organisations of the radical right 'as the by-products of forces outside their own control, in contrast they should be viewed as engineers of their own success'.[10] In a similar vein, Martin Schain, Aristide Zolberg and Patrick Hossay have argued in the introductory chapter of a seminal volume on the radical right in Western Europe that 'causal conditions do not develop in isolation or exist separately from the radical right parties that exploit them: the conditions which facilitate the success of the right are entwined with the party's own agency'.[11] Following this interest in actors and agency, a recent volume from social anthropologists on the emergence of far-right movements has asked 'how far is neo-nationalism to be understood as a socio-cultural process introduced and performed, but also opposed and negotiated, by more or less creative agency?'[12]

This also echoes recent trends in historical research which have gradually moved away from the predominance of structural history to a perspective that devotes more attention to actors as driving forces in the social and political processes of the past, and to human agency which plays a key role in the reproduction of social structures. Inspired by constructivism in social science and going along with the 'cultural turn' in historiography, structural settings are no longer regarded as the steadfast and all-determining conditions of history but rather as shifting contexts of historical development in which sufficient space exists for individual and collective actors to engage in activities and develop ideas. In addition, what some call 'new cultural history' has brought a revival of hermeneutic approaches in the history of politics and has again directed research interest onto ideas, as well as the distinct agents who communicate these ideas.[13] In summary, taking account of these tendencies in different academic disciplines, new research on the radical right must bring organised and individual actors, as well as ideas, back into focus.

The plead for more actor-oriented research resonates with the deficiencies addressed by some experts on the radical right who have complained for quite some time about how little attention has been paid to the ideology and intellectual inspirations of the radical right, and how even less focus has been drawn to individuals, groups and publications who develop and propagate theses ideas.[14] To overcome this shortage empirically, it is claimed that research should invest more in the analysis of the radical right's worldview formulated by party leaders, intellectuals and propagandists and expressed in writings, speeches and policy proposals. Focus on the ideological profile would particularly help to capture more consistently the role played by the intellectuals and authors affiliated with the New Right in the drafting of ideas and concepts and the supply of arguments and ideological inputs to political parties and other organised actors. However, as Jens Rydgren has noted in a recent article on the state of the art in the study of the radical right, 'there has been conspicuously little research on the nonparty sector of the new radical right: the think tanks and more informal circles of intellectuals, the party press and radio stations, and civil society organizations ... associated with the new radical right'.[15] Finally, the need to attach more importance to supply-side factors also calls for comprehensive and in-depth investigations of the radical right's organisational structures, political and intellectual leadership, processes of internal decision making and its resources in terms of membership, partisan commitment and finances.

Main Arguments and Structure of the Book

Following the research agenda expressed in recent literature on the radical right and challenging the above-mentioned notion of Swiss exceptionalism, my argument presented in this book is threefold. First, drawing on primary historical research, I argue that there exists a long and established tradition of the radical right in postwar Switzerland. As is revealed by the investigation of party writings, parliamentary minutes, partisan literature, press reports and other publications, a wide variety of radical right-wing organisations have consistently promoted exclusionist thinking inspired by the idea that people coming from outside the country are unequal because of their cultural differences, and have thus helped these beliefs to find their way into Swiss political and intellectual debates. In addition to an ideology of exclusionism, the Swiss radical right's political, intellectual and cultural agenda is inspired by a conception of society that is built on authoritarian and hierarchical principles and traditionalist values. As will be shown, this has made the radical right the most vigorous opponent to those ideas of '1968' that were driven by the quest for a multicultural and more egalitarian and emancipatory society.

Second, I make the case in this book that, empirically and analytically, the Swiss radical right represents a political family and collective actor. As part of the same political family, the various members are bound together by common ideas. Following this perspective, it is shown that circles and publications associated with the New Right played a key role in providing ideas and concepts for the common ideological ground of the Swiss radical right as a political family. This approach corroborates the presumption that ideas matter. In addition, as a collective actor, the Swiss radical right is engaged in different forms of activities and its various exponents assume distinct positions in Swiss politics and society. Although the collaboration and linkage between the groups and individuals are usually rather loose and in most cases simply informal, I show that there were specific moments of mobilisation when the partnership became closer and more straightforward, which made it possible to achieve common goals more effectively.

Third, I argue that, as in most Western democracies, Switzerland accounts for a number of the contextual conditions that foster the emergence and consolidation of the radical right. To go further, certain features of the Swiss political system such as direct democracy and consociationalism, and specific aspects of the Swiss national discourse such as the long-standing notion of so-called overforeignization have produced a considerable degree of structural and ideological openness in which it has been possible for the radical right to form organisations and promote its ideas.

The focus of my study stretches over the period from 1945 to 2000. While Switzerland had not been ruled by a fascist regime and the end of the Second World War was merely a starting point of profound changes in domestic policies, 1945 represents a clear break in the history of the Swiss radical right. As the true nature of the atrocities committed by National Socialism was revealed to the greater public, in Switzerland, as elsewhere in Europe, the radical right was genuinely disgraced in the period immediately after the end of the war. As a consequence, isolated individuals and groups of the extreme right were active at some remove from the public at large, throughout an initial period that ran from the mid 1940s to the early 1960s. In the 1960s, however, radical right-wing populist parties emerged with some force and succeeded in consolidating, albeit as fringe parties, at the margin of the Swiss party system. In addition, the first circles and publications of the New Right were founded in the late 1960s, not least as a reaction to the events of 1968. While radical right-wing populism continued to exist as a fragmented party camp into the 1990s, it was during the course of this decade that the Swiss People's Party embarked on a process of profound transformation which was completed by the late 1990s and made the SVP the most powerful representative of the Swiss radical right ever seen. Having achieved an unprecedented success in the National Council elections of 1999, it entered the new millennium as the strongest of all Swiss political parties.

The book is organised into nine chapters. Chapter 1 presents the theoretical and conceptual framework. It develops an ideology-centred definition of the radical right and conceptualises the radical right as a political family and collective actor comprised of three main family members: the radical right-wing populist parties, the New Right and the extreme right. Chapter 2 identifies contextual factors in Switzerland such as national traditions, socioeconomic changes, political institutions and discursive opportunities which help to explain the persistence of the Swiss radical right. In addition, it gives a brief overview of the different members of the political family of the radical right in Switzerland. The next three chapters present a historical survey of Swiss radical right-wing populist parties since the 1960s. While chapters 3 and 4 deal with the development of fringe parties at the margins of the party system from the 1960s to the 1990s, chapter 5 focuses on the transformation of a mainstream party, the Swiss People's Party, into a radical right-wing populist party in the 1990s.

Chapters 6 and 7 examine the New Right by looking separately at the German-speaking and French-speaking parts of Switzerland. The examination of developments since the late 1960s shows that the New Right can be divided into six different currents inspired by distinct intellectual legacies. Chapter 8 concentrates on the development of the Swiss extreme right since the end of the Second World War. It shows that, while acting at the margins of politics, the extreme right has evolved from a small underground scene into a larger, diversified subculture. The chapter draws a main distinction between ideologues and propagandists on the one hand and combative and violent groups on the other, allowing us to differentiate between the variety of objectives and means of action which exist among the heterogeneous extreme right in Switzerland. Finally, the conclusion chapter presents a number of key organisational and ideological features characteristic of the radical right in Switzerland. While it assesses the Swiss radical right as a collective actor dominated by political parties and held together by linkages and interactions, it shows the main patterns of the radical right's exclusionist worldview and intellectual agenda.

Acknowledgments

This book is the result of a transnational journey between continents, countries and places that has taken place over the period of a couple of years, accompanied by many friends, colleagues and academic institutions. First of all, I would like to express my gratitude to Urs Altermatt, director of the Department of Contemporary History at the University of Fribourg, for giving me the opportunity to develop my scholarship on the subjects examined in this study. I am also greatly indebted to Martin A. Schain, former director of the Center for European Studies at New York University where I greatly appreciated the stimulating environment during my stay as a Visiting Scholar from 1999 to 2002. This book would not have been possible without the numerous conversations and academic exchanges with colleagues who work in the field of the radical right. They have inspired me with their thoughtful ideas and have given me advice on how to tackle and examine a country case like Switzerland which has hitherto received so little attention. In particular, I would like to mention Hans-Georg Betz, Roger Eatwell, Piero Ignazi, Hanspeter Kriesi, Oscar Mazzoleni, Michael Minkenberg, Cas Mudde, Jens Rydgren, Marc Swyngedouw, Jack Veugelers and Ari Zolberg. Giving seminars and lectures at different universities and presenting papers at various conferences and workshops, I have very much appreciated the invaluable feedback and comments received from colleagues and students on the topics presented in this book. Moreover, special thanks go to Marion Berghahn, Ann Przyzycki, Melissa Spinelli and Cecilia Busby at Berghahn Books for their professional support and excellence throughout the publication process.

There is great advantage in Switzerland in the fact that academic research can benefit from the funding provided by the Swiss National Science Foundation (SNSF). I am no exception, since in one way or another, the research that has already been undertaken on issues that I deal with in this book has been generously funded at different stages by the SNSF. I made my first explorations into the ideological realm of

Swiss politics while working from 1997 to 1999 as a scientific collaborator on the project 'Racism and Politics in the Nineties', which was part of the Swiss Priority Program (SPP) 'Switzerland: Towards the Future'. My subsequent stay at the Center for European Studies in New York was initially made possible by a SNSF grant for young researchers. My most recent SNSF research project, 'Radical Right-Wing Populist Parties and Politics of Migration in Switzerland', which I codirected from 2004 to 2007 as a part of the National Research Program 40+ 'Right-Wing Extremism – Causes and Countermeasures', allowed me to examine more systematically the migration agenda of political parties belonging to the radical right.

The collection of sources and literature was gathered in a variety of archives and libraries. For their helpful assistance, I would like to thank collaborators from the Swiss National Library in Bern, the Research Centre for Swiss Politics at the University of Bern, the Social Archive in Zurich, the Archive for Contemporary History at the Swiss Federal Institute of Technology in Zurich, the Bobst Library at New York University, the New York Public Library, the Wiener Library in London, the Hoover Institution Library and Archives at Stanford University and the Central European University Library in Budapest.

I owe a particular debt of gratitude to Christina Späti, who read and commented on the entire manuscript. As a demanding reader and truly supportive friend, she was of enormous help at the different stages of my study. I am also very grateful to Roger Karapin and Ted Perlmutter who commented on earlier drafts of one or more of the chapters. Among the friends who have proofread earlier versions of the manuscript and helped to edit the text into polished English, I would particularly like to thank Bruce Campbell and Vanessa Nornberg. With appreciation for his thoroughness and feeling for language, I am most grateful to Duncan Brown, who has edited the final version of the book manuscript. I would also like to express my deep gratitude to Rita Matus who has displayed great patience over the years, while helping and encouraging me in many ways to accomplish this book. Last but not least, I would like to thank my parents for their lifelong support.

1

The Concept of the Radical Right

Distinctions and Boundaries

An array of varied terms is employed to define political parties and groups whose ideology, program, discourse and policies locate them on the right margin of the political spectrum. In the literature we find labels such 'radical right', 'extreme right', 'neo-fascist', or 'far right', as well as 'national-populism', 'right-wing populism', 'radical right-wing populism', or 'new populism'. While distinct parties or groups are scrutinised and categorised according to identical definitional criteria, they are often differently labelled.[1] Despite this variety in terminology, most authors continue to agree on the indispensability of using the concepts of 'right' and 'right-wing' as analytical tools in social science. This also proves the aptness of the conventional left–right spectrum for understanding contemporary politics, especially when it comes to ideological aspects. Drawing on Norberto Bobbio's distinction between right and left, anti-egalitarian and exclusionist ideology represents the key feature in defining the radical right.[2]

Considering the diversity of the right, it also important to distinguish and demarcate the radical right from other right-wing currents such as conservatism or traditionalism. Frank Decker, for example, argues that both right-wing populists and conservatives embrace principles of anti-egalitarianism and hierarchy in their worldview, but while the former refute, first and foremost, cultural equality and socioeconomic equality of opportunity for the 'culturally different', the latter promote political elitism and the hierarchical organisation of the state.[3] On the other hand, one must bear in mind that a number of political and intellectual currents are rather difficult to categorise as being part of the radical right, since some of their ideological and political characteristics reflect right-wing orientations, while others lean more to the left.[4]

Radicalism vs. Extremism

In recent years, we note the increasing use in research literature of the concepts 'radical right' and 'extreme right', or 'right-wing radicalism' and 'right-wing extremism', terms which are often used as synonyms. There are a number of studies and edited volumes in which authors alternate between the two terms, without distinguishing between them.[5] It is necessary, however, to make clear the distinction between them by pointing out essential differences between the concepts of 'radicalism' and 'extremism' and by examining the reasons for preferring to use one concept over the other.

First of all, the use of 'radicalism' or 'extremism' is dependent on distinct academic traditions. In research conducted in the German language, 'radicalism' was for a long time the concept commonly employed in the study of political groups and attitudes at the margin of the political spectrum.[6] In the 1970s, there was a shift in the approach of the German authorities and particularly the Federal Office for Protection of the Constitution who started to distinguish between 'radicalism', which denotes criticism of the constitutional order without the rejection of democratic rules, and 'extremism', which is used to label groups who reject the democratic and constitutional state and can therefore be banned by authorities.[7] As a result of this normative approach and because of research on totalitarianism in particular, the latter became the concept of reference in a large part of German-language research.[8] This normative position is open to major criticism, however. Some authors point to political motivations behind the use of the concept of 'extremism' and denounce it as a leftover from cold-war debates on totalitarianism. Others argue that the presupposed equivalency between left-wing and right-wing extremism leads to erroneous conclusions, because it takes no account of basic differences between the left and the right, such as the egalitarian objectives of left-wing politics, for example.[9]

In contrast to the German literature, there is a tradition in English-language research which refers to the concept of 'extremism' in a broader sense, that does not limit its use to anti-democratic and anti-constitutional politics that endanger democratic rules and order. From this perspective, the main goal of extremists is to attack and undermine basic principles of the democratic process, such as the commitment to political pluralism and social heterogeneity.[10] On the other hand, Anglo-Saxon and especially U.S. scholars have long been more comfortable operating with the concept of 'radicalism' and examining the politics and ideas of 'radicals' who basically aim at changing all or part of the social order. Since Daniel Bell's 1963 volume 'The Radical Right', the term 'radicalism' has been widely used in academic research into politics at the right-wing margin.[11] As Jeffrey Kaplan and Leonard Weinberg point out, the 'term radical right is of American origin having come into use during the 1950s as part of an effort by scholars to understand the

McCarthy experience and the anticommunist crusades of the post-war era'.[12] Cas Mudde, who had long advocated the concept of 'extreme right' in his research has now also opted for use of the term 'radical right' in his most recent study, pointing out that 'the term *radical* is defined as opposition to fundamental values of liberal democracy, while *right* is defined as the belief in a natural order with inequalities'.[13]

One can also distinguish between 'extremism' and 'radicalism' at the level of substance and conception. Generally speaking, 'extremism' implies the notion that extremists are anti-democratic and aim to implement basic changes by using extreme means and methods. This perspective denotes, as Hans-Georg Betz puts it, that the extreme right is characterised by 'the fundamental rejection of the democratic rules of the game, of individual liberty, and of the principle of individual equality and equal rights ... and the acceptance, if not [the] propagation, of violence as a necessary means to achieve political goals'.[14] On the other hand, in the conceptualisation of 'radicalism' and 'radical', which both have their etymological foundation in the Latin word 'radix' (root), the term 'radical' characterises someone who is going to the roots of something.[15] Such understanding of the term allows the inclusion of a broad range of political movements.[16] Their common characteristic remains criticism of the existing socioeconomic and sociocultural system and the demand for basic transformations of the status quo to be carried out. In contrast with the concept of extremism, the conception of radicalism does not denote that all means are acceptable in pursuit of this goal. It might even be called a reformist position which therefore distinguishes it from the rather revolutionary rationale of extremists.[17]

Distinguishing the Radical Right from the Extreme Right

When we take into account these differences between 'radicalism' and 'extremism', the radical right needs to be distinguished from the extreme right on a number of different levels. Unlike the extreme right, the radical right accepts the rules of the democratic game and does not reject the political and legal system of postwar democracies. While the radical right embraces ideological traits characteristic of the extreme right's worldview, e.g., nationalism, (neo)racism and xenophobia, it does not share other key ideological features of the extreme right, in particular a total hostility towards liberal democracy and its basic foundations, such as the electoral system, parliamentary decision making and the notion of a pluralistic society.[18] Features more central to the radical right's critique would include, for example, the achievements of 'what has come to be known as the social-democratic consensus', in particular the social welfare state and the multicultural society.[19] One last important point to note is that, in contrast to the extreme right, the radical right is not characterised by strategies and activities that would advocate the use of all means necessary in order to achieve its objectives.

The clarifications developed for distinguishing between 'radical right' and 'extreme right' have consequences in terms of how these two concepts are applied in the present study. First, I use 'radical right' as an overarching concept. This makes it possible to capture different organisational subcategories, which draw on different strategies and methods and yet share certain of the ideological features and political objectives that are presented in the following section. Second, the extreme right is seen as a subcategory of the radical right and therefore the term 'extreme right' is exclusively applied for organisations, individuals and activities characterised by the threat or use of violence, the rejection of democratic rules and/or extreme versions of an exclusionist ideology. Following this perspective, the extreme right is treated as being situated, organisationally and ideologically, at the margin of the radical right. Thus, the concept of 'radical right' is intended to be inclusive, covering a wide range of appearances and manifestations of the phenomenon of right-wing radicalism, while the term 'extreme right' is deliberately applied in a limited and exclusive way.

Third, the understanding of 'radical right' applied in this study does not label this phenomenon as anti-democratic and does not attempt to marginalise the radical right from a normative perspective and present it as a pariah political actor. As the examination of the Swiss case will show, the vast majority of radical right-wing actors accept the rules of democracy and apply methods and strategies within the constraints of liberal democracy. Thus, being radical does not mean a rejection of the democratic and constitutional system, but rather represents disagreement with or rejection of the established party system, with particular policies and with values shared by large segments of the polity and society.

The Ideology and Politics of Exclusionism

There is a growing consensus in the research literature that 'radical right' denotes, first and foremost, a form of political ideology.[20] In order to adopt this approach, ideology is understood, as suggested by Roger Eatwell, as 'a relatively coherent set of empirical and normative beliefs and thoughts, focusing on the problems of human nature, the process of history, and socio-political arrangements. It is usually related to a programme of more specific immediate and short-run concerns.'[21]

Drawing on this conception of ideology, one must start from the point that the radical-right's ideology basically consists of a frame of reference which provides certain actors with criteria for choices and decisions. As many authors further stress, the radical right can hardly be said to have a coherent worldview or a consistent belief system. Its ideology is fairly heterogeneous and includes distinct features that can vary in each national setting. Taking into account variations over time and space, it is not surprising that we observe paradoxes and conflicting positions in the political programs of many radical right-wing actors, in the quest, for example, for both more state activity (security issues) and less state activity (economy and tax policies).[22]

From this perspective, the persisting debate over definitions also serves as a reflection of the actual state of the radical right in Western democracies. The variety that can be seen in the attributed ideological features has led to a situation where definitions of the radical right resemble a shopping list containing a number of different elements.[23] As Cas Mudde and Ulrich Druwe both demonstrate, when examining the use of definitions in this specialised literature, there is an astounding amount of disagreement in academic research, which operates with a large number of definitional criteria.[24] According to Mudde: 'In twenty-six definitions of right-wing extremism that can be derived from the literature no less than fifty-eight different features are mentioned at least once'.[25]

Despite variation in definitions of the radical right, one can still distinguish key features of ideology inherent in some sort of 'radical right minimum'. The core ideology, which provides the frame of reference for various actors of the radical right, consists primarily of manifestations of an exclusionist ideology. They serve the radical right as the foundation for a worldview based on demarcation, both internally, within a collective group, and externally, towards the outside of the group. In other words, the exclusionist ideology is expressed in the radical right's quest for separation and segregation within the nation-state and isolation from the outside world. All radical right-wing actors are united in their commitment to some sort of national, ethnic or cultural exclusionism and can thereby be distinguished from conservative or other contemporary political strands.[26] The core of the radical right's ideology is based around the principle of fundamental human inequality and inegalitarian beliefs and 'divides society into those who belong and those who do not'.[27] As pointed out by Elisabeth Carter, 'institutionalized social and political inequality may be based on a number of different criteria, but those overwhelmingly favoured by parties and movements of the extreme right have been nationality, race, ethnic group and/or religious denomination'.[28] Following this perspective, the radical right's exclusionist worldview is most commonly characterised by ideological toolkits of nationalism, (neo)racism, anti-Semitism and xenophobia.

Nationalism: A Key Ideological Feature

Nationalism represents a key feature of the radical right's worldview. The radical right refers to an exclusionist conception of nation-state and nationhood which serves as a counter-concept to the culturally pluralist society. Particularly in periods of crisis, real or subjectively perceived, it is the preferred tactic of nationalist movements to present the nation and the nation-state as a sanctuary where longings for clarity, stability and safety are satisfied. As the study of nationalism acknowledges, the concepts of nation and nation-state aim at binding people to a political organisation and achieving integration within a large group. In essence, the nation-state provides the framework for individuals with differing interests and from different social classes to accept the norms and rules of a political system. Political culture, historical references and cultural categories such as language, religion and myths are taken as characteristics of a unique national identity, which distinguishes one's own nation from other nations and cultures and serves to yoke people together.[29] While the conception of nation goes back to Greek antiquity, where the nation was mainly linked to the understanding of a people as *demos*, the concept of nation-state gained momentum in the nineteenth century, as it served as the foundation to a large wave of nation-building processes in Europe.[30]

Nationalism and the quest for national identity rely on the dialectical process of identity building. On the one hand, by emphasising the sense of group belonging and collective identity, the nationalist ideology has an inclusive purpose and aims at integrating the members of the nation into a culturally, if not ethnically, homogeneous community. On the other hand, nationalism has an exclusionist effect, as it promulgates the view that the exclusivity of citizenship and its associated political and social privileges must be vigorously defended and that non-members of the community should be excluded from these rights. These tendencies, aimed at buttressing the society against the outside and at pursuing a homogenisation within it, together produce far-reaching discriminatory effects. Ultimately, the strengthening of one's own identity and the construction of the identity of the 'other' are part of the same political strategy and discourse.[31]

Drawing on a primordial understanding of collective identity and essentialist ideas of 'natural differences', the radical right's conception of nationhood and national identity offers patterns of interpretation premised on the idea that sociocultural, political, or historical differences between human groups are based on natural distinctions. Thus it promotes a nationalism which assumes the existence of naturally given divisions and puts emphasis on the native national and cultural profile.[32] As pointed out by Roger Griffin, the radical right 'takes on highly culture-specific forms, largely because it draws on nationalist myth, whose contents are by definition unique to each cultural tradition in question (and pose particularly grave problems of translation and comprehension to other nationals)'.[33]

Research literature points to the distinction between ethnocultural nationalism and civic nationalism. This draws on a conceptualisation of nation and nation-state which depends on the two classic models of culture-nation and state-nation. On the one hand, in the understanding of state-nation, the emphasis is on a sense of voluntarily belonging to a political community and on common citizenship as the base of nationhood. On the other hand, the concept of culture-nation highlights the symbolic feeling of group belonging, kinship and a collective identity that draws on real or constructed cultural and historical commonalties.[34] The use of ethnocultural references is applied by a large majority of the radical right.[35] However, it is important to take into account that the radical right is also keen to emphasise the distinct origins, historical particularities and political culture of the nation and hence seeks to underscore the individuality and uniqueness of one's own nation-state. More often than not, the radical right merges the concepts of both state-nation and culture-nation in order to draw boundary lines and substantiate its exclusionist notion of membership in the political community. Thus, the case of the radical right demonstrates the analytical weaknesses of the definitional antithesis between culture-nation and state-nation, since in most cases the conception of nationhood combines civic and ethnocultural components.[36]

From Racism to Neoracism

Traditionally, racism has been another ideological feature most commonly associated with the radical right and its ideological realm. The emergence of the radical right was often seen in relation to the appeal of its racist political program.[37] Classical racism draws upon nineteenth century pseudoscientific 'race' theories and on anti-egalitarian assumptions of Social Darwinism.[38] As it presumes biological and genetic differences between human beings, classical racism promulgates the idea that a natural inequality exists between human groups. It justifies a biological and immutable natural order of ranking among human groups based upon socially constructed or phenotypic characteristics (such as skin colour) which are used to define differences between groups. In classical racism, distinct features, either real or supposed, that are attributed to individuals or groups, are essentialised and seen as being determined by nature. From this deterministic perspective, both social behaviour and cultural traditions are expression of inherited, deeply imprinted characteristics of human beings.[39]

After the crimes that were committed by the National Socialist regime in the name of racist ideology, racism has been largely discredited and an anti-racist taboo has been achieved as most West European countries have passed anti-racist laws, with the result that statements expressing overt, classical racism are hardly ever made in public.[40] However, it has been pointed out that an important shift has occurred in the area of racism and the rhetoric of exclusion. While some have called this transformation of racism and its discourse 'neoracism' or 'new racism', others describe it as 'differentialist racism'.[41] Most authors agree that the doctrinal work of the New Right has contributed to a large extent to these reformulations within racist discourse.[42]

In contrast to inegalitarian racism, neoracism exalts the 'right to be different' and thus pretends to support egalitarian assumptions, but emphasises a presumed incommensurability of different cultural identities. As pointed out by Pierre-André Taguieff, racist thinking and discourse is not only, as many might believe, affected by *heterophobie* but also by *heterophilie*. Hence, in his view, the fear of difference and of being different has increasingly been replaced by an appraisal of difference and diversity.[43] Or, in the words of Douglas Holmes, neoracism 'creates a potentially invidious doctrine of difference, which holds that cultural distinctions must be preserved among an enduring plurality of groups and provides, thereby, a discriminatory rationale for practices of inclusion and exclusion'.[44]

From the perspective of neoracists, culture and cultural characteristics – whether attributed to nation, ethnic group, or *Volk* – are viewed as a static and natural category and become the determining feature of differentiation. Consequently, neoracists substantiate their position with an essentialist notion of culture or way of life. Particularly in debates on various issues of migration policy, a discourse of culture and ethnicity is commonly used, where these are seen as deterministic categories. As the neoracist position uses the slogan 'right to be different' in order to preserve ethnic and cultural identity and difference, the homogenisation of the group within, as well as its isolation from without, become important objectives. Cultural unity and ethnic homogeneity are presented as basic conditions for the preservation of one's own identity or group.[45] In some ways, these ideas closely resemble those of nativism, which according to Cas Mudde, represents a core ideological feature of the radical right and is defined 'as an ideology, which holds that states should be inhabited exclusively by members of the native groups ("the nation") and that non-native elements (persons and ideas) are fundamentally threatening to the homogenous nation-state. The basis for defining 'nativeness' and 'non-nativeness' can be diverse, e.g. ethnic, racial or religious, but will always have a cultural component.'[46]

Embracing a pronounced view of cultural differentialism, neoracism joins ethnopluralism in placing emphasis on cultural differences and the separate development of different cultures. Developed by the *Nouvelle droite* in France and adopted by the German New Right in debates on national identity, the concept of ethnopluralism presumes that there is 'differential plurality of primordial collective identities' and hence stresses the fundamental incompatibility between cultures that will inevitably clash. From this point of view, there can be no possibility of overcoming cultural difference and so immigrants and refugees should stay in, or at least return to, their homelands. At the same time, both ethnopluralist and neoracist positions presuppose the superiority of the home culture by pointing out the differences between cultures, in a radical ethnocentric stance.[47]

The Persistence of Anti-Semitism

Anti-Semitism is another feature expressed in the ideas and discourse embraced by the radical right. Generally speaking, anti-Semitism is defined as those views and attitudes which are directed against Jews, that are based upon prejudices and stereotypes and apply a deterministic attribution of negative characteristics.[48] While modern anti-Semitism, parallel to classical racism, originated in the pseudoscientific 'racial theories' of the nineteenth century, religiously motivated anti-Judaism is entrenched in the history of Christianity and substantiated with theological arguments taken from the New Testament and the distorted image of Jews as the 'killers of Jesus'.[49]

After the Second World War, overt statements of modern anti-Semitism, making use of blunt racist categorisations, have largely vanished from the public sphere and have become confined to marginal extreme-right groups. Thus, in much the same way as racism, many believed that anti-Semitism would fade away as a doctrine and patterns of thought once its exterminationist nature had been revealed in the murderous crimes of the National Socialists. However, what some have termed 'post Holocaust' or 'post fascist' anti-Semitism has remained a potent force of anti-Jewish hostility in contemporary societies and is most commonly found among political and intellectual actors associated with the radical right.[50] The existence of this variant of anti-Semitism basically means that while anti-Semitism has lost its importance as a coherent ideology, except among propagandists and activists of the extreme right, it still continues to exist in the form of prejudices, stereotypes and resentments prevalent in most postwar societies. Moreover, German literature has pointed to the evocative emergence of 'secondary anti-Semitism', which is basically the product of the examinations and debates about the Shoah throughout the postwar era, in which long-standing patterns of prejudices and stereotypes, such as references to conspiracy theories or finance capitalism, demonstrate their persistence.[51]

Xenophobia: The 'Other' Perceived as a Threat

Xenophobia is another feature usually attributed to the ideology of the radical right. In a strict sense, the term refers to the fear of the 'other' or the 'stranger', eventually resulting in a condensed attitude of hostility and hatred towards the 'stranger'. Common definitions describe xenophobia as attitudes that are founded on latent, often unconscious prejudices and expressed in everyday life through mistrust and scepticism towards immigrants.[52] It is seen as a basic element of xenophobic assertions that 'they impute to all people labeled as members of an outgroup the actions of some members that have been considered a threat to the ingroup'.[53] Since the concept of xenophobia denotes rather diffuse and emotionally founded feelings, some criticise it as a 'somewhat vague psychological concept' that 'has only a very limited analytical value'.[54]

However, in recent years there has been a notable shift in the approach to xenophobia, as observed by Michael Banton: 'Once regarded as a psychological condition – to describe persons who feared or abhored [sic] groups regarded as 'outsiders' – its more recent application has been in the context of attacks on immigrants and asylum seekers in western Europe'.[55] He argues that the increased use of xenophobia might also be related to the fact that in Germany, the term racism is associated with the era of National Socialism and hence 'German institutions are more ready to refer to *Fremdenfeindlichkeit* and to translate this into English as xenophobia. This is one factor underlying the increased reference to xenophobia in internationally-agreed documents.'[56] Overall, it appears that the strict, psychological conception of xenophobia has been expanded, not least because of the increasing use of the term to describe anti-immigrant attitudes and actions and discriminatory policies proposed by the radical right.[57]

In recent years, as with xenophobia, so too has the concept of Islamophobia been used to capture the growing hostility and hatred towards Muslims, in particular Muslim immigrants, in most West European societies. Although the term has been criticised for its reductionist emphasis on faith and religion instead of people, it describes prejudices and stereotypes that picture Islam and Muslims as irrational, aggressive and hostile to the Western world. Without considering the diversity of Islam and the differences between Muslim societies, Islamophobic attitudes take Islam as one monolithic and static bloc and stress the cultural, religious and political incompatibility of Muslims with Western societies.[58]

Authoritarianism, Anti-'68' Attitudes and Neoliberalism

In addition to the exclusionist ideology, the anti-egalitarian tradition of the radical right is also revealed in its strong belief in the importance of an authoritarian and hierarchical structured order. In most cases, the authoritarian tendency of the contemporary radical right differs from fascist authoritarianism's conception of a non-democratic, total state based on omnipotent leadership and keeping watch over all spheres of social life. Today's authoritarian beliefs imply moral dimensions, for instance, such as those that are seen when the radical right complains that 'the modern society is in decline because of crime, moral decay and narrow self-interest' and that it is therefore necessary to reinstall moral order and social cohesion.[59] To this aim, the radical right usually proposes the notion of an organic society based on traditional values and ethics. From this view, the preservation of the family as the natural nucleus of society, the belief in the traditional role of women and the rejection of abortion and homosexuality are placed on top of the list of moral priorities.[60] The exaltation of a strong state and the strict rule of law also disclose the radical right's unconditional belief in authorities and its proximity to authoritarianism and to hierarchical conceptions of society. The emphasis on internal security and the urge to improve enforcement of the law at all levels, including policing and the judicial and penal systems, are blatant examples of the prominent role that the radical right has advocated for the state.[61]

The rejection of egalitarianism, cosmopolitanism and emancipatory conceptions of society makes the radical right the main carrier of the 'silent counter-revolution', as Piero Ignazi calls it.[62] This view suggests that the radical right, with its anti-egalitarian, hierarchical and anti-pluralistic ideology, stands against the basic changes in sociocultural values that have taken place in Western societies since the 1960s: symbolically represented by the events of 1968. The radical right thus has developed an ideological counter-model to egalitarian and multicultural principles of the 1968 generation on issues like migration, social welfare, cultural policy and education, and it forms a counter-weight to left-libertarian and ecological movements. While the left and particularly the New Left is criticised as the defender of modernity, universalism and immigration society, the radical right advocates the return to traditions, cultural relativism and nationally defined communities.[63] After the collapse of communism in 1989, which had traditionally been the radical right's main adversary, the radical right succeeded in filling the gap by reinforcing its already pronounced positions against the New Left.[64]

In the last decade or so, a number of authors have emphasised that the neoliberal element has become one of the most important features of the radical right's ideology, since its economic program prominently advocates a free market economy, individual achievement and a drastic reduction of state expenditure, in order to guarantee the economic and social well-being of large segments of the population.[65] By combining an individualistic, neoliberal message with the rejection of particularistic claims, especially those coming from disadvantaged and marginalised groups, the radical right advocates the Social Darwinist idea of a social stratification in which the fittest are rewarded and the less fit assume a subordinate role.[66] The neoliberal quest for less state, more market and individual self-reliance also emerges from the basic principles of populism, a genuine characteristic of the newly emerging radical right-wing parties. The populist strategy aims at combining defiance and resentments towards the political elite with anti-state sentiments. Populists denounce the state and its bureaucracy as being alienated from the people and representing only the interest of the current power holders.[67]

Considering the nationalist nature of the radical right, its support for neoliberalism, which entails the pursuit of global capitalism and economic globalisation, seems to be something of a paradox. By linking together liberalism and nationalism, however, the radical right offers a socioeconomic concept that suggests the possibility of reducing the negative effects of a liberal market by emphasising the national components. In this logic, the program of the radical right combines neoliberalism with nationalism and xenophobia and insists that the nation's 'own people' should benefit first and foremost from the fruits of the national economy.[68] Consequently, Roger Eatwell argues that: 'The issue is not simply one of free markets versus statism: the central debate concerns what is in the interests of the "true" community.'[69] On the other hand, authors such as Michael Minkenberg point out that 'market liberalism was never a key component of right-wing ideology' and that the promotion of neoliberalism should rather be seen, first and foremost, as 'a tactical tool' used by radical right-wing parties in the light of electoral competition.[70] Moreover, the quest for liberation from state limitations in terms of economy and bureaucracy contrasts essentially with the above-mentioned advocacy of a strong state, which many authors see as a key feature of the radical right.

The Predominance of Identity Politics

Based on its ideology of exclusionism, the radical right has a distinct political agenda and pursues concrete goals in politics and society, even though its policy choices sometimes just reflect the salience of present-day debates in a specific national context.[71] Most consistently, the radical right seeks to challenge the premises of a world that is increasingly globalised in terms of economy, politics and culture. In this way, it belongs to those 'reactive movements that build trenches of resistance on behalf of God, nation, ethnicity, family, locality, that is, the fundamental categories of millennial existence now threatened under the combined, contradictory assault of techno-economic forces and transformative social movements'.[72] By putting emphasis on clearly defined identities, it promises guidance through concrete points of reference that counter the alleged loss of identity in postindustrial societies.

While various forces of globalisation cut across the boundaries of national states and decrease the influence of national institutions, the radical right proposes a 'radical delineation of society in which "cultural" idioms as opposed to abstract interests serve as instruments for expressing meaning and for deriving power'.[73] As a result, identity politics has become a key characteristic of the contemporary radical right's political agenda and strategy, through which its notion of nationally and culturally defined collective groups is transformed into concrete policies. Its identity politics is based around the fundamental distinction between 'we' and 'them', between 'us' and the 'other', and essentially promotes the basic principle of natural inequality as an inherent product of existing differences between social groups and individuals.[74]

In today's Western Europe, the central focus of the radical right's identity politics is on migration. Its aim is to support the proliferation of a form of kinship illusion that constructs an imagined community along national and cultural lines and strives for the exclusion or expulsion of non-members of one's own community.[75] According to Hans-Georg Betz and Carol Johnson, the 'main argument behind this is that certain groups cannot be integrated into society and therefore represent a fundamental threat to the values, way of life and cultural integrity of the "indigenous" people'.[76] Following this purpose, a variety of policies related to migration – such as rates of immigration, integration policies, or citizenship laws – are addressed as key issues. They represent the main contentious debates in which radical-right rhetoric is employed to undermine liberal policies towards migrants and the accommodations that are made to facilitate integration.[77] For example, the politics of citizenship today, as Rogers Brubaker argues, 'is first and foremost a politics of nationhood. As such, it is *politics of identity*, not a *politics of interest* (in the restricted, materialist sense). It pivots more on self-understanding than on self-interest.'[78]

The radical right's identity politics in Western Europe gained further prominence in the growing debates on the concept of the welfare state. As the welfare state seems to be losing its influence as the model of social solidarity that was dominant throughout the postwar period, it is increasingly viewed as a national achievement and an expression of solidarity reserved for the national community, or the *Volksgemeinschaft*.[79] As a result, the feeling of belonging to a national community gains a concrete component of vested interest, as the exclusive national community replaces the inclusive social community. This sort of identity politics, termed 'welfare chauvinism' by some, implies that non-members of the nation, e.g., migrants and asylum seekers, should be excluded from the social protection of the welfare state.[80]

Integration into the supranational institutions, especially the process of European integration, is a further area where identity politics play a crucial role. In most European countries, the radical right is a principal advocate of Euroscepticism and one of the driving forces in campaigns opposed to European unification. It highlights the loss of national sovereignty and identity and hence argues that European integration undermines national integrity.[81] European integration is criticised for being part of the recent economic, political and cultural developments associated with globalisation and internationalisation and many radical right leaders like to refer to it as part of the new 'mondialist' ideology.[82]

The radical right in Western Europe also shows great interest in debates over history and the ways in which politics and society should deal with their pasts. As pointed out by Tzvetan Todorov and Annick Jacquet, 'the memory of our past is a large part of our present identity, and one may not touch it without scandalous consequences'.[83] As a result, at different moments of the 1980s and 1990s, the radical right tried to intervene in virulent debates over the role that respective European countries had played during the period of fascism. The purpose of most radical right-wing groups, excepting factions of the extreme right, is not so much to clear or deny the responsibility of fascism and National Socialism for crimes committed and the establishment of totalitarian regimes. Rather, they show a reluctance to review disturbing aspects of national history and have rejected the deconstruction of certain collective myths that have persisted for almost fifty years and profoundly shaped the conception of national identity in each country. By applying a fair amount of anti-intellectualism, the radical right strove to delegitimise these efforts to shed full light on the past.[84]

Finally, the issues of anti-racism and anti-racist legislation became another great concern for the radical right, which managed to incorporate these issues into its identity politics. This was supported by the fact that anti-discriminatory laws were increasingly applied to anti-immigrant propaganda after the 'legal repression of extreme-right parties has shifted its ideological foundation from anti-fascism to anti-racism' in most Western European countries in the 1970s and 1980s.[85] While '[o]utlawing freedom of expression ... presents a challenge to the self-legitimating basis of liberal democracies, and a dilemma that is not easily resolved',[86] the purpose of the radical right's critique is rather to denounce anti-racist policies as a further example of pro-immigrant politics that undermine the individual character and homogeneity of the national community. In such arguments, anti-racist legislation is denounced as discrimination against one's own nation, and the so-called immigration lobby is made responsible for foreigners purportedly receiving more legal protection and public attention than native citizens.[87]

A Political Family and a Collective Actor

Having focused on the ideological and political aspects inherent in defining the radical right, it is now time to discuss the high degree of organisational variety and structural heterogeneity of the radical right. Following this purpose, the concept of 'political family' has lately gained importance in the comparative study of political parties of the radical right.[88] As Piero Ignazi notes, the centrality of ideological criteria as defining elements for understanding the radical right, 'revives Duverger's suggestion when he assessed the existence of *"familles spirituelles"*, identified on the basis of the ideological reference of the party'.[89] In their conception of political families, Maurice Duverger and others have stressed the ideological and historical similarities between political parties from a national and cross-national perspective.[90]

One part of the study of the radical right has carried the concept of 'political family' beyond the party system and applied it to other types of social and political actors. It was Michael Minkenberg, foremost, who introduced a modified model of political family into research on the radical right. Minkenberg first used the model – that he refers to as 'ideological family' – in a comparative study that developed typologies to capture the organisational variation of the radical right in Germany, France and the United States. He argued that the radical right should best be described as an ideological family of political groups that are characterised by populist ultranationalism, but are divided below this common ground into various branches featuring different degrees of relationship.[91] In the same vein, authors such as Paul Hainsworth maintain that the radical right can be understood 'as a political family whose constituent parts exhibit certain things in common, but that also may be divided into subtypes'.[92]

This understanding of a political family of the radical right bears resemblance to what some term the 'national camp' (*camp national* in French; *nationales Lager* or *rechtsextremes Lager* in German), which describes a current or movement that has a common political vision and is composed of a network of parties, organisations, periodicals and individuals.[93] Overall, the concept of 'political family' attempts to go beyond the limited view of separate types of radical right-wing actors by pointing to convergences at the level of distinct ideological references and sociocultural principles. From this perspective, the different organisational forms of the radical right rely upon those key ideological features, political views and sociocultural values which comprise the radical-right worldview. At the same time, the concept means that these actors may have different opinions on specific issues, or in the style they use to translate their views into public and political discourse. Moreover, the organisational variants of the radical right are bound together, not only by shared ideological features and common intellectual–historical references, but also by networks, interactions and instances of mobilisation.[94]

In order to further conceptualise the radical right, some authors draw on social-movement research, where the concept of 'collective actor' helps to better understand the relationships and interactions between the different subtypes of the radical right. The term 'collective actor' allows us to grasp the structural and organisational aspects of the radical right, whilst also appreciating the possibility for variations in the contentious actions it may pursue in mobilising for a common objective. The concept of political family, on the other hand, places importance on the realm of ideas and beliefs espoused by the radical right.[95] In this view, the radical right expresses itself as a collective actor through a broad repertoire of collective actions, ranging from participation at elections and public campaigns to random acts of violence.[96] While organisational and mobilising structures are important resources for strengthening the cohesion and identity of the entire movement, they are also part of the multi-organisational field of the movement, which is characterised in reality by competing groups and conflicting interests.[97] This is reflected, for example, in the commonly observed factionalism of radical right-wing movements and in the different positions that radical right-wing actors hold in the political system.

Most commonly, social movements are defined as mobilised networks of individuals, groups and organisations which strive to produce or impede social change by using various forms of actions and protest.[98] Based on such a definition, it is necessary to focus on three distinct, though often overlapping, dimensions of social movements in order to capture the nature and dynamics of the radical right.[99] First, although the radical right is characterised by organisational and structural variations, the concept of network points to a discursive and communicative convergence between the variants of the movement. For instance, the commitment to common ideological references and sociocultural values strengthens the structural network, produces collective identity and solidarity, and ultimately holds the movement together.[100] Second, actions and protests are contentious means of expression through which people mobilise against something or someone and manifest their strong disagreement with certain political and social conditions or oppose particular social and political groups.[101] Consequently, the dynamics of the radical right's collective action imply aspects of opposition and struggle, on the one hand, and the promotion of alternative ways that politics and society might work, on the other. Third, closely related to the purpose of protest is the idea of producing or impeding social change, which implies, ultimately, that radical right-wing movements are not only interested in specific social and political issues, but also strive for basic changes in society and politics.

Following this perspective, I conceive the radical right as a collective actor composed of networks of individuals and organisations. While the 'variants can be seen as components of an inter-related system of collective action, which centres on the ideological core of right-wing radicalism',[102] they also depend upon structural resources and persuasive forces to get public resonance, and use different sorts of methods and forms of action to promote their political agenda and their sociocultural program, as well as to mobilise public support.

More specifically, the radical right consists of organisations such as political parties, intellectual circles and combative groups, on the one hand, and political entrepreneurs, ideological suppliers and militant activists, on the other. The various actors hold distinct positions in the political system and therefore have different impact in terms of public support or public resonance. Since the different actors use a variety of means of action and forms of mobilisation, and because they address various though often overlapping audiences, there appears to be a wide-ranging division of labour within the radical right.[103]

The political family of the radical right is basically comprised of three main members: the radical right-wing populist parties, the New Right and the extreme right. As shown in this study, each of these three categories is further divided into organisational subtypes. This reflects the high degree of organisational variation within the radical right. While their ideology is inspired by exclusionist ideas and their agenda is marked by identity politics, these three types of actors differ in their methods of action as well as in the intellectual sophistication they display in their ideological and programmatic work. Most importantly, perhaps, the various actors assume different positions in the political system and the public sphere, which ultimately have repercussions in terms of the diverse levels of support they receive and the respective level of impact they are able to exert on politics and public debates.

Figure 1.1 | *The Radical Right as Political Family and Collective Actor*

Dimensions of Convergence

Ideological Features and Intellectual References (Doctrine)
Political Views and Sociocultural Values (Program and Agenda)

Radical Right-Wing Populist Parties	New Right	Extreme Right

Dimensions of Distinctions

Means of Action (Division of Labour)
Intellectual Sophistication (Discursive and Ideological Performance)
Position in Political System (Systematic Integration and Policy Effects)
Position in the Public Sphere (Public Resonance and Support)

The Radical Right-wing Populist Parties: Key Actors in the Political System

The radical right-wing populist parties play the predominant and most influential role within the political family of the radical right. In terms of public resonance and ability to effect policy, these parties deserve the most attention. As the main public actors of the radical right, they engage in political campaigns, run for office and participate in decision-making processes, etc. Since they tend to be integrated within the political system and to participate in electoral competition, they basically accept the rules of democracy and adjust their ideology and radical-right agenda to the constraints of realpolitik.

The concept of 'radical right-wing populism' accurately captures the essence of these parties.[104] Above all, the term 'radical right' denotes ideological and political aspects. It points to the exclusionist worldview of these parties, which is shaped by nationalist, neoracist and xenophobic ideas, finds expression in their political program and agenda, and is translated into their identity politics. The concept 'populism' describes both ideological and strategic dimensions. On the one hand, populism points to a Manichean worldview which divides politics and society 'into two homogenous and antagonistic groups, "the true people" versus "the corrupt elite". It is further argued that politics should be an expression of the *volonté générale* (general will) of the people'.[105] It follows from this view that populism stands in basic conflict with the pluralism and heterogeneity of contemporary politics and societies. Since populism is a 'thin-centred ideology',[106] it is commonly linked to other ideologies and political demands, as shown for example by the radical right with its exclusionist ideology and identity politics.

On the other hand, the concept also refers to the political strategies and techniques of political parties striving to get popular legitimation against the established elites. Their populist nature is disclosed in their appeal to the 'common man', which evokes the notion of 'the people' in the everyday sense of the word, and finds expression in their stated conviction of running against established parties in order to return power to 'the people'.[107] They all 'involve some kind of revolt against the established structure of power in the name of the people' and hence consistently try to evoke and mobilise resentments against the alleged holders of power in politics and society.[108] With their anti-establishment rhetoric and resentments, however, radical right-wing populist parties also aim to transform the foundations of the existing socioeconomic system and sociocultural values. They promote their own program as a popular alternative to the prevailing system of elites, institutions and political agreements. Consequently, they ask for more direct democracy, claiming that popular will and popular decision should be taken into account in concrete policy making and that this would return political power to the people.[109]

Radical right-wing populist parties are characterised by specific constituents related to their leadership and party organisation.[110] First of all, many of the successful parties of the radical right in Europe have a charismatic and personalised leadership.[111] As the examples of Jean-Marie Le Pen, Jörg Haider, Umberto Bossi, Pim Fortuyn and others demonstrate, strong leaders have been an important reason for increased public resonance and electoral growth. Conversely, the cases of Haider and Fortuyn also show that these parties can lose much of their public attention and electoral support as soon as their leader figures leave the political stage. Thus, while charismatic party leaders illustrate the personification of the party, they also epitomise the general personalisation of politics.[112] They skilfully demonstrate what it takes to build a mass following in an era where television has become the most important device for winning voter support. They often move their political stage from traditional venues such as parliamentary debates and party meetings to TV shows where controversial debate, demagogic rhetoric and charismatic appearance are more important than content and factual accuracy.[113] Moreover, as Margaret Canovan argues, since populist leaders like to 'celebrate both spontaneous action at the grassroots and a close personal tie between leader and followers', they basically hold their parties together and contribute greatly to the internal cohesion within their parties.[114] Also closely related to a strong party leadership are the efforts to establish a centralised and authoritarian party apparatus, which serves as a counter-model to the traditional type of bureaucratic catch-all mass party. Control over the party organisation allows for effective adaptation of the political agenda and strategies, as well as improving the effectiveness and proficiency of political work and campaigning.[115]

For many radical right-wing populist parties, the establishment of an organisational network is of major importance because it helps to integrate a wider circle of sympathisers and followers and to create a 'countersociety or counterculture' which goes beyond the scope of party politics.[116] This network includes not only the associated organisations, groups and publications, but also a number of informal ties to other members of the radical right-wing political family. Another type of linkage consists of party members whose socialisation and politicisation were shaped by former membership of non-partisan groups, for example in study circles of the New Right or in subcultural groups of the extreme right. As shown by some studies, while the degree of formal and informal interactions and the strength of links may vary considerably from country to country and from party to party, it seems that the parties are most successful in integrating followers of the New Right.[117] The relationship to the extreme right is obviously the most troubling part of the parties' external links and hence comes under constant and vigilant scrutiny from the public. In general, it seems that despite attempts to appeal to extreme-right groups and to integrate them, most radical right-wing populist parties are relatively careful to avoid being seen as seeking overt collaboration with the militant extreme right.[118]

The New Right: Initiators and Suppliers of Ideas

The New Right represents both an ideological strand that embraces distinct intellectual and sociocultural concepts and a collective actor that relies on an organisational network of organisations, study groups, journals and individuals, primarily seeking to exert influence at the level of ideas and discourses[119] Unlike the radical right-wing populist parties, the New Right uses means other than the ballot box and parliamentary representation to express their ideas and views. Since some factions of the New Right attempt to reach a certain level of ideological sophistication, they concentrate on the world of intellectuals and culture and develop arguments wrapped in scholarly language in order to influence public discourse. Others display their ideological and political objectives more openly and simply choose propagandistic means of action in order to move public debates to the right.

In their role as initiators and suppliers of ideas and intellectual concepts, the followers of the New Right produce a gradual rather than an immediate political impact. Their aim is to shape, in the long run, a whole variety of the political, cultural and social issues that are discussed in politics and society. However, some followers of the New Right are also involved with political parties and in everyday politics. They serve as advisers to political leaders, contribute articles to party papers, or even run for public offices. Overall, arguments and policy proposals put forward by radical right-wing populist parties are inspired, more often than not, by ideas and concepts developed by the New Right.[120] On the other hand, one section of New Right intellectuals associate themselves with the extreme right, particularly its negationist faction, and thereby engage in its propaganda campaigns, attend rallies and meetings, or supply its periodicals with articles and essays.

Since a large part of the literature on the New Right draws from single-country research, we are still missing a general, cross-nationally applicable definition of the 'New Right'. A common distinction is made between, on the one hand, the Anglo-Saxon New Right, based mainly in the United States and Great Britain, and on the other, the continental European New Right with its strongholds in France and Germany and its offshoots in most other European countries. The main difference between the Anglo-Saxon New Right and that of continental Europe is the latter's belief that the economic system should be subordinated to the domain of ideas, culture and politics. This puts a large majority of the continental New Right in sharp opposition to insurgent neoliberalism and its free market doctrine, whereas the Anglo-Saxon New Right defends neoliberal ideas on economic matters and expresses fierce criticism of the welfare state.[121]

In spite of differences from a cross-national perspective, as well as ideological variations within national contexts, the continental New Right in Europe has pursued, since the late 1960s, a strategic and intellectual renewal of the radical right. In France, for example, this renewal is shaped, as pointed out by Pierre-André Taguieff, by different intellectual currents inspired by distinct ideological traditions.[122] Among them, the *Nouvelle droite*, a new organisational formation and intellectual current that emerged in the late 1960s and reached the peak of its public resonance in the late 1970s and early 1980s, represents the strategically most inventive and intellectually most influential current of the New Right.[123]

The *Nouvelle droite* promotes, for example, the concept of so-called metapolitics which it endorses as a prime strategic choice that New Right intellectuals should make. The purpose here is to emphasise the importance of culturally and intellectually oriented activities which aim to win over the minds of the people and to gain thematic leadership in public debates. Inspired by Antonio Gramsci's concept of cultural hegemony, the *Nouvelle droite* believes that the struggle should be led in the realm of ideas and culture.[124] Consequently, some authors argue that by stressing the ascendancy of discourse and cultural politics, the strategy of the New Right follows that of the New Left and particularly the postmodernist cultural left.[125] The reference to the Italian Marxist theorist Antonio Gramsci is a revealing example of the eclecticism that the New Right has adopted in its theories and strategies. In spite of Gramsci's adherence to Marxism and the emancipatory and egalitarian foundation of his work, the *Nouvelle droite* incorporated what it dubbed 'right-wing Gramscianism' (*gramscisme de droite*) into its strategy.

The New Right in general pursues a strategy of 'scientification'. Since most adherents to the New Right show great interest in theoretical questions and intellectual debates, they try to conceptually develop and ideologically renew some key features of radical-right thought.[126] As mentioned above, theorists of the *Nouvelle droite* are responsible for cultural differentialism becoming an important factor in the shift from biological to cultural racism. The strategy of scientification is also revealed in the importance that the German New Right gives to the research current in the study of ethology which was influenced by Konrad Lorenz and his disciple Irenäus Eibl-Eibesfeldt. This research tradition argues for so-called neo-instinctivism and presents the socioaffective behaviour patterns of individuals as indelible marks of the animal aspect of the human being. Based on comparisons between different cultures, it is claimed that sceptical reactions and mistrust towards 'strangers' are part of the genetic heritage of the genus and not the result of social life and culture.[127] Hence, arguments drawing on ethological research basically conclude that a mistrustful relation toward foreigners has to be seen as an anthropological constant, which gives us the notion of a 'homo xenophobicus'.[128]

Since the New Right is ardently opposed to ideas promoted by the activists of the 1968 movement and their offspring, the New Left and the new social movements, it plays a key role in 'the "counter-revolution" to the "revolution" of 1968'.[129] It is a driving force in the overall struggle of the radical right against the multicultural, feminist, or otherwise emancipatory and egalitarian concepts of the 1968 generation which gained momentum in the 1970s and 1980s and underpinned general sociocultural and political change in most West European societies. As the New Right denounces egalitarianism as Enemy Number One, it seeks to return to a hierarchical, organic social order in which community is held together by nation and family and by essential bonds of traditional values such as honour, virtue and duty.[130] One consequence of this, for example, was the peculiar move from the French *Nouvelle droite* to put such investment in reviving the Indo-European roots of European societies and presenting ancient societal concepts as counter-models to what they saw as atomistic and mechanistic conceptions of modern society. Opposition to the traditions of Judeo-Christianity and biblical monotheism resulted in the embrace of neo-paganism and polytheism, both of which, according to the *Nouvelle droite*, adequately translate the rootedness and ancient rituality of European religious belief.[131]

Finally, the New Right seeks to increase interest in authors of the so-called Conservative Revolution during the Weimar Republic.[132] In contrast to the generally accepted academic literature, the New Right regards the Conservative Revolution as a truly homogenous intellectual current of German conservatism and emphasises that its work is of great strategic and ideological value for contemporary intellectual and cultural struggles.[133] The New Right also dismisses the view, widely shared in academic scholarship, which argues that the intellectuals of the Conservative Revolution 'helped prepare the ground for National Socialism'.[134] In terms of an ideological and intellectual legacy, the New Right draws upon the Conservative Revolution's total critique of democracy and liberalism and the often-cited attitude of cultural despair that is best reflected in Oswald Spengler's 'Decline of the Occident'.[135] Referring to Carl Schmitt, considered one of the intellectual godfathers of the contemporary European New Right, and his denunciation of democracy as a symbol of political weakness and excessive pluralism, the New Right proposes concepts based on an organic and hierarchical order of politics and society, which would adequately honour – in the eyes of the New Right – the vital quest of the national community for unity and homogeneity.[136]

On the whole, the ideological mélange of the Conservative Revolution serves the New Right well by helping it to denounce, on the one hand, egalitarianism, globalisation and the Americanisation of European culture, whilst simultaneously substantiating the ethnopluralism and new nationalism expressed in its quest for nationally and culturally homogenous communities. Such selective amalgamation fits with Walter Laqueur's assessment that 'an examination of the New Right's ideology is like a visit to a supermarket (or a cemetery) of ideas and ideologies that have been selected in an attempt to produce a new synthesis'.[137]

The Extreme Right: Pariah Actors at the Fringe of Politics and Society

The extreme right, the third member of the political family of the radical right, differs from radical right-wing populist parties and New Right intellectuals in its style, appearance and objectives. The extreme right is, organisationally and structurally, perhaps the radical right's most autonomous and isolated member and represents the 'micro-mobilisation' of the radical right-wing political family.[138] When compared with the political parties and intellectual circles, the extreme right is characterised by a pronounced aggressiveness and severity of purpose and activity. Consequently, extreme-right activists and groups hold marginal positions in public space and act at the fringe of politics and society. They are generally stigmatised as pariah actors by the news media and perceived as deplorable contestants by other political groups. By engaging in militant and extremist activities, such as acts of violence or overtly racist propaganda, the extreme right often places itself outside the legal system.[139] Other members of the extreme right prefer to act within the legal frame and pursue a wide array of activities, mainly characterised by radical rhetoric and disruptive purposes. The ideological and intellectual foundations of verbal attacks, propaganda campaigns and conspiracy theories are rarely elaborate, particularly when they refer, often straightforwardly, to 'racial theories' or when they reveal anti-democratic purposes.[140]

As a member of the political family of the radical right, the extreme right embraces the radical-right worldview, marked by exclusionism and identity politics. It is also true, however, that its supporters promulgate more extreme versions of the ideological corpus than followers of radical right-wing populist parties and the New Right. For example, most extreme-right groups advocate classical racism or biologically founded anti-Semitism and refer openly to the ideological foundations of National Socialism and fascism as part of their intellectual legacy.[141] Of the three members of the radical right-wing political family, the worldview of the extreme right displays perhaps the most typically 'paranoid style' and conspiracist beliefs. They are conveyed in conspiracy theories asserting that various groups such as Jews, Freemasons or capitalists constitute evil forces and are the secret rulers of the world.[142]

In many ways, the contemporary extreme right takes on the appearance of a rebellious subculture that seeks to appeal outside the frame of conventional politics and culture. Like other subcultures, the extreme right aims at drawing a symbolic and cultural boundary between itself and the political and sociocultural environment and as a consequence creates a collective identity as a counterculture. References to an array of codes and symbols taken from fascist and National Socialist iconography and the celebration of ancient cults and festivities inspired by old Nordic and Germanic mythology all help to generate a common symbolic and cultural framework.[143] On the other hand, their collective stigmatisation as pariah actors by state authorities, media and the general public is perceived by the extreme right as a hostile expression of demarcation from mainstream society and ultimately reinforces its conception of itself as a marginalised subculture.[144]

2

SUCCESS CONDITIONS AND ORGANISATIONAL VARIATION IN SWITZERLAND

The radical right plays a significant role in Swiss politics and has been characterised by a remarkable continuity that extends throughout the postwar era. As in most Western European democracies, the Swiss radical right has evolved in a variety of organisational formations which can best be captured by the concepts developed above, of political family and collective actor. In order to explain the persistence of the Swiss radical right, it is necessary to examine variables identified by the comparative literature, which focus on the contextual factors including national traditions, socioeconomic changes, political institutions and discursive and cultural opportunities. They are considered to be possible success conditions in explanations of the emergence of radical-right politics in contemporary democracies. An examination of these factors challenges the argument that Switzerland should be seen as an exception and undermines the idea that conditions facilitating radical right-wing activities and mobilisation have been much less relevant in the particular case of Switzerland.

National Traditions: The Front Movement in the 1930s

As the literature on the postwar radical right correctly maintains, the political and economic conditions of the postwar era differ profoundly from the period of fascism and National Socialism and it is rather difficult, therefore, to elucidate similarities between the old fascist movements of the interwar years and the new radical right-wing movements which have emerged in postwar Europe.[1] However, the existence of successful radical right-wing movements in the past can still be a factor in explaining the success or failure of the contemporary radical right. As most country cases demonstrate, a radical right which draws, ideologically and organisationally, a direct line back to precursors from the 1930s and the 1940s and then presents them as historical models tends to lose much of its reputation and limits its potential appeal to a wider constituency. On the other hand, the radical right can claim legitimacy for its demands when advocates of nationalist and exclusionist ideas have a long tradition in a country's history, even when they are tied to the interwar period.[2]

In the 1930s, Switzerland, like most European countries, accounted for a range of radical right-wing and ultranationalist parties and groups, known under the umbrella term of the Front Movement (*Frontenbewegung*). While some tried to present themselves as a Swiss version of contemporary authoritarian and anti-democratic movements rejecting the liberal and pluralistic order, others referred directly to National Socialist and fascist ideologies and extolled the virtues of the neighbouring totalitarian regimes. When a number of newly founded groups and parties forcefully emerged in the political arena in spring of 1933, it was branded as the Springtime of Fronts (*Frontenfrühling*).[3] At the national level, however, the Fronts counted only one notable electoral success, when they won a single seat in the cantons of both Zurich and Geneva in the National Council elections of 1935. They were more successful at the cantonal and local government level and in the 1930s they held a number of seats in cantonal and municipal parliaments. In terms of social stratification, the Fronts received their electoral support from a range of social groups, including workers, employees, farmers, entrepreneurs and academics. The Fronts' candidates for public office also came from different social backgrounds. This variety contrasted starkly with most other political parties at the time, who mainly recruited their candidates from within distinct social strata.[4]

In 1940, the Swiss authorities began to issue orders to ban some of the more extremist organisations. After the end of the Second World War, the federal government hastened to draw a line under the history of domestic fascism and released a report in 1946 on anti-democratic activities in Switzerland during the war. In the report, which was, as some suggested, an example of 'a particularly favorable form of "controlled management of the past"',[5] it was argued that fascist and National Socialist groups had not represented a real threat to the country's stability and public order and that Swiss democracy had never really been put at risk. The report acknowledged, however, that at certain moments the groups' potential for subversion had been substantial, also due in no small part to the support they had received from National Socialist and fascist regimes in Europe.[6]

Overall, in comparison with most other European countries at the time, the groups and parties of the radical right in Switzerland did not succeed in rising up into a mass movement, and their political impact was rather ephemeral. Reasons for this failure can be found in the country's party system as well as in the internal structure of the parties. The composition of the mainstream centre-right parties in Switzerland, which are structurally and ideologically rather diversified, has facilitated the integration of more radical factions, eventually pulling the carpet from beneath the feet of the Front Movement. The weakness of the Front Movement was also the result of its organisational fragmentation in relation to the federalist structure of the Swiss party system, on the one hand, and of the power struggles and ideological disagreements that took place within the movement, on the other. Moreover, in comparison to many other European countries, the socioeconomic crisis of the 1920s and 1930s produced less political and social unrest in Switzerland of the kind which the radical right might otherwise have instrumentalized.

Finally, one should also not forget that, as historical studies have revealed in recent years, exclusionist ideas resulting in discriminatory attitudes and policies were anchored not only at the margins but also at the centre of Swiss politics and society.[7] This suggests that while an important radical right-wing potential existed in terms of attitudes and ideas, political actors at the far-right margin failed to translate it into large-scale political behaviour.

As we will see, to make direct or overt reference to the Front Movement was not an option in the postwar era for those on the radical right who sought to engage in the parliamentary arena and maximise their electoral support. At the same time, however, it is worth noting that some protagonists of the postwar radical right had previously been involved in groups that were part of the Front Movement. In addition, exclusionist and anti-pluralist patterns of thoughts that were drafted in the interwar years served as an intellectual legacy to the various currents of the postwar radical right.

Social Changes and the Support for the Radical Right

Like most Western European societies, Swiss society has undergone a course of profound transformation throughout the postwar period. The process of individualisation as a consequence of sociocultural modernisation has produced cleavages similar to those seen in other postindustrial societies. Swiss society has experienced the liberation of alignments from traditional social ties and political institutions, which has eventually resulted in a fragmentation of social life and in social disintegration. In the last twenty years or so, social fragmentation has been reinforced by basic economic changes, and by the accelerated flexibilization of labour structures in particular.[8] An important part of the research on the radical right in postwar Western Europe suggests that these changes in the social environment should be taken into account as macro-contexts for understanding the emergence of the radical right. By presenting rigid and closed systems of thought and counter-concepts that have drawn, above all, on the idea of a homogenous, nationally defined community and the return to traditional roles, the radical right has sought to respond to growing insecurity and a longing for greater clarity.[9] This becomes particularly salient at times when structural conflicts are increased by economic problems and material grievances, for example due to high unemployment or poor housing. It is therefore suggested that 'the dissatisfaction of the losers of the modernization process is being mobilized by the movements of the radical right'.[10] This line of argumentation would seem to be confirmed by electoral studies which show that political parties of the radical right in Western Europe tend to attract disproportionate numbers of socially disoriented and educationally disadvantaged people and find large support among the lower social classes and the unemployed.[11] One must consider, however, that while individualisation, social disintegration and economic uncertainty affect a large part of the population, only a minority is prepared to vote for the radical right or to espouse radical-right views.

As this study will show, parties of the radical right in Switzerland do indeed find electoral support from economically disadvantaged voters and people with limited exposure to formal education, as well as from sections of the working class. On the other hand, however, such parties traditionally appeal to a diverse electorate and tend to recruit their supporters across the lines of social class. Some attract an electorate that is composed of voters who are fairly well off and in good positions of employment. Moreover, the rise of Swiss radical right-wing populist parties has not necessarily correlated with times of economic crisis or recession. In the beginning of the 1970s, at the time when they made their first major electoral breakthrough, the economic situation in Switzerland was actually very good and the oil crisis and the economic slump had not yet happened. Conversely, the Swiss People's Party enjoyed dramatic electoral growth in the 1990s, while the Swiss economy was experiencing recession with rising rates of unemployment. Since 1991, the lingering economic crisis has resulted in unemployment rates higher than they have been since the 1930s. Examples of this were seen in 1994 and 1997, for example, with rates of 4.7 per cent and 5.2 per cent respectively, though these were still much lower than average unemployment rates of 8–11 per cent that were seen in countries of the

European Union.[12] Overall, it appears that the Swiss case shows the limitation of explanatory theories that seek to draw on social-structural and economic variables.

In the study of the radical right, theories of economic interest and material grievance also emerge in the debate concerning whether levels of voting for the radical right is higher among people who feel threatened by high rates of immigration or who associate immigration with growing unemployment and job competition.[13] Some argue that there is no correlation between immigration and levels of voting for these parties or the strengthening of hostile attitudes towards immigrants.[14] Others hold that the increase in the number of immigrants or the spatial concentration of immigrants represent favourable conditions for radical right-wing populist parties.[15] Following the latter argument, one might assume that the fact that Switzerland has, since the 1960s, accounted for one of the highest percentages of immigrant populations among Western European countries, would represent a contextual factor of major significance for the radical right. The number of immigrants living in Switzerland has risen from 9.3 per cent in 1960, to 15.9 per cent in 1970 and 14.1 per cent in 1980, and then to levels as high as 16.4 per cent in 1990 and 19.3 per cent in 2000. In addition, as can be seen in numerous opinion polls of the 1990s, a considerable section of the Swiss population reveals sceptical and discriminatory attitudes towards foreigners. A survey from 1995 shows, for example, that 39 per cent of the people interviewed said that the Swiss ought to have better opportunities than foreigners.[16] The present study will also give evidence that a large majority of the electorate of radical right-wing populist parties embraces attitudes that are hostile towards immigrants. It is still essential, however, to raise the question as to whether or not these parties construct and politicise the so-called 'immigration problem' and thereby evoke and reinforce anti-immigrant sentiments among the population. Moreover, a study supports the argument that the percentage of foreigners in particular areas of Switzerland does not correlate with the degree of xenophobia to be found among the local population.[17]

Some also argue that the parties of the radical right benefit from a decline in party identification and growing political alienation, as well as from decreasing confidence in political institutions.[18] Following this vein, electoral surveys show that volatile voters and those who distrust government and established parties are particularly well represented among radical right-wing constituencies. These processes of alienation and growing mistrust have also been noted in Switzerland during the last thirty years, potentially providing advantageous conditions for parties of the radical right. While the percentage of voters who identified themselves with a political party dropped from 59 per cent in 1975 to 42 per cent in 1995, the proportion of people who approved of how the government was doing its job decreased from 70 per cent in the mid 1970s to 40 per cent in the mid 1990s.[19] Another indication was the consistent fall-off in turnout at federal elections and popular votes, which reached an average of around 40 per cent, an all-time low, in the 1990s, although referendums on some particularly controversial issues like membership of the European Economic Area in 1992 brought up to 78 per cent of the voters to the ballot.[20]

Finally, there is also a tendency to explain the rise of the radical right in terms of the postmaterialist turn in the 1970s and 1980s, through which material concerns as well as traditional values lost much of their importance and gave rise to what is called 'new politics'.[21] Following this line of argumentation, the radical right is supposed to appeal to segments of the population that are opposed to the postmaterialist agenda and to those ideas of grass-roots democracy, emancipation and equality which are promoted by the New Left and new social movements.[22] Switzerland belonged to the group of West European countries where an array of new social movements made a forceful breakthrough in the 1970s and 1980s, addressing issues of ecology, women's emancipation, pacifism, issues of civil and human rights and alternative culture.[23] In addition, while postmaterialist values found considerable support amongst the population, the issues and concerns of 'new politics' entered onto the stage of Swiss mainstream politics, not least with the consolidation of the Greens in the Swiss party system.[24]

As the present study will show, it is a prime goal of the radical right, vividly expressed in the New Right's ideological endeavours, to counter the postmaterialist agenda and sociocultural legacy of the 1968 movement. Thus, the radical right both supplied and benefited from the process in which postmaterialist values have lost much of their salience in Swiss society in the last fifteen years. As recent studies on value change emphasise, the postmaterialist/materialist cleavage seems to have been replaced in the 1990s by a new, so-called opening/traditional cleavage, which favoured the rise of the SVP and basically opposed two constituencies: on the one hand, those who support Switzerland opening up to the outside world, who defend emancipatory values and embrace a tolerant attitude towards foreigners; and on the other, those who reject both the country's international involvement and equality of opportunities for Swiss citizens and foreigners, who emphasise the defence of Swiss traditions, and who hold up the concepts of authority and order.[25]

The Openness of the Swiss Political System

Another set of explanatory theories employed in the study of the radical right addresses the structures of political opportunity, including the institutional setting and political context in which the radical right undertakes political mobilisation. It is argued that the degree of openness of the political system provides conditions which foster or impede the evolution of the radical right into a serious political competitor. A key question to consider would be the matter of which institutional channels might be available for the radical right to articulate political claims and intervene in policy-making processes.[26] In the case of Switzerland, it is essential to bear in mind that the political system is based on direct democracy which offers the most powerful means of action to the radical right and hence allows a considerable degree of openness in the political system.

At the national level, there are three institutions of Swiss direct democracy. First, the popular initiative calls for a partial revision of the constitution and must be signed by one hundred thousand eligible voters. Second, international treaties and many legislative acts are subject to an optional referendum, meaning that they must be submitted to a vote if so requested by fifty thousand eligible voters. Third, revisions of the constitution and membership in organisations for collective security or supranational communities are subject to a mandatory referendum.[27] Most significantly, the system of direct democracy allows the Swiss radical right to lead political campaigns with the result that large sections of the public become more familiar with the goals and ideology of the radical right. Small parties of the radical right can ensure their political survival by focusing on direct democratic opportunities without having to direct the bulk of their efforts to election and parliamentary work.[28] For them, the means of direct democracy represent a remarkable opportunity structure by which to mobilise constituencies, exert continuous pressure on the formation of public policy, and to weaken mainstream parties.[29] Since popular votes represent the most meaningful channels 'for venting voter dissatisfaction with the state and with the behavior of political leaders', the parties of the radical right are keen to use direct-democratic instruments in their populist campaigns against the political establishment.[30] Finally, as this study will show, since direct-democratic activities bring together various factions of the radical right and generate specific mobilisation events, they are essential for the radical right to function as collective actor.

Federalism is another key institutional setting of the Swiss political system and it also serves the radical right as an opportunity structure.[31]

Although federalism weakens national parties, making it difficult for them to develop strong party organisation and internal cohesion, it strengthens parties at the cantonal level and enables them to put issues on the national agenda which might only be advocated by a minority in the national party.[32] This is evocatively demonstrated by the role that the cantonal SVP party of Zurich played in the process of transformation undergone by the national SVP in the 1990s. The federalist structure of the Swiss party system also provides good conditions for the emergence of the radical right in the form of fringe-based, sometimes regionally-based parties. A common assumption related to federalism is the notion that proportional representation encourages the electoral rise of radical right-wing populist parties.[33] In Switzerland, the proportional system is applied in elections to the National Council, the Swiss parliament's lower chamber of two hundred members. This offers relatively easy access because it has no formal threshold that applies countrywide. In fact, since each canton represents an electoral district of highly different population size, the threshold in large cantons is much lower than in cantons with a small population. In cantons with a large population such as Zurich, Bern, Geneva and Basel, small parties of the radical right have good prospects of winning seats in the National Council. On the other hand, members of the Council of States, the upper chamber of forty-six members, are elected by majority rule in most cantons and therefore representatives of small parties have very little chance of being elected.[34]

As many studies of radical right-wing parties argue, the potential emergence of these parties has much to do with the strategic convergence of mainstream parties. When major left-wing and right-wing parties cluster around the centre, the political space opens to parties from the radical right and gives them the opportunity to apply a strategy of delegitimization against the political establishment.[35] The convergence of major left-wing and right-wing parties can appear in a well-established mode, such as the consociational system of governance, which in the case of Switzerland, represents a key characteristic of the political system.[36] The country's consensual politics and remarkable postwar political stability strongly relate to the establishment of the 'magic formula' in 1959 as the guiding principle of Swiss governance. For more than forty years, the grand coalition was comprised of two members each from the Liberal Democratic Party (*Freisinnig-Demokratische Partei* – FDP), the Christian-Democratic People's Party (*Christlichdemokratische Volkspartei* – CVP) and the Social-Democratic Party of Switzerland (*Sozialdemokratische Partei der Schweiz* – SPS), plus one member from the Swiss People's Party (SVP).[37]

Only the 2003 election of Christoph Blocher brought to an end this informal rule of the governmental coalition. His election made him the second representative of the SVP in the seven-headed Federal Council, thereby replacing one of the two members previously taken from the CVP. The system of consociational governance consistently served as a target of the anti-establishment rhetoric applied by parties of the radical right which sought to appeal to the increased number of Swiss voters expressing dissatisfaction and mistrust towards parties and political institutions. On this matter, in the 1990s, the SVP started to play its particular role of 'oppositional co-governance' by challenging the concordance policy between government parties from the left and right, while remaining in the government coalition.[38]

National Identity, Swiss Exceptionalism and Fears of 'Overforeignization'

In recent studies on the radical right, some argue that the political opportunity approach fails to take into account the broader cultural and discursive determinants of political mobilisation. They propose the concept of discursive or cultural opportunity structure to capture how the radical right mobilises symbolic and cultural resources in order to set forth their proposals. This corresponds to reflections made by historians who emphasise that public resonance and the success of political actions depend upon cultural and ideological frameworks that already exist in society.[39] In recent years, this approach has mainly drawn attention to the significance that conceptions of nationhood and citizenship have for the radical right, suggesting that it basically 'mobilizes an ethnic-cultural framing of national identity against the idea of the nation as a political or civic community'.[40]

Typically, Switzerland is described by leading scholars of nationalism as a 'voluntary nation' (*Willensnation*) and a classic example of a state-nation founded on political institutions.[41] The Swiss federal state unites four ethnoculturally distinct regions, each with its own language and culture. This is seen as one of the main pillars of Swiss national identity, along with the institutional mixture represented by the three core elements of direct democracy, federalism and neutrality.[42] It could be argued, therefore, that it is difficult for the Swiss radical right to exploit civic nationalism, because its ultranationalist discourse relies on the concept of a homogenous ethnic and cultural nation. However, it is important to take two crucial points into consideration when discussing the Swiss radical right's way of referring to Swiss national identity and nationhood.

First, the country's self-perception as a national community is shaped by a long-term process of inventing national traditions that emphasise the Swiss people's common mentality, as well as shared historical and geographic experiences, which have collectively generated some kind of organically grown national culture.[43] Following this line of argumentation, Didier Froidevaux claims that the continuous construction of national ideas and myths contributed to 'an ethnic construction relying on a perception of Switzerland as an exceptional or insular case'.[44] This view is supported by studies on Swiss citizenship, which point to the highly exclusionist basis of the country's nationhood. From this perspective, Swiss citizenship policy comes close to an ethnic-assimilationist model and is more comparable to Germany than to France or Great Britain. Not only are there high institutional and cultural obstacles to the process of naturalisation, but migrants are also required to give proof of the degree of their assimilation in the public sphere, while their cultural differences enjoy very little recognition.[45] Such a framing of Swiss nationhood represents a historically and culturally determined opportunity structure that the radical right is able to draw on in its nationalist agenda and exclusionist migration policies.[46] Second, in the voluntarist conception of Swiss nationhood, political institutions assume an exalted, almost naturalised meaning when they are conceived of as a constant foundation of the country's 'civic exceptionalism' whose origins go a long way back in history. In this respect, the radical right present the country's institutional settings as distinctive and unique features of Switzerland's authenticity that must be preserved in times of changes, come what may.[47]

The radical right firmly believes in its mission to defend Switzerland against alleged threats from external forces and to demarcate the country from the outside world. Applying the notion that Switzerland represents an 'exceptional case' (*Sonderfall*) that is constantly at risk, the radical right is able to rely on the longstanding conception of what has been described as a national identity based on a 'negative identity'.[48] From this view, many Swiss national myths refer to fights of liberation from foreign powers (William Tell), or to the call for a strong will to defend the country against foreign invaders (Second World War). In a similar way, neutrality, a long-standing doctrine of Swiss foreign policy, is utilised by many to demarcate the country from the external world and this consequently reinforces the country's isolated position.

As some of the constituents of Swiss exceptionalism came under increasing scrutiny in the 1990s, the radical right assumed the role of presenting itself as the upright defender of the country's national identity. For example, the reference to Switzerland as an exceptional case served as an effective cultural and discursive resource in the area of foreign policy, when the federal government began to redefine its policy of neutrality and to seek international integration, particularly in terms of Switzerland's move towards the European Union.[49] In fact, the successful campaign against EEA membership, rejected in a popular vote in December 1992, represented a turning point for the radical right, which has managed to keep foreign policy as a contentious issue on the national agenda ever since.

The controversy over Switzerland's role during the Second World War was another debate of the 1990s where the notion of Switzerland as a special case was at stake. Throughout the postwar period, large sections of the polity and general public had consistently ignored the critical assessments made by historical studies into Switzerland's wartime past, preferring to draw the picture of a country that was courageously steadfast and independent.[50] But when the issue of 'unclaimed' Jewish assets in Swiss banks received a great deal of international and domestic attention in 1996 and 1997, the country began to face growing criticism, for its refugee policy in particular, as well as its economic and financial ties to the Third Reich.[51] During this unprecedented public discussion, large parts of the Swiss radical right invested heavily in an attempt to preserve a collective memory shaped by the notion of Swiss exceptionalism and based around the idea that neutrality and a well-prepared army were the key reasons for the country not being invaded by Hitler.

Another important discursive and symbolic frame in Switzerland is represented by the 'discourse of overforeignization', which is unique in Europe for its persistence throughout the twentieth century and has consistently been utilised by the radical right to construct and to politicise the boundary between 'us' and the 'other'. Initially developed by Swiss intellectuals and politicians before the First World War, the term 'overforeignization' is used as a sociocultural code to express the perception and exclusion of socially segregated groups supposed to have distinguishing cultural features that set them apart. In the interwar years, the notion of alleged 'overforeignization' served as a foundation of the newly implemented migration legislation and as a tool in anti-Semitic arguments for limiting the numbers of Jewish refugees.[52] In the 1960s, the term 'overforeignization' was revived, and it became a frame of reference for large parts of Swiss politics, including state authorities, left-wing parties and trade unions. While the emerging parties of the radical right were able to benefit from this widely touted discourse of exclusion, they also radicalised it with their demands for restriction on immigration and channelled it into political action in the 1960s and

1970s.[53] In the two decades that followed, while the focus of their anti-immigration agenda shifted from so-called 'guest workers' (i.e., the citizens of southern European countries) to asylum seekers and refugees from the former Yugoslavia, from Turkey and from Asian and African countries, the parties of the radical right continued to stir up fears of 'overforeignization'.[54]

The persisting effect of this type of exclusionist discourse is revealed in numerous surveys which indicate that a considerable section of the Swiss population has been receptive to xenophobic attitudes and expressions of mistrust towards immigrants. A comparison of two identically constructed surveys among men living in the city of Zurich notes that 56.7 per cent of those interviewed in 1969 said that Switzerland is 'overforeignized', while in 1995 this view was still being expressed by 38 per cent.[55] According to an opinion poll conducted during the 1995 national elections, 39 per cent of people interviewed said that the Swiss ought to have better opportunities than foreigners.[56] As indicated by a poll from 1994, 24 per cent of those interviewed insisted that the 'mixing of peoples' was something to be avoided and that the purity of 'Swissness' (*Schweizertum*) was something that must be considered.[57]

Prejudices and stereotypes directed against Jews fuelled another exclusionist discourse that has an extended tradition in Switzerland. After the Second World War, the issue of anti-Semitism was long seen as a taboo in public discussions and an ideological feature linked exclusively to German National Socialism and pariah groups of the extreme right.[58] During the historical debate over the 'unclaimed' Jewish assets in Swiss banks and the country's role in the Second World War, Switzerland experienced a visible rise in public expressions of anti-Semitic sentiments, which appeared in the form of conspiracy theories asserting Jewish influence over the economic and financial world and in allegations about Jews' greed for money.[59] As shown by an opinion poll carried out in 2000, 16 per cent of persons interviewed and 33 per cent of those who said they voted for the Swiss People's Party expressed anti-Jewish attitudes. The survey further indicates that 39 per cent of the respondents said that Jews were exploiting remembrance of the Shoah for their own interests and 32 per cent believed that Jews show more loyalty towards Israel than towards Switzerland.[60]

The Political Family of the Radical Right in Switzerland

As shown, the case of Switzerland presents a variety of conditions on the demand and the supply side that are potentially favourable for the emergence and consolidation of a radical right. However, these explanatory approaches largely fail to take into account the central role that political actors play in the multi-dimensional relationship between context and attitudes, between institutions and mobilisation, between discourse and actions. They also tend to overlook the fact that radical-right politics and attitudes gain relevance when they are translated into political process and public debates by organised actors.[61] This becomes evident when we ask, for example, what is the role that political actors play in the construction and politicisation of the so-called immigration problem, how do they shape the perception of 'times of crisis', and what kind of solutions are they presenting?[62] We also need to consider that the actual experience of social disintegration or economic problems is often less relevant than the subjective dimension and many 'merely' believe themselves to be menaced by ongoing socioeconomic and cultural changes, or display a tendency to perceive unfair distribution and unachieved expectation as relative deprivation.[63] Following this reasoning, the present study emphasises the significant role played by organised actors, both political and intellectual, in the processes which determine how political issues are constructed, defined and perceived. With this in mind, our prime focus here is therefore to examine the different members of the political family of the Swiss radical right.

By assuming a dominant position in the political family of the radical right in Switzerland, radical right-wing populist parties have proved their astounding persistence, despite notable structural and electoral changes that they have encountered since the 1960s. From a cross-national perspective, there are several reasons why the development of Swiss radical right-wing populism appears to be particularly interesting. First of all, Switzerland was a forerunner of radical right-wing populism in Western Europe. With the emergence of the parties of the Movement against Overforeignization in the 1960s, Switzerland was one of the first countries to account for a new type of radical right-wing party that conspicuously avoided drawing on a fascist legacy. Moreover, since the end of the Second World War, Switzerland has seen seven different radical right-wing populist parties that have at some point been represented in the National Council. Among the democracies of Western Europe, therefore, Switzerland has recorded the largest number of radical right-wing populist parties to have elected national MPs. Another notable feature is the fact, that with the rise of the new Swiss People's Party (SVP) in the 1990s, Switzerland has produced one of the most electorally and politically important parties in what has been described as the third wave of West European radical right-wing populism since the Second World War. Despite its radicalisation in the 1990s, the SVP has managed to remain in the government coalition and so it also provides a prominent example of a European right-wing populist party in national executive office.

The postwar history of radical right-wing populist parties in Switzerland can be divided into three main phases. The first phase, from the early 1960s to the mid 1980s, witnessed the creation of four fringe parties from the Movement against Overforeignization. They received just a small share of the vote in elections and remained at the margin of the Swiss party system, but managed to exert considerable pressure on government and polity by using the instruments of direct democracy. The second phase, from the mid 1980s to the early 1990s, was characterised both by the emergence of new parties and a persisting fringe status within the party system. The continuity of the Movement against Overforeignization was assured by the oldest party of the Swiss radical right, while the new parties reinforced the traditional fragmentation of the radical right-wing populist party camp and added new elements to its political agenda, such as neoliberal economy policies and regionalist identity politics. Since the early 1990s, the third phase has been marked by fundamental changes and none have had greater repercussions than the shift which occurred at the core of the SVP. The 'old' SVP had enjoyed a long-established tradition as a mainstream right-wing party and coalition partner in government. With this historical capital still exerting an influence, the party's transformation and radicalisation in the 1990s had the effect of bringing a major radical right-wing populist party to the very heart of mainstream Swiss politics and also made it possible for the party to absorb a considerable amount of support from the fringe parties on the right-wing margin. Hence, by the late 1990s, the long-standing diversification had largely faded and the new SVP became the dominant party in Swiss radical right-wing populism.

The New Right in Switzerland consists of various currents that supply ideas and discourse to the radical right and to radical right-wing populist parties in particular. While most adherents to the New Right avoid using this term and prefer to call themselves 'conservatives' or 'right-wing bourgeois' (*Rechtsbürgerliche*), from a comparative perspective, it is appropriate to use 'New Right' to describe an intellectual current which is embedded in a transnational network and characterised by common ideas. Some followers of the New Right are mainly interested in the world of culture and ideas and pursue a cultural and 'metapolitical' strategy. They provide support to the ideological realm of the radical right in the form of intellectual 'legitimacy' and discursive tools. Others are deliberately involved with everyday politics and often even directly associated with political parties. As what we could call parapolitical actors, they also engage in direct democratic and other political campaigns and aim at addressing a larger public.

In terms of organisation, in much the same way as has been seen in other Western European countries, the Swiss New Right has made itself felt in an organisational array of study groups, associations, publications and intellectuals since the late 1960s. In terms of organisational variation and sources of intellectual inspiration, there are significant differences between the New Right factions in the respective German- and French-speaking parts of Switzerland. These factions rarely collaborate with each other and have only a small number of organisational links. Moreover, in contrast to its counterparts in France and Germany, the Swiss New Right has so far failed to form a prolific intellectual movement capable of developing innovative theories and sophisticated concepts, or of establishing an intellectually spirited current of thought. To some degree, the Swiss New Right confines itself to reproducing and referencing ideas and work produced by theorists from abroad and applying them to Swiss discussions. Unlike the radical right-wing populist parties, therefore, the Swiss New Right is far more integrated in an international environment of ideas and debates and is consequently inspired by counterparts in other European countries. On the other hand, however, some of the German-speaking currents of the Swiss New Right seek to demonstrate their independence from external intellectual influences. They are keen to present arguments and ideas which draw on a Swiss intellectual legacy, for example, when it comes to casting conceptions of the country's national identity or emphasising the extraordinary significance of the Swiss 'special case'.

As in most European countries, the extreme right has managed to establish itself in Switzerland, as a subculture occupying a position at the outermost fringe of politics and public discourse. Membership in the extreme right is limited, with the core of active members and supporters not exceeding one thousand in the late 1990s. Characterised by organisational variation and a diverse repertoire of action, the extreme right mainly confines its activities to the extraparliamentary domain. Some members of the extreme right act outside the legal system by committing violent acts and by circulating overtly racist propaganda. The extreme right, especially in its combative and violent forms, regularly provokes criticism and indignation in the Swiss public. A long-standing feature of the Swiss extreme right lies in its international ties and relationships. This was considerably reinforced in the 1990s by the increased globalisation of international right-wing extremism and the emergence of new communication technologies.

The development of the Swiss extreme right since 1945 can be roughly divided into three phases. The first phase, from the mid 1940s to the mid 1980s, was characterised by the underground nature of the Swiss extreme right. A number of isolated individuals and groups were active and they addressed a small community dedicated to the realm of neo-fascism. Compared with other European publics, namely those in Germany, Italy, Austria and France, the Swiss public was rarely confronted by the propaganda or organisational manifestations of the extreme right. In the second phase, from the mid 1980s to the early 1990s, the Swiss extreme right underwent major changes, similar to those seen in other West European countries. It developed into a new, diversified subculture and went public by disseminating propaganda and organising an array of actions. The insurgency of militant, mainly young activists brought a new dimension of violence into extreme-right activities, predominantly directed against asylum seekers and their lodgings. The third phase, which began in the early 1990s, is characterised by a consolidation of the Swiss extreme-right subculture. Despite loose structures and fluctuations in organisation and personnel, the extreme right succeeded in sustaining a network of groups, publications and activists. While the number of violent acts declined after 1991, the propensity for violent offences continued to characterise the extreme right.

The reactions of the authorities and law enforcement agencies towards the Swiss extreme right have changed notably since the 1980s and reflect the changing nature of the extreme right, as well as the changing repertoire of actions used by extreme-right groups, such as the increased use of violence. However, the authorities often lagged behind the pace of actual developments in their evaluations of right-wing extremism and it was not until the late 1990s that their policies were properly enshrined in terms of legislation and law enforcement, or fully took account of the labour and expertise of the various social institutions with experience at the sharp end of extreme-right activity, such as researchers, educationalists and social workers.

The three members of the political family of the radical right in Switzerland have developed a set of interactions and linkages which help to hold the different factions together and allow them to function as a collective actor. There are distinct points of intersection in the areas of mobilisation contexts, organisational and personal contacts and joint activities. The closest relationship exists between the political parties and the New Right. Some party officials contribute to New Right publications, participate in events organised by the New Right, or are members of New Right circles and groups. Conversely, a considerable number of New Right followers consistently engage in party politics, speak at party assemblies, or take party offices. In some ways, the shifting borders between commitment to intellectual and cultural endeavours and engagement in partisan activities have been more fluid among the Swiss New Right than they have among their West European counterparts. Similar types of structural and personal linkages also exist between the New Right and the extreme right in Switzerland, but to a much lesser extent. Some New Right followers began their career in militant factions of the extreme right, before moving to intellectual and ideologically oriented activities. Others try to serve as ideological masterminds that operate behind the scenes of the extreme right and seek to raise levels of intellectualisation in young activists. On the other hand, some of the extreme-right groups are keen to invite members of New Right circles to give talks, or make reference to writings by authors from the New Right in their own propaganda.

As is confirmed by most research on the radical right in Western Europe, it is more difficult to capture the linkage between radical right-wing populist parties and the extreme right. In terms of organisation and activity, the extreme right usually prefers to act autonomously and typically rejects cooperation with existing political parties. Moreover, by expressing overtly racist and fascist views and/or by committing acts of violence, the extreme right relegates itself to the outermost fringe of the political scene and puts itself into the position of a pariah actor.[64] On the other hand, 'radical right-wing populist parties have been rather careful to distance themselves from the extreme Right' and conspicuously attempt to apply strategies of demarcation with respect to the extreme right, since the public reacts with outrage to any kind of association with the extreme right.[65] As a consequence, a central difficulty inherent in examining these linkages relates to methodological questions and the character of available information and it appears to be difficult to gather publicly accessible sources and documentation for research.

Unlike most other European countries, postwar Switzerland has not seen the establishment of a larger political party that emerged as the direct product of extreme-right political endeavours, or was otherwise closely associated with the extreme right. For many members of the extreme right, the lack of alternative options ensured that the only way to engage in party politics was to join radical right-wing populist parties. In this way, numerous structural linkages have been developed between radical right-wing populist parties and the extreme right. In view of the afore-mentioned methodological difficulties, the present study does not produce a systematic inquiry or conclusive assessments regarding all the potential points of intersection. Instead, it presents an examination based on a typology of potential linkages, substantiated by selected examples and pointing to key features of identified interactions within the political family of the radical right. To begin with, the typology draws on the general distinction between instances where extreme rightists involve themselves with radical right-wing populist parties, on the one hand, and the participation of members of radical right-wing parties in extreme right activities, on the other.

The first set of instances of involvement includes cases where extreme-right ideologues and activists have experienced a political socialisation within radical right-wing populist parties, as well as specific mobilisation events (e.g., popular initiatives, rallies, public meetings), at which radical right-wing populist parties are joined by extreme-right groups. Another type of relationship shows extreme-right groups and publications making distinct endorsements for political parties and their policies. The second set of linkage types presents those collaborations and activities that members of radical right-wing populist parties undertake in the context of the extreme right, including organisational collaboration, isolated activities and personal contacts. Investigation of these involvements takes into account the position that respective party members hold in the party hierarchy. While the links of low-ranking party members to the extreme right obviously bears less weight, the involvement of leading party officials is of great political significance and often provokes fierce reactions from the media and the public.

The following chapters examine organisations, activities and mobilization patterns that the Swiss radical right has developed since the end of the Second World War. The Swiss radical right has been able to take advantage of socioeconomic conditions in Switzerland that were not fundamentally different from those seen in other Western European countries, as well as additional contextual factors such as the relative openness of the political system and certain types of national discourse. While looking separately at the three main members of the political family, the study consistently pays attention to the commonality of ideological features and sources of intellectual inspiration, as well as to the linkages that exist between the three family members.

3

AN EARLY PRECURSOR: THE MOVEMENT AGAINST OVERFOREIGNIZATION IN THE 1960S AND 1970S

The first expression of radical right-wing populist parties in postwar Switzerland was the Movement against Overforeignization which made its appearance on the political stage in the early 1960s. When the movement emerged, its numerous and constant anti-immigrant campaigns were unique in Europe. Together with the Poujadist movement, a short-lived populist movement from the mid 1950s in France, it represents in many ways the political precursor to today's radical right-wing populism in Western Europe.[1] Although leading figures of the Movement against Overforeignization had already been active in the Front Movement of the 1930s, they conspicuously avoided making reference to this interwar movement.

The label 'Movement against Overforeignization' is used as a blanket term for four fringe radical right-wing populist parties that were founded between the early 1960s and the mid 1970s. These included National Action (founded in 1961), Vigilance (1964), the Swiss Republican Movement (1971) and the Swiss Democratic Union (1975). When viewed collectively as a movement, these parties were bound together by strong anti-immigrant sentiments and a common political agenda that aimed at toughening the country's policies towards immigrants and foreign residents. When the first groups were founded, they had few organisational resources and stressed that they sought to maintain a position outside the established party system. To a greater degree than other Swiss parties, they relied on street propaganda, public meetings and mass events for their public campaigning. Overall, the parties from the Movement against Overforeignization showed particular interest in mobilising support beyond the conventional channels of political participation.

A Divided Movement of Fringe Parties

National Action against Overforeignization of People and Homeland (*Nationale Aktion gegen die Überfremdung von Volk und Heimat* – NA) was founded in 1961 by Fritz Meier and advanced to become the main political force in the Movement against Overforeignization.[2] While NA was initially intended to be a fairly unstructured anti-immigrant group, it began to reinforce its organisational structures and to build up a well-organised party apparatus. In 1966, NA launched the party paper *Nationale Aktion* and released one hundred thousand copies of a promotional issue. Two years later, the paper was rechristened *Volk + Heimat* (People and Homeland) and ultimately came to play a vital role in the party organisation. According to NA's own information, the paper had a circulation of twenty-two thousand in the mid 1970s. In 1967, NA made its first major political breakthrough at the national level, when James Schwarzenbach was elected to the National Council and the party got its first parliamentary seat. The large public debate over the 'Schwarzenbach Initiative' (*Schwarzenbach-Initiative*), the first federal initiative launched by NA (see below), and its narrow defeat in 1970, gave the party an enormous political boost and by 1969–70, NA had succeeded in establishing itself as a serious political force on the Swiss political scene.

With James Schwarzenbach (1911–1994), the Movement against Overforeignization produced the first radical right-wing populist politician of the country's postwar era and one of Switzerland's best-known political leaders of the twentieth century.[3] He came from a well-known industrialist family in Zurich and converted to Catholicism at the age of twenty-two. In 1940, he graduated from the University of Fribourg with a PhD in history. In the early 1930s, Schwarzenbach was a member of the National Front, a group from the Front Movement, and he wrote articles for its party organ. In 1934, he played a leading role in a riot organised by the National Front that targeted a renowned cabaret house in Zurich and he was subsequently arrested by the police. In his later years, he stated that he used to have sympathies with the regimes of Franco in Spain and Dollfuss in Austria. In 1947, Schwarzenbach took over the publishing house Thomas–Verlag, which, among other titles, carried extreme-right books on its publisher's list. Alongside his publishing activities, Schwarzenbach worked as a journalist, and in 1961 he acquired the *Schweizerische Republikanische Blätter* (Swiss Republican Papers), a newspaper whose origin dates back to the end of the eighteenth century. He renamed it *Der Republikaner* (The Republican) and thanks to his activities as a publisher, journalist and writer, as well as his lecture tours as an anti-communist campaigner, Schwarzenbach was a well-known public figure before he embarked upon his second career in 1967, this time as a political leader.

In the 1960s, Schwarzenbach became the 'charismatic personification'[4] of the emerging Movement against Overforeignization and his radical right-wing populist manner demonstrated similarities to contemporaries like Jean-Louis Tixier-Vignancour in France and Enoch Powell in the U.K. In his political style and technique, he was a truly modern populist politician who made skilful use of the mass media to suit his purposes, especially where the newly emerging medium of television was concerned. His populist leadership and strategy were important factors that allowed the movement to attract great public attention and considerable electoral support, particularly in the late1960s and early 1970s.

After 1970, developments within the Movement against Overforeignization were characterised by power struggles and doctrinal quarrels. Most importantly, after internal disagreements over the party's future course of action, James Schwarzenbach left NA in late 1970 and went on to found the Swiss Republican Movement (*Schweizerische Republikanische Bewegung* – SRB) in 1971. Exerting authoritarian leadership, Schwarzenbach built up a hierarchical party organisation and provided the official party paper, *Der Republikaner*.[5] According to its own figures, the paper had 3,500 subscribers in March 1971. While Schwarzenbach made reassurances that all he intended was simply to establish a patriotic movement advocating a political agenda based upon Christian-conservatives values, the exclusionist tendency of the party was evident from the very beginning. The first manifesto, published in late 1970, noted that the fight against the 'overforeignization' of Switzerland in terms of politics, economy, population and culture should represent a guiding principle.[6] Hence, it became clear that the SRB would retain the tradition of the Movement against Overforeignization and act as a competitor to NA in the area of migration policy.

Despite their rivalry, the SRB and NA experienced great success in the National Council elections of 1971. The SRB received more than 4 per cent of the vote straight off, conquering seven seats in the National Council (tables 3.1 and 3.2). NA increased its vote share from 0.6 to 3.2 per cent and thus had four representatives on the National Council.[7] As noted by Urs Altermatt, no outsider party had achieved such a breakthrough into the traditional party system of Switzerland since 1935.[8] Among the elected NA members was Walter Jäger-Stamm, a former member of the National Front in the 1930s.[9] As election surveys suggest, NA and the SRB were disproportionately supported by voters living in the suburbs of larger cities. Though the SRB found more supporters among voters from the middle class, the two parties drew most of their support from the workers, employees and voters of the lower social classes. To some degree, this corresponds to the voter profile commonly described by the electoral study of parties of the radical right. Surveys of the 1971 elections also show that it was only in a few regions that there was a correlation between the proportion of foreign residents living in the area and the vote for NA and the SRB. It is further suggested that the voters of NA and the SRB displayed a fairly high degree of scepticism towards the political elite and that they had previously given their support to left-wing parties.[10]

Table 3.1 | *Results of NA and SRB in National Council Elections, 1967–1987*

	1967	1971	1975	1979	1983	1987
National Action	0.6	3.2	2.5	1.3	2.9	2.5
Republican Movement[1]	–	4.3	3.0	0.6	0.5	0.3

Note: [1] Includes Vigilance's share of vote in the canton of Geneva
Source: Die Bundesversammlung – Das Schweizer Parlament, http://www.parlament.ch/d/dokumentation/statistiken/Documents/wa-nr-nationalratswahlen-waehlerstimmen-1919.xls, retrieved 31 August 2008.

Table 3.2 | *Seats of NA, SRB and Vigilance in the National Council, 1967–1987*

	1967	1971	1975	1979	1983	1987
National Action	1	4	2	2	4	3
Republican Movement	–	7	3	–	–	–
Vigilance	–	–	1	1	1	–

Source: Die Bundesversammlung – Das Schweizer Parlament, http://www.parlament.ch/d/dokumentation/statistiken/Documents/ed-rueckblick-47-leg-mandate-nr.pdf, retrieved 31 August 2008.

Success in the elections of 1971 turned out to be the high point for the Movement against Overforeignization. In the two national elections that followed, both parties lost much of their electorate and their combined number of MPs declined from eleven in 1971 to three in 1979.[11] After Schwarzenbach retreated from politics for health reasons in June 1978, the SRB suffered a devastating defeat in the 1979 National Council elections and lost all of its MPs, while NA managed to hold on to its two MPs. As a result, some leading SRB members deserted to the Swiss People's Party and the party's agonising decline was set in motion, a process which was to end with the dissolution of the SRB in 1989.[12]

There are two main reasons for the party's electoral decline after the initial success of the early 1970s. First, the setbacks reflected the fact that the migration issue had lost much of its salience. In the 1970s, the Swiss government gradually implemented restrictive measures to stabilise and eventually reduce the percentage of immigrants and foreign residents in Switzerland.[13] By the mid 1970s, the country had started to be affected by the worldwide economic crisis and the government reacted by reducing the number of foreign workers allowed to enter the country.[14] Some authors argue that the Swiss government has, to a certain degree, 'exported' the expected increase in rates of unemployment by limiting immigration.[15] In so doing, the government made it difficult for anti-immigrant parties to exploit the migration issue in the context of economic recession.

Second, dissension and conflict between and within NA and the SRB played a major role in the way that broad sections of the parties' electorate lost political faith in the Movement against Overforeignization and in the parties' own failure to present much in the way of common policy proposals. Moreover, Schwarzenbach's authoritarian leadership regularly attracted strong criticism from other leading members of the party. Within NA too, party leadership and cohesion were regularly jeopardised by the kind of squabbling among senior party members that occasionally came to an end only in court.[16]

With the Geneva-based Vigilance party, another anti-immigrant political force made its appearance on the national stage in the mid 1970s and won its first seat in the National Council elections of 1975.[17] Vigilance had been officially associated with the Republican Movement at the national level since 1972 and presented an electoral alliance with the SRB in the National Council elections of 1975. It received 6.9 per cent of the vote in the canton of Geneva, leading to the election of Mario Soldini, a former member of the National Union and close collaborator of the interwar Front Movement leader Georges Oltramare.[18] Soldini was twice reelected and remained a member of the National Council until 1987.

The Vigilance party had already been in existence at cantonal level since 1964.[19] When Vigilance gained a clear 10 per cent of the vote in the 1965 elections in the canton of Geneva and conquered ten of the hundred seats in the Great Council, it was viewed as a political sensation.[20] In the two decades that followed, the party basically consolidated its electoral base in the canton of Geneva (1969: 5.9%; 1973: 9.3%; 1977:

8.0%; 1981: 7.7%). With its monthly party paper *Vigilance*, established in 1964 and renamed *Le Vigilant* in 1978, the party had a forceful public voice at its disposal. The paper had a circulation of some eight to ten thousand, which even rose as high as sixty thousand in times of elections.[21] The main goal of Vigilance was to play an oppositional role in the politics of the city of Geneva, challenging the established political parties on matters related to tax issues and the privileged status of international organisations and their employees based in Geneva. In a party manifesto from 1965, the Vigilance party also declared that the struggle against immigration represented one of its political priorities.[22] Accordingly, the party supported the 'Schwarzenbach Initiative' in 1970 and from this moment on, it started to collaborate closely with the parties from the Movement against Overforeignization.[23]

In the first half of the 1980s, National Action made an astonishing electoral comeback. The party shifted its focus to asylum policy and was hence 'able to gain advantage from the restrictionist sentiments in the Swiss electorate'.[24] In the National Council elections of 1983, NA more than doubled its vote share from 1.3 to 3.0 per cent and gained two more seats in the National Council, allowing the party to establish, for the first time since 1971, a parliamentary group in alliance with the MP from Vigilance (tables 3.1 and 3.2). Four years later, however, NA's share of the vote decreased from 3.0 to 2.5 per cent and the party lost one of its four seats. As the Vigilance deputy was not reelected, the representation of the Movement against Overforeignization in the National Council was reduced to three seats. At the cantonal and municipal level, NA went through similar electoral developments: while the party experienced a number of remarkable electoral successes in the first half of the 1980s, it had lost much of its support by the late 1980s.[25]

There were four reasons for the changing electoral fortune of NA in the 1980s: first, as early as the late 1970s and early 1980s, NA politicised the issue of asylum and demanded restrictive measures in the country's asylum policy. By the mid 1980s, most centre-right parties were advocating restrictions and limitations on the right of asylum, and the Swiss authorities had begun to expedite the procedures of granting asylum.[26] As Christopher Husbands put it: 'The Swiss government moved to restrict the entry of asylum-seekers and thereby co-opted, at least temporarily, the NA's major issue'.[27] In this way, it became more difficult for NA to exploit the asylum issue in political campaigns. Second, since NA achieved remarkable successes in those federal referendums of the first half of the 1980s addressing classical issues of migration (see below), the party was able to take advantage of this plebiscitary boost in elections. Conversely, in the second half of the 1980s, NA was less involved in direct-democratic campaigns and the only NA initiative that reached the ballots received little popular support. This plebiscitary weakening was accompanied by a considerable electoral decline.

Third, NA continued to suffer internal conflicts among its leadership. There was major disagreement between a radical faction on the one hand, which was led by NA founder Fritz Meier and aimed at reinforcing the party's anti-immigrant agenda, and a more moderate faction on the other, which sought to widen the party's agenda by including ecological and economic issues. The latter faction was most prominently represented by Valentin Oehen, party president since 1972 and next to James Schwarzenbach the second leadership figure generated by the Movement against Overforeignization.[28] Born in 1931, Valentin Oehen grew up in the rural region of the canton of Bern and graduated in agronomy from the Swiss Federal Institute of Technology in Zurich. In 1958, Oehen began his political career in the Conservative Christian-Social People's Party (*Konservativ-Christlichsoziale Volkspartei* – KCVP), the precursor to today's CVP. Two years after leaving the KCVP in 1965, he joined a party named Young Bern (*Junges Bern*).[29] In 1970, Oehen left Young Bern and attached himself to National Action. In the National Council elections of 1971, he was elected as deputy for the canton of Bern. During his party presidency, Oehen significantly shaped the policy direction and political agenda of NA, adopting a combination of ecological concerns, nationalist ideas and anti-immigrant sentiments. While Oehen did not enjoy the same charismatic posture and populist style as Schwarzenbach and attracted less public and media attention, he was considered the father figure of NA throughout the 1970s. Within NA, the faction led by Oehen gained a brief victory in 1977, when the term 'overforeignization' was removed from the party name. From this point on the party was called National Action for People and Homeland. In the long term, however, the radical line prevailed and Valentin Oehen resigned as party president in 1980.

Fourth, following these internal disagreements and power struggles, NA underwent a significant radicalisation of rhetoric and policies, which eventually took some considerable shine off the party's public image. Most prominently in this respect, the party organ *Volk + Heimat* radicalised its editorial line after Jean-Jacques Hegg became editor-in-chief in 1980, and published articles drawing overtly on racially and biologically based ideas.[30] At leadership level, Markus Ruf strengthened his position of power. Elected to the National Council in 1983 at the age of twenty-four, he became notorious for his uncompromising statements and demands. It was also Ruf who delivered a speech in 1985 at the congress of Le Pen's National Front in Versailles, where he passed on official greetings from NA and its executive committee and made a vivacious appeal for mutual support.[31] Moreover, NA was involved in a number of court cases in the mid 1980s, which were seen in the eye of the public as evidence of the party's increased radicalisation and political crisis. In a widely noted court case, NA sued a journalist who had written that NA had increasingly evolved towards a 'Nazi-like racism' (*nazihaften Rassismus*). Hearings at different levels of the judiciary system rejected the party's lawsuits. This included the Federal Tribunal, which stated in 1987 that 'the statements made by NA politicians and articles published in the party organ *Volk + Heimat* do bear, in parts, an alarming resemblance to the National Socialist doctrine'.[32] Eventually, NA was forced to try and cope with the substantial financial costs of the court cases and with growing internal discord.[33]

The electoral performance of Vigilance in the 1980s mirrored the unstable electoral development of the Movement against Overforeignization during this period. In the cantonal elections of 1985, Vigilance advanced to become Geneva's strongest party, gaining 19 per cent of the vote and almost tripling its number of seats in the Great Council, from seven to nineteen.[34] The year 1985, however, was also the turning point in Vigilance's history. From this date on, the party experienced internal disagreement, causing the deterioration of party cohesion and resulting in its significant electoral decline. For example, Eric Bertinat was elected as party president in 1985 at the age of twenty-eight and later became an important New Right figure in the French-speaking part of Switzerland. He came under sharp criticism from his party fellows for attending a meeting of the National Front in Paris in the spring of 1987, where he paid public tribute to Jean-Marie Le Pen.[35] In the cantonal elections of 1989, Vigilance's vote share was reduced by 8 per cent and the party lost ten of its nineteen seats in the Great Council.

In the early 1990s, Vigilance made a desperate attempt to rise up against its electoral decline and considerably radicalised its rhetoric in proposals made on issues related to migration and internal security.[36] However, two developments led to the fragmentation of the radical right-wing populist party camp and made it very difficult for Vigilance to sustain its electoral support: the creation of a new political group, the Geneva Patriotic Movement (*Mouvement patriotique genevois* – MPE) and the emergence of the Automobilist Party, which arrived on the stage of local politics in Geneva under the banner of the Union for the Defence of Liberties (*Union pour la défense des libertés*, or UDL).[37] Following the loss of all seven of its seats in the cantonal elections of 1993, Vigilance withdrew from political life. A couple of years later, former leading members of the Vigilance party, such as Eric Bertinat and Pierre

Schifferli, became the driving forces behind the establishment of the cantonal party of the SVP in Geneva (see chapter 5).[38]

The Power of Direct Democracy

Since the parties from the Movement against Overforeignization were fringe electoral parties whose joint performance never took them beyond the 8 per cent mark in National Council elections, they have had little significance in Swiss politics in terms of their showing in elections and representation in parliament. However, the parties have been proficient in taking advantage of the power of direct democracy and in that way have played a remarkable role in the Swiss political system. As Patrick Ireland maintains: 'Weak and fragmented as a political party and hardly a bona fide social movement, National Action and similar groups have nonetheless managed to affect public policy profoundly with the tools of direct democracy'.[39] They have managed to submit seven federal initiatives and have had two successes when calling for referendums on policy change (tables 3.3 and 3.4). Even though none of the seven federal initiatives has successfully overcome the hurdle of the popular vote, the parties have succeeded in influencing public and political debates by continually thematizing and expounding the so-called 'foreigners problem'. Recent studies of Swiss migration policy agree that the movement's strategy of contentious plebiscitary politics has made things considerably easier for the federal government, with scant opposition, to push through restrictions on what had once been relatively liberal migration policies.[40]

The first federal initiative from National Action, launched in 1968 and voted on in 1970, was a political milestone for the then nascent Movement against Overforeignization and it laid foundations for the movement within the country's political system. Officially titled the initiative 'Against Overforeignization' (*Gegen Überfremdung*), the proposal was known in the vernacular as the 'Schwarzenbach Initiative', taking its name from the indisputable leader of NA at that time. The party launched the initiative after the Democratic Party in the canton of Zurich had withdrawn, in 1968, a successfully submitted initiative that had followed a similar purpose. The aim of the NA initiative was to limit the percentage of foreign residents in Switzerland to 10 per cent of the population, which would have meant that more than one-third of the foreign population would have had to leave the country.[41] Following an extensive and very controversial public debate over the initiative, 74.7 per cent of the voters turned out at the ballots in June 1970,

Table 3.3 | *Federal Initiatives and Referendums by National Action, 1968–1988*

Subject	Year of Launch	Submitted	Year of the Vote	Objective Achieved[1]
Initiative 'Against Overforeignization'	1968	yes	1970	no (46.0%)
Initiative 'Against Overforeignization and Overpopulation'	1971	yes	1974	no (34.2%)
Initiative 'For the Reorganisation of the Referendum on State treaties'	1971	yes	1977	no (21.9%)
Initiative 'For the Limitation of Naturalisations'	1973	yes	1977	no (33.8%)
Initiative 'Against the Selling-Off of the Homeland'	1978	yes	1984	no (48.9%)
Referendum on the revised alien legislation	1981	yes	1982	yes (50.4%)
Initiative 'For the Limitation of Immigration'	1983	yes	1988	no (32.7%)
Initiative 'Against Overforeignization'	1986	no	–	–

Note: [1] Indicating whether and with what percentage voters supported the party's objective
Source: http://www.admin.ch/ch/d/pore/va/index.html, retrieved 31 August 2008.

the highest number since 1947. With 54 per cent voting against, the NA proposal was narrowly defeated; but in almost one third of the cantons a majority of voters had accepted the initiative.[42]

According to post-vote surveys, supporters of the initiative mostly belonged to the lower social classes and the elderly.[43] The initiative received disproportional support in German-speaking Switzerland, particularly in rural areas and working-class districts of industrialised centres. The latter was also reflected in the fact that 55 per cent of the members of the Swiss Trade Union Federation (*Schweizerischer Gewerkschaftsbund* – SGB), the umbrella association of the Swiss trade unions, approved NA's proposal.[44] On the other hand, the initiative found very little support in frontier areas, or in the French- and Italian-speaking regions. The voters who rejected the initiative were largely from groups with medium or high incomes, and typically those with better educa-

Table 3.4 | *Federal Initiatives and Referendums by the Swiss Republican Movement, 1972–1985*

Subject	Year of Launch	Submitted	Year of the Vote	Objective Achieved[1]
Initiative 'For the Defence of Switzerland'	1972	yes	1977	no (29.5%)
Referendum on the loan to the IDA	1975	yes	1976	yes (56.4%)
Initiative 'For the Limitation of the Reception of Asylum Seekers'	1985	no	–	–

Note: [1] Indicating whether and with what percentage voters supported the party's objective
Source: http://www.admin.ch/ch/d/pore/va/index.html, retrieved 31 August 2008.

tional qualifications. As the surveys further show, while there was some correlation in certain urban regions between acceptance of the initiative and the number of foreign residents, the younger generations living in areas with a high proportion of foreign residents tended to reject the initiative.

The high levels of support for the NA proposal 'made such an impression that vigorous and effective political action became imperative'.[45] Yet, even in the run-up to the vote, the Swiss government had decided to apply a policy of stabilisation and to introduce the so-called 'global ceiling' by implementing strict quotas on annual immigration. This represented a major shift in the country's migration policy from a model of rotation to one of stabilisation. It is still a matter for dispute, however, as to whether or not the Swiss government took advantage of the pressure brought to bear by the initiative in order to implement measures which had in fact already been planned since the 1960s.[46] Whatever the case may be, it was clear to James Schwarzenbach that 'stabilisation was a first and irrefutable partial success of our initiative, a measure taken by the government to take the wind out of the sails of initiative II'.[47]

After the stunning plebiscitary result in 1970 and the subsequent electoral breakthrough in the National Council elections of 1971, the parties from the Movement against Overforeignization managed to maintain a high degree of mobilisation and a strong position on the Swiss political scene. Within two years, they successfully launched four federal initiatives, three of them asking for restrictions on the government's immigration and integration policy. While the three anti-immigrant initiatives were turned down by large margins at the polls, they still caused intense debates and shaped the way that issues of migration were discussed.[48] To take the example of the NA initiative 'Against Overforeignization and Overpopulation' (*Gegen Überfremdung und Übervölkerung*): launched in 1971, the proposal set off a controversial debate as Social Democrats and trade unions tried without success to force the government to present a counter-proposal to the voters that would include some measures of limitations to immigration. Thus, it was not surprising that the turnout of 70.3 per cent of the vote in 1974 was the third highest of the postwar era. However, only 34.2 per cent supported the policy presented by NA. There were two basic reasons why voters of the time rejected the anti-migrant proposals by such large margins: first, the government's restrictive handling of migration, particularly during the economic crisis of the mid 1970s, 'proved sufficient to take the edge off the grassroots movements'.[49] Second, migration was no longer the most salient issue for voters who were becoming increasingly concerned about issues related to economic, social and employment policies.[50]

In addition to migration policy, the Movement against Overforeignization was interested in matters of foreign policy and astonishingly enough it experienced some plebiscitary success in this respect. So far, this has largely been ignored by studies in the field. While the migration theme undoubtedly lay at the heart of the movement's political agenda, the parties also used the tools of direct democracy to shape the country's foreign policy, a strategy that became one of the main objectives of the Swiss radical right in the 1990s. In 1971, NA launched the initiative 'For the Reorganisation of the Referendum on State Treaties' (*Über die Neuordnung des Staatsvertragsreferendums*), which demanded that international treaties should be placed on the ballots and that a petition, signed by thirty thousand citizens, could ask for a vote on treaties that had been concluded in the past. While the latter request was clearly directed against the 'Italian Treaty' (*Italienerabkommen*) of 1964, which had bilaterally regulated the legal and social status of Italian immigrants in Switzerland, the overall objective of the initiative was to strengthen direct democracy in the process of decision making on foreign policy.[51] Although the NA initiative was clearly rejected in the vote of 1977, that saw a turnout of 45 per cent, the government's counter-proposal was actually approved by 61 per cent of the voters. Henceforth, certain issues of foreign policy would have to be decided at the polls. Most significantly, in 1992, the government put the disputed EEA treaty to a popular vote by referring to the change in the ratification procedure of international treaties that had previously been approved in 1977.[52]

The second direct-democratic intervention relating to foreign policy was carried out in 1975–76 by the SRB, in alliance with Vigilance, and ended with a remarkable success at the ballots. The two parties successfully demanded a referendum on the government's proposal to give a loan of 200 million Swiss francs to the International Development Association (IDA) of the International Monetary Fund (IMF).[53] In the referendum campaign, Schwarzenbach denounced the government's active involvement in favour of the loan as indoctrination of the people and as an act of 'brainwashing' paid for with tax money.[54] According to Kenneth Pitterle, in the 'campaign, one of the Republicans prime motivations was their ethnocentric disinclination to help people who were not like the idealised Swiss themselves'.[55] Eventually, the government's proposal was rejected in June 1976 by 56.4 per cent of the voters, with a turnout of 34.5 per cent. As Kris Kobach points out, '[t]his outcome did not augur well for a referendum on UN membership', which had, at the time, been forecast by the Swiss government.[56]

In the early 1980s, the parties from the Movement against Overforeignization also achieved astounding results in federal votes on some of the movement's classical issues related to policy regarding foreigners. For instance, the parties had decried from early on that foreigners owned too much property in Switzerland.[57] Following through on this logic, in 1979 NA submitted the initiative 'Against the Selling-Off of the Homeland' (*Gegen den Ausverkauf der Heimat*), requesting a total halt to the acquisitions of properties and vacation apartments by foreigners who did not have a permanent residence permit in Switzerland. Despite the fact that the national parliament passed a Federal Statute in 1983, the *Lex Friedrich* which contained significant legal restraints on such matters, the NA initiative was, to the surprise of many, only narrowly defeated by 51.1 per cent of the voters in May 1984, with a turnout of 42.5 per cent. As shown by polls taken after the voting, among those who had accepted the initiative, 23 per cent said that foreigners should not own property in Switzerland, and 17 per cent stated that they were against foreigners in general.[58]

Integration policy represented another focus of interest for parties from the Movement against Overforeignization. In the late 1970s, they started an aggressive campaign against the 'Togetherness Initiative' (*Mitenand Initiative*) that had been submitted by socially oriented Christian groups demanding that certain measures of legal and social integration should be taken in favour of immigrants.[59] While the Movement against Overforeignization was the first political force to oppose the proposal, by the early 1980s most centre-right parties had expressed their disapproval and even the Social Democrats and trade unions showed little support for the initiative. Eventually, at the ballot box in April 1981, only 16.2 per cent of voters approved the first pro-immigrant initiative, with a voter turnout of 39.9 per cent. This was one of the lowest approval scores that a federal initiative has received in the postwar era. As suggested by a post-vote survey, the fear of alleged 'overforeignization' was the main motive for voters rejecting the initiative and, overall, there was significant resemblance to the kind of voting behaviour that had been seen in the 1970 referendum on the 'Schwarzenbach Initiative'.[60]

The Movement against Overforeignization achieved its most spectacular victory so far in 1982, when NA successfully undermined the revision of the Federal Statute of Abode and Settlement of Foreigners (ANAG). After parliament had approved the comprehensive reform of the ANAG, which dates back to 1931, NA collected over 84,000 signatures in three months, thereby forcing the new Federal Statute to a popular vote. As Patrick Ireland notes, 'the legislation had not included enough restrictions on immigration to satisfy the xenophobes. The government, they felt, had subordinated protection of Switzerland's national identity to certain employers' need.'[61] In June 1982, the revised alien legislation was rejected by a narrow margin of 50.4 per cent of the voters, with a small turnout of 35.2 per cent. The NA party organ *Volk + Heimat* celebrated the outcome as a great victory over 'the conspiracy of forces hostile to the Swiss people'.[62] The survey taken after the voting shows that the 'fear of overforeignization' was the main reason for voter disapproval and that voters knew very little about the legislation's real content. As it goes on to stress, the rejection rate was disproportionately high among older people and those with no more than a primary education. Moreover, the law was rejected by those living in rural areas and by a very large majority of workers and farmers.[63]

In line with their electoral decline in the second half of the 1980s, the parties lost much of their ability to mobilise. They shifted their focus to matters of asylum, in an attempt to take advantage of the emergence of this new issue on the Swiss migration agenda. With the initiative launched in 1983, 'For the Limitation of Immigration' (*Für die Begrenzung der Einwanderung*), which the authorities also dubbed the sixth 'Overforeignization-Initiative' (*Überfremdungsinitiative*), NA established a close link between immigration policy and asylum policy. While the initiative called for a limit on the number of immigrants coming each year to Switzerland, it demanded that refugees should also be included in this quota.[64] Accordingly, NA stressed in its campaign that the initiative would significantly contribute to a solution to the problem of asylum. In December 1988, 67.3 per cent of the voters rejected the initiative, with a turnout of 52.8 per cent. Once again, the surveys indicate that the large majority of the voters who accepted the initiative were driven by xenophobic sentiments. In a similar way to the previous votes, it was further shown that age, education and occupation were important determinants of support for the initiative.[65]

The next two initiatives failed at the earlier stage of signature collection: first, a faction of NA, led by the party founder Fritz Meier, launched the initiative 'Against Overforeignization' (*gegen Überfremdung*) in 1986, which demanded that the number of foreign residents in Switzerland, including refugees, should not exceed 500,000.[66] Second, in 1985, the SRB launched the initiative 'For the Limitation of the Reception of Asylum Seekers' (*Für eine Begrenzung der Aufnahme von Asylanten*) and made the fruitless attempt to rise from the political insignificance to which the party had plunged since the late 1970s. James Schwarzenbach was the head of the initiative committee.[67] The initiative contained very radical demands, including for example, the request that asylum should basically only be granted to refugees from European countries, demands that were supported by Vigilance and by factions from the Swiss extreme right.[68] These two last attempts to reemerge as a plebiscitary challenger in the 1980s reveal the difficulties faced by the Movement against Overforeignization in its attempt to gather support and resources, as well as the degree of radicalisation to which its anti-immigrant demands had stretched.

Populist Strategy and Exclusionist Ideology

The parties and party leaders from the Movement against Overforeignization have consistently pursued a strategy of presenting themselves as a popular voice while evoking resentment against the so-called political and social elite. Based on their Manichaean worldview, they have stressed that there is a large gap between the 'common people' and the 'power holders', such as political authorities, mainstream parties, economic interest groups and intellectuals. They have linked their criticism of unrestrained economic growth and materialistic thinking with accusations laying the blame for unrestrained immigration at the door of the 'political establishment' and 'big business'.[69] While the parties have emphasised that the fissure between 'the people' and the political and economic elite is particularly discernible in policies related to migration and foreign residents, they have also complained of a lamentable situation in Switzerland generally, that is characterised by the estrangement of the political elite from the people. For instance,

James Schwarzenbach deplored that 'there is a fissure, from the bottom to the top, between the people and the authorities' and that 'lobbyists are sitting as the people's representatives in our parliament'.[70] As a consequence of this concern, Schwarzenbach proposed that the Federal Council should be elected by the people. Consequently, the SRB launched a federal initiative in 1972 demanding that the elected members of the government should be approved by popular vote, but the party failed to collect the necessary number of signatures to realise its goal.[71]

Given the movement's anti-establishment attitude and populist appeal, some authors emphasise that support for its radical-right populist agenda was in reality an expression of voter dissatisfaction and discontent with the established parties and their policies.[72] Others argue that the Movement against Overforeignization was the result of disenchantment in a period of increased modernisation and rapid socioeconomic changes.[73] Both views imply that the movement was short of a coherent ideology that would appeal to its supporters, since anti-modernist views, protest appeal and political discontent represent rather diffuse attitudes. Yet the parties and leaders from the Movement against Overforeignization presented an elaborate ideology that was based on exclusionist ideas and expressed in clear arguments and a distinct political program.[74]

The exclusionist ideology espoused by the parties from the Movement against Overforeignization was, above all, displayed in a political agenda that was directed first against immigrants and foreign residents living in Switzerland, and later against asylum seekers and refugees. In their anti-immigrant campaigns, the parties employed a set of arguments that all had the basic aim of inducing xenophobia and hostility towards foreign residents and of presenting immigration as a threat to Switzerland. However, the initial upswing of the movement's anti-immigrant appeal must be put in the context of the general revival of the 'overforeignization' theme in the 1960s. Much like the Social Democrats and trade unions, the parties applied economic and labour market arguments to make their points. They argued that industry was in favour of mass immigration because it wanted to reduce the wages of Swiss workers, and that, eventually, Swiss workers would be the victims of the inevitable restructuring and rationalisation of the economy.[75] In their view, foreigners would inundate Switzerland with their families and the country would be overwhelmed by 'an avalanche of foreigner births'.[76] The parties aimed at inducing xenophobic sentiment in the population by evoking what Andreas Wimmer describes as 'the fear of being "inundated" by foreigners and estranged from one's own culture'.[77] In addition, the parties have regularly linked themes such as environmental problems and protection of nature to migration issues (see also chapter 6). As a matter of fact, NA was the first Swiss political party which consistently incorporated, as early as the 1960s and 1970s, ecological and environmental policy in its manifesto.[78]

As early as the 1960s, the parties from the Movement against Overforeignization began to highlight the importance of culture and cultural identity in their anti-immigrant campaigns. The parties' evocation of culturalist arguments has to be seen, however, in the context of a general shift from the economic to the cultural aspects of so-called overforeignization, which occurred in the debates on migration in the 1960s. As Gaetano Romano argues, the 'foreign workers' question' changed into the 'foreigners' question' in the 1960s.[79] At this point, the notion of 'overforeignization' began to imply that Swiss identity was culturally and ethnically under threat from immigrants and their culture. In the context of this type of cultural protectionism, the parties set forth essentialist notions of culture, values and ways of life, and sought to emphasise a cultural incompatibility between the Swiss and foreign residents. The culturalist discourse became of particular significance, first in debates on integration and then, as it was called in the 1960s and 1970s, on 'assimilation'.[80] As the anti-immigrant parties relied on the conception of culture as an unchangeable constant in the development of individuals and society, they rejected the concept of 'assimilation' of foreigners or argued that it was simply impossible. The immigrants, they claimed, would never really be assimilated, especially considering their alleged national pride in deeply rooted traditions, a pride that the anti-immigrant discourse would describe as a fundamental, inborn and inherited characteristic.[81] Consequently, the parties opposed any policies which might lead to a political integration of foreigners and urged for restrictive naturalisation procedures, arguing that the granting of citizenship to foreigners would remove foreigners only from the statistics, and not from Switzerland.[82]

In the late 1970s and early 1980s, the emphasis on cultural identity and difference was then transferred into the emerging debate on asylum seekers coming in from non-European countries.[83] Thereby, NA was one of the first Swiss parties to espouse cultural-differentialist and ethnopluralist views. For example, as early as 1979, the party manifesto stated that, of refugees whose life and limb is threatened, only those should be received who come from 'one's own cultural sphere'.[84] In its campaigns against asylum seekers, NA greatly emphasised an assumed cultural and ethnic distance from Swiss culture and nationhood and stressed a fundamental incompatibility between cultures that would inevitably clash.[85] By the mid 1980s, however, large parts of the established centre-right parties – as well as parts of the government – showed an understanding for the alleged antipathy among the Swiss population towards asylum seekers of what began to be called 'foreign cultural spheres'. For example, the Federal Councillor Elisabeth Kopp, member of the FDP, declared in June 1985 during a parliamentary debate on asylum seekers, that 'their skin colour, their cultural differences arouse fear in us'.[86] NA went a step further and argued in a neoracist fashion that there exists no possibility of overcoming cultural difference.[87] Senior NA members combined an ethnopluralist view, which highlighted cultural differences and the separate development of different cultures, with the claim that refugees should stay in or at least return to their homelands. Markus Ruf, for example, submitted a parliamentary initiative in February 1985 demanding that asylum seekers coming from non-European 'cultural spheres' should be extradited within twenty-four hours.[88]

Until the early 1980s, only a few NA officials had drawn on biologically based arguments and classical racism was only occasionally expressed in the party papers of the three parties associated with the Movement against Overforeignization.[89] In the 1980s, NA considerably radicalised its rhetoric in the debates on asylum policy, and senior party officials made reference to 'racial theories' and disclosed overtly racist views. As the discourse of NA became increasingly 'racialised', authors of articles published in *Volk + Heimat* repeatedly used terms such as 'race' or 'race problems' and based them upon biologically grounded conceptions of 'race differences'.[90] During this period, the NA party organ also contributed to ensuring that the sociobiological ideas of the human ethology research school surrounding Konrad Lorenz and his disciples such as Irenäus Eibl-Eibesfeldt were well received among the Swiss radical right.

It was Jean-Jacques Hegg in particular, psychiatrist by profession and leading ideologist in the Movement against Overforeignization, who propagated these ideas and attempted to move NA toward the discourse of the European New Right.[91] As early as 1974, Hegg published a long essay in the mainstream newspaper *Neue Zürcher Zeitung*, in which he claimed that the quest for hierarchical order must be seen as part of the biological heritage of human beings and that it corresponds to the law of nature that hostile reactions emerge when masses of strangers intrude into one another's territory.[92] In the 1980s, Hegg wrote numerous pseudoscientific articles in *Volk + Heimat* in which he made extensive reference to literature written by authors of the European New Right.[93] His articles were also reprinted in periodicals of the

German extreme right such as *Nation Europa*. But Hegg also made a career in public office. After running without success for the Republican Movement in the 1971 National Council elections in the canton of Zurich, he was elected on an NA ticket in the same canton in 1983. He resigned after just one year as a national MP and later became an NA deputy in the cantonal parliament of Zurich.

Nationalism was another core feature of the ideology embraced by the parties from the Movement against Overforeignization. They expressed nationalist views not only in their anti-immigrant campaigns, but also in their opposition to Switzerland's involvement in the international community.[94] In numerous public campaigns, they defended the notion of Switzerland as an exceptional case and as a national community of common origins. As they maintained, the country's national homogeneity and distinctiveness should be protected, particularly by keeping away foreigners who, supposedly, would never be able integrate into Swiss society and thus could never be true members of the national community. In their nationalist rhetoric, the parties were fond of referring to the country's distinct culture, religion and historical origins. Historical references were mainly made to the period of the Old Confederation that preceded the establishment of the federal state in 1848, a time when – in their view – the country had been wholeheartedly preserved from modernity, technology and urbanity.[95]

As the parties from the Movement against Overforeignization continuously warned that Switzerland would lose its individuality and authenticity, they followed essentialist notions of Switzerland as a culture-nation. The main features of the Swiss culture and the Swiss people's collective mentality were described as a love of liberty, a desire for independence, a rootedness in the native soil and a strong sense of tradition. They emphasised that Switzerland and the Swiss are deeply rooted in a culture whose characteristics do not change throughout the entire life of a human being or indeed the whole history of a country. This idea of Swiss nationhood came into play in 1972, when the government planned to sign a free trade treaty with the European Economic Community, and Valentin Oehen warned of unifying the historically developed European Nations with all their different cultures into one big market melting-pot.[96] In the late 1980s, shortly before the great battles relating to Switzerland's stance toward European integration had begun, the NA president Rudolf Keller reconfirmed this position by denouncing the new Europe for its destruction of local distinctiveness, cultures and traditions and by declaring that NA stood for a Europe of the fatherlands.[97] In the nationalist discourse, the parties from the Movement against Overforeignization were also keen to make reference to Switzerland's political institutions and political culture. In their view, federalism, neutrality and direct democracy were the central, everlasting foundations of the country's national identity and nationhood. They were presented as key elements of the country's uniqueness and distinctiveness and the main reason why it had to be accepted that Switzerland represented an exceptional case.

Overall, the Movement against Overforeignization failed to produce a larger and electorally stable party. Internal conflicts and leadership disputes caused a high degree of factionalism and radical political statements seriously damaged the public image of the parties. While they challenged policies relating to Swizerland's integration in the international community, they were ultimately single-issue parties focusing predominantly on issues of migration. Thus, the government's shifts in migration policy and the changing conditions for anti-immigrant politics also contributed to the movement's setbacks in elections and referendums. However, with their fairly elaborate, exclusionist ideology drawing on xenophobic, neoracist and nationalist ideas, they chalked out the path of an ideology and a political agenda which became the main frame of reference for the radical right-wing populist parties that followed.

4

OUTSIDERS IN THE PARTY SYSTEM
Fringe Parties in the 1980s and 1990s

The decline and disappearance of some parties from the Movement against Overforeignization did not bring an end to the presence of parties of the radical right in the Swiss party system. On the contrary, from the mid 1980s on, a new phase of radical right-wing populism began, bearing witness to the organisational persistence of the already existing parties and to the emergence of new parties. However, they continued to act as fringe parties at the margin of the Swiss party system and to be perceived as pariah parties by most of the established parties. Moreover, the foundation of new parties underlined the traditionally high degree of fragmentation and factionalism in the camp of radical right-wing populist parties. This diversity was also the product of the political priorities and ideological prefererences that each party adopted in its own political agenda.

The Swiss Democrats (*Schweizer Demokraten* – SD), the successor party to National Action, was the direct continuation of the Movement against Overforeignization and so gained some benefit from its long-standing position in the Swiss party system. As the party continued to act as a cadre party and to radicalise its agenda and political demands – a process NA had begun to undergo in the early 1980s – organisational and ideological sectarianism seriously undermined the party's popular appeal, in a manner that makes the SD a typical example of a radical right-wing party. As for the Swiss Democratic Union (*Eidgenössisch-Demokratische Union* - EDU), which also had its origins in the Movement against Overforeignization, it had gradually transformed itself during the 1980s into a party of religious orientation. As the quest for the restoration of moral order based on Christian values became the party's central goal, the EDU came to represent a fundamentalist party-type among the parties of the Swiss radical right. Among the newly founded parties was the Car Party/Freedom Party (*Autopartei/Freiheits-Partei* – APS/FPS), originally launched as an anti-ecological party aiming to challenge the postmaterialist tendencies in Swiss politics. Since the party combined anti-establishment rhetoric and neoliberal economic ideas with radical exclusionist demands in policy areas to asylum, it corresponded to the kind of new, radical right-wing populist party seen in other Western European countries since the late 1980s. In style and agenda, the second newly created party, the *Lega dei Ticinesi,* also resembled the new radical right-wing populist parties, but it was strongly marked by its ethnoregionalist ideological profile and was confined by its geographical limitation to the canton of Ticino.

The Swiss Democrats: Survivors of the Movement against Overforeignization

In June 1990, National Action changed its party name to the Swiss Democrats. This new name was meant to express the party's intention to extend its policy agenda and to rid itself of the tag of being a single-issue party that was only concerned with migration policy and the theme of 'overforeignization'. Accordingly, the SD started to pay more attention to foreign policy, in particular to issues related to the country's projected membership in supranational organisations. The new party name was also intended as a signal to party supporters that new issues, such as national identity and foreign policies, had become more salient for the country's future.[1] As party president, Rudolf Keller, emphasised at the party assembly in 1990, in view of the forthcoming debates over the country's EU membership, the new party name should point to the distinct character of Switzerland and express the party's desire to fight for the preservation of the country's democratic institutions.[2] Another purpose of the name change lay in the party leadership's intention to revise the public image of the SD as a political party with extreme-right and racist tendencies.[3] Although the party tried hard to widen the scope of its policies and to de-radicalize its rhetoric, the SD belongs to the group of radical right-wing parties in Western Europe, such as the National Front in France and the Vlaams Blok in Belgium, which have most consistently combined drastic exclusionist views with a right-authoritarian and anti-system appeal.[4]

Gradual Decline in the Elections of the 1990s

As in the 1970s and 1980s, the SD continued to retain its status as a fringe party in elections through the 1990s and played a marginal role in the national parliament and in most cantonal parliaments. The party's development in the national elections of the 1990s was characterized by steady decline (table 4.1), but in contrast, the SD succeeded in strengthening its

Table 4.1 | *Results of National Action/Swiss Democrats in National Council Elections, 1987–1999*

Cantons[1]	1987		1991		1995		1999	
ZH (35/34)[2]	5.0	2	5.2	2	3.3	1	1.5	–
BE (29/27)[2]	3.2	1	6.0	2	5.5	1	3.7	1
BL (7)	6.2	–	9.1	1	11.0	1	10.1	–
BS (6)	4.5	–	3.2	–	6.9	–	3.8	–
AG (14/15)[2]	4.5	–	4.5	–	4.5	–	2.7	–
SG (12)	2.1	–	3.1	–	2.0	–	1.4	–
LU (9/10)[2]	1.5	–	2.8	–	2.2	–	0.8	–
VD (17)	2.8	–	2.9	–	1.8	–	0.9	–
NE (5)	3.4	–	6.4	–	2.5	–	2.3	–
TG (6)	–	–	3.5	–	4.8	–	2.5	–
FR (6)	–	–	1.4	–	0.9	–	0.3	–
GE (11)	1.1	–	2.0	–	2.4	–	–	–
SO (7)	–	–	–	–	2.8	–	–	–
SZ (3)	–	–	–	–	3.1	–	–	–
NW (1)[3]	–	–	–	–	–	–	(8.0)	–
Total[4]	**2.5**	**3**	**3.4**	**5**	**3.1**	**3**	**1.8**	**1**

Notes: First column: share of the vote; second column: number of seats
Turnouts: 46.5% (1987), 46.2% (1991), 42.2% (1995), 43.4% (1999)
[1] Total of cantonal MPs in National Council
[2] 1995 change of the number of MPs in National Council per canton
[3] Majority electoral systems
[4] Total national share of the vote and number of MPs in National Council
Sources: *Année politique suisse 1987*, Bern 1988, p. 50, 52; *Année politique suisse 1991*, Bern 1992, appendix; *Année politique suisse 1995*, Bern 1996, appendix; *Année politique suisse 1999*, Bern 2000, appendix; W. Seitz, *Nationalratswahlen 1995*, Bern. 1995, pp. 44–71; W. Seitz, *Nationalratswahlen 1999*, Neuchâtel, 1999, pp. 56–80.

position in cantonal parliaments. The party had twenty-four cantonal MPs in the period covering 1992 to 1995, but it was able to increase this figure to the level of twenty-nine for the period from 1996 to 1999.

At the national level, the National Council elections of 1991 were by far the most successful. The SD received 3.4 per cent of the vote and increased the number of MPs from three to five. This allowed the party, for the first time in its history, to establish its own parliamentary group. In their election campaign of 1991, the SD particularly thematised the issues of asylum, drug policy and European integration.[5] In order to stress the central focus of its election program, the party launched the federal initiative 'For a Reasonable Asylum Policy' (see below). Moreover, the party tried to increase its appeal to female voters and established, for the first time, a women's candidate list in the canton of Basel Country.[6] In the 1995 National Council elections, the Swiss Democrats suffered their first significant losses at the polls. While the electoral support dropped only slightly from 3.4 to 3.1 per cent, the party lost two of its five MPs, one each in the cantons of Bern and Zurich.[7] Migration policy and rejection of Switzerland's EU membership remained the central issues of the SD election campaigns.[8] Once again, the party sought to boost its election campaign by launching a federal initiative; this time directed against the alleged 'overforeignization' of the country.

The National Council elections of 1999 were a major defeat for the SD after which the party basically lost significance as a parliamentary actor at the national level. The party's share of the vote went down from 3.1 to 1.8 per cent and two of the three National Councillors failed to be re-elected.[9] During the election campaign, the SD promulgated those claims that the party had already put on the top of the political program it had developed in early 1998: 'Stop the destructive immigration, overforeignization and overpopulation of our homeland'; 'Stop the discrimination against the native Swiss in the workplace'; 'Stop the insidious internationalisation of our country – no joining of EU, UN or NATO'.[10]

Because of the limited survey data available, it seems difficult to make a full assessment of the constituency of the Swiss Democrats.[11] As a rare account reveals, the social base of the SD electorate largely corresponded to what we have come to know from the electoral studies of traditional radical right-wing parties in Western Europe, studies which point to the male, working-class background of such parties' constituencies. The large majority of SD voters were men (72.5 per cent) and many were between twenty and thirty years old (25 per cent). It is also suggested that blue-collar workers and low-status employees were disproportionately over-represented among supporters of the SD (table 4.2). The same account indicates that the concern of law and order issues was a characteristic of the SD electorate, while economic issues such as unemployment, competition for jobs and the growth of the economy seemed to bother SD supporters less than was the case for voters of other parties (table 4.3).[12]

A Cadre Party without a Leader

In contrast to the 1970s and 1980s, when National Action was performing at its best and had fairly good organisational structures in place,

Table 4.2 | *Occupational Profile of Swiss Democrats Supporters, 1995*

	SD	Other Parties
Farmers	3.9%	6.9%
Blue collar workers	38.2%	18.9%
Low-status employees	21.1%	10.9%
Middle-status employees	19.7%	32.6%
Old middle class[1]	15.8%	26.6%
Pensioners	1.3%	3.9%

Notes: n (SD) = 76; n (other parties) = 7,654
[1] Includes professionals, craftsmen and shopkeepers
Source: P. Gentile and H. Kriesi, 'Contemporary Radical-Right Parties in Switzerland: History of a Divided Family', in *The New Politics of the Right*, eds H.-G. Betz and S. Immerfall, New York, 1998, p. 136.

the Swiss Democrats actually lost some of their structural base during the 1990s. While the party had fourteen cantonal sections in 1980, the number of cantonal parties decreased to eleven in 1997.[13] With electoral decline in the late 1990s, several cantonal sections disappeared, and in 2002, the party had only seven sections left.[14] Moreover, compared to other Swiss parties, the SD was traditionally less established at the local level and hence had local sections in less than half of its cantonal parties. It was suggested that the SD counted around five thousand party members in 1997, a number which has most likely decreased since.[15] In terms of membership, the party mainly drew on the country's German-speaking part, particularly in the cantons of Zurich and Bern, as well as in Central Switzerland. In the past, the party had been quite well established in the francophone part of Switzerland, holding party sections in

Table 4.3 | *Priority Issues of Swiss Democrats Supporters, 1995*

	SD	Other Parties
Unemployment	31.5%	41.1%
Law and order	23.9%	10.8%
Free speech protection	12.0%	8.0%
Growth and competition	7.6%	8.1%
Protect the environment	22.8%	26.8%
No answer, no idea	2.2%	2.9%

Note: n (SD) = 92; n (other parties) = 8,222
Source: Gentile and Kriesi, 'Contemporary Radical-Right Parties', p. 136.

the cantons of Neuchâtel, Vaud and Geneva. Yet in the 1990s, the party lost a lot of ground in the French-speaking part of Switzerland. Overall, the SD increasingly took on the appearance of a cadre party that was forced to rely on the commitment of a small number of party officials to ensure the survival of the party organisation.

Compared to the early years of the Movement against Overforeignization, when leaders such as James Schwarzenbach and Valentin Oehen helped to gain popular appeal, the leadership of the SD lacked strong and charismatic political figures in the 1990s. In addition, the party continued to be shaken by internal conflicts and disputes, which were often carried out in public and eventually resulted in changes in party leadership. In 1991, for example, two local MPs in Zurich resigned from the SD and joined the parliamentary group of the SVP.[16] Another prominent example was the case of Markus Ruf, made National Councillor in 1983, who was well known in the 1980s as the youngest national MP and the talking head of the new generation of young radicals within the SD. In 1998, Ruf resigned from the party after the executive committee of the cantonal party of Bern had decided that he would not figure on the candidate list for the 1999 National Council elections.[17]

Internal cohesion was also weakened by the party's federalist structure which facilitated the increase of conflicts between cantonal sections. This was illustrated in 1990, when some cantonal sections refused to adopt the party name change which had been decided at the national party assembly.[18] Moreover, internal disputes emerged because francophone cantonal sections regularly challenged the German-speaking predominance at the level of national leadership. This resulted, for example, in a major conflict in 1998, when the central committee harshly criticised leading party officials from the two cantonal sections of Geneva and Vaud.[19]

However, the party paper, *Schweizer Demokrat* (Swiss Democrat), allowed the party to ensure at least some degree of party stability and cohesion. In fact, the monthly published paper represented the main link between leadership and members. Originally founded in 1966 under the title of *Nationale Aktion*, the name was changed to *Schweizer Demokrat* in September 1990. After the name change, the paper also included the subtitle 'Paper for a Free and Independent Switzerland' (*Zeitung für eine freie und unabhängige Schweiz*), which was supposed to reflect the programmatic shift of 1990, when the party leadership declared that foreign policy and national identity would become major concerns for the party.[20] In the late 1990s, the paper had a circulation of 11,500.[21] The counterpart in French had been published between 1976 and 1990 under the name of *peuple + patrie* (People and Fatherland), which included translated articles taken from the German-written paper as well as its own editorial contributions. Since the late 1970s, many of the editorial articles were written by Martine Boimond and Mary Meissner; both of whom are rare examples of women represented in NA and in the Swiss radical right in general. The French paper has appeared as an integrated section of *Schweizer Demokrat* since January 1991.[22]

The Continuity of Plebiscitary Strength

In spite of internal conflicts and electoral decline, the SD continued to make frequent use of the instruments of direct democracy and even achieved two plebiscitary successes. Considering the decrease in membership and the limited organisational resources, it seems somewhat surprising that the party was still able to carry out campaigns of signature collection and achieve an astounding record of two submitted popular initiatives and three successful requests for a referendum (table 4.4). Given the SD's long tradition of using direct-democratic means, the party was able to depend on organisational know-how and the party members' strong commitment to leading signature collection campaigns. The party organ, *Schweizer Demokrat*, also made it possible to reach out efficiently to party members and sympathisers. Moreover, the close collaboration with the *Lega dei Ticinesi* facilitated the organisational task of collecting the required number of signatures. At the same time, the SD continually criticised the Swiss People's Party and its leader Christoph Blocher for the lack of support they offered to initiatives launched by the SD, particularly those related to issues of migration and European integration.[23]

In the 1990s, the direct-democratic activities of the SD basically focused on the two poles of identity politics: in line with its exclusionist ideology, the party urged for restrictive measures on migration policy, whilst simultaneously pursuing its inclusive intentions with policies aimed at strengthening the country's national identity and preserving the conception of Switzerland as a special case. In the area of migration policy, the attempts of the SD to promulgate their exclusionist agenda and regain political strength by using the tools of direct democracy turned out to be unsuccessful: all three federal initiatives launched by the SD failed to make it to the ballots. The first initiative, named the initiative 'Against the Mass Immigration of Foreigners and Asylum Seekers' (*Gegen die Masseneinwanderung von Ausländern und Asylanten*), was launched in 1990 by party founder and National Councillor Fritz Meier. It was launched without the official approval of the party leadership and did not receive the necessary number of signatures.[24]

Table 4.4 | *Federal Initiatives and Referendums by the Swiss Democrats in the 1990s*

Subject Achieved[1]	Year of Launch	Submitted	Year of Vote	Objective
Initiative 'For the Day Off on the Federal Holiday' (1st August Initiative)	1989	yes	1993	yes (83.8%)
Initiative 'Against Mass Immigration of Foreigners and Asylum Seekers'	1990	no	–	–
Initiative 'For a Reasonable Asylum Policy'	1991	yes[2]	–	–
Initiative 'EC/EU Membership Negotiations: Let the People Decide!'[3]	1992	yes	1997	no (25.9%)
Referendum on the Federal Statute on Swiss forces for peacekeeping operations[3]	1993	yes	1994	yes (57.2%)
Referendum on Federal Statute on buying property by people living abroad	1994	yes	1995	yes (53.6%)
Initiative 'Exercising Moderation on Immigration'	1995	no	–	–
Referendum on sectoral agreements between Switzerland and the EU[3]	1999	yes	2000	no (32.8)

Notes: [1] Indicating whether and with what percentage voters agreed with the party's proposal
[2] The initiative was declared invalid by parliament in March 1996
[3] Launched and submitted together with the *Lega dei Ticinesi*
Source: http://www.admin.ch/ch/d/pore/va/index.html, retrieved 31 August 2008.

The second proposal, called the initiative 'For a Reasonable Asylum Policy' (*Für eine vernünftige Asylpolitik*), was successfully submitted in 1992 and demanded, among other things, that asylum seekers who came into the country illegally should be expelled without further notice.[25] Parliament decreed, however, that the initiative was invalid because its purpose was not in accordance with international law and that in the event of its acceptance, Switzerland would be forced to withdraw from the Geneva Convention on refugee and human rights.[26] Finally, in 1995, the party launched the initiative 'Exercising Moderation on Immigration' (*Masshalten bei der Einwanderung*), which asked that the annual quota of immigrants should not exceed the number of people who had left the country the previous year. For this initiative too, the party failed to collect the required number of signatures.[27] At the local level, however, the SD was more successful. In 1996, for instance, the party celebrated an astounding plebiscitary success in the city of Zurich. After the SD had asked for a referendum on certain directives aimed at adjusting municipal rules to the cantonal and federal legislation on naturalisation, voters backed the claims of the SD and rejected the official proposal with 62 per cent in June 1996.[28]

At the national level, the SD was successful in an area of policy that was linked to the theme of foreigners and migration. Since its initiative 'Against the Selling-Off of the Homeland' had been narrowly defeated in 1984, NA and then the SD had acted as the main political force opposed to any policies which would make it easier for foreigners to purchase property and real estate in Switzerland. Following this line, the SD successfully launched a referendum challenge in 1995, against the change of a Federal Statute limiting the opportunity for foreigners to buy real estate, the *Lex Friedrich*. Although almost all major political parties, except the Greens, were in favour of the law change, 53.6 per cent of the voters rejected the modified Federal Statute in June 1995, with a turnout of 40.3 per cent.[29] The SD celebrated the result as a victory for David over Goliath.[30] As shown by a post-vote survey, the xenophobic and exclusionist sense of purpose evoked in the SD's referendum campaign was the main reason for voters rejecting the Federal Statute. The argument that too many foreigners were living in Switzerland was by far the most important factor among those voters who disapproved of the liberalisation of the law.[31]

The SD also had some success in popular votes on issues related to Swiss national identity. In 1990, the party submitted the initiative 'For the Day Off on the Federal Holiday' (*Für einen arbeitsfreien Bundesfeiertag*), also termed the '1st of August Initiative' (*1. August Initiative*). The party used this as way to stress its concern about the country's national identity and national consciousness.[32] However, the course taken by the initiative was in many ways an exception among the different direct-democratic activities pursued by the SD. For the first time in its history, the party was able to celebrate a victory. In September 1993, the SD proposal was overwhelmingly approved with 83.8 per cent of the vote, the highest approval rate ever achieved by a federal initiative. The turnout was a low 39.9 per cent. During the referendum campaign, the proposal was supported by the government and by all political parties, which argued that the national holiday is a public holiday in almost every other country and that it was necessary to standardise the practice at the federal level, since the 1st of August was already a public holiday in some cantons.[33] Only a few members from the Social Democratic Party expressed their uneasiness with the fact that the initiative had been submitted by a right-wing nationalist party.[34] With this initiative the SD actually managed to enhance its policies related to foreigners and migrants – the traditional focus in the party's direct-democratic endeavours – with themes of national identity and patriotic feelings. This certainly struck a chord with one section of the voters, since a post-vote survey indicates that patriotic aspects were the essential motivation for fifteen per cent of the voters who agreed with the initiative. To put this into perspective, twenty-two per cent who backed the initiative cited the simple need for a national holiday as the main motivation for their support.[35]

After shifting political priorities to foreign affairs in the early 1990s, the SD started to oppose policies involving the country's international integration and consistently strove for a strengthening of isolationist positions in Swiss politics. Accordingly, the SD staunchly supported the *Lega dei Ticinesi* which, in 1993, asked for a referendum on the Federal Statute regarding the employment of Swiss troops in peacekeeping operations. Assisted by various small groups, the two parties achieved the collection of more than ninety thousand signatures, thereby forcing the Federal Statute to the ballot. The opponents argued that providing troops to the UN would be in fundamental breach of Swiss neutrality.[36] Despite near-unanimous support for the Federal Statute in the national parliament, it was defeated by 57.2 per cent of voters in the referendum of June 1994, with a turnout of 46.8 per cent. While the proposal was accepted in the four French-speaking cantons, it was largely rejected in the German-speaking regions.[37] As shown by a post-vote survey, only 18 per cent of the followers of the Swiss People's Party, and only 13 per cent of the supporters of the Swiss Democrats and the Car Party accepted the Federal Statute.[38] Although the SD and the *Lega* claimed full credit for the popular rejection, the success was largely due to the substantial campaign support of the Swiss People's Party and its satellite organisation, the Campaign for an Independent and Neutral Switzerland (see chapter 6).

The SD disclosed its isolationist attitude most consistently in opposing the country's involvement in the process of European integration. In 1992, the party fervently supported the opposition campaign against Switzerland's membership in the EEA and proclaimed that it amounted to a matter of survival for the people and the nation.[39] In the same year, the SD launched, together with the *Lega dei Ticinesi*, the federal initiative 'EC Membership Negotiations: Let the People Decide!' (*EG-Beitrittsver-*

handlungen vors Volk!).⁴⁰ The party emphasised that launching the initiative was an immediate reaction to the government's declaration that the country would apply for EC membership. While the proposal demanded that the government should consult the voters before opening any negotiations with Brussels, its main aim was to show fundamental opposition to any attempts at joining the European Community.⁴¹ As well as senior members of the SD and the *Lega dei Ticinesi*, the initiative committee was joined by members of the Car Party/Freedom Party, the Catholic People's Party and the Swiss Democratic Union. Conversely, the government and all parties forming the government coalition were opposed to the initiative, arguing that the proposal contradicted the idea of constitutional power-sharing. This logic was also largely followed by the voters in June 1997, when they rejected the initiative with 74.1 per cent of the vote.⁴² The turnout of 35.4 per cent was very low and commentators stated that 'this vote was only marginally about European integration'.⁴³

At the end of the 1990s, the SD made another attempt to obstruct the country's overtures towards the European Union. Joined, once more, by the *Lega dei Ticinesi*, the SD challenged the sectoral agreements between Switzerland and the European Union. After EEA membership had been rejected by voters in 1992, the Swiss government sought to make a move toward the European Union and hence started negotiations in 1994 regarding bilateral agreements in various policy domains. These negotiations were brought to an end in June 1999, and a couple of months later, both houses of parliament overwhelmingly approved the agreement which included seven policy sectors.⁴⁴ However, the SD and the *Lega di Ticinesi* successfully called for a referendum. The two parties were soon joined by an array of small groups, which helped to ensure that a fairly large number of signatures was collected. Some of these groups were known for their association with the New Right or even the extreme right, such as the *Presseclub*, led by the notorious negationist Ernst Indlekofer (see chapter 8). The most substantial support came from a committee called A Switzerland for Our Children (*Eine Schweiz für unsere Kinder*), which contributed over twenty-two thousand signatures (more than the Swiss Democrats), and was closely associated with the New Right group, Society for Advancing the Psychological Knowledge of Human Nature (see chapter 6).⁴⁵

In their voting campaign, the SD denounced the bilateral agreements as a dictate of the European Union and put emphasis on the alleged devastating consequences that freedom of mobility would bring to the country.⁴⁶ In the run-up to the vote, the SD distributed two hundred thousand copies of its paper *Schweizer Demokrat*.⁴⁷ Despite these efforts, a large majority of 67.2 per cent of the voters accepted the agreement in the referendum of May 2000, with a turnout of 48.3 per cent.[48] One of the main reasons for so clear a defeat lies in the fact that the SVP and the Campaign for an Independent and Neutral Switzerland, who represented the leading forces in the anti-European camp, failed to give their full support to the referendum campaigners.[49]

Exclusionist Ideology Drawing on (Neo)Racism and Nationalism

Compared to other parties of the Swiss radical right in the 1990s, the Swiss Democrats had more difficulty in applying a populist strategy and presenting themselves as the 'voice of the people'. After the resignation of prominent party leaders in the 1970s and the process of radicalisation in the 1980s, the SD found itself increasingly at the margin of the party system and was generally perceived as a pariah party. In view of this, the party made repeated efforts to reshape its public image and reclaim the status of a popular tribune. The SD sought to emphasise their traditional role as a political party that had not been corrupted by political power and consensual agreements, and they further insisted that they were the only remaining political force which was concerned about the well-being of the homeland. The party stressed that the government and the parties forming the government coalition had failed miserably to solve the key problems facing Switzerland at that time, and that they were responsible for the gloomy situation of Swiss society generally, a malaise best illustrated by 'the dreadful state of affairs regarding asylum seekers [*Asylanten*]; the overforeignization; the criminality; and the selling out of our country to the EU governors in Brussels'.[50]

Most commonly, the SD adopted an anti-establishment rhetoric in campaigns related to issues of migration and asylum. On this matter, the SD succeeded most consistently in combining the Manichean worldview of a populist party with a radical right-wing, exclusionist ideology. For example, the party regularly criticised the government and political elite for betraying the people, because they had supposedly failed to solve the so-called 'foreigners problem'. In addition, foreign policy, and particularly the issue of European integration, became main areas of policy where the SD sought to evoke resentment towards the political establishment in the 1990s. During the 1992 debate over the country's EEA membership, the SD denounced the *'classe politique'* for losing touch with the people and criticised the people's representatives for no longer representing the people, but 'big money' and 'internationalism' instead.[51] The party complained that social agents such as the media and the trade unions supported European integration and were thereby betraying the country's independence.[52]

In the 1990s, the political agenda of the SD was still profoundly marked by an exclusionist ideology. This was most consistently demonstrated in the party's migration policy, which continued to be at the top of its political agenda. The SD regularly intervened on issues related to immigration, asylum, naturalisation procedures and what the SD insisted on calling 'assimilation'. This ensured that they enjoyed regular opportunities to advocate discriminatory policies towards migrants, asylum seekers and foreign residents. Despite attempts in the early 1990s to display some moderation in its public appearance, the SD continued to put forward radical demands and to favour harsh language when it came to any kind of migration matters. As repeatedly stressed in party manifestos, there were too many immigrants and foreigners living in Switzerland and therefore, the reduction of foreigners would have to be seen as an unavoidable prerequisite for a healthy, stable and social 'living space' for the Swiss people.[53] The party also continued to point to the alleged overforeignization of the country and complained that Switzerland suffered from a high 'demographic overforeignization' and that it was no longer possible therefore, to proceed with the 'assimilation' of the people who had immigrated.[54] This situation would cause the creation of 'ghettos for foreigners' and the increasing demarcation between foreigners and the 'Swiss people' which would eventually result in social tension, hostility against foreigners and a profound security risk.[55]

The SD also embraced ethnopluralist and neoracist views, as shown, for example, in the response drafted by the local section from Zurich opposing the model of integration policy proposed by the local authorities in Zurich. Therein, the SD section put emphasis on the dramatic changes in immigration: whereas most immigrants had previously come 'from neighbouring countries or at least from countries which belong to the European cultural sphere [*Kulturkreis*]', in recent years Zurich had, they claimed, been 'flooded with newcomers coming from exotic countries' and their 'assimilation is almost impossible'.[56] It was clear for the SD that all these immigrants should ultimately return to their home country. Thus, it was no surprise, in 1998, when the SD local section of Zurich launched its initiative 'Swiss first!' (*Schweizer/innen zuerst!*) with the party demanding that the authorities should ensure that the city of Zurich retained a Swiss character and that there should be no more immigration of foreigners from 'non-European cultural spheres' who were hardly able to assimilate.[57] In November 2003, after a long-running controversy over the validity of the initiative, the Federal Tribunal upheld the decision of the cantonal government of Zurich, declaring that the initiative was invalid.[58]

Another main concern of the SD was the growing number of Muslim migrants living in Switzerland, which was allegedly leading to the increasing 'Islamisation' of the country.[59] As early as 1990, the SD paper published an article by Beat Christoph Bäschlin, who became notorious for his contributions in publications associated with the extreme right and the New Right in Germany and Switzerland.[60] Bäschlin argued that 'Islamic immigrants cannot assimilate', and claimed that 'smuggling-in of Muslims [*Musulmanen*] is a conscious and planned attack on our European-Christian and Swiss independence'.[61]

The SD also resolutely rejected the conception of multiculturalism, presenting it as a threat to the cultural identity of the national community and as the reason for violent outbursts in the inner cities.[62] Jean-Jacques Hegg, who served as an editor on the SD paper in the 1990s despite the controversies related to his writings in the 1980s, even went one step further in a front-page article on multiculturalism: he maintained that the purpose of using the term 'multiculturalism' is to keep the people calm and prevent them from getting upset about the fact that their 'living space' was becoming increasingly overpopulated and 'overforeignized' with immigrants from all around the world, and that native inhabitants who should otherwise be enjoying full benefit of their own cultural identity would disappear, die out, or themselves be forced to assimilate because of this 'mass of intruders'.[63] He then made the racially motivated claim that a multicultural society would reflect 'a dying out of the native peoples of European origin, the Europides [*europiden Völker*], and their replacement by a mish-mash of peoples [*Völkermischmasch*] from all the other parts of the world'.[64] It was also Hegg who was mainly responsible for the fact that *Schweizer Demokrat* continued to publish articles in which references were made to theories of ethology and sociobiology.[65]

Nationalism was another key feature of the political program of the SD in the 1990s. The SD coined the slogan 'Switzerland for us, the Swiss!'[66] and warned that 'the loss of one's own culture threatens our own self-conception and undermines our will for national self-assertion'.[67] For this reason, the party stressed the importance of safeguarding Swiss cultural possessions and customs and of cultivating Swiss historical consciousness. In addition to the nationalistic views expressed in statements on migration policy, the SD voiced their nationalism through numerous campaigns against European integration. In 1992, for example, the editor-in-chief of *Schweizer Demokrat*, Dragan Najman, argued that accepting EEA membership would mean a betrayal of 'our ancestral values, our culture, our customs and traditions, and particularly the abandonment of our independence and liberty'; this process would start with EEA membership and conclude with joining the EC.[68] In the interest of consistency, the SD claimed that the concept of Europe should draw upon the principle of a Europe of the fatherlands reserved only for Europeans.[69]

In the debate over the country's role during the Second World War, the SD also revealed their nationalist attitude and opposed any reappraisal of Switzerland's history. The party insisted that fully applied neutrality and a strong army were the main reasons why Switzerland had not been invaded and occupied during this difficult period of time. In line with this point of view, the SD condemned the report on Swiss refugee policy that was released by the Independent Commission of Experts Switzerland – Second World War, a report which they accused of being one-sided, self-righteous, biased and the product of left-wing historians at home and foreign historians generally.[70] In the debate over the 'unclaimed' Jewish assets in Swiss banks, SD president and National Councillor Rudolf Keller had already denounced 'the unprecedented dirty campaign of the international and national press which is dragging our country and particularly our Second World War generation through the mud'.[71] It was also Keller, in July 1998, who signed a call launched by the Swiss Democrats to boycott 'all American and U.S. Jewish goods, restaurants and vacation offers' until there was a halt to the attacks against Switzerland.[72] As the statement bore resemblance to 'Do not buy from Jews' – the notorious call for a boycott that had been issued by the National Socialists – Keller was arraigned on charges of breaking the anti-racism law, although the Council of States ultimately refused to lift Keller's parliamentary immunity.[73]

Finally, it is worth noting that the economic program of the SD was somewhat different to other parties of the Swiss radical right. The SD regularly pointed to the negative aspects of a free market economy, a consumer society, unlimited economic growth and the expansion of the big corporations. It also stressed the importance of a national market economy that should be in the interest of the national community and not for the profit of multinational corporations. As the party criticised the increasing dismantling of the social state, it demanded that 'the rich should not get always richer and the poor always poorer'.[74] From the view of the SD, the economy should not be an end in itself, but should fulfil the real needs of the Swiss people.[75] Moreover, by emphasising the importance of an efficient environmental policy, by tradition a concern of the SD, the party asked for state interventions to regulate energy and transportation policies and thereby restrict the forces of the free market. The SD's conviction that the state should assume a strong role was particularly expressed on issues related to internal security and crime. For example, when the party argued that a sense of fear had increased among the population and that the rise of crime and violence was the result of more immigration, it urged state authorities to reinforce security and policing and to restrict immigration laws.[76]

In conclusion, the Swiss Democrats were the only direct survivors of the Movement against Overforeignization and hence typified the persistence of a traditional party of the radical right in the Swiss party system. However, the party failed to produce truly populist leaders with a mass appeal, or to mobilize greater popular support with a campaigning style that bordered on the old-fashioned. As a cadre party, it had its base in a relatively small membership and continued to be a fringe actor in elections and parliaments, yet it still managed to exploit its proficiency and experience in direct-democratic activities. Compared to the other fringe parties of the radical right that will be addressed in the following sections, the political program of the SD combined the most consistently exclusionist and nationalist ideas with an authoritarian belief in a strong state.

The Swiss Democratic Union: A Fundamentalist Party and its Exclusionist Worldview

The Swiss Democratic Union (*Eidgenössisch-Demokratische Union* – EDU) was founded in 1975 as a splinter party from the Movement against Overforeignization. In the 1980s, the religiously oriented faction gained predominance within the national party. Under the leadership of the cantonal party from Bern, the EDU ultimately developed into a political party that was turned towards the fundamentalist current of the Protestant-Conservative movement in the German-speaking part of Switzerland and its main aim was 'to promote biblical values and to oppose the influence of other cultures in Swiss society'.[77] The EDU shared similar views with other radical right-wing populist parties on a number of issues, particularly on policies related to migration and European integration. In some ways, the EDU bore resemblance to the New Christian Right in the United States which has established a network of think-tanks, single-issue groups and religious organisations since the 1970s.[78] As a counterpart to the EDU, in the mid 1990s, some tried to build a Catholic party in the German-speaking part of Switzerland and formed the Catholic People's Party (*Katholische Volkspartei* – KVP). The party aimed at attracting Catholics with a fundamentalist orientation and a pronounced conservative worldview.[79] The KVP participated at several cantonal elections, but failed to gain any support worthy of note or any lasting political significance, not least because of its internal squabbling.[80]

From Dissident Group to Political Party with a Stronghold in Bern

Dissident senior officials from the Republican Movement and National Action played a key role in the foundation of the EDU in 1975.[81] When the EDU presented its first political program, the *Neue Zürcher Zeitung* wrote that the party was a splinter group with a 'right-wing national ideology', and so bore certain similarities to Schwarzenbach's Republicans and to National Action.[82] Nonetheless, in its party writings, the EDU conspicuously avoided any reference to its origins in the Movement against Overforeignization. For example, the official publication of the party's 25th anniversary stated that 'the EDU has its origins in the Christian circles of protestant Switzerland and was founded by visionary representatives from the cantons of Bern, Zurich and Vaud'.[83] This point of view presents the EDU as an entirely new party creation formed as the result of a split from the long-established Protestant People's Party (*Evangelische Volkspartei* – EVP).[84] The EVP was founded in 1917 as a political party that sought to act as a counterbalance to the Catholic Conservatives, promoted conservative and religious values and had electoral strongholds in the cantons of Zurich and Bern.[85]

In the early years, it was Zurich section in particular which continued to be characterised by its proximity to the Movement against Overforeignization. This was still the case in 1995, when the EDU section established an electoral alliance with the SD cantonal party for the National Council elections in Zurich. On this occasion, the Zurich section of the EDU issued a statement declaring that the two parties shared the same views on important issues such as abortion, European integration, family policy and drug policy.[86] It is also worth noting that some early senior members of the EDU in Zurich, who had left the party in the early 1980s, later gained notoriety for their involvement in the Swiss extreme right. One example was Max Wahl, first president of the section of Zurich and editor-in-chief of the paper *Eidgenoss* (Swiss), founded in 1975 and closely associated to the EDU (see chapter 8).[87] Wahl was expelled from the EDU in 1981 because of his neo-Nazi attitude and anti-Israel statements.[88] After Wahl's expulsion, the EDU launched the paper *EDU-Standpunkt* as its official party organ in September 1981.[89]

The most important section of the EDU was the cantonal party of Bern, which also went on to become the dominant force in the party organisation at the national level. Under the leadership of Peter Rüst, president of the national party from 1979 to 1989, and his successor Werner Scherrer, the cantonal section gradually succeeded in establishing itself in the cantonal party system of Bern. The cantonal party was influenced by religious circles and aimed at attracting Protestant voters living in the canton of Bern. In its early years, the cantonal section of Bern also espoused an intransigent standpoint towards Catholicism, as displayed, for instance, in the programmatic writing of Peter Rüst.[90] According to some authors, this anti-Catholic position gave the EDU the opportunity to attract supporters from the EVP who were still opposed to the revocation of the Jesuits article in the Swiss constitution, which had long restricted the activities of Jesuits in Switzerland and was eventually lifted in a popular vote in 1974.[91]

In the 1978 elections in the canton of Bern, the EDU conquered its first seat in the Great Council, the cantonal parliament of one hundred members. It took until 1990 for a second EDU representative to be elected to the parliament, when the party gained 2.3 per cent of the vote. In 1994, the EDU received 3.3 per cent of the vote and added a third seat. In 1998, when the EDU increased its share of the vote to 4.6 per cent, the party counted four MPs in the cantonal parliament of Bern. In the late 1990s, in addition to its stronghold in Bern, the EDU succeeded in conquering one seat each in the cantonal parliament of Aargau (1997), Zurich (1999) and Thurgau (2000). The EDU also made use of direct-democratic tools to promote its agenda. By these means, the cantonal section of Bern tried in the 1980s to defend the moral and religious order against alleged impunity and profanity.[92] Another goal was to denounce the fraudulence of the political elite in Bern. In 1986, for example, the cantonal party of Bern submitted an initiative demanding that members of the cantonal government should no longer be allowed to hold a second public office.[93]

A Fringe National Party and its Far-reaching Mouthpiece

At the national level, the EDU was a fringe party and received only little support in elections. It scored 1 per cent of the vote in the National Council elections of 1991. Four years later, the party managed to slightly increase its support to 1.3 per cent and maintained this score in 1999. Almost half of all the votes received by the EDU in the 1999 elections came from the canton of Bern.[94] In 1991, the party won its first seat in the National Council with Werner Scherrer, representative from the canton of Bern. Scherrer was reelected in 1995 and then resigned in 1997. He was then succeeded by Christian Waber, who consolidated his position in the National Council elections of 1999.

The EDU has occasionally been engaged in extra-parliamentary activities, mainly by waging petitions and calling for referendums on issues related to moral order and drug policy. In 1991, the EDU successfully requested a referendum on the new federal legislation on sexual offences. The party argued that the law would basically put homosexuality on an equal footing with heterosexuality and that it would also legalise soft pornography.[95] The law was accepted, however, by a large 73.1 per cent majority in the popular vote of May 1992, with a 39.2 per cent turnout. In 1999, the EDU demanded a referendum on the Federal Decree on the medical prescription of heroin, arguing that the party felt deeply disturbed by the way that drug policy was developing in Switzerland.[96] Once again, the voters did not share the EDU's view and accepted the decree with 54.4 per cent in June 1999. The turnout on this occasion was 45.7 per cent. In 1995, the party achieved its greatest degree of mobilisation to date, as it collected over eighty-eight thousand signatures for a petition that opposed the granting of equal rights to homosexual couples.[97]

In the 1990s, the EDU improved its organisational structures and expanded its party apparatus. It established, for example, new party offices in several regions of the country. The party made considerable further increases in its number of cantonal parties. In 1991, the EDU had sections in nine cantons, but by 2003 it was represented in as many as twenty-three cantons.[98] Nonetheless, the EDU remained a fringe party with a small membership of some three thousand in 1995.[99] On the other hand, the EDU produced the party paper *EDU-Standpunkt* (EDU Standpoint), founded in 1981, which has been published monthly since 1990. The paper not only played a vital role in the enhancement of the party's cohesion, but also ensured that the party was known beyond the inner circles of party members. In addition to party information, the paper published longer feature articles on a variety of religious, political, social and cultural themes. The circulation ranged from thirty-one to forty-five thousand, and in times of national elections it even increased to five hundred thousand.[100] In addition, the EDU founded the four-page French-language paper *impulsion* in 1995, with a circulation of ten thousand. This was part of a larger campaign that aimed to improve the party's position in the French-speaking part of Switzerland.[101]

From Solidarism to Fundamentalism and Exclusionism

The first party program of the EDU in 1975 was strongly influenced by revolutionary nationalism and its solidarist current in particular. Solidarism draws mainly upon the ideas of Otto Strasser, the well-known German national-revolutionary from the 1930s. From a solidarist standpoint, the combination of socialism and nationalism should represent the third way that would go beyond the communist and capitalist conceptions of society which had both proved insufficient.[102] Following this line of thinking, the EDU used the term 'patriotism' rather than 'nationalism' in its 1975 party program and stated that the solidarist synthesis of patriotism and socialism was precisely the ideology the Confederation should aspire to. According to the EDU, solidarism is the ideological unity of the national and social propellant of human beings, both of which can be proven scientifically. The public should meticulously apply the three principles of solidarity, sovereignty and legality in order to renew, morally and ethically, what the EDU referred to as the 'sick Confederation'. This was deemed necessary because 'the uneasiness of the people (corruption in state, economy and political parties; indebtedness; inflation; overforeignization; unemployment; increase in crime) requires the reordering of conditions'.[103] It was also demanded that immigration be handled in a more selective way and that only a limited number of citizens from foreign countries, those who 'are educated and able to assimilate', should be allowed to receive Swiss citizenship.[104] Finally, it is worth noting that the EDU program claimed that since life is indivisible, biopolitics represented an entity that would include the different areas of society, economy and politics.[105]

Religion played a minor role in this first political program of the EDU. It was only in the early 1980s that Christianity and the bible started to become the key references of the party's worldview. For example, in the first issue of *EDU-Standpunkt* from 1981, Peter Rüst declared that it must be the goal of the EDU to ensure that 'our Swiss politics are imbued with true Christian and biblically grounded thought'.[106] From that moment, the Christian doctrine began to serve as the basic foundation of the party's views on political and social life. Senior members declared that they felt first obliged to God, the Bible and the Christian faith, and then to the party and their program. They also maintained that the ethical and moral aspects of biblical principles should be the central inspiration of any political commitment and activity.[107] According to Werner Scherrer, since Switzerland had witnessed growing godlessness and the deterioration of values, it would be the mandate of the EDU to confront these godless forces with the positive alternative of the gospel.[108] Consequently, the party program from 1999 noted that the party would do everything possible to make Christian values stronger in politics.[109]

The party's religious fundamentalism also generated strong criticism of modernity and liberal attitudes, which were both perceived as destructive forces of social and moral order and cultural tradition. According to Christian Waber, president of the EDU since 1995, social decline started with the French Revolution, when God was deposed and the human being became the measure of all things. In his view, the deterioration of values has subsequently been triggered by the emergence of humanism, evolution, industrialisation and materialism.[110] In view of such criticism, the EDU faced up to the development of modern society – or the *Zeitgeist*, as party officials liked to call it – with a sense of cultural despair, and so responded with the espousal of a profoundly conservative value system. Most significantly, the party held uncompromising positions on family policy, abortion, drug abuse, AIDS and homosexuality. It was argued that family, marriage and children should be the building blocks of society and that any alternative ways of living together should be dismissed.[111] Based on this line of reasoning, the EDU sharply rejected homosexuality and thereby also expressed a homophobic attitude.[112] When it came to the issue of AIDS, the disease was presented as the logical and direct result of 'illicit sexual relations, whoring, homosexuality and drug abuse'.[113]

Aside from its religiously fundamentalist orientation, the nature of the EDU corresponded in large part to the profile of other parties of the Swiss radical right. In its approach to the party system, the party applied a populist line of reasoning. In election campaigns in the canton of Bern, for example, the EDU claimed that it was the sole party that was free of scandals and not associated with the disastrous sinecure of 'package politics'.[114] When it came to issues of international integration, the party accused power holders of being subverted by internationalist forces. Moreover, the political and social elite were regularly made responsible for casting Switzerland in an unfavourable light.[115]

The EDU was also left in no doubt that the left and the offspring of the 1968 movement played an influential role in politics, media and culture and that they had greatly contributed to the moral decline of Swiss society. For example, Friedrich Külling, a cantonal MP from Bern and a historian renowned for his pioneering study of Swiss anti-Semitism, argued in a series of articles dealing with the Swiss media that the ultimate goal of those supporters of the 1968 movement who were now employed in editorial positions, was to destroy the order of family, society and the state.[116] Following this line of argument, the party paper of the EDU made the left consistently responsible for any problems which occurred that related to policy areas such as asylum, drug abuse, or internal security.[117]

The positions taken by the EDU regarding migration and migration policy were characterised by exclusionist attitudes. The EDU supported most of the measures that were taken in the 1990s to restrict

Swiss asylum policy. Moreover, senior party officials were engaged in the campaign for a federal initiative, which had been launched by a small committee composed of politicians from the centre-right and radical right-wing populist parties and which was led by the FDP party member, Philipp Müller.[118] The proposal aimed at limiting the number of foreigners to 18 per cent of the population. Müller enjoyed the regular opportunity to present his xenophobic and cultural-differentialist views on migration in the EDU paper. In an article published in 1994, for example, he talked about understandable 'fears of overforeignization' and that the government should take these fears seriously 'in view of the massive immigration from countries which for us are of foreign culture (for instance, the tripling of the number of Muslims in Switzerland within ten years)'.[119]

Müller's allusion to the immigration of Muslims corresponded to the EDU's view on Islam and Muslims, which was marked by rejection and hostility. In fact, *EDU-Standpunkt* published a number of articles that disclosed radical Islamophobic views and evoked the danger of the growing 'Islamisation' of Europe. While Islam was pictured as a militant and invasive religion with contempt for humanity, it was lamented that Europe had lost its Christian faith and hence was more vulnerable to the alleged invasion of Islam.[120] Accordingly, a French missionary stated in an interview that every mosque built on European territory meant that occidentals accepted de facto the superiority of the 'Dar-al-Islam' (Islamic land).[121] In one of the harshest Islamophobic articles published in *EDU-Standpunkt*, Kurt Spörri, a regular contributor to the paper, complained about 'a latent infiltration of the "Christian" occident by an Islam which is getting increasingly virulent', and stated that this infiltration is 'reinforced by an unrestrained "flood of children" descendant from immigrants who were already resident (on average 4 to 6 children per family). They want to "kill Europe by giving birth", as one of their choicest phrases tried to claim.'[122] In the same article, the author made the following comparison: 'Just as Adolf Hitler, who was met with an ironic smile, once revealed his goals so unmistakably in "Mein Kampf", so too are the goals of Islamic fundamentalism disclosed with equal clarity.'[123] While the party's genuinely exclusionist views certainly supported a position of such pronounced Islamophobia, there might also be further explanations for this statement. On the one hand, hostility towards Islam may have been motivated by the party's Christian fundamentalism; on the other, it might be related to the EDU's distinctly pro-Israel attitude that had been laid down in the party program and was typically represented by Werner Scherrer, who was president of an association called Pro Israel.[124]

Finally, the EDU consistently opposed any involvement of Switzerland in supranational organisations. The party was very supportive of isolationist campaigns that were directed against European integration and the country's attempted rapprochements towards the United Nations. Accordingly, *EDU-Standpunkt* published one-page interviews with Christoph Blocher and Ulrich Schlüer, the two most prominent proponents of isolationist positions within the SVP.[125] As the EDU National Councillor Christian Waber pointed out, there is a far-reaching strategy of attacking the various pillars of what made Switzerland a special case. These pillars are represented, according to Waber, by the fatherland, democracy, diligence, labour, banks, discipline and faith. He assumed that the goal of these attacks was to break the country's resistance against membership of the EU, UN and NATO.[126] Some anti-European statements also contained conspiracy-type insinuations stressing that the European Community represented the first step towards a world domination of the Antichrist,[127] and that a united Europe would be a breeding ground and springboard for the emerging 'anti-Christian empire'.[128]

In summary, the EDU remained a fringe party at the national level, but managed to establish a fairly strong base in the canton of Bern and also produced a party paper of significant circulation, through which the EDU could disseminate its political views to a larger audience. As the EDU was transformed into a religious fundamentalist party, the party showed deep concern over the alleged threat that modernity posed to social order, family values and sexual morality – particularly in the form of libertarian ideas coming from the left. In view of its origins in the Movement against Overforeignization, the party also maintained its exclusionist ideological profile, most prominently expressed in its position on issues related to migration and in its harsh Islamophobic attitude. When compared to the two parties that are about to be described, the EDU was somewhat more restrained in its public appearance and political style, but it still employed a populist and defiant anti-establishment rhetoric.

The Car Party/Freedom Party: Rise and Fall of a New Radical Right-wing Populist Party

The Car Party of Switzerland (*Auto-Partei der Schweiz* – APS) was founded in 1985 by Michael Dreher, a legal consultant from Zurich, together with seven former members of the SVP and the FDP. At that time, many believed that the party would be a short-lived political experiment.

Others, particularly observers from abroad, looked upon the party and its peculiar name as a curiosity of Swiss politics.[129] With the remarkable success in the National Council elections of 1991, however, it became clear that the APS would be more than a brief political episode. The party was a good example of the new wave of radical right-wing populist parties that had emerged in Western Europe since the late 1980s and was interpreted by some authors as a response to the emergence of the libertarian left.[130] By combining exclusionist ideas, neoliberal demands and anti-establishment rhetoric, the party adopted a 'winning formula' that typically corresponded to parties like the Austrian Freedom Party and the Progress Parties in Scandinavia, which are considered distinct examples of a new type of radical right-wing populist parties.[131]

From Citizens' Action Group to Political Party

The precursor to the APS was the Citizens' Action Group for Less State (*Bürgeraktion für weniger Staat*), which was founded in Zurich in 1981. The group attracted public attention by placing ad campaigns in newspapers, mainly focusing on issues related to cantonal and local politics.[132] In the ad campaigns, the promoters embraced a neoliberal and anti-statist agenda that latter became the programmatic basis of the APS. Reducing taxes and state expenditure, facilitating private traffic, and abolishing state monopoly of television and radio broadcasting were some of the central demands propagated by the group in their ads. The group also notably criticised the large number of asylum seekers and illegal immigrants, asking: 'Why do they always come to Switzerland? Why, for example, do the supposedly persecuted Tamils not go to neighbouring South India, where they would fit in with the religion, culture and climate?'[133]

At its very beginning, the APS was seen as a reaction to growing concerns about ecological issues and the increasing influence of green politics.[134] After the emergence of ecological movements in Switzerland in the 1970s and the subsequent establishment of green parties in the early 1980s, ecological demands such as the reduction of air pollution, the restriction of individual motorised transportation and programs of economy measures regarding energy became principal themes in the domestic political agenda. All mainstream parties began to include ecology and environmental protection in their political programs and election campaigns.[135] When, in 1983, the dying of the forest was at the centre of public debates, with the Swiss government adopting a number of emergency measures, opposition instantly materialised against what opponents called the results of 'Eco-war' and the hysteria about the dying of the forest. In this context, the APS presented itself as a protective organisation for motorised consumers and claimed that it would act as an interest group in favour of free private transportation. Michael Dreher, co-founder and leading figure of the APS, declared that the party would lead the counter-reformation to hit back at the reformation of the Greens.[136]

Thus, the APS was initially a single-issue party whose political program was essentially based upon 'anti-attitudes' that appealed to voters who were aggravated by the increased importance of ecological issues and postmaterialist politics.[137] In addition, by espousing neoliberal positions, the party sought to distinguish itself from National Action, the other party of the radical right at the time. The APS criticised NA for being green, hostile to the economy and against free private traffic, as well as for often voting overtly with the socialist and 'eco-communists'.[138] Yet, just two years after its foundation, the APS shifted more and more toward exclusionist politics and added the themes of asylum and refugee policy to its political agenda, making them central issues of its campaign for the National Council elections of 1987.[139] When James Schwarzenbach, former leader of the Movement against Overforeignization, joined the APS section of Graubünden in July 1989, the APS underscored its intention to reach out to the radical right-wing segments of the Swiss electorate.[140] The programmatic shift in the late 1980s also aimed at transforming the party's outlook from a single-issue party to a neoliberal catch-all party, covering a wide range of issues and policies. This shift was underlined in 1990, when the party added the heading 'The Liberals' (*Die Freiheitlichen*) to its name, and again in 1994, when the party name was changed to the Freedom Party of Switzerland (*Freiheits-Partei der Schweiz* – FPS).

From the Peak to the Depths in Electoral Support

After remarkable growth in national elections in the second half of the 1980s and the first half of the 1990s, the APS/FPS suffered numerous electoral setbacks after the mid 1990s and the loss of all its parliamentary seats in the National Council elections of 1999 eventually put the party in serious disarray. While the electoral rise of the APS in the late 1980s and early 1990s can be seen to some extent as a counter-reaction to the salience of ecological issues and the emergence of the Greens, the decline of the APS in the second half of the 1990s was mainly due to the new electoral competition that came from the Swiss People's Party.[141]

In terms of electoral support, the APS/FPS was largely based in the German-speaking regions of Switzerland, with strongholds in the cantons of Aargau, St. Gallen, Thurgau, Solothurn, Schaffhausen and Appenzell Outer-Rhodes. On several occasions, the APS/FPS made efforts to find its grounding in the French-speaking regions of Switzerland, but failed to attract enough supporters and voters. Some commentators have argued that its concentration in decentralised and suburban regions of German-speaking Switzerland reflects the fact that voters in those regions tended to be commuters who were therefore more concerned about issues related to cars and transport as well as being more politically dealigned from the established parties.[142] In cantonal elections during the peak period from 1991 to 1995, the APS/FPS succeeded in adding twenty-seven new seats in cantonal parliaments and even outdid the SVP, which increased the number of cantonal MPs during the same period by twenty-two.[143] At the local level, it is worth noting that from 1992 to 2008, Jürg Scherrer, twice party president (1990–1994; 1998–), has been a member of the municipal executive for the town of Biel. So far, he is the only FPS member to have held executive public office.

When the APS presented candidate lists for the National Council elections in ten cantons in 1987, most observers doubted that the party would gain any seats. However, the party received 2.6 per cent of the vote straight off and won two seats, one each in the cantons of Zurich and Bern (table 4.5). Senior officials of the APS talked of an electoral success, which they believed might have been even better had the right-wing parties, in particular the FDP, not refused to establish electoral alliances with the APS.[144]

Four years later, the APS made a major electoral breakthrough in the National Council elections of 1991. The party almost doubled its share of votes from 2.6 to 5.1 per cent and quadrupled the numbers of MPs in the National Council from two to eight. Commentators were stunned by the success of the APS and viewed it principally in terms of being the result of a large protest vote.[145] In the run-up to the elections, the APS established election alliances with the Swiss Democrats in four cantons (BL, AG, TG and ZH), despite disagreement on some questions of political agenda. If asylum and drug policy were the key issues of the APS election campaign, other issues such as traffic and the environment were confined to the background.[146] Much like the Swiss Democrats, the APS began to use the phrase 'the boat is full' to denounce the government's asylum policy.[147] As post-election polls show, the strategy turned out to be successful. For a large majority of APS voters the theme of asylum and refugees was by far the highest priority, followed by the drug issue.[148]

After the remarkable success in 1991, the renamed FPS experienced slight losses in the National Council elections of 1995. While the share

Table 4.5 | *Results of Car Party/Freedom Party in National Council Elections, 1987–1999*

Cantons[1]	1987		1991		1995		1999	
ZH (35/34)[2]	3.8	1	5.9	2	3.5	1	0.8	–
BE (29/27)[2]	3.2	1	6.8	2	5.9	1	2.7	–
AG (14/15)[2]	5.3	–	13.2	2	11.3	2	1.4	–
SG (12)	5.1	–	12.6	1	10.2	1	1.0	–
SO (7)	4.9	–	9.1	1	10.6	1	1.3	–
TG (6)	6.4	–	8.7	–	8.0	1	2.7	–
BL (7)	2.6	–	4.3	–	1.3	–	0.3	–
SH (2)	–		11.4	–	8.6	–	–	
AR (2)	–		15.8	–	8.9	–	–	
SZ (3)	4.9	–	–		2.8	–	–	
LU (9/10)[2]	3.4	–	–		–		0.3	–
BS (6)	–		–		2.5	–	–	
VD (17)	–		2.5	–	–		–	
GE (11)	–		3.0	–	–		–	
UR (1)[3]	–		(1.7)	–	–		–	
OW (1)[3]	–		–		(3.8)	–	–	
Total[4]	**2.6**	**2**	**5.1**	**8**	**4.0**	**7**	**0.9**	–

Notes: First column: share of the vote; second column: number of seats
Turnouts: 46.5% (1987), 46.2% (1991), 42.2% (1995), 43.4% (1999)
[1] Total number of representatives in National Council per canton
[2] 1995 change in the number of MPs in National Council per canton
[3] Majority electoral system
[4] Total national share of the vote and number of MPs in National Council

Sources: *Année politique suisse 1987*, Bern 1988, p. 50, 52; *Année politique suisse 1991*, Bern 1992, appendix; *Année politique suisse 1995*, Bern 1996, appendix; *Année politique suisse 1999*, Bern 2000, appendix; Seitz, *Nationalratswahlen 1995*, pp. 44–71; Seitz, *Nationalratswahlen 1999*, pp. 56–80.

of the vote was reduced by 1.1 per cent, the party lost only one of its eight seats in the National Council. Most commentators agreed that the FPS declined at the expense of the SVP, the clear election winner in 1995.[149] The APS had continued to prefer the Swiss Democrats as an electoral ally, eventually forming alliances in seven cantons (SZ, SO, BS, BL, SG, AG and TG). Once again, the issues of migration, asylum and drug policy dominated the election campaign of the FPS, though this time the party noticeably radicalised it style and rhetoric.[150]

In 1999, the FPS was the main loser in the National Council elections. The party's share of the vote decreased dramatically from 4.0 to 0.9 per cent and the party lost all seven deputies in the National Council, among them Michael Dreher who had been an MP since 1987. There was wide consent among election analysts that the FPS was ousted by the SVP, which eventually absorbed most of the electorate that had supported the radical right-wing populist splinter parties.[151] This time, the FPS had entered into electoral alliances with the SD in twelve cantons. The FPS led an election campaign whose issues were more wide-ranging than in previous times, demanding that more freedom be given to the individual private motorist; that borders should be closed to asylum seekers; that the government should improve internal security by reinforcing law and order; and that the social security system should be made more secure.[152]

In their educational and occupational profile, large parts of the APS voters could hardly be said to represent what some liked to call 'modernisation losers'. Rather, they resembled the diverse electorate of several of the newly emerging radical right-wing populist parties in Europe of that time, in particular the Northern League in Italy, the Progress Party in Norway and New Democracy in Sweden.[153] The most comprehensive set of data shedding light on the constituency of the APS/FPS emerges from the survey carried out after the National Council elections of 1991. While gender and religion were not categories that distinguished the social base of the APS from other parties, factors such as age groups, level of education and place of residency appeared to be of greater significance (table 4.6). What seems to be likely is that the APS attracted younger people and voters who had a fairly good education and were living in urban areas. While the party recruited its supporters across social classes, it did particularly well among blue-collar workers as well as among professionals in executive positions.[154]

Another electoral account states more precisely that the APS especially appealed to members of the older middle class, including professionals, craftsmen and shopkeepers. The account also points to differences between the electorates of the APS and the Swiss Democrats and argues that in the case of the APS: 'Liberal nationalism draws the older middle class more strongly, whereas social nationalism [of the Swiss Democrats] is more attractive for blue-collar workers and low-status employees who might have to rely on the welfare state'.[155] As shown by the survey from 1991, APS voters were particularly concerned with the issue of asylum and refugees (table 4.7). Moreover, in comparison with other parties, the APS electorate revealed strong dissatisfaction and mistrust of the political authorities (table 4.8). Although

Table 4.6 | *Social Profile of Car Party Supporters, 1991*

	APS	Sample
Gender		
Female	46%	46%
Male	54%	54%
Age		
18–39 years	46%	36%
40–64 years	42%	45%
65–84 years	12%	19%
Religion		
Protestant	56%	51%
Catholic	40%	42%
Education		
Low	12%	13%
Medium	76%	62%
High	12%	25%
Occupation		
Executives	36%	23%
Medium-level employees/civil servants	29%	39%
Lower-level employees/civil servants	7%	13%
Workers	29%	19%
Farmers	0%	6%
Employment		
Full	56%	49%
Part time	4%	15%
Unemployed	40%	36%
Residency		
Large Cities	48%	28%
Small and Medium-Sized Cities	24%	27%
Rural Area	28%	45%

Source: C. Longchamp and S. Hardmeier, *Analyse der Nationalratswahlen 1991*, Adliswil, 1992, p. 22.

Table 4.7 | *Priority Issues of Car Party Supporters, 1991*

	APS	Sample
1. Priority: Asylum rights/refugees	48%	21%
2. Priority: Drugs	8%	5%
3. Priority: Traffic questions	8%	2%

Source: Longchamp and Hardmeier, *Nationalratswahlen 1991*, p. 23.

Table 4.8 | *Trust of Car Party Supporters in Federal Council and Parliament, 1991*

	APS	Sample
Federal Council	24%	49%
National Council	20%	45%
Council of the States	24%	45%

Source: Longchamp and Hardmeier, *Nationalratswahlen 1991*, p. 23.

Table 4.9 | *Self-placement of Car Party Supporters on the Left–Right Continuum, 1991*

	APS	Sample
Far right	24%	5%
Right	44%	27%
Center	20%	31%
Left	8%	27%
Far left	0%	3%

Source: Longchamp and Hardmeier, *Nationalratswahlen 1991*, p. 23.

some authors have recently argued that a self-assessment of where voters believe they sit on the left–right continuum actually says little about the attitudes of radical right-wing voters, it is nonetheless striking that, in 1991, almost a quarter of APS voters assessed themselves as being at the far right of the political spectrum (table 4.9).[156]

Weak Party Organisation and Little Direct-democratic Activity

Because the APS had been launched as a loose interest group and was subsequently held together by a couple of political entrepreneurs, the early years of the party were characterised by weak organisational structures and a low degree of membership. For the 1987 National Council elections, the APS was barely able to present lists of candidates in ten of the twenty-six cantons. Some of the first cantonal party sections were solely founded with a view to participate in the upcoming cantonal elections.[157] But as the party multiplied its successes in cantonal and local elections, it began to build a network of cantonal sections and managed to make a significant increase in the number of party members in the late 1980s. While in 1989, the APS had thirteen cantonal sections, this number grew to sixteen in 1997.[158] In January 1989, the party claimed that to have over ten thousand members who were resident across almost all of the Swiss cantons.[159] In 1997, the number of party members was generously estimated to be around six thousand, and since then membership may well have dropped again significantly.[160] Overall, it is tempting to agree with Andreas Ladner, who concludes: 'The FPS did not succeed in establishing a party organisation in the traditional sense or binding members in great number to the party'.[161]

Initially, the organisational looseness of the APS was also reflected in the simplicity and limitations of its political program and in its party literature. During the first six years of its existence, the so-called Political Guidelines represented the party's principal policy document and included nothing more than political slogans and short statements on different policy issues.[162] In 1991, the party presented a complete, 21-page party program for the first time, which contained extensive coverage of a wide range of policy areas, including transportation, asylum, environment, energy, economy and finances, social affairs, drugs, etc.[163] The subsequent program editions of 1995 and 1999 were even more comprehensive and elaborate, suggesting that the party was seeking to ameliorate its public image from that of merely a low-profile political party.[164]

The paper *Tacho* (Speedo) was an important publication of the APS/FPS, since it consistently promoted the party's political agenda.[165] Although *Tacho* was not the official party organ, the paper steadfastly assumed the role of being the political and public voice of the APS/FPS. Michael Dreher, the party's long-time leading figure, was owner and editor-in-chief of the paper. *Tacho* appeared eight to ten times per year, was available through subscription and was also distributed in a free copy format. The paper reached fairly high circulation figures, ranging typically from fifty-one to sixty-two thousand. In the beginning, *Tacho* had enjoyed even higher circulation numbers: in 1987, 150,000 copies of the first issue were released and two years later, in the run-up to the National Council elections, the circulation of a promotional copy reached a high of 1,750,000.[166] In terms of style, layout and content, *Tacho* resembled common tabloid papers and articles were often written in simple language with large-font headings.[167] The paper also contained a large number of ads from the car industry. As *Tacho* was not a party organ in the strict sense of the word, politicians from other political parties regularly contributed articles to the paper. Among the contributors were senior officials from the FDP and the SVP in particular. For example, during the debate over EEA membership, Christoph Blocher published articles in *Tacho*.[168] The paper *Tacho* ceased publication in 1999, following the devastating defeat of the FPS in the National Council elections.

The APS/FPS was not characterised by strong leadership, nor was the party led by an uncontested, charismatic leader. In the beginning, it seemed that Michael Dreher would take full control over party leadership, but his role became more like that of the party's chief ideologue than that of its charismatic leader, and he tended to gain notoriety with his provocative rhetoric and controversial style.[169] However, Dreher's presidency came under scrutiny in the late 1980s, when some critics condemned his authoritarian leadership. As a result, he resigned as party president in 1990, but continued to be one of the party's leading figures. Party cohesion was also regularly impaired by internal conflicts over the programmatic and political course of the party line. These disputes shaped many internal debates and frequently put the unity of the party in jeopardy.[170] When the party experienced electoral losses in the second half of the 1990s, heated debates reemerged about the programmatic direction of the FPS and this ultimately contributed to the party's further disintegration.[171]

In the second half of the 1990s, the FPS recorded a significant drop in membership, in particular at the leadership level. With the exit in 1996 of Ulrich Giezendanner, National Councillor from the canton of Aargau, and of Roland Borer in 1998, National Councillor from the canton of Solothurn and former party president (1994–98), the FPS lost two prominent party members.[172] Both joined the Swiss People's Party and were reelected on an SVP ticket in the National Council elections of 1999. Michael Dreher, too, had deserted from the FPS by the end of 2000 and one year later joined the SVP of the canton of Zurich.[173] At the cantonal and the municipal level, a large number of MPs left the FPS and joined other parties, most of them becoming members of the Swiss People's Party.[174]

Weak party organisation and limited resources had detrimental consequences for the direct-democratic engagement of the APS/FPS. Compared to the Swiss Democrats, the party made much less use of the instruments of direct democracy (table 4.10). Thereby, the APS/FPS confined itself to issues of transportation policy. In 1992, with the support of traffic associations and an employers' group from the French-speaking part of Switzerland, the APS demanded a referendum on the Federal Statute regarding new petrol taxes and managed to collect almost a hundred thousand signatures.[175] However, in the popular vote of March 1993 – which saw a turnout of 51.3 per cent – voters accepted the government's proposal to increase tax on petrol by a small majority of 54.5 per cent.[176] With respect to federal initiatives, the party's record

Table 4.10 | *Federal Initiatives and Referendums by Car Party/Freedom Party in the 1990s*

Subject	Year of Launch	Submitted	Year of Vote	Objective Achieved[1]
Initiative 'For the Abolition of the Direct Federal Tax'	1990	no	–	–
Referendum on the Federal Statute on gas tax increase[2]	1992	yes	1993	no (45.5%)
Initiative 'Second Gotthard Tunnel Pipe'[2]	1998	no	–	–
Initiative 'Enlargement of the Highway A1 Zurich-Bern to Six Lanes'[2]	1998	no	–	–
Initiative 'Enlargement of the A1 Geneva-Lausanne Highway to Six Lanes'[2]	1998	no	–	–
Initiative 'For the Abolition of the Right of Associations to File Complaints at the Federal Level'[2]	1998	no	–	–

Notes: [1] Indicating whether and with what much percentage voters supported the party's proposal
[2] Initiative committee also included members of transport associations and other political parties
Source: http://www.admin.ch/ch/d/pore/va/index.html, retrieved 31 August 2008.

turned out to be even less successful. All five attempts to submit initiatives failed straight away at the stage of signatures collection.

Populism, Exclusionism and Neoliberalism

The populist nature of the APS/FPS was clear to see in the party's consistent strategy of evoking resentment and mistrust towards government, state administration and the party system. It was clear that the party perceived an antagonistic relationship between the political establishment and 'the people', whom they saw as being betrayed by government, politicians and other political parties. This view drew on two basic lines of reasoning: on the one hand, the APS/FPS was convinced that the left and the Greens had subverted the state administration and the party system to eventually build up a position of dominance in Swiss politics and society; on the other hand, the party took a strong anti-state attitude, which resulted from the party's commitment to neoliberal views on economic matters and were gradually transformed into a far-reaching anti-system attitude.

As early as 1988, Michael Dreher argued that voters supported the Car Party because they were fed up with the conformist politics of the government parties and their willingness to compromise.[177] In 1995, the FPS delegates adopted a resolution at the tenth anniversary party assembly which accused both the government and right-wing parties of mismanagement, and demanded that the principle of concordance and the 'magic formula' should finally be brought to an end.[178] The party also argued that while a grand coalition might be the optimum solution in most countries, this was not generally the case in Switzerland, where left-wing and green parties would be able to dictate who would be elected into government, eventually leading to a situation which the FPS regarded as a 'perversion of democracy'.[179]

The party also launched attacks against other social agents, particularly against the media, intellectuals and academics, whom they believed to exert too much influence in the political and public life of the nation.[180] Most commonly, the criticism was directed against the so-called 'political class', including both established parties and government, the latter of which was described by Michael Dreher as 'degenerate' and 'wrecked' and no longer able to run the country.[181] As shown by numerous parliamentary speeches, press releases and articles published in *Tacho*, such harsh language and polemical rhetoric were significant traits of the party's political style. Occasionally, the Swiss public reacted with strong indignation to these kinds of statements. The most notorious example was the inflammatory words of Michael Dreher at a reception of the Swiss Academy of the Humanities in 1988, when he reportedly said that left-wingers and Greens should be nailed against the wall and then torched with a flame-thrower.[182]

Shortly after the foundation of the APS in 1985, asylum and refugee policies became one of the party's programmatic and political priorities. From this moment on, the APS/FPS started to reveal bluntly xenophobic sentiments, presenting asylum seekers as 'spongers', 'bogus asylum seekers', 'asylum tourists', 'criminals' or 'drug dealers'. During the campaign for the National Council elections of 1995, for example, the FPS section of the canton of St. Gallen distributed two hundred thousand copies of a brochure that referred to the 'unrestricted immigration of bogus asylum seekers and Tamil tourists'.[183] Moreover, the party consistently emphasised the allegedly negative aspects of the right to asylum and sought to make asylum seekers responsible for any kind of socioeconomic problem. Reinforced by its neoliberal criticism of increasing state expenditure, the party's program was, as Hans-Georg Betz put it in his survey of radical right-wing populist parties in Western Europe, 'perhaps the most blatant appeal to the public's perception that immigration represents a growing financial burden on West European societies'.[184]

Drawing on xenophobic attitudes, the FPS proposed drastic policy measures to stop what the party called the growing flood of asylum seekers. It demanded that Switzerland should denounce the 1951 Geneva Convention on Refugees; that no more immigrants should enter the country as long as there were unresolved cases of asylum application; and that all asylum seekers who have entered the country illegally should immediately be deported without going through the interviewing procedures.[185] In its critique of migration and asylum policy, the APS/FPS also took the position that it was the immigrants' and asylum seekers' own fault if they encountered xenophobia and hostility from the Swiss population. Conversely, the party showed great concern that criticism of migration and asylum policy would be sanctioned by law and fiercely opposed, therefore, the anti-racism legislation of 1994. According to Walter Steinemann, FPS National Councillor, it would be highly disturbing if a patriotically motivated opposition to obvious and proven misuse of the right to asylum should be equated with racism.[186]

The APS/FPS also vigorously rejected notions of Switzerland as a country of immigration or a multicultural society. The FPS claimed that the notion of a multicultural society represents a threat to Switzerland because it 'makes us Swiss strangers in our own country' and that 'unhindered immigration would systematically undermine and destroy the Swiss people's [*Schweizervolks*] conception of itself and its distinctiveness.'[187] History, they claimed, could provide plenty of evidence for the fact that conflicts were unavoidable when there was mass immigration of people of foreign cultural origins.[188] On this matter, the party drew a clear distinction between Europeans and immigrants who came from other countries. As early as 1987, an article published in *Tacho* warned of 'an unrestrained immigration of exotic peoples into little Switzerland' and proclaimed 'Asia for the Asians'.[189] Following this reasoning, the party argued in a neoracist fashion that immigrants, particularly those from non-European countries, were not able to integrate in Switzerland since they came from a different culture, and that they should be repatriated.[190] Some party members even employed biologically and racially based language. Jürg Scherrer, for example, declared in an interview that 'there is a long-term aim to extinguish the distinctiveness of the Swiss people and to promote the mixing of races, to the point that

Swiss people themselves will feel that they no longer exist in their own self-image'.[191]

The party also linked the theme of asylum to issues of internal security and law and order. They claimed that serious crimes were committed in disproportionately high levels by immigrants from a different 'cultural sphere' and that the increase in drug crimes was the consequence of the government's failed asylum policy.[192] The party demanded that fingerprints, photographs and/or DNA analysis should be taken of all asylum seekers whose request for asylum had been rejected.[193] Generally, the issue of law and order represented a principal theme of the party's political agenda. On several occasions, the party demanded very drastic measures in the fight against crime. In the first half of the 1990s, some party sections sought to launch a demand for the reintroduction of the death penalty.[194] Moreover, party president Jürg Scherrer demanded that petty criminals should be publicly exposed and that those that sprayed graffiti should be imprisoned with nothing more than bread and water. Party delegates integrated some of his suggestions into their propositions for a statement paper on law, order and security that was released in February 1998.[195]

Throughout the 1990s, the APS/FPS repeatedly supported campaigns that opposed the country's international involvement, expressing thereby its nationalist views. While the party somewhat moderately backed the campaign against EEA membership in 1992, by putting the emphasis on financial and economic questions, the party later became more intransigent and rejected any step towards a European integration of Switzerland.[196] National Councillor René Moser, for example, argued that EU membership would mean, amongst other things, not only that the people would lose their democratic rights, but that the country would experience unrestrained immigration which would ultimately result in 'total overforeignization'.[197] Furthermore, when the *Lega dei Ticinesi* and the SD launched the campaign for a referendum on UN peacekeeping forces, the APS National Councillor Walter Steinemann joined the campaign by accepting a position as co-president of the referendum committee.[198]

When Switzerland's role during the Second World War came under scrutiny, the FPS also disclosed its nationalist attitudes. The party defied any criticism and argued that there was no reason for the country to review its past. According to National Councillor Jürg Scherrer, the campaign aimed at systematically dismantling the country's self-confidence and national pride.[199] From the FPS's point of view, the new historiography was primarily politically motivated and sought to play down the importance of the country's military defence during this difficult period of history.[200] Moreover, the FPS criticised the Swiss government for giving in to blackmailing, and denounced the settlement reached between the Swiss banks and claimants in the United States as the 'Munich agreement'.[201]

The APS/FPS was anxious to present neoliberalism as a main feature of its ideological foundation and an irrefutable principle of its political agenda. The party argued that individual liberty and personal initiative were the vital forces of economy and society. In terms of social policy, the party demanded that the social security system should not be a hammock for people who were not willing to perform. It also disapproved of the establishment of a minimum income that would be guaranteed for everyone.[202] According to Hans-Georg Betz, no other party in Western Europe 'has brought the maxims of the new era as succinctly to the point, has celebrated the dawn of individualism and egoism as enthusiastically as the Swiss Automobile party'.[203]

The party's neoliberal position was predominantly expressed in harsh critiques of welfare policies and in demands for tax cuts. From the APS/FPS viewpoint, the balancing of the state budget should be achieved by limiting state interventions to a minimum and by reducing state expenditures. The market economy would not bear permanent state interventions which, the party claimed, had increasingly become the rule in Switzerland because of the extreme levels of faith that right-wing government parties had expressed in the state.[204] One would be mistaken, however, to see the party as a genuine liberal party. In contradiction to principles of liberalism, the APS/FPS expected the state to significantly reinforce its presence in some public domains, such as drug policy, illegal immigration and internal security. As the party highlighted the importance of law and order and constantly thematised alleged failures of internal security, it eventually promulgated the notion of a strong state and the necessity of reinforcing the role of the state in security matters.

In conclusion, while initially conceived as a single-issue pressure group concerned with transportation issues and making anti-ecological claims, the APS/FPS very quickly developed into a populist party with anti-establishment rhetoric and a marked radical-right agenda. The neoliberal agenda served primarily as a foundation of the party's strategy of invoking resentment toward state administration and the party system. Since the party failed to build up a well-structured party organisation and neglected to invest sufficient resources in partisan activities and party work, it experienced difficulties in achieving broad, long-term political mobilization and, ultimately, organisational consolidation. The persistence of internal factiousness and leadership conflicts also weakened the already fragile party cohesion. Thus, the APS/FPS turned out to be an ephemeral actor in the Swiss party system and was eventually absorbed – both electorally and in terms of personnel – by the new SVP.

The Lega dei Ticinesi: A Regionalist, Anti-establishment Party

The *Lega dei Ticinesi* was founded in 1991 in the Italian-speaking canton of Ticino.[205] It emerged as a protest movement that opposed the consensual politics and agreements of the cantonal political elite and thereby adopted a fierce anti-establishment rhetoric. Most authors view the emergence of the *Lega* as the expression of an anti-party revolt in the canton of Ticino.[206] In addition, as Paul Taggart argues, the *Lega dei Ticinesi* 'established itself as an anti-establishment party' by taking advantage of its charismatic and popular leadership.[207] While an examination of its political style and agenda suggests that the *Lega* featured most characteristics of a radical right-wing populist party,[208] it also represents a good example of a regionalist party that pursued its identity politics and populist strategy on multiple levels. As Oscar Mazzoleni put it, 'the *Lega dei Ticinesi* cannot be said to be a purely regionalist, localist or nationalist party, but is simultaneously regionalist, localist, and nationalist'.[209]

While the *Lega dei Ticinesi* made some early explicit references to the Northern League (*Lega Nord* – LN) and its predecessor, the Lombardic League (*Lega Lombarda*), its organisational and political ties to the leagues in Northern Italy were in fact rather loose and limited to a few mutual approaches.[210] One reason for this lies in the fact that the institutional context in Switzerland is fundamentally different from that in Italy, where the League's prime objective was to establish a federalist system. In Switzerland, federalism was already a solid pillar of the political and institutional system, and therefore the *Lega*'s criticism directed towards the central power in Bern was primarily integrated as part of the party's all-purpose anti-establishment and anti-system program. Another reason should be seen in the scepticism and mistrust that has traditionally marked the relationship between Ticino and Lombardy.

Electoral Successes: Diverse Electorate or Protest Voters?

Although the *Lega dei Ticinesi* was fond of highlighting the movement aspect of its character and frequently used unconventional means of action, it was most successful as a political party running for public office.[211] As some authors argue, in the arena of electoral competition, the *Lega*'s 'political effect can even be compared to an earthquake'.[212]

In April 1991, three months after its creation, the *Lega dei Ticinesi* took part in its first elections and promptly won 12.8 per cent of the vote and twelve seats in the Great Council, the cantonal parliament of ninety members (table 4.11). Six months later, the *Lega* received 23.5 per cent in the National Council elections thereby doubling its share of the vote in the canton. Flavio Maspoli, the movement's leader figure, and Marco Borradori were both elected to the National Council. Moreover, in the Council of States elections, the *Lega* won one of the two seats assigned to the canton. In the local elections of 1992, the party continued its triumphant progress and conquered 17.2 per cent of seats in municipal parliaments and 17.6 per cent of those in municipal executives. Most significantly, the *Lega dei Ticinesi* conquered two of the five seats in the local executive of Lugano, the canton's largest city.[213]

In the cantonal elections of 1995 and the municipal elections one year later, the *Lega dei Ticinesi* reinforced its electoral position. Many observers began to realise that the *Lega* was more than a temporary outburst of protest and discontent. The *Lega* was able to raise its number of cantonal MPs to sixteen and managed to maintain its position in most of the municipalities. In 1995, the National Councillor Marco Borradori was elected to the cantonal government of five members. This was a significant break with the long-held tradition that only members of the Liberal, Christian-Democratic or Social-Democratic parties were able to reach this public office.[214] It was also a shift in the *Lega*'s strategy of acting primarily as a protest movement. In the national elections of 1995, however, the party experienced a severe setback and lost one of its two seats in the National Council as well as its representative on the Council

Table 4.11 | *Results of the Lega dei Ticinesi in Great Council and National Council Elections, 1991–1999*

	Great Council		National Council	
1991	12.8%	12	23.5%	2
1995	17.9%	16	18.6%	1
1999	18.1%	16	18.5%	2

Note: First columns: share of the vote; second columns: number of seats
Sources: *Année politique suisse 1991*, Bern 1992, appendix; *Année politique suisse 1995*, Bern 1996, appendix; *Année politique suisse 1999*, Bern 2000, appendix; O. Mazzoleni, *Nationalisme et populisme en Suisse*, Lausanne 2003, p. 28; *Neue Zürcher Zeitung*, 9 April 2003.

of States. To many, the electoral defeat was the result of the rather extravagant public conduct of MPs from the *Lega* in Bern.[215]

In the cantonal elections of 1999, the party succeeded in consolidating its position and defended the sixteen seats in parliament and its one deputy in the government. In the National Council elections of the same year, the *Lega dei Ticinesi* even regained a second seat and was now represented in Bern by Giuliano Bignasca and Flavio Maspoli, the two founders and leaders of the *Lega*. But as commentators have pointed out, the *Lega* came under significant pressure from the SVP, which noticeably strengthened its position in the canton. Ultimately, the *Lega* won the second seat simply because of the electoral alliance it had struck with the SVP.[216]

Early accounts of the party's constituency suggest that the voters of the *Lega dei Ticinesi* were hardly unprivileged persons and that this contradicts to some extent the thesis of 'modernisation losers' that are attracted by a protest movement of the radical right. As a survey taken in the summer of 1991 shows, the *Lega* supporters appeared to have a better education and a higher income in comparison with some left-wing voters and were more likely to own their own house and business. Based on these findings, René Knüsel and Julian Hottinger conclude that 'it seems excessive to qualify the *Lega* voters as merely "desperation" voters, with downwardly mobile categories or in a difficult position willing to express their discontent, like the "Swiss Democrats" for example. Rather, they have some cultural and economic resources, and socially they are upwardly mobile or stable more than downwardly mobile.'[217]

However, data provided by a survey taken after the 1999 National Council elections paints a slightly different picture of the *Lega*'s electorate and confirms the view that there is a proletarisation in the electorate of radical right-wing populist parties. Most significantly, the survey shows that the party was disproportionately represented among workers and employees without professional qualifications (30.0 per cent), while employees in executive positions were under-represented (10.0 per cent). At the same time, the *Lega dei Ticinesi* was made up of the following constituent groups: independent professionals (12.5 per cent), employees in mid-level positions (35.0 per cent) and workers and employees with professional qualification (12.5 per cent). The survey further indicates that the attitudes of *Lega* voters on a number of issues did not significantly differ from those of the two centre-right parties, the FDP and the CVP. For instance, 85.4 per cent of *Lega* supporters pleaded for the protection of traditions, while 84 per cent of FDP voters and 80 per cent of CVP voters took the same position. The data regarding self-placement on the left–right continuum demonstrates that while 43.6 per cent of the *Lega* voters saw themselves as being to the right; this was also the case for 52.5 per cent of the FDP electorate.[218] However, a significant difference between the constituencies of the three parties is revealed when we examine the issue of confidence in political institutions. As aggregated survey data from 1995 and 1999 show, 47.3 per cent of *Lega* voters expressed little or no confidence in political institutions, while only 17.4 per cent of the CVP and 19.6 of FDP supporters took the same stance.[219] This would confirm the view that the *Lega*'s message of mistrust towards political institutional has was of significant appeal to the party's constituency.

The differing results of the surveys certainly have to do with the variable quality of the data sample used. Whatever the case may be, the findings suggest that although the *Lega dei Ticinesi* was able to depend on more support from the lower socioeconomic strata, it did succeed in finding support among all social classes. The higher proportion of underprivileged voters and the low levels of confidence in political institutions would support the thesis that the *Lega* should be viewed as a typical protest party. However, the voters' pronounced right-wing worldview and, as we will see, the party's elaboration of a typical radical-right political program and the growing integration into the political system raises doubts as to what extent the protest thesis explains the electoral success of the *Lega dei Ticinesi*.

Between Movement and Political Party

Compared to traditional parties, the *Lega dei Ticinesi* was more engaged in direct, sometimes unconventional activities and its organisation was less structured, more personalised and more centred on leader figures. This showed not only the movement character of the *Lega*, but also helped it to play the role of a political actor outside the party system of Ticino. Outsider status was also disclosed by the fact that the origins of the *Lega* lay in the free Sunday paper *Il Mattino della domenica* (The Sunday Morning). The tabloid-style paper was launched in March 1990 and run by the editorial director Flavio Maspoli and the publisher Giuliano Bignasca.[220] With a circulation of forty-five to sixty thousand, the paper served as the powerful public voice of the *Lega* and assumed a hub function for the movement. Special issues of the paper even had considerably higher circulation figures. For instance, one hundred and twenty thousand copies were circulating in the run-up to the National Council elections of 1991.[221] This shows the significance that the paper had in the canton of Ticino, that had a total population of around 307,000.

The leadership of Maspoli and Bignasca, 'both of them popular and charismatic', was another important factor in making the *Lega* attractive to the public, and in enabling it to be perceived as a grassroots movement.[222] In 2000, the daily paper *Corriere del Ticino* voted Giuliano Bignasca, life president of the *Lega*, as Ticino's second most important politician of the twentieth century, after Giuseppe Motta, former Federal Councillor and foreign minister.[223] On the other hand, the integrity and credibility of the two leaders were regularly jeopardised, as they were involved in a number of legal proceedings.[224] Moreover, internal conflicts and leadership struggles have also regularly put at risk the cohesion of the *Lega dei Ticinesi*. Particularly in its early years, the *Lega* initiated various forms of popular protest and sought to raise its degree of mobilisation by organising rallies and public events which often caused great public stir.[225] In July 1991, for example, when the *Lega dei Ticinesi* was practically unknown to the public, it caused a sensation when the *Lega* organised a go-slow on the highway to protest against the planned speed limit on Swiss roads. Over five hundred cars participated and succeeded in bringing the traffic to a standstill for a couple of hours. As a consequence, Giuliano Bignasca was sentenced to three months in prison.[226] In addition, on several occasions, the *Lega* launched cantonal initiatives and asked for referendums in order to underline its discontent with the established parties.[227]

At the same time, however, Oscar Mazzoleni shows that the *Lega* went through a process of political integration in the second half of the 1990s. After entry into the cantonal government in 1995, the *Lega* had become a more integrated part of the canton's political system which was based on the principles of concordance and consensus. When Giuliano Bignasca, fierce proponent of the party's role as a protest movement, was elected to the local government of Lugano in 2000, it was seen as a further indication of the *Lega*'s political integration. This process of integration was accompanied by internal disputes between hardliners and moderates over which strategy and course of action the party should take. It was also controversial as to whether or not the *Lega dei Ticinesi* should support the required rule of governmental collegiality.[228] The founders in particular insisted on maintaining the public image of an opposition force fighting against the cantonal *partitocrazia*, a term commonly used by radical right-wing populist parties 'to indicate the fusion of state, party, and the economic elites in politico-economic networks characterised by patronage, clientelism, and corruption'.[229]

At the federal level, the *Lega dei Ticinesi* functioned as a fringe political party which played a rather insignificant role in the parliament, but managed to use the tools of direct democracy as important means of opposition. In both the electoral and the direct-democratic arenas, the *Lega dei Ticinesi* has, since its inception, been closely tied to the Swiss Democrats and on several occasions the two parties have acted as political comrades-in-arms. In the National Council, the *Lega* first formed a parliamentary group with the SD between 1991 and 1995. After the 1995 National Council elections, Flavio Maspoli, the only MP left from the *Lega*, had briefly joined the parliamentary group of the Freedom Party. But in late 1996, he returned to the 'Democratic Fraction' (*Demokratische Fraktion*), which included three MPs from the SD, Maspoli, and an independent MP from the canton of Ticino.[230]

Most significantly, the *Lega dei Ticinesi* and the SD worked in close collaboration as plebiscitary forces. Already in June 1992, the *Lega* had given, for the first time, its unreserved support to the plebiscitary activities of the SD when it organised a last minute collection of signatures in the canton of Ticino in support of the federal initiative 'For a Reasonable Asylum Policy'.[231] As described above, the two parties later collaborated mainly on issues related to Switzerland's international integration. The relationship between the *Lega* and the SD was, however, not without divergence, since the two parties were of a different opinion regarding certain issues of policy. In view of that, the parliamentary group agreement, concluded between MPs from the SD and the *Lega* in 1991, stated that the *Lega* MPs would commit to refraining from fighting in public against the politics of the SD.[232] Most significantly, the two parties disagreed when it came to environmental and transportation policy. The *Lega dei Ticinesi* was also a fierce critic of regulations limiting foreigners' purchase of real estate and hence took an opposing stance to the SD in the 1994 referendum on the revised Federal Statute.[233] Nonetheless, it appeared that for most of the time the *Lega* was a reliable partner of the SD and its national political campaigns.[234]

Between Regionalism and Radical Right-wing Populism

Most authors argue that the *Lega dei Ticinesi* should be categorised as an 'ethnoregionalist' or 'regionalist party'.[235] From this perspective, it makes sense to examine the *Lega* under the aspect of the periphery–centre cleavage.[236] Generally speaking, the defining feature of ethnoregionalist parties is the 'demand for political reorganisation of the existing national power structure, for some kind of "self-government"'.[237] In the case of the *Lega dei Ticinesi*, the party combined a regionalist and populist appeal in order to take advantage of the distinct periphery–centre cleavage that exists in the canton of Ticino. The regionalist purpose of the *Lega* was basically confined to a sort of protectionism within

Swiss federalism, and included cultural, institutional and economic aspects. Thereby, the *Lega* came close to those ethnoregionalist parties which 'endorse a nationalism whose core is based on ethnic distinctiveness'.[238]

As the canton of Ticino forms a linguistic entity – where almost the entire Italian-speaking minority of Switzerland is concentrated – and a geographical insularity behind the Gotthard, it was the purpose of the *Lega* to strengthen, culturally and linguistically, the regional identity. This goal was well-expressed in the slogan 'Ticino for the Ticinesi'.[239] In the debate over a new cantonal constitution, Giuliano Bignasca argued that, in view of growing globalisation, there is a need for local and regional identity and self-government and that the independence, autonomy and identity of Ticino should be explicitly stated in the new constitution.[240] The *Lega dei Ticinesi* also applied rhetoric with ethnic-linguistic overtones, when it criticised what it alleged to be the increasing degree of cultural influences being exerted from within the German-speaking cantons.[241] The *Lega* also fought against too much intervention from the Federal State and from Bern, whilst endeavouring to preserve distinct prerogatives at the level of cantonal politics and administration. On the other hand, the *Lega* complained about the peripheral location of Ticino and the way that the canton is discriminated against by the country's powerful economic centres. This type of argument was particularly salient in the 1990s, when the canton was struck by economic crisis and unemployment, and the population showed great concern about economic matters.[242]

The populist aspect of the *Lega dei Ticinesi* was most compellingly disclosed in its anti-establishment attitude, a key principle of its political program. The prime targets of the *Lega*'s attacks were the established parties to the right and to the left in the canton of Ticino, both of which would supposedly undermine the canton's political culture with their family clans, favoritism and nepotism. The political program for 1995–1999 noted that 'the ruling class of bigwigs' had lost touch with the common people and their problems, and that the strength of the *Lega* lay in its proximity to real and everyday life.[243] To substantiate this type of argument, leading figures of the *Lega* used very aggressive and polemical language. Giuliano Bignasca, for example, called Ticino's party system a *'partitocrazia banditocratica'* and claimed that the *Lega dei Ticinesi* has brought 'a creative wind to the fossilised and sclerotic political mood' established by the traditional parties.[244] Moreover, in numerous articles published in *Il Mattino della domenica* the dollar sign was inserted into words like socialist and socialist party (e.g., 'partito $ocialista').[245]

The *Lega dei Ticinesi* took a pronounced anti-system attitude, which was particularly expressed through a defiant perception of political institutions. For example, Giuliano Bignasca complained that parliament had degenerated into 'a cash register' and 'a chat room'.[246] He also proudly declared that the populism of the *Lega* aimed at giving a face to the silent majority who had always had to suffer under the democratic system. In his view, this democratic system was simply the continuation of the famous feudal monarchies, where the noble families had now been replaced by political parties which were themselves controlled by the wielders of economic power.[247]

Compared to the other radical right-wing populist parties in Switzerland, it appears that, in the early years at least, the issue of migration policy was of less importance for the political agenda of the *Lega dei Ticinesi*. In the political program from 1991, the party even demanded that the status of seasonal workers should be abolished and that familial reunion should be allowed to foreign workers.[248] Both claims were diametrically opposed to the positions taken by the Swiss Democrats. In the second half of the 1990s, however, the issue of asylum became one of the *Lega*'s main priorities. In so doing, the party regularly took positions marked by exclusionist and xenophobic sentiments. In the paper *Il Mattino della domenica*, asylum seekers were usually presented as bogus refugees, most of whom had come to Switzerland illegally and simply out of economic motivations.[249] Significantly, the *Lega* was in favour of the two asylum initiatives launched by the SVP. By using the phrase 'the boat is full', *Lega* also endorsed the initiative launched by Philipp Müller and others, which demanded that the number of foreigners should be limited to 18 per cent of the population.[250]

When the debates over the 'unclaimed' Jewish assets in Swiss banks emerged, *Il Mattino della domenica* published articles with anti-Semitic overtones.[251] Anti-Semitism was overtly displayed in an article written by Giuliano Bignasca. The article was about the emissaries of the 'Volcker Commission',[252] who were exploring the archives of the Cantonal Bank of Ticino at the time. Bignasca noted that they were accommodated in a luxury hotel in Lugano and wrote the following line: 'For these gentlemen ... one should pay for two weeks vacation in the Hotel Buchenwald of Dachau, which is run by a congenial gentleman with a little mouth.'[253] For the article, Bignasca was eventually sentenced under anti-racism legislation.[254]

Identity politics and a call for the uncompromising protection of Swiss national identity were further core features of the political agenda promoted by the *Lega dei Ticinesi*. This was reflected in the isolationist stance on issues related to Switzerland's international involvement. Throughout the 1990s, the party was continually engaged in the struggle against the process of European integration. According to the *Lega*, the country's independence, neutrality and democracy would be put at serious risk if Switzerland were to join the European Union. Concurrently, the *Lega* pictured the EU as a supranational organisation characterised by undemocratic, centralistic and bureaucratic features.[255]

In its economic program, the *Lega dei Ticinesi* embraced neoliberal principles of free market economy and deregulatory policy. Consequently, the demands for tax cuts, reduced expenditure, fewer regulations and the 'de-bureaucratisation' of the public sector were high on the party's political agenda.[256] Moreover, the *Lega* emphasised the importance of Switzerland and the canton of Ticino as places where financial affairs represented a vital economic sector, and hence the party rejected any plans to relax the banker's duty to maintain confidentiality. On the other hand, the *Lega* was eager to present itself as an advocate of the common man's interests. For example, it regularly defended the interests of both car drivers and commuters using public transport, or demanded that social policy should be improved, for example by reducing health insurance costs or by increasing retirement pensions.[257] Comparable to other radical right-wing populist parties, the *Lega dei Ticinesi* combined neoliberal demands with social policy concerns and hence applied an electoral strategy aimed at attracting constituencies from different socioeconomic backgrounds.

In summary, while the *Lega dei Ticinesi* was first and foremost a radical right-wing populist party, it also featured ethnoregionalist characteristics and hence represented an exception in the contemporary Swiss party system. In its populist view, the *Lega* viewed not just the cantonal elite but also the federal government in Bern as adversaries, both of which they saw as being dealigned from the people of the canton. With the exception of the Swiss People's Party, the *Lega* was the sole party of the Swiss radical right in the 1990s that could claim strong and charismatic leaders whose popular appeal and contentious style had contributed to the party's success. While the *Lega* had a widely distributed press organ, it failed to build an efficient party organisation capable of helping the party to consolidate its place in the cantonal party system. In the late 1990s, the *Lega dei Ticinesi* came under pressure for both internal and external reasons: the popular attraction of its leaders faded away and the persistent conflict over the anti-system nature of the party jeopardized its internal cohesion. On the other hand, and more importantly, the *Lega* was put in serious trouble by the dynamic emergence of the new Swiss People's Party as a competitor in the canton of Ticino and elsewhere in Switzerland – an emergence we will examine in the next chapter.

5

ENTERING THE MAINSTREAM
The Emergence of the New SVP in the 1990s

Up until the early 1990s, radical right-wing parties remained at the margins of the Swiss party system. This situation changed radically in the 1990s, with the transformation of the Swiss People's Party, a fundamental change which allowed a radical right-wing populist party to enter the mainstream of Swiss politics. In the history of the Swiss party system throughout the twentieth century, the SVP has long played the role of a right-wing, mainstream party that stood for marked conservative viewpoints and represented the electorate of farmers and small business people. As a member of the Federal Council since 1929 and a steadfast partner in the so-called bourgeois bloc, which included the CVP and the FDP, the SVP acted as a reliable, long-term companion that consistently helped to build Switzerland's postwar consensual system.

In the 1990s, however, the SVP entered a new phase in its history and it is in this context that we can speak of the emergence of a new SVP.[1] While the party underwent significant political and ideological radicalisation, adopting an agenda and a rhetoric comparable to other radical right-wing populist parties in Western Europe, the SVP managed to substantially improve its party organisation and enormously expand its constituency. In some ways, this process of transformation resembles the case of the Austrian Freedom Party in the years after Jörg Haider assumed the leadership in 1986. In the history of postwar Western Europe, therefore, together with the FPÖ, the SVP represents a prime example of an established, right-wing party which was transformed into a radical right-wing populist party.

Taking these changes into account, the study of the radical right in Western Europe has paid increasing attention to the SVP in recent years and a number of studies that take a cross-national perspective have included the Swiss party.[2] Referring to the electoral performances of the FPÖ, the SVP and the Northern League, Hans-Georg Betz notes that in the 1990s, 'Austria, Switzerland, northern Italy became home to three of Western Europe's politically most successful exclusionary populist parties'.[3] In her comprehensive study of radical-right parties, Pippa Norris writes: "In the 1999 election the Swiss Schweizerische Volkspartei also saw a substantial advance in voting support, from 14.9% in 1995 to 23.3%, under the more radical ultranationalist, anti-EU, and isolationist rhetoric of their leader, the billionaire industrialist Christoph Blocher'.[4] Finally, according to Jean-Yves Camus, the SVP must be seen as part of the third postwar wave of nationalist and xenophobic parties, which has hit Western Europe since the 1990s.[5] These assessments from leading experts in the field are shared by some Swiss scholars who have worked on analyses relating to recent developments of the SVP.[6] In view of that, the edited volume regarding the National Council elections of 1999 includes an article by the two U.S. scholars of the radical right, Herbert Kitschelt and Anthony J. McGann, in which they draw a comparison between the SVP and the Austrian Freedom party.[7]

On the other hand, however, a significant section of Swiss scholarship does not allow for conceptualizations drawn from comparative research on the radical right and prefers to use terms such as 'national-conservative' or 'conservative-right' in defining the SVP.[8] In particular, 'national-conservative' has gained prominence among the definitions used in Swiss research on the SVP, although a thorough explanation of the concept, which would allow comparison from a cross-national perspective, is still lacking. A sketchy characterisation is provided by Claude Longchamp, who argues that national-conservatism gives emphasis to traditions, advocates isolationism in the area of foreign policy and highlights privileges that should be granted to Swiss citizens.[9] This understanding, however, takes into account neither the exclusionist politics of the SVP, nor its shift towards a populist strategy and rhetoric. In addition, some authors put emphasis on the factionalism within the SVP and resist seeing the SVP as a united national party with a common strategy and agenda.[10] The disagreement in Swiss scholarship has led to a situation where the study of the SVP has included a variety of different concepts and terms; this has been prominently revealed by a recent edited volume on the electoral emergence of the SVP since the mid 1990s.[11]

The Old SVP: The History of a Right-wing, Mainstream Party

The origins of the Swiss People's Party extend back to the late 1910s, when a number of farmers' parties were created in agrarian cantons of Protestant, German-speaking Switzerland.[12] Prior to the First World War, large numbers of Swiss farmers felt well represented by the Liberal Democratic Party, but they began to be alienated during wartime, because the party had mainly defended the interests of industrialists and consumer circles.[13] As a result, in the aftermath of the First World War, farmers' parties were founded in different Swiss cantons and immediately received significant electoral support after the introduction of proportional representation in 1919. Among them were the two farmers' parties in the cantons of Zurich (1917) and Bern (1918), which eventually grew to be powerful cantonal party organisations. In particular, the farmers' party from the canton of Bern became an influential political force, not only at the cantonal but also at the national level.[14] When Rudolf Minger was elected to the federal government in 1929, it began the long-standing tradition of the party from Bern having a member in the Federal Council. In spite of the membership in government and the fact that the cantonal farmers' parties were well represented in the national parliament, it was only in 1936 that the national party was founded under the name of the Farmers, Artisans and Citizens Party (*Bauern-, Gewerbe- und Bürgerpartei* – BGB), acting as an 'umbrella organization for various cantonal parties representing the interests of small trades and, above all, farmers'.[15]

Once integrated in the 'bourgeois bloc', the BGB consolidated its position in the government and in the mainstream of Swiss politics throughout the difficult period of the 1930s. In its role as a pronounced right-wing, conservative party, the BGB condemned any kind of socialist ideas, as well as internationalism or anti-militarism, as concepts that were unpatriotic and disloyal to Switzerland. Designed to appeal to the middle classes, the political program of the BGB was meant to form a spearhead against big business and international capital, both of which were seen as a threat to soil-grounded Swiss farmers and locally oriented tradesmen.[16] With its emphasis on Swiss rural traditions deeply rooted in the country's history and by representing the political epitome of the Swiss farmers' community, the party made a vibrant contribution to the establishment of a national ideology, framed in the so-called Spiritual Defence of the Nation (*Geistige Landesverteidigung*) and largely responsible for the country's growing sociocultural and political cohesion in the period after the mid 1930s.[17]

As historical studies reveal, sections of the Swiss farmers' community showed ideological affinity to ideas of fascism and even National Socialism and some BGB officials voiced understanding, if not support for fascism, especially for its concepts of an authoritarian state and its fight against left-wing ideologies.[18] Others failed to take clear distance from the emerging fascist movements, not least because of their strict opposition to socialism and communism. Take the example of Markus Feldmann, National Councillor (1935–45, 1947–51) and Federal Councillor (1952–58) from the BGB. As his recently published diaries show, in the early years of his career, he showed very little criticism of the emerging Front Movement in Switzerland.[19] From 1928 to 1945, while editor-in-chief of the *Neue Berner Zeitung*, the BGB party organ in the canton of Bern, Feldmann failed to intervene when the paper published articles in which some attraction was expressed towards the Front Movement or even the National Socialist regime.[20] A more controversial figure was the physician and army colonel Eugen Bircher, BGB National Councillor from 1942 to 1955, who was involved in politics at the far-right margin and showed a 'particularly fascism-friendly attitude'.[21] Moreover, in 1935, the Young Farmers' Movement (*Jungbauernbewegung*) split away from the BGB party of Bern and, while it supported left-wing ideas on economic policies and differed from the fascist farmers' movements seen in other European countries at that time, it was led in a authoritarian fashion by Hans Müller, who cherished a leader cult and demonstrated attraction for the National Socialist regime.[22] In the 1960s, Müller became involved in the Swiss League for Biological National Defense (*Schweizerische Liga für biologische Landesverteidigung* – SLfbL), an early proponent of right-wing environmentalism in Switzerland (see chapter 6).[23]

It is also worth noting that the BGB representatives in the Federal Council considerably reinforced the authoritarian and right-wing tendency within the Swiss government. In 1933, in the early days of the Front Movement, Rudolf Minger, head of the Federal Military Department from 1930 to 1940, emphasised that the movement and the BGB pursued the same goals and that the party should therefore seek to integrate this new political force.[24] He also showed a somewhat ambiguous attitude towards National Socialism in 1933, when he told the German ambassador, von Weizsäcker, that he thought National Socialism, while an obvious development for Germany, with which he had a personal sympathy, represented a danger to the existence of Switzerland.[25] Eduard von Steiger, Minger's successor in the Federal Council, was head of the Federal Department of Justice and Police and hence in charge of the Swiss refugee policy during the Second World War. He became known for coining the phrase 'the boat is full', which gained notoriety as the catchphrase for the country's restrictive policy towards Jewish refugees during this period.[26]

After the end of the Second World War, the BGB contributed to the establishment of the consensual politics, social agreements and policies of economic growth that characterised postwar Switzerland. Despite minor disagreements, especially regarding the importance of agricultural policy, the BGB continued to act as a reliable partner of the two parties with whom they shared political and ideological principles: the Swiss Conservative People's Party (*Schweizerische Konservative Volkspartei* – SKVP), known since 1957 as the Conservative Christian-Social People's Party (*Konservativ-Christlichsoziale Volkspartei* – KCVP), and the Liberal Democratic Party.[27] When the 'magic formula' was introduced in 1959 as the guiding principle of Swiss governance, the BGB ensured its steadfast place in the governmental coalition. As a junior coalition partner holding one seat in the Federal Council, the party was largely supportive of the government's policies. Without taking any radical views, the party promoted, for example, unspectacular slogans such as 'courage for conformism' and 'assemble the positive forces' in its campaign for the 1967 National Council elections.[28] In terms of electoral support, the BGB showed remarkable stability, which persisted until the early 1990s. Throughout the postwar era, the party has received between 10 and 12 per cent of the vote in National Council elections and the number of its MPs in the National Council has fluctuated between twenty-one and twenty-five.[29]

Like all Swiss parties, the party organisation of the BGB was marked by federalist and decentralised structures. By the end of the 1950s, the party had sections in ten cantons and its national party organisation remained fairly unstructured. The autonomy of cantonal sections was disclosed in the variety of party names, political agendas and constituencies. Among the cantonal parties, the party from Bern persisted in holding the position of the predominant political force. Of all the cantons, the party enjoyed the strongest electoral support in its home canton and was by far the most influential BGB section at the national level.[30] The Bern section also continued to successfully adapt the dual electoral strategy of addressing voters from rural areas and from the cities, particularly Bern. This entrenched attachment to the middle class and the bourgeoisie laid the foundation for the conservative tendency of the Bern party.

The cantonal party of Zurich was the second strongest force of the BGB. In National Council elections, the two cantonal parties of Zurich and Bern have continually received more than the half of the BGB's countrywide share of the vote. While the Zurich party had traditionally drawn its support from farmers, it began to increase its efforts to address people living in the suburban areas of Zurich.[31] This became evident in 1962, when the paper *Die Mitte* (The Middle) split away from *Der Zürcher Bauer* (The Zurich Farmer), the long-established party organ which also served as the professional paper of the farmers' community in the canton of Zurich.[32] When, in 1968, the city of Zurich found itself in the spotlight on account of the student movement's rallies, the Zurich section of the BGB began to notably revive the ideological tools of law and order and patriotism, demanding that the state take firm measures against the protesters. On the other hand, like all the mainstream parties at the time, the Zurich BGB distanced itself from the Movement against Overforeignization and criticised the vicious anti-immigrant tendency of the movement's proposals and initiatives.[33]

The second defining moment of the party's history, after the foundation of the national party in 1936, was the merger in 1971 with the two Democratic Parties from the cantons of Glarus and Graubünden. That same year, the party changed its name to the Swiss People's Party (SVP). Since the agricultural sector and the two socio-professional groups forming the BGB constituency, namely farmers and rural inhabitants, lost ground in the postwar period, the party's goal was to attract other social groups, in particular employees, workers and people from the lower middle class.[34] This is the context in which to view the merger with the two Democratic Parties, whose origins date back to the late nineteenth century and which both enjoyed significant electoral support in their respective cantons, from workers and employees in particular.[35] Since the two Democratic Parties have traditionally espoused social-liberal ideas and tended toward the political centre, it became evident that the fusion would be followed by internal debates over the new political direction that the SVP should take. The subsequent debates resulted in a shift toward the centre, prominently expressed in the new party program of 1977, which included, among other statements, general considerations regarding human rights, ecology and consumer protection.[36] This tendency toward the political centre was expressed in the French name for the SVP, *Union démocratique du centre* (Democratic Union of the Centre).

However, the programmatic opening and an electoral strategy designed to appeal to a wider range of voters failed to help the electoral performance of the SVP to improve and the party continued to stagnate around the 11 per cent mark.[37] In addition, debates over the SVP's programmatic course, which started in the mid 1970s and recurred regularly in the years that followed, revealed early signs of disagreement between different factions and set off centrifugal forces within the national party.[38] Eventually, this gave rise to growing differences in the 1980s between the cantonal parties of Bern and Zurich. While the former was a main advocate of the shift toward a centre position, the latter started to look for niches to squeeze itself into, by putting new issues on the political agenda and reshaping the style of political campaigning in order to raise the party's electoral appeal.[39]

Towards the New SVP: The Process of Structural Transformation

In the early 1990s, the nature of the SVP continued to be characterized by the antagonism that existed between the two most powerful cantonal parties of Bern and Zurich, which together accounted for more than 65 per cent of all SVP party members.[40] They stood for two opposing factions within the national party: on the one side, the Bern-oriented faction which represented the old SVP with its right-wing, conservative politics and moderate style; on the other side, the Zurich-oriented faction, or the 'Blocherite wing', as Clive Church calls it, because of the leading role played by Christoph Blocher,[41] as the proponent of a new SVP drawing on a radical-right agenda and adopting a populist strategy. This conflict became evident in the early 1990s when the Zurich party set out to controversially politicise asylum issues and the question of European integration started to dominate Swiss political debates. In the following years, the intransigent style and exclusionist agenda of the Zurich SVP evoked regularly harsh criticism from other cantonal sections. In particular, the cantonal parties of Bern and Graubünden, backed by the francophone sections of Vaud and Jura, denounced the conflict-ridden style of the Zurich-oriented faction and insisted that the SVP should commit to moderate right-wing politics and show responsibility as a governmental party.

However, as the Blocherite wing managed to strengthen its position of power in the national party, the Bern-oriented faction gradually lost ground and with it the standing of the national SVP in the political centre. Although the remaining minority faction from the old SVP continued to be represented in the federal government body, it had very little influence on the political course of the national party, given that those factions supporting the turn towards radical-right politics produced an excellent electoral record. Consequently, under the guidance of the Zurich-led faction and its leader Christoph Blocher, the SVP went through a process of structural transformation and nationalisation which resulted in both organisational centralisation and increased ideological cohesion of the national party. This unity was also reflected in the growing homogeneity of the SVP constituency across different cantons.[42]

Overall, the process of transformation was a major reason for the remarkable electoral success story of the new SVP in the 1990s, not least because it gave a great advantage to the SVP over other traditionally 'low profile' Swiss parties, characterised by factionalism, loose organisation structures and weak central power. However, when Christoph Blocher was voted out of government in December 2007 and replaced by Eveline

Widmer-Schlumpf, a representative from the more moderate cantonal party of Graubünden, antagonistic dynamics again emerged within the SVP. The conflict over the election of Widmer-Schlumpf to the Federal Council and the following expulsion of the cantonal party of Graubünden resulted in the founding during the summer of 2008 of a breakaway party named the Bourgeois Democratic Party (*Bürgerlich-Demokratische Partei –* BDP) in the cantons of Bern, Graubünden and Glarus.

Many of the policies, strategies and organisational tools adapted by the new SVP in the 1990s were initially developed by the cantonal SVP party of Zurich in the late 1970s and the 1980s. The high level of autonomy assumed by cantonal parties in Switzerland made it possible for the Zurich SVP to set its own political agenda and work on its party organisation in a manner that was relatively independent of the national party. In some ways, the Zurich SVP served as a laboratory and training ground for the new SVP.

The Preliminary Work of the Zurich SVP in the 1970s and 1980s

In May 1977, Christoph Blocher, a young entrepreneur and party member of just five years standing, was elected to the presidency of the cantonal party of Zurich. This signalled the beginning of a new era for the Zurich section, and from a long-term perspective, for the national SVP.[43] After his election, Blocher declared that he planned to oversee significant change in the political line and style of the Zurich SVP, and that he would bring to an end the debates of recent years which had aimed at opening the SVP to a wide variety of opinions and interests. Blocher consolidated his position of power in the cantonal party in a short time and so began a period in which he consistently strove to renew and transform the organisational structures, activities, campaigning style and political agenda of the Zurich SVP party. As a result, the SVP section also began to express increasing criticism of the reorientation that the national party had taken. The cantonal party managed to get across its strong conviction that the Zurich party should pursue a different political line from that of the national party.

It became an important objective of the Zurich party to expand its radius of action and reinforce its presence at different levels of everyone's political life. There was particular concern about giving a boost to the party youth, thereby allowing it to gain importance as a training ground for new party cadres and counter the attraction of the groups emerging from the New Left.[44] The cantonal section of the Young SVP (*Junge SVP* – JSVP) was created in Zurich in 1977 and this was followed by the foundation of many other local sections in the canton of Zurich. The group began to organise special training courses in rhetoric for young members. Numerous SVP members who later became prominent political figures had previously been active in the Young SVP. Another way to improve cohesion in the Zurich section was by establishing private cadre conferences, which sought to reinforce networking within the party and ameliorate the ideological and political education of senior party members. The Zurich party further organised, on a regular basis, different types of public events and manifestations. The idea was that these public events, which could be attended by anyone interested, should address a wide range of political questions and eventually increase the mobilisation of SVP voters.

Under the leadership of Christoph Blocher, the Zurich section also started to refashion its campaign style in the late 1970s. As senior officials stressed, in order to assure electoral success, the party should not only address programmatic questions more rigorously and modernise the way that election campaigns are run, but also reinforce ideological and political polarisation in the arena of party competition. As was shown in the municipal, cantonal and national election campaigns of the following years, the party repeatedly employed an aggressive style and harsh rhetoric to encounter political adversaries. The efforts to improve the electoral performance of the Zurich SVP paid off as early as the National Council elections of 1979: the party increased its share of the vote in the canton of Zurich from 11.3 to 14.5 per cent, the best showing thus far for fifty years. On the other hand, in the cantonal elections of the same year, the SVP augmented its electoral support by only 1 per cent. In the 1980s, the electoral results of the cantonal party stagnated. It was only in the early 1990s that the party experienced a dramatic electoral breakthrough in the canton of Zurich, as elsewhere in Switzerland.

The most striking element of the party's renewal under the leadership of Christoph Blocher was certainly the transformation of its political agenda and ideology. Many political principles and ideological references, which later became main characteristics of the national SVP in the 1990s, had already been developed earlier within the Zurich party. Issues such as asylum, drug policy and law and order became central points of the party's political agenda in the 1980s. Leading figures of the Zurich party, most prominently Christoph Blocher, espoused a rigorous isolationist attitude and played a central role in the successful campaign against the country's membership of the United Nations in 1986.[45] The shift towards the right-wing margins was underscored by the strategy of integrating the remnants of the Swiss Republican Movement, which had been in a state of total disintegration following James

Schwarzenbach's retreat from politics in 1978.[46] This purpose was illustrated by the party switch of the Republican National Councillor, Hans Ulrich Graf, who deserted in 1978 to join the Zurich SVP.[47] Another example is to be found in the fate of *Der Republikaner*, Schwarzenbach's paper and the party organ of the Republican Movement. When the paper ceased publication in 1978, a new paper called *Schweizerzeit* was launched in close association with the Republican Movement, in March 1979.[48] The editor-in-chief was Ulrich Schlüer, former private secretary of James Schwarzenbach, and the paper soon turned into a powerful voice of the SVP in the canton of Zurich (see chapter 6).

The Campaign of the Zurich Party to Gain Control within the National SVP

The cantonal SVP party of Zurich was not only the driving force behind the process of structural transformation and nationalisation undergone by the national SVP in the 1990s but was also the main beneficiary since it was able to considerably reinforce its position within the national party. This process must be understood against the background of the Swiss party system which is characterised by a so-called vertical segmentation, which gives great importance to the sub-national level. As a result of the country's socio-cultural heterogeneity, national parties have a highly federalized structure and are divided into a large number of cantonal and local sections. Altogether, Switzerland numbers over 180 cantonal parties and the major parties have cantonal sections in almost all of the twenty-six cantons. In addition, there are almost 6,000 local party sections, 70 per cent of which are represented by sections of the four governing parties.

Since national parties are more like umbrella organizations than centralized, firmly organised party units, cantonal parties often show more unity in terms of programmatic work and taking political action. They are able to play an autonomous role that is independent from the national party, for example, when making policy proposals or recommendations on federal votes.[49] While the cantonal SVP party of Zurich took advantage of this highly federalised party system in its campaign to gain control of the national party organisation on different levels, it also contributed to the manner in which a number of these settings within the system were altered, by inducing a process of nationalisation in the SVP.

From the outset, the Zurich party had the distinct advantage of being able to rely on significant financial resources. Since Swiss parties at all levels are usually rather low on finances, this was an important prerequisite for the Zurich party's strategy of becoming a political actor capable of pursuing a wide range of political activities and getting attention from the national public. The Zurich party used most of the money for organising public events, placing ad campaigns in newspapers and distributing party material. In the election year of 1995, for example, the annual budget of the cantonal SVP party of Zurich was 1.8 million Swiss francs, a greater sum than even the 1.6 million Swiss francs that the national SVP had at its disposal.[50] In the period from 1996 to 1998, the cantonal SVP section of Zurich spent 5.4 million Swiss francs on ad campaigns, while the expenditures of the FDP were 1.9 million and those of the Social Democrats 1.8 million.[51] As Leonhard Neidhart has pointed out, the considerable financial resources of the Zurich SVP were the result of a remarkable strategy of political sponsoring, which the country had never witnessed before.[52]

Organisationally, the SVP expanded enormously in the 1990s and effectively became a true national party with representation in all the Swiss cantons. Between 1991 and 2001, the number of cantonal sections increased from fourteen to twenty-six.[53] Since most of the newly founded cantonal parties were fully supportive of the agenda and style promoted by the cantonal party of Zurich, they helped the Zurich section to alter the balance of power within the institutions of the national party, whereas the cantonal party of Bern lost its long-standing predominance.

Take the example of the national assembly of delegates, which plays a central role in the process of internal decision making in the national party. The assembly elects the party leadership, issues endorsements for federal votes and decides whether federal initiatives should be launched and whether referendums should be requested.[54] The number of cantonal delegates depends upon the share of the vote that the respective cantonal party received in the National Council elections. In 1995, when the Zurich SVP received a higher share of the vote than the cantonal party of Bern, it meant that the Zurich party had, for the first time, more delegates in the assembly than the Bern party. To gain a majority in the assembly, the Zurich party needed assistance from other cantonal sections. This support was provided by the old allies of the Zurich party and most of the twelve new cantonal parties. The shift to the right within the assembly of delegates was illustrated in August 2000, when the delegates decided to endorse a federal initiative demanding that the number of foreigners living in Switzerland should be limited to 18 per cent of the population. Ironically, with this endorsement, the assembly embarrassed the cantonal party of Zurich, together with the national party executive and a large majority of senior officials, who all opposed the federal initiative, mainly for economic reasons.[55]

Since the mid 1990s the cantonal party of Zurich was also able to place devoted followers in senior party positions. By so doing, the party not only reinforced step by step its position of power in the national party organisation, but also helped to increase internal cohesion in the national party. By tradition, the important party offices, such as president and secretary, had tended to be held by deputies of the cantonal party of Bern and its moderate right-wing allies. This was still very much the case in 1988, when Hans Uhlmann, Councillor of States from the canton of Thurgau, was elected to the party presidency and his appointment was interpreted as a clear sign of the SVP maintaining its unyielding position in the political centre.[56] In 1996, however, Ueli Maurer, associate of Christoph Blocher and National Councillor from the canton of Zurich since 1991, was elected to the party presidency. Maurer, born in 1950 and long-time secretary of the Zurich farmers' association, was a member of the cantonal parliament of Zurich from 1983 to 1991. His election to the presidency was understood as an indubitable concession to the Zurich-oriented faction within the party.[57] The choice of general secretaries followed a similar course and resulted in the 2001 appointment of Edgar A. Rutz, who had been a member of the Liberal Democratic Party of the canton of Zurich before joining the SVP in 1998 and gained notoriety in 1993–94 as co-president of a campaign committee against the anti-racism law (see chapter 6).

While the Zurich-oriented faction proved adept at filling important party posts throughout the 1990s, it failed to obtain the only SVP seat in the Swiss government. This proved possible on account of the fact that the National Council and the Council of States, which are united in the Federal Assembly, elect each member of the Federal Council by secret vote and do not have to follow party instructions. In general, the parliament chooses one of usually two candidates that are presented by the party that is entitled to the seat. On several occasions, however, the Federal Assembly refused to elect candidates supported by the Zurich-oriented section of the SVP. With Adolf Ogi (1988–2000) and Samuel Schmid (2001–2008) both representing the centrist and moderate conservative faction, the Bern section was twice able to send one of its members to the Federal Council. This exclusion from governance was skilfully exploited by the Zurich-oriented faction, who used it to their advantage by playing the double game of acting as both governmental and opposition force.[58] It was only in December 2003 that Christoph Blocher was elected into government and the SVP received a second seat in the seven-headed Federal Council at the expense of the CVP. Nonetheless, the SVP continued to assume its role as a government party while also filling the role of an oppositional party. When the majority of the Federal Assembly decided not to re-elect Christoph Blocher to the government in December 2007 and the two remaining SVP Federal Councillors joined the newly founded BDP, the largest Swiss party was a party in opposition for the first time since the late 1920s. Then again, when Samuel Schmid stepped down as Federal Councillor in December 2008, the parliament elected Ueli Maurer, as his successor, thereby conceding to the SVP its representation in the federal government.

Direct Democracy: Setting the Agenda and Playing Opposition Party

The system of direct democracy helped the cantonal SVP party of Zurich and its allied sections to impose their political agenda on the national party. In addition, direct democracy made it possible for the national SVP to play the role of an opposition party and undermine the consensual rules of Swiss governance. In the early 1990s, a first major conflict emerged around the question of Switzerland's European integration. Within the SVP it was the turning point in the antagonism between the Blocherite wing and the Bern-oriented faction, and the starting point for the emergence of the new SVP. In 1990, the cantonal party of Bern and a majority of the national SVP leadership still backed the government in its plan to join the European Economic Area (EEA), but disapproved of the prospect of Switzerland's membership of the European Community.[59] Conversely, a group of senior SVP officials, led by Christoph Blocher, began to voice their strong opposition to any policies of integration and vehemently rejected the project of Switzerland participating in the EEA.[60] As this faction increased the pressure on the national leadership, the SVP began to show increasing reservation over the idea of Switzerland being more closely tied to the EC.

In the run-up to the popular vote on membership of the EEA in December 1992, the polarisation within the party reached its peak. While the party committee and the assembly of delegates decided to endorse the rejection of the EEA, the cantonal parties of Bern and Vaud took the opposite stance. The subsequent rejection of EEA membership in the popular vote, with 68 per cent of SVP supporters voting against,[61] considerably strengthened the position of power of the Zurich-oriented faction and particularly its leader, Christoph Blocher. Five years later, Blocher pointed out that in retrospect the EEA vote had been of vital importance for the further development of the SVP.[62] The outcome of the EEA vote was also a major success for the SVP as an opposition and challenger party, since government and most political parties had expressed their support for joining the EEA. Since then, the SVP has used European integration as a main issue with which to emphasise its oppositional role in Swiss politics.

In the late 1980s and early 1990s, the SVP started to give a great deal of attention to asylum policy and to present it as a controversial political issue. In 1989, Christoph Blocher filed a parliamentary interpellation demanding that the government should institute emergency law in order to bring abuse of the right of asylum to an end. With his interpellation, Blocher took over a demand which had been proposed a short time before by the Campaign for an Independent and Neutral Switzerland (CINS) and been widely advertised in Swiss newspapers. In the past, demands over the institution of emergency law on asylum policy had already been put forward by National Action (1984) and the Freedom Party (1987).[63] The cantonal party of Zurich made an important move in 1991, when it launched a petition – which is primarily of symbolic value in Swiss politics – demanding emergency measures against the misuse of asylum. Although the Zurich party was only supported by the cantonal sections of Aargau and Glarus, it was able to gather 106,000 signatures for the petition.[64]

Following this success in mobilisation, the cantonal party of Zurich increased its pressure on the national party to launch a federal initiative on asylum policy. In 1992, in spite of strong resistance from the cantonal section of Graubünden, the party executive agreed to launch the federal initiative 'Against Illegal Immigration' (*Gegen die illegale Einwanderung*) which was geared to implement severe restrictions on the right of asylum.[65] In fact, it was the first time ever that the SVP had launched a federal initiative. Among other demands, the initiative stipulated that people who entered the country illegally should no longer be able to get asylum, and that the right to appeal against asylum decisions should be restricted.[66] While the cantonal SVP parties of Graubünden and Vaud rejected the initiative, as did Federal Councillor Adolf Ogi, the Bern section refrained from giving any endorsement to its voters. On the other hand, it was backed by all the radical right-wing populist splinter parties, including the FPS, the SD, the *Lega dei Ticinesi* and the EDU. In the popular vote in March 1996, the SVP proposal was thrown out by a fairly narrow majority of 53.7 per cent, with a turnout of 46.8 per cent.

As shown by a survey carried out after the voting, the SVP proposal was largely supported by its own constituency, while voters from the three other large parties expressed their disapproval by a majority. In fact, 75 per cent of the SVP supporters approved the initiative, and while only 20 per cent of the SPS supporters and 24 per cent of the CVP supporters agreed with the initiative; the approval rate was much higher among the FDP supporters, with 42 per cent voting in favour. The survey also notes that the majority of voters perceived the initiative in a very general way, without knowing the specific points of the proposed policy change. This suggests that for many voters, it was the government's asylum policy as a whole that was at stake. To a large extent, this met the intentions of the SVP which had tried throughout its campaign for the initiative to be perceived less as a specific modification of asylum law than as a mark of general discontent with the current asylum policy and as an expression of resentment towards asylum seekers and foreign residents generally. The survey further indicates that the initiative was approved by voters between the ages of fifty and sixty-nine years old. The initiative also found disproportional support among those who were living in the suburbs of small and middle-size cities and those who had a low or medium level of education.[67]

After the 1996 vote, the asylum policy firmly remained the focal point of the SVP's political agenda. Once more, in late 1997 and early 1998, senior officials from the cantonal party of Zurich initiated another federal initiative on asylum policy.[68] Since the national parliament was debating revision of the asylum law, their goal was to put the law makers under pressure to consent with restrictive measures on asylum policy. The initiative 'Against the Misuse of the Right of Asylum' (*Gegen Asylrechtsmissbrauch*) was submitted in November 2000, and contained demands still more drastic than the previous (for instance, that asylum would be denied to anyone arriving overland via a country that Switzerland considers a safe haven).[69] This time, there was almost no disagreement within the SVP on the necessity of the initiative. The assembly of delegates endorsed the initiative by unanimous vote and all cantonal sections supported the proposal. Only the Federal Councillor Samuel Schmid expressed his disapproval and was therefore criticised by his fellow party colleague Christoph Blocher.[70] In November 2002, the SVP initiative was rejected with 50.1 per cent voting against and a turnout of 48.1 per cent. The 'No' vote won out by just 4,200 ballots, one of the narrowest margins ever in the history of Swiss direct democracy.[71]

The example of the federal initiative 'Surplus of Gold Reserves to the AHV-Fund – Gold-Initiative' (*Überschüssige Goldreserven in den AHV-Fonds – Goldinitiative*) shows how Christoph Blocher was able to set the political agenda of the SVP and reinforce the idea that the SVP played an oppositional role in the Swiss political system. In January 1998, Blocher launched the idea that the surplus of gold reserves accumulated by the Swiss National Bank should be used for the country's social security system.[72] With this proposal he sought to underpin his fierce rejection of the Swiss Solidarity Foundation (*Stiftung Solidarität Schweiz*), which had been initiated by the government during the debates regarding 'unclaimed' Jewish assets in Swiss banks and Switzerland's role during the Second World War and sought to use a part of the gold reserves for humanitarian projects.[73] Blocher had consistently objected to the Foundation and denounced it for being compliant in a blackmailing campaign that was allegedly led by various organisations from abroad.[74]

Table 5.1 | *Federal Initiatives by the SVP in the 1990s*

Subject	Year of Launch	Year of the Vote	Objective Achieved[1]
Initiative 'Against Illegal Immigration'	1992	1996	no (46.3%)
Initiative 'Against the Misuse of the Right of Asylum'	1999	2002	no (49.9%)
Initiative 'Surplus of Gold Reserves to the AHV - Gold-Initiative'	1999	2002	no (46.4%)

Note: [1] Indicating whether and with what percentage voters supported the party's objective.
Source: http://www.admin.ch/ch/d/pore/va/index.html, retrieved 31 August 2008.

Shortly after Blocher had presented his proposal, the SVP leadership expressed its positive reception and hence, convened an extraordinary assembly of delegates in April 1999 in order to discuss the issue of gold reserves. As a final point, the federal initiative was launched in August 1999, one year and a half after Blocher had came forward with this idea, and was submitted in October 2000 with over 125,000 signatures. The popular vote of September 2002 saw a turnout of 45.2 per cent and the SVP initiative was rejected with 46.4 per cent voting in its favour. The same fate was shared, however, by the government's counter-proposal which included the project of a Swiss Solidarity Foundation and was supported by all governmental parties except the SVP.[75]

Christoph Blocher: A National and Populist Leader

The establishment of a strong and efficient leadership was another major factor in the process of nationalisation and transformation undergone by the SVP. While Christoph Blocher formally confined his political offices to the presidency of the cantonal party of Zurich and membership of the National Council, he effectively became the true national leader of the SVP and one of Switzerland's best-known politicians. Comparable to Jörg Haider, Carl I. Hagen and Umberto Bossi, it is the name of Christoph Blocher which comes to mind when the SVP is mentioned.[76] For many SVP voters, Blocher symbolised the SVP and represented an important motivation to vote for the party. As electoral studies show, the so-called Blocher effect goes some way to explaining the remarkable electoral successes of the SVP since the mid 1990s.[77]

The leadership of Blocher bears particular significance, since Swiss politics tends to lack national leaders who assume positions of dominance in their respective parties, or who appeal to a nationwide public. In addition, Blocher was both mastermind and driving force for the process of transformation undergone by the SVP in the 1990s. In this respect, there is some similarity with the Freedom Party of Austria (FPÖ), where 'it has been the leadership of Jörg Haider that has in fact transformed the party into being a New Populist party'.[78] Blocher played the kind of highly integrative role that was required in order to carry out his agenda of transforming the SVP. Moreover, Blocher was able to draw on his experience of transforming the Zurich cantonal party of the 1980s into a centralised and more professionalized party organisation.

Christoph Blocher was born in 1940 as one of eleven children in a protestant pastor family. He graduated in law and received his PhD in 1971 from the University of Zurich.[79] After that, he worked as a manager of *Emser Werke*, a chemical company located in the canton of Graubünden. In 1983, he acquired the majority of the company shares and became owner and CEO of *Emser Werke* and eventually one of Switzerland's wealthiest people.[80] During his student years at the University of Zurich, Christoph Blocher was already showing an interest in politics. He was actively involved in opposing the 1968 students' movement and co-founded the Students' Ring (*Studentenring*) at the University of Zurich.[81] The aim of the student organisation was to oppose the alleged increase in left-wing influence in university politics. After joining the SVP in 1972, Blocher became president of the district section of the town of Meilen in 1974. One year later, he was elected to the cantonal parliament of Zurich. From 1979 to 2003, he was a member of the National Council. On 10 December 2003, the Federal Assembly elected Christoph Blocher to the Federal Council, and he took charge of the Federal Department of Justice and Police. However, since he regularly showed reluctance to comply with the rules of collegiality and consociational governance, he was voted out by the parliament after only four years in December 2007.

Christoph Blocher gained public prominence and political success by bringing in 'a whole series of personal resources: unrivalled media skills, highly effective organisational skills and a deep pocket'.[82] As a flamboyant, populist leader, he succeeded in mobilising support in election and voting campaigns and in skilfully demonstrating what it takes to build a mass following in an era where media, especially television and Internet, have become an important vehicle for winning voter support. He was one of the first Swiss politicians to recognise the importance of the Internet for the purpose of political propaganda and public relations. In October 1996, he established his personal website which presented the main lines of his political program and carried his public speeches, interviews and articles. The website was designed and maintained in a professional fashion and edited in the four languages of German, French, Italian and English.[83]

Blocher also was responsible for the fact that the so-called *Albisgüetli* meeting, which has been held annually in January in Zurich since 1989, has become one of most important political meetings in Swiss politics. The meeting is staged as a large media event, where Christoph Blocher presents a detailed speech, which is often widely distributed in a written version later on. Through these meetings, Blocher has managed to receive extraordinary levels of public attention and to set for the coming year the political agenda not just of the SVP, but also, to some extent, the agenda of national politics too.[84] In many ways, he can be described as a modern political entrepreneur who not only ran the cantonal party of Zurich in a business-like fashion, but also regularly funded his own campaigns as well as those of his party. On several occasions, Blocher used his own resources to finance the distribution of a printed version of his speeches to all Swiss households. According to some reports, Blocher spent more than one million Swiss francs on the campaign against EEA membership.[85]

Blocher's rhetoric and style were typically characterised by the populist appeal to the people. While he was a very wealthy businessman, he presented himself as a politician with a common touch, who tried hard to show understanding for the worries, concerns and problems of the people. Blocher further emphasised that he had, in contrast to most of the other politicians, a sense of the mood of the people, and hence voiced popular grievances. In an almost folkloric fashion, he has regularly stressed that he has very close ties with his native soil of Switzerland. According to Margaret Canovan, what marks politicians like Blocher as populists is not only that they employ simple and direct language in the way they address political issues, but that they offer 'political analyses and proposed solutions that are also simple and direct'.[86]

Blocher has also exhibited traits that are commonly attributed to charismatic leaders, although the concept of 'charisma' remains a debated issue in the analysis of political leadership. In common with other charismatic leaders, he has shared the exceptional public relations skills, the emphasis on identity politics, and the sense of a special mission intended to save the country from harmful forces.[87] On the other hand, Blocher has also contributed to the fact that the Zurich SVP as well as the national SVP both resemble 'entrepreneurial issue parties', similar to the Progress Parties in Denmark and Norway.[88] While the leader is the main message for charismatic parties, the entrepreneurial issue parties 'emphasize issues in the message the leader creates'.[89]

Blocher could reckon on the unconditional support of the cantonal party of Zurich which had evolved under his leadership into a party organisation with an authoritarian, leader-oriented structure.[90] Criticism from within the party was usually dismissed and internal critics were often pushed out of the way. As Blocher established a leader-oriented structure within the Zurich section, some senior party members gained prominence as his lieutenants and close associates. As a result, like many radical right-wing populist parties where important political and programmatic decisions are made by a circumscribed circle of high-ranking party members,[91] the political agenda of the Zurich party and eventually of the national party was set by an inner circle of decision makers, gathering around Christoph Blocher, and then promoted with a very professional style of political marketing.

Members of this inner circle included party president and National Councillor, Ueli Maurer, as well as the two National Councillors Hans Fehr and Ulrich Schlüer. Fehr was party secretary of the cantonal party of Zurich from 1985 to 1998 and has been secretary of the powerful Campaign for an Independent and Neutral Switzerland (CINS) since 1998. Schlüer is a former member of the Republican Movement, has been a National Councillor since 1995, and is editor-in-chief of the New Right paper *Schweizerzeit*. Whereas Maurer's task mainly consisted of ensuring and strengthening the position of the Blocherite wing at the leadership level of the national party, Fehr and Schlüer, both intensely engaged in policies of migration and foreign affairs, were known for their populist rhetoric and uncompromising views.[92] Another member of Blocher's inner circle was Christoph Mörgeli, National Councillor since 1999 and professor of History of Medicine at the University of Zurich. While Mörgeli has often been presented as the party's approved intellectual, his political style and rhetoric were rather provocative and confrontational.[93]

Improving the Party Organisation, Political Campaigning and Means of Mobilisation

Taking the cantonal party of Zurich as a model, the national SVP made efforts to improve its party organisation and to professionalise its political activities. This is all the more significant considering that the organisational structures of Swiss parties are generally rather loose and the degree of professionalisation is fairly low. Swiss parties have relatively few resources, in terms of full-time staff and finances, while the public funding of parties is virtually non-existent.[94] The low level of professionalisation also relates to parliament with its long tradition of the 'militia' system, which implies that political work should be done on a voluntary basis.[95] By overcoming some of these shortcomings, the SVP was able to bring about a remarkable organisational improvement in the 1990s.

First of all, the party professionalized its administrative apparatus, in particular by involving experts in internal decision making processes. The party established specialised services and expert committees, which advise party functionaries and senior party members on distinct policy issues. For example, the SVP created, as part of the party's general office in Bern, a specialised office focusing on migration policy. It also assigned a Working Group on Migration (*Arbeitsgruppe Migration*), which was composed of lawyers, academics, cantonal government members and professionals, and met on a regular basis to evaluate current developments and policies related to migration. Both the office and the working group had the task of advising the party leadership on distinct strategies regarding upcoming decision-making processes or possible political campaigns related to migration issues.

The areas in which the SVP made the most effective improvements were in matters of political campaigning and public relations.[96] In order to address a nationwide public, the party invested heavily in poster campaigns as well as in ad campaigns in the Swiss printed press. Of the four mainstream parties, the SVP spent by far the most on its ad campaigns. In the period from 1996 to 1998, the SVP paid out 8.8 million Swiss francs on ads and posters, while the FDP spent 5.8 million Swiss francs, the SPS 4.6 million and the CVP 2.8 million.[97] Once again, the national party was able to take considerable advantage from the professionalism and campaigning know-how that the Zurich section had acquired since the 1980s. Once the Zurich party had utilised concepts and methods developed by a Zurich-based advertisement agency, the national SVP later used the same Zurich-based PR agency for some of its national campaigns and adopted a similar campaigning style.[98] In 1996, the national SVP commissioned the agency to take charge of the voting campaign for the asylum initiative and to take care of the entire communication strategy (e.g., information concepts, press conferences and ad campaign).[99] Another important aspect was the direct support of Christoph Blocher, who himself undertook, on several occasions, the nationwide distribution of vast numbers of his propaganda brochures, which considerably helped the national SVP to increase its presence in the national public arena.

Like most major Swiss parties, the SVP lacked a strong party press at the national level, but was able to rely on fairly important party papers at the cantonal level. In 1987, the national SVP had founded the monthly publication *SVPja* (SVP Yes), a simply made paper which had a circulation of sixty thousand in 2003 and was mainly intended for party members. While the paper contained sections run by the national party and dedicated to national politics, the cantonal parties were prominently represented with their own sections. In 1997, the SVP launched the French-language party paper *Le Pays romande* (The Romand Country), which merged with the paper of the cantonal party of Vaud. This ceased publication after less than a year, on account of low rates of subscription.[100]

In contrast, the Zurich SVP had a fairly strong presence in the press arena within the canton of Zurich. This included the party organ, *Der Zürcher Bote* (The Zurich Messenger), a paper which was also published as *Der Zürcher Bauer* (The Zurich Farmer). It featured an additional agriculture section and served as the official mouthpiece of the Zurich Farmers' Association. Together they had a circulation of twelve thousand. In addition, the party could count on a number of other publications, which showed their support for the SVP. In particular, Walter Frey, president of the local SVP section of Zurich from 1982 to 2001 and a shareholder in several media companies, played an influential role in the Zurich media scene. Moreover, with the bi-monthly paper *Schweizerzeit* (Time of the Swiss), the SVP took advantage of another important public voice, whose significance went beyond the borders of the canton of Zurich (see chapter 6).[101]

The SVP also tried to improve its means of mobilisation and in this drew on the experience of the cantonal party of Zurich which had developed what some call a strategy of 'steady campaigning'.[102] This strategy aims to establish a constant presence in the public sphere by holding public events, launching controversial debates and creating partisan organisations. By these means, the Zurich SVP also sought to present itself as a political movement, characterised by continuous mobilisation as well as having appeal to a variety of social groups. The party gave itself, in the words used by Margaret Canovan to describe populist parties, 'the revivalist flavour of a movement, powered by the enthusiasm that draws normally unpolitical people into the political arena'.[103] The characteristics of a movement were displayed, for example, in September 1995, when Christoph Blocher, the cantonal SVP party of Zurich and associated groups organised a rally in Zurich against joining the European Union. The rally was attended by over ten thousand people, one of the highest numbers of participants to be seen at a political demonstration in the 1990s.

The strategy of 'steady campaigning' was most successfully adopted by the party of the city of Zurich. Since the 1980s, the local party continually organised a wide range of public events all around town, seeking to mobilise sympathisers and potential voters and to show the party's proximity to the common people and their everyday life. The range of public events organised by the SVP local section of Zurich included 'seniors' afternoons', with free coffee and cake; matinees; local regulars' table; information events; or the widely known 'farmers' breakfasts', with free sausages and popular music. Most of these events were accompanied by a cultural program, including music and a catering service.[104] The party was also able to in reinforce its steady presence in the public sphere by constantly placing ads in the local newspapers, which either announced party events or promulgated the party's views on controversial political issues.

The establishment of a network of satellite organisations was yet another aspect of the SVP's mobilisation strategy and its desire to act as a ubiquitous and national political force. At the level of membership and leadership, these satellite organisations were closely linked with the SVP. By addressing distinct policy issues, the satellite organisations aimed to appeal to different voter segments and to take advantage of the Swiss political system where direct democracy provides an opportunity structure to interest groups.[105] These activities were supposed to help to strengthen the bonds of solidarity between members, voters and sympathisers of the SVP. This network is significant, not only for the political intentions that lie behind it, but also for the sociocultural dimension. In some ways, the SVP sought to create a counter-movement and counterculture with the capacity to cover different spheres of political, cultural and social life. On this matter, the circles, publishing houses and publications associated with the New Right also played an important role, since they made a considerable contribution to the establishment of an intellectual counterculture for the right. Although the Zurich section was again the driving force in the creation of these groups, their range of activity went far beyond the cantonal frontiers.

To illustrate the purpose of these satellite organisations, take the following example: in 1995, the Federation of Tax Payers (*Bund der Steuerzahler* – BdS) was founded, having sections in several German-speaking cantons and a predominance of SVP politicians in its executive committee.[106] According to its own information, the group had 3,500 members in 2000.[107] It embraced a strong anti-state attitude and launched a municipal initiative in Zurich, demanding that the salaries of the members of the municipal executive of Zurich should be cut. To the surprise of many, the initiative was approved by 53 per cent of the voters in May 2000.[108]

The Society for Active Seniors (*Verein für aktive Senioren*) was another group which had close affiliations to the SVP section of Zurich. The group won two seats in the 1999 cantonal parliament elections of Zurich. In December 1999, it submitted a cantonal initiative demanding lower taxes for retired people, which was approved by 50.6 per cent of the voters in September 2002.[109] A final example is a group named Security for All (*Sicherheit für alle* – Sifa), which was founded by SVP National Councillor Ulrich Schlüer and focused mainly on issues related to security and law and order. As the group put it in its adverts, these issues were of major concern, since the city of Zurich had become the 'capital of crime'.[110] At the national level too, the SVP took the opportunity to increase its mobilisation potential by setting up a variegated network of different satellite groups. The most prominent example was the powerful Campaign for an Independent and Neutral Switzerland (CINS), which is examined in detail in chapter 6.

The Extraordinary Electoral Rise of the New SVP

'The success of the Swiss People's Party (SVP) in the 1990s is probably the most striking in the whole electoral history of the Swiss party system', notes Andreas Ladner in his overview of Swiss political parties.[111] The party owed its electoral growth predominantly to gains in parliamentary elections at both the national and the cantonal level. In the National Council elections of 1991, the SVP still emerged as the smallest of the four parties forming the governing coalition and was therefore still considered the junior partner. In the elections eight years later, however, the SVP advanced to become the largest Swiss party after celebrating a historic victory (table 5.2).

In elections to the Council of States, the SVP also experienced some increase in support, yet the success was minimal compared to that which was seen in the National Council elections. Consequently, the Council of States continued to be heavily dominated by the FDP and the CVP, who together held thirty-two of the forty-six seats in 1999. The poor performance of the SVP was mainly to do with the fact that different rules apply in elections to the Council of States than is the case in those to the National Council. In most cantons, Council of States elections are based on a majority electoral system and therefore the personality of the candidates and agreements made between party elites in the run-up to elections are important factors that determine vote behaviour.[112] This made it more difficult for the SVP to push through their candidates. Similar explanations are given for the failure to substantially increase the party's representation in cantonal governments, since in a large majority of the cantons the election of the executive follows a

Table 5.2 | *Results of all Parties in National Council and Council of States Elections, 1987–1999*

Parties	1987 NC		1987 SC	1991 NC		1991 SC	1995 NC		1995 SC	1999 NC		1999 SC
SPS	18.4	41	5	18.5	41	3	21.8	54	5	22.5	51	6
CVP	19.6	42	19	18.0	36	16	16.8	34	16	15.9	35	15
FDP	22.9	51	14	21.0	44	18	20.2	45	17	19.9	43	17
SVP	11.0	25	4	11.9	25	4	14.9	29	5	22.5	44	7
NA/SD	2.5	3	–	3.4	5	–	3.1	3	–	1.8	1	–
APS/FPS	2.6	2	–	5.1	8	–	4.0	7	–	0.9	–	–
EDU	0.9	–	–	1.0	1	–	1.3	1	–	1.3	1	–
Lega dei Ticinesi	–		–	1.4	2	1	0.9	1	–	0.9	2	–
LPS	2.7	9	3	3.0	10	3	2.7	7	2	2.3	6	–
LDU	4.2	8	1	2.8	5	1	1.8	3	1	0.7	1	–
GPS	4.9	9	–	6.1	14	–	5.0	8	–	5.0	9	–
Others	10.3	10	–	7.8	9	–	7.5	8	–	6.3	7	1
Total	100%	200	46	100%	200	46	100%	200	46	100%	200	46

Notes: NC: National Council (first column: share of the vote; second column: number of MPs)
SC: Council of States (only number of MPs)
Sources: Die Bundesversammlung – Das Schweizer Parlament, http://www.parlament.ch/d/dokumentation/statistiken/Documents/ed-rueckblick-47-leg-mandate-nr.pdf, retrieved 31 August 2008; Die Bundesversammlung – Das Schweizer Parlament, http://www.parlament.ch/d/dokumentation/statistiken/Documents/wa-nr-nationalratswahlen-waehlerstimmen-1919.xls, retrieved 31 August 2008.

simple majority system. This relatively low representation in both the cantonal executives and the upper house of the federal parliament hindered the SVP in its efforts to directly translate electoral success into policy making.

Doubling its Support in National Council Elections

For a period of more than sixty years from the 1930s to the early 1990s, the BGB and then the SVP stagnated around the 11 per cent mark in elections to the National Council. After this long dry spell, the party almost doubled its electoral support over the course of the two elections of 1995 and 1999. In so doing, the SVP did particularly well in cantons where the respective parties adopted the agenda and style of the Blocherite wing, as well as in cantons where new SVP sections had been founded.

The results of the 1991 National Council elections were consistent with the electoral performances of the SVP throughout the postwar period. The party received 11.9 per cent of the vote, a scant 0.9 per cent more than in the elections of 1987. It also failed to increase the number of their MPs in either the National Council or in the Council of States, yet for all that, the SVP was still the most successful of the four parties that composed the government. The real winners in the 1991 elections, which some commentators called 'elections of protest' and 'elections of fear', were the fringe parties from the radical right, including the Swiss Democrats, the Car Party and the newly founded *Lega dei Ticinesi*.[113] In the canton of Zurich, the SVP advanced to become the strongest party for the first time, with 20.2 per cent of the vote and two more National Councillors. In the canton of Aargau, too, the SVP received the highest share with 17.9 per cent of the vote, even though the APS, the SD and the EDU together scored more than 19 per cent.[114] In the run-up to the elections, the cantonal SVP party of Zurich considered establishing an electoral alliance with the Car Party, but the centre-right parties in Zurich reacted with harsh criticism and eventually forced the SVP to drop the idea. On the other hand, the SVP and the APS formed an electoral alliance in the canton of Geneva, after the party's national executive gave it authorisation on the grounds that it constituted an exceptional case.[115]

The SVP did not organise an election campaign in 1991 at the national level, which would have been supported by all cantonal sections. By far the most coherent and broadest campaign was conducted by the cantonal party of Zurich. In this way, the Zurich party was able to set the election agenda of the national party and to receive the largest amount

Table 5.3 | *Results of the SVP in National Council Elections, 1987–1999*

Cantons[1]	1987		1991		1995		1999	
ZH (35/34)[2]	15.2	6	20.2	8	25.5	9	32.5	13
BE (29/27)[2]	27.8	9	26.3	8	26.0	8	28.6	8
AG (14/15)[2]	15.7	3	17.9	3	19.8	3	31.8	5
TG (6)	21.7	2	23.7	2	27.0	2	33.2	3
GR (5)	20.0	1	19.5	1	27.0	1	27.0	2
SH (2)	23.5	–	19.2	–	20.4	–	26.0	–
SZ (3)	7.6	–	9.2	–	21.5	1	35.9	1
BL (7)	12.0	1	12.3	1	10.8	1	18.0	1
FR (6)	8.9	1	9.7	1	8.3	–	11.4	–
VD (17)	6.2	1	7.3	1	7.7	1	10.7	2
TI (8)	1.3	–	1.0	–	1.5	–	5.3	–
AR (2)	–		–		22.0	1	37.5	1
SG (12)	–		–		8.4	1	27.6	3
LU (9/10)[2]	–		–		14.1	1	22.8	2
ZG (2/3)[2]	–		–		15.2	–	21.4	1
SO (7)	–		–		6.7	–	18.6	1
BS (6)	–		2.0	–	–		13.6	1
GE (11)	–		1.1	–	–		7.5	–
VS (7)	–		–		–		9.0	–
JU (2)	–		–		–		7.2	–
AI (1)[3]	–		–		–		(25.7)	–
GL (1)[3]	(85.6)	1	(42.8)	–	–		–	
Total[4]	11.0	25	11.9	25	14.9	29	22.5	44

Notes: First column: share of the vote; second column: number of seats
Turnouts: 46.5% (1987), 46.2% (1991), 42.2% (1995), 43.4% (1999)
[1] Total number of representatives in National Council per canton
[2] 1995 change of the number of cantonal MPs in National Council per canton
[3] Majority electoral system
[4] Total national share of the vote and number of MPs in National Council

Sources: *Année politique suisse 1987*, Bern 1988, p. 50, 52; *Année politique suisse 1991*, Bern 1992, appendix; *Année politique suisse 1995*, Bern 1996, appendix; *Année politique suisse 1999*, Bern 2000, appendix; W. Seitz, *Nationalratswahlen 1995*, Bern. 1995, pp. 44–71; Seitz, *Nationalratswahlen 1999*, pp. 56–80.

of media coverage. Asylum and drug policy were the two dominant issues of the election campaign. By submitting a petition and announcing the launch of a federal initiative in the election year, both of which demanded restrictions of the current asylum policy, the Zurich party underlined its leading role in the election campaign. In addition, while the established parties conspicuously tried to avoid European integration becoming an important theme of the election campaign, the issue was consistently thematised by the SVP and especially by the cantonal party of Zurich. Ultimately, the campaign strategy developed by the SVP turned out to be successful, since SVP voters considered the issues of asylum and European integration as the most pressing problems facing Switzerland.[116]

In the National Council elections of 1995 the SVP emerged as one of the two winners, making gains of 3.0 per cent and reaching a new high of 14.9 per cent. The second winner was the Social-Democratic Party, which increased its share of the vote by 3.3 per cent.[117] Commentators pointed out that both parties succeeded in attracting voters who had previously given their support to parties positioned at the two opposite margins of the political spectrum.[118] According to Daniele Caramani, 'the shift towards the right of the Swiss People's Party catalysed the extreme-right vote to the detriment of the right-wing protest parties'.[119] The SVP gained five new seats in the National Council (ZH, LU, SG, SZ and AR) and lost just one in the canton of Fribourg, thereby increasing the number of their MPs from twenty-five to twenty-nine. In the elections to the Council of States, the SVP was only able to increase its seats by one, from four seats to five. The outcome of the National Council elections brought significant change in the cantonal distribution of electoral votes within the SVP. With 29.6 per cent, this was the first time that the cantonal party of Zurich contributed more votes to the overall SVP result than the cantonal party of Bern (24.8 per cent) and so, electorally speaking, they became the strongest cantonal party of the SVP. Moreover, the newly founded cantonal sections (LU, SG, AR, ZG and SO) enjoyed significant electoral gains right away and altogether they added more than 2 per cent to the total vote of the SVP. This strengthened the position of the Zurich-oriented faction and its political agenda still further.[120]

The election campaign in 1995 gave evidence once again that the Zurich section occupied a position of predominance within the national party.[121] In January 1995, the SVP assembly of delegates decided that the party program should include the phrase 'joining the EU is not a goal of Swiss foreign policy'.[122] This decision was understood as a clear triumph for the Zurich-oriented faction and as a signal for the upcoming election campaign. In addition, the cantonal party of Zurich got strong support from the Campaign for an Independent and Neutral Switzerland (CINS), which made great efforts to influence the voters with its extensive advertising campaign in the Swiss media. In September 1995, the cantonal party of Zurich and the CINS also co-organised a rally, which took place in Zurich under the motto 'Yes for Switzerland – No to joining the EU/EEA' and was attended by more than ten thousand people.[123] In its election campaign, the SVP party consistently associated issues like economic crisis, unemployment, immigration, asylum policy and drug problems with the European question, suggesting that all these problems would get worse if the country were to open its borders toward the outside world. The SVP's intention of integrating voters from the right-wing margin was also demonstrated by the fact that several cantonal sections of the SVP established electoral alliances with the FPS (ZH, SH and SO) and the SD (LU, SO).[124]

The National Council elections of 1999 turned out to be a sensational triumph for the Swiss People's Party.[125] The SVP advanced to become Switzerland's strongest party, receiving slightly more votes than the SPS. The SVP won 22.5 per cent of the vote, raising its share by an astounding 12.6 per cent.[126] Since the establishment of the proportional electoral system in Switzerland in 1919, no single party had ever been able to make so big an increase in its share of the vote. On the one hand, the SVP succeeded in integrating the radical right-wing electorate and in virtually driving out the splinter radical right-wing parties from the Swiss party system. On the other hand, the SVP also took votes from the CVP and FDP, whose share of the vote had been in constant decline since 1987.[127] Since cantons represent the election districts in Switzerland, the increase in votes was not fully translated into gains of parliamentary seats. Nevertheless, the SVP augmented its number of MPs from twenty-nine to forty-four. While the party won four new seats in the canton of Zurich and two more in the canton of St. Gallen, it conquered one new seat in seven cantons (AG, LU, SO, TG, ZG, BS and VD). In addition, the two former FPS National Councillors who had deserted to the SVP (see chapter 4) were both reelected in their respective home cantons of Aargau and Solothurn. In contrast, in the elections to the Council of States, the SVP failed to make a major breakthrough and increased its number of MPs by only two, now having seven deputies in the upper house.

The 1999 election campaign of the SVP was again largely shaped by the Zurich-oriented faction and was more uniform across the country than was the case in previous elections, despite the fact that some cantonal parties continued to pursue their own campaign activities. The national assembly of delegates opened the election year in January 1999 and put European integration and asylum policy at the forefront of the party's agenda.[128] The party's main concern over the asylum issue was shown in both the launching of the federal initiative 'Against the Misuse of the Right on Asylum' and in a highly controversial poster campaign. In addition, the SVP emphasised its neoliberal positions by demanding vigorous tax cuts and a decrease in state expenditure. As election analysts point out, the SVP and its Zurich section in particular managed once again to dominate the election year debates by leading a well-organised campaign and employing a provocative and resentful style.[129] Moreover, its election agenda turned out to be very effective, since many SVP voters stated that refugee policy and foreigners were pressing problems which needed to be solved.[130]

Accumulating Victories in Cantonal Elections

During the 1990s, the SVP displayed an astounding electoral dynamism in most of the Swiss cantons and scored significant gains in cantonal parliament elections.[131] Within twelve years, the SVP almost doubled its number of cantonal MPs, from 297 in 1991 to 570 in 2003. Nonetheless, the SVP still came in fourth among the four governmental parties in 2003, behind the FDP (671 cantonal MPs), the CVP (620) and the SPS (582).[132] At the level of cantonal executives, the SVP found it much more difficult to strengthen its position in public offices. Between 1999 and 2003, the party was unable to increase its number of representatives in cantonal governments. With just seventeen cantonal executives from a total of one hundred and sixty, the SVP took last place among the four governmental parties in 2003 (CVP: 49; FDP: 44; SPS: 29).[133]

The SVP's record in cantonal elections is characterised by several trends, which basically reflect the results seen in the national elections of the 1990s. In general, the SVP scored their best electoral results in those cantons where the respective cantonal party adopted the populist style and the radical-right agenda of the cantonal section of Zurich.[134] In the canton of Aargau, for example, the SVP absorbed the electorate of the FPS and almost doubled its share of the vote between 1993 and 2001, growing into the largest party of the cantonal parliament.[135] In the canton of Zurich, Switzerland's largest canton and home canton to the driving force behind the transformation process of the national SVP, the party's share of the vote in cantonal parliament elections rose steadily from 19.4 per cent in 1991, to 21.1 per cent in 1995 and 28.9 per cent in 1999. During this period, the party almost doubled the number of its cantonal MPs, from thirty-seven in 1991 to sixty in 1999. In contrast, those cantonal parties which were more restrained in their style and stood for a moderate political course experienced electoral setbacks. Most significantly, the two cantonal parties of Bern and Graubünden lost electoral ground in the second half of the 1990s. Between 1991 and 2000, the SVP lost almost a quarter of its deputies in the cantonal parliament of Graubünden.

The SVP was also able to expand its representation in cantonal parliaments as a consequence of having founded twelve new cantonal sections since 1991. As was also the case in the National Council elections, some of these newly founded cantonal parties immediately experienced spectacular election successes. For example, in the canton of St. Gallen, the newly founded SVP section straight away won 9.8 per cent of the vote in the cantonal elections of 1996 and then 22.6 per cent in those of 2000, which helped them advance to become the second largest party in the canton. As was the case in the National Council elections, the SVP made a remarkable breakthrough in Catholic cantons, where the CVP had held an almost hegemonic position for more than a century (e.g., LU, ZG, OW and NW). In the canton of Lucerne, where the SVP section was founded in 1992, the party won 7.6 per cent of the vote in the parliament elections of 1995 and 17.0 per cent in those of 1999.[136]

While the SVP continued to be a party predominantly anchored in the German-speaking part of Switzerland, it made great efforts to increase its support in the French-speaking cantons. Eventually, this resulted in some initial electoral gains. In the canton of Geneva, for example, the newly created cantonal section, which drew on the legacy of Vigilance, immediately received 10.4 per cent of the vote in the cantonal parliamentary elections of 2001. Finally, it is worth noting that the SVP experienced little success in elections to cantonal governments. This reflects the rather unsuccessful performances of the SVP in the Council of States elections of the 1990s. The majority electoral systems, the personality of the candidates and arrangements made between the major parties played an important role in elections to cantonal executives and had a rather detrimental effect on the SVP.

Diversity of Social Bases and Consistency in Political Attitudes

Like many radical right-wing populist parties in Western Europe, the SVP attracted a socially diverse constituency in the 1990s and it is difficult, therefore, to apply the individual sociostructural approaches used in research literature to capture the electorate of these parties. This becomes particularly evident, when we look at the significant changes indicated by surveys that have looked into the occupational composition of the SVP electorate throughout the 1990s (see table 5.4). While in 1991, 26 per cent of the SVP voters were farmers, the representation of this particular professional group among the SVP electorate decreased to 6 and 9 per cent in 1995 and 1999 respectively, but was still disproportionately well represented. In addition, the party consolidated its traditionally strong position among the self-employed and succeeded in increasing its support among pensioners. On the other hand, the SVP attracted a significantly larger proportion of blue-collar workers and low-level employees in 1999 than was the case in 1991.[137] Since these two electoral groups were disproportionately well-represented among those voters who chose the SVP for the first time in 1999, some noted that the new SVP was significantly shaped by ordinary employees and workers.[138]

As exit polls of the 1999 National Council elections suggest, the SVP also significantly increased its electoral support among young voters and, as a matter of fact, advanced to become the party most favoured by people under the age of forty. Moreover, while female voters strengthened their representation in the SVP's constituency, the party continued to display a slight gender gap in its support: of the four established parties, the SVP attracted the highest proportion of male voters in the National Council elections of 1999.[139] In this respect, the party holds to the tradition of the Swiss Democrats and the Freedom Party, which have both received disproportionately high support from younger male voters in the past.[140]

In contrast to the Swiss Democrats, however, the SVP gained ground among voters with a high level of education and fairly good income. While the SVP was significantly under-represented among highly educated voters in 1991, the party did much better among voters of this stratum of the electorate in the 1995 and 1999 elections. In 1999, 14 per cent of all voters with a high level of education supported the SVP and thus, the party received more support from this electoral stratum than the CVP (11%), though this was still much less than the SPS (32 per cent) and the FDP (23 per cent). At the same time, in 1999, the SVP became the strongest party among voters with a low level of education, in spite of the fact that there was no notable increase in the proportional representation of this electoral group in the SVP constituency between 1991 and 1999.[141] Moreover, of the four governmental parties, the SVP had the highest proportion of voters who belonged to the second highest income class (five to nine thousand Swiss francs per month per household). Fifteen per cent of the SVP voters are individuals who earn more than nine thousand Swiss francs, compared to 29 per cent of the SPS voters and 33 per cent of the FDP voters.[142]

As is shown by the survey taken after the 1999 elections, the SVP significantly increased its number of supporters who were resident in the larger cities and particularly in the suburbs. At the same time, the SVP continued to be well-represented among voters living in the countryside and was able to maintain its position as the strongest electoral force in villages. Another trend can be discerned in terms of religion.[143] By tradition, the SVP has drawn heavily from the support of Protestant voters; Catholics, on the other hand, were poorly represented in the electorate of the SVP. Significantly, this gap eroded throughout the 1990s and the SVP made a major breakthrough among Catholic voters in the 1999 elections.[144]

Furthermore, in the late 1990s the great majority of the SVP's electoral support was to be found in the German-speaking part of Switzerland. Despite the SVP's far-reaching efforts to establish cantonal sections in the French-speaking regions, the party failed to gain substantial support in the French-speaking part of Switzerland in the 1999 national elections. One of the reasons was the party's intransigent rejection of the European Union, which was less commonly shared in the French-speaking regions than in the German-speaking regions. Another reason can be found in the difficulties faced by the SVP leadership and Christoph Blocher in particular, in trying to exert the same public attraction in the French-speaking districts, not least because of the language barrier. Finally, in many of the francophone cantons, the process of building-up the organisational structures was still a work in progress and it was too early, therefore, for it to show the expected results.[145]

To conclude, the social composition of the SVP's constituency changed significantly throughout the 1990s. While the SVP continued to attract voters from the older middle classes and from people living in rural areas, both of which are traditionally well-represented sections of the SVP electorate, the party increased its electoral support among younger, well-educated and well-off voters, as well as people living in urban areas. These changes in the socio-structural profile can be described as a rejuvenation and dynamisation of the SVP's constituency. There is, however, some disagreement among pollsters and electoral analysts as to whether the SVP succeeded in increasing its appeal to socially and economically advantaged voters.[146] While some note that the SVP attracted both privileged and underprivileged social classes,[147] others point to the rather low representation of well-educated and well-off voters in the SVP's constituency.[148] As Andreas Ladner stresses: 'Traditional working-class voters of the Social Democrats have changed to the right-wing Swiss People's Party'.[149] Some conclude, therefore, that together with lower ranking employees, blue collar workers were the

Table 5.4 | *Social Profile of SVP Supporters, 1991–1999*

	1991	1995	1999
Language Regions			
German	–	93%	95%
French	–	7%	4%
Religion			
Protestant	81%	60%	54%
Catholic	16%	29%	34%
Others and no Religion	–	11%	12%
Gender			
Female	47%	46%	46%
Male	53%	54%	54%
Age			
18–39 years	36%	26%	27%
40–65 years	48%	49%	52%
65 years and more	16%	25%	21%
Education			
Low	13%	28%	15%
Medium	74%	57%	62%
High	13%	28%	23%
Occupation			
Farmers	–	6%	9%
Self-Employed	–	12%	14%
Managers (with high education)	–	11%	11%
Managers (with low education)	–	22%	–
Craft Specialists	–	2%	10%
Technical Specialists	–	2%	4%
Socio-cultural Specialists	–	4%	3%
Administrative/Commercial Specialists	–	5%	7%
Skilled Workers/Employees	–	16%	20%
Unskilled Workers/Employees	–	5%	7%
Income per Household			
Less than 3,000 Swiss francs per month	–	8%	10%
3,000 to 5,000 Swiss francs	–	30%	31%
5,000 to 9,000 Swiss francs	–	41%	44%
More than 9,000 Swiss francs	–	16%	15%
Residency			
Large Cities	23%	18%	38%
Small and Medium-Sized Cities	20%	49%	29%
Rural Areas	58%	33%	33%

Sources: C. Longchamp and S. Hardmeier, *Analyse der Nationalratswahlen 1991*, Adliswil, 1992, p. 20; C. Longchamp et al., *Hin zur Tripolarität im Parteiensystem der Schweiz*, Bern, 1995, p. 32; P. Farago, *Wahlen 95*, Bern, 1996, p. 20; H. Hirter, *Wahlen 1999*, Bern, 2000, p. 21; data from the 1995 and 1999 samples compiled by Swiss Electoral Studies (Selects).

new constituencies that the SVP succeeded in attracting with its programmatic shift to the right.[150] In summary, by the end of the 1990s, the social profile of the SVP electorate could be said to resemble the constituencies of other radical right-wing populist parties in Western Europe, particularly those of Scandinavia and Austria. In these countries too, such parties have increasingly attracted young voters, people living in an urban environment and voters from both lower and higher social classes.[151]

According to the surveys taken after the National Council elections of 1995 and 1999, the political attitudes of SVP voters did not change noticeably in the second half of the 1990s (table 5.5), despite the fact that the party almost doubled its number of supporters. Generally speaking, the attitudes of the SVP electorate tended to be the mirror image of those disclosed by voters of the Social-Democratic Party.[152] On a number of issues, such as law and order and the need for a strong army, the views of SVP voters came close to those shared by the electorate of the two centre-right parties, the FDP and the CVP. On the other hand, the electorate of the SVP was closer towards the right-wing pole in terms of its exclusionist and isolationist standpoint on issues of identity politics (Swiss traditions, opportunities of foreign residents, EU membership).[153]

A vast majority of SVP voters shared the neoliberal criticisms of the welfare state, and the proportion of their voters who took these views was even higher than was the case within the electorate of the FDP, the party which tends by tradition to express strong scepticism toward state expenditure. As pointed out by Herbert Kitschelt and Anthony McGann, the views of the SVP electorate were extremely to the right in 1999, on issues related to the free market economy, sociocultural conservatism, national demarcation and opposition to European integration. They also argue that on these issues, the electorate loyal to the SVP – meaning voters who had already cast a previous vote for the SVP – was ideologically more to the right than was the newly attracted constituency. Accordingly, it appears that the party's neoliberal and exclusionist program found substantial support among those voters who are commonly regarded as the long-standing constituency of the SVP.[154]

As electoral studies show, the self-placement of SVP voters on the left–right continuum represents a significant variable in explaining their voting behaviour.[155] By large margins, SVP voters saw themselves as being to the right side of the political spectrum (table 5.6). Although the percentage somewhat declined following a high in 1995, compared to voters of the FDP and CVP who heavily clustered themselves in the

Table 5.5 | *Attitudes of SVP Supporters on Political Issues, 1995 and 1999*

	1995				1999			
Issues	**SVP**	FDP	CVP	SPS	**SVP**	FDP	CVP	SPS
For EU membership	**11%**	64%	53%	76%	**18%**	66%	60%	86%
For the preservation of Swiss traditions	**88%**	67%	68%	42%	**84%**	53%	65%	37%
For an emphasis on law and order	**85%**	80%	75%	50%	**84%**	77%	85%	47%
For equal opportunities for foreigners and Swiss	**31%**	41%	49%	70%	**27%**	44%	39%	71%
For increased tax on high incomes	**57%**	50%	60%	81%	**55%**	45%	72%	84%
For increased federal spending on social security	**22%**	29%	23%	64%	**16%**	20%	34%	56%
For a strong army	**83%**	69%	64%	23%	**71%**	60%	69%	26%
For the prioritization of environmental protection	**37%**	38%	45%	62%	**37%**	41%	45%	64%
For a Switzerland free of nuclear energy	**40%**	43%	51%	72%	**48%**	49%	52%	79%

Note: Those interviewed could answer on a 5-point scale ranging from 'I entirely agree' to 'I entirely reject'. The percentage above reflects how many people fully or largely agree with the statement.
Sources: Farago, *Wahlen 95*, p. 26; Hirter, *Wahlen 99*, p. 25; data from the 1995 and 1999 samples compiled by Swiss Electoral Studies (Selects).

Table 5.6 | *Self-placement of SVP Supporters on the Left–Right Continuum, 1991–1999*

	1991	1995	1999
Right	45%	71%	58%
Centre	47%	25%	39%
Left	6%	4%	3%

Sources: Longchamp and Hardmeier, *Nationalratswahlen 1991*, p. 21; Farago, *Wahlen 95*, p. 24; Hirter, *Wahlen 99*, p. 23.

political centre, the SVP attracted an electorate in which a majority of 58 per cent placed themselves to the right.[156] In comparison with the constituency of the Austrian Freedom Party in 1998, of whose voters a large majority (some 68 per cent) considered themselves to be politically to the centre, while only 21 per cent situated themselves to the right, the SVP voters showed a much stronger tendency to the right.[157]

Confidence in political institutions declined significantly among voters of the SVP during the 1990s (table 5.7). In 1991, their confidence in the federal government and the two chambers of the parliament was still very high and actually above average. With 66 per cent of their voters expressing confidence in the Federal Council, the electorate of the SVP exhibited the highest level of confidence of all the established parties. This changed noticeably in the following years and by 1999 the Swiss political institutions enjoyed little confidence among SVP voters.[158] Moreover, in 1995, only the voters of the SVP showed more confidence in the national parliament than they showed in the Federal Council.[159]

It is worth noting that the SVP owed much of its election success of 1999 to both floating voters and newly mobilised voters.[160] As a matter of fact, 33 per cent of those voting for the SVP in the National Council elections of 1999 had not voted for the party in the previous elections, and 22 per cent did not even go to the ballots in 1995. At the same time, compared to the other governmental parties, the SVP succeeded in having the highest percentage of loyal voters: 78 per cent of the 1995 electorate voted again for the SVP in 1999, while only 63 per cent of the voters who chose to vote for the CVP in 1995, for example, voted the

Table 5.7 | *Trust of SVP Supporters in Federal Council and Parliament, 1991–1999*

	1991	1995	1999
Federal Council	66%	43%	40%
National Parliament	56%	46%	44%

Note: The comparison between the three data sample is somewhat problematic. For example, while the data for 1991 do not allow a multiscale comparison, 1995 and 1999 interview answers were given on a scale from zero (no trust) to ten (full trust), with the above table samples reporting the percentage total of responses six through ten. Moreover, the 1991 data include two separate questions for the National Council and State Council, while the 1995 and 1999 data relate to the parliament as a whole.

Sources: Longchamp and Hardmeier, *Nationalratswahlen 1991*, p. 21; data from the 1995 and 1999 samples compiled by Swiss Electoral Studies (Selects).

same way in 1999. Having taken advantage of the political dealignment that has taken place in Swiss politics as it has in most Western democracies in the last twenty years, the SVP has gradually succeeded, as some argue, in generating a process of realignment and should be seen in this respect not so much in terms of a protest party, but rather a party which voters choose because of its ideology and its programmatic course.[161]

Political and Ideological Radicalisation

The radicalisation of the new SVP in the 1990s resulted in the adoption of a program and a strategy similar to those of other radical-right populist parties in Western Europe. As we have shown, this redesign of the party's ideology and politics mainly took place under the guidance of the Zurich party and its leader, Christoph Blocher. The new programmatic course and numerous campaigns and statements bearing the stamp of a provocative and resentful rhetoric, directed not only against the elite but also against a variety of marginalised groups, all revealed a new party ideology profoundly marked by populism and exclusionism. As a result, identity politics, expressed in a variety of forms and different policy areas, became a key feature of the new SVP. Last but not least, the SVP espoused a neoliberal doctrine which provided the frame of reference for both the economic program and the populist anti-establishment strategy.

The SVP's politics of resentment, particularly those propounded in its anti-establishment strategy, suggest that the new SVP exhibits the defined features of protest parties. Following this point of view, the SVP would especially appeal to voters discontented with the established parties, and the party's electoral success would be seen as another example of the 'radical populist right's rise to political prominence … in the wake of a profound and diffuse dissatisfaction and disenchantment with the established parties throughout western Europe'.[162] To some extent, this explanation could be supported by the fact that the new SVP found support among voters who expressed their mistrust towards government and political institutions. However, in line with recent studies suggesting that the protest voting thesis does not sufficiently explain the electoral support for radical right-wing populist parties and that their electoral attractiveness should been seen in relation to the appeal of their ideology, it is more crucial to examine in detail the ideological bases of the new SVP and how they were applied in various policy areas.[163]

Politics of Resentment and Ideology of Populism

The SVP persistently adopted the strategy of evoking resentments.[164] The first purpose of its politics of resentment was to induce animosity and mistrust and to create a general climate of discontent and alienation. It included the use of defiant rhetoric and harsh language and aimed to generate polarisation and division in Swiss politics. As the SVP president, Ueli Maurer, put it in an interview: 'Polarisation helps us in any case; it allows us to make our own positions clearer'.[165] This was in line with the style adopted by most radical right-wing populist parties when they emphasise 'agitation, spectacular acts, exaggeration, calculated provocations, and the intended breech of political and sociocultural taboos'.[166] Accordingly, public opinion was in an uproar on several occasions over the highly provocative character of advertising campaigns conducted by the SVP. Describing the campaigning style of Christoph Blocher, the *Neue Zürcher Zeitung* ran the following headline in 2001: 'Opposition means provocation'.[167] The strategy of mounting resentful attacks was of special significance in the context of the Swiss consensual system, since political competition in Switzerland had not really been marked by a confrontational style for many years, and particularly not from a party forming part of the government coalition.

The government and the established parties were the most common targets of the SVP's campaigns. The SVP liked to use the term 'political class' to denounce the government and the mainstream parties and to imply that the political elite represented an enclosed circle which had lost touch with the common people. This was in line with the party's populism and based on the dichotomist idea that society and politics can be separated into two homogenous groups, the 'political class' and 'the people'. In this manner, the SVP was inspired by the belief of most populists who 'see themselves as true democrats, voicing popular grievances and opinions systematically ignored by governments, mainstream parties and the media'.[168]

When the voters rejected a Federal Statute in June 1994, which would have allowed the Swiss provision of UN peacekeeping troops and was supported by all major parties except the SVP, Ulrich Schlüer called the outcome of the popular vote 'the Waterloo of the political class'.[169] In the late 1990s, the SVP took the election of government members as an opportunity to complain that the established parties would not grant the SVP a second seat in the government, instead following agreements made behind the scenes and not reflecting, therefore, the people's will as expressed at the ballots.[170] The party also regularly threatened to launch a federal initiative demanding that the Federal Council should be elected by way of a popular vote. In 1998, for example, Christoph Blocher made such a proposal by arguing that 'so long as the Federal Council is not elected by the people, it remains uncertain whether the Federal Council is backed by the majority of the people. But democracy means nothing if not governing with the majority! The Federal Council should have the mandate of the people'.[171]

The attempts of the Swiss government and the majority of the mainstream parties to achieve greater integration of Switzerland in the international community was one of the main policy areas where the SVP's populist ideology found expression and where the party presented itself as the voice of the ordinary people, purportedly disaffected from political decision-making processes. The policies towards the European Union were at the centre of many SVP campaigns of the 1990s and were preferably linked to sweeping criticism of government and mainstream parties for disregarding the people's will on the issue. In 1992, the campaign against Switzerland's membership in the EEA was profoundly marked by anti-establishment rhetoric. Christoph Blocher, who virtually personified the anti-EEA position at the time and played a ubiquitous role in the media and in public,[172] denounced 'the lack of leading politicians capable of identifying themselves with their own country, with their own people, and with their own duty. Yes, if one reads some articles, if one listens to some speeches, this lack of identification culminates, not infrequently, in a contempt for one's own country and one's own people'.[173] The strategy of exposing the government turned out to be successful, since distrust of the Federal Council was a major factor for voters who disapproved of EEA membership: 73 per cent of those expressing distrust of the government voted against the country's membership of the EEA.[174] In 1995, the Zurich SVP denounced the left-wing and other parties for being 'tired of the homeland' (*heimatmüde*) in its campaign for the National Council elections, suggesting that the established parties intended to sell-off Switzerland by guiding the country straight into the arms of the European Union.[175] While the slogan was widely criticised, it became an idiomatic expression for the party's anti-establishment stance.

Among political adversaries and those who were purported not to represent the people, the Social Democrats were the target most often chosen by the SVP. In 2000, Christoph Blocher instigated a highly controversial campaign against the Social Democrats, when he published the brochure 'Freedom not Socialism' and distributed it in vast numbers. He basically drew on the thesis that there is little difference between National Socialist and Communist regimes. His aim was to take the debate which had emerged after the publication of Stéphane Courtois' 'The Black Book of Communism' and adapt it to the Swiss political context.[176] In the brochure, Blocher argued that the common intellectual roots of National Socialism, Fascism and Socialism 'are the causes of totalitarianism and they reside in the aim of wanting the state to have powers as far-reaching as possible in every facet of life (etatism), the overemphasis of the community (collectivism) and the disrespect for the freedom of individuals (anti-individualism, anti-liberalism)'[177]. He further condemned the Social Democrats for refusing to admit these commonalities and asked polemically: 'What, I wonder, is the difference between playing down or denying Red mass-murders and denying the Brown mass-murders?'[178]

The media, as well as intellectuals and academics, particularly those who were denounced for being on the left, were also prominent targets of the SVP's politics of resentment and were presented as a part of the elite deeply detached from the people. One year after the rejection of EEA membership, the Zurich SVP complained in an ad campaign that left-wing intellectuals and those who had lost the vote were now trying to enter the EC through the back door.[179] The debates over Switzerland's role during the Second World War serve as a particularly good illustration of how the SVP depicted alleged left-wing intellectuals and historians as untrustworthy and opportunistic, as well as showing how the SVP attempted to evoke popular resentment generated by the reappraisal of the country's national history. On several occasions, intellectuals were accused of being 'moralists' and 'hypocrites' and historians were criticised for drawing a false picture of Switzerland's history. In one of the harshest attacks related to this issue, Christoph Blocher declared that:

> The current discussion is far too strongly influenced by moralists. With hypocritical self-righteousness, they pick on the Swiss people, the decision-makers of the 30's and 40s [sic], on our forefathers. It is above all the young representatives of the left, a few theologians, numerous sociologists, professors, artists and journalists who are sure that they know – in detail and from a safe distance – what we should have done better in the difficult situation of half a century go [sic]. In bigoted, loud-mouthed, hypocritical manifestos, these people extol their own highly sensitive sense of humanity, their flawless character, their deep concern, and they are quick to point a finger at the guilt-laden decision-makers.[180]

In the controversy over the 'unclaimed' Jewish assets in Swiss banks and the country's role in the Second World War, the SVP and its leader Christoph Blocher in particular stirred resentment against interest groups from abroad, particularly against Jewish organisations, which he claimed would jeopardise Switzerland's integrity. Blocher complained that 'we are being threatened, ridiculed and blackmailed by organisations and their representatives in New York' and he attacked the Federal Council on the grounds that '[i]t acquiesced to the pressure of foreign Jewish organizations and allowed itself to be blackmailed into payments out of national assets!'[181] On another occasion, Blocher declared that the Jewish organisations were solely interested in money and that Switzerland should firmly reject any attempt at blackmail, stressing that it should not be forgotten that 'it was the boycott of Jewish business in Germany that initiated the atrocious extermination of the Jewish people'.[182] For this speech, the district attorney's office of Zurich sought to indict Christoph Blocher under the anti-racism law and asked for the lifting of Blocher's parliamentary immunity,[183] but in 2001, both houses of the national parliament rejected the request.[184]

In numerous campaigns and statements, the SVP sought to incite resentful sentiments against marginalised groups. As discussed below, the party most consistently evoked xenophobic sentiments against migrants and particularly against asylum seekers. In addition, the SVP regularly struggled against the idea that, in a pluralistic society, efforts should be made to socially integrate marginalised groups. It was the powerful local SVP party of Zurich, in particular, which led the way for policies directed against minority groups, or 'groups at the margin' (*Randgruppen*) as they were called by the SVP.[185] Among them, drug users were particularly targeted by the local party of Zurich. While the Zurich section and the national SVP both admitted that prevention measures and therapy facilities needed to be integrated parts of a comprehensive drug policy, they also emphasised the outstanding importance of law enforcement, repression and prohibition.[186] Since the mid 1980s, the SVP in the city of Zurich has treated drug policy as a matter of law enforcement and internal security, thereby exploiting fear and anxiety among the population and evoking resentment against drug users.[187]

The Exclusionist Migration Agenda

In the 1990s, the SVP became increasingly preoccupied with migration issues. In the party program from 1999, the SVP stated categorically that Switzerland is not an immigration country.[188] In the 1980s, migration was not high on the SVP's list of priorities, but it went on to become a key issue in the activities and campaigns carried out by the new SVP in the 1990s. In this way, the party changed its focus and adapted its policy to the general shift in debates on migration which occurred during the 1990s.[189] Until the 1980s, the SVP and most of Swiss politics had discussed migration policy mainly in terms of immigration rates, competition in the job market and the percentage of foreign residents living in Switzerland. In its program of 1987, the SVP argued that Switzerland was not solving the 'foreigner problem' and that the majority of the Swiss who were worried about their jobs would like to see the percentage of foreigners reduced.[190] In the 1990s, the issues of integration and multiculturalism gained prominence in public debates. This shift from policies of immigration control to policies concerned with immigrants and integration also found expression in the changing lines of argumentation being used in some debates on migration. While arguments based on economic concerns and crafted in terms of economic stabilisation were common in the 1980s, conceptions of culture and identity were the issues most frequently debated in the 1990s.[191]

The exclusionist ideas of the new SVP were most consistently expressed in statements regarding policy areas related to migration and were typically directed towards immigrants and foreign residents, in particular asylum seekers. In some ways, the SVP took the direct legacy of the Movement against Overforeignization and continued to evoke the alleged danger of overforeignization in its approaches to migration, implying both economic and cultural aspects. The party talked about 'heavily overforeignized zones' in urban areas,[192] and Christoph Blocher claimed that in the case of Switzerland joining the EU and the country opening its border, the 'overforeignization' and the unemployment rate would increase.[193]

The SVP embraced the view that immigrants, in particular those coming from countries outside Europe, can be characterised by their cultural distance from the Swiss culture and nation. In statements on asylum policy and integration, the party assumed that the immigrants' cultures and ways of life would have to be seen as distinctive characteristics, which were immutable and uniform. Senior party officials drew on the idea that there was a high degree of incompatibility between cultures that were bound to clash and that there was little chance of overcoming cultural difference.[194] It was stressed that Muslim immigrants were particularly unable to integrate in Swiss society and that Islam should be viewed as a real obstacle to integration. The SVP local section of Zurich took a pronounced anti-Islamic stance and used it to argue that leftwing and liberal people, who had traditionally fought and struggled in the name of emancipation and religious freedom, were now supporting a migration policy which actually represented a threat to the basic values of the occident.[195]

Some voices from the SVP combined an ethnopluralist view, which highlighted cultural differences and the separate development of different cultures, with the claim that refugees should remain in their homelands, or at very least return as soon as possible. This ethnopluralism bears resemblance to the differentialist views of what some have called neoracism.[196] Following this line of reasoning, SVP officials regularly denounced multiculturalism as a threat to the occidental value system, which would ultimately lead to the decline of Swiss culture.[197] In 1998, the SVP local section of Zurich drafted a position paper on integration policy, producing a compelling example of an ethnopluralist and cultural-differentialist view. The local party firmly rejected the concept of multicultural society and argued that the great majority of foreigners, who had recently moved to Switzerland and were 'of foreign culture', had absolutely no desire to assimilate and instead they insisted that their national and cultural identity should be respected.[198] The party also highlighted the vital importance of cultural identity and claimed that:

> He who has lost the legacy of his culture, also loses his firm ground. The current wave of immigrating people of foreign culture, which has been washing over us for several years now, and, closely linked to this wave, the mixing of cultures which are alien to each other, all result in references to history, tradition, culture, religion and ancestry becoming lost.[199]

The SVP also conceded that one could not expect foreign residents to give up their 'cultural specificities', a route which would eventually lead to assimilation.[200] Nonetheless, the party insisted that the efforts of social and cultural integration must be made in the first instance by the foreign residents. Following this point of view, the SVP expressed its opposition to state-subsidised measures of accommodation and integration,[201] particularly for immigrants coming from the Balkans and from non-European countries. Take the example of an integration project for immigrants from Kosovo, which the local section of Zurich was able to defeat in a popular vote of 1998 after the party had made use of a poster in its voting campaign that had provoked widespread criticism among the public. The poster was designed in such a way that the phrases 'Kosovo Albanians' and 'No' were written in large font, while the text regarding the integration project remained small and hence of less apparent relevance. The people responsible for the campaign were accused of inciting racial discrimination under the anti-racism law.[202] The case was later dismissed, however, by the appeals court in December 2002.

Over the course of the 1990s, the SVP made a remarkable shift in policies related to citizenship. The party program from 1991 still welcomed the facilitation of naturalisation procedures for the second and third generation of immigrants.[203] Following this point of view, the SVP supported the respective Federal Decree in the popular vote of 1994.

By the end of the 1990s, however, the party was handling issues related to citizenship with a great deal of reservation and was very critical of naturalisation policy, complaining that many foreign residents who received Swiss citizenship were neither integrated nor assimilated.[204] According to the SVP, obtaining Swiss citizenship should be seen not as a means of integration, but as the final stage of the integration process.[205] In this way, the party opposed any liberalisation of naturalisation procedures. The SVP also rejected dual citizenship and the government's proposal that *jus soli* should be introduced for the third generation of immigrants.[206] In addition, the party played a major role in campaigns promoting the idea that the decision over whether foreigners could become Swiss should lie in the hands of the Swiss people. Consequently, a number of SVP sections demanded that the popular vote on the conferring of citizenship should be introduced in several municipalities. For example, the local SVP section of Zurich submitted a popular initiative in October 2001 demanding that the voters should decide on the conferring of citizenship. The municipal executive and legislative, as well as the Zurich cantonal government, decreed that the initiative was not valid. In July 2003, the Federal Tribunal confirmed this decision.[207]

The issue of asylum and refugee policy was a further focal point of the SVP's migration agenda in the 1990s, especially if one considers the main issues that the party put forward in its federal initiatives and election campaigns. On this matter too, the SVP somewhat shifted its policy positions from those it had held in the 1980s. Overall, in the 1980s the SVP had continued to be supportive of most of the asylum policies proposed by the government,[208] even though pressure from critics inside the party had already started to emerge.[209] As early as 1982, SVP National Councillors had begun to use the term 'economic refugees' (*Wirtschaftflüchtlinge*) and to point out that asylum policy needed to be seen as part of the debate over 'overforeignization'.[210] In 1985, Christoph Blocher had criticised the authorities' asylum policy, arguing that small countries like Switzerland develop high levels of anxiety about 'overforeignization'.[211] Then, in the early 1990s, the national SVP made a dramatic entrance on the stage of asylum policy, assuming the role of a harsh oppositional force.[212] This criticism was largely the result of the increased influence of the cantonal party of Zurich, which took a particularly intransigent view on asylum and refugee policies.

The SVP advanced to become the prime political force that consistently pursued the strategy of putting the asylum issue on the agenda of national politics and ensuring it remained politicised as a controversial topic. In numerous campaigns related to the issue of asylum, the SVP aimed at evoking xenophobic attitudes and hostile sentiments towards asylum seekers. This was done, for example, by pinpointing asylum seekers as a security threat and a socioeconomic burden. In a similar vein, the party was fond of thematizing the alleged abuse of the right of asylum and associating the presence of asylum seekers with a variety of problems in Swiss society, such as the rise in crime, drug problems, insufficient security in inner cities, violence in schools and among young people generally, the increase in state expenditure and the financial problems of the welfare state.[213] In addition, the SVP took the view that the abuse of the right to asylum and the large number of foreign residents in general were main reasons for the emergence of racism and xenophobia in Switzerland. Following this line of reasoning, the SVP program for 1999–2003 noted that hostility towards foreigners and racism could only be effectively confronted with a consistent fight against abuse of the right to asylum and a stabilisation of the number of foreigners.[214]

Identity Politics, Isolationism and the Struggle for Swiss National Identity

The SVP put great emphasis on identity politics and issues associated with the question of Swiss identity. The party presented itself as the last true defender of the sovereignty and identity of Switzerland, which they alleged to be facing increased threats from the outside world. Accordingly, the SVP emphasised in its party program of 1999 that the party's prime goal was to give a sense of security and to create identity.[215] It is of no surprise that identity politics gained momentum in the debates on migration issues, as the party argued that there was real danger that Switzerland would lose its national identity and cultural distinctiveness in the case of there being no strict restrictions on immigration. In its party program released in 2002, the cantonal party of Zurich declared that:

> There is a threat to the national identity of a country, which brings together four languages and is characterised by direct democracy and federalism, and to the balanced relationship between the Swiss population and the population of foreign residents. The roots of Western and occidental culture are in danger. This is why Switzerland needs a restrictive policy regarding foreigners in order for it to become less attractive as an immigration country.[216]

The identity politics of the SVP implied both the national cohesion of the group within, as well as its isolation from the world outside. The party's idea of Swiss national identity was basically built upon demarcation and defence against the outside world and stabilised through the belief that there were external threats to the country.[217] This corresponded to what some have described as Switzerland's long-standing conception of 'negative identity'.[218] The SVP propounded its identity politics most significantly, therefore, in debates over the country's foreign policy, in particular on questions related to international integration and membership of supranational organisations.

As was shown by numerous SVP campaigns against possible European integration, the sense of delimitation from the outside world was grounded in the conception of Switzerland as a special case, characterised by historical and cultural peculiarities.[219] In his critique of the planned UN membership, the party president Ueli Maurer referred to Switzerland's national hero, William Tell, and argued that 'myths are of crucial significance for a people. The will of independence and the unbridled urge to be free have shaped the history of our people and our country to the present day. They are the pillars that support the cohesion of the voluntary nation of Switzerland.'[220] It was emphasised that the Swiss are members of a national group held together by common historical experiences and a common mentality and that, as Christoph Blocher put it:

> For us, 'Heimat' means not just a patch of earth but also the history that came to pass there, the community of people who live their [sic] and know one another, the feeling of 'being at home' in the countryside, in the villages and towns. Anyone who tries to disparage or take away our homeland is committing a despicable crime, for he is murdering a part of our soul and poisoning the spiritual air we breath [sic].[221]

The SVP also referred to a conception of national identity that drew on political and institutional constituents. For instance, it was argued that membership in the EEA or EU would put an end to the country's exceptional institutional framework combining direct democracy, federalism and neutrality.[222] By pinpointing in particular the extraordinary significance of the well-established traditions of Swiss neutrality, the SVP sought to maximise the isolationist tendency in struggles over international involvement. To this end, the party played a key role in almost all opposition campaigns against the attempts of the Swiss government to achieve wider international involvement. After the successful 1992 campaign against EEA membership, the party regularly voiced a fierce rejection of any policy which would imply future bids for membership in the European Union. In 1993, the SVP also joined the opposition against the plan for Swiss forces to take part in UN peacekeeping operations. After NA and the *Lega dei Ticinesi* had initiated the signature collection to force the provision of UN peacekeeping troops to a referendum, the very active SVP campaign under the leadership of

Blocher substantially contributed to the rejection of the proposal in the popular vote of 1994.[223]

As national history and collective memory were important constituents in the SVP's conception of Swiss national identity, the party was a fierce critic of any attempt to review Switzerland's role in the Second World War and urged that the country's integrity be defended against any criticism from inside or outside the country. According to Christoph Blocher, 'on the whole, Switzerland deserves respect, esteem and admiration for its policies in those years. There is nothing to apologise for.'[224] When the Independent Commission of Experts Switzerland – Second World War published its final report in March 2002, the SVP criticised it as 'state historiography' and stated that, in the judgment of Switzerland's past, one should not criticise the 'military readiness of a small democracy squeezed between totalitarian neighbours'.[225]

Neoliberalism and Anti-statism vs. the Call for a Strong State

Like other Western European radical right-wing populist parties, the SVP put forth an economic program that drew on neoliberal demands for less state and more private enterprise. A number of senior SVP officials liked to make reference to well-known economists such as Milton Friedman, Friedrich A. von Hayek and Ludwig von Mises, who had, in recent decades, become iconic proponents not just of 'free market doctrine' but also of the neoliberal current of the Anglo-Saxon New Right.[226] In some of his speeches, Christoph Blocher referred prominently to von Hayek and Wilhelm Röpke, the German conservative thinker. For Christoph Mörgeli too, von Hayek, Friedman, von Mises and Röpke, as well as the influential Mont Pèlerin Society, all represented important points of reference.[227]

The SVP's neoliberal agenda was based on the idea that a free market ideology guarantees the economic and social well-being of large segments of the population and supports individual self-responsibility and the spirit of entrepreneurship. To achieve this goal, there should be less state intervention, lower taxes and a reduced state bureaucracy and state expenditure.[228] As the cantonal section of Zurich proclaimed in its party program: 'The future belongs to a free, healthy and slimline state, with low public expenditure and low taxes'.[229] The state should limit its activities to definite policy areas, particularly those related to asylum, foreign relations, social welfare, transportation and state bureaucracy and it should also make substantial budget cuts in these areas. The SVP also insisted on tax cuts for the middle class, in particular for small and medium-sized businesses, entrepreneurs and families with children.

While the party pleaded for a socially sustainable market economy, it also denounced the so-called exuberant welfare state, in which private initiative and a sense of effort would lose ground.[230] However, the party did not urge for a dismantling of the social security system and the welfare state but asked instead for concrete economic measures and rejected the increase in individual contribution rates.

The SVP's belief in the forces of free market economy and the principles of laissez-faire was closely linked with strong criticism of the role of the state. The party's anti-state criticism was not solely a manifestation of true free-market beliefs or an all-encompassing neoliberal doctrine. It also drew on populist anti-establishment sentiments and on the conviction that the state was mainly beholden to power holders that belong to the left. For the SVP, therefore, the state basically served as battleground for populist attacks, which were in fact directed against the political class as a whole. In its fight against interventionism and bureaucracy, the SVP was predisposed to denounce the left for being responsible for Switzerland becoming a socialist state.[231] From this it would seem, that for the SVP, as is the case for many other radical right-wing populist parties, 'the neo-liberal program is only secondarily an economic program. Primarily, it is a political weapon against the established political institutions and their alleged monopolisation of political power which hampers economic progress and suppresses true democracy'.[232]

Even if the SVP asked for a reduction in state intervention in most of the public sector, there were policies areas in which the party favoured substantial state activity. For example, since the SVP continued to defend the interest of the agrarian milieu, it demanded massive state interventions in the agricultural policy. The party also opposed any budget cuts on national defence and military affairs. However, the discrepancy between the neoliberal doctrine and the notion of a strong state is most strikingly illustrated by the standpoint that the SVP took on issues related to internal security and law and order. According to the party program of 1999, the protection of law and order is the central and basic task of the state.[233] As a matter of fact, when it came to public security issues, the SVP proposed a quasi-authoritarian view regarding the omnipotence of the state. As the increase in crime, the deficiency of public security and drug-related criminality were consistently presented in political campaigns as the pressing problems facing present-day Switzerland, the SVP demanded that law enforcement should be improved, that the police should show a greater public presence and that perpetrators should be sentenced more severely and more jails should be built.[234]

Reasons for the Success of the New SVP

The most intriguing question regards the nature of the factors that accounted for the extraordinary electoral rise of the SVP in the 1990s. Certainly, changing socioeconomic conditions and the growing salience of the asylum theme, as well as new policy issues such as Switzerland's international integration and the reexamination of the country's role in the Second World War provided a fertile environment. It is important, however, to point to the new SVP's successful strategy of constructing new cleavages and reinforcing those already in existence. Perhaps most significantly, the new SVP played a central role in the political construction of issues such as migration, asylum seekers and international integration by presenting them as a threat to Swiss national identity. In this way, the party greatly contributed to the emergence of sociopolitical cleavages in Swiss society that revolved around the subject of identity politics.[235] These divisions were reinforced by the new SVP's adoption of a new style of provocation and confrontation that starkly contrasted with the mode of consensual politics that was characteristic of the country's political system.

In order to explain the success of the SVP, it is first important to remember that the SVP was not a *new* party and did not actually have to go through the difficult initial phase of party formation. Because of the SVP's status as a long-established mainstream party that was represented in the government and many other public offices, the new SVP was also able to rely on a 'historical capital' and could not simply be dismissed as an untrustworthy pariah party. These factors differentiated it from the fringe radical right-wing populist parties who never succeeded in transcending their outsider status. Another set of explanatory factors draws on the remarkable improvement in organisation, campaigning and leadership that the party made in the 1990s. Organisationally, the SVP expanded enormously in this decade. It almost doubled the number of cantonal parties and finished by contesting elections in all the Swiss cantons. The new SVP also went through a process of institutionalisation and nationalisation which resulted in both organisational centralisation and increased ideological cohesion, in stark contrast to the fragmented, fringe, radical right-wing populist parties. A further key difference in respect to the fringe parties was the fact that the SVP was able to count on considerable financial resources, including the contributions from Christoph Blocher, who repeatedly financed public campaigns.

The new SVP built up an efficient election and propaganda apparatus, and with professional marketing and a controversial campaigning style, it increased its presence in the media and in public debates. Establishing a wide-ranging network of satellite organisations also helped the new SVP to become a ubiquitous force in Swiss political and public life. This was reinforced by the popular appeal of Christoph Blocher, who followed James Schwarzenbach to be the second right-wing populist leader of postwar Switzerland. In a time of growing media influence and personalization of politics, Blocher acted as a leader figure with charisma and rhetoric skills. With his authoritarian leadership, he gained a dominant position in the new SVP and arguably became the most influential political leader in Swiss politics.

Moreover, the new SVP took advantage of its dual role as an opposition and government party. While the party applied an anti-establishment rhetoric and used direct democratic instruments to undermine consensual politics, it was also keen to demonstrate its capability and experience in holding executive power, considered by many as being necessary for effectively carrying out policy changes. Until 2003, when Christoph Blocher was elected into government, the Zurich-oriented faction skilfully took advantage of its exclusion from governance by presenting itself as a trustworthy critic of the political establishment and as a popular voice not corrupted by political power.

Finally, as the new SVP applied the three-fold 'winning formula' of combining neoliberalism with exclusionism and nationalism, it enabled the party to enlarge its electorate and to attract a diverse constituency.[236] Most consistently, the party presented itself as the last true defender of the sovereignty and identity of a Switzerland that the party alleged to be facing increased threats from the outside world. As a result of the process of programmatic and ideological transformation that it went through in the 1990s, therefore, identity politics and issues associated with the question of Swiss identity became the core of the new SVP's programmatic course. In developing its new ideological profile and political agenda, the party referred to ideas, concepts and discourses that, as we will see in the next two chapters, have been produced by a variety of circles, intellectuals and publications of the New Right since the late 1960s.

6

A SUPPLIER OF IDEOLOGY
The New Right in the German-speaking Part of Switzerland

In the German-speaking part of Switzerland, most intellectuals are traditionally more engaged in academia and culture and the world of ideas and aesthetics than in politics and public affairs. One reason is that the political and public culture in the German-speaking part of Switzerland is somewhat marked by anti-intellectualism, and intellectuals receive little recognition from the public. The rather anti-elitist climate, reinforced by the egalitarian impetus of direct democracy, brings about a situation where intellectuals whose interests and engagements focus on the sphere of ideas, theories and knowledge are regarded as being detached from the everyday life of society. As a consequence, intellectuals rarely tend to intervene in political discussions as individual public figures, and there are few intellectual publications and circles in existence which deal with political questions or address a wider public. This low profile of intellectuals in the public sphere is also fuelled by an intellectual self-image that models the situation in Germany, where intellectuals maintain a fairly elitist stance and keep to the tradition of the *Bildungsbürgertum* (educated bourgeoisie).

In order to overcome their limited public authority, however, a number of intellectuals in the German-speaking part of Switzerland choose not to limit themselves to the world of academia, arts and culture and to address a larger audience more frequently and intervene in public and political debates more directly. In order to come to the forefront of public discussion and to act as public figures, these intellectuals are determined to assume partisan engagement and become involved in party politics. They affiliate themselves more directly with political parties, or engage in party politics behind the scenes by acting as advisers on programmatic and ideological questions. While this type of 'committed intellectual' is found among the left and the right, it appears that the New Right has forcefully revived the tradition of a right-wing intellectualism that shows a firm dedication to political and public engagement.

As was the case in other European countries, right-wing intellectuals in Switzerland at the turn of the twentieth century were greatly inspired by the nationalist, racist and authoritarian ideas of theorists and authors from the European radical right.[1] During the period between the First and Second World War, fascist intellectuals acted at the margin of political and cultural life in Switzerland, while intellectuals advocating a so-called New Conservatism were affiliated with the established political right and hence exerted a remarkable influence on mainstream politics. With an attitude of cultural despair, a fierce anti-modernism and a sharp criticism of liberal and pluralistic society as well as parliamentarian democracy, New Conservatism might in some ways be said to represent the Swiss version of the German Conservative Revolution. New Conservatives contributed to the national renewal of Switzerland, best expressed in the so-called Spiritual Defence of the Nation (*Geistige Landesverteidigung*), as a newly engineered ideological and cultural concept of 'Swissness'.[2]

The Spiritual Defence of the Nation was influenced by authoritarian and nationalist thought and highlighted the distinctiveness of the Swiss national community, which stems from exceptional cultural and historical experiences. By putting a strong emphasis on the national community and absorbing the existing 'discourse of overforeignization', the Spiritual Defence of the Nation incorporated exclusionist ideas and considerably reinforced the distinction between 'us' and 'them'.[3] On the other hand, since the concept aimed to underscore the country's independence from the surrounding totalitarian regimes and to promote a policy of demarcation from the racist ideology of those regimes, it had the effect of integrating the Swiss national community and was also supported by Social Democrats and trade unionists.[4]

The new conservative current of the interwar period was prominently represented by the influential Swiss writer and historian, Gonzague de Reynold, and by Philipp Etter, Federal Councillor (1934–1959) from the Swiss Conservative People's Party and main architect of the Spiritual Defence of the Nation.[5] If most New Conservatives were opposed to National Socialism and pleaded for Switzerland's independence from the neighbouring dictatorships and a cultural renewal based on Swiss national traditions, other intellectuals such as the well-known writer Jakob Schaffner were clearly attracted to National Socialism and its new European order.[6] In addition, fascist ideas were embraced by a circle of young academics and intellectuals in Zurich who founded the National Front and New Front in the early 1930s, two leading groups of the Front Movement.[7] After the end of the Second World War, a few intellectuals affiliated with the Front Movement were brought to justice and eventually punished with imprisonment. Others were spared legal action and were portrayed by the authorities as good patriots, albeit somewhat misled.[8]

While some authoritarian intellectuals became engaged with groups that acted as precursors to the Swiss New Right, most made a smooth transition into Switzerland's postwar order. They played an important role in shaping the new national consensus of the Cold War era, which was marked by a high degree of political and social cohesion and a remarkable convergence between the right and the left.[9] Organisations that were created in the prewar climate of national renewal survived in the form of parapolitical groups and intellectual circles and these continued to attract a wide range of right-wing intellectuals, as well as representatives of the left.[10] At this point, the main objective of the ever persistent Spiritual Defence of the Nation shifted to a desire to combat alleged communist subversion. While anti-communism hardly represented a coherent ideology, driven as it was by a real or imagined communist threat, it served the right as a general ideological tool of integration and was skilfully exploited in order to achieve political stabilisation domestically.[11] In the late 1960s, the anti-communist attitude of the right received a new boost with the events of 1968 and the emergence of the New Left. At the same time, new patterns of an exclusionist ideology were provided by the insurgent Movement against Overforeignization and its nationalist and xenophobic program.

In the late 1960s, James Schwarzenbach, considered by contemporaries from the right to be both a political leader and a spirited intellectual, prominently personalised the merger of conservative thought with a radical-right agenda. His emergence marked the beginning of the New Right in the German-speaking part of Switzerland. Schwarzenbach combined a belief in the continuing authority of religion and family with a critique of modernity and mass society and with the search for social equality, while placing emphasis throughout on the national community as the key frame of reference.[12] He inspired a number of young intellectuals who aimed at reshaping and revitalising conservative thought. They complained about the blind faith that a large part of conservative intellectuals seemed happy to show in the march of progress and materialistic improvement and bemoaned the high prevalence that egalitarian and emancipatory principles of Enlightenment had taken in society at the expense of values, traditions and authority. With the value-oriented current of Swiss conservatism, they shared an attitude of cultural pessimism and a concern 'with the survival of the traditional values of Western civilisation which, influenced by Christian thought, do not subordinate people to progress and technology but seek to make universal self-realisation the ultimate ethico-political criterion'.[13]

In addition, their criticism of egalitarianism included the view that, as Robert Antonio put it, 'Enlightenment universalism is equated with cultural homogenisation, the destruction of community, and the evaporation of cultural autonomy'.[14] Thus, the intellectuals of the Swiss New Right began to put high emphasis on aspects of national and cultural identity, which, in their view, would help the people to find their way in a modern, disoriented society. Another important goal of the emerging New Right was to counter and ultimately go beyond the progressive and anti-authoritarian ideas of the 1968 movement. It was argued that with the 'cultural revolution' of 1968, the left was well on the way to refining its cultural and intellectual concepts to a level at which the right had very little with which to answer. For the decades to follow, therefore, it became a key objective of the New Right in the German-speaking part in Switzerland, as for most of their counterparts in Western Europe, to strive for a strategic renewal based on the idea that the right would seriously need to expand its cultural and intellectual engagements.

Organisationally, what has taken place in the German-speaking New Right of Switzerland since the late 1960s resembles to some extent the developments in Germany, where the New Right has been described as an 'organised confusion'.[15] While different groups and publications have emerged and disappeared, the New Right has basically held itself together in a loosely organised network containing a variety of study groups and periodicals. Surveying the developments since the late 1960s, the New Right in the German-speaking part of Switzerland may be grouped around three ideological currents: the neo-conservatives, the ecologists and the nationalists. While such categorisation draws on distinct historical, ideological and organisational characteristics, there are also overlaps between the three currents, particularly in the form of

Figure 6.1 | *Ideological Typology of the German-speaking New Right*

Common Exclusionist Ideology

Neo-Conservatives	Ecologists	Nationalists
Renewal of Conservatism	Right-wing Environmentalism	Isolationist and Nationalist Agenda

Distinctive Intellectual Legacy and Ideological Priorities

multiple membership, collaborations and alliances, and common ideological features.

The Neoconservatives: Renewing Conservatism and Approaching the New Right

The term 'neoconservatives' is used in different national contexts to denote a distinct current of intellectuals, authors and academics which has aimed, since the 1970s, at renewing conservative thought and restoring the appeal of conservatism to new constituencies.[16] In the United States, neoconservatives, grouped around Irving Kristol, Norman Podhoretz and Daniel Bell, along with journals such as *The Public Interest* and *Commentary*, have sought to revitalise those moral, cultural and religious foundations of American society which are purportedly jeopardised by the predominance of liberalism and the New Left.[17] In Germany, neoconservatism challenged the sociocultural premises of the 1968 student movement and was represented by well-known academics like Hermann Lübbe, Odo Marquard, Günter Rohrmoser and Helmut Schelsky. They pursued a 'modernisation of German conservatism', by combining traditional, illiberal concepts with ideas of economic growth and technological progress.[18]

The most important faction of German neoconservatives looked for what some have called the 'reconstruction of conservatism'.[19] To this end, they embarked on the enterprise of launching a cultural revolution from the right by putting themes such as a 'reevaluation of the past' and 'national identity' on the mainstream agenda. Since they rejected universalistic values and egalitarian and emancipatory ideas, while emphasising the need for a secure sense of authority, traditions and national pride, neoconservatives became an important ideological current of the New Right.[20] The ideological and organisational move towards the New Right was the consequence of increasing criticism of the Christian Democratic Union (*Christlich-Demokratische Union* – CDU) and the established right. Soon after the right-wing government took office in 1982–83, Günter Rohrmoser, for example, complained that the CDU did not have a philosophy, nor a concept or strategy with which to accomplish a real intellectual and moral change in Germany. He claimed that it was necessary to reorientate conservative thinking in order to accomplish such change and to integrate a constituency located on the right of the CDU.[21] Intellectuals like Rohrmoser and Gerd-Klaus Kaltenbrunner, as well as political figures like Hans Filbinger, a CDU member who had had to resign as minister-president of Baden-Württemberg in

1978 because of his role as a naval judge in the National Socialist regime, all played an influential role in the move towards the New Right. Conferences and lectures organised by think tanks like the Weikersheim Study Centre (*Studienzentrum Weikersheim*) became gathering places for intellectuals from the different currents of the German New Right. In particular, the Weikersheim Study Centre, which was founded by Hans Filbinger in 1979, served as a bridge between neoconservative intellectuals and the New Right.[22] In addition, neoconservative authors regularly contributed to the periodicals *Criticón, Mut* and *Junge Freiheit*, thereby underscoring their conformity with the efforts of the New Right.[23]

In a similar way to Germany, the neoconservative current of the New Right in the German-speaking part of Switzerland has developed a highly variegated network of groups, intellectual circles and publications since the late 1960s and has thereby attracted a diverse range of intellectuals, authors and politicians. Most followers were very critical of egalitarian and emancipatory conceptions of society, a criticism which stemmed from the genuinely strong belief of neoconservatives in organic society based on authority, hierarchy and moral order. Often driven by traditional Christian values, they saw the preservation of the family, as the natural nucleus of society, the preservation of traditional education methods, and the rejection of abortion and homosexuality as moral priorities which had to be defended in modern society, which they claimed to be characterised by declining values, permissiveness and moral disorder. While in the early years their ideology was marked by the legacy of conservatism, a pronounced anti-communist attitude and the rejection of Enlightenment philosophies, in the 1980s and 1990s, features of radical-right ideology such as exclusionism and nationalism became increasingly key characteristics of the neoconservative program.

Strategically, one part of the neoconservative current put into practice the idea that political conquest should be preceded by ideological and sociocultural action. In accordance with the 'metapolitical' strategy of the continental European New Right, these neoconservatives were fond of picturing the world as a battlefield of ideas and hence put emphasis on cultural politics and intellectual debates. Other protagonists of the neoconservative current were steadily engaged in everyday politics and affiliated with political parties. They acted as parapolitical actors and were involved in direct democratic activities. While the party membership of neoconservatives has extended to centre-right parties, the SVP has been the party with which they have most commonly been affiliated since the late 1980s and early 1990s. Another important characteristic of the Swiss neoconservatives were the strong links to counterparts in Germany. In fact, it is thanks to them that some of the most important authors, periodicals and books associated with the German New Right found an interested audience in Switzerland.

Herbert Meier and the Paper Abendland:
From Conservative Revolution to the New Right

Herbert Meier has been perhaps the most prolific publishing director, author and parapolitical entrepreneur of the New Right in the German-speaking part of Switzerland. Since the 1960s, he has engaged in a range of intellectual and political groups, edited and published several periodicals, and written a large number of articles. From the earliest days of his activities, he was involved with right-wing Catholicism, a tendency which developed a strong presence in postwar Switzerland in the form of traditionalist, integrist and anti-abortion groups.[24] Meier was an editor of the periodical *Timor Domini*, launched in 1972; an executive member of Pro Ecclesia, which was founded in 1984; and a publishing director of *Schweizerische Katholische Wochenzeitung* (Swiss Catholic Weekly Paper), created in 1987 as successor to the Catholic traditionalist weekly *Das Neue Volk* (The New People).

In 1970, Meier also helped to found the short-lived Wilhelm Röpke Society (*Wilhelm-Röpke-Gesellschaft*), which was dedicated to the work of the German theorist of early neoliberal conservatism and mainly attracted traditionalist Catholics.[25] Born near Hannover in 1899, Wilhelm Röpke taught at the Institute of International Studies in Geneva from 1937 until his death in 1966. Considered as a student of the Austrian Economic School, he emphasised the close relationship between culture and economic system, and fiercely opposed the idea of collective wealth in social, political and economic theory. Along with Friedrich A. von Hayek and Ludwig von Mises, Röpke co-founded the influential Mont Pèlerin Society in 1947.[26] Another Swiss co-founder of the Wilhelm Röpke Society was Martin Rhonheimer, who became a member of the right-wing Catholic group Opus Dei in the early 1970s and received a PhD in philosophy from the University of Zurich in 1977, with Hermann Lübbe as thesis director. In 1974, Rhonheimer published an essay on the theory of conservative thinking in an important volume which was edited by Gerd-Klaus Kaltenbrunner and included leading German intellectuals from the New Right, such as Armin Mohler, Caspar von Schrenck-Notzing and Klaus Hornung.[27]

Herbert Meier has also been involved in party politics and in a number of political campaigns. From 1972 to 1985, he was member of the cantonal parliament of Aargau, for the first two years as a representative of the Republican Movement and then later for the Swiss People's

Party.[28] In 1987, he ran without success for the National Council, on an SVP ticket in the canton of Aargau.[29] So far, his most important political engagement was the support he gave in the campaign opposing anti-racism law in 1993–94. In September 1993, Meier founded the Committee for Freedom of Speech and Thinking (*Komitee für Freiheit im Reden und Denken* – KFRD), which helped to collect signatures for bringing the law to a popular vote. Meier's committee was comprised of eight National Councillors, five from the FPS and one each from the SD, the SVP and the FDP. Other committee members were associated with New Right groups and publications.[30] In its campaign, the KFRD sought to present more elaborated arguments than other opponents of the law who were associated with the extreme right (see chapter 8). For example, references were drawn from the cultural-differentialist ideas developed by Olivier Delacrétaz, in his booklet *L'universel enraciné*, which was intellectually and conceptually perhaps the most articulate work written by an opponent of the anti-racism law (see chapter 7). In addition, the KFRD argued that the concept of anti-racism represented just another form of 'political correctness' and hence just another way that the left was seeking to control the minds of the people and pursue its cultural revolution. According to Meier's committee, the anti-racism law was an example of the cultural hegemony assumed by the left and its implementation would have the consequence that legitimate demands for the preservation of Swiss identity would automatically be associated with racism.[31]

Herbert Meier's most important contribution to the New Right in the German-speaking part of Switzerland is to be found in the role he played in developing both a Swiss publishing network and a close relationship with German authors and intellectuals. He served as a publisher of the *Schweizerische Akademiker- und Studenten-Zeitung* (Swiss Academics and Students Paper) which aimed at countering the alleged influence of the 1968 movement within Swiss universities and had an estimated circulation of forty thousand in the 1980s.[32] More significant for the development of the Swiss neoconservative current was Meier's position as publisher of the paper *Abendland* (Occident). Founded in 1964 as a college paper, *Abendland* represented the earliest mouthpiece of Swiss neoconservatism and served as a publishing vehicle for Meier's goal of renewing the Swiss right intellectually and culturally. While the paper was released monthly until the early 1980s, publication became less frequent in the 1980s and 1990s, usually four times per year. In 1994, the editors of *Abendland* claimed to have a circulation of thirty thousand, a number which has most probably dropped significantly since then.[33] The *Abendland* was made in a simple newspaper-like style and included four to eight A3 format pages. The paper published long feature-length articles on a regular basis concerning political, cultural and historical issues and sought thereby to fulfil intellectual pretensions.

While Herbert Meier was responsible for the editorial policy, a range of Swiss and German authors have published in *Abendland* throughout the last four decades. In the 1990s, the paper brought out texts written by prominent proponents of Swiss radical right-wing populism, including Christoph Blocher, Hans Fehr and Luzi Stamm, the latter a National Councillor since 1991, who deserted from the FDP to the SVP in 2001 and authored a number of books on Swiss politics.[34] Several articles on immigration were written by Philipp Müller, FDP member and chief promoter of an anti-immigrant initiative demanding a limit on the number of foreigners to 18 per cent of the population. Another prominent contributor was Pirmin Meier, a historian, novelist and journalist who had co-founded *Abendland* in 1964. He had helped to found the Swiss Republican Movement in 1971 and was its executive committee member for the following two years. Pirmin Meier became an acclaimed book author in the 1990s and in 2000 he received the literary prize of the New Right circle Foundation for Occidental Consciousness.

A general aim of *Abendland* was to make German intellectual and cultural debates better known to the Swiss audience. For that reason, numerous German authors have published in the Swiss paper since the 1960s. The most frequent German contributor to *Abendland* was Gerd-Klaus Kaltenbrunner, who mainly wrote on issues of philosophy, art and literary history. Another important author was Christa Meves whose work was also regularly reviewed in *Abendland*. Meves has published extensively in periodicals of the German New Right and was known in Switzerland for her contributions to the paper *Schweizerzeit*, as well as for her association with religious fundamentalist groups.[35] In March 1993, *Abendland* also reprinted an article written by Klaus Hornung, a leading author of the German New Right, which had originally published in *Criticón*.[36] Meier, for his part, had already contributed an article to the German magazine *Criticón* in 1974.[37]

Abendland provides a good example of the key objective of the New Right to strive for strategic renewal and an expansion of its cultural and intellectual engagements. This purpose was well illustrated in a 1987 article by Herbert Meier, in which he argued that:

> The rightists [*Bürgerlichen*] thought for all too long that the job was done and dusted once they were able to fill key positions in economy and finance, and they neglected areas such as education, culture and media. The filling of key positions in economy and finance might represent success in the short run. Yet the areas of education, culture and the media

are the places where the kind of long-term development and creation of greater consciousness take place which eventually have the potential to change an entire society.[38]

In the 1960s and early 1970s, *Abendland* published a number of ambitious articles which give an idea of the paper's strategic intentions and intellectual references.[39] The paper complained that contemporary society was going through a profound crisis that was mainly caused by the legacy of the Enlightenment. The proliferation of Enlightenment ideas had, they claimed, eventually resulted in the critical prevalence of human rights, total democratisation and the levelling of social structures. Other indications of the contemporary crisis were the common belief in progress and rationalism, and the denial of the past and traditions, both of which should actually be seen as expressions of tried and tested experience. Herbert Meier was never tired of emphasising that large parts of the established right had complied with this type of thinking.[40] He was convinced, therefore, that it was time that nonconformist conservatives rose up, to prompt a regeneration of conservative ideas and form an avant-garde of 'revolutionary conservatism' that would represent the 'only real alternative to the bankrupt Zeitgeist'.[41]

Another characteristic of the early *Abendland* was the passionate plea for the strengthening of Europe's consciousness and identity. In accordance with the self-styled aim to promote values of the Christian-occidental legacy, the editors emphasised the importance of reviving European history and culture. Europe was pictured as the leading intellectual and cultural force in the world, or, as Pirmin Meier put it in a markedly Eurocentric way: 'What takes place today in Asia, Africa and Latin America, is nothing other than an enormous adjustment to the superior European mind'.[42] It was also demanded that Switzerland be part of Europe's process of unification which would eventually result in a European federal state; it would be a matter of necessity, therefore, for the country to get rid of its outdated neutrality policy.[43]

From the beginning, *Abendland* took a pronounced anti-left view and regularly gave anti-communist groups the opportunity to express their views during the cold war.[44] It also became a prime goal of the paper to denounce the alleged dominance of the left and the 1968 generation in politics, media, culture and education. In addition, under the influence of Herbert Meier, Catholic traditionalism and Christian values were an integrated part of the worldview that was promoted by the paper. This was probably the main reason that Meier expressed his disagreement with the French-influenced New Right. In an article from 1995, he declared that the Christian-occidental thought of conservatives is 'diametrically opposed to the neo-pagan and nominalistic intellectual approaches, which [are] supposedly "new-right" but in truth neo-fascist'.[45] As a consequence of his rejection of the *Nouvelle droite*, he published a harsh critique of Alain de Benoist and his work one year later.[46]

In the early years, the editors of *Abendland* saw the Movement against Overforeignization and particularly James Schwarzenbach as natural allies in their political and intellectual struggle.[47] Arguing that the 'Schwarzenbach Initiative' from 1970 had managed to mobilise supporters across party lines, Herbert Meier strongly believed that the time had come to create a large coalition of conservatives factions which would be able to counter the progressive forces dominating Swiss politics and media.[48] Soon after, however, the paper distanced itself from the Republican Movement and in 1973, Pirmin Meier published a harsh three-page critique of Schwarzenbach's movement denouncing the 'nationalistically polluted patriotism' and the authoritarian structure of the SRB.[49]

Later, in the 1990s, *Abendland* showed a lot of agreement with the agenda and strategy of the SVP and published many articles aimed at evoking resentments towards the political class, including the established centre-right parties. Such anti-establishment criticism was applied, for example, on issues related to Europe's unification where *Abendland* made its most noticeable shift from the positions of its early period.[50] The European Union was now being rejected for being preoccupied with economics while neglecting the people's connection to the country. As Pirmin Meier argued in an article published after the rejection of EEA membership, 'the deeper the roots and the greater the level of embodiment in the national customs and traditions [*Volkstum*], not to forget the religiosity, the less prone German-speaking Switzerland was to exterior influences'.[51] It is therefore of little surprise that many articles published by *Abendland* rejected the reappraisal of Switzerland's role in the Second World War and denounced critics as people that were guilty of fouling their own nest.[52]

Another trait of *Abendland* in the 1980s and 1990s was the sharp criticism of the government's migration policy and the regularly expressed hostility towards foreigners and asylum seekers in particular. As early as 1985, the paper published an article which discussed the danger that Swiss asylum policy might be handled in a way that was contrary to the will of the people.[53] For the paper it was clear that Switzerland simply could not be allowed to be an immigration country and that everything should be done to stop to immigration. In the 1990s, cultural-differentialist views became a key feature of articles published on immigration. In an article from 1994 it was argued that 'the immigrants are increasingly coming from world regions which are very foreign to us – integration is hardly possible any more'.[54] Another example was Philipp Müller who claimed that the mixing of different, even opposing cultures would lead sooner or later to an excessive hostility toward foreigners in Switzerland. He further maintained that the watering down or even the loss of one's own identity could not possibly be the point of Swiss migration policy.[55] Or as Herbert Meier put it, while everyone, including the Swiss, has the (human) right to identity and to be 'native to a place' (*Beheimatung*), this is seriously jeopardised by mass immigration. Efficient counter-measures are not taken, however, because the Federal Council and most of the politicians are intimidated by 'the dogged multiculti-ideologues'.[56] These examples show the long ideological journey that Herbert Meier and his periodical *Abendland* have taken, from an early revolutionary mission of renewing conservative thought, to a radical-right ideology marked by exclusionist and nationalist views – positions that were consistently fuelled, however, by a determined anti-left attitude.

The Foundation for Occidental Consciousness: An Established Cultural Circle

The Foundation for Occidental Consciousness (*Stiftung für Abendländische Besinnung* – STAB) represents an intellectual and cultural circle committed to the strengthening of occidental culture and values. It was founded in 1968 by Hans R. Jenny (1912–1996), who held a PhD in economics from the University of Zurich and gained some reputation by publishing books on Africa.[57] He was a former member of the National Front, a leading group of the Front Movement in the 1930s.[58] During the Second World War, he published two essays in which he showed understanding for Germany's expansion into south-eastern Europe.[59] Jenny was the driving force of the STAB and long-time president of its board. In 1995, he was succeeded by Eduard Stäuble, who advanced in the 1990s to become a prolific journalist and author of the Swiss New Right. Born in 1924, Eduard Stäuble received a PhD in literature from the University of Zurich and authored a number of books on literary topics. From 1965 to 1986, he was in charge of the department of Culture and Society at the Swiss German national TV network. Between 1975 and 1999, Stäuble was a regular contributor to the regional daily paper, *Badener Tagblatt*, and its successor, *Aargauer Zeitung*.[60]

The STAB had important financial resources at its disposal, mainly thanks to donations from a small group of supporters. After the foundation was founded with capital of twenty-five thousand Swiss francs, donations from the founders and a small circle of friends – as well as returns on capital – had raised the fortune of the STAB to 3.5 million Swiss francs by 1993.[61] This provided the means with which to award an annual literary prize of twenty-five to fifty thousand Swiss francs, the '*STAB-Preis*' (STAB Prize). With this literary prize, the circle gained some recognition not just in Switzerland's cultural and intellectual milieu, but also among the prominent political figures of the right.

In the 1990s, former Federal Councillor, Rudolf Friedrich (1992), Hermann Lübbe (1993) and the former mayor of Zurich, Sigmund Widmer (1998) gave the laudatory addresses for the prize winners. The selection of prize winners was eclectic and comprised writers, scholars and intellectuals who had published writings on philosophy, literature, religion, science, medicine, etc.[62] Moreover, the circle edited the *STAB-Schriftenreihe* (STAB Publication Series), part of which has been released in recent years by the publishing house Arbora-Verlag. By 2001, thirty-seven volumes had been published in the series. Most of the brochures were the written versions of speeches held at the award ceremonies. The STAB also provided important funding for a range of social, cultural and religious institutions and associations, whose political and ideological orientation did not really correspond to the New Right profile of the STAB. Between 1968 and 1993, the foundation allocated funds to the tune of 1.5 million Swiss francs.[63]

The STAB was created with the purpose of presenting an intellectual and cultural counter-project to the 1968 student movement, which had cast doubt on the whole of occidental culture, according to the founders of STAB.[64] Convinced of the destructive impact that emancipatory and pluralistic concepts wreak on society and individuals, the circle believed that a revitalisation of occidental values and traditions would bring ultimate salvation from cultural and moral decadence. By exploring the sources of occidental culture inspired by Christian faith and Greek philosophy, the circle sought to contribute to the moral and cultural renewal of the occident. Following this purpose, the STAB stated in its foundation document that it aimed to promote the consciousness of occidental tradition, culture and morality, and the intellectual unification of Europe.[65] As a result, many writings published by the STAB passed judgment on growing social, moral and cultural alienation in contemporary society and a general loss of orientation. Eduard Stäuble complained that 'we live in a time of a distracted *pluralism* (where everything is possible) and *permissively* decomposing values (where everything is permitted)'.[66] Among the pressing problems that society has increasingly had to face since the 1970s, Hans Jenny, for his part, identified a loss of transcendence and religious aspects. According to Jenny, both these elements have been challenged by a number of developments, such as Islamism, materialist thinking, economic Darwinism, individualisation and social discrimination against families.[67]

The STAB demonstrated a markedly elitist self-understanding and insisted, in its basic principles of July 1969 (later revised in September 1977), that elites had been in charge since the beginning of the occident in order to uphold tradition, culture and morality. In view of this, the circle embraced an anti-egalitarian worldview and advocated a hierarchical concept of society because 'no better age begins from a position of absolute equality'. They maintained that the majority of humankind would accept an order of precedence based on performance and responsibility, and that people would do well not to forget the fact that nature had created differentiation of its own with reference to gender, descent, language, character and social position.[68] Following this view, a letter from 1973 sent to the members of the circle claimed that the ethologist and Nobel Prizewinner Konrad Lorenz and his book 'Civilised Man's Eight Deadly Sins' laid bare the 'misconception of equality' (*Irrglauben der Egalität*).[69]

In the second half of the 1990s, authors and scholars associated with the German New Right were awarded the STAB annual prize. The psychologist Christa Meves and the pedagogue Wolfgang Brezinka jointly received the '*STAB-Preis*' in 1995.[70] Both were well-known for their long-standing commitment to the struggle against the alleged influence of the New Left in pedagogy and the education system. The daily paper, *Neue Zürcher Zeitung*, which occasionally covered the awarding of STAB prizes, criticised both prizewinners by noting that their speeches drew on concepts of the enemy which could hardly be said to create a sense of community.[71]

Two years later, the STAB honoured the controversial German ethologist and disciple of Konrad Lorenz, Irenäus Eibl-Eibesfeldt, who is criticised by many for his pronounced xenophobic positions on migration issues. Drawing on research into sociobiology and ethology, Eibl-Eibesfeldt examines the socio-affective behaviour patterns of individuals in terms of them representing indelible marks of the animal sides of human beings. In his work, he argues that the presupposed human instincts for territory and aggression would naturally lead to repulsive attitudes toward foreigners. He consequently claims that human beings were naturally distant, mistrustful and even frightened of 'strangers'.[72] When Eibl-Eibesfeldt received the STAB award, Eduard Stäuble remembered in his introduction that Eibl-Eibesfeldt had made it very clear what to expect from unrestrained population growth, from threats to the environment, from xenophobia and hatred towards strangers, from the utopia of a multicultural immigration society, from aggressiveness, violence and aspiration for power, and from the meaning of the national state.[73]

In his award address, Eibl-Eibesfeldt denounced the failure of current immigration and asylum policies and warned of the danger that 'we induce our own ousting' if immigrants coming from far-away cultures are encouraged to nurture their cultural distinctiveness in their new homeland.[74] He further embraced an ethnopluralist view and pleaded for the 'cultivation of our own occidental and national identities to serve as Europe's contribution to the multicultural world community'.[75] According to Eibl-Eibesfeldt, an equalised world state with a homogenised world population will probably never exist because life pushes for variety, not only at the level of animal and plant types but also at the level of human populations and cultures.

A similar cultural-differentialist view had already been embraced by Hans Jenny, when he noted, in a text published posthumously, that the STAB considered the cultivation of cultural identity to be a way of preserving ethnic diversity.[76] He further stressed that based on recent experience, it was questionable if the integration and assimilation of people of foreign cultures could ever be achieved and that 'immigrants from Islamic countries, in particular, are not prepared to give up their particular nature or even their faith'.[77] According to Jenny, it would be an illusion to imagine that the second generation of immigrants would assume and in turn pass on our culture. So we see, therefore, that if the STAB could be said to have espoused an anti-egalitarian ideology since its inception, in the 1990s the circle increasingly promoted views that corresponded to the exclusionist and ethnopluralist ideas that were both characteristic of the worldview embraced by the New Right.

The Schweizerzeit: A Bridge to the World of Politics

Founded in 1979, the paper *Schweizerzeit* (Time of the Swiss) represents the most important mouthpiece of the neoconservative current of the Swiss New Right and provides a good example of the strategy of combining intellectual and cultural interests with political partisanship. The paper succeeded *Der Republikaner*, the party organ of the Republican Movement, which had ceased publication in 1978. *Schweizerzeit* played a central role in the changes that had occurred in the Movement against Overforeignization since the late 1970s and contributed to the transfer of personnel and ideas from the old radical right-wing populist parties to the new SVP.[78]

A key figure in this process was Ulrich Schlüer, a historian and former private secretary to Schwarzenbach, who has been the editor-in-chief of *Schweizerzeit* since its inception. Having run for the National Council without success in 1979, on a ticket of the Republican Movement, he was subsequently elected with the Zurich SVP in 1995 and became a close ally of Christoph Blocher.[79] In the beginning, *Schweizerzeit* was affiliated to the Republican Movement in terms of personnel and party preference. Franz Baumgartner, who was president of the SRB at the time, was the first head of the publisher's board of directors. In an editorial article from 1979, he recommended for readers to vote for the SRB in the National Council elections.[80] For his part, Schwarzenbach retained his role as a model for the paper and its editorial staff. It is of little surprise, therefore, that in the obituary he penned in 1994, Ulrich Schlüer praised Schwarzenbach as an exceptional politician and intellectual.[81]

Schweizerzeit began with two thousand subscribers in 1979 and had increased this number to twenty-three thousand by 2003, with a publication that appeared thirty-four times per year. Occasionally, the paper circulated as a promotional tool, attaining a mass print run of up to 530,000 copies.[82] *Schweizerzeit* usually consisted of eight A3 pages and was styled in a professional way. It contained various types of contributions, including feature articles, commentaries, book reviews, caricatures, letters to the editor, etc. The articles covered a large variety of themes, ranging from domestic and international politics to history and culture. Particularly in articles on domestic politics, the language often appeared to be quite polemic. *Schweizerzeit* was released by the publishing venture, "Schweizerzeit"-Verlag AG, which also published and distributed books and other writings. For example, forty-four brochures had been released in the publishing series *"Schweizerzeit"-Schriftenreihe* by 2003.

The mail order service, which also allowed online shopping, offered more than one hundred books covering a wide range of issues. The choice was extensive and included publications from many different authors, among them Alain de Benoist with his book *Schöne vernetzte Welt* (Nice Interlinked World), published by the German Hohenrain-Verlag, a sister company of the extreme-right publishing house Grabert-Verlag.[83] In addition, the publishing venture held annual general meetings, to which outside speakers were invited, and it also sponsored conferences, *"Schweizerzeit"-Tagungen,* which featured speeches by politicians, academics and intellectuals from Switzerland and abroad. At the 1993 meeting, for example, Manfred Brunner, founder of the German-based Eurosceptic party, the Federation of Free Citizens (*Bund Freier Bürger –* BFB), appeared together with Christoph Blocher.[84]

The group of contributors to *Schweizerzeit* has fluctuated considerably through time and the list of guest authors from Switzerland is rather diverse. In terms of party affiliation, *Schweizerzeit* has published articles by prominent political figures from both centre-right parties and radical right-wing populist parties. In the 1990s, however, the newspaper gradually developed into a mouthpiece of the Blocherite wing of the SVP and became part of the party's network of satellite organisations. Leading officials of the cantonal SVP section of Zurich have consistently used *Schweizerzeit* as public platform to disseminate their ideas and policies. Since the early years, Christoph Blocher has written articles in *Schweizerzeit* and he also became a shareholder of the "Schweizerzeit"-Verlag AG in 1982.[85] But the paper continued to attract authors from other political parties, namely the FDP. In addition, a number of Swiss academics and essayists have been published in *Schweizerzeit*.

Since its beginnings, *Schweizerzeit* has demonstrated an affinity with the German New Right. The paper contributed to the import and proliferation of ideas promoted by the German New Right and to the fact that segments of the Swiss public became acquainted with intellectuals associated with the New Right in Germany. *Schweizerzeit* supplied the poorly equipped Swiss right with theoretical ideas and concepts that emanated from the German New Right and it engaged in the debates which took place in the German intellectual community. For this purpose, the paper paid particular attention to the work of German authors and published numerous, sometimes detailed book reviews, as well as book excerpts, speeches and original articles written by German intellectuals and academics. Most regularly, *Schweizerzeit* published articles by neoconservatives who had moved towards the German New Right and had eventually become an integrated part of the scene of New Right intellectuals in the 1980s and 1990s. Usually, they were the authors and collaborators of German periodicals like *Criticón*, *Mut* and *Junge Freiheit*. Surveying the issues of *Schweizerzeit* from 1979 to 2000, the list of authors who have published in both the Swiss paper and the three German periodicals includes Wolfgang Brezinka, Hans Graf Huyn, Gerd-Klaus Kaltenbrunner, Hans-Ulrich Kopp, Gerhard Löwenthal, Christa Meves and Günter Rohrmoser.[86]

From the 1980s to the late 1990s, Gerd-Klaus Kaltenbrunner wrote a number of feature articles on issues related to international politics, contemporary history and culture. Günter Rohrmoser was the German author who arguably contributed the largest number of ideologically elaborated articles in *Schweizerzeit*. On the occasion of his seventieth birthday, the paper published a one-page interview with Günter Rohrmoser.[87] Other regular contributors were Hans Filbinger and Hans Graf Huyn; the latter served as a long-time author in *Criticón* and was appointed collaborator of *Schweizerzeit* in 1993.[88] In February 1994, the Swiss paper published a front-page article by Hans-Ulrich Kopp, influential editor of *Junge Freiheit* from 1990 to 1995,[89] in which he denounced the social and cultural impact of the 1968 generation and celebrated the intellectual legacy of the Conservative Revolution.[90] On the other hand, the affiliation with *Junge Freiheit*, the true flagship of Germany's New Right, was underscored in February 1996, when the German weekly published a one-page interview with Ulrich Schlüer.[91] Moreover, a list of authors who had published in *Junge Freiheit* by October 2003 included four Swiss authors from *Schweizerzeit*: Thomas Meier, former party secretary of the SVP of the city of Zurich; Mauro Tuena, former president of the Young SVP; Ulrich Schlüer; and Philipp Müller.[92] The Swiss paper also regularly published articles based on lectures held at the Weikersheim Study Centre. Ulrich Schlüer talked at the annual meeting of the study centre in 1994.[93] Finally, it is worth noting that *Schweizerzeit* reviewed books released by German publishers such as Universitas, Herbig and Langen Müller, which are part of Herbert Fleissner's publishing company.[94]

The worldview expressed in *Schweizerzeit* was characterised by a rejection of the philosophies of the Enlightenment and a sharp opposition to egalitarian and emancipatory conceptions of society. As stated in a book review, the bottom line was that all politics of equality stand in the way of human nature.[95] In line with this reasoning, many authors argued that, in the previous three decades, egalitarian and anti-authoritarian traditions had been taken up and noticeably reinforced by the 1968 movement and the New Left. In their view, this had affected most areas of society, and ultimately produced 'cultural environment devastation'.[96] For German academics like Christa Meves, Wolfgang Brezinka and Heinz-Dietrich Ortlieb, the anti-authoritarian education of the 1968 generation was responsible for the disintegration of the youth, the decline of family values, an increase in drug problems and the suicide rate, and a growing acceptance of homosexuality. Christa Meves took a marked homophobic attitude when she claimed that concealing the high percentage of homosexuals that were affected by AIDS was designed to overshadow the need to see homosexuality as a perversion.[97]

Authors like Günter Rohrmoser and Hans-Ulrich Kopp saw the alleged sociocultural crisis as a chance for right-wing intellectuals to regenerate philosophical concepts of conservatism. According to Kopp, like the supporters of the Conservative Revolution in the 1920s, a small group of thinkers and intellectuals should develop and present ideas which would eventually find a breeding ground in the disoriented youth of today.[98] In the view of Rohrmoser, since the French Revolution conservatives have developed a sense of historical catastrophes and are therefore the only ones who are able to stir up new forces in the human being, when faced with the current postmodern catastrophe of hedonism and the loss of Christian values. It is crucial, therefore, he argues, to understand the individual as a cultural being and in the ways that he belongs to national and other collectivities. As Rohrmoser further claimed, a renewed conservatism must be conscious of its liberal and Christian roots because only such a version of conservatism would be able to separate itself from the flourishing New Right.[99] His testimony also gives evidence to the tendency among neo-conservatives to draw a distinction between themselves and the New Right, which they commonly associated with the French-influenced *Nouvelle droite*.

From the beginning, *Schweizerzeit* combined criticism of the left with a neoliberal doctrine on issues of the economy and public affairs. As declared in the publisher's statement for the first issue in 1979, the aim of the paper was to defend the freedom and responsibility of the individual and oppose socialist egalitarianism. In a leading article from the same issue, Ulrich Schlüer made a passionate plea for the need to pursue a renewal of the right. He presented an agenda which would later form the basis for the belief system assumed by the neoliberal orientation of Swiss radical right-wing populism. Schlüer criticised right-wing parties for not drawing a clear line between themselves and socialists and urged them to express their rejection of the welfare state and take firm measures against a bloated state bureaucracy. According to Schlüer, it was the duty of the right to guarantee that free economic forces could develop and create the ideal conditions for everyone to take their own fate into their own hands.[100]

As stated in this first issue of *Schweizerzeit*, another prime concern of the paper was to discuss the various aspects of national identity and to do what it could for the independence of the Swiss Confederation, in political, intellectual and cultural terms, and to obstruct internationalist compliance in the federal government.[101] Following this purpose, many authors in *Schweizerzeit* were keen to present themselves as the only true advocates of the Swiss national community and as guardians of the country's national heritage. Based on a culturalist, almost ethnic conception of nationhood, a number of articles published in *Schweizerzeit* pieced together historical, cultural and institutional features and presented them as the primordial ingredients of Switzerland's national identity.[102] In an article from 1979, James Schwarzenbach argued that a community like the Swiss Confederation could only make improvements when its development was derived from the primary substance, from the nature of the community.[103] As the country's political institutions, particularly those of direct democracy, federalism and neutrality, were presented as the real 'substance of the Swiss', they took on an exalted, mythical significance for the binding together of the national community. Neutrality, for example, was described by Schwarzenbach as Switzerland's own best feature and a creative force so great that even in periods of the sharpest division it was more than sufficient to ensure and cement a federation threatened by disintegration.[104]

While such exaltations of national distinctiveness more or less followed the lines of Swiss mainstream politics in the 1980s, they became more contentious in the 1990s when a large part of Swiss polity began to adopt a more open-minded view on Switzerland's role in international relations. *Schweizerzeit* continued to consistently oppose any international involvement and was very much engaged in the campaigns against the country's membership of the EEA, EU, or UN. In a special issue for the 1995 National Council elections, Ulrich Schlüer declared that the voters should opt for the defence of freedom, democracy, self-determination and neutrality and that they should therefore elect those candidates who categorically rejected EU membership.[105] In another article, it was suggested that the Brussels regime saw 'historically evolved structures, national characteristics as obstacles which have to be eradicated'.[106] One should bear in mind that, as the popular Swiss comedian Walter Roderer put it in a front-page article, 'we are the oldest and best democracy in the world, and we are today the *richest country of the world*. As if this is not a special case!'[107] Considering such an attitude, it is not surprising that in the historical debate over Switzerland's role in the Second World War, *Schweizerzeit* vigorously denounced the hostilities of 'ideologically driven young historians', media workers and all sorts of other activists, who have waited a long time for the opportunity to reckon with the neutrality and independency of the country.[108]

In the 1990s, migration and particularly asylum policy were issues extensively covered by *Schweizerzeit*. Most authors showed an exclusionist attitude and often expressed hostility towards foreigners, especially asylum seekers. In a number of articles, a cultural-differentialist view was taken, sometimes marked by neoracist ideas. As early as 1990, the paper participated prominently in a campaign demanding a policy of restriction on asylum and released 225,000 copies of a special issue on the subject of asylum, which included, among others, a front-page article discussing Jürgen Graf's bluntly xenophobic views.[109] Graf, who was to become the most prolific Swiss negationist in the years that followed (chapter 8), had just published his book *Das Narrenschiff* (The Ship of Fools), in which he described in a hostile way how asylum seekers undergo the application procedures for granting asylum, a book which was advertised in almost every issue of *Schweizerzeit* over the course of 1990.[110] *Schweizerzeit* also supported the two asylum initiatives launched by the SVP and regularly gave senior SVP members the opportunity to present their views on the issue. For the campaign of the first asylum initiative in 1996, 280,000 copies were released of a single edition.[111] The paper was also supportive of the federal initiative which aimed at limiting the number of foreigners to 18 per cent, and on several occasions it gave an opportunity to Philipp Müller, the promoter of the initiative, to convey his anti-immigrant messages.[112]

In his regular column, Heinz Allenspach, FDP National Councilor from 1979 to 1995 and director of the Central Association of Swiss Employers Organisations from 1970 to 1993, made a number of pronounced xenophobic and discriminatory statements, for example when he wrote: 'Our foreigner problem is – let's say it openly – first of all a Yugoslavian problem, a Turk problem and an asylum seeker problem.'[113] In another of his columns, he stated that most of those ex-Yugoslavians and Turks who were not ready to integrate in Switzerland live in the German-speaking region and that it was understandable that 'fears of overforeignization' should be more common in these regions.[114] Drawing on such thinking, Allenspach and other authors regularly argued that foreigners were themselves responsible for the hostility they faced from people who felt threatened in their cultural identity and the basis of their livelihood. For example, Eduard Stäuble put it in the following terms: 'Should we be surprised that existential fears become apparent here and there when an excessively unrestricted flow of asylum seekers and strangers floods our country'.[115]

In addition, *Schweizerzeit* regularly presented multiculturalism as a threat that was posed to the Western value system, ultimately leading to the decline of Swiss culture. Thomas Meier, senior SVP official from Zurich and a collaborator of *Schweizerzeit* at the time, wrote an article that was marked by neoracist beliefs.[116] He argued that belonging to a culture is of existential significance to every person. If a person could not identify himself or herself with certain traditions and culture, he or she would not have a real identity. It is a fundamental problem, therefore, according to Meier, that 'overforeignization results in a loss of identity in the hosts' and that, 'as a result, multi-culture means the decline of culture. As history shows, the cohabitation of people of different nationality, race, skin colour and religion has always created problems and been ridden with conflict, in all countries.'[117]

All in all, *Schweizerzeit* assumed a dual role in the neoconservative current. On the one hand, the paper incessantly sought to supply the Swiss New Right – otherwise rather poorly equipped in terms of theory – with the ideas and concepts with which to engage in the debates taking place in the right-wing intellectual communities of both Germany and Switzerland. On the other hand, *Schweizerzeit* was consistently involved in Swiss party politics, expressing unreserved support for radical right-wing populist parties, first in the form of the Swiss Republican Movement, and later the Swiss People's Party.

The JES: The Intellectual Struggle on Swiss Campuses

The Young European Pupils and Students Initiative of Switzerland (*Junge europäische Schüler- und Studenteninitiative der Schweiz* – JES) was created in 1980. According to a Swiss executive member, the main purpose of the JES was to renew right-wing thinking and to challenge the New Left which supposedly held a dominant position within Swiss schools and universities.[118] In the early 1980s, JES sections existed in Germany, Austria and Italy.[119] In Austria, the JES was active on several university campuses in the 1990s, and JES members were involved in activities of the Austrian New Right.[120] The Swiss section, for its part, was in contact with the German New Right and featured in a brief article published by the magazine *Criticón*.[121]

During the 1980s, the Swiss JES section was part of the Swiss anti-communist network and engaged in the organisation of seminars and panel discussions relating to communism and the peace movement.[122] Since 1990, the group has released the small bulletin *Spectrum*, which consisted of four A4 pages and was mainly distributed at university campuses. Every now and then, the bulletin extended its audience and was enclosed as a supplement in other periodicals.[123] Between 1992 and 1996, the JES published six brochures on a variety of themes, such as immigration, Eastern Europe, education policy and drug policy. Although there are no reports on membership, one can assume that the number of members was quite small, since the group was basically run by a couple of young devoted members. It also seems likely that the JES had lost much of its significance by the end of the 1990s.

In an article of principle from 1982, the JES stated that the group intended to strive for an intellectual and cultural renewal of the right, since the weak pragmatism of the right-wing parties and their disorientation in terms of content could not claim to represent a credible alternative to left-wing ideas. The article deplored the rapid internal decline of democratic forces and Christian, occidental culture. It also pleaded for young people to rediscover conservatism as an ideology. According to the JES, conservatism should not imply a slowing down of developments, nor should it make one afraid of new things, but it should rather lead politics in a new direction and open new views on the future of society.[124] As the JES guidelines from 1982 reveal, typical neoconservative views such as these were also firmly grounded in a vigorous rejection of any kind of egalitarian conception of society.[125]

In the 1990s, many articles published in the JES bulletin *Spectrum* focused on migration policies and demanded, above all, more restrictive measures on asylum policy. In accordance with the JES founding principles of safeguarding occidental and Christian culture and values in Europe, the group presented immigrants and asylum seekers, especially those coming from 'countries of foreign cultures', as serious threats facing Switzerland and its national identity.[126] In addition, the paper showed an attitude that was generally xenophobic, since more often than not, its coverage of asylum and migration raised other issues such as crime, drug dealing, high financial expenses, the misuse of asylum rights and illegal immigration.[127]

In 1996, the JES released the booklet, *Islam im Vormarsch. Gefahr für das Abendland?* (Islam Gains Ground. A Threat to the Occident?), for which the group received funding from the STAB.[128] Excerpts were published in *Bürger und Christ* (Citizen and Christian), a Christian fundamentalist periodical.[129] As JES executive member Emil Schreyger chose to put it in the preface, the Western world was experiencing an identity crisis with the collapse of communism and the main representatives of Islamic fundamentalism were taking advantage of this crisis by trying to fill the vacuum with Islamic faith. He expressed hope, therefore, that the JES booklet would help to bring a better understanding of the new developments emerging from the increased immigration of Muslims into Switzerland.[130] The booklet presented a markedly Islamophobic perspective, however, by giving the impression that Islam and Muslim immigration should be seen as threats to Europe and its occidental values.

Introduced as an expert on politics and religion, Robert Rudin claimed that there was a great difference between those former immigrants who came from Italy, Spain and Portugal, who 'socially, culturally, ethically and religiously belong to the same cultural sphere as we', and the new immigrants from Muslim countries. He claimed that the majority of the Muslims in the West neither wanted nor were able to integrate themselves, because for them to assume the social, cultural, ethical and religious values of the West would entail them mixing down and eventually obliterating their principles, something their religious leaders would never allow. Rudin also maintained that religious and ethnic conflicts are inevitable, and that the communities of Muslims in the West were therefore comparable to 'ticking time bombs'.[131]

A similar cultural-differentialist view, implying ethnopluralist conceptions of today's immigration society, was developed in another publication of the JES, entitled *Einwanderungsland Schweiz – wohin?* (Immigration Country Switzerland – Where Will It Lead?), in which the main essay was a contribution from Peter Stadler, the historian and key figure of the nationalist current of the Swiss New Right (see below).[132] While it was a small group in terms of membership, it is clear when we consider these publications that the JES succeeded in publishing some of the most important and more elaborated literature of the German-speaking New Right in Switzerland and in spreading its intellectually and discursively oriented strategy on Swiss university and college campuses.

Association Pro Libertate: A Transformed Cold Warriors' Group

The Association Pro Libertate (*Vereinigung Pro Libertate*) was founded in 1956 after the invasion of Hungary and saw its main dedication in fighting communism.[133] Also known as the Swiss Association for Freedom, Democracy and Human Dignity (*Schweizerische Vereinigung für Freiheit, Demokratie und Menschenwürde*), the group had its stronghold in the canton of Bern and counted more than two thousand members in 2000.[134] Four to seven times annually, since 1987, it has published the bulletin *Pro Libertate Mitteilungen* (Pro Libertate News). This is a well-printed, A4 format publication comprising four to twenty pages. The group also edited the publication series *Schriftenreihe Pro Libertate*, some sixteen volumes of which had been published by 2002. A number of external authors have contributed articles to the bulletin and published brochures in the publication series.

During the Cold War era, Pro Libertate was an integrated part of the wider network of anti-communist groups and publications in Switzerland.[135] It was primarily engaged in denouncing the oppressive communist regimes in Eastern Europe and attacking the Swiss left for its alleged subversion of Swiss society. The group's struggle against alleged threats from both outside and inside Switzerland was well received by National Action, whose party organ published reports on Pro Libertate.[136] The group also showed particular interest in military affairs and fiercely defended the view that Switzerland should have a strong and well-equipped army. As a non-partisan group, Pro Libertate counted prominent members of established centre-right parties among its ranks and was supported by conservative intellectuals and authors. In retrospect, Pro Libertate declared that since its creation in 1956 the association had been 'neutral in terms of party politics and religion, and continuously in the service of the Spiritual Defence of the Nation'.[137] After the collapse of communism in 1989, the group went through an ideological transformation and intellectual reorientation. While the group continued to appeal to conservative intellectuals and members of mainstream centre-right parties, it increasingly attracted senior officials of the Swiss People's Party, particularly from the canton of Bern. In 1999, prominent members numbered, among others, the national SVP MPs Simon Schenk, Walter Schmied, Hanspeter Seiler and Samuel Schmid (who went on to become Federal Councillor one year later), as well as EDU National Councillor Christian Waber and FDP National Councillor Luzi Stamm.[138]

In the 1990s, Pro Libertate began to address issues that the new SVP had put on the political agenda, in particular those related to migration and foreign policy. Articles published in *Pro Libertate Mitteilungen* demanded severe restrictions of the current asylum policies and often expressed bluntly xenophobic views. The May 1991 issue gave an account of a public talk delivered by Jürgen Graf and thereby reported Graf's statement on Muslim immigrants who he claimed would never assimilate and who – under the spell of fundamentalist Mullahs – 'will destroy our intellectual values and bases'.[139] Another article from the same year assessed that if 'the flood of immigration' was not taken care of, Switzerland would fall in a deep crisis 'because social and religious peace, as well as the national identity of our state in general, are being put at risk'.[140] Pro Libertate also fiercely opposed the anti-racism law. In the run-up to the 1994 referendum, the bulletin published a long article by Jean-Jacques Hegg, former editor-in-chief of *Volk + Heimat*, in which he denounced the law as a legal tool being used against those people who oppose more immigration, 'overforeignization' and overpopulation.[141]

While the bulletin mainly focused on specific domestic policies, writings released in the publication series *Schriftenreihe Pro Libertate* dealt in a more general way with issues related to military affairs, Second World War history, media and culture. Some of the volumes in the publication series were published in collaboration with other groups such as the Media Curiosities Association (*Vereinigung Medien-Panoptikum*), or a group called Society and Church, Where Now? (*Gesellschaft und Kirche wohin?*), both organisational remnants of the anti-communist network of the 1980s.[142] Most importantly, publications in this series shaped the Swiss New Right's criticism of 'political correctness'. Initially, the term 'political correctness' was meant to denounce the use of discriminatory language in the United States, before it became a highly debated issue at U.S. universities in the 1980s and 1990s. The German New Right began to employ the term 'political correctness' in the 1990s, in order to complain about restrained freedom of speech and to expose alleged taboos in debates over Germany's past and assessments on the new role in world politics that the country should assume after reunification.[143]

In *Schriftenreihe Pro Libertate* a fifty-page brochure on 'political correctness' was released in 1997, which supplied the Swiss debate on the issue with arguments taken from the German New Right.[144] The author, Paul Ehinger, was member of the FDP and editor-in-chief of the regional newspaper *Zofinger Tagblatt*. The brochure reached significant circulation figures of fifteen thousand copies and also found high levels of appreciation among publications from the Swiss New Right and extreme right.[145] In his text, Ehinger referenced writings by authors from the German New Right, as well as articles published by the German periodical *Nation & Europa*, considered by the German Federal Office for the Protection of the Constitution as the most important extreme-right theory organ in Germany.[146] He extensively quoted Jürgen Hatzenbichler, a leading figure of the New Right in Germany and Austria, and endorsed the highly controversial book *Die Faschismuskeule* (The Fascism Cudgel) by Hans-Helmuth Knütter,[147] an emeritus professor of political science from the University of Bonn and an author who published in German periodicals like *Junge Freiheit, Ostpreussenblatt, Aula* and *Deutsche National-Zeitung*.[148]

Ehinger noted that he had first become aware of the phenomenon of political correctness when learning that the word 'Negro' could not be used anymore.[149] He further argued that in Switzerland, like in Germany, 'race', gender and coming to terms with the past are the key themes in which the principle of political correctness is applied, and that the anti-racist law in particular was a paradigmatic example of political correctness in Switzerland and the result of the egalitarian principle. In racially marked language and presupposing the existence of 'races', Ehinger stated that it would be wrong to believe that everyone is equal and that 'this is not even correct for human beings of the white race. The differences between the individual races are even larger, which is not to assert that either one is of greater value or better than the other.'[150] He further claimed that the aim of political correctness is to level all cultural differences by using the concept of multiculturalism, which ultimately has the effect that cultures become alike and that the autochthonous, the country's own culture disappears.

In another brochure published in the Pro Libertate series, Eduard Stäuble sought to make a further contribution to the Swiss debate on political correctness. He asserted that his text would critically review the use of political language and distinct terminology in public debates, and in the media in particular. Stäuble picked out terms such as racism, nationalism, fundamentalism, multiculturalism and populism, to demonstrate how the meanings and implications of words had supposedly been changed for political purposes. He argued, for example, that the term 'multiculturality' hides a questionable cultural relativism which seeks to make us believe that all cultures are equivalent. This would imply that no culture has produced norms and values which might be more highly estimated in relation to other cultures. In an ethnopluralist fashion, Stäuble then drew the conclusion that the mixing and levelling of all cultural differences, as propagated by multiculturalism, must be rejected.[151]

The criticism of political correctness that was promoted by the New Right gained unexpected significance in June 1999, when the daily paper *Neue Zürcher Zeitung* published an essay by the German author Claus Nordbruch on the issue.[152] Nordbruch has published extensively in periodicals of the New Right and extreme right in Germany.[153] In the July/August 1999 issue of a journal released by the negationist Institute for Historical Review, he wrote an article on political correctness.[154] In his article in the *Neue Zürcher Zeitung*, Nordbruch defended Ernst Nolte and 'revisionist historiography', as he called it, as examples of a critical examination of previous research findings. He further quoted Horst Mahler, a former lawyer of the Red Army Fraction (RAF) who had turned into a leading ideologue of the German extreme right, and who, as Nordbruch noted, complained that there were more political prisoners in Germany than there had been in the GDR one year before the fall of the Berlin wall.[155] The article in the *Neue Zürcher Zeitung* also gives full reference to Nordbruch's book *Sind Gedanken noch frei? Zensur in Deutschland* (Are Thoughts Still Free? Censorship in Germany),[156] which the German Federal Office for the Protection of the Constitution called an example of 'right-extremist publications' in which the theme 'is the complaint over the perceived loss of free speech'.[157] As is shown by the example of the debate over the issue of political correctness, the radiation of publications and authors from the New Right was able to go beyond the inner circle of members and sympathisers and expand to fit the pages of a mainstream paper like the *Neue Zürcher Zeitung*.

The VPM and Its Transnational Network

Founded in Zurich in 1986, the Society for Advancing the Psychological Knowledge of Human Nature (*Verein zur Förderung der Psychologischen Menschenkenntnis* – VPM) played a significant role as both parapolitical actor and supplier of concepts related to various sociocultural issues. It also served to give a boost to the neoconservative current of the Swiss New Right in the 1990s. The VPM had sister organisations in Germany and Austria.[158] When the VPM was dissolved in March 2002, the group claimed that it had achieved a significant part of its objectives.[159] Some observers argued that the VPM was most probably struck by financial problems and that its activities had somewhat petered out.[160] According to press reports, however, former VPM members continued to be active in other groups and publications and engaged themselves with issues related to education and drug prevention.[161] Initially, the VPM was founded as a group of psychologists and pedagogues who sought to promote the ideas and practices of the libertarian thinker and psychoanalyst Friedrich Liebling (1893–1982). The group made its first public appearance in debates over drug policy in the city of Zurich in the late 1980s.[162]

The VPM's prime concern regarding drug policy and education stemmed from its belief that contemporary society was undergoing a moral and ethical decline. Driven by the cultural pessimism of a modern world in crisis and disorder, the VPM saw drug policy and education as the sociocultural areas where a loss of values, traditions and authority has shown its disastrous effects most noticeably. Or, as the VPM stated in a 1994 position paper, the group was troubled by the fatalistic laissez-faire attitude of educators and the mentality of young people who conceived of no future, as well as by the decline of performance, the breakdown of relations, social alienation and a loss of orientation in schools and studying.[163] Wrapped in educational theories and therapeutic concepts, the VPM basically advocated a return to the anti-egalitarian thinking of authority and hierarchy. In a neoconservative fashion, the group pleaded for the regeneration of a society in which the emphasis on family values, traditions and moral order, as well as on prohibition and abstinence, would save both the individual and the collectivity from disarray and decadence. For the VPM, the 1968 generation and the New Left were the main culprits responsible for the decline in values and moral order and the increasing disorientation of the youth. Consequently, the members of the VPM were strongly convinced that the New Left had taken control of political and cultural institutions, that it dominated public debates and consistently undermined the educational and social system with anti-authoritarian and progressive concepts.[164]

Under the leadership of Annemarie Buchholz-Kaiser, technical director and driving force of the VPM, and her cousin Ralph Kaiser, longtime VPM president, the group mainly attracted people who were from the middle class and had an academic education, such as physicians, teachers, pedagogues, psychologists and students. By the end of the 1990s, estimates talked in terms of about two thousand supporters, two-thirds of which came from Switzerland.[165] Critics have regularly exposed the rigid way in which the VPM was organised internally and have chosen to describe the VPM as a 'psycho-sect'.[166] According to the Professional Association of German Psychologists (*Berufsverband Deutscher Psychologen*), 'a friend–enemy thinking predominates in the VPM, which grows to the levels of a conspiracy theory as soon as criticism is expressed about structure, psychological expertise or ideology'.[167] On different occasions throughout the 1990s, the group filed law suits against its critics.[168]

In Switzerland, the VPM and its members were involved in a variety of activities. The VPM ran the publishing house, Verlag Menschenkenntnis (Publisher for the Knowledge of Human Nature), issued the monthly journal, *Menschenkenntnis*, and published writings on subjects related to drug policy, education, pedagogy and psychology.[169] The group also organised conferences and meetings on an international level. In 1990, for example, the VPM organised in Zurich the 'Ist International Symposium against Drugs in Switzerland' (*I. Internationales Symposium gegen Drogen in der Schweiz*), attended by well-known experts from the U.S. administration and the UN from the field of drugs policy.[170] In addition, VPM members acted as authors and editors of publications not directly affiliated with the VPM. A prominent example was Alexander Segert, who was appointed in 1993 as both part-time editor of *Der Zürcher Bote*, the party organ of the SVP in the canton of Zurich, and part-time collaborator of *Schweizerzeit*.[171] VPM members also co-founded or were engaged in advisory bodies, interest groups and ad-hoc committees that launched initiatives and petitions and also ran public campaigns. Since the late 1980s, the VPM strategy of placing its members in schools, university departments and state advisory bodies has repeatedly provoked critical reactions from media and authorities.[172]

Observers have pointed out that the VPM has consistently worked on far-reaching coalition building and thereby acted as a powerful parapolitical group.[173] Certainly, the best example of such a policy of alliances is the federal initiative 'Youth without Drugs' (*Jugend ohne Drogen*), which was submitted in June 1993 with over 140,000 thousand signatures. The initiative demanded that Swiss drug policy must be based on prohibition, repression and abstinence and hence any measures of survival aid (e.g., medically controlled heroin prescription, methadone programs, handing out free injections) should be stopped. As Peter Niggli and Jürg Frischknecht have meticulously described, in terms of logistics, resources and ideological supply, the VPM acted as leading force in the launching of the initiative and the subsequent campaigning.[174] The VPM received active support from various small groups, as well as senior party officials affiliated with both centre-right and radical right-wing populist parties.[175] In the vote recommendations, left-wing and centre-right parties recommended a rejection of the initiative, while the SVP, the FPS, the SD and the EDU endorsed the proposal. In September 1997, the federal initiative was defeated by 70.7 per cent of the voters, with a turnout of 40.8 per cent. As indicated by a survey carried out after the voting, the proposal found support among sympathisers of the FPS (75 per cent), the SD (75 per cent) and the SVP (53 per cent), but was not backed by supporters of the CVP (42 per cent), the FDP (25 per cent), or the SPS (3 per cent). Moreover, 73 per cent of those who rejected a more egalitarian conception of society and were against equal opportunity for everyone approved the initiative.[176]

In Germany, a number of intellectuals associated with the New Right were supportive of the VPM, which also ran under the name of *Gesellschaft zur Förderung der psychologischen Menschenkenntnis* (GFPM).[177] In 1993, when the German Federal Minister for Women and Youth thought to include a section on the VPM in a brochure on sects and psycho cults, an advertisement criticising the ministry's decision was published in the *Frankfurter Allgemeine Zeitung* and signed by almost two hundred academics, authors and politicians. Among the signatories were well-known followers of the German New Right and particularly its neoconservative current.[178] In addition, the Weikersheim Study Centre collaborated with the VPM and the centre's leading functionary, Günter Rohrmoser, participated at conferences that the VPM had organised.[179] In Austria, the Institute for Advancing the Psychological Knowledge of Human Nature (*Institut zur Förderung der psychologischen Menschenkenntnis* – IPM), founded as early as 1983, served as a subsidiary organisation of the VPM and even changed its name to VPM in 1994. In the early 1990s, the IPM began to multiply its public interventions on issues of drug policy, releasing flyers, articles and brochures. IPM/VPM members also presented papers at meetings of groups interested in drug policy.[180]

The paper *Zeit-Fragen* (Current Questions), published since October 1993, has been on close terms with the VPM.[181] With the paper, the group established an important publishing vehicle and pursued the goal of intellectual and cultural networking. Many authors in *Zeit-Fragen* signed with their initials and hence were, most likely, members of the paper's editorial staff.[182] A large number of articles were written by members and supporters of the VPM, in particular articles dealing with issues of drug policy, pedagogy, the education system and AIDS prevention. *Zeit-Fragen* regularly published interviews with experts and scholars from abroad, as well as articles written by Swiss guest authors, for example by the well-known Swiss professor of economics, Silvio Borner.[183] *Zeit-Fragen* was released in Zurich, but also addressed readers in Germany and Austria. The paper was initially issued monthly for more than six years, but has been run as a weekly publication since January 2000. According to its own information, *Zeit-Fragen* had a circulation of forty thousand, which is most probably an overestimate.[184] The editors also maintained a website, which included a selection of the articles that were published in the current issue, as well as those taken from back issues.[185] The paper usually included sixteen pages (A3 format) and was made in the style of a professional newspaper. Almost every issue contained feature articles of one or more pages in length. Since December 1998, a monthly English edition has been published under the name of 'Current Concerns', including original articles in English and translated articles taken from *Zeit-Fragen*.[186] Since 2000, a French-language edition of *Zeit-Fragen* has been released six times per year under the name of *Horizons et débats* (Horizons and Debates), which mainly consists of articles translated from the German edition.[187]

Zeit-Fragen extensively covered Swiss domestic policy. In addition to drug policy, AIDS prevention and education reforms, on which the paper basically followed the position of the VPM, a large number of articles raised the issue of Switzerland's international integration. Thereby, European integration and Switzerland's participation in international organisations such as the UN and WTO were met with harsh criticism. After the success of the SVP in the national elections of 1999, *Zeit-Fragen* wrote that the voters had rewarded the credibility of the SVP and its rearing up against the attempted blackmail from abroad.[188] After the bilateral agreements were approved by the voters in 2000, *Zeit-Fragen* published an excerpt from *Die europäische Dimension der Schweiz* (The European Dimension of Switzerland), a book that was highly critical of the EU and written by Wolfgang von Wartburg, a former professor of history at the University of Basel.[189] In the introductory remarks to von Wartburg's article, it was warned that in the case of further Swiss integration in the European Union, the diversified culture of four languages would become entirely impoverished, the economy would produce social chaos rather than prosperity, and the system of direct democracy would be completely destroyed.[190]

The significance of the paper lies in its association with intellectuals from the German New Right and in the interest that the paper showed for debates and issues launched by the New Right in Germany. Among the regular German authors were the two specialists on the Cold War and Eastern Europe, Helmut Bärwald and Friedrich Wilhelm Schlomann, along with two important figures of the German New Right, Klaus Hornung and Gerhard Löwenthal, the latter of which was a particularly devoted supporter of *Zeit-Fragen*.[191] In addition, the paper was closely connected to intellectuals associated with the Study Centre of Weikersheim and frequently reported on conferences held at the centre.[192] In an article from 1995, Klaus Hornung complained that the 1968 generation had created a climate of the witch hunt, in which conservative critics were continuously denounced as extreme rightists and fascists. In a time of such left-wing cultural hegemony, Hornung claimed that it was good to see that there were still writers like Botho Strauss, author of the essay *Anschwellender Bockgesang* (Swelling Songs of the Buck), who could demonstrate the courage of their convictions.[193] Strauss' essay had first been published by the German magazine *Der Spiegel* in February 1993 and provoked extensive criticism for reviving the ideology of the interwar Conservative Revolution. An extended version was reprinted as the key essay in the edited volume *Die selbstbewusste Nation*,[194] which was considered the main manifesto of the German New Right 'for domestic policy and cultural criticism'.[195]

When Rainer Zitelmann, a key representative of the German New Right's young generation of historians, was dismissed as an editor of the German daily paper *Die Welt*, an article in *Zeit-Fragen* denounced the decision as another result of widespread political correctness in Germany. The article quoted the historian Ernst Nolte, who had maintained that radical right-wing intellectuals have as much of a legitimate and necessary place in a pluralistic democracy as radical left-wing intellectuals, so long as they do not cross the clear line into extremism, which means that they should not demand or tolerate the use of violence.[196] Finally, it is worth noting that *Zeit-Fragen* published in 1997 a three-part series of articles authored by Roger Scruton, who was considered a leading intellectual of the British New Right and had served as an editor of *The Salisbury Review* from 1982 to 2000.[197] Scruton's series of articles in *Zeit-Fragen* focused on the alleged failure of left-wing intellectualism. He attempted to draw a picture of hope for the future of the right because left-wing intellectuals had purportedly lost most of their supporters and found themselves isolated and alone on the campus.[198]

Another important activity initiated by the VPM is the annual three-day conference 'Courage to Take a Moral Stance' (*Mut zur Ethik*). This has taken place since 1993 and is a remarkable example of the international networking strategy developed by the Swiss New Right.[199] The event was intended to carry on from the 1978 conference 'Courage for Education' (*Mut zur Erziehung*) which had appealed at the time to those neoconservative academics who sought to counter the alleged education revolution that was supposedly inspired by the emancipatory and egalitarian ideas of the 1968 movement.[200] Officially, the conferences have been organised by the European Working Group, 'Courage to Take a Moral Stance' (*Europäische Arbeitsgemeinschaft 'Mut zur Ethik'* – EAME) which consists of thirty organisations from nine European countries and the United States.[201] Until its dissolution in 2002, however, the VPM was the leading group in the organisation. It ran the conference office in Zurich and was in charge of coordinating the activity of the EAME.[202] After the dissolution of the VPM in 2002, the conference office stayed in Zurich, where most likely it was still run by former VPM members. According to the organisers' own information, the conferences were usually attended by up to one thousand participants.[203] Prior to 1998, papers and notes presented at the conferences were published in edited volumes. The VPM was responsible for the editorship and released the books in its publishing house Menschenkenntnis.

The lists of speakers and participants included academics, authors and politicians from all around Europe and the United States. Among them were well-known authors and intellectuals associated with the German New Right. For instance, the honorary chairmen of the first conference in 1993 were Günter Rohrmoser and Gerhard Löwenthal.[204] Löwenthal has been a regular speaker at the conferences since the beginning. Another regular was Lothar Bossle, professor of sociology at the University of Würzburg and functionary at the Weikersheim Study Centre. The 1994 conference, which was also advertised by the German magazine *Criticón*, counted Klaus Hornung and Hans-Helmuth Knütter among its speakers.[205] To the 1996 conference on the theme of society and democracy were invited Konrad Löw, professor of political science at the University of Bayreuth, *Criticón* contributor and interview partner in *Junge Freiheit*, as well as the two political scientists Klaus Hornung and Walter Pfeifenberger. From Switzerland, VPM members regularly took part in the conferences and contributed articles to conference volumes. In addition, the list of invited Swiss participants and speakers included members of small groups and collaborators from assorted publications, most of whom were associated with the New Right, as well as senior officials from both centre-right and radical right-wing populist parties.[206] As many of the participants presented scholarly developed concepts and arguments at the conferences, they tried to serve as the supply line for the academic and intellectual struggles of the New Right on various sociocultural issues and to reinforce the authority of traditional institutions such as family, religion and state.

The Ecologists: A Right-wing Version of Environmentalism

Since the 1960s and 1970s, most Western European countries have experienced right-wing versions of environmentalism, thereby challenging the dominance of the left in this area. In their conception of environmentalism, these ecologists on the right identify ecological-biological determinants, in which attachment to geographical places and embedment in distinct cultures play a crucial role as key references of human identity.[207] Following this line of reasoning, right-wing ecologists seek to protect and preserve nature, environment and natural resources because they are organic parts not only of the ecological system, but also of the national community. Protection of the natural environment means protection of the homeland, limited to a defined geographical and cultural space and a particular national community.[208] By naturalising the sense of belonging to nature into a notion of deeply rooted identity, right-wing environmentalism combines ecological survival with questions of cultural and national identity. Such biologically determined links between territory and ethnic group are often substantiated with the ethology research of Irenäus Eibl-Eibesfeldt and Konrad Lorenz.[209]

Drawing on the experience of the ecological catastrophes of the 1970s and 1980s, environmentalists associated with the New Right began to raise the issues of overpopulation and population growth. They sought to exploit concern with those ecological problems that are related to population density for their own anti-immigrant agenda and to counter the progressive tendencies of ecological politics with the exclusionist demands of their radical-right program.[210] In their environmental policies, ecologists of the New Right point to the alleged danger that immigration poses for the ecological equilibrium and natural 'living spaces', and they emphasise that any interference from the outside would disturb the natural environment and ecology of the national community. Moreover, by taking an ethnopluralist view, they often plead for the segregated development of certain defined ecological entities which are marked by natural as well as national and cultural characteristics. In their vision of the world, all cultures should not only have sovereignty over themselves, but also over their environment.[211]

Germany provides a good example of the significance and persistence of New Right ecologists in the debates on environmental issues since the 1970s. Most prominent here is, Herbert Gruhl (1921–1993), who was a CDU member until 1978, a German MP from 1969 to 1980, and author of the best-selling book, *Ein Planet wird geplündert* (A Planet Is Plundered).[212] Gruhl played a central role in the efforts that came from the right and sought to undermine the German Greens as they came into existence in the late 1970s and early 1980s. After his failed attempt to gain influence in the German Green Party, Gruhl co-founded the Ecological Democratic Party (*Ökologisch-Demokratische Partei* – ÖDP) in 1982 and greatly influenced the party's pronounced anti-immigration and nationalist program until his resignation in 1990.[213] In his conception of ecology, Gruhl combined authoritarian and Social Darwinist thought with biologist and national-ecological ideas.[214] One ecological group that had direct links with the German extreme right was the World Federation for the Protection of Life (*Weltbund zum Schutze des Lebens* – WSL), founded by the Austrian neo-fascist Günther Schwab in 1958. Under the leadership of Werner Georg Haverbeck, a former NSDAP functionary, founder of the educational centre *Collegium Humanum* in 1963, and WSL president from 1974 to 1982, the WSL advanced to become an influential organisation within the ecologist current of the New Right in Germany.[215]

Ideas of right-wing environmentalism have been disseminated in Switzerland since the 1960s and concepts developed by ecologists from the German New Right have played an important role in this process. The ecologist current of the New Right has not only been present in Swiss political parties, but has also emerged in the form of non-partisan organisations and scientific working groups of intellectuals. Thus, it serves as a telling example of how to combine an engagement in party politics with ideological and scientific work. From early on, its environmental concern was marked by anti-immigrant sentiments and its ecological policy was closely associated with an anti-immigration agenda. Typically, high immigration rates were made responsible for different aspects of environmental pollution and destruction and particular emphasis was placed on the connection between ecology and overpopulation. By pointing to alleged cultural and social problems of immigration, ecologists from the Swiss New Right also sought to link environmental issues to questions of cultural and national identity and to equate a balanced ecological system with a state of mental and cultural equilibrium of the national community. Such national-ecological views operated more often than not with biologically determined conceptions of both ecology and cultural identity and were regularly fuelled by the ethnopluralist belief that every nation requires its own natural environment which is to be preserved from outside interference.

The Movement against Overforeignization: Forerunner and Protagonist

The Movement against Overforeignization played an important role as both forerunner and protagonist of right-wing environmentalism in

Switzerland. As early as the 1960s, the founding members of the movement expressed concerns about the preservation of nature and protection of the environment and they linked environmental problems with issues of immigration and 'overforeignization'.[216] In one of the first programmatic writings of National Action it was stated that 'overforeignization' caused huge levels of construction and made entire landscapes disappear.[217] The early anti-immigrant campaigns were backed by leading figures of the Swiss movement for nature conservation.[218] There were different reasons for this support. By tradition in Switzerland, the preoccupation with environmentalist matters and the quest to safeguard the natural environment have been fuelled by nationalist ideas. The Swiss nature conservation movement took the view that nature and the natural environment must be seen as magnificent parts of the national heritage and as aesthetical manifestations of the country's distinctiveness. With a status comparable to that of the country's history and culture, nature was presented as an important constituent of Swiss national identity. Moreover, in the postwar period, rapid economic growth and accelerated technical progress were criticised as being causes of the construction boom and overpopulation, and as a burden on the country's limited natural resources. Thus, since the 1960s, the efforts of the nature conservation movement to reduce environmental pollution and to rescue nature from destruction have also included demands for limiting and reducing the number of foreigners living in Switzerland.[219]

Significantly, a key figure of the nature conservation movement revealed markedly xenophobic views as early as the start of the 1960s. Jakob Bächtold was twice a National Councillor (1959–75, 1978–79) of the Alliance of Independents (*Landesring der Unabhängigen* – LDU) and from 1960 to 1969, he was also president of the Swiss Federation for Nature Conservation (*Schweizerischer Bund für Naturschutz* – SBN), the country's largest organisation committed to the protection and conservation of nature. In an article from 1962, he criticised the alleged 'overforeignization' of Switzerland, arguing that 'apart from the noticeable increase in sexual and other types of offences, overforeignization has further consequences that are usually too little considered. We think only of the increasing demand for housing, of land speculation, of increased water and energy consumption, and of larger demands for the service sector.'[220] When he resigned as SBN president in 1969, he declared in his farewell address that the Swiss who cherished the traditional clod, the cultural values, the beauty and the laws of nature just as highly as he cherished material prosperity – and who recognised the right to life of all creation – was increasingly becoming a minority in a land of the stranger, the one without tradition.[221] Bächtold also played a leading role in the creation of the Swiss League for Biological National Defence (*Schweizerische Liga für biologische Landesverteidigung* – SLfbL) in 1964, an early representation of right-wing environmentalism in Switzerland.[222] In the late 1960s, the SLfbL collaborated with the World Federation for the Protection of Life (WSL) and its senior members were in contact with WSL founder Günther Schwab.[223] In the early 1970s, Schwarzenbach's paper *Der Republikaner* also published articles by Bächtold, in which he linked immigration with environmental issues and warned of growing 'overforeignization'.[224]

In the 1970s, National Action put environmental issues high up on its political agenda and was the first Swiss party that consistently brought ecology into the political arena.[225] In the anti-immigrant campaigns, the party linked issues of overpopulation and pollution with demands relating to immigration policy. NA argued, for example, that Switzerland's ecological balance was put at risk by the large number of immigrants and the reckless immigration policy promoted by the government and various economic interest groups.[226] The Republican Movement too, made the connection between environmental issues and immigration and declared in its manifesto from 1971 that 'our small state with its limited space cannot become a country of immigration' and that the party would fight against 'any kind of foreign seizure, especially against land speculation, and the pollution of air, water and land which all are in part the results of overforeignization'.[227]

Valentin Oehen, NA party president from 1972 to 1980, was the chief architect of the ecological program promoted by NA in the 1970s.[228] Drafted by Valentin Oehen and the scientist Pierre-André Tschumi, the party's declaration of principle from 1971 stated that the party would fight for a change of general politics in the way that our people, in its limited 'living space', prepared itself to confront the expected crisis in biological nature. The document further emphasised that population policy should take central stage in the ecological agenda, since the uncontrolled explosion of the world population was continuing unchecked, even as human civilisation daily put more pressure on the biosphere. The document further concluded that the situation of the Swiss people was becoming increasingly more dangerous as the result of today's economic and population policy.[229] Together with the German ecologist Herbert Gruhl, Oehen co-founded the European Working Group for Ecological Politics (*Europäischer Arbeitskreis für ökologische Politik* – EAföP), in 1977. The group aimed at exerting influence on the environmental policies of governments and could count on the collaboration of prominent academics and MPs from Switzerland, Germany and Austria. After Oehen resigned for personal reasons in 1979, the EAföP dissolved without the state authorities ever showing real interest in the proposals submitted by the group.[230] Herbert Gruhl, for his part, remained in close touch with NA and made contributions in the early 1980s at a public event in Bern and in the party paper.[231]

When the resistance to nuclear power-plants was considerably heightened in the 1970s and Switzerland experienced the forceful emergence of the left-wing ecological movement, National Action and especially Valentin Oehen made attempts to proliferate their national-ecological ideas among the followers of the insurgent movement.[232] NA party members also joined with protesters in 1975 when they occupied the construction area of the planned nuclear plant of Kaiseraugst.[233] After Oehen deserted from National Action in 1986, he founded the Ecological Libertarian Party of Switzerland (ÖFP). The party championed Oehen's biologist and national-ecological ideas and stated in its principles that to be ecological means to fit our way of thinking and our activities within the laws of nature.[234] In the end, however, the ÖFP did not have any political success or significant influence on right-wing environmentalism in Switzerland.

Of more influence was the *Heidelberger Manifest*, signed by a group of German professors and ecologists, among them Werner Georg Haverbeck, and published by the NA party paper *Volk + Heimat* in November 1982.[235] In fact, the Swiss paper published the first, more radical version of the manifesto which was revised after strong criticism and then reissued.[236] The manifesto is considered to be the most important writing of the German New Right on the theme of ecology.[237] Drawing on the idea of ethnopluralism, the text condemned the growing 'overforeignization' of Germany and argued that the return of foreigners to their home country would constitute a source of social and ecological relief for Germany. The manifesto was also an articulated example of what some have coined 'ecological racism',[238] since it described peoples as '(biological and cybernetic) living systems of a higher order, with differing system characteristics that are passed on genetically and by way of traditions'.[239]

In the 1980s, the NA party paper published a number of articles on overpopulation and population policy that drew upon classical racism.[240] In addition, under the intellectual guidance of Jean-Jacques Hegg, NA, and in particular its party paper, revitalised the biologically grounded approaches to ecology and consistently referenced the German New Right's literature of sociobiology and human ethology. Hegg regularly addressed the issue of overpopulation, arguing that human beings need sufficient space in which to live and that under conditions of overpopulation, people are stricken by numerous physical and mental sicknesses.[241] In the 1990s, Hegg continued to endorse the ethology work of Konrad Lorenz and Irenäus Eibl-Eibesfeldt and argued that high population density would inevitably cause aggression and damage to health.[242] In 1994, Hegg took over the editorship of the column entitled 'Life and Environment' (*Leben und Umwelt*) in the party paper of the Swiss Democrats, initially established in the 1970s under the name of 'Green Page' (*Grüne Seite*). On this occasion, he stated that the preservation and protection of the natural life basis of our state territory, of our 'living space', had become a vital issue which amounted to more than simply the protection of the natural environment.[243] As these examples show, the Swiss Democrats retained the tradition of the Movement against Overforeignization in disseminating the ideas of right-wing environmentalism and combining the quest for ecological sustainability with immigration issues.

ECOPOP: An Anti-Immigration Group in Ecology and Population Growth Debates

Officially, the Swiss Working Group for Population Questions (*Schweizerische Arbeitsgemeinschaft für Bevölkerungsfragen* – SAfB) was founded in 1971, having existed in the form of a loosely organised group since 1967. The name was changed to the Ecology and Population Association (*Vereinigung Umwelt und Bevölkerung/Association Ecologie et Population* – ECOPOP) in 1987.[244] The conceptions of ecology and population growth promoted by ECOPOP came close to the anti-immigrant and nationalist thinking that was advocated by the German ecologist Herbert Gruhl. Accordingly, the group acknowledged the decisive influence that Gruhl had exerted on the ecological movement generally, and declared that it would foster an exchange of ideas with the Herbert Gruhl Society (*Herbert-Gruhl-Gesellschaft*), a German group founded in 2001 and committed to preserving the legacy of Gruhl.[245] In Switzerland, ECOPOP assured the continuity of right-wing environmentalism and managed to establish itself as an ecologist group with significant intellectual and organisational resources.

The creation of the SAfB in 1971 was initiated by Jakob Bächtold and Gottlieb Flückiger, a director of the Federal Veterinary Office until 1957 who has also lectured at the Faculty of Medicine and Veterinary Medicine at the University of Bern.[246] The driving force and first president of the SAfB was the biologist Pierre-André Tschumi, who was appointed Professor of Zoology at the University of Bern in 1971. In the same year, the NA paper *Volk + Heimat* published a one-page summary of a speech

Tschumi had held in Bern on overpopulation and environmental problems.[247] Just one year later, he resigned as SAfB president, but has remained on the support committee of ECOPOP until this day.[248] Tschumi also worked with Valentin Oehen on the drafting of the party literature of NA.[249] Oehen for his part had joined the study circle in 1967 and helped to draft the first statutes of the SAfB. He became vice-president and remained on the executive committee until 1979. Oehen took advantage of the fact that the SAfB had renowned natural scientists among its ranks, by asking them to review the programmatic writings of NA and to give presentations at meetings organised by NA.[250]

In the 1980s and 1990s, the group continued to attract academics, mainly from natural science and economics. For example, Hans Christoph Binswanger, renowned professor of economics at the University of St. Gallen from 1969 to 1994 and author of several acclaimed books on ecology, economy and monetary theory, is still to this day a member of the ECOPOP support committee. He actually took part in the founding meeting of the EAföP in March 1977.[251] On the other hand, ECOPOP has also appealed to ideologues from the extreme right, as the example of Ernst Indlekofer shows. He was a notorious Swiss negationist (see chapter 8) who was expelled from ECOPOP in the mid 1990s because of his extreme-right activities.[252]

ECOPOP engaged in a wide range of activities, for the most part on issues related to environment, population growth and immigration.[253] From time to time, its activities were covered by the mainstream press.[254] The group placed ads in the printed press, released statements on policy reports drafted by the government and issued recommendations on federal votes. In 1972, the SAfB submitted a petition with ten thousand signatures to the Federal Council which demanded an environment-friendly population policy. The group regularly organised conferences and discussion rounds and set up exhibitions which toured the country. For schools and other educational purposes, it provided information and didactic material and produced movies and slide shows. ECOPOP has also published a number of elaborate information brochures. Since 1990, the group has issued the *ECOPOP-Bulletin* three times per year, a simply made bulletin comprising four A4 format pages. While there is no information on the number of members, a print run of one thousand copies for the second edition of a brochure which was released on the twenty-fifth anniversary of ECOPOP, gives an idea of the partisan support the group may receive.[255]

As noted in the ECOPOP statutes, the goal of the group was to make the general public aware of the causal connection between population density and the alleged threat that it posed to the environment.[256]

Hence, ECOPOP sought to present means and ways with which to combat the developments that destroy the natural environment, and in the long run, to reduce the population in Switzerland to a level that was environmentally and socially sustainable. It claimed that Switzerland had lost the so-called bioeconomic balance and that its ecological sustainability had been greatly exceeded. This means that more natural resources were being used than could be reproduced, and that more waste was being produced than nature was able to absorb. In the long run, according to ECOPOP, this disproportion could only be solved by a significant decrease in the population. In the view of ECOPOP, the reduction of population would have to be achieved by lowering the birth rate and by putting a halt to the excess of births over deaths.[257]

ECOPOP argued, however, that it was even more important to focus on the issue of immigration as the most significant contributing factor behind the population growth in postwar Switzerland.[258] The group therefore invested much of its efforts in developing arguments and leading campaigns which promoted the view that immigration was the main source of ecologically critical population growth. On many occasions, ECOPOP conspicuously emphasised that its concern regarding the limiting of immigration was different from the anti-immigrant demands of the Movement against Overforeignization, or extreme-right groups.[259] ECOPOP took the view that the number of immigrants living in a densely populated country like Switzerland would first need to be stabilised and then, in the long run, reduced. As stated in the group's most comprehensive publication on migration policy, *Thesen zur schweizerischen Migrationspolitik* (Theses on Swiss Migration Policy), 'from an ecological perspective Switzerland can no longer be a country of immigration.'[260] Moreover, an article published in the *ECOPOP-Bulletin* argued that migration causes undesirable additional mobility and hence contributes to environmental pollution and the waste of natural resources. It argued, therefore, that official migration policy and the idealisation of a multicultural society would need to be questioned and that it was wrong to assume that settling down in other countries should represent a human right.[261]

But ECOPOP did not confine itself to ecological and demographic arguments, but also gave social and cultural arguments in favour of a reduction in immigration. For example, as the group noted in its brochure on migration policy, each society has only a limited ability to assimilate immigrants and exceeding this limit was bound to create social tension between natives and immigrants.[262] According to ECOPOP, the persistence of initiatives demanding a limitation of immigration would demonstrate the degree to which the population was uneasy with this issue. This unsettled situation would also stem from the fact that media, parties and environmental groups preferred to treat the issue of immigration as taboo instead of proposing firm measures.[263] In addition, the ECOPOP bulletin proposed the argument that the number of asylum seekers undoubtedly played a decisive role in the growth of hostile attitudes towards foreigners and in feelings of insecurity among the population.[264] Such views corresponded to the assumptions made by researchers into ethology and sociobiology. Therefore, it is of little surprise that ECOPOP included the writings of Konrad Lorenz and Irenäus Eibl-Eibesfeldt in a list of reference books.[265]

ECOPOP showed a highly critical attitude towards multicultural societies that would permit the integration of immigrants. A front-page article in the *ECOPOP-Bulletin* presented the concept of multicultural society as a 'model for disorder', and suggested that the United States served as a good example of a society where multicultural living together meant cultural struggle on a broad front. The article claimed that it was crucial that everyone who leaves his or her territory must assimilate in the new place, and that assimilation is easier where there are less pronounced ethnical differences, in terms of way of life, conception of legality, religion, etc.[266] Overall, the significance of ECOPOP lies in the fact that the group's publication of information brochures and teaching material had a remarkable effect through dissemination. In this way, a wider public became acquainted with scientifically substantiated ecological arguments for opposing population growth which ECOPOP claimed to be a driving force for the destruction of the natural environment. In this line of argumentation, immigration was presented as a key reason for overpopulation and an issue that was particularly critical in Switzerland, one of the most densely settled countries on earth.

The Neo-nationalists: For the Defence of Swiss Exceptionalism

Nationalism and the spreading of nationalist ideas are characteristic of most actors associated with the New Right. For the neo-nationalist current of the New Right, however, nationalism represents the main motivating force and a nationalist agenda is at the forefront of most activities. In addition, this current must be seen as the main advocate of a so-called neo-nationalism which reflects 'the re-emergence of nationalism under different global and transnational conditions'.[267] With the end of the Cold War, various forms of political and sociocultural transformations have created new contexts to which neo-nationalists have responded. Most noticeable are their critical stances towards immigration and processes of transnational integration, but also the positions they assume with regard to the increasingly globalised notion of historical memory that became most evident in public debates over the role that different countries had played during the era of National Socialism. Overall, neo-nationalists are convinced that the nation-state is increasingly jeopardised through globalisation and supranational organisations and that immigration predictably destroys the national and cultural identity of a nation.[268]

While these recent changes set a new framework for claims and discourses, neo-nationalists continue to refer to earlier variants of nationalism and thereby ensure that the traditions of nationalist patterns of thought have stayed alive.[269] They see the preservation and strengthening of national identity as the most important objective of political and intellectual ambition, in order to maintain national unity and cohesion. From their perspective, divergent 'individual interests' in a national community must be subordinate to the 'common interest' of the nation. Driven by a strong sense of community, neo-nationalists continue to plead for the homogenisation of one's own group and are fond of drawing up boundaries in order to preserve the national character against the outside world. With emphasis on the particularity and exclusivity of each national group, neo-nationalists seek to defend the idea of a distinct national culture, history and mentality. In this way, a common origin and a shared historical and cultural heritage serve to construct the national myths, symbols and value systems which provide the 'identity card' of the 'imagined community'. Moreover, presenting political culture as a unique, deep-rooted feature of national history and culture implies a primordial and essentialist meaning in the process by which national identity is formed. By idealising and mythologizing political institutions and considering them as key constituents of national identity, neo-nationalists elevate the preservation and defence of institutional and political specificities to a question of national survival.

Since the end of the Cold War, neo-nationalists have been the most vigorous forces within the New Right in Switzerland, in terms of reacting to the changing contexts of the Swiss nation-state. As the country's long-standing role as a reticent actor in international affairs increasingly came under scrutiny and as the speeding up of the process of European integration called for a rethinking of the country's external relations, neo-nationalists fiercely sought to uphold Swiss exceptionalism and to reinforce the notion of Switzerland as a special case in terms of history, culture and political institutions. They fought against the supposedly homogenising forces in the processes of globalisation, international integration and migration, which they presented as perilous threats to the country's distinct national and cultural identity. From a perspective of organisation building, the controversies over European integration and the history of the Second World War were particularly important moments in the 1990s, since both initiated the emergence of the neo-nationalist current within the New Right and prompted the creation of new organisations. In addition, the neo-nationalist current closely collaborated with neoconservative groups and publications, as well as with radical right-wing populist parties. This partnership materialised in active collaboration and association, in joint parapolitical and publishing activities, and in dual membership. Unlike the other two currents of the New Right in the German-speaking part of Switzerland, neo-nationalists had no connection to the New Right in Germany and barely referenced the literature of their European counterparts.

The CINS: A Powerful Parapolitical Organisation

Created in 1986, the Campaign for an Independent and Neutral Switzerland (CINS) acted as a parapolitical group and represented by far the most important organisation of the neo-nationalist current of the New Right.[270] Among the groups of the Swiss New Right, the CINS had particular status since it was a mass organisation which was consistently involved in everyday politics, yet a group which also sought to gain thematic leadership by engaging in publishing activities. The CINS emerged out of the campaign against Switzerland's membership in the United Nations in the mid 1980s. Its precursor, the Swiss Campaign Committee Against UN Membership (*Schweizerisches Aktionskomitee gegen den UNO-Beitritt* – SAKU), founded in 1982, opposed the government's proposal to join the UN and was led by Christoph Blocher and Otto Fischer, FDP National Councillor from 1970 to 1993 and former director of the Swiss Association of Traders from 1963 to 1979. The opponents of UN membership prevailed in the referendum of March 1986. Shortly after the vote, the CINS was founded and took over most of the organisational resources from the SAKU; more than half of the senior members joined the executive committee of the CINS.[271]

Initially, the CINS attracted a rather small number of some two thousand members, but the group experienced a remarkable growth in membership in the 1990s and eventually developed into a true mass organisation.[272] As a matter of fact, the membership increased from sixteen thousand in 1992 to over forty-three thousand members in 2003.[273] Since the mid 1990s, the CINS has also made great efforts to expand into the French-speaking part of Switzerland and in 1999 it launched the French-language bulletin *La Lettre verte* (The Green Letter), with a circulation of eight thousand.[274] The editor was Eric Bertinat, a key figure of the New Right in the French-speaking part of Switzerland, who joined the CINS in 1992 and was member of its executive committee from 2000 to 2003. The general meetings of the CINS, usually held once a year, were attended by more than a thousand members and were set up as large popular events that were covered extensively by the media. Often, academics, politicians and other public figures were invited to present a speech to the assembly.

The group also had large financial resources, mainly allocated by membership subscriptions.[275] While the group spent just 920,000 Swiss francs in 1997, its expenses went up to over 4.6 million Swiss francs in 2001.[276] These were significant figures in the context of Swiss politics, where financial resources for public campaigning are rather low. In addition, the CINS managed to put into operation a very well-structured organisation and effectively professionalised their political campaigning and public relations. It created a full-time secretary position in 1998, organised training courses for speakers and offered them sample speeches to use in their campaigning. The group also maintained its own website which was edited in the four languages of German, French, Italian and English.[277] The CINS released the member bulletin *Grauer Brief* (Gray Letter), which was issued every two months. The bulletin counted a circulation of over forty thousand in 2002. In addition, the group has published a number of brochures, featuring speeches delivered at the general meetings and often authored by Christoph Blocher.[278] The CINS also set up its own mail-order service and offered a large range of propaganda material, including brochures, leaflets, T-shirts, pins, stickers, etc. By carrying out large distribution and ad campaigns, the aim was to go beyond the circle of members and reach a broad audience. In 1997, for example, the CINS distributed Blocher's brochure *Die Schweiz und Europa. 5 Jahre nach dem EWR-Nein* (Switzerland and Europe. 5 Years after the No to the EEA) to all Swiss households.[279] While distribution costs came to 840,000 Swiss francs, Christoph Blocher himself contributed 600,000 Swiss francs.[280]

Christoph Blocher was CINS president from 1986 to 2003 and acted as unchallenged leader. With the CINS, he managed to establish a major power base outside the party system. Following his election to the government in December 2003, he resigned as CINS president. The CINS executive committee displayed a party political diversity in the 1980s and was mainly comprised of senior officials from the SVP, the CVP and the FDP.[281] Mario Soldini, member of the National Union in the 1930s and Vigilance National Councillor from 1975 to 1987, was also a member of the executive committee from 1986 to 1993. In the first half of the 1990s, significant changes took place at leadership level. As the CINS started to take an intransigent position on the issue of European integration, most members of the FDP and CVP resigned from the executive committee. Following this shift, by the mid 1990s, the leadership largely reflected the group's partisanship for radical right-wing populist parties.[282] In addition, some executive committee members made contributions to periodicals associated with the New Right and the extreme right. For example, Heinrich Schalcher, EVP National Councillor from 1968 to 1984 and driving force in the above-mentioned Swiss League for Biological National Defence, contributed articles to Emil Rahm's paper *Prüfen + Handeln*, the successor publication of the conspiracist paper *Memopress* (see chapter 8).[283] Since the CINS has never released official lists of its members, it is difficult to make assessments on the links of individual members to other groups of the radical right.[284] However, in May 1995 the press exposed the fact that Gaston-Armand Amaudruz, a notorious Swiss neo-fascist (see chapter 8), had been present at the general meeting of the CINS. Soon after, the executive committee expelled Amaudruz from the CINS.[285]

The CINS leadership was keen to present the organisation as a popular movement that integrated all the social classes and voiced the grievances of the common people. Adopting a marked anti-establishment rhetoric, leading CINS members complained that the power holders in Switzerland would not respect the will of the people and only pursued their own interests. Intellectuals, academics and the media were also to be counted among those who had lost touch with the common people.[286] This corresponds to the established strategy of radical right-wing populist parties which consistently evoke resentments against government, established parties and social elites. The main goal of the CINS, as stated in the statutes from 1986, was the 'fight for a federal foreign policy which respects integral and traditional neutrality and therefore guarantees the independence and security of the country'.[287] Following this purpose, the CINS opposed any changes in foreign policies initiated by the Swiss government. In 1992, the CINS participated in the opposition against EEA membership with large ad campaigns in newspapers and with numerous public appearances of leading members, in particular Christoph Blocher. As some argue, the involvement of the CINS and its president made a substantial contribution to the fact that the opposing forces were omnipresent in the public space and succeeded in shaping the public debate on the issue.[288] Another example was the key role played by the CINS in the 1994 referendum campaign that was launched by the Swiss Democrats and the League of Ticino against the Federal Statute on the use of Swiss troops for peacekeeping operations.

In these campaigns, the CINS mainly drew on arguments which had already been developed in the struggle against UN membership in 1986. At that time, opponents argued that the country's distinctiveness and sovereignty was at stake and that Swiss neutrality would be seriously endangered if the country became a UN member.[289] Despite the significant changes in international relations that occurred since 1989, the CINS continued to defend the conception of integral neutrality and consequently opposed any international involvement on the part of Switzerland. When, in the early 1990s, the CINS shifted the focus from the United Nations to the European Union, 'satellitization' (*Satellisierung*) became a catch-all term intending to suggest that Switzerland would lose its independence to foreign powers and become a satellite of the European Union.[290] To underscore such argument, the CINS was fond of pointing to the foundation myth of the Old Confederation and presenting it as excellent proof of the country's will to fight for its independence.[291] Swiss neutrality was another key point of reference. By presenting neutrality as the main foundation of the Swiss national community and the most precious national heritage, the CINS attributed a mythical meaning to the conception of neutrality. As the historian Peter Stadler argued in his address to the CINS general meeting in 1996, neutrality provides, both externally and internally, the steadfastness of historical location and therefore the compass which has worked as a point of orientation throughout the centuries of modern times.[292] In addition, senior CINS members maintained on numerous occasions that neutrality has determined the distinctiveness and uniqueness of Switzerland and that it hence serves as a key constituent in the conception of the Swiss special case.[293]

For the CINS, immigration represented a further serious threat being posed to Switzerland's national identity and cohesion. Consequently, the group showed great concern over migration policy, in particular those issues related to asylum and refugee policy. In the early 1990s, a large number of statements published in the member bulletin *Grauer Brief* revealed a fierce hostility towards asylum seekers. For example, an article from 1990 put the following question:

> Is it not understandable that someone who is Swiss, who has been looking for an apartment for months without finding anything, might wish that asylum seekers would go to hell when he sees that these ladies and gentlemen are taken care of and that apartments and houses are provided to Tamils, Turks and Yugoslavs, but not to the Swiss?[294]

The CINS also supported the two asylum initiatives that the Swiss People's Party launched in the 1990s. According to the CINS, the main problem was that Switzerland faced the immigration of people from foreign 'cultural spheres'. As early as 1987, the CINS warned that immigration of people coming in from other continents would produce ghettos of residents of different colour and result in situations similar to that seen in former colonial states.[295] It was further argued that one should take the fear of Swiss people as a 'natural reaction' against 'the foreigner of a different kind [*fremdartigen*]'.[296] The CINS was also very critical of the new anti-racism law, arguing that expanding criminal prosecution to include statements made verbally would result in an exceptional position for 'residents of another race', one which could not be justified, and which would in fact promote racial discrimination.[297]

The CINS regularly referred to the notion of 'overforeignization', implying a menacing danger from those who are of foreign origin and culture. In 1990, vice-president Otto Fischer urged the Federal Council to agree with the assessment that 'in our place, we cannot tolerate any overforeignization by Muslims or people of other cultural spheres and races'.[298] It was then argued that with respect to the flow of asylum seekers, 'nobody could really deny the fact that the term overforeignization is appropriate, not least in the ethnic way'.[299] The term 'overforeignization' was also a buzzword in the 1992 ad campaigns directed against EEA membership.[300] This shows that CINS sought to play the role of an ideologically and discursively active purveyor of exclusionist and nationalist ideas exhibited in the areas of both immigration and foreign policy. Due to a large membership, substantial resources and well-organised campaigning, the group was able to become a powerful parapolitical challenger in the Swiss system of direct democracy.

The Historian Peter Stadler: An Emeritus Professor as Intellectual Vanguard

Peter Stadler, born in 1925, was professor of history at the University of Zurich from 1970 to 1993 and the author of several reference books on the nineteenth century.[301] In the 1990s, he began to supply the neo-nationalist current of the German-speaking Swiss New Right with essays, newspaper articles and speeches, in which he basically argued that immigration and new multiculturalism now represented the most serious threats to Switzerland's national identity. The New Right, for its part, was fond of stressing Stadler's reputation as a scholar and former university professor and claimed the academic respectability of his reflections. Some of his writings were published in acknowledged periodicals and the mainstream press, thereby reaching a broader audience. Even if Stadler avoided making explicit reference to the literature of the New Right, his explanations drew on concepts of cultural differentialism and neoracism, as developed by the French *Nouvelle droite* in particular. He combined an essentialist conception of identity with the assumption of cultural and ethnic incompatibility between members of the host society and foreigners and consequently took the position that a new multiculturalism with immigrants is doomed to failure.

Prior to the 1990s, his academic work on the history of asylum and refugees in Switzerland had rarely included the current state of migration. However, there is an example from 1988, when he wrote a short essay entitled *Die Schweiz als Exilland* (Switzerland as a Country of Exile) in an edited volume on the subject of Germany and its neighbouring countries. He stressed that there was a difference between recent developments and the situation in past centuries, when Switzerland had been a host country for many religious and political refugees. Stadler wrote that, from the 1980s on, immigration growth would mainly consist of economic refugees arriving from Third World countries. Faced with this new development, he warned that on account of its limited space, Switzerland could hardly be a country of immigration without ultimately losing its identity.[302]

In the 1990s, Stadler multiplied his writings on migration and Swiss national identity and tried to reach a public outside academia. In 1992, with Stadler's permission, the front page of *Schweizerzeit* featured a shortened version of an article he had originally written for the renowned monthly *Schweizer Monatshefte*.[303] The original article was also reissued in a 2001 collection of his essays.[304] In the *Schweizerzeit* version, Stadler argued that history has witnessed 'race and class struggles' and 'while no one can assume the superiority of a particular race, one can simply assume that races have *their own areas of settlement* and that there are legitimate reasons for resistance if *they should spread out into other regions*'.[305] Stadler's use of the term 'race' appears all the more astonishing considering that he noted in another controversial essay, published four years later by the CINS, that the term 'race' had lost its meaning for the science of history. According to Stadler, the reason for this lay in the fact that the pseudoscientific 'race doctrine' of the late nineteenth century had been misused for the elimination of the Jews.[306]

In a 1994 article published in the history journal *Freiburger Geschichtsblätter*, Stadler reminded his readers that Oswald Spengler had forecast in 1933 'that one day class struggle and race struggle will join together and could put an end to the "white world" (as he called it)'.[307] Stadler made reference to *Jahre der Entscheidung* (Years of Decision) by the late Oswald Spengler, a German author aligned with the Conservative Revolution.[308] In this book, Spengler had complained about the decline of the occident because of both the 'white world revolution' of liberalism and socialism and the insurgent 'coloured revolution' emerging from developing countries.[309] According to Stadler, what still seemed unimaginable – on account of colonialism – at the time when Spengler wrote his text, had meanwhile come much closer to reality. With regards to Switzerland, Stadler stressed his sense of alarm that a country of limited space which had already witnessed a rather difficult set of relationships between minorities, was now entering a situation where the numbers of 'certain peoples' (*bestimme Völkerschaften*) was actually larger than the population of a middle-sized canton. Stadler suggested that one should think what the reaction might be like if a mass immigration of Swiss, Austrians, or Germans were to take place in an Afro-Asian or Balkan country.[310]

In another essay which eventually appeared in different versions in a number of publications and therefore enjoyed significant circulation, Stadler conveyed his strong disapproval of the multiculturalism that had followed recent immigration. Once again, it was *Schweizer Monatshefte* which published the first version in 1992. The JES then edited a brochure that included Stadler's article three years later.[311] Abbreviated versions were published by *Der Zürcher Bauer*, the party paper of the cantonal SVP section of Zurich, and by *Schweizerzeit*.[312] In the version released by the JES, Stadler argued that the independence of a nation is reflected in its ability to remain constant throughout periods of historical transformation and sudden change, and its ability to preserve its national identity. Regardless of what may happen in terms of modernisation, identity should be seen as the cornerstone of human experience.[313] Furthermore, he claimed that immigration was able to rapidly transform the ethnic composition of the host society and that 'foreign influence' (*Fremdeinwirkung*) and 'foreign settling down' (*Fremdfestsetzung*) are almost always perceived as threats and only rarely as enhancements. Stadler argued that not every 'foreign mentality' would fit well in Switzerland and complained that while direct democracy gave the Swiss the opportunities to vote on many things, they were not able to vote on key problems like the mass immigration of 'immigrants who do not belong here'.[314] From Stadler's point of view, the implementation of naturalisation procedures granting faster and easier citizenship would not solve the problem of an immigration society. It would instead simply conceal the real symptoms, 'because the most important obstacle is not simply that of citizenship – nor that of language since children are able to learn the language of the host country quickly – but it is rather the mentality of people from different socio-cultural and religious backgrounds'.[315]

While this article and its reprinted versions were still little noticed by the general public, Peter Stadler's above-mentioned address to the general meeting of the CINS in May 1996 elicited quite a reaction from the public and the printed press.[316] In the written version of the speech, Stadler argued that the historically-proven Swiss neutrality should be maintained in its integral form, and denounced European integration as peaceful attempts at 'bringing into line' (*Gleichschaltung*). He further maintained that the immigration of the previous two decades had literally produced an 'ethnic revolution' in Switzerland which was marked not only by the 'so-called multicultural society', but also by an imported criminality that Switzerland had not seen since the occupation by French troops in 1798–99. Stadler also stated that EEA membership would increase Switzerland's attractiveness as a country of asylum and immigration and that the ensuing immigration would 'mobilise the lower classes in particular, North Africans of French nationality, for example, and all the potential for conflict they would bring'.[317]

Despite the criticism provoked by Stadler's explanations, he continued to be published in mainstream papers. In 2000, for example, the *Neue Zürcher Zeitung* featured his article 'Geschichte als Gewalttat' (History as an Act of Violence), in which he looked in a general way at the relationship between war and peace throughout history.[318] Once again, however, he claimed that new tides of refugees were turning the host countries upside down and that they represented a 'new, permissive form of the migration of peoples [*Völkerwanderung*] and an invasion from the bottom up'.[319] The fact that Stadler's views were published in the mainstream press and thus reached a broader audience demonstrates the particular significance that this renowned Swiss historian had for the neo-nationalist current of the New Right.

The Guardians of the National Consciousness:
A Battle over Collective Memory

In 1996 and 1997, the search for 'unclaimed' Jewish assets in Swiss banks not only made headlines in the global news media but also generated a broad domestic debate over various aspects of Switzerland's conduct during the time of National Socialism. The debate was propelled to the top of the political agenda and included issues such as the Swiss National Bank's gold trade with Germany, the government's refugee policy, art trade, transit transport through the Alps for the Axis powers, export of war material to Germany, and so on. Soon after it began in 1996, the discussion developed into a controversy which produced some degree of division in the Swiss public. The debate gave rise to a variety of groups and authors forming an intellectual front against the efforts to reevaluate the country's conduct during the Second World War. Their main goal was to preserve the picture of a blameless and untainted past in which there was little room for mistakes, weakness or self-questioning. By presenting national cohesion and steadfastness, combat readiness and neutrality as decisive factors of the country's self-survival and independence during the Second World War, they sought to hold on to a self-assuring formulation of the country's national identity and hence to strengthen the basis of contemporary national consciousness and self-confidence. Specific targets of their criticism included in particular the reports and findings that the Independent Commission of Experts Switzerland – Second World War (ICE) had presented since the late 1990s.[320] Known as the Bergier Commission, the ICE was appointed by the Federal Council in late 1996 and was headed by the Swiss historian Jean-François Bergier.

As I have shown in the previous chapters, radical right-wing populist parties and their leaders have, from the beginning, taken a prominent role in the disputes over Switzerland's wartime history and have presented themselves as advocates of the national interest and self-confidence. In 1996 and 1997, when the criticism first arose revealing how Swiss banks had been handling 'unclaimed' accounts in the postwar era, radical right-wing populist parties reacted promptly and denounced it as an outrageous campaign that was being led by left-wing media and foreign interest groups. In public campaigns, they stirred resentments against intellectuals, historians and journalists, as well as against Jewish organisations who were all presumed to want to expose Switzerland and challenge its integrity. These campaigns were fuelled by statements from high-ranking politicians, not only from the radical right, but also from centre-right parties, who by 'equating Jewish creditors with "blackmailers" opened a floodgate for old anti-Semitic clichés (conspiracy, usury, greed for money …)'.[321] For example, Jean-Pascal Delamuraz, FDP member and Federal Councillor from 1984 to 1998, said in a newspaper interview that listening to certain people made him wonder if Auschwitz was actually in Switzerland. When Jewish organisations called for a compensation fund to benefit Shoah victims, he equated their claims with blackmail.[322]

Outside the party sector, groups and authors aligned with the New Right were also engaged in the historical debate from early on. They showed particular concern with the ongoing review of Swiss history, since, according to the JES bulletin *Spectrum* from Spring 1997, it was obvious that the understanding of one's own history shapes and determines the present, the condition and the self-confidence of a people.[323]

Following this reasoning, 'dealing with our own history as a fundament of our Swiss identity', as the group Pro Libertate put it, was high up on the intellectual agenda of the Swiss New Right.[324] When Kaspar Villiger, then Federal President, apologised in his commemoration speech of May 1995 for Switzerland's policies towards Jews persecuted by National Socialism, authors from the New Right quickly began to voice objection to the government's intention to revise the country's role in the Second World War. Eduard Stäuble, for example, rejected the need for a fresh review of Switzerland's conduct and urged that the time had come to forgive and reconcile. As Stäuble further maintained, it should not be forgotten that Switzerland was in a very difficult situation at that time.[325]

While most followers of the Swiss New Right shared such disapproval, critics associated with the neo-nationalist current mainly belonged to groups that were created or had reemerged in 1997 and 1998.[326] They attracted, above all, members from the so-called active-service generation (*Aktivdienstgeneration*), which consisted of elderly people who had experienced wartime, some of whom had carved high-profile careers as politicians, diplomats, academics and army officers in the postwar period. They rejected the view that the country had had ties with the National Socialist regime in its role as a financial and economic centre, and hence disapproved of a reexamination of Switzerland's stance as a neutral country. Conversely, they acted as the guardians of a national ideology that continued to draw a heroic, prevailing picture of a country that had kept its independence from National Socialism mainly because of the will to resist displayed by its army, population and its political and social elite. Moreover, while most findings and assessments of the ICE confirmed the findings of historical research carried out previously and hence met little disagreement among academic historians, those members of the 'active-service generation' went on to become the main critics of the historical reports presented by the ICE.

The most important voice was the Living History Working Group (*Arbeitskreis Gelebte Geschichte* – AGG) which was founded in the summer of 1998. According to its statutes, the main goal of the group is to bring personal wartime experiences into the historical debate and to examine and comment on reports issued by the ICE.[327] In addition, the group was determined to address the insecurity of the people and to strengthen their self-confidence. Among its executive members were retired diplomats, high-ranking army officers, former politicians and academics. The AGG was co-presided by Elisabeth Bürki-Flury and Hans-Georg Bandi, an emeritus professor of prehistory at the University of Bern who had supported the paper *Schweizerzeit* in its early years.[328]

Leading AGG members also published articles in periodicals associated with the neo-conservative current of the Swiss New Right.[329] The group counted over five hundred members in 2003 and released a number of press statements on issues related to the ongoing historical debate. In May 2000, the AGG initiated the creation of the Interest Group: Switzerland – Second World War (*Interessengemeinschaft Schweiz – Zweiter Weltkrieg* – IG), which served as an umbrella organisation of nineteen groups with almost twenty thousand members. In a petition addressed to the Federal Councillor in 2000 and presented to the media by the historian and AGG executive member Sigmund Widmer (1919–2003), the IG complained that Switzerland had been heavily humiliated in recent years and urged for a restoration of the country's self-confidence. The petition demanded that the Federal Council should react to the ICE reports by publishing an account that took an opposing point of view.[330]

In 2002, the AGG published the book *Erpresste Schweiz* (Blackmailed Switzerland), a collaborative work bringing together authors who were members or sympathisers of the AGG. Dedicated to the former Federal Councillor, Jean-Pascal Delamuraz, the volume compiled original articles, excerpts from press articles and historical studies, and other documents. The first edition had a circulation of eight thousand, the second five thousand. As the introduction noted, all contributors to the book had done what they could for their homeland and for the preservation of the freedom and independence of the country – not only during wartime, but also later in professional life. The publication defended the picture of an innocent Switzerland, surrounded by enemy powers, which had had no choice in how to conduct its refugee policy or how to manage its economic and financial relations with Germany. The book stressed that its authors deemed it particularly reprehensible that Switzerland had been humiliated in a perfidious way in recent years, in a manner not seen since the invasion of the French revolutionary army at the end of the eighteenth century.[331]

In their description of a campaign being led against the country, the authors fell back on anti-Semitic prejudices and stereotypes, including theories of Jewish conspiracy, as well as of associations of Jews with influence and power. For example, it was denounced that the media campaign against Switzerland had been meticulously orchestrated by Jewish organisations in the United States, namely the World Jewish Congress.[332] It was also argued that the campaign of Jewish-American organisations had helped to awaken anti-Semitism in Switzerland. Here, the authors followed the old anti-Semitic pattern that Jews themselves are responsible for the rise of anti-Semitism. The AGG made this kind of argument in a letter addressed to the U.S. ambassador to

Switzerland.[333] In her answer, the ambassador wrote perspicuously: 'I am very troubled by your description of growing anti-Semitism and anti-Americanism. I am sure you agree that there is no justification for anti-Semitism regardless of what justification anti-Semites might think they have'.[334] Despite the fact that *Erpresste Schweiz* contained these types of arguments, the book was rather favourably reviewed in the *Neue Zürcher Zeitung* and acknowledged as a valuable supplement to the reports that were published by the ICE.[335]

In addition to the book from the AGG, a number of other publications were released that followed the same purpose. They met with strong resistance a critical reexamination of Switzerland's conduct during the Second World War. Among these publications were books by Ernst Leisi, emeritus English professor at the University of Zurich, and Luzi Stamm, FDP Councilor, to mention just two.[336] Both were well received by publications associated with the New Right and radical right-wing populist parties.[337] Most of these writings came out of publishing houses that have published books in the recent past by authors associated with the Swiss New Right, such as Schweizerzeit Verlag, Novalis, Th. Gut Verlag and L'Age d'Homme. A revealing example was the publisher Rothenhäusler, which put out a brochure in 1999, entitled *Nun lügen sie wieder* (Now They Are Lying Again), extensively documenting the alleged lies about Switzerland that were circulating in English-language publications.[338] The second edition included a short review of Norman Finkelstein's controversial book *The Holocaust Industry*,[339] presenting it as a work about 'the shameless misuse of the Brown Holocaust as a moral coat for greed'.[340] On the whole, the debate over Switzerland's role during the Second World War gave the New Right a new boost in terms of personal and publishing activity. A network of groups, authors and publishing houses emerged in the late 1990s and received support from constituencies that had been only marginally engaged with activities of the New Right in previous years.

As this chapter has shown, the German-speaking New Right in Switzerland had its origins in the late 1960s, when the anti-communist attitude of the old right was supplemented by new ideological components which were directed against the rising emancipatory and egalitarian ideas of the 1968 movement. At the same time, with its nationalistic and xenophobic program, the Movement against Overforeignization and its political and intellectual leader, James Schwarzenbach, provided a set of new patterns of thought that were marked by an exclusionist ideology. It was also a period when intellectuals to the right began to voice self-criticism and denounced the alleged politics of convergence between the left and the right. Subsequently, a considerable part of the German-speaking New Right became involved in everyday politics and started to play its role as supplier of ideology for political parties, most evocatively demonstrated in recent years by the case of the new SVP. Many followers of the New Right strove to increase the popular appeal of their ideas and their work and were therefore fond of addressing a wider public. In its quest for a renewal of strategy and ideology, the New Right in the German-speaking part of Switzerland was stimulated by the model of the New Right in Germany. Conversely, it largely dismissed theorists of the *Nouvelle droite* in France for their anti-Christian beliefs and their proximity to the extreme right in France. Nonetheless, central premises of the *Nouvelle droite* found reception among followers of the Swiss New Right, like the concepts of ethnopluralism and radical cultural differentialism, for instance, or the strategic objective to influence opinion-forming groups in order to achieve sociocultural changes.

7

AN INTELLECTUAL ELITE
The New Right in the French-speaking Part of Switzerland

The radical right in the French-speaking part of Switzerland has traditionally been characterised by the influential role of its intellectuals and the strong affinity for reflection developed by French theorists and authors.[1] During the interwar period, a number of intellectuals felt that a political climate that was critical of liberalism and democracy suited their efforts to promote authoritarian and anti-democratic visions of politics and society. At the time, French theorists and authors like Charles Maurras, Léon Daudet and Maurice Barrès were well received by the radical right-wing intellectual community in the French-speaking regions of Switzerland.[2] Compared to their counterparts in the German-speaking part of Switzerland, the francophone intellectuals of the 1930s were more involved in the world of culture and academics. They saw themselves as a part of the intellectual and cultural elite which, like the intellectuals in France, assumed a non-partisan position in public life and was more concerned with the world of ideas, arts and literature than with the lowly spheres of everyday party politics.

Nevertheless, a number of Swiss francophone intellectuals were also engaged in politics and made attempts to gain influence in party politics. For example, Georges Oltramare, a theatre writer, journalist and leader of the National Union, was active both culturally and politically and stood as a symbol of a Swiss version of fascism.[3] Marcel Regamey, a lawyer who founded the Vaud League, was also engaged in politics, where he advocated an anti-democratic and nationalist ideology that was greatly inspired by the thinking of Charles Maurras.[4] Gonzague de Reynold, the aforementioned writer, university professor and admirer of authoritarian dictatorships in Italy and Portugal, played the role of a political adviser and influential ideologue in the French and German linguistic regions of Switzerland.[5]

As in other European countries, following the collapse of National Socialism, fascism and the Vichy regime, most of the intellectuals of the radical right in the French-speaking part of Switzerland went into internal exile or pursued their activities away from the public eye. The general rejection of nationalist and anti-democratic ideologies made it difficult for radical right-wing intellectuals to maintain the same level of public presence that they had during the prewar years. Nevertheless, some followers adapted to the postwar conditions and achieved remarkable integration in political and intellectual life. Without a doubt, the far-reaching anti-communist climate made such an ideological and political integration possible and this was an important reason why the French-speaking regions of Switzerland did not experience the wave of epuration that swept through France in the immediate postwar period and brought numerous suspected collaborators of the Vichy regime before the courts.[6] The widespread anti-communist attitude was also a reason why an international organisation like the World Anti-Communist League (WACL), for example, was able to attract prominent public figures from the centre right and the radical right in Switzerland, particularly in the French-speaking part.[7] Founded in 1966, the primary aim of the WACL was to bring together anti-communists from all around the world. At the same time, however, the WACL 'provided a Euro-American network for anti-Semites, racists, and other right-wing extremists'.[8]

In the 1970s and 1980s, a new period of radical-right intellectualism began in the French-speaking part of Switzerland. It was characterised by the emergence of the New Right and included both the creation of new groups and periodicals and the reshaping of existing organisational and publishing structures. In contrast to the German-speaking part of Switzerland, where large parts of the New Right were rooted in the conservative intellectual milieu and sought to revitalise conservatism in a reformist way, this new period was marked, in the French-speaking part, by the rejuvenation of long-standing intellectual traditions in the radical right and a renewal of anti-democratic thinking that was particularly critical of parliamentary democracy. This made the French-speaking New Right more open to a revolutionary mood. This is demonstrated, for example, by the strong influence that national revolutionary ideas had on followers of the New Right. With its anti-egalitarian and anti-pluralistic conceptions of social and political order, the New Right was also a counter-reaction to the events of 1968 that had given rise to an intellectualisation of the left and the promotion of pluralistic, egalitarian and multicultural concepts. Moreover, since the francophone intellectual community continued to be the main point of reference, the New Right closely followed the developments and debates that were unfolding in France, namely the appearance of the *Nouvelle droite*. In many ways, the francophone New Right in Switzerland was influenced by the ideas and concepts developed and advocated by the French New Right.

The renewal and reorientation of radical-right thinking in the French-speaking part of Switzerland since the 1970s and 1980s produced a new intellectual and ideological landscape. To some extent, this corresponded to developments in France, where the New Right had pursued a renewal of radical-right ideology since the late 1960s, which ultimately aimed to reorient political and cultural life.[9] In francophone Switzerland, this renewal was shaped by three different intellectual currents: the counter-revolutionaries, the integrists and the *Nouvelle droite*. All three currents shared the exclusionist and anti-egalitarian ideas of a radical-right worldview and there was often an overlap in terms of membership and collaboration in certain areas of activity. While all three were greatly inspired by their counterparts in France, each of the three currents referred to a distinct intellectual and ideological legacy and was grouped around particular circles, groups and periodicals.

The Counter-revolutionaries: Contesting Pluralistic and Parliamentarian Democracy

The counter-revolutionaries profoundly disagree with the legacy of the Enlightenment and the achievements of the French Revolution. The principle of equality, the declaration of human rights and the rule of pluralistic democracy are seen as the manifestations of repugnant modernity and the causes of social and political disarray. In their critique of liberalism and individualism, they promote an anti-modernist

Figure 7.1 | *Ideological Typology of the Francophone New Right*

Common Exclusionist Ideology

Counter-Revolutionaries	Integrists	*Nouvelle droite*
Opposition to Parliamentary and Pluralistic Democracy	Authoritarian and Anti-modernist Concepts	Neo-paganism and Cultural-differentialism

Distinctive Intellectual Legacy and Ideological Priorities

conception of a society of people who are bound by long-lasting traditions and customs and know precisely where they belong in the well-structured collectivity. Instead of market economics and individual choice, the counter-revolutionaries advocate corporatist models of professional and economic order. Their elitist and aristocratic attitude also stirs in them a deep-founded belief in authority and strong political leadership. For counter-revolutionaries, therefore, the answer to modernity would be the return to an ancien régime, an idealised past in which the natural social and political order is based on authoritarian, hierarchical and organic principles. The counter-revolutionary current has enjoyed a particularly lively tradition in France over the last two centuries. Its initial intellectual inspiration came from the nineteenth century classics of counter-revolutionary thought represented by Joseph de Maistre and Louis de Bonald and their aristocratic and monarchist counter-program to the French Revolution.[10]

In the twentieth century, the French author and leader of the French Action (*Action française*), Charles Maurras (1869–1952), was by far the most important theorist of counter-revolutionary thought. As John McClelland states, 'Charles Maurras' great service to the French right was to exercise an intellectual domination so complete that right-wing thinking which was different from his always looked incomplete by comparison'.[11] Maurras and French Action combined the concept of 'integral nationalism' with anti-egalitarian, monarchist and anti-Semitic ideas to become the leading intellectual of the interwar nationalist and radical right-wing movements in France.[12] After the war, Maurras' writings remained a key inspiration to various factions of the intellectual radical right and, in particular, the counter-revolutionary current in France.[13] For example, the weekly *Rivarol*, founded in 1951 by ex-Vichyites, drew on Maurrassian ideas in its criticisms of parliamentary democracy and became one of the most important periodicals of the postwar extreme right in France.[14]

In the French-speaking part of Switzerland, a close and long-time association has existed with French counter-revolutionaries and their attempts to combat the purportedly dreadful legacy of the French Revolution. Maurras' ideas of defiance towards party politics and parliamentarianism have been cultivated for a long time by Swiss counter-revolutionaries. In addition, the reemergence of traditionalist and integrist Catholic groups following the Second Vatican Council was a forceful expression of the traditional relationship between counter-revolutionary thought and Catholicism, best illustrated in Maurras' work and also adopted by Swiss counter-revolutionaries. Another influence came from the *Nouvelle droite* in France which began to renew and revitalise radical-right thinking in the 1970s and 1980s. This had a delayed effect on counter-revolutionaries in French-speaking Switzerland, when some of the ideas and concepts developed by the French *Nouvelle droite* were well-received by counter-revolutionaries in the 1990s and integrated into their worldview shaped by anti-egalitarian and anti-pluralistic ideas. Most notably, cultural differentialism became characteristic of arguments advanced during debates on immigration, multicultural society and national identity. However, the strong commitment that Swiss counter-revolutionaries had to Christian values and traditions placed a limit on support for the *Nouvelle droite* and its neopagan and anti-Christian orientation.

The Vaud League: Guardians of the Maurrassian Legacy

The Vaud League (*Ligue vaudoise*) was based in the canton of Vaud and had its origins in the 1930s. At that time, the group's worldview was marked by pronounced anti-democratic convictions. Despite political and intellectual metamorphoses, the group has maintained its fundamental criticism of egalitarian and pluralistic principles. After the Second World War, the League's aversion to democracy shifted to a distrust of the system of electoral and parliamentary democracy. In distinctive counter-revolutionary fashion and still inspired by Maurrassian thought, the group continued to reject the egalitarian premise of the French Revolution and to advocate an authoritarian and corporatist view of political and social order. The League drew liberally from nationalist ideas and viewed territory, history and culture as the primordial components forming the regional identity of the canton of Vaud. In addition, since the 1980s, the group has kept a close eye on the intellectual and ideological renewal undertaken by the New Right in France.

Originally, the Vaud League was founded in 1933 to oppose a federal tax statute on alcoholic beverages.[15] It was the successor of a small intellectual circle named Order and Tradition (*Ordre et Tradition*) created by a couple of students from the University of Lausanne in 1926.[16] From the beginning, the League was committed to the anti-democratic and nationalist ideas of Charles Maurras, who regularly travelled to the French-speaking part of Switzerland in the 1930s. The leader and chief ideologue of the Vaud League, Marcel Regamey (1905–1982), promulgated fervent opposition to democracy and liberalism and sought to install an authoritarian political order based on strong leadership. Ultimately, in 1941, Regamey also signed the 'Petition of the 200', thereby demonstrating his willingness to adapt, to a certain extent, to the new European order.[17] Regamey's worldview was also characterised by anti-

Semitism, as illustrated by his infamous anti-Semitic article, 'Défie-toi du Juif!' (Distrust the Jew), written in 1932.[18] A number of anti-Semitic articles were also published in the League's paper, *La Nation*.[19] In the 1930s, the League approached the insurgent Front Movement and joined the anti-democratic efforts to recast Swiss democracy in an authoritarian mould. On the other hand, the League did show a fair degree of caution in its attitude toward the centralism and the militaristic style of some of the fascist groups associated with the Front Movement.[20]

By assuming a strong federalist stance and combating the central power of the federal government in Bern, the League succeeded in gaining allies among the centre-right groups in the canton of Vaud. Further support in this respect was provided by the manner in which the League's program highlighted the distinct nature of the canton of Vaud, a premise which promoted a nationalist style of discourse at the regional level, in a manner that was consistent with Maurrassian thought. After the war, the Vaud League moderated its anti-democratic zeal – but without denying its Maurrassian legacy of authoritarianism and traditionalism – thereby achieving integration in the political life of the canton of Vaud. As argued by Roland Butikofer, it was the Vaud League's devotion to federalism and anti-communism and its transformation into a non-subversive group that made it possible for the League to establish itself in the political and intellectual life of the canton of Vaud.[21]

In recent decades, the group has continued to affirm its non-partisan stance and has consequently exhibited a great deal of scepticism towards party politics. On the other hand, the League praised direct democracy as an expression of the people's common sense and has regularly participated, therefore, in direct democratic campaigns. For example, in the 1990s, the Vaud League was actively engaged in campaigns which dealt with Switzerland's membership of international organisations. During these campaigns, the League advocated an isolationist position and fervently rejected membership of the EEA and the UN.[22] In addition, its senior members were unrelentingly engaged in discussions covering a wide range of cultural, historical and literary themes.

The League has edited the publication series *Cahiers de la Renaissance vaudoise* (Notebooks of the Vaud Renaissance), which has covered a variety of themes, including history, culture, literature and politics. By 2003, 142 volumes had been published in the series, usually in editions of one thousand copies, but sometimes reaching a print run of up to ten thousand. The League also published the paper *La Nation* (The Nation), founded in 1931 and released bi-monthly with a circulation of around four thousand.[23] The paper usually consisted of four A3 pages and its style and language aimed to address a more intellectual readership.

The list of contributors to the two publications has been quite diverse and has included senior members of various political parties. For example, Georges-André Chevallaz, FDP member from the canton of Vaud and Federal Councillor from 1974 to 1983, wrote an article in the volume entitled *Mélanges Marcel Regamey* (Marcel Regamey Collection), which was published in 1980 in the publication series and paid tribute to the long-time leader of the Vaud League, who was still alive at the time.[24] One of the reasons that the League appealed to a wide variety of authors was the claim that it placed primary importance on defending the identity of the canton of Vaud, or the *'pays de Vaud'* (Land of Vaud), as it was commonly called. As a result, the Vaud League succeeded in convincing some that its primary role was as a true promoter of federalism and a trustworthy advocate of the canton's cultural and historical traditions.

Following the death of Marcel Regamey in 1982, Olivier Delacrétaz assumed the presidency and became the driving force of the Vaud League. Delacrétaz, a member of the Association of the Friends of Robert Brasillach (see below), was also the most prolific contributor to *La Nation* and wrote the majority of the League's programmatic texts. When seeking to present the League as a non-partisan group that should be able to appeal to members from different political parties, he expressed a strong aversion to electoral competition and partisan quarrels. He argued, with an undercurrent of anti-pluralism, that while all political systems consist of different factions dividing up the country, a political system based on electoral ballots is the only one which acclaims this division as a founding principle.[25]

In another programmatic article published in 1997, Delacrétaz demanded, in authoritarian fashion, the establishment of a strong cantonal government and a corporatist system composed of representatives from communes, professional groups, trade unions, employer associations, churches and universities.[26] This corresponds to what Delacrétaz wrote about the necessity of establishing a hierarchically structured community that individuals could build upon in their desire for liberty, equality and unity.[27] He also underscored his counter-revolutionary stance when he declared in the November 2002 issue of *La Nation* that France had witnessed the revolution and suffered – was suffering still – from the injuries inflicted upon itself at that time.[28] With great admiration, *La Nation* dedicated this issue to Charles Maurras to commemorate the fiftieth anniversary of his death, thereby demonstrating that the French author remained a major source of inspiration for the Vaud League.

In 1993, Delacrétaz supplied the referendum campaign against the anti-racism law with a booklet entitled *L'universel enraciné* (The Deep-

Rooted Universal), which was published in the series *Cahiers de la Renaissance vaudoise*.[29] As an official referendum committee, the Vaud League also actively supported the signature collection for the petition demanding a referendum on the anti-racism law.[30] Delacrétaz's publication presented a comprehensive critique of anti-racism which, according to him, had become today's secular religion. In his text, Delacrétaz made a clever move when he claimed that the critique of anti-racism presented by Pierre-André Taguieff in his 1988 book *La force du préjugé* (The Power of Prejudice) was an important source of inspiration.[31] It is true that Taguieff exposed the trap into which anti-racists with essentialist conceptions of culture and cultural difference might fall, which is why Taguieff's arguments are often used by authors of the New Right. However, these same authors deliberately avoid presenting Taguieff's thorough analysis of racism, in particular his perspicuous examination of the cultural-differentialist arguments that are characteristic of the neoracist discourse of the New Right.

Delacrétaz's text was inspired by arguments developed on the issue of anti-racism by the French *Nouvelle droite* and it drew on differentialist and neoracist ideas common to the discourse of the *Nouvelle droite*. In the introductory chapter, Delacrétaz quoted extensively from *La lettre de Magazine Hebdo* (The Letter of the Magazine Hebdo), a magazine directed by Jean-Claude Valla, former general secretary of the Group for the Research and Study of European Civilisation (*Groupement de recherche et d'études pour la civilisation européenne* – GRECE). The citation, which basically constructs an equivalency between racism and anti-racism, served as a point of reference for Delacrétaz in his essay. He stressed that the idea of an incommensurability between 'races', ethnic groups and nations was promoted both by racist theorists and those authors of the *Nouvelle droite* who took anti-universalistic and anti-Christian positions. He then declared that anti-racism should be seen as an evocative example of an ideology based on universalistic values, or 'the universal' (*l'universel*), as he preferred to call it.[32] As Delacrétaz further argued, universalism rejects any kind of biological, historical, social and familial individuality and hence seeks to suppress 'the individual' (*le particulier*) and to glorify its 'eradication' (*déracinement*). Hence, the ultimate objective of anti-racism is to establish a globally unified cultural and political framework based on human rights, by denying the differences that exist between communities.[33]

According to the Vaud League president, the concept of 'race' is exclusive in nature, while the nation's ability to assimilate foreigners gives it an inclusive character.[34] He consistently referred to the scientifically refuted category of 'race' and thereby applied racially grounded concepts. He denounced the UNESCO declarations on 'race' as ideological derivations which simply denied scientific evidence.[35] In addition, he talked about the social and cultural features of human beings which were the alleged results of 'race' and 'biological inheritance'. For instance, he gave the example of the purported Mediterranean temper, whose fervour, in the words of Delacrétaz, had cooled after a few generations had lived their lives in the canton of Vaud.[36] For Delacrétaz, assimilation was the only way in which a country could host and accept immigrants, since attempts to apply the concept of integration would inevitably lead to ghettos. Assimilation was not always possible, however, he argued, either because the nation was not enough strong to assimilate the newcomers, or because the newcomers – immigrants of Islamic faith, for example – were incompatible with the host societies.

Delacrétaz went on to claim that xenophobia should be seen as a social fact which was both a vital and a blind reaction of the social body.[37] In his view, xenophobia was simply a symptom of disorder that was mainly due to the failure of immigration policy and the lack of national self-confidence. He quoted extensively from a speech by Uli Windisch, a sociology professor at the University of Geneva, whose work on issues related to migration and xenophobia had become increasingly controversial in recent years, pleading that it would be better to understand the fears and worries of individuals espousing xenophobic views instead of stigmatising and excluding them.[38] While Delacrétaz's booklet on anti-racism was certainly the most comprehensive account of issues related to anti-racism, migration and xenophobia, many articles published in *La Nation* expressed the same views.[39]

The influence that authors and debates of the continental New Right exerted on the Vaud League was demonstrated in an article by Eric Werner regarding a widely criticised book that had been written by Ernst Nolte. In this article, Werner referred to a conversation between Ernst Nolte and Dominique Venner, a well-known historian of the *Nouvelle droite* in France. The conversation had been published in *Éléments*, a key periodical of the *Nouvelle droite* in France. Werner presented an argument introduced by Venner in which he basically argued that the emergence of National Socialism should be seen in terms of a reaction to both communism and the Anglo-Saxon ideology of liberal democracy.[40]

Despite a similarity to ideas of the French *Nouvelle droite*, however, some of the writings revealed the distance that existed between the League and the neo-pagan and anti-Christian current of the *Nouvelle droite*.[41] So while the Vaud League was attracted to the reformulated arguments of an anti-egalitarian and anti-universalistic discourse based on essentialist and differentialist conceptions of identity and developed by the *Nouvelle droite* in France, the group demonstrates, above all, the persistent legacy of counter-revolutionary thought in the French-speaking part of Switzerland.

Le Pamphlet: A Bridge between New Right and Extreme Right

The periodical *Le Pamphlet* (The Pamphlet) was founded in 1970 by Claude Paschoud, Mariette Pache and members of the student fraternity *Zofingue*.[42] The significance of the paper lies in its function as a bridge between the New Right – as represented by the counter-revolutionary current – and factions of the extreme right. In fact, the periodical provides a good example of the shifting ideological borders that existed between the New Right and the extreme right. Published ten times per year and available by subscription, it had a circulation of some two thousand in the 1970s and 1980s.[43] By the mid 1990s, its circulation figures had dropped to less than one thousand.[44] Since then, *Le Pamphlet* has created its own website which carries the current issue as well as an archive of back issues published since 1995.[45] The periodical appears to have been published on the Internet in reaction to the difficulties that it experienced in recent years in finding a sufficient number of subscribers. The periodical usually consisted of four pages, slightly larger than A4 in size. It often featured articles that were one or more pages in length and most contributions were written in well-crafted language. The articles covered a variety of themes, ranging from politics and culture, to history and religion.

The editors of *Le Pamphlet* emphasised that the periodical had been founded in reaction to the 1968 student movement and sought to provide a counter-force to the allegedly streamlined public opinion in francophone Switzerland. Their goal was to provide a voice for the non-partisan intellectual milieu in the French-speaking regions of Switzerland which takes a position on the right and yet opposes the conformist attitude of the established right.[46] The result was that *Le Pamphlet* was able to establish itself as a small periodical that advocated counter-revolutionary and traditionalist thought and referred to ideas taken from both the New Right and the extreme right. Moreover, as shown in chapter 8, the fact that the debates of French negationism were being noticed in the French-speaking part of Switzerland was in large part due to the activities undertaken by *Le Pamphlet* since the 1980s, with its editors taking the view that negationist endeavours should be seen as valuable scientific attempts to revise the history of the Second World War and of the Shoah in particular.[47]

The editorial line was mainly determined by Claude and Mariette Paschoud who were both members of the Association of the Friends of Robert Brasillach (see below).[48] They also contributed many of the articles published in *Le Pamphlet*. Claude Paschoud, who had had contacts with the extreme right since the 1960s,[49] was the editor-in-chief from 1970 to 1988, at which time he was succeeded by his spouse. When Claude Paschoud was appointed as a lawyer to the cantonal office of foreigners in Vaud in 1988, the public reacted with indignation and protest.[50] Nonetheless, the cantonal government refused to give in to public pressure and Paschoud remained in his job until 1990, when the head of the cantonal department was replaced.[51] Mariette Paschoud, a language and history teacher, as well as an army officer, gained notoriety in 1986 when she expressed her doubts about the existence of gas chambers in concentration camps (see chapter 8). She subsequently had to resign from her position as a grammar school teacher in Lausanne and her promotion in the Swiss army was blocked. Until the mid 1990s, Mariette Paschoud pursued legal proceedings against journalists and critics who accused her of having sympathies for National Socialism.[52] In 1995, the Federal Tribunal exonerated a journalist who had used the title 'brown Mariette' (*braune Mariette*) in a newspaper article on Mariette Paschoud.[53]

In addition to the Paschoud couple, in the last three decades the list of authors in *Le Pamphlet* has included, among others: Michel de Preux, an integrist Catholic who wrote the anti-statist pamphlet *Une Suisse totalitaire* (A Totalitarian Switzerland), published by L'Age d'Homme;[54] Claude-Alain Mayor, who was forced to resign his position as party secretary of the Liberal Democratic Party in the canton of Vaud in 1981, after publishing a newspaper editorial containing anti-Jewish statements;[55] Giuseppe Patanè, a long-time author in the Swiss neo-fascist paper *Courrier du Continent* (see chapter 8) and former member of the Italian Social Movement (*Movimento Sociale Italiano* – MSI);[56] and Eric Werner, who co-authored a small booklet with Jean-Philippe Chenaux in 1988, denouncing the criticism of Claude Paschoud's appointment to the cantonal office of foreigners in the canton of Vaud.[57] *Le Pamphlet* liked to demonstrate its close relationship with the Vaud League and proudly noted that Marcel Regamey had strongly encouraged the founders of the periodical to launch a new publication.[58] Accordingly, *Le Pamphlet* acknowledged *La Nation* as 'our eminent fellow-member' and frequently reviewed publications released by the Vaud League.[59] The National Front in France was a further point of reference, with the periodical continually reporting on Le Pen's party. Some authors displayed great admiration for the French party leader. Michel de Preux, for instance, called Le Pen the only politician leading a political group that was worthy of the name in France and someone who has a vision of French politics, as well as a vision of world politics.[60] *Le Pamphlet* also demonstrated its proximity to the publishing world of the extreme right in France. For instance, the periodical *Rivarol* was praised as an excellent weekly from Paris and excerpts taken from the French periodical were also reproduced.[61]

On several occasions, the editors insisted that *Le Pamphlet* brought together authors of various political convictions and could not therefore be said to follow a particular ideological line.[62] However, the rejection of contemporary democracy and the electoral system was certainly shared by most editors of *Le Pamphlet*, or, as an editorial from 1986 put it, the editors 'are all allergic to electoral politics, if not disgusted by it'.[63] According to Michel de Preux, a hatred of modern democracy is the beginning of political wisdom.[64] Consequently, he declared that it was the duty of state authorities to respect the natural hierarchical structure of all human, public and private societies.[65] For this purpose, de Preux endorsed a biologically based conception of hierarchy developed by the Italian fascist philosopher and theorist Julius Evola. According to this viewpoint, hierarchy should be based on the principle that those who are by nature inferior should be subordinate to those who are superior.[66] It is therefore no surprise that philosophies of Enlightenment and the declaration of human rights were regularly presented in *Le Pamphlet* as being detrimental to the natural and traditional order of human society.[67]

Many articles published in *Le Pamphlet* expressed xenophobic and neoracist views and drew on a biologically based conception of culture and 'race'. Roland Reichenbach discussed the 'irreducible dissimilarity' between ethnic groups that resulted from the fact that these concepts are 'inscribed in mental structures solidified by customs stretching back thousands of years'.[68] Quoting from the work of the social anthropologist Claude Lévi-Strauss, he argued that contact between different groups living in a small area, or an overlap of these groups, would inevitably give rise to aggressive reactions.[69] Xenophobic and racist attitudes were presented as anthropological constants, embedded in human history and therefore impossible to remove from social life.[70] In racially marked language, so went the complaint, 'one constantly collides with people of race, colour and religion who are foreign to our manners and habits'.[71] In another article, Michel de Preux made a fervent plea for maintaining the biological concept of 'race'.[72] Moreover, integration, or assimilation as the editors preferred to call it, was received with great scepticism. An article published in 1982 noted that while assimilation 'can be positive when dealing with people of the same race, this is less certain where children of colour or another race are concerned'.[73] In a 1997 article, Michel de Preux stated that 'the defence of race, ethnic group, identity (of nations and provinces, as well as that of individuals, families, trades and the liberal arts) belongs to the advanced guard in the battle for the survival of the whole of Europe.'[74]

The Jewish community in Switzerland was the target of some articles published by *Le Pamphlet*. Most commonly, the editors denounced the alleged influence that the 'Jewish milieus' were said to have on the authorities and public opinion.[75] Moreover, in debates concerning the 'unclaimed' Jewish assets in Swiss banks and Switzerland's role during the Second World War, it was argued that the arrogance displayed towards Switzerland would inevitably provoke the rise of anti-Semitism. Claude Paschoud noted that if the survivors of the Shoah had the right to receive compensation, then why was not the Israeli state paying any compensation to Palestinians?[76] Some articles were also expressions of blunt anti-Semitism. For example, Michel de Preux, notorious for taking anti-Judaist views, wrote that 'the negation of the genocide of six million Jews by the Nazis is nothing, yes, nothing, in comparison to the negation by the Jews of the crucifixion of the God-man, Christ'.[77]

Since the editors declared that the quest for a true Christian church represented a central objective of *Le Pamphlet*, some authors exhibited a strong attraction to integrism (see next section). Most prominently, Michel de Preux was a fervent critic of ecumenism and the Second Vatican Council and wished to reestablish the Catholic Church's traditional role in society. His religious fundamentalist views included the intransigent rejection of abortion, euthanasia, emancipation and modern democracy.[78] While displaying great sympathy for the integrist aims of Marcel Lefebvre and his Society of Saint Pius X, de Preux remained critical towards the schism that the integrist movement had brought about.[79] *Le Pamphlet* also published a one-page interview with Gustave Thibon, a symbol of the continuity of the Catholic fundamentalist movement in France since the Vichy regime.[80] In view of its devotion to Christianity, it is not surprising that *Le Pamphlet* showed little understanding for the neo-pagan, anti-Christian currents of the *Nouvelle droite*. When Alain de Benoist was invited to speak at the University of Geneva by the Proudhon Circle in November 1985 (see below), Michel de Preux wrote a critical report denouncing de Benoist's rejection of Europe's Christian past.[81]

Le Pamphlet also extensively covered debates on issues of domestic policy. Most significantly, it supported the campaign against the anti-racism law and published a large number of articles on the matter. The editorial in the September 1994 issue, which was entirely dedicated to the anti-racism law, argued that the prime objective of the law was to ban 'historical revisionism', as the editors liked to label negationism.[82] Referring to assessments made in a book by Eric Delcroix, who was associated with French negationism and a contributor to the *Revue d'histoire révisionniste* (Review of Revisionist History), the editorial reminded the readership that a similar law in France, the so-called *Loi Fabius-Gayssot* of 1990, had produced a disastrous effect on the public and intellectual climate.

The editors also made it clear that they rejected Switzerland's membership of supranational organisations. As early as 1977, Claude-Alain Mayor defended the idea that the uniqueness of Switzerland's case must categorically be retained and that the UN was a politically useless and discredited institution.[83] In the early 1990s, Christoph Blocher was welcomed by Claude Paschoud as the leader of the anti-European campaign. At the same time, Paschoud denounced the French-speaking media of Switzerland for using the SVP leader as a new scapegoat in their 'euro-maniac' campaign.[84] However, with the CINS about to expel Mariette Paschoud in 1995 because of her supposed extreme-right and negationist partisanship, support for the German-speaking populist leader diminished noticeably.[85]

Overall, *Le Pamphlet*, which had emerged with such zeal to counter the emergence of left-wing intellectualism after 1968, came to represent the radical faction within the counter-revolutionary current. While the periodical displayed a fundamental distrust of democracy and egalitarian principles and defended traditionalist views on social and political questions, its racially shaped language and anti-Jewish statements, as well as the regular references to extreme-right publications and negationist propaganda, moved *Le Pamphlet* into proximity with the extreme right.

The Integrists: Catholicism and Politics

For integrists, or Catholic fundamentalists, as some prefer to call them, Catholic faith defines human and social life in an integral manner.[86] Integrist thought is based on the three guiding principles of an intransigent version of Catholicism: immutability, intangibility and integrality.[87] By tradition, integrism has attracted intellectuals and political figures who have sought to translate their integrist views on religion and Catholicism into conceptions of social and political order and, as a consequence, often joined the counter-revolutionary current of thought.[88] Integrists firmly believe that religion and politics are closely related spheres of life and therefore associate a hierarchical and authoritarian type of political project with their own religious model.[89] Or, as expressed by Étienne Borne:

> The religion of integrism is basically authoritarian and pessimistic; it emphasises the disciplinary, hierarchical and dogmatic aspects of Catholicism and especially the absoluteness of a truth which cannot be opposed by the rights of man; this religion looks to the theology of original sin for reasons to reject modern ideas of democracy and progress.[90]

Historically, integrism emerged very early in the twentieth century as a reaction to modernism and its efforts to use scientific methods taken primarily from the disciplines of archaeology and philology to gain understanding of the Holy Scripture. Integrism essentially meant the rejection of attempts to comform Catholic faith and doctrine with the modern world of science, democracy and progress. It had its golden age under the pontificate of Pius X (1903–1914), when it served as a foundation for the Church's struggle against democracy, liberalism and modernism.[91] In France, the integrist current of thought found great political and intellectual support in French Action (*Action Française*) and its leader Charles Maurras, despite the fact that the Vatican had issued an interdiction against the group in 1926, which was only lifted in 1939. Despite being an agnostic, Maurras viewed Catholicism as the main force with the potential power to reinstall hierarchical order and combat egalitarian and democratic principles.[92] After the war, integrists found themselves on the sidelines of the Catholic Church and intellectual life. However, the creation of the group Catholic City (*Cité Catholique*), its two organs *Verbe* and *Permanences* and the journal *Itinéraires*, allowed integrism to preserve organisational continuity in France. Catholic City was directed by Jean Madiran, a pseudonym of Jean Arfel, who was a devoted disciple of Charles Maurras.[93]

The Second Vatican Council, where the Catholic Church decided to take a more open-minded stance towards the modern world, was a turning point in the history of integrism. Opposition to the Council's decrees included criticism that was both traditionalist and integrist in nature. Traditionalist critics opposed ecclesiastic and liturgical changes, such as a move towards a celebration in the vernacular instead of the traditional Latin mass, but they ultimately accepted the authority of the Catholic Church. Integrists went a step further. They categorically rejected the renewal of the Catholic Church and the new concepts promoted by the Council, such as ecumenism and freedom of conscience, while refusing to bow to the will of the Vatican.[94] In many ways, however, the integrist and traditionalist movements have maintained their close association. They succeeded in establishing a network of communities, groups and periodicals, and have undergone a process of organisational and intellectual revitalisation since the 1970s.[95]

Together with Jean Madiran, Bernard Antony, who also likes to call himself Romain Marie, played a central role in the traditionalist movement of the post-Council era in France.[96] Antony's relentless political and publishing activities have played a part in the increasing politicisation of one segment of the traditionalist current since the 1970s and its movement toward Le Pen's National Front. In 1975, he founded the monthly *Présent* which was transformed into a daily paper in 1982 and was co-edited by Jean Madiran and Pierre Durand, the latter a member of the FN political bureau. Antony also founded the Centre Henri and André Charlier in 1979 and a network of local groups named Christendom Solidarity Committees (*Comités Chrétienté-Solidarité*) in 1982. In 1984, he joined the National Front and was elected to the European Parliament. In the 1990s, Antony was the FN political bureau member for cultural affairs.

Since the late 1960s and 1970s, the establishment and consolidation of the integrist movement in the French-speaking part of Switzerland has led to a strengthening of relations with France, in which the leaders of the traditionalist movement in France have been acknowledged by Swiss intellectuals and political figures. In the French-speaking regions of Switzerland, integrists succeeded in developing an organisational network that consisted of a religious movement, political and cultural groups and a periodical. In a similar way to the counter-revolutionaries, they played a role in the upswing in anti-egalitarian and authoritarian ideas and the ideological revitalisation of the intellectual current of the radical right. While some devotees of the integrist cause displayed their exclusionist convictions by directing them primarily against immigrants, others operated with anti-Jewish conspiracy theories.

The Priestly Society of Saint Pius X: The Integrist International

Archbishop Marcel Lefebvre (1905–1991) founded the Priestly Society of Saint Pius X (*Fraternité sacerdotale Saint-Pie X; Priesterbruderschaft St. Pius X* – SSPX) in Switzerland in November 1970. The SSPX represents the most important organisation committed to the cause of integrism. While the congregation has had a global sphere of action, it has used Switzerland as a base for its activities. It has advocated the authoritarian, counter-revolutionary and anti-modernist tradition of Catholicism. Although the SSPX was a religious community concerned with spiritual and ecclesiastic matters, a number of prolific intellectuals, authors and politicians have been attracted by the Society and its integrist cause.[97]

The origins of the SSPX extend back to the late 1960s.[98] Its founder Archbishop Marcel Lefebvre, born in France in 1905, was the first archbishop of Dakar in 1947 and superior general of the congregation of Holy Ghost Fathers from 1962 to 1968. In 1969, he came to Switzerland to direct a priest seminary in Fribourg.[99] During the Second Vatican Council from 1962 to 1965, Lefebvre gained prominence as a fierce critic of the reforms that the majority of the Council members were ready to reach agreement on, namely the idea of ecumenism and of tolerance in a pluralist world of religions. In 1970, Lefebvre moved the seminary from Fribourg to Ecône (VS) and created the SSPX, which very shortly thereafter received canonical approval from François Charrière, bishop of Lausanne, Geneva and Fribourg. In the years that followed, Lefebvre ordained priests in defiance of the orders of the Vatican and continued to celebrate the traditional Latin mass. In 1982, he stepped down as superior general of the SSPX and handed its direction over to the German abbot Franz Schmidberger, who was in turn succeeded by the Swiss Bernard Fellay, in 1994. When Lefebvre ordained four bishops in June 1988, the Vatican reacted by excommunicating Lefebvre, the ordained bishops and all the Catholics who followed the SSPX.

While the headquarters of the SSPX were located in Menzingen (ZG), the priest seminary in Ecône in the canton of Valais was considered to be its spiritual and religious centre and served as a site of pilgrimage for international integrism. In 2002, the Society had more than 650 members, numbering 401 priests, as well as 132 branches, 600 chapels and more than forty schools in over twenty countries.[100] Lefebvre's movement enjoyed its greatest support in France, where estimates placed the number of faithful at around one hundred thousand. In Switzerland, the number of faithful was estimated at ten thousand.[101] The SSPX has published bulletins and journals in various languages in a number of countries. In France, it was represented by the bimonthly journal *Fideliter*. Since 1978, the congregation has published the monthly bulletin *Mitteilungsblatt der Priesterbruderschaft St. Pius für den deutschen Sprachraum* (Newsletter of the Priestly Society of Saint Pius X for the German-Speaking Language Area), for its readership in German-speaking countries, including the German-speaking part of Switzerland,

According to Lefebvre's declaration of 1974, the SSPX refuses 'to follow the Rome of neo-modernist and neo-protestant tendencies which were clearly evident in the Second Vatican Council, and after the Council, in all the reforms which issued from it'.[102] While the conflict with Rome mainly concerned doctrinal and liturgical questions, some argued that Lefebvre's intransigent stance had primarily political origins and was fuelled by concerns that the clergy was losing its influence in society and among the faithful.[103] The schism between the Catholic Church and Lefebvre's congregation caused a split within the integrist movement. A large number of clerical leaders and prominent faithful refused to follow the rupture with Rome. For example, Bernard Antony and Jean Madiran distanced themselves from Lefebvre and continued with their own, traditionalist criticism of the Catholic Church.[104]

While the goals of the SSPX were of a religious nature and primarily targeted Rome's authority, its leader, Marcel Lefebvre, has been very critical of modern democracy and has also defended exclusionist and xenophobic views.[105] In 1989, for example, he harshly criticised Muslim immigration, arguing that it would be better for Muslims if they returned home. One year later, a French court convicted Lefebvre on charges of defamation of the Muslim community for this statement.[106] Although the SSPX never engaged directly in the activities of the National Front in France, Lefebvre expressed his support for the party when he declared in a 1985 interview with the daily paper *Présent*, that 'insofar as Mr Jean-Marie Le Pen defends God's laws, the Decalogue, which should, in principle, guide the people and form the basis of all societies, one can only encourage him and agree with him'.[107] In the same interview, Lefebvre also said that 'the ideas of Jean-Marie Le Pen – except, perhaps, those concerned with religious freedom ... – are in conformance with the moral code and doctrine of the Church'.[108] Moreover, Lefebvre showed his sympathy for authoritarian regimes on various occasions, namely, the dictatorships of Franco in Spain and of Salazar in Portugal.[109]

In a 1993 interview with the Swiss weekly *Das Magazin*, Franz Schmidberger, Lefebvre's successor as superior general, took strong positions on a number of political and social issues. According to the journalist who conducted the interview, Schmidberger criticised Switzerland's existing policy on asylum and demanded that the borders be closed to stop the flood of foreigners. Schmidberger further held that the Swiss must remain Swiss, that one had to accept that people are different and that this difference must be preserved because mixing would only produce bad results. As the article further reveals, the superior general maintained that it was necessary to stop the inundation and infiltration of Islam. Finally, Schmidberger also complained that what was happening today with abortion was worse than Hitler's completely horrifying acts in the concentration camps.[110] Schmidberger's interview in a Swiss mainstream magazine shows that with their traditionalist and exclusionist ideas, leading SSPX members were not only addressing a rather closed circle of faithful adherents who were dedicated to the cause of integrism, but a larger public as well. In addition, the significance of such a large, globally acting religious movement as the SSPX lies in the fact that it was able to build up an organisational network and cultural-religious exchange at the transnational level.

The Canton of Valais: Stronghold of the Political Wing of Integrism

To date, the most significant political wing of the integrist movement has emerged in the canton of Valais, traditionally a stronghold of conservative Catholicism in Switzerland. Since the early days, Marcel Lefebvre and the Priestly Society of Saint Pius X received support from prominent political figures in the canton, namely senior members of the CVP.[111] These included Roger Lovey, Guy Genoud and René Berthod, all of whom showed great admiration for the integrist cause. Roger Lovey, a friend of Bernard Antony, was general secretary of the CVP in the canton of Valais and a district attorney from 1977 to 1989. Lovey was recognised by Michel de Preux as the most renowned representative of Catholic traditionalists in the canton of Valais.[112] Guy Genoud was a member of the cantonal government from 1969 to 1985 and a representative of the canton of Valais in the Council of States from 1975 to 1987. René Berthod, teacher, district prefect and a contributor to regional newspapers, declared that he saw Lefebvre as a pivotal figure and that he had enormous veneration for him as a bishop who did his duty.[113] Roger Bonvin, Federal Councillor from 1962 to 1973, was another prominent CVP member who supported Lefebvre's integrist congregation. In 1970, Bonvin, Genoud and Lovey had helped Lefebvre to establish his seminary in Ecône by providing the necessary premises. In 1975, they were also among the signatories of a letter to Pope Paul VI, demanding reconciliation between the Vatican and Lefebvre's congregation.

In 1981, Roger Lovey, Guy Genoud and René Berthod were involved in the creation of the group called Renewal of the Rhône (*Renouveau rhodanien*), which had several hundred members in 1985. As stated by the group, it did not intend to engage in party politics but would instead seek to appeal to people who were concerned about the future of their children and their homeland.[114] The group received great public attention when it invited Jean-Marie Le Pen to deliver a speech in the town of Sion in November 1984. The public event included a talk by Bernard Antony and was attended by close to a thousand people.[115] In his address, Le Pen mainly focused on issues of family values, immigration and national patrimony, arguing that the Europe of today should be built around the vital cells of family and fatherland. His speech was published in its entirety by the regional daily paper *Le Nouvelliste et*

Feuille d'Avis du Valais.[116] The only French-language daily paper in the canton of Valais, this had a circulation of forty-two thousand and, according to Isabelle Raboud, has given followers of the integrist movement the opportunity to express their views since the early 1970s.[117] In his introduction to Le Pen's text, the paper's director noted that he personally agreed with the FN leader and that Le Pen was saying today what he himself had been writing for the last thirty-six years.[118]

The Valais Conservative and Liberal Movement (*Mouvement conservateur et libéral valaisan* – MCLV) was created in February 1985, just three months after Le Pen's public appearance. Once again, Roger Lovey, Guy Genoud and René Berthod were among its founding members. Since the group was more oriented towards party politics, it sought to address issues that would complement the culturally active Renewal of the Rhône.[119] The group's aim was to establish a dissident right-wing group within the CVP, which was alleged to have drifted to the left. The leading members were committed to Lefebvre's integrism and consequently maintained that they rejected the decrees of the Second Vatican Council, which, in their view, would represent a theological justification of human rights.[120] In the end, the group had little political or public significance and disappeared following the death of Guy Genoud in 1987.[121]

In 1995, the canton of Valais witnessed the emergence of another group associated with the integrist movement: the Valais Christian Conservative Movement (*Mouvement chrétien-conservateur valaisan* – MCCV). The two founders were Paul Germanier, a former school director, and René Berthod, who gained prominence in 1994 with his harsh attacks against the anti-racism law. As noted by Eugenio D'Alessio, Germanier and Berthod were greatly inspired by *Lepénisme* and Maurrassian thought and are 'both hardened militants of the Ecône school', while the MCCV group 'serves as a sort of political manifestation of their religious pursuits'.[122] The group appeared to represent the resurgence of the defunct MCLV. It was better organised this time around and succeeded in attracting one hundred and ninety members and more than four hundred sympathisers.[123] According to the MCCV president Paul Germanier, the most urgent issues of our time were immigration, the increase in crime and the liberalisation of abortion.[124] Faced with these problems, the group intended, as the MCCV statutes note, to reinforce the respect for natural order and Christian principles in public life.[125] While the group's program greatly resembled the political agenda of the Swiss radical right-wing populist parties (strict neutrality in foreign policy, restriction of immigration, economic neoliberalism and anti-statist demands), it also emphasised the importance of family policies and the struggle against abortion.[126]

When the CVP showed little interest in collaborating with the MCCV, the group attempted to work together with the newly emerging SVP cantonal section in the canton of Valais. As Paul Germanier stated, he met with Christoph Blocher for negotiations in 1997 and Blocher himself addressed a meeting of the MCCV in 1998.[127] Although a partnership agreement was concluded between the two groups, it appears that the cantonal SVP party subsequently distanced itself from the MCCV in the run-up to the 1999 National Council elections.[128] Since that time, the group has lost much of its importance and has disappeared from the political stage in the canton of Valais.

Journal Controverses: The Admirers of Lefebvre and Pétain

Journal Controverses was the most important publishing vehicle of the intellectual and political wing of integrism in francophone Switzerland.[129] It presented a compelling vision of the political and ideological realm of the intellectuals and authors devoted to Lefebvre's integrist movement. The paper also showed the close relationship that existed between Swiss and French integrism. Published from 1988 to 1997, *Journal Controverses* was professionally styled and written in sophisticated language. Between 1988 and 1995, the paper was published ten times per year and contained eight A3 format pages. During this period, the editor-in-chief was Eric Bertinat, a devotee of Marcel Lefebvre and a key figure in the attempts to combine activities of the New Right with party politics in the French-speaking part of Switzerland.[130] Bertinat, who was president of the Vigilance party from 1985 to 1988, shifted his sphere of activity in the 1990s to the CINS and the SVP and became party secretary of the cantonal SVP section of Geneva in 2002.[131] After 1995, *Journal Controverses* was released monthly, in a slightly smaller format and with the number of pages gradually increasing to twenty-four. In July 1995, Olivier Rouot became the new editor-in-chief.

The paper also published two supplements, *Les cahiers du journal Controverses* (The Notebooks of Journal Controverses; 1991–1994) and *Carnets spirituels* (Spiritual Notebooks; since 1995), both of which mainly dealt with religious and spiritual themes. *Journal Controverses* was affiliated with the integrist distribution venture *Tradiffusion*, co-founded by Eric Bertinat in 1989. It offered books written by well-known authors of the French extreme right, such as Henry Coston and François Brigneau.[132] Emmanuel Allot, alias François Brigneau, is considered one of the most prolific activists and authors of the French extreme right in the postwar era. He was associated with a large number of periodicals, including *Rivarol, Minute, Présent* and *National Hebdo*.[133] When *Journal Controverses* set up a stand at the Geneva international book fair in 1989, Brigneau came to autograph his writings.[134]

In addition to many articles from clergymen, contributions to *Journal Controverses* were written by authors associated with the New Right in the French-speaking part of Switzerland, including Eric Werner, Jean-Philippe Chenaux and René Berthod, who wrote under his alias Rembarre. Mary Meissner, NA member and editor of the NA party paper *peuple + patrie*, contributed a number of articles in the early 1990s. *Journal Controverses* also published articles written by prominent members of the French New Right and extreme right:[135] Pierre de Villemarest, an author in the journal *Défense de l'Occident* in the 1960s; Serge de Beketch, editing director of the weekly *Minute*, a central newspaper of France's radical right; Suzanne Labin, contributor to *Militant* and an anti-communist propagandist well-known in Switzerland;[136] and Yves Chiron, author of an apologetic biography on Charles Maurras.[137] The Swiss paper also reprinted caricatures from the French periodicals *Rivarol* and *Présent*.[138]

Journal Controverses contained ongoing reports on developments in the integrist and traditionalist movement in France. It published long articles on the Catholic City, for example, and Bernard Antony's Centre Henri and André Charlier.[139] In 1990, the editorial staff released a front-page letter to Jean Madiran expressing deep disappointment that Madiran had turned away from Lefebvre after the Vatican declared the schism in 1988. The open letter also included a lengthy quotation from a critical remark that Charles Maurras had made to Madiran in 1948. It was therefore no surprise that the paper's editor-in-chief acknowledged Maurras as an important intellectual point of reference.[140] In 1991, E.B. [Eric Bertinat] wrote that Maurras' project of nationalist politics had retained its topicality today because the main problem was still being 'caused by the global politics of the big Judeo-Masonic and communist internationals'.[141] Following this line, *Journal Controverses* published a large number of articles denouncing globalisation and supranational organisations, such as the UN and European Union. They also warned of growing Jewish and Freemason influence. The paper also demonstrated a pronounced anti-Jewish orientation by publishing an article that was very critical of the agreement between the Vatican and Israel. The article was packed with anti-Judaist statements and citations taken from the bible.[142]

It was also E.B. [Eric Bertinat] who underscored the counter-revolutionary line of the paper by writing a front-page article on the bicentenary celebrations in France in 1989. Among other claims, he argued that the French Revolution had been incited by Freemasons and that its aim was primarily anti-Christian. In the same article, E.B. [Eric Bertinat] enthusiastically endorsed the monthly publication *L'Anti-89* and in particular its editor-in-chief, Francois Brigneau, when he wrote: 'I am overwhelmed every time I read this fellow's powerful writing'.[143] In 1991, on the fortieth anniversary of Marshal Pétain's death, the paper published a veritable hymn of praise written by a clergyman in honour of the Vichy leader. Pétain was presented as an 'authentic head of State devoted to the service of the common good', who became a 'victim of Freemasonry and communism'. The article further emphasised that Pétain's message of adherence to Christian and traditional values of work, family, fatherland and church fully retained its validity and that Pétain should therefore not be seen as a martyr of the past but of the future.[144]

A significant number of articles dealt with issues related to Swiss politics. For example, with regard to the asylum issue, while admitting that the number of asylum seekers was relatively small compared to the total number of foreigners living in Switzerland, the paper stated that the main problem was largely due to the inability of asylum seekers to assimilate because of their cultural origins.[145] In 1992, the editorial board expressed a fierce rejection of Switzerland's membership of the EEA, arguing that the agreement symbolised the growing importance of secularism, materialism and socialism.[146] The paper consequently paid tribute to Christoph Blocher and his anti-European campaign. Blocher was presented as a comrade who shared the same views and was combating European integration which sought 'to erase all distinctive national characteristics in the name of economic effectiveness and the construction of a new, egalitarian and supposedly peaceful world order'.[147]

The editors of the paper were also fundamentally opposed to the anti-racism law and published a number of articles denouncing the government's proposal as another step in the anti-Swiss campaign. One of these articles complained about the difficulties that publications such as *Rivarol, Minute* and *Présent* had to face after the new anti-racist law had been implemented in France in 1990. Eric Werner for his part compared the proposed Swiss anti-racist law to certain criminal laws which had been implemented during National Socialism to punish those with convictions and ideals.[148]

This series of engagements in political debates by *Journal Controverses* evocatively shows the close links that are to be found in integrism between the spheres of religious beliefs and politics. Most importantly, the publication promoted views that combined authoritarian and anti-modernist thought characteristic of integrism with conspiracist and anti-Judaist ideas. *Journal Controverses* also gives evidence of a consolidated Swiss integrist movement that was interested in domestic politics and yet also had close relations with France, in which Charles Maurras, Marshal Pétain and Jean Marie Le Pen were the figures most frequently referenced.

The Nouvelle droite: Importing the French Legacy

The *Nouvelle droite* in France and other European countries has made the greatest contribution to the renewal and rejuvenation of radical-right thinking that has taken place since the 1970s. Arguably, in a strategic and intellectual sense, the *Nouvelle droite* represents the most innovative current of the New Right. By focusing on the domains of cultural politics and intellectual debates, its strategy is to influence the minds and the thinking of the people, thereby countering the alleged dominance of left-wing ideas. The *Nouvelle droite's* aim is to gain ideological and political influence by achieving cultural and intellectual hegemony, not through elections and party politics. The ideology of the *Nouvelle droite* is far from homogenous. Instead, it combines various currents of thought and creates new syntheses of different ideological legacies. References are made to counter-revolutionary, traditionalist and national-revolutionary ideas and inspiration is taken from authors associated with the Conservative Revolution, fascism and neo-paganism.[149]

One of the central tenets of *Nouvelle droite* thinking is a rejection of Judeo-Christianity and a critique of monotheism as an alleged reason for the significance that totalitarianism has had in world history. Judeo-Christian traditions are also made responsible for the predominance of egalitarianism and the decadence of European civilisation. In this way, the *Nouvelle droite* developed an agenda in which a return to the original European identity, purified of egalitarian and monotheistic elements, becomes the focus of intellectual and historical interest. This also includes the demand for a return to paganism and polytheism and the quest to uncover the rituals and roots of ancient Europe.[150] As a result, the *Nouvelle droite* invests a great deal in the study of Indo-European culture and history. From the early 1970s, a number of scholars associated with France's *Nouvelle droite* have been involved in presenting archaeological, anthropological and linguistic works on Indo-European origins, often by employing – and distorting – the work of the renowned historian of religion, Georges Dumézil.[151]

The *Nouvelle droite* also finds great inspiration in the writings of the Italian author and philosopher Julius Evola (1898–1974).[152] Referred to as 'our Marcuse, but only better' by Giorgio Almirante, the first leader of the Italian Social Movement, Evola was devoted to Italian fascism even though he never joined the Fascist Party.[153] Evola's racism was marked by cultural rather than biological characteristics and his 1941 book *Sintesi di dottrina della razza* (Synthesis of the Doctrine of Race) became fascism's official statement of 'spiritualist' racism.[154] Moreover, his 'synthesis of metaphysical idealism, primitive mythologies, and what he called a "metaphysics of history"' serves as a point of reference to many intellectuals of the *Nouvelle droite*.[155] They therefore like to take Evola's pagan views, his mission to rejuvenate European roots and culture and his rejection of Judeo-Christianism and egalitarianism as intellectual precursors to their own thinking.[156] As research into the *Nouvelle droite* has emphasised, replacing the idea of 'race' with the concept of culture represents a resourceful intellectual move on the part of theorists affiliated with the *Nouvelle droite*. By claiming that every cultural group has the right to search for its roots and to be different, followers of the *Nouvelle droite* emphasise the primacy of cultural identity and advocate cultural-differentialist and ethnopluralist concepts.[157] They have therefore contributed to the fact that 'the move from a discourse of race to one of culture and the embrace of a non-hierarchical, differentialist racism proved a crucial strategy in rehabilitating a right-wing discourse of ethnopolitics that had long been discredited'.[158]

Organisationally, the *Nouvelle droite* started off in France in 1968 in the form of the Group for the Research and Study of European Civilisation (GRECE), which became the most important group promoting the thought of the *Nouvelle droite*.[159] Founded by intellectuals, writers and students, GRECE adopted a discursively and culturally oriented strategy and was particularly engaged in organising seminars, workshops and conferences as well as publishing the two well-known periodicals *Éléments* and *Nouvelle École*.[160] Leading figures of the GRECE also became increasingly involved in party politics, mainly by joining the National Front at a very high level. In the late 1970s and early 1980s, at the peak of its public resonance, GRECE could count on more than three thousand members and had gained some influence in French public life, especially by placing devoted followers onto the editorial boards of mainstream right-wing journals such as *Le Figaro Magazine*.[161] Among its leading members, Alain de Benoist is perhaps considered the most influential intellectual of the European New Right. Born in 1943, de Benoist started his career as a theorist and author in France's extreme-right and nationalist subculture of the 1960s. He was a founding member of GRECE and published a large number of books, articles and essays, many of which were translated into other languages. In 1978, he received the French Academy award for literature, for his book *Vue de droite* (Seen from the Right).[162] Since the 1980s, de Benoist has significantly expanded his contacts with New Right strands in other countries, particularly in Germany, Russia, Italy, Belgium, the United States and Switzerland.[163]

In the French-speaking part of Switzerland, the *Nouvelle droite* began its activities in the early 1980s.[164] Former members of national-revolutionary groups associated with the extreme right (see chapter 8) shifted towards a more discursive and culturally oriented strategy and laid the foundation for a lively intellectual scene. For Swiss followers, the *Nouvelle droite* in France served as a model and a close relationship was developed with French theorists and authors. As the Swiss *Nouvelle droite* also sought to copy the strategy of metapolitics developed by the French *Nouvelle droite*, its activities were concentrated on cultural, literary and academic subjects. A small group of devoted followers organised meetings and cultural events and established a network including circles and bookstores, as well as a publishing house and mail order service. In keeping with its conception of itself as an elite group, the organised events only sought to appeal to a small audience. On the other hand, the various kinds of publications arguably reached a larger circle of people, although it is difficult to make a precise estimate of their circulation. Some protagonists of the Swiss *Nouvelle droite* have also shown an interest in party politics and have run for public office on the ticket of radical right-wing populist parties. Moreover, since its beginnings, the *Nouvelle droite* has been associated with groups, publications and propagandists of the extreme right and has attracted adherents to negationism and neo-fascism. On the other hand, the cultural and literary activities of the *Nouvelle droite* have also appealed to conservative intellectuals.

Compared to its French counterpart, the Swiss *Nouvelle droite* has produced little in terms of theoretical and conceptual work. There were almost no Swiss theorists or authors who were acknowledged by the *Nouvelle droite* in Europe. It appears that the Swiss *Nouvelle droite* confined itself to publishing and distributing the writings of authors from other countries and preferred to take on the role of receptive audience and readership. As a result, the *Nouvelle droite* in the French-speaking part of Switzerland was exposed to a diversity of ideological influences and inspirations, leading to a worldview that was far from coherent and homogeneous.

The New Forces Circle: A First Attempt at Intellectualisation

Founded in 1979, New Forces (*Forces nouvelles*) stands as the first attempt in the French-speaking region of Switzerland to launch an intellectual circle in direct imitation of France's *Nouvelle droite*.[165] The goal was to create an elitist circle attracting only the best members, and accordingly the membership fee was extremely high.[166] While there are no reports on the public activities that New Forces engaged in, its significance lies in the fact that it was the first time a Swiss circle had explicitly taken the French *Nouvelle Droite* as a model and looked to Alain de Benoist for intellectual inspiration.

New Forces was also the first group created by Pascal Junod, who built an exemplary career in the Swiss *Nouvelle droite*. Junod, a Geneva-based lawyer, was involved in most of the activities of the *Nouvelle droite* during the 1980s and 1990s. As early as 1976, at the age of nineteen, Junod took part in a show on Swiss French-language TV presenting the group Culture and Liberty Circle, which was associated with the national-revolutionary movement (see chapter 8).[167] Junod was also a member of GRECE and a Swiss correspondent for the journal *Nouvelle École*.[168] *Elemente*, a magazine of the German *Nouvelle droite*, listed Junod as a contributor in its 1985–86 issue and introduced him as one of the most important representatives of the 'New Culture' in Switzerland.[169] Moreover, in the mid 1980s, he sat on the editorial committee of the Belgian journal *Orientations*, which was directed by Robert Steuckers, a key figure of the Belgian *Nouvelle droite*.[170] In the late 1990s, Junod became more and more involved in party politics. He was appointed party secretary of the revived cantonal SVP section of Geneva. However, his political career was brought to an abrupt end as he made ready to run for the SVP in the 1999 National Council elections. After some initial hesitation and under strong pressure from the media, which emphasised Junod's alleged links to the extreme right, the national SVP called for him to leave the party in September 1999. In December, Junod resigned from the SVP.[171]

New Forces presented an ideologically sophisticated program in the form of both a ten-page manifesto and a two-page document of political principles.[172] In the manifesto, the circle presented itself as representing the emerging *Nouvelle droite* in the French-speaking part of Switzerland. Quoting Alain de Benoist, the manifesto declared that 'in a period when everyone (or almost everyone) describes themselves as being on the left, "being on the right" is still the best way to be elsewhere'.[173] The circle's ideology was very much marked by national-revolutionary thought and, in particular, solidarist conceptions of society. Thus, the New Forces' manifesto noted that a society should be built on naturally defined collectivities such as family, professional grouping and local community. These 'organs of the Nation' would make it possible to establish 'a new, authentic democracy: the organic democracy'.[174]

According to the manifesto, a renewed democratic order of this nature would provide a distinct contrast to the current form of democracy run by 'sclerotic parties with their stupid elections'.[175] In the manifesto, it was further argued that inegalitarian order should be seen as the core principle of all human and social relations and that one should support the inequality of all beings because this enriches novelty and quality. The manifesto also endorsed ethological research as a science which would provide convincing proof that all communities were determined by the three bio-political principles of hierarchy, territory and perpetuation. Referring to the particular importance of the so-called 'principle of perpetuation,' the manifesto stated that it was essential for all communities to pass on their genetic and cultural inheritance to ensure their survival.[176] It was also argued that the different European regions and ethnic groups represented the natural communities of Europe, a Europe which was intended to be the place of rebirth for the entire occidental civilisation, which – so went the claim – still dominated the world of today 'through its genius'.[177] As the manifesto shows, New Forces sought to underline its attraction to the *Nouvelle droite* in France and to adapt its sophisticated rhetoric, but fundamentally, it was principally influenced by an extreme right ideology that drew upon biologist ideas and national-revolutionary traditions.

Thule Circle: Its Enduring Role as a Supplier of Publications

The Geneva-based Thule Circle (*Cercle Thulé*) was created in 1983 and was directed by Pascal Junod.[178] Also operating under the name of the National Centre of European Thought (*Centre national de la pensée européenne*), the circle liked to present itself as part of a Europe-wide network of New Right think tanks, including GRECE in France and the Thule Seminar (*Thule-Seminar*) in Germany. Consequently, the German Thule Seminar listed the Thule Circle as its Swiss branch.[179] In 1980, Pierre Krebs had founded the Thule Seminar as the German counterpart to GRECE in France. He wanted to establish an elitist circle which would promote the ideas and concepts of the French *Nouvelle droite* in Germany. However, the circle largely failed to gain significant notice in intellectual debates and attracted only a few followers among the German New Right.[180] In Germanic mythology, the name 'Thule' refers to a mystical island in the North Sea. It also alluded to the Thule Society (*Thule-Gesellschaft*), which was founded in 1918 as a neo-Germanic secret society and attracted figures such as Alfred Rosenberg, Rudolf Hess and Hans Frank, who later played a key role in the National Socialist regime.[181]

According to Claude Cantini, the Thule Circle had close links with the Fribourg-based publisher Les Trois Nornes, operated by the Swiss historian Jean-François Mayer in the 1980s.[182] In Lyon, in 1976 and 1977, Mayer was responsible for the distribution of the neo-fascist periodicals *Défense de l'Occident* and *Horizons européens* (European Horizons), the latter primarily inspired by the ideas of Julius Evola.[183] In the following year, Mayer was in charge, again in Lyon, of the Odinist publication *Skuld*. He joined the NOS in 1979 after returning to Switzerland. In 1986, he wrote a book review for GRECE's literary bulletin *Panorama des idées actuelles* (Panorama of Current Ideas). In 1991, Mayer resigned from the scientific board of the controversial Study Centre on New Religions (*Centre d'études sur les nouvelles religions* – CESNUR) which was known for its association with members of the New Right. In the 1990s, Mayer became a prolific academic expert on new religions, in particular, on the issue of sects.

The main goal of the Thule Circle was to supply adherents of the *Nouvelle droite* in the French-speaking part in Switzerland with the literature and periodicals that were circulating among the continental European New Right, and its French branch in particular. The wide selection of publications promoted by the circle reflected the variety in intellectual and historical influences which characterised the *Nouvelle droite* in most European countries. However, the Thule Circle showed particular interest in those factions of the New Right who were committed to reviving the neo-pagan and Indo-European legacy. By referring to Celtic legacies, the circle emphasised the importance of tracing back regional and local identities in order to strengthen European identity. This also corresponded to the goals of the circle's German counterpart, the Thule Seminar: when it launched the magazine *Elemente* in 1986, the Thule Seminar declared that the publication's goal was to attack the so-called transatlantic community of values and to develop a pagan and metaphysical alternative to Judeo-Christianity.[184]

The Thule Circle established a large mail order service and issued a promotional bulletin at irregular intervals throughout the 1980s and 1990s.[185] The bulletin contained annotated lists of books, brochures, periodicals, comics and recordings. The mail order service was intended to appeal to a variety of different sections of the New Right audience in the French-speaking regions of Switzerland, each of which was interested in specific cultural, historical and intellectual themes. The list of offered publications included writings of key contemporary and classic authors of the New Right and the extreme right, among them Maurice Barrès, Léon Degrelle, Julius Evola, Alain de Benoist, Guillaume Faye, Giorgio Freda, Hans F. K. Günther, David Irving, Jean-Gilles Malliarakis, Charles Maurras, Alfred Rosenberg, Saint-Loup and Georges Sorel. The bulletin also promoted authors who were associated with the German Conservative Revolution and whose books had been translated into French: Ernst Jünger, Carl Schmitt, Oswald Spengler, Arthur Moeller van den Bruck and Ernst Niekisch. Moreover, the bulletin offered current and back issues of *Nouvelle École*, *Éléments*, *Études et Recherches*, *Krisis*, *Vouloir* and *Orientations*, all publications connected with the French or Belgian *Nouvelle droite*. The bulletin also promoted national-revolutionary periodicals such as *Troisième voie*, *Totalité* and *Partisan*, as well as neo-pagan magazines such as *Combat païen* and *Sol invictus*.[186]

In addition to its distribution activities, the Thule Circle organised two major cultural meetings in the late 1980s which demonstrated that the Swiss *Nouvelle droite* was very well-connected with its counterparts in Europe. In the summers of 1987 and 1988, in the small village of Vaulion (VD), the circle held what they called a 'European folk feast Lugnasad' – a name which refers to the Celtic celebration of the sun-god Lug.[187] Both events were attended by several hundred people, who came from all points across Europe and represented a wide spectrum of organisations and periodicals associated with both the New Right and the extreme right.[188] As is shown by the program of the 1988 Lugnasad event, the cultural festivities were greatly influenced by pagan and Celtic traditions, including a fire ceremony in the closing evening.[189]

While the first Lugnasad event in 1987 went almost unnoticed by the general public, the media gave extensive coverage to the second meeting in 1988, which eventually produced a public outrage.[190] Following this fierce public reaction, the Thule Circle withdrew from organising larger gatherings and essentially confined itself to distributing publications and organising lectures with speakers associated with the French *Nouvelle droite*. For example, in 1996, the Thule Circle organised a lecture with Jean-Marc Vinvenza, publishing director of the monthly *Volonté futuriste* (Futurist Will) and expert in the history of Italian futurism.[191] This was supposed to ensure that supporters and sympathisers of the New Right were able to follow the intellectual and literary developments taking place in the publishing world of the continental European New Right, or more precisely, of the *Nouvelle droite* in francophone countries.

Proudhon Circle and European Synergies: An Intellectual and Academic Strategy

The Proudhon Circle (*Cercle Proudhon*) was founded in 1984 and was based in Geneva. Again, Pascal Junod played a central role.[192] According to information given by a leading member, the circle had five hundred associates in the late 1980s, a number which was almost certainly an overestimate.[193] The Proudhon Circle took GRECE as a model and primarily sought to engage in intellectual debates in the academic world. The circle therefore mainly organised conferences and lectures. It also had links to the extreme right, namely, the negationist faction (see chapter 8).[194] The circle's name referred to the French Proudhon Circle which was founded in 1911 by Georges Valois, a leading member of French Action and an influential forerunner of French fascism. The circle unified French revolutionary-syndicalists with the nationalists of Charles Maurras' French Action. Valois contributed greatly to the dissemination of Pierre-Joseph Proudhon's anarcho-syndicalist ideas and was responsible for Proudhon's thought finding its way into the nationalist movement at the time.[195]

Inspired by the thinking of Julius Evola, the Swiss Proudhon Circle attempted to set up what it called a silent resistance in the form of a small elite group designed to provide new relationships and values for society. In a programmatic text, the circle argued that the modern world had become a monstrous anomaly and that the moment had come to set in place the transcendent foundations of a new spiritual island and to apply the metapolitical principles of a cultural rebirth. It would therefore be necessary to enter into total combat against all the manifest or occult forces determined to finish the process they had started long ago: the complete uprooting of Europe, the Europe they hoped to consign to the museum of history. The Indo-European legacy, with its principle of engaging in spiritual, political and cultural combat, would provide an appropriate framework for this purpose and help to strengthen the common European identity. According to the circle, Switzerland, with its Celtic history and federalist structure, could play an important model role in this combat by supporting efforts to reveal the traditions and roots of European culture.[196]

In the second half of the 1980s, the Proudhon Circle organised a number of high-profile conferences and lectures at the University of Geneva. In doing so, the organisers sought to appeal not only to their own followers but also to a larger academic public. On several occasions, the circle succeeded in bringing well-known New Right theorists and authors to Geneva. These events were also vivid examples of the increased interest that key figures of the European New Right, particularly its *Nouvelle droite* current, had for the insurgent *Nouvelle droite* in Switzerland. In March 1985, the Circle invited a number of prominent theorists of the *Nouvelle droite* to the conference entitled '*Europe: Le droit à l'identité*' (Europe: The Right to Identity). The invited speakers included the four leading GRECE members, Alain de Benoist, Guillaume Faye, Pierre Vial and Pierre Brader; as well as Robert Steuckers, publisher of the Belgian journals *Orientations* and *Vouloir;* Michael Walker, publisher of the British magazine *The Scorpion;* Marco Tarchi, leading figure of the Italian New Right; and Jean-Gilles Malliarakis, national-revolutionary leader and theorist.[197] In a public debate on the 'Usefulness of the State' held in November 1985 at the University of Geneva, Alain de Benoist confronted the Swiss sociologist Jean Ziegler, who was renowned for his commitment to third world liberation movements.[198]

In March 1988, a conference on the topic of '*Héritages indo-européens*' (Indo-European Heritages) was attended by more than a hundred people. Jean Haudry, Jean-Paul Allard, Jean Varenne and Pierre Vial were among the speakers invited to the Geneva conference.[199] Haudry was a member of the National Front's scientific council and Allard chaired the dissertation committee at the University of Nantes, which had approved Henri Roques's negationist dissertation in 1983 (see chapter 8). Both were affiliated with the Institute of Indo-European Studies (*Institut d'études indo-européennes*) at University Lyon-III, whose faculty members have made considerable contributions to the French *Nouvelle droite*'s efforts to use the Indo-European legacy for its own purposes.[200]

After the press had begun to expose the presence of the *Nouvelle droite* at the University of Geneva, the Proudhon Circle was forced to move its activities outside the campus in the 1990s.[201] Despite the somewhat unfriendly public environment in Geneva, the circle continued to bring key figures of the French *Nouvelle droite* to the French-speaking part of Switzerland, giving them the opportunity to talk about current intellectual and political debates in France. In February 1997, the circle invited Bernard Notin, economics professor at University Lyon-III and member of the National Front scientific council, to talk on the issue of freedom of speech.[202] In 1990, Bernard Notin had come under fierce criticism because of the negationist theses he had presented in an article that was published in a renowned journal of economic science.[203] Another speaker was Pierre Vial, who addressed the subject '*France: où va la droite nationale?*' (France: Where Is the National Right Going?) in February 1999.[204] Pierre Vial, former secretary of GRECE, joined the National Front in 1988, where he entered the political bureau in 1994.[205] As a final example, it is worth noting the May 1999 lecture by the French author Roger Garaudy (see chapter 8), who became notorious for his 1995 negationist book *Mythes fondateurs de la politique israélienne* (The Founding Myths of Israeli Politics).[206]

In the late 1990s, a Swiss section of European Synergies (*Synergies européennes*) appeared in the French-speaking part of Switzerland in close association with the Proudhon Circle.[207] European Synergies was founded in 1993 by Robert Steuckers, a prolific publisher and author of the Belgian *Nouvelle droite*. It aimed at setting up a European network of intellectual circles to defend national-revolutionary ideas. After disagreeing with Alain de Benoist concerning the ideological orientation that the *Nouvelle droite* and, more specifically, GRECE should take, Steuckers aimed at creating an intellectual movement. His strategy turned out to be fairly successful, since European Synergies established sections in a number of European countries, most significantly in Germany and Russia.[208]

For the centennial anniversary of Julius Evola, the Swiss section organised a conference at the University of Geneva in November 1998.[209] Although the conference was allegedly attended by only twenty people, the event demonstrated the following that Evola's work enjoyed in the francophone *Nouvelle Droite*. In fact, Swiss authors and publishers made significant contributions to the revival of Evola's thought that was brought about during the last three decades as a result of the publishing efforts of the European New Right. Among other things, in 1991, L'Age d'Homme (see below) published what was probably Evola's most influential book, *Rivolta contro il mondo moderno* (Revolt against the Modern World), originally published in Italian in 1934.[210] In this book, Evola basically denounces modernity and democracy as the consequences of decadency. The new edition included a 24-page afterword by Alain de Benoist, who also presented a comprehensive French bibliography of Evola.[211] Moreover, Jean-François Mayer has written the afterword to the new French translation of Evola's *Masques et visages du spiritualisme contemporain* (Masks and Faces of Contemporary Spiritualism; originally published in 1932), which was published in 1991 by Éditions Pardès.[212]

These publications on Evola evocatively portray the close relationship that existed between the *Nouvelle droite* of Switzerland and France, a relationship that the Proudhon Circle has intensively cultivated since the 1980s by organising conferences and cultural events. It can be said that the academically and scholarly oriented activities of the Proudhon Circle served to supplement the Thule Circle's distribution of literature. The fact that Pascal Junod played a central role in both circles suggests a close collaboration and association among the followers of the *Nouvelle droite*. The primary aim of the Proudhon Circle, as well as the Swiss section of European Synergies, was to acquaint its supporters with key figures from the Europe's *Nouvelle droite*. In keeping with their conception of themselves as elite groups of intellectuals dedicated to the strategy of metapolitics, the circles only appealed to a small audience and exerted little influence outside the literary and academic world.

The Excalibur and Libre R. Bookstores: Difficulties in the Public Space

From the start of the early 1980s, the promotion and distribution of publications was one of the main activities of the *Nouvelle Droite* in the French-speaking regions of Switzerland. With mail order services, advertisements and bookstands at conferences and lecture events, it primarily addressed a closed circle of followers and sympathisers. However, the francophone *Nouvelle droite* also made attempts to stimulate the interest of a larger audience in the literature of the European New Right. A bookstand was set up at the annual international Geneva book fairs of 1988 and 1993 for this purpose. While the bookstand was sponsored by the Proudhon Circle in 1988, in 1993 it was run by a circle named the Hagal Cultural Circle (*Cercle culturel Hagal*), which also became involved with the *Excalibur* bookstore.[213] When the *Excalibur* bookstore opened in Geneva in December 1993, this strategy of targeting a wider audience reached a new level, with the *Nouvelle Droite* seeking to create a stable and publicly accessible base for the promotion and distribution of its literature.

Excalibur was established by the Association of the Friends of Robert Brasillach (see below) and the Hagal Cultural Circle.[214] *Excalibur* had previously been the name of GRECE's official bookstore in Paris at the end of the 1980s.[215] Once again, Pascal Junod acted as a driving force in setting up the new store.[216] *Excalibur* offered a large assortment of books and journals issued by the major New Right publishers in France, Belgium and Switzerland. It also offered a number of other items, including posters, records, CDs, videotapes, jewellery and badges. Moreover, *Excalibur* aimed to be a cultural centre where lectures and discussions could take place. For the December 1993 opening, *Excalibur* hosted, among others, Pierre Vial, Eric Delcroix, who has written in the French negationist journal *Annales d'histoire révisionniste* (Annals of Revisionist History), and Eric Werner, Swiss author and philosopher.[217] At the same time, however, the bookstore was also connected with the neighbouring store, *Eagle exportation*, which sold paramilitary items, such as knifes, handcuffs and army shirts. In April 1994, several newspapers reported on *Excalibur*, revealing its spatial proximity to a store offering extreme-right merchandise.[218] Pascal Junod publicly defended the bookstore and the selection of publications being offered.[219] However, a growing public movement forced the bookstore to close in April 1994.

Following the experience in Geneva, the establishment moved to the canton of Vaud in February 1995, to a bookstore called *Libre R* which was opened in the town of Montreux. *Libre R* took over the inventory of *Excalibur* and was closely affiliated to the Association of the Friends of Robert Brasillach. As the members newsletter of the Association expressed it, 'we hope that the climate in the canton of Vaud will be more favourable than the one in the town of Calvin'.[220] When the authorities confiscated Roger Garaudy's *Les mythes fondateurs de la politique israélienne* in the summer of 1996, the public's attention turned to the *Libre R* bookstore, since it had distributed copies of Garaudy's negationist book. The case for a violation of the anti-racism law was opened against Aldo Ferraglia, who was in charge of the bookstore.[221] Associated with the negationist scene since the 1980s, Ferraglia had disseminated negationist theses and promoted negationist literature in his capacity as editor of the advertising magazine *Bourse-Autos*, which occasionally had a print run of thirty thousand.[222] Based on a Federal Tribunal decision, the cantonal court of Vaud sentenced Ferraglia to twenty days' conditional imprisonment in 2000.[223]

The *Libre R* bookstore moved to other locations in the French-speaking regions of Switzerland; first to the town of Romont (FR) in 1997, then to the small village of Vuadens (FR) in the summer of 1999.[224] It therefore appears that the *Nouvelle droite* had little success in its efforts to establish a bookstore that could act as a stopping point for its followers, and perhaps also for a larger audience. If the first bookstore was launched in the major city of Geneva, the last one was located in a small country village, far from the intellectual centres of French-speaking Switzerland.

L'Age d'Homme: Contributions of a Renowned Publisher

In the publishing world of the *Nouvelle droite*, the Lausanne-based Swiss publisher L'Age d'Homme (The Age of Man) played a significant role which extended beyond the French-speaking regions of Switzerland. In fact, it not only acted as a distributor of various New Right publications in the French-speaking part of Switzerland, but also as a publisher of French writings addressed to the continental European New Right. Founded in 1966 by the Yugoslavian émigré Vladimir Dimitrijević, L'Age d'Homme also operated bookstores in Lausanne and Paris.[225] It is important to note, however, that the vast majority of books on the publisher's list are not works that were written by adherents of the New Right.[226] In the literary and academic world, L'Age d'Homme is recognised for its publication of contemporary literature and its translation of great works of Slavic literature, including those of writers such as Ivo Andrić, Aleksandr Pushkin and Aleksandar Tišma. On the other hand, the publishing venture and its director, Vladimir Dimitrijević, came under increasing public scrutiny in the 1990s for overtly taking the side of Serbian nationalism.[227]

Vladimir Dimitrijević was involved in the activities of the *Nouvelle droite* in France. For example, he was honorary president of the Association of the Friends of Pierre Gripari (*Association des amis de Pierre Gripari*).[228] The society was created in 1990 after the death of the well-known author of children's books, Pierre Gripari, a close friend of Dimitrijević. Gripari had been involved with France's *Nouvelle droite* since the 1970s.[229] Most of the adult books he wrote were published by L'Age d'Homme. Moreover, in 1991, Dimitrijević delivered a speech at the Summer University of the Centre Henri and André Charlier. In the same year, other speeches were delivered by several prominent figures of the French radical right, including the European MP of the National Front, Jean-Marie Le Chavallier, the editor of the traditionalist periodical *Présent*, Alain Sanders, and the two Catholic traditionalists, Jean Madiran and Gustave Thibon.[230] The reputation that Dimitrijević enjoyed among the French *Nouvelle droite* was reflected by the fact that he was invited to take part in the roundtable '*Rébellion et pensée unique*' (Rebellion and Unique Thought) at the 35th GRECE colloquium in Paris in January 2002.[231]

Launched in 1987, the annual journal *Politica Hermetica* is an illustrative example of the role played by Dimitrijević and L'Age d'Homme in the *Nouvelle droite*'s attempts to gain respectability in the academic world.[232] While the journal was published by L'Age d'Homme, Dimitrijević acted as its publishing director and Jean-François Mayer was the journal's Swiss correspondent.[233] The journal essentially dealt with the relationship between esoterism and politics and covered themes such as hermetism, Freemasonry, mysticism and occultism. It generally consisted of papers presented at the annual conference, which was usually held at the Sorbonne University in Paris. The list of authors and academics supporting the journal was quite varied. The renowned historian Victor Nguyen wrote the declaration of principles of the Association Politica Hermetica in 1984.[234] Distinguished scholars such as Emile Poulat, who was also a member of the journal's editorial board, Pierre-André Taguieff and Franco Ferraresi all contributed to *Politica Hermetica*.

On the other hand, the journal published articles authored by prominent intellectuals of the *Nouvelle droite*, including Alain de Benoist, Alexandre Douguine, a key figure of the Russian *Nouvelle droite*, and Philippe Baillet, a contributor to *Nouvelle École* and translator of Evola's writings. Moreover, the journal attached great interest to the thought of Evola. For this reason, some authors pursued an intellectual and political rehabilitation of Evola, while seeking to minimise the influence that Evola's work had on the militant extreme right. For example, the first issue of *Politica Hermetica* included a controversial debate between Franco Ferraresi, an expert on Italian neo-fascism, and others who made an attempt to play down Evola's significance for the postwar extreme right.[235] In the 1998 issue, Christophe Boutin presented a short historical survey of French and Italian intellectual currents that had been inspired by Evola's thinking.[236] In the same issue, Philippe Baillet described the reception of Evola's work in France's publishing world and emphasised the important role of the publishing house Éditions Pardès and the journal *Totalité*, both of which were directly linked with the French *Nouvelle droite*.[237]

L'Age d'Homme also played the role of supplier for the *Nouvelle droite* by publishing a number of books written by authors closely associated with the *Nouvelle droite*. For example, Thomas Molnar published a fierce critique of the United States in 1991, which bore the title *L'Américanologie*.[238] Molnar had contributed to the neo-fascist periodical *Défense de l'Occident* until 1982 and was associated with both the integrist movement and the *Nouvelle droite* in France.[239] In recent years L'Age d'Homme has also published two books written by Alain de Benoist.[240]

So far, the most important contribution by the Swiss publisher to the body of literature of the *Nouvelle Droite* was the edited volume *Aux sources de la droite* (To the Origins of the Right) in 2000. The book was laid out as a kind of encyclopaedia, with articles dealing with the relationship between 'the right' (*la droite*), as the authors call it, and twenty-five different topics, including cinema, ecology, the elite, the family, identity, morals, democracy, tradition, etc.[241] It was edited by Arnaud Guyot-Jeannin, a contributor to the magazine *Éléments*, president of the French neo-pagan circle Sol Invictus and editor of a book on Evola published by L'Age d'Homme.[242] The significance of *Aux sources de la droite* lies in the fact that the book brought together a group of key authors of the New Right, who were inspired by different currents of thought that ranged from neo-paganism, the Conservative Revolution and integrism to revolutionary nationalism. The contributors included, among others: Alain de Benoist; Charles Champetier, editor-in-chief of *Éléments* and *Nouvelle École*; Jean Mabire, historian and influential neo-paganist of the *Nouvelle droite*; Jean-Paul Lippi, who authored two books on Evola; and Luc Saint-Etienne, who occasionally contributed to the periodicals *Éléments, Nouvelles synergies européennes* and *Combat*. As expressed in the introduction by Guyot-Jeannin, despite such diversity, the book intended to present a base level of common understanding, shared by all authors, on various different subjects related to social issues and issues of identity. He further pointed out that, as could be seen in this volume, the right is anti-globalist and anti-Jacobin and therefore '*identitariste*'; it is anti-statist and anti-liberal and therefore supports the values of the community; it is anti-materialist and therefore challenges the ravages of contemporary rationalism.[243]

L'Age d'Homme also ensured that writings published by the *Nouvelle droite* in France would be distributed in the French-speaking regions of Switzerland. For this purpose, the publisher entered into an agreement with the proprietary company of the French publishing and distribution house Labyrinthe, the home publisher of GRECE.[244] Moreover, L'Age d'Homme published the writings of Swiss authors associated with the New Right. Significantly, it published a total of six books by the Swiss philosopher and essayist, Eric Werner, who was possibly the most prolific author of the *Nouvelle Droite* in the French-speaking part of Switzerland. In the 1980s and 1990s, Werner lectured at the University of Geneva and wrote a number of books on history, philosophy and politics.[245] In some of his publications, Werner referred extensively to authors of the New Right in France and Germany and showed that he was very familiar with the literature and debates of the New Right. For example, in his book *De l'extermination* (About the Extermination), he referenced the writings of Hellmut Diwald, Ernst Jünger, Armin Mohler, Henry Coston, Maurice Bardèche, François Brigneau, Alain de Benoist and Jean-Gilles Malliarakis, as well as articles published in periodicals such as *Défense de l'Occident, Criticón, Valeurs actuelles* and *Revue d'histoire révisionniste*.[246]

In his 1998 book *L'avant-guerre civile* (The Pre-Civil War), Werner took strong anti-immigrant positions. Among others things, he presented the argument that European governments were greatly supporting immigration from non-European countries in order to govern more effectively by dividing the nation, applying the strategy of *divide ut impera*.[247] Such views are unsurprising, since Werner was directly engaged in anti-immigrant politics in the French-speaking regions of Switzerland in the 1980s and was a contributor to the party paper *Le Vigilant*.[248] In 1986, Eric Werner was elected on a Vigilance/National Action ticket to the cantonal parliament of Vaud. In 1988, he also published a brochure on the 'Paschoud affaire' (see chapter 8) in which he presented a variety of revisionist and negationist arguments.[249]

In 1992, L'Age d'Homme launched the series *La Fronde* (The Fronde), giving New Right authors another opportunity to present their ideas. While the series covered a variety of areas, including religion, theology, history, literature and politics, its publishing policy was to provide an outlet for writers whose thought was profoundly anti-conformist for their time.[250] To this end, the first volume in the series was the booklet

Rembarre (Rebuff), which was written by René Berthod, a journalist and supporter of the integrist movement in the canton of Valais. The booklet brought together columns that Berthod had written for the newspaper *Le Nouvelliste et Feuille d'Avis du Valais*. In this collection of polemic writings, Berthod not only praised dictatorships in Latin America, but also assumed an anti-Jewish attitude, claiming that the continuing Russian hatred of National Socialism was able to rely on the perpetual renewal of the Jewish grudge for revenge.[251]

In conclusion, part of the publishing program of the renowned publishing house L'Age d'Homme played an important role for the New Right, and particularly for the *Nouvelle droite* in francophone countries. This was also reflected in the reputation that its director, Vladimir Dimitrijević, enjoyed among the French *Nouvelle droite*. With its publication of the edited volume *Aux sources de la droite*, one of the most important reference books of recent years, and with the latest books by Alain de Benoist, L'Age d'Homme strengthened its position in the publishing world of the *Nouvelle droite*. In addition, the publisher gave Swiss New Right authors the possibility of having their writings published by an established and well-connected publishing house.

The Brasillach Literary Circle: Safe Haven in Postwar Switzerland

Founded in 1948, the Association of the Friends of Robert Brasillach (*Association des amis de Robert Brasillach*, ARB) was an intellectual circle based in Geneva.[252] It claimed that to be primarily interested in the literary legacy of the French writer Robert Brasillach and to have only cultural and intellectual objectives.[253] The ARB sought to present Brasillach as a poet and novelist, not a fascist and anti-Semitic propagandist. In this way, the circle's untiring activities throughout the postwar era contributed to 'the myth of a martyred, innocent Brasillach' and to the fact that 'Brasillach is more marked politically today than he has been at any time other since the Occupation'.[254] This was of particular importance, since Brasillach's work was increasingly being used by parties, groups and publishers to refresh the intellectual and literary genealogy of the radical right.

Robert Brasillach (1909–1945) was a devoted supporter of fascism and the Vichy regime and his views 'included a virulent and often expressed anti-Semitism'.[255] A graduate of the *École normale supérieure*, Brasillach started his career as a journalist and novelist in the early 1930s and joined the newspaper of Charles Maurras' French Action as a literary critic. From the mid 1930s, he began to publicly praise fascism and to show admiration for German National Socialism. According to

Alice Kaplan: 'The scandal of Brasillach's concept of fascism was that he relied on the reference points and vocabulary of a literary critic – images, poetry, myths – with barely a reference to politics, economics, or ethics'.[256] In 1937, Brasillach was appointed editor-in-chief of the notorious antisemitic newspaper *Je suis partout*, which was the main collaborationist paper during the wartime Occupation and whose 'line was hardcore pro-Nazi'.[257] He kept his position as editor-in-chief until 1943 – with a break in 1940–41 when *Je suis partout* was not published and Brasillach was first conscripted and then imprisoned in a German camp. Moreover, as pointed out by Alice Kaplan, the publication of Brasillach's best-known novel *Les sept couleurs* (The Seven Colours), in 1939, definitively made Brasillach a 'fascist novelist'.[258] After the liberation in 1944, Brasillach was arrested and indicted for collaboration and treason. Jacques Isorni, later the defence attorney of Marshal Pétain, took on Brasillach's legal defence.[259] After a court trial, Brasillach was executed in February 1945.[260]

After Brasillach's death, his brother-in-law and close friend, Maurice Bardèche, played a 'controlling role in research on Brasillach' and was highly influential in transforming the literary legacy of Brasillach into a 'remarkable case of ideological distortion' and a revealing example of 'how revisionism around a literary figure works'.[261] Bardèche, a self-professed French neo-fascist and a key theorist of the postwar extreme right in Europe, is considered 'a pivotal actor in the articulation of extreme-right ideas, be it in the immediate aftermath of the war or more recently with the formation of the Nouvelle Droite in France and the Euro-right in Spain, Italy and France'.[262] Brasillach and Bardèche co-authored the two books, *Histoire du cinéma* (History of Cinema) and *Histoire de la guerre d'Espagne* (History of the Spanish War).[263] According to Ian Barnes, following the death of his brother-in-law, Bardèche 'considered himself to be Brasillach's literary executor, defending him against all comers, and establishing a cult that smacked of unhealthy and intellectually inflexible idolatry'.[264]

The Association of the Friends of Robert Brasillach was founded in Lausanne on 18 December 1948 and played an important role in this apologetic crusade. The Brasillach devotees chose Switzerland as a safe haven for their endeavour, since the intellectual and political climate in France was hostile to this kind of revisionism immediately after the war.[265] Since the circle's goal was to appeal to the francophone cultural and literary world, most members were from French-speaking countries and two branches of the ARB existed in France and Belgium. In the 1980s, the ARB had some seven hundred to seven hundred and fifty members, or '*amis*' (friends), as they were called, around the world.[266]

Prominent intellectuals of the New Right in Switzerland, France and Belgium joined the circle in the 1970s and 1980s. As a result, the ARB has gradually been transformed into a cultural and literary circle of the *Nouvelle droite*. This was also reflected in the fact that Pascal Junod became president of the ARB in 1992.

In postwar Switzerland, the ARB remained largely unnoticed by the general public and there were only very few reports that dealt with the circle's activities. For instance, the Swiss Federation of Jewish Communities released a ten-page report after Brasillach's play *Bérénice* was aired on a French-language radio station and performed at the Avenches theatre festival in 1957. The report extensively documented anti-Semitic passages in Brasillach's writings and pointed out the apologetic purpose of the ARB.[267] In the late 1960s, journalistic accounts of the Swiss extreme right reported on the ARB, exposing, in particular, the circle's association with the intellectual world in the French-speaking part of Switzerland.[268]

The formation of the ARB was initiated by Swiss citizen Pierre Favre and a few of his friends, who, as was noted in the circle's bulletin, were supported from the beginning by political refugees living in Switzerland.[269] Favre was ARB president from 1948 to 1989 and greatly contributed to the circle's appeal to intellectuals from outside the world of neo-fascism.[270] In the 1930s, Favre was involved in the Front Movement.[271] After the war, he made a professional career in Lausanne as the director of a large Swiss advertising company. Favre went so far in his admiration for Brasillach that he named his private residence *Les sept couleurs*. He also succeeded Maurice Bardèche as director of the Paris-based publishing house Les sept couleurs, which published, among other things, Bardèche's *Nuremberg – ou la Terre promise*, the first French-language negationist book (see chapter 8), as well as François Duprat's *L'ascension du M.S.I.* (The Ascension of the MSI).[272] After Pierre Favre's death in 1989, Maurice Bardèche wrote a long obituary in *Rivarol*, which was reprinted in the ARB bulletin soon thereafter.[273]

Two other key members of the ARB were Maurice Bardèche, 'the soul of the ARB', as Pascal Junod described him in his first editorial as the new ARB president,[274] and Jacques Isorni. They also drafted the first statutes of the ARB.[275] Because of his involvement with postwar neo-fascism, the Swiss authorities issued an entry refusal order for Bardèche in 1950, which was only lifted in 1973.[276] In spite of the entry refusal order, it was reported that Bardèche attended the performance of Brasillach's play *Bérénice* in Avenches in July 1957.[277] In February 1973, right after the entry refusal order was lifted, Bardèche was scheduled to address the annual ARB meeting.[278]

The ARB has engaged in a variety of literary activities which have ultimately demonstrated remarkable continuity over time. The circle has been publishing the book series *Cahiers des amis de Robert Brasillach* (Notebooks of the Friends of Robert Brasillach) since 1950. The edited volumes, which were published once a year until 1999/2000 and then biannually, contained contributions that dealt with Brasillach's work and evocatively reflected a strategy of rehabilitating Brasillach as a literary and intellectual figure. They also included the ARB's annual reports and other accounts of the activities undertaken by the circle. Some articles in the volumes were written by key figures of francophone neo-fascism. For example, on the twentieth anniversary of Brasillach's death in 1965, an edited volume was published as part of the book series and included articles written by well-known neo-fascists such as Maurice Bardèche, François Brigneau, Marc Augier (alias Saint-Loup), and by Karel Dillen, who later became the leader of the Flemish Block (*Vlaams Blok* – VB) in Belgium.[279] In the 1995 edition, Alain de Benoist contributed an article on the purge of collaborationist intellectuals in the France of the immediate postwar period.[280] In the 1999–2000 volume, he presented the most complete bibliography to date on Robert Brasillach.[281] The *Cahiers des amis de Robert Brasillach* also included reedited texts of Brasillach which supplemented the *Oeuvres complètes* of Brasillach that had been edited by Maurice Bardèche in the 1960s and contained 'sanitized' versions of Brasillach's original writings.[282] By comparison with the originals, Alice Kaplan shows in detail how Brasillach's work had been distorted by Maurice Bardèche's reediting in the *Oeuvres complètes*.[283] Finally, it is worth mentioning that in 1975, the ARB created the annual award *Prix Brasillach* for scholars and writers who performed research on Brasillach or had been inspired by his work.

The circle has been issuing the *Bulletin de l'Association des amis de Robert Brasillach* (Bulletin of the Association of the Friends of Robert Brasillach) since 1958, which was published in A4 format using a very simple layout. Until the 1980s, the bulletin was almost always published three times a year. After the 1980s, the bulletin came out more irregularly and since 1995 it has been issued once a year. As Pierre Favre stated in the second issue, the main goal was to ensure 'internal information and the links between all of us and between each of you and the presidency'.[284] The bulletin typically contained an extensive literary survey of articles, periodicals and books that had mentioned Robert Brasillach and his work. A broad selection of publications was cited, including journals and books associated with the extreme right and the New Right. A survey of the 108 bulletins published between 1958 and 2001 that are available in Swiss public libraries shows that the bulletin regularly cited periodicals such as *Rivarol, Défense de l'Occident, Valeurs actuelles, Lectures françaises, Nouvelle École, Europe réelle, Éléments* and *Totalité*.

As the bulletin regularly reviewed books and other publications written by ARB members, it also made mention of reference literature from the postwar extreme right, such as the second volume of Henry Coston's *Dictionnaire de la politique française* (Dictionary of French Politics).[285] In the 1970s, the bulletin welcomed newly founded Swiss publications such as the two national-revolutionary periodicals *Renaissance* and *Le Huron* (see chapter 8), as well as *Le Pamphlet*. In 1973, the circle's growing association with the *Nouvelle droite* was expressed in its praise of the journal *Nouvelle École*, founded in 1968 and directed by Alain de Benoist, which it described as the best contemporary journal of knowledge.[286] After Pascal Junod assumed the presidency in 1992, the bulletin added a section which reported extensively on a variety of circles and periodicals belonging almost exclusively to the New Right and, in particular, the *Nouvelle droite* in francophone countries. It appears that the bulletin took on the role of being the main supplier of information for the *Nouvelle droite* in the French-speaking regions of Switzerland. The bulletin continued, however, to advertise publications released by the extreme right, namely its negationist faction.[287]

The ARB proved that it was able to appeal to intellectuals, writers and scholars of diverse political and ideological backgrounds and to bring together different generations of the postwar radical right.[288] The annual ARB meetings, most frequently held in Lausanne, gave ARB members from different countries the opportunity to meet. Since the ARB never issued an official membership list, there are two ways to discover who the members of the ARB were. First, the ARB bulletin referred to its members as '*amis*' (friends) and published a variety of reports on them with respect to becoming an ARB member, book reviews, marriage and birth announcements, death notices, obituaries, etc. Based on this source, one can conclude that the ARB included the following among its members: Francis Bergeron, Henry Coston, Eric Delcroix, Jean Mabire, Alain Sanders, Dominique Venner and Noël de Winter. Second, the official website of the ARB posted a list of persons who have supported the circle. Some of the many names included on this list are: Raymond Abellio, Jean Anouilh, Alain de Benoist, François Brigneau, Karel Dillen, Jean Madiran, Pierre Monnier, Saint-Loup, Jean-Louis Tixier-Vignancour, Pierre Vial, etc.[289]

In Switzerland, the ARB succeeded in attracting prominent public figures, such as Gonzague de Reynold (1880–1970), a key intellectual of Helvetic authoritarianism, and Olivier Reverdin (1913–2000), professor of classical philology at the University of Geneva, LPS National Councillor from 1955 to 1971 and member of the Council of States from 1972 to 1979.[290] When Reverdin was awarded the Robert Schumann Medal in 1974, the ARB bulletin congratulated him and expressed gratitude for the strong friendship he had shown towards the ARB.[291] On the other hand, Swiss ARB members included, for example, Eric Werner, Olivier Delacrétaz, president of the Vaud League, René-Louis Berclaz, head of the negationist group Justice and Truth (see chapter 8), Mariette and Claude Paschoud, both associated with the paper *Le Pamphlet*, and Roger Pache. As Pache was an editor of *Journal de Payerne*, the local newspaper has regularly published very favourable reports on the ARB.[292] He was also the author of autobiographical writings presenting a partisan picture of the right-wing intellectual world in the French-speaking regions of Switzerland since the 1930s.[293] Notorious Swiss neo-fascist Gaston-Armand Amaudruz also attended the annual ARB meetings and reported on them in his paper *Courrier du continent* (see chapter 8).[294]

Overall, the ARB assumed a special role in postwar intellectual life in the French-speaking part of Switzerland. It appealed to a variety of intellectual milieus and a number of prominent figures in Swiss public life, despite the fact that prominent French neo-fascists were part of the circle's leadership and the members newsletter consistently referred to neo-fascist publications. As an international circle, the ARB managed to maintain an organisational network connecting groups and intellectuals and it acted as a bridge between different ideological currents, including those of neo-fascists, New Rightists and conservatives. As the circle's goals were well aligned with the cultural and 'metapolitical' strategy adopted by the *Nouvelle droite* since the 1970s and 1980s, the ARB has become a well-organized instrument used by the francophone *Nouvelle droite* to influence debates on (literary) history.

As we saw in this chapter, the beginning of the francophone New Right dates back to the late 1960s and early 1970s, when a number of new groups and publications sought to renew long-standing traditions of radical-right intellectualism in the French-speaking part of Switzerland. They were able to benefit from an intellectual milieu and from organisational structures which had existed since the interwar period, or had been established in the postwar era. As they managed to build up a diversified network of associations, circles, periodicals and publishing houses, they were able to sustain a fairly dynamic intellectual scene. Their aim was to rejuvenate thinking that was critical of parliamentary democracy and to react to the intellectualisation of the left, particularly of the New Left, and its advocacy of pluralistic, emancipatory and multicultural concepts. Some prioritised the counter-revolutionary and authoritarian aspects of a radical right ideology, while others sought to revive neo-pagan and Indo-European legacies, but both promoted pronounced anti-egalitarian and exclusionist ideas.

Until the late 1980s, large parts of the francophone New Right preferred to stay in the background of the world of culture rather than take up a position at the forefront of politics and the media. In most cases, they chose an elitist approach and avoided attracting large audiences. They limited themselves to organising events of a cultural and academic character and to circulating publications for an interested public. This largely corresponded to the intellectual and cultural strategy of the New Right in France, which exerted a great influence on the New Right in the French-speaking part of Switzerland. The Swiss intellectuals did not only make extensive reference to the work of French authors and theorists, but also collaborated continually with the intellectual community of the French New Right, in the form of associations, conferences, edited volumes and periodicals.

In the 1990s, a considerable part of the francophone New Right abandoned – at least partially – the 'metapolitical' approach of 'just' acting as potential suppliers of ideology and looked instead for opportunities for direct political intervention. They moved towards the realm of politics and became increasingly involved with party politics. Where followers of the New Right had previously shown some degree of attraction for Vigilance and National Action, by the 1990s the SVP was being seen as the main political ally and this was the party that a number of key figures from the New Right in the French-speaking part of Switzerland chose to join. At the same time, the francophone New Right maintained its long-standing tradition of close relationships with the extreme right at the level of organisations and personnel. As will be shown in the following chapter on the Swiss extreme right, some of the ideologues and groups associated with the extreme right have also collaborated with the New Right.

8

AT THE MARGINS OF SOCIETY AND POLITICS
The Subculture of the Extreme Right

Since the end of the Second World War, the extreme right in Western Europe has transformed itself from a small underground scene into a larger, diversified subculture. While the extreme right is not ideologically homogenous, most variants of its worldview feature blunt versions of racism, anti-Semitism, xenophobia and nationalism. They are also characterised by anti-democratic conceptions of the political system. Until the 1970s, the extreme right was typically comprised of old fascists and National Socialists, neo-fascist groups and periodicals, and militant *groupuscules* that were sometimes terrorist-like in nature.[1] Since the 1980s, it has undergone major changes which have ultimately resulted in the establishment of a subculture that includes a wide-ranging network of organisations and a high degree of potential mobilisation. Figures indicate that 171 extreme-right groups were active in sixteen different European countries in 1996. While the conclusiveness of the statistics would appear to be somewhat diminished because the figures do not include short-lived groups or those not publicly visible, they do give us an idea about the relative degrees of concentration in different countries. For instance, relative to their population size, Austria, Belgium, Norway and Sweden have a disproportionably high number of extreme-right groups, while France, Germany, the Netherlands and Switzerland take a middle position. Estimates which draw on the same figures suggest that membership of the extreme right in the mid 1990s was a little under twenty-five thousand individuals across the whole of Western Europe.[2]

The transformation that has taken place within the extreme right in Western Europe since the 1980s is basically characterised by four distinct features and this pattern largely corresponds to the development of the extreme right in Switzerland. First, there has been a rejuvenation of the extreme right, in part due to the emergence of the racist faction of the skinhead movement. Adherence to the extreme-right subculture became 'an alternative way of life' for a number of predominantly male young people, by which they sought to underscore their autonomy from their parents' generation and to exhibit their rebellious attitude towards mainstream society.[3] Second, the globalisation of the extreme right has been supported by new means of communication technology and has reinforced the international ties between organisations and individuals.[4] It seems that '[t]he massive expansion of racist and neo-fascist sites on the Internet and in other arenas of electronic communication points to a new pattern of social and political communication that is likely to shape racist and neo-fascist politics for some time to come'.[5] Third, the diversification of the extreme right is particularly reflected in its organisational variation and in the diversity of its action repertoire. The range of organisational forms stretches from well-organised paramilitary groups, which run training camps and are characterised by authoritarian leadership, to loosely structured gangs that team up by wearing the same clothes or going to the same neighbourhood bar.[6] Fourth, the growing use of violence became a key characteristic of the extreme right in the 1990s. Anti-immigrant violence, hate crimes and attacks against symbolic objects like Jewish cemeteries are typical elements of the new wave of extreme-right mobilisation in Europe.[7]

For the examination of the development in Switzerland since the end of the Second World War, the Swiss extreme right has been divided into two main categories, with ideologues and propagandists on the one hand, and combative and violent groups on the other. Such a distinction makes it possible to depict the differences at the level of action, means and objectives. It also allows us to consider that there is a difference between aggressive rhetoric and militant action, between hate speech and violent act and, for example, between the ideological masterminds who operate behind the scenes and the combative and violent perpetrators who act in the forefront. While extreme-right ideologues and propagandists have a long history in Switzerland that dates back to the immediate postwar years, most of the combative and violent groups have emerged since the mid 1980s.

To distinguish between the actors in terms of ideological preferences, historical origins and purpose of activity, each of the two main categories must be further divided into different subtypes: the ideologues and propagandists include neo-fascists, negationists, conspiracists and national-revolutionaries; the category of combative and violent groups consists of fronts and skinheads.[8] While some overlap exists between these subtypes in terms of membership and ideology, this typology permits the identification of distinct categories and the development of a comprehensive framework in which these categories can be deployed to illustrate the complexity of the Swiss extreme right.

Figure 8.1 | *Typology of the Extreme Right in Switzerland*

Common Ideological Features

Classical Racism and Anti-Semitism, Radical Nationalism, Xenophobia, Anti-democracy

Idealogues and Propagandists	Combative and Violent Groups
Neo-fascists, Negationists Conspiracists, National-revolutionaries	Fronts, Skinheads

Distinctive Objectives and Means of Action

Dissemination of Ideas and Ideology (Publications, Meetings, Lectures, etc.)
Mobilisations, Confrontation, Disruption (Demonstrations, Symbolic Actions, Violent Attacks, etc.)

Ideologues and Propagandists: Disseminating Thought and Ideas

Ideologues and propagandists are primarily engaged in disseminating thought and ideas. They provide the ideological and intellectual underpinning of militant acts and confrontational activities of the extreme right. Their propagandistic work consists of publishing and circulating books, brochures and other writings; of organising meetings, conferences and talks; of giving speeches to audiences of like-minded people; and of developing and maintaining websites. In other words, they are more likely to publish and propagate than to engage in direct action on the streets. From time to time, ideologues and propagandists create organisations and act as members of organised groups. In most cases, however, they prefer to act individually as author, publisher, or organiser. In most cases, Swiss extreme-right ideologues and propagandists are enterprising individuals who are fervently and zealously dedicated to the cause of right-wing extremism. They resemble ideological movement entrepreneurs who play a crucial role in both the production and promotion of ideas and propaganda. Since these ideologues and propagandists are prolific writers, they produce a significant amount of the propaganda that constitutes the ideological realm of the Swiss extreme right. In addition, by periodically taking a coordinating role in the organisation network, they seek not only to develop and strengthen the links between the various domestic groups, but also to reinforce the collaboration with counterparts in other countries.

The Neo-fascists: Ancestors of the Extreme Right

The neo-fascists (or neo-Nazis) expressly refer to the ideology and the historical model of fascism and National Socialism. Their ultimate, utopian goal is the resurgence of a fascist or National Socialist regime. In their statements, writings and propaganda campaigns, neo-fascists draw upon theories of classical racism and incorporate the racist and anti-Semitic literature that provided the intellectual and ideological foundations of National Socialism. They edit books glorifying the National Socialist period or employ an array of emblems, codes and symbols taken from the iconography of fascism and National Socialism. Thus, neo-fascists are mainly responsible for the fact that 'international cultural production has grown up since the war dedicated to keeping alive Nazism as an ideology'.[9]

Historically, the neo-fascist current in Europe emerged shortly after the end of the Second World War, when former collaborators of fascist and National Socialist regimes founded clandestine organisations and circulated propaganda material.[10] They established an underground of European neo-fascism in the 1950s and aimed at developing a 'European neofascist "International"', as Roger Eatwell calls it.[11] Newly founded organisations such as European Social Movement (ESB), European New Order (*Nouvel ordre européen* – NOE), Young Europe (*Jeune Europe*) and periodicals such as *The European, Nation Europa* and *Europa Nazione* strove for a new European order based on the idea of Europe as a cultural and historical unity and hence Europeanization has become 'a striking feature of the post-1945 fascist radical right'.[12] Equally, the first transcontinental organisations were created in order to internationalise the network of contacts and collaboration.[13] However, due to personal rivalry and ideological conflicts, most postwar groups were short-lived and factionalism became the key characteristic of Europe's postwar neo-fascism.[14]

In the 1960s and 1970s, neo-fascist organisations mainly surfaced in national settings and hence reinforced the fragmentation of the European extreme right. Moreover, as *groupuscules* of the militant underground were responsible for highly planned acts of violence and some of them were banned by the authorities, the extreme right became increasingly associated with terrorism.[15] In the 1980s and 1990s, the presence of partisans of the old predecessor groups faded and new leader figures emerged. There were also increased efforts to integrate skinheads in well-structured and politicised neo-fascist organisations. This was shown, for example, by the French and European Nationalist Party (*Parti nationaliste français et européen* – PNFE), an extreme-right group founded by Claude Cornilleau in 1985 with up to thousand members.[16] In more recent years, the creation of party-like structures and attempts to participate in elections have characterised some of the new neo-fascist groups.[17]

In Switzerland, the first generation of neo-fascists emerged in the immediate postwar years. Some were former members of the Front Movement in the 1930s; others had started their political activity during the Second World War. Founded in 1951, the People's Party of Switzerland (*Volkspartei der Schweiz* – VPS) was the first significant neo-fascist organisation in Switzerland.[18] Among the leading members was Erwin Vollenweider, who had been involved with Young Guard (*Junge Garde*), a small group that took part in the 1946 local elections in Winterthur but with very little success. The VPS's aim was to structure and unify the Swiss neo-fascist scene. As stated in its political program, the VPS was dedicated to defending the European people and the 'white race'.[19] In 1952, the VPS joined the ESB, which brought together some forty organisations from all over Europe.[20] The group also had in mind to take part in the 1955 National Council elections, but lack of financial resources and growing internal frictions undermined the group's activity and eventually led to the party's dissolution in 1958.

More important from a cross-national perspective, and so far largely ignored in the study of postwar European neo-fascism, is the fact that a number of Swiss neo-fascists took part in the early efforts to create a 'fascist international' and were firmly integrated in the organisational structures of the neo-fascist underground of postwar Europe.[21] The key figure was Gaston-Armand Amaudruz (born 1920), who went on to become a driving force in the development of a European neo-fascist network.[22] While most early Swiss neo-fascists were only active for a short period in the 1950s, Amaudruz has remained active right up to the present day and stands for the notable continuity of Swiss postwar neo-fascism.

At the international level, Gaston-Armand Amaudruz assumed influence on European neo-fascism in two ways. First, he co-founded the above-mentioned European New Order (NOE) in 1951, an organisation that espoused a pronounced racist and anti-Semitic program in order to counter the course of the ESB, which was purported to be too moderate.[23] In the late 1950s, the NOE headquarter moved to Lausanne in Switzerland, and Amaudruz subsequently became the driving force of the NOE. The NOE developed into an international umbrella organisation, assembling as many as fifty groups from twenty European countries in its early years. Counting some two hundred and fifty supporters in the early 1960s, the NOE organised a large number of meetings and attracted an array of well-known European neo-fascists. From 1957 to 1971, the NOE released its own organ called *Europe réelle* (Real Europe) in Brussels, which was alleged at some point to have a circulation of fifteen thousand. In the early 1970s, the NOE experienced internal squabbling and personal rivalry, and eventually lost much of its significance for the European extreme right. By the late 1980s, according to its own information, the NOE had a membership of three hundred and fifty. In order to underline the international significance of Amaudruz and the NOE, one may also take note of the Montreal-based Institute of Psychosomatic, Biologic and Racial Sciences (*Institut des sciences psychosomatiques, biologiques et raciales*), founded by the NOE in 1969. Amaudruz acted as the so-called Rector of the institute. The institute became known for awarding Alain de Benoist with an honorary doctorate and for founding the publishing house Éditions Celtiques (Celtic Publications) whose publisher's list contained some of the more notorious racist writings to have been published after the Second World War.[24]

Second, Amaudruz made important contributions to European neo-fascism by launching and editing periodicals and by writing several books of his own. He started his writing career in 1945 with an essay in the periodical *Le Mois suisse* (The Swiss Month), a periodical closely associated with the neo-fascist current.[25] Amongst other claims, Amaudruz raised doubts in the article about whether Germany had sole responsibility for the outbreak of the Second World War.[26] In 1951, Amaudruz became the editor of the *Courrier du Continent*, which was the party organ of the VPS at the time. Over the years, this very simply made paper, which was typewritten and Xeroxed in A4 format, developed into Amaudruz's personal voice. In the late 1980s, it supposedly had a circulation of four hundred.[27] The *Courrier du Continent* contained a large amount of information about organisations, activities and publications, most of which were associated with the extreme right. The significance of the paper rests primarily in its coordinating function for the extreme right in Europe.[28] Amaudruz was also the author of four books, some of which are considered to be key writings of postwar racist and neo-fascist literature. In his books, Amaudruz developed a biologistic and racist worldview in which he made key reference to the pseudo-scientific concept of 'race' and notions of 'racial inequality' and social order based on organic principles. By drawing consistently on various types of conspiracy theories, Amaudruz denounced so-called *mondialists* – media, finance lobbies, political parties, Jews and other groups – for being responsible for the moral and social decadence and the economic and political decline of the Western world.[29]

In Switzerland, Amaudruz has played the role of *éminence grise* in the extreme right of the last three decades. Because of his long-standing reputation as a neo-fascist ideologue and publisher, he has been able to provide support since the 1970s to several groups that were founded by a new generation of Swiss extreme rightists. During the so-called Small Springtime of Fronts (*kleiner Frontenfrühling*) in the late 1980s and early 1990s (see below), Amaudruz showed ambition to take the leadership, but eventually confined his role to that of a purveyor of extreme-right ideology.[30] In the late 1980s and early 1990s, he sought to stay in touch with the new generation of young activists, namely skinheads. He reported extensively in the *Courrier du Continent* about ongoing extreme-right activities in Switzerland and also organised training courses at his home. It seems, however, that by the late 1990s, the veteran Amaudruz had lost influence among the new generation of extreme-right activists.[31]

Perhaps Amaudruz's most significant contribution to the Swiss extreme right was the leading role he played in the National Coordination (*Nationale Koordination* – NK). The NK was founded in 1983 as an umbrella organisation which aimed to facilitate the countrywide coordination of the different extreme-right groups.[32] The group released press statements that were published in the *Courrier du Continent*, but also in the party papers of National Action and the Republican Movement.[33] In 1986, an NK section took part in the local elections of Zurich, but did not receive any significant electoral support.[34] In the late 1980s, the NK meetings in the town of Fribourg were attended by representatives from most of the active extreme-right groups. In the early 1990s, the NK sought to organise the campaign against the anti-racism law among the extreme right, but was eventually pushed aside by the two campaign committees of Herbert Meier and Emil Rahm (see below). Surprisingly enough, Amaudruz's *Courrier du Continent* participated in the preparliamentary consultation procedure and was, along with the CINS and the Vaud League, the only non-party actor to reject the anti-racism law.[35] Amaudruz also coined the term 'muzzle law' (French: '*loi muselière*', German: '*Maulkorbgesetz*'), which eventually became a buzzword that was widely used in the campaign against the anti-racism law. Eventually, Gaston-Armand Amaudruz and the Vaud League gathered, according to some reports, 2,200 signatures in the francophone regions of Switzerland.[36] Once the new anti-racism law was implemented in 1995, the NK disappeared from the extreme-right stage.

François Genoud (1915–1996) was another prominent proponent of Swiss neo-fascism. Compared to Amaudruz, he was more independent (not to say isolated) and hardly ever engaged directly with organised extreme-right groups. As Anne-Marie Duranton-Crabol notes, he almost represents an international association in himself.[37] While Genoud was a member of the National Front in Switzerland in the 1930s, he continued to express his sympathy for National Socialism after the war. Genoud played a minimal role in the Swiss extreme right, but assumed a remarkable position at the international level, primarily because of his financial activities and personal networks. Genoud possessed the copyright for Goebbels' diaries and some of Hitler's writings. He was also in close contact with prominent figures of the European extreme right, such as Léon Degrelle, and he supported Klaus Barbie during his trial.[38]

In the 1970s, a number of small neo-fascist groups were created in the German-speaking part of Switzerland. In 1971, the psychiatrist Heinz Manz (1924–1994) revived the Zurich-based fraternity Arminia (initially founded in 1946) and gave the group a marked neo-fascist orientation. The group made reference to National Socialism in its symbols and ideology and showed an overt admiration for Hitler. Under the authoritarian leadership of Manz, Arminia attracted fifty to a hundred members of all ages, some of which came from Germany and Austria. Among the German members was the leader of an extreme-right terrorist group, Manfred Roeder, who was sentenced in Germany to thirteen years of prison in 1982.[39] As a split-off from Arminia, the National Basis of Switzerland (*Nationale Basis Schweiz* – NBS) was founded in 1974 by the pastor Gerd Zikeli (born 1937), a devoted National Socialist and anti-Semite. The NBS edited a paper named *Visier*, which had two to three hundred subscribers and published articles by Swiss and European extreme-right authors. The group had close ties to Austrian and German neo-fascists, and made efforts to establish a close collaboration with the scene in the French-speaking regions of Switzerland and with Amaudruz's *Courrier du Continent* and the New Social Order (*Nouvel ordre social* – NOS) in particular. By the end of the 1970s, however, Arminia and the NBS had disappeared from the scene.[40]

At the turn of the 1980s, a new generation of young neo-fascists made attempts to set up new organisational structures. In 1978, for example, Jürgen Künzli (born 1957) founded the People's Socialist Party of Switzerland (*Volkssozialistische Partei der Schweiz* – VSP). This minute group published two small papers before 1981, but failed in their project to establish a party-like organisation.[41] In 1981, another ephemeral neo-fascist group was created under the name of Comradeship Eyrie (*Kameradschaft Adlerhorst*), attracting a handful of young people, among them Switzerland's first extreme-right skinheads.[42]

Since the mid 1980s, most of the elderly Swiss neo-fascists have passed away and no authentic neo-fascist group has been founded in Switzerland in the meantime. However, the absence of organisation building did not mean that neo-fascism had disappeared from the Swiss extreme right scene. The key role of passing on neo-fascist ideas to new extreme-right groups continued to be played by Gaston-Armand Amaudruz, the last survivor of the old generation and the guardian of the legacy of neo-fascism in Switzerland. Neo-fascist orientation became primarily a concern of the emerging extreme-right skinhead movement and associated groups. In their worship of leader figures and diffuse worldview, skinheads were often fond of incorporating symbolic and ideological references to fascism and National Socialism. Moreover, as is described in the following section, attempts to rehabilitate and revive fascism still play a fundamental role in underpinning the activities of negationists.

The Negationists: Pioneer Role in Europe and their Recent Globalization

Negationists are genuinely anti-Semitic and seek to relativize and deny the Shoah and other crimes and atrocities committed by the National Socialist regime. Since the Shoah is recognised as the most malicious crime in history, it is the main goal of negationists to present the genocide of Jews as a myth, and thereby remove the largest moral obstacle impeding a resurgence of National Socialism.[43] While authors in German studies commonly refer to the term 'revisionism',[44] Anglo-Saxon scholars prefer to use 'Holocaust denial'.[45] However, there are conceptual problems inherent in both terms. In historical science, the term 'revisionism' is applied when existing interpretations of historical events need to be reexamined and revised because new sources have been discovered.[46] On the subject of Shoah, historians have indeed revised certain aspects but 'their revision entails *refinement* of detailed knowledge about events, rarely complete denial of the events themselves, and certainly not denial of the cumulation of events known as the Holocaust'.[47] Moreover, negationists themselves insist on using the term 'revisionism' for their endeavours, with the intention of underscoring the legitimacy of their historical work and putting themselves in the long tradition of revisionism in historical science.[48] The term 'Holocaust denial' also seems to be problematic, since it reduces the perspective by confining it to one part, albeit the most barbaric, of the atrocities committed by National Socialism. As a consequence, it fails to capture the fact that negationists also intend to deny and relativize other crimes committed by the National Socialist regime, for example the murdering of gypsies, socialists, communists and members of religious groups. In view of these deficiencies in the terms 'revisionism' and 'Holocaust denial', I prefer to use the term 'negationism', which better captures the real intentions of this current of the extreme right.[49] In France, the term 'negationism', initially introduced by Henry Rousso in his seminal study *Le Syndrome de Vichy*,[50] has since become the accepted term of reference.[51]

In their arguments, negationists deny or play down the three defining aspects of the Shoah: the killing of six millions Jews; the systematic fashion of the extermination, including the use of gas chambers; and the Nationalist Socialist regime's intention to exterminate Jews.[52] By writing articles packed with references, editing academic-sounding journals and organising historical conferences, they seek to give their endeavours a scholarly look. Negationists attempt to make their case by applying three different basic methods.[53] First, without even delivering any supposedly scientific evidence, negationists bluntly deny the existence of concentration and death camps. Second, they present fabricated forgeries and faked documents as alleged counter-evidence to what they call the official version of history written by the winners of the war under the alleged influence of Jewish interests. Third, by making a selective and biased choice of evidence, negationists 'disregard any convergence of evidence; instead, they pick out what suits their theory and ignore the rest'.[54]

The origins of negationist propaganda go back to the late 1940s in France, when Maurice Bardèche, a key figure of postwar neo-fascism, and Paul Rassinier, a former member of the Communist Party, began to publish the first writings raising doubts about the anti-Semitic crimes committed by the National Socialist regime.[55] Recently, however, Michael Shermer and Alex Grobman have taken the view that the first author to deny the Shoah was a Scotsman named Alexander Ratcliffe who in late 1945 and in 1946 claimed that the Shoah was invented by Jews.[56] Whatever the case may be, a number of propagandists espousing the same purpose emerged very soon in an array of countries, such as the United States, Great Britain, Germany, Belgium and Switzerland. It became clear from the very beginning that negationism was of international scope. Even though the publications circulated in fairly large numbers, at that time authorities and the general public only occasionally took notice of the growing negationist literature.[57]

In the late 1970s, a new phase of negationism started up, which was characterised by four main aspects. First, to deny the extermination of Jews, the negationists started to use forged evidence based on natural-science methods.[58] Second, at regular intervals, they succeeded in generating discussions in the public domain, demonstrated most vividly by the numerous negationist affairs that have taken place in France over the last twenty-five years – the 'Faurisson affair' in 1978–79, the 'Roques affair' in 1985–86 and the 'Garaudy affair' in 1996.[59] Third, an international network based around publishers, institutes and conference events was firmly reinforced in the 1980s, and received a major boost in the 1990s with the establishment of the Internet.[60] Within this international network, the California-based Institute for Historical Review (IHR), founded in 1978, and its periodical, *The Journal of Historical Review* (JHR), play a key role.[61] Fourth, as various countries have passed laws that make statements denying the Shoah illegal, negationists seek to turn their denial activities into an issue of 'free speech'.[62] More recently, this has been seen in the campaigns of negationists who fiercely oppose the closing down of their websites by authorities.[63]

In Switzerland, negationism has a long tradition and its origins go back to the immediate postwar years.[64] To date, the study of the history of negationism has largely failed to acknowledge that Swiss propagandists were among the first generation of negationists. One exception amongst the scholars of negationism is Pierre-André Taguieff, who noted that Gaston-Armand Amaudruz was the author of one of the first 'revisionist texts' written in French.[65] In his book from 1949, *Ubu justicier au premier procès de Nuremberg* (Ubu Avenger at the First Nuremberg Trial), Amaudruz largely drew on an article he had published as early as 1946 in the *Courrier du Continent*, a paper edited at the time by Paul Gentizon, a sympathiser of Italian fascism.[66] In these early publications, Amaudruz had developed lines of reasoning that later became key arguments of negationist propaganda. Among other claims, he condemned the Nuremberg tribunal as nothing more than victors' justice that had simply been imposed by the winners of the Second World War and, consequently, he denied the tribunal's legal legitimacy. Amaudruz urged that all evidence presented at Nuremberg should be critically examined. He claimed that the Allies had fabricated documents in order to provide support for the charges they had raised.[67]

Another important Swiss contribution to this initial phase of international negationism was the German translation of Maurice Bardèche's 1948 book, *Nuremberg ou la Terre promise* (Nuremberg or the Promised Land). It was translated by the Swiss neo-fascist Hans Oehler (1888–1967), and released in 1949 by the Zurich-based publisher Kommissionsverlag.[68] The paper *Turmwart* (Tower Guard) was also an example of early negationist endeavours in Switzerland. Published by the former follower of the Front Movement, Werner Meyer (1909–1981), the paper appeared from 1947 to 1953 with a circulation of two thousand and was closely associated with the international neo-fascist network. The list of contributors to *Turmwart* included the following: Paul Gentizon; Hans Oehler; Pierre Hofstetter, author of the foreword in Amaudruz's 1949 negationist book; Otto Strasser, key figure of German revolutionary nationalism; Theodor Fischer, former member of the Front Movement; and the colonel Gustav Däniker, former high-ranking Swiss army officer.[69] Some articles published in *Turmwart* relativized the crimes committed by National Socialism by comparing them to activities of the Allies after the end of the Second World War. It was further argued that the number of Jews killed in the Shoah remained uncertain.[70]

The continuity of negationist propaganda in postwar Switzerland was ensured by Amaudruz's paper *Courrier du Continent*. From the 1950s on, the paper has published anti-Semitic and negationist propaganda and advertised negationist literature.[71] As early as 1953, the paper released a number of articles condemning Germany's reparation payments to Israel and claiming that the figure of six millions Jews killed by National Socialism was one that had been invented by the Allies.[72] While the *Courrier du Continent* had limited distribution and was only available by subscription, it served as a platform for international communication among negationists and neo-fascists until the 1990s.[73]

Despite these numerous publishing and literary activities, Swiss postwar negationism remained a clandestine activity. This changed for a short time in the second half of the 1960s, when the Swiss public was alerted, perhaps for the first time, to the existence of negationist propaganda. The reason was the so-called 'Mathez affair.' In 1968, the authorities issued a legal ban on the book by James-Albert Mathez, *Le passé, les temps présents et la question juive* (The Past, Present Times and the Jewish Question), which was published in 1965.[74] The following year, the author was forced to stand trial for incitement to crime and the disturbance of religious freedom and he was eventually sentenced to one month's imprisonment. The book contained numerous negationist and extreme anti-Semitic statements. Four thousand copies were published of this book that was 728 pages long and included an 80-page summary in English.[75] The book was enthusiastically reviewed in Amaudruz's *Courrier du Continent*, and widely acknowledged by the European neo-fascist scene.[76]

Despite this legal ruling, Swiss negationists continued to produce propagandistic material. In the mid 1970s, negationist premises were supported in the neo-fascist paper *Visier*, the organ of the National Basis of Switzerland. For instance, the paper propagated the view that the only crimes committed systematically during the Second World War were those of the English, American and Soviet armies.[77] More significantly, in the early 1980s, the former member of the Swiss Democratic Union, Max Wahl (born 1923), transformed the paper *Eidgenoss* (Swiss), founded in 1976, into an inflammatory negationist and anti-Semitic publication. *Eidgenoss* had a print run of ten thousand in 1985, and was hence the most far-reaching vehicle for negationism in the 1980s.[78] In 1992, the paper declared that it could now look back on '12 years of refuting the lies about gas chambers and the holocaust'.[79] Max Wahl had close ties to the Swiss extreme right as well as to groups in Germany and Austria, where he made speeches at meetings and conferences. In 1992, an appeal court in Munich imposed a fine of twenty-five thousand German marks on Wahl, for disseminating negationist propaganda.[80] Although *Eidgenoss* went out of circulation in late 1994, just before the anti-racism law came into effect, Wahl continued to send newsletters to some of the subscribers.[81]

Almost twenty years after the 'Mathez affair', negationism provoked public reactions once again in the mid 1980s. At this moment, negationists in the French-speaking regions of Switzerland changed their practice of only addressing those who believed in what they did, to one that actively strove to command public attention. They managed, within the space of four months, to address the public on three occasions.[82] The main objective of the campaign was to spread doubts about the existence of the gas chambers and so too about the systematic fashion in which the National Socialists had exterminated the Jews. This corresponded to the shift that French negationists had made under the guidance of Robert Faurisson in the 1980s, when they began to deny certain technical elements related to the carrying out of the Shoah.[83]

In August 1986, Mariette Paschoud (born 1947) took part in a press conference held in Paris by the French negationist Henri Roques. On this occasion, she raised doubts about the existence of gas chambers in concentration camps, a view she later sustained in a reader's letter published in a Swiss newspaper.[84] In January 1986, Paschoud had already published a favourable review of Henri Roques' 1985 dissertation *Les confessions de Kurt Gerstein* (The Confessions of Kurt Gerstein).[85] Together with an article in the French periodical *Rivarol*, her review was a factor in Roques' negationist dissertation receiving some degree of public attention.[86] What became known in the vernacular as the 'Paschoud affair' stirred widespread public protest and put the cantonal government under great pressure to impose sanctions on Paschoud, who was teaching history at a cantonal grammar school at the time. Eventually, she was removed first from her position as history teacher, and then as a teacher at the grammar school.[87]

In October 1986, the best-known French negationists Robert Faurisson and Pierre Guillaume took part in a roundtable discussion organised at the renowned documentary film festival in Nyon. According to a press report, Faurisson declared in the discussion that he wanted to show that those who claimed that the Germans had committed a crime without precedent, using an instrument without precedent, were uttering a historical lie.[88] Finally, in November 1986, a press conference with Henri Roques and Pierre Guillaume was held in Geneva that dealt with the theme of 'the Mariette Paschoud affair and the revisionist debate'. As reported by a newspaper, Guillaume claimed on this occasion that Soviet and American propaganda had invented the issue of the gas chambers, and that a maximum of one million Jews had been killed during the time of National Socialism.[89]

When mainstream media in the French-speaking part of Switzerland covered the coming-out of the negationists in 1986, there was practically unanimous public condemnation of the negationist theses. Among the New Right, however, some voices insisted on the importance of freedom of speech.[90] They took the view that theses put forward by negationist authors should be discussed as openly and publicly as any other assessments made by serious historians. This position was most prominently advocated by the counter-revolutionary paper *Le Pamphlet*, whose editor-in-chief at the time was Claude Paschoud, the spouse of Mariette Paschoud.[91]

In the early 1990s, Swiss negationism entered into a new phase. These changes were characterised by five distinct features that ultimately gave a new quality to negationist endeavours. First, a new generation of negationists emerged in German-speaking Switzerland, including Jürgen Graf (born 1951), Bernhard Schaub (born 1954) and Andres J.W. Studer (born 1936).[92] They substantially enlarged the body of negationist literature produced by Swiss authors and their publications consistently drew on the premises of international negationism.[93] Jürgen Graf has been by far the most prolific Swiss negationist. He wrote a number of books that were distributed around the globe and translated into many other languages. For example, one of his books was translated into English in 2001 and is distributed by the publisher Noontide Press, which is closely associated with the Institute for Historical Review and run by its founder Willis Carto.[94] In his writings, Graf systematically referenced the literature of international negationism and espoused the view of those who denied the existence of the extermination machinery.[95] Bernhard Schaub also took negationist views and had already referred to a 'classic' of negationist literature, the oft-cited pseudoscientific *Leuchter-Report*, in his own book, *Adler und Rose* (Eagle and Rose), which was published in 1992.[96]

Second, the development of organisational structures was another feature of the 1990s. For this purpose, Swiss negationists founded new groups and periodicals. Most significantly, in 1994, the new generation of negationists joined Arthur Vogt (1917–2003) in creating the Working Group for Breaking the Taboo on Contemporary History (*Arbeitsgemeinschaft zur Enttabuisierung der Zeitgeschichte* – AEZ).[97] In its statutes, the AEZ declared that the study group's aim was 'the discovery of the historical truth by exposing the politically motivated falsification of history'.[98] By 1999, the AEZ had released eighteen issues of the paper *Aurora*, which had a circulation of one to two hundred. The AEZ president, Arthur Vogt, had been convicted in Germany in 1994, for denigrating the memory of deceased people.[99] Another group was founded in 1999 under the name of Truth and Justice (*Vérité et Justice – Wahrheit und Recht*), and was co-directed by Jürgen Graf. Since there was little collaboration between negationists from the French-speaking and German-speaking regions of Switzerland, the group's prime aim was to bring followers from the two linguistic regions together.[100] Truth and Justice also promoted the sale of negationist publications and organised a number of lectures and conferences. As the result of a court order, the group was forced to dissolve in March 2002 and its assets were confiscated by the authorities.[101] Another example of the increase in publishing activities is the paper *Recht + Freiheit* (Law + Freedom), which has been in circulation since June 1995. It was published by Ernst Indlekofer (born 1929) from Basel and had a print run of four thousand in 1998, occasionally attaining a mass print run of eleven to sixty thousand.[102] The paper hosted negationist authors and reported extensively on legal cases related to the anti-racism law.[103] Finally, when Neue Visionen (New Visions), was founded in 1994, under the direction of former *Wehrmacht* officer Gerhard Förster (1920–1998), it became the first Swiss publishing house that systematically included negationist books in its list of publications.[104]

Third, Swiss negationists increased their efforts to receive public attention and to evoke public debates. They sought to enlarge the readership of their publications and to reach a broader audience. The significance of the negationists' strategy of addressing a larger public should not be underestimated. As shown by a 2000 survey on anti-Semitism in Switzerland, 65 per cent of those asked said that they had heard about the denial of the Holocaust. Conversely, 94 per cent assessed that there was no doubt that the extermination of the Jews by National Socialists had really happened.[105] An example of this propaganda strategy comes from 1993, when Jürgen Graf sent unsolicited copies of his publications to different addressees, and to federal MPs and history departments at Swiss universities in particular.[106] Moreover, when complaints were filed for infringement of the anti-racism law, Swiss negationists sought to generate public debate. One strategy was to promote discussion of the freedom of expression that was purportedly being jeopardised by the anti-racist legislation. It was expected that some intellectuals would show their support for the cause of free speech. This sort of debate emerged in French-speaking Switzerland in 1996, when the police confiscated copies of Roger Garaudy's book, *Les mythes fondateurs de la politique israélienne* from several bookshops. Elements of public opinion expressed their disagreement with such measures, by arguing that freedom of speech should be sacrosanct.[107]

Another strategy was to use the public trials as an opportunity to both gather together fellow negationists and to publicly express negationist views. As Meindert Fennema put it, negationists are keen to use such trials to 'present themselves as the underdog and the defenders of freedom of historical research', while the form of the trial itself 'suggests that there are two different interpretations of Nazi history'.[108] This strategy was most prominently applied during the 1998 trial of Jürgen Graf and Gerhard Förster, director of Graf's publishing house Neue Visionen. Thirty to forty supporters showed up in the courtroom, among them Robert Faurisson, the Austrian negationist Wolfgang Fröhlich, Gaston-Armand Amaudruz and Andres J.W. Studer.[109] The trial was extensively covered in print and electronic media and it attracted not inconsiderable public attention.[110] However, while a new generation of negationists increased their efforts to generate a public discussion of their issues, negationism remained an affair of isolated propagandists.

Fourth, the implementation of the anti-racism law in January 1995 had major consequences for Swiss negationism. With this law, negationism, and more specifically the denial of the Shoah, became subject to legal persecution.[111] The denial of the Shoah was explicitly declared a crime in paragraph four of the new Article 261[bis] of the Swiss Criminal Code. It prescribes that anyone who publicly denies, grossly downplays, or seeks to justify genocide or other crimes against humanity should be punished by fine or imprisonment. Many of the notorious Swiss negationists were charged for violating the anti-racism law and some were ultimately convicted. The Federal Tribunal also issued a number of final decisions which clarified several legal issues.[112] As the figures released by state authorities have shown, between 1995 and 2000, fifteen final verdicts were pronounced under the ruling on negationism in the anti-racism law (see table 8.1). Nevertheless, Swiss negationists have continued to publish and disseminate their propaganda. Some have moved their activities to other countries where legislation is less restrictive. Others have used the Internet as a tool to propagate negationist views – taking advantage of the fact that it has proven difficult to develop and enforce legal measures related to Internet activity.[113]

Table 8.1 | *Final Verdicts against Negationist Propaganda under the Anti-racism Law, 1995–2000*

1995–1997	4
1998	2
1999	3
2000	6
Total	15

Source: *Staatsschutzbericht 2000*, published by the Federal Department of Justice and Police, Bern, 2001, p. 36.

Among the negationists charged and convicted on the basis of the anti-racism law, two that are particularly noteworthy are the cases of Jürgen Graf and Gaston-Armand Amaudruz, the two most prominent and prolific representatives of Swiss negationism. In the above-mentioned trial of 1998, Graf was sentenced to fifteen months' imprisonment without probation. He lodged an appeal that was eventually rejected by the Federal Tribunal in March 2000.[114] With Graf due to begin the sentence in October 2000, he fled the country and according to some reports, found refuge first in Iran and then in Russia.[115] In April 2000, Amaudruz was initially sentenced to one year in prison by the criminal court of Lausanne, for having published articles that denied the Shoah. The cantonal court of Vaud later reduced the sentence to three months. After the Federal Tribunal had rejected Amaudruz's appeal in October 2001, he served this sentence in early 2003.[116]

Fifth, increased internationalisation had become a distinctive characteristic of Swiss negationism, reflecting the worldwide development that negationism that has taken since the 1990s. Swiss negationists also reacted to the tougher legal situation in Switzerland by looking for opportunities to engage in propaganda abroad. Their international network and areas of collaboration covered three main areas: conferences and lectures; publications; and the Internet. In addition, Swiss negationists took part in the increasing efforts to find allies on the issue of negationism among radical Islamist groups.

In the 1990s, several negationists from abroad were invited to give lectures in Switzerland. In July 1992, the Avalon circle (see below) organised a lecture by Robert Faurisson in Bern that was attended by fifty to seventy people.[117] The same circle organised a lecture in 1995 by the U.S. negationist Robert H. Countess, who was at the time a member of the editorial board of the JHR.[118] On the other hand, Swiss negationists frequently took part in conferences and lecture events held abroad.

Bernhard Schaub has given numerous talks in Germany since the late 1990s and in 1994, Arthur Vogt and Jürgen Graf attended the twelfth IHR conference in California.[119]

At the level of publications, the international exchange increased significantly in the 1990s. In Switzerland, the promotion and circulation of negationist literature was ensured through the papers *Courrier du Continent* and *Aurora;* the groups AEZ and Truth and Justice; and the publisher Neue Visionen. The Thule Circle and bookstores associated with the *Nouvelle droite* in the French-speaking part of Switzerland also played an important role in the distribution of negationist literature. On the other hand, Swiss authors also contributed articles to international negationist journals and distributed publications for circulation abroad. Jürgen Graf and Bernhard Schaub were authors in JHR.[120] Articles by Jürgen Graf and Andres J.W. Studer were also published in *Vierteljahreshefte für freie Geschichtsforschung* (Quarterly Notes for Free Historical Research), the journal of the Flemish negationist group Free Historical Research (*Vrij Historisch Onderzoek* – VHO), which has been edited since 1998 by the notorious German negationist Germar Rudolf.[121] In the 1990s, Jürgen Graf's books and brochures became part of the body of negationist reference literature.[122]

The Internet represented a further domain where Swiss negationists enjoyed considerable international attention. Once again, Jürgen Graf appeared to be the best-known Swiss author and was featured on numerous negationist websites.[123] The VHO site, which perhaps carries the most complete database on negationist literature written in the German language, contained a large number of writings by Gaston-Armand Amaudruz, Jürgen Graf, Arthur Vogt, Bernhard Schaub and Andres J.W. Studer.[124] Swiss negationists also developed their own website named *Wilhelm Tell* (William Tell), featuring articles written in German, English, French and Italian.[125]

A final aspect of the growing internationalisation was the quest for alliance with radical Islamist factions. Since the publishing of Roger Garaudy's book in 1995, this development has become a prominent feature of international negationism.[126] Once again, Jürgen Graf appeared to be a driving force. For instance, he sought to organise an international negationist conference in Beirut in April 2001, which was meant to be a joint collaboration between the IHR and the group Truth and Justice. After international protest, the Lebanese government prohibited the holding of the conference.[127] Among the invited speakers were Roger Garaudy, Robert Faurisson and the Swiss journalist (and convert to Islam) Ahmed Huber.[128] Ahmed Huber (1928–2008) played a key role in efforts to bring the European extreme right and radical Islamists closer together.[129] In Switzerland, Huber was a long-time contributor to several mainstream newspapers and until 1993, he was member of the Social-Democratic Party, despite the fact that he had published, as early as the 1960s and 1970s, texts in which anti-Zionist claims were fuelled by anti-Semitic sentiments.[130]

To sum up, Swiss negationists were at the forefront of the very early endeavours of postwar European extreme rightists to relativize the crimes and atrocities committed by National Socialism. Since the late 1940s, they managed to maintain a remarkable continuity by circulating and producing propagandistic writings. After decades of mainly underground activities, they started to shift their strategy in the mid 1980s and began to address a wider public with their propagandistic work. Since then, among extreme-right ideologues, negationists would appear to have been the most active, as they account for a small number of prolific propagandists who publish and circulate negationist literature. By developing a global network of contacts, based around publishers and journals outside Switzerland and increasingly through the Internet, they also became the faction of the Swiss extreme right with the strongest international links. Since their worldview was based around conspiracy theories and anti-Semitism, negationists had things in common with the conspiracists, a further current of ideologues and propagandists in the Swiss extreme right, described in the following section.

The Conspiracists: Political Propaganda, New Age and Animal-rights Activism

Conspiracy theories nourish the worldview of groups and individuals from different political and ideological backgrounds.[131] Typically, conspiracists embrace the reasoning that there is a 'suppressed knowledge' that is 'allegedly known to be valid by authoritative institutions but ... suppressed because the institutions fear the consequences of public knowledge or have some evil or selfish motive for hiding the truth'.[132] While extreme-right conspiracists share the view, in common with other believers in global conspiracies, that the world is controlled by powerful subversive forces, they put particular emphasis on the theme of a Jewish and Zionist conspiracy. Hence, anti-Semitism expressed around the theme of a 'world Jewish conspiracy' forms an integral part of extreme-right conspiracist propaganda. When extreme-right conspiracists identify Freemasons, Illuminati, or groups belonging to global finance and multinational corporations as conspirators, they often either see them as closely associated with Jewish and Zionist groups, or use them literally as substitutes for Jews and Zionists.[133] Other versions of extreme-right conspiracy theories are fuelled by nationalist and xenophobic sentiments and thereby point to evil forces who 'work insidiously to subvert independent nations' or ethnic groups.[134] Whereas conspiracy theories are espoused in one way or another by most factions of the Swiss extreme-right, they represent the key characteristic of the worldview and propaganda of those groups and publications that this study subsumes under the category of conspiracists.

Extreme-right conspiracists in Switzerland were typically represented by the paper *Memopress* published by Emil Rahm (born 1930). The paper appeared from 1966 to 1999 and was usually published several times a year with a print run of twenty to forty thousand in the 1980s and 1990s.[135] Most of the time, the paper amounted to only a few unbound photocopied sheets. In 1998, Rahm launched the paper *Prüfen + Handeln* (Check + Act), which subsequently replaced *Memopress* in 1999. Rahm played an important role in the campaign against the anti-racism law in 1993–94 and was the leading figure of the Campaign for Freedom of Speech – Against the Imposition of the UN's Will (*Aktion für freie Meinungsäusserung - Gegen UNO-Bevormundung* – AfM), which gathered over forty thousand signatures for the petition demanding a referendum on the law. The founding members of the AfM were: Walter Fischbacher (president), anti-Semitic author and FDP member until January 1995 (see below); Ernst Indlekofer (vice-president), SVP member until 1996 (see below); Emil Rahm (secretary, spokesperson); Reto Kind (adviser), FDP member and president of the nationalist group Identity Switzerland (*Identität Schweiz*), founded in 1991 – and also editor of a quarterly bulletin with the same name; and Wolfgang von Wartburg (adviser). Fischbacher and Indlekofer resigned from the committee after the media exposed their radical views.[136] Von Wartburg, on the other hand, managed to publish articles attacking the anti-racism law in the Swiss mainstream press.[137] In comparison with the other groups which were also opponents of the anti-racism law and associated with the New Right, Rahm's committee applied a rather crude style and language in its propaganda. The committee warned, for example, that the International Convention on the Elimination of all Forms of Racial Discrimination 'fosters the mixing of peoples, races, cultures and religions'.[138]

As declared in a 1976 issue of *Memopress,* the purpose of the paper was to point toward things that are little known about, even if the truth cannot always be identified.[139] This resembles the claims of conspiracists, who emphasise that they hold 'stigmatized knowledge' and intend to share it with those who live in ignorance.[140] Another example of a conspiracist statement was one posted on the *Memopress* website, denouncing critics of the paper's editor-in-chief Emil Rahm: 'New extremists, who seek a world government with a world religion, try over and over again – by applying the strategy of totalitarian rulers – to put the libertarian and patriotic minded Emil Rahm into an extremist corner and to isolate him. But many have and will see through this, particularly the readers of *Memopress*.'[141] Rahm applied the method of collage in *Memopress* to try and achieve his goal, piecing together different types of texts, including original and reprinted articles, book reviews, book excerpts and simple quotes. In this endeavour, the paper drew on world conspiracy theories and made reference to extreme-right publications.[142]

The most frequently used source of articles published in *Memopress* was the German magazine *CODE*, which was associated with the extreme-right and negationist scene in Germany.[143] As early as 1983, Emil Rahm recommended his readers to subscribe to the precursor of *CODE*, the journal *Diagnosen*. According to Rahm, the journal 'reports comprehensively on state-endangering machinations in politics, finance and economy'.[144] In 1993, *Memopress* reprinted a four-page article taken from *CODE* and written by the Swiss physician Walter Fischbacher. He denounced the anti-racism legislation as a product of 'a catastrophic ideology that wants to mix peoples [*Völker-Durchmischungs-Ideologie*]' and declared that the law 'corresponds to the mono-racist [*monorassistischen*] world population mania supported by progressive circles'.[145] Fischbacher had already published racist texts in the 1980s in the NA party paper *Volk + Heimat*, but first provoked public outrage with his anti-Semitic statements in the 1990s.[146] In 1997, a lower court sentenced Fischbacher to two months' conditional imprisonment because he had circulated a text that was reportedly anti-Semitic. Fischbacher filed an appeal.[147] Later, in 1998, Fischbacher wrote an article in the supplement of Ernst Indlekofer's negationist paper *Recht + Freiheit*.[148]

Memopress advertised books and other publications that were offered for sale by a publisher of the same name (Memopress-Verlag). Some of the publications advocated world conspiracy theories, in which Jews, Freemasons, Illuminati and financiers were presented as secret rulers of the world. *Memopress* had already been exposed to public criticism in the 1980s, when it promoted Heinz Scholl's *Von der Wallstreet gekauft* (Bought by Wall Street).[149] In his anti-Semitic writing, Scholl developed the theory that Zionists and international finance groups had sponsored Adolf Hitler, and that they should therefore be made responsible for the Second World War and the Shoah.[150] In 1978, E.R. [Emil Rahm] wrote a three-page review of Scholl's book; in 1993, the book was still being offered for sale by the Memopress-Verlag.[151] Another book distributed by Memopress-Verlag was *Wer regiert die Welt* (Who Rules the World), written by the U.S. conspiracist Des Griffin, whose writings were distributed in the United States by Noontide Press, which was run by Willis Carto, the founder of IHR.[152] Published in Germany by Diagnosen-Verlag, Griffin's book contained a 75-page excerpt from 'The Protocols of the Elders of Zion'.[153] First published in Russia in 1903, 'The Protocols' represent a forgery and 'the most important anti-Semitic text of modern times'.[154] The text claims that Jews had outlined a plan of world domination at a secret meeting. In 1935, a trial was held in Bern which received a great deal of international attention and confirmed that the document was a forgery.[155] Nonetheless, in Switzerland and elsewhere, some persist in disseminating the text, or making claims for its authenticity.

In 1996, *Memopress* advertised the book, *Geheimgesellschaften und ihre Macht im 20. Jahrhundert* (Secret Societies and Their Power in the Twentieth Century), published by the German conspiracist author Jan van Helsing, alias Jan Udo Holey, in 1993.[156] For selling van Helsing's book, a fine of five thousand Swiss francs was imposed on Emil Rahm under the anti-racism law in 1997.[157] According to some reports, one hundred thousand copies of van Helsing's books were sold and ten thousand in Switzerland alone. These figures include copies of the second volume, *Geheimgesellschaften 2* (Secret Societies 2), which was published in 1995.[158] Helsing integrated a great deal of the common conspiracy propaganda into in his writings and referred to conspiracy theories such as those developed in 'The Protocols of the Elders of Zion'.[159] In early 1996, authorities in Germany and Switzerland confiscated the two books, which were subsequently withdrawn from most bookshops, but still remained available through the Internet.[160]

Van Helsing's publications were particularly well-received by audiences interested in the esoteric and New Age thinking.[161] In fact, they were evocative examples of the way in which disparate elements of conspiracy theories can address different audience segments and hence 'lift conspiratorialism out of the realm of right-wing political ideology and instead link it to occultism, alternative science and healing, New Age spirituality, and allied subjects'.[162] In the 1990s, Switzerland witnessed the emergence of this type of conspiracism in the form of a religious association and a magazine which were both of esoteric and New Age orientation and espoused antisemitic conspiracy theories.[163] While the association claimed that it spoke primarily to a limited circle of followers and true believers, the magazine addressed a larger audience that was interested in esoteric and occult issues.

The religious association was the Universal Church (*Universale Kirche* – UK), a group inspired by theosophical principals combining occultism and Eastern religions.[164] The UK was founded in the United States in 1981, by Peter Leach-Lewis (born 1938), who acted as a spiritual leader of the association. In the late 1990s, the global membership was estimated at two thousand, half of which were to be found in the three German-speaking countries of Germany (600), Switzerland (300) and Austria (100).[165] The association counted a number of managers, lawyers and local politicians among its Swiss members. While the UK had its headquarters in Virginia, USA, the European centre was in the small Swiss town of Walzenhausen (AR). The Universal Church published internal circulars addressed to its members, containing references to conspiracy theories and making verbal attacks on Jews. In the July 1993 circular, 'Inner Light', sent to four hundred German-speaking members, Peter Leach-Lewis stated that 'the Jews are a cancer in the body of mankind'.[166] Another circular from July 1995, which was sent to four hundred Swiss, German and Austrian members, included the following statement: 'Driven by their satanic cupidity, the Jews fomented the Second World War, in the same way that they were responsible for the start of communism.'[167] In addition, according to some reports, a new English–German translation of 'The Protocols of the Elders of Zion' was set about at the European centre of the Universal Church in Walzenhausen. After a while, however, the project was called off.[168] In his role as the administrator of UK's European centre in Switzerland, the German citizen Reimer Peters was charged under the anti-racism law. At the trial, held in the village of Trogen (AR), in July 1996, two hundred and fifty UK followers dressed in cowls showed up to show their solidarity with the defendant.[169] Peters was sentenced to four month's conditional imprisonment and a fine of five thousand Swiss francs. The verdict was upheld by the appeal court in March 1997 and the Federal Tribunal in December 1997.[170]

Closely associated with the Universal Church was the esoteric magazine *ZeitenSchrift* (Times Script), which was launched in 1993 and circulated in Switzerland, Germany and Austria.[171] The magazine tackled a variety of conspiracist topics, including Freemasonry, UFOs and National Socialism, and the links between the Illuminati and the New World Order. According to a systematic analysis of articles published in *ZeitenSchrift*, the magazine combined a conservative Christian-Puritan morality with theosophical and esoteric principles. It also propagated anti-Semitism and world conspiracy theories as well as anti-democratic and theocratic political concepts.[172] *ZeitenSchrift* also covered events organised by the Universal Church and published a twenty-four-page interview with Peter Leach-Lewis in 1996.[173]

In the context of anti-Semitic conspiracist propaganda, there is also a need to mention the Society Against Animal Factories (*Verein gegen Tierfabriken* – VgT) and its president, the animal-rights activist Erwin Kessler.[174] As noted on the VgT's own website, the group (founded 1989) had a membership of twenty-six thousand in 2003.[175] The VgT published its own paper, which ran as *Tierschutz-Nachrichten* (Animal Protection News) from June 1993 to January/February 1996 and has been issued under the title *VgT-Nachrichten* (VgT News) since March/April 1996. According to its own information, the paper usually had a circulation of one hundred thousand copies and sometimes attained a print run of up to two hundred thousand.[176] All issues of the paper were posted on the Internet. The VgT president, Erwin Kessler, was an ardent opponent of the ritual slaughter of animals, and thereby expressed anti-Jewish, as well as anti-Muslim sentiments.[177]

In 1995, Kessler wrote in *Tierschutz-Nachrichten:* 'When the Jews kill large numbers of animals during ritual slaughters, they are no more worthy than the Nazi executioners of old …'[178] Articles published in *VgT-Nachrichten* regularly thematised the alleged 'power of the Jews'.[179] For example, one article denounced Jews for manipulating the ritual slaughter of animals and argued that they could do this because 'our government barely dares to draw breath' whenever Jewish circles want to achieve something in Switzerland.[180] According to Erwin Kessler, in their strategy for gaining influence, Jews would often deny that they belonged to Jewry. He attacked an animal-rights lawyer for spending years 'as a covert Jew' (*verdeckter Jude*) playing down the ritual slaughter of animals.[181] In the July/August 1997 issue of *VgT-Nachrichten,* Kessler quoted sections taken from a book by Jürgen Graf, whom Kessler presented as 'a victim of political persecution'.[182] Ernst Indlekofer's negationist paper, *Recht + Freiheit,* published articles by Kessler in 1996 and 1998.[183] Since 1997, Kessler has been involved in a number of legal proceedings.[184] In 2000, the Federal Tribunal upheld a court decision which had sentenced Kessler to forty-five days' imprisonment for violating the anti-racism law.[185] In a 2002 decision, the Swiss Federal Tribunal declared that it was permissible to say, 'with specific reference to the antisemitically motivated polemic on the ban on the ritual slaughter of animals, … [that Kessler had] contacts with the neo-Nazi and revisionist scene'.[186]

In summary, while conspiracists had been represented since the 1960s by a publication with elevated levels of circulation, they emerged with new confidence in the second half of the 1990s and this was particularly true of those who propagated anti-Semitic conspiracy theories. Organisationally, one section of the Swiss conspiracists consisted of isolated authors and publishers with significant means of publishing at their disposal. This enabled them to circulate their publications widely and to address larger audiences. Another section included a religious association which chose to limit its dissemination of conspiracist and anti-Semitic propaganda to an inner circle of followers. The conspiracists were mainly based in the German-speaking part of Switzerland, not least for reasons of publishing and for the organisational links they were able to maintain with their counterparts in Germany and Austria. This contrasts with the national-revolutionaries, examined in the following section, who were concentrated in the francophone regions of the country and primarily looked to neighbouring France for inspiration.

The National-revolutionaries: Between Intellectualism and Street Militancy

National-revolutionaries draw on the legacy of the national-bolshevist and national-revolutionary intellectuals of the 1920s and 1930s that are associated with the German Conservative Revolution.[187] Since the 1970s, there has been a revival of national-revolutionary ideology in Europe and, in particular, in its renewed version of radical nationalism. National-revolutionaries advocate the idea that the national or ethnic community should form the main foundation of all societies. Their guiding principles therefore include the conception of individuals as firmly integrated parts of the national collective as well as the search for a strong national identity. Since national-revolutionaries stress the centrality of national and cultural identity, they are highly active in the dissemination of ethnopluralism, a key concept in the New Right's differentialist racism. In a clever strategic move, national-revolutionaries combine their emphasis on national identity and self-determination with support for national liberation movements in the Third World. The emphasis on anti-imperialist and anti-capitalistic aims is an attempt to join together with left-wing and libertarian groups, and national-revolutionaries are keen to stress that ultimately, the right and the left have common objectives. In addition, they refer to the concept of a so-called 'third way.' In the 1970s and 1980s, national-revolutionaries prominently promoted the view that a feasible alternative to capitalism and communism exists and that both the superpowers, the United States and the Soviet Union, had to be opposed.[188]

National-revolutionary ideas have served as a point of reference for both the extreme right and some currents of the New Right. In France, the *Nouvelle droite* was inspired by national-revolutionary authors from the interwar period, namely the German, Ernst Niekisch.[189] Organisationally more important, however, was a militant national-revolutionary movement that emerged in the 1970s under the leadership of Jean-Gilles Malliarakis and went on to become part of the extreme right in France.[190] After the movement was struck by numerous divisions in the 1970s and early 1980s, the Nationalist Revolutionary Movement (*Mouvement nationaliste révolutionnaire*) of Malliarakis, together with other groups from the extreme right, founded the organisation Third Way (*Troisième voie* – TV).[191] Featuring decentralised organisational structures, Third Way allowed the different local and regional sections a high degree of autonomy and counted around four hundred supporters in 1991. The strategy to attract members from the skinhead movement was illustrated by the group Nationalist Revolutionary Youths (*Jeunesses nationalistes révolutionnaires* – JNR), founded in 1987 and closely associated with the Third Way. In 1991, a further splitting led to the creation of the group New Resistance (*Nouvelle résistance* – NR), headed by the former GRECE member Christian Bouchet. Eventually, this division proved to be the reason for the dissolution of the Third Way in 1992.

In Switzerland, national-revolutionaries were centred in the French-speaking regions. In the early 1970s, a national-revolutionary movement emerged as a new variant of the extreme right. It was a time of upheaval for a young generation of ideologues and propagandists. Significantly, some of them were to form Switzerland's francophone *Nouvelle droite* a few years later. The first national-revolutionary group was New Social Order (NOS), which existed from 1972 to 1979.[192] It numbered around fifty members and one hundred sympathisers, most of them college and university students. In the beginning, Gaston-Armand Amaudruz acted as an ideological godfather, acquainting the young activists with the realm of European neo-fascism, while his paper *Courrier du Continent* regularly reported on the NOS.[193] In addition, George Oltramare, leader of the Front Movement, also served as a role model for the NOS, as has been noted by Daniel Cologne, himself a prominent member of the NOS.[194] In the 1970s, the NOS was responsible for a number of propaganda campaigns, namely the distribution of pamphlets, posters and stickers. NOS members were also involved in militant acts, including street fights and Molotov cocktail attacks. The group organised gatherings with national-revolutionary leaders. For example, together with a group called Culture and Liberty Circle (*Cercle culture et liberté*), it invited Jean-Gilles Malliarakis to a lecture that took place in Geneva in December 1976.[195] Most NOS activities, however, consisted of issuing publications and periodicals.[196]

The NOS managed to publish three papers: *Renaissance* (1973–74), *Le Huron* (The Boor; 1974–1976) and *Avant-Garde* (1978–1979, 1981). Each of them was available for a short time only, with their print quality and style of layout resembling relatively amateurish fanzines. Most of the articles published in *Renaissance* and *Avant-Garde* were written in simple and often polemic language. On the other hand, the two papers also included a number of more elaborated and intellectually ambitious contributions, authored either by editors or outside authors. *Renaissance* was supposed to have had a circulation of one thousand and was founded by a member of the Association of the Friends of Robert Brasillach.[197] As shown by the references made in the NOS papers, the group was associated with the extreme right, in particular with neo-fascist groups. *Renaissance* published, for example, a communiqué released by Amaudruz's neo-fascist group European New Order (NOE) and referred to organisations and periodicals of the French extreme right.[198] It also brought out a four-page chronology on the deterioration of the French neo-fascist group New Order (*Ordre nouveau* – ON).[199] *Avant-Garde* reported extensively on debates concerning conflicts occurring in the French national-revolutionary movement and contained a number of articles contributed by French authors (e.g. Yves Bataille, Jean Thiriart). It also published a one-page presentation of *Cahiers européens Hebdo* (European Weekly Notebooks), the newest national-revolutionary paper in France at that time.[200] In addition, *Avant-Garde* was the place where growing interest for the French *Nouvelle droite* found expression.[201]

Another publication of the NOS was launched in January 1979 under the name of *Le Rat noir* (The Black Rat).[202] While the editors expressed their goal to lie in the creation of a sophisticated periodical, the paper remained a sort of culture and information bulletin. In fact, *Le Rat noir* was again more of a fanzine than an intellectual magazine. The paper was published in A4 format, had a grim appearance and used rather sloppy language. *Le Rat noir* contained a large number of cartoons and used a Celtic cross and a furious rat as logos, the latter being a symbol commonly used by the extreme right in France. The paper also included a mail order service, offering a wide range of items such as books, journals, stickers and posters. As shown by the articles and advertisements published in *Le Rat noir,* the paper sought to bring together different ideological currents. For instance, the paper also acknowledged negationist authors and collaborated with the French neo-fascist paper *Notre Europe* (Our Europe), which was directed by the notorious extreme-right activist Marc Frederiksen.[203] At the same time, *Le Rat noir* also referred to writings of the French *Nouvelle droite* and presented an extensive survey of New Right periodicals published in France, Germany, Great Britain, Italy, Belgium and Spain.[204]

When *Le Rat noir* was launched, the NOS had already lost much of its significance and the national-revolutionary movement had split up into a variety of small groups. By the end of the 1970s, five different groups existed and each recruited its members more or less from the same milieu: Europe-Youth (*Europe-Jeunesse*), Occident 2000 Viking Youth (*Occident 2000 Viking Jeunesse*), Odal Rune (*Odals Rune*), New Forces (*Forces nouvelles*) and New Social Order.[205] The division was the result of major conflicts which had emerged over the question of which strategy national-revolutionaries should choose to adopt. In reference to these disagreements, the editorial of the first issue of *Le Rat noir* noted that unanimously accepted slogans such as 'USA–USSR Same Struggle' remained valid at the level of street militancy, but were certainly insufficient for building a strong and structured ideology. The paper should try to hold these two factions of the movement together, by continuing to elaborate on ideological foundations in particular, and by reinforcing the commitment to a program marked by revolutionary nationalism.[206]

In the 1980s and 1990s, the name and logo of *Le Rat noir* appeared in the context of a number of actions carried out in the French-speaking part of Switzerland.[207] In 1985, posters were put up in the city of Geneva depicting a Celtic cross and a rat bearing a cudgel and helmet, with a speech-balloon attached containing the slogan: '*Touche pas à mon peuple*' (Don't Touch My People).[208] The slogan became well known as a result of the National Front's anti-immigrant campaigns in France. In 1987, a promotional campaign was launched under the name of *Le Rat noir*, which included an advertising leaflet offering Alfred Rosenberg's *Le mythe du XXème siècle* (The Myth of the Twentieth Century), the reference book of the racist ideology of National Socialism. In an outrageous expression of foul humour, which revealed the group's malicious racism and anti-Semitism, the book was also offered as a luxury edition, bound in the skin of Elie Wiesel.[209]

In the late 1980s, a Swiss branch of the French-based Third Way was founded in Geneva and had close links with the paper *Le Rat noir*. In the beginning, Pascal Junod, the leading figure of the *Nouvelle droite* in the French-speaking part of Switzerland was engaged in the Third Way, along with another member of the Proudhon Circle.[210] According to some reports, the Geneva group counted around thirty members in the early 1990s, among them skinheads and other young militants.[211] The group demonstrated evocatively the influence that the French extreme right exerted on the national-revolutionary scene in francophone

Switzerland. Following the above-mentioned split that took place in the French movement in 1991, the Geneva branch had difficulties taking sides. The section initially called itself Third Way/New Resistance, but changed the name in 1992 to New Resistance. The Geneva section was particularly tied to the French strongholds in Grenoble and Lyon. At the same time, however, it also sought to bridge the linguistic border between the French and German-speaking regions by bringing together groups which had emerged in different parts of the country during the Small Springtime of Fronts (see below). For this purpose, the group organised a meeting in Geneva in October 1990, to which several groups of the Swiss extreme right were invited.[212]

Since it was the aim of the Swiss branches of Third Way and New Resistance to contribute to the ideological sophistication of the extreme-right scene in the French-speaking regions of Switzerland, it established a mail order service for journals issued by the French national-revolutionary movement, such as *Revue d'histoire du nationalisme révolutionnaire* (Review of the History of Revolutionary Nationalism) and *Lutte du peuple* (Struggle of the People). In 1993, the group was also present with its own promotion stand at the Geneva book fair.[213] At the same time, the Geneva section pursued street propaganda activities in the French-speaking regions of Switzerland, including the circulation and posting of flyers and stickers, which had often been produced by its French counterpart. As the group demonstrated a willingness to ally with the left and with the green movement, the circulating flyers and stickers often used symbols and wordings taken from left-wing and ecological groups. Moreover, in 1988, the group was allegedly responsible for a vicious campaign in which razorblades were hidden behind posted stickers bearing racist slogans.[214] Since the mid 1990s, the Geneva New Resistance has not made any public appearances.

In summary, national-revolutionaries have managed to develop organisational and publishing structures since the 1970s. They have founded a variety of groups and publications, even though they mobilised only a small numbers of followers and sympathisers. On the one hand, national-revolutionaries sought to improve the level of intellectual and ideological sophistication in the extreme-right scene. In terms of personnel and ideological positions, they are also considered as forerunners of the *Nouvelle droite* in the French-speaking part of Switzerland. On the other hand, many Swiss national-revolutionaries were attracted to militancy and committed to street propaganda. They also recruited activists from those combative and violent groups which represented an important part of the Swiss extreme right and are described in the following section.

Combative and Violent Groups: Emergence and Consolidation since the Mid 1980s

The use of direct, confrontational, or violent action is characteristic of combative and violent extreme-right groups. Although some members of these groups are engaged in propagandistic and ideologically-oriented activity, a propensity for militancy and violence remains the key feature of their actions and mobilisations. Some combative and violent groups implement organisational structures, including formal membership, strong leadership, training courses and coordinated action, but others, particularly those associated with the skinhead scene, are characterised by a rather low degree of organisation. More often than not, attempts to establish strong leadership turn out to be short-lived.

In Switzerland, the emergence of combative and violent groups in the second half of the 1980s noticeably transformed the nature of the extreme right. It brought dimensions of militancy and violence into extreme-right activities, and, as a consequence, these activities attracted far more attention from the public and the authorities then had previously been the case. In addition, there has also been a significant increase in the degree of mobilisation and activity since the period prior to the mid 1980s. In fact, it is fair to say that right-wing extremism emerged from the underground and began to make its presence felt in the public space. The racist and nationalist ideology of the extreme right received a new dimension since asylum seekers, foreigners and members of other minority groups were now being physically exposed to the threat or use of violence.

Extreme Right Violence: Switzerland in the Midst of Europe

Until the mid 1980s, there were few media reports on violent acts committed by extreme-right militants in Switzerland.[215] During this period, extreme-right violence was largely viewed as a problem facing other European countries, especially France, Germany and Italy, where well-organised underground groups committed terrorist-like acts. In 1980, however, the Swiss public was shocked by the killing of a border guard and a police officer by an extreme-right activist from Germany.[216] The mid 1980s saw the first appreciable spread of extreme-right violence taking place. The media began to report more frequently on violent acts committed randomly by skinheads and soccer hooligans, and analysts warned of the new threat coming from a transformed extreme-right scene that was mainly attracting young activists.[217]

It was during the Small Springtime of Fronts in the late 1980s and early 1990s that the country witnessed a genuine wave of extreme-right violence. A comprehensive data set was gathered during this period which has allowed the production of consistent analyses. Between 1988 and 1993, the extreme right was held responsible for 378 violent acts, which ranged from setting fire to the lodgings of asylum seekers, physical attacks against the person and Molotov cocktail attacks, to violent demonstrations, profanity, harassments and threats.[218] During this period, Switzerland reached a level of heavy violence (e.g., bombings, arson and shootings) that was comparable to Germany. Fourteen people were killed and one hundred and forty-five injured in extreme-right attacks and therefore, 'on a per capita basis the number of deaths in Switzerland has been far higher' than in Germany.[219] Unlike extreme-left violence, which was mainly directed against symbolic objects and property, almost half of all extreme-right violent acts were targeted against persons, either through physical attacks, or in assaults against asylum seekers' accommodation.[220] As pointed out by Pierre Gentile, the 'massive use of threats and direct violence aiming at frightening enemies is quite new in Swiss political life and characterises the contemporary radical right strategy'.[221]

After 1994, the available data regarding the development of extreme-right violence is less consistent. There is an annual chronology keeping a record of racist acts (see tables 8.2. and 8.3.), but this also includes acts which are not necessarily carried out by the extreme right or its sympathisers. In addition, the chronology presents a very inclusive data set which incorporates all kinds of acts and mobilisations, including violent and non-violent, as well as legal and illegal forms of activity.[222] On the other hand, the official figures published in the *Staatsschutzbericht* (State Protection Report) are limited to acts of violence against asylum seekers' accommodations (see table 8.4). Somewhat randomly selected, the state reports also present a documented list of violent acts in which extreme-right activists were involved, most of them attributed to skinheads.[223] Thus, in contrast to Germany, where the annual *Verfassungsschutzbericht* (Protection of the Constitution Report) by the Federal Ministry of the Interior publishes complete data sets on criminal offences and violent acts attributable to the extreme right, the Swiss authorities do not provide such comprehensive figures.

Despite the lack of consistent data, it is possible to determine tendencies of extreme-right violence in Switzerland since the mid 1990s, at least of those with a racist background. After a fall in racist violence in 1996 and 1997, the number of racist acts then increased in the two fol-

Table 8.2 | Violent Racist Acts, 1992–2002

	1992	1993	1994	1995	1996	1997	1998	1999	2000	2001	2002
Threats, Harassment	1	5	13	13	6	3	6	10	12	2	6
Damage to Property, Graffiti	23	4	9	10	7	10	7	18	7	8	10
Physical Assaults	9	6	19	15	6	3	17	23	19	19	12
Arson Attacks, Gunshots	20	13	15	–	5	2	1	8	5	2	3
Total	**53**	**28**	**56**	**38**	**24**	**18**	**31**	**59**	**43**	**31**	**31**

Source: http://chrono.gra.ch/chron/chron_index.asp, retrieved 31 August 2008.

Table 8.3 | Non-violent Racist Acts, 1992–2002

	1992	1993	1994	1995	1996	1997	1998	1999	2000	2001	2002
Verbal Racism	5	5	6	10	16	9	25	12	12	18	21
Discrimination	1	4	6	6	6	5	4	6	3	5	4
Circulation of Racist Writings and Recordings	1	3	5	11	20	16	9	5	6	10	6
Holocaust Denial	1	6	3	2	2	4	2	2	3	1	–
Extreme-Right Parades, Appearances, Meetings	1	1	2	1	5	6	13	14	26	15	15
Total	**9**	**19**	**22**	**30**	**49**	**40**	**53**	**39**	**50**	**49**	**46**

Source: http://chrono.gra.ch/chron/chron_index.asp, retrieved 31 August 2008.

Table 8.4 | *Violent Acts against Asylum Seekers' Accommodations, 1990–2000*

	1990	1991	1992	1993	1994	1995	1996	1997	1998	1999	2000
Bomb Attacks	2	3	2	–	–	–	–	–	1	–	–
Cases of Arson	6	39	16	3	7	2	6	2	1	3	4
Shotgun Assaults	4	8	2	–	2	1	–	–	–	2	–
Threats	4	15	1	4	–	–	–	1	–	3	–
Damage to Property	11	12	21	2	1	3	–	–	1	3	–
Total	**27**	**77**	**42**	**9**	**10**	**6**	**6**	**3**	**3**	**11**	**4**

Sources: *Staatschutzbericht 1993/94*, published by the Federal Department of Justice and Police, Bern, 1995, p. 42; *Staatschutzbericht 2000*, published by the Federal Department of Justice and Police, Bern, 2001, p. 34.

lowing years, with a peak in 1999, before the figures stabilised at something like the level of 1995 (see table 8.2.). Compared to the first half of the 1990s, it appears that certain types of heavy racist violence, such as arson attacks and gunshots, have noticeably decreased. This observation is also confirmed by official figures, which recorded four acts of violence against asylum seekers' accommodations in 2000, compared to seventy-seven in 1991, when extreme-right violence was at its worst to date (see table 8.4). On the other hand, considering the growth in non-violent racist acts that has been seen since 1996, particularly at parades and other public gatherings, it seems that the extreme right has striven to reinforce its organised, non-violent presence in the public space (see table 8.3.).

The characteristics of extreme-right violence in Switzerland bear similarities to those observed in other European countries.[224] For the period between 1984 and 1993, Swiss studies have shown that 51 per cent of extreme-right violent acts were committed by organised groups. While the majority of violent offences (69 per cent) involved instrumental actions with a defined political aim, 31 per cent of the violence was expressive, its main intention being to strengthen the collective identity of the extreme right.[225] The relatively high level of organisation and politicisation certainly reflects the transformed nature of the extreme right during the Small Springtime of Fronts, in the late 1980s and early 1990s, which saw the emergence of a significant number of well-organised groups.

In recent years, however, it appears that extreme-right violence has included a larger number of non-organised, spontaneous acts, which are often committed by racist skinheads.[226] As studies of the skinhead violence suggest, with their militant attitudes and violent offences, these predominantly young perpetrators are looking to impress their fellows or to establish status in the scene.[227] In Switzerland, too, their violence is boosted less by coherent political ideas than by situative, instant factors such as group dynamics and the effects of alcohol.[228] Nonetheless, since most violent acts are directed against foreigners, asylum seekers and their hostels, an exclusionist ideology, namely racism and xenophobia, serves to underpin much of the violence. In recent years, moreover, attacks on left-wing and anti-racist groups have also become part of the common pattern of extreme-right violence in Switzerland.

The Reactions of the State: From Restraint to Counter-measures

Research on right-wing extremism emphasizes the important role that the state plays as a force for intervention and prevention against extreme-right mobilization. While it is a matter for debate how far legislation and authorities should intervene in the areas of propagandistic activities and ideological endeavours – an issue which is handled in various ways in different countries – there is unanimous agreement that authorities must take the most effective measures to prevent and persecute criminal offences and violent acts.[229] In Switzerland, the reactions and countermeasures adopted by the state have changed considerably since the early 1980s. More often than not, the responses to right-wing extremism, and its combative and militant representatives in particular, have been made as a consequence of increased public pressure and have represented delayed adjustments to de-facto situations.

Surveying the counter-measures that have been taken by state authorities since the early 1980s, it is possible to distinguish four phases. The first phase between 1980 and 1989 was characterized by an attitude of inattention and restraint. Security services, especially those concerned with the so-called Protection of the State (*Staatsschutz*) – the Swiss equivalent to the German Protection of the Constitution (*Verfassungsschutz*) – considered right-wing extremism an insignificant issue. A main reason for this was the fact that the political left had been considered the primary and most likely source of potential subversion throughout the Cold War period. While the services dealing with political extremism and security issues carried out extensive policing of the left, including surveillance and other preventative measures, a fact which was exposed in 1989 in the secret files scandal known as the *Fichenaffäre*, they paid little attention to the extreme right and were poorly documented on its organisations and activities.[230] As a result, large parts of the police were logistically unprepared and politically insensitive when militant groups of the extreme right emerged and their violence dramatically increased in the late 1980s. In addition, the Swiss federalist system made it often difficult for police forces to pursue a coherent policy and to coordinate cantonal and local activities.[231]

The second phase, which covered the first half of the 1990s, can be defined as a period of growing public pressure which ultimately prompted a reaction on behalf of the authorities and resulted in institutional measures. With the significant increase in racist and extreme-right violence that was seen in the late 1980s and early 1990s, the general public and political officials were eventually becoming aware of the considerable presence of militant right-wing extremism in Switzerland. As a consequence, the federal government released the 1992 report on extremism in Switzerland, launched the publication of an annual *Staatsschutzbericht* and commissioned a study on the Swiss extreme right.[232] Some critics argued, however, that the shift of focus had much to do with the need for the security services and particularly the Federal Police to reclaim legitimacy in the public eye, after they had largely been discredited by the *Fichenaffäre*.

The third phase, covering the second half of the mid 1990s, was marked by the expansion and consolidation of the penal and administrative measures taken by authorities. With the implementation of the anti-racism law in January 1995, authorities received a legal instrument with which to combat any racist speech or act. Although they showed some restraint in applying the law in a repressive way, the number of criminal prosecutions and sentences increased in the late 1990s, many of them involving members of the extreme right. In 1995, the government appointed the Federal Commission against Racism (*Eidgenössische Kommission gegen Rassismus* – EKR) which was designed as a specialized body against racism, but was also much concerned with right-wing extremism. Moreover, police authorities were now closely watching the development of the extreme right and in 1996 the Federal Police published a detailed report on skinheads in Switzerland.[233] At the cantonal level, police forces demonstrated that they had somewhat increased their determination to prosecute the militant activities of the extreme right.

Finally, in the fourth phase (since 2000), the authorities have increasingly applied a comprehensive approach to right-wing extremism. It appears to have been acknowledged that policies designed to deal with right-wing extremism should not only be a matter of criminal law and policing. For example, the authorities welcomed the suggestions made by two study groups of experts that were set up, to intensify scientific research on Swiss right-wing extremism, and as a consequence, the Federal Council took the decision to allocate funding for a research program on right-wing extremism in June 2001.[234] The view which was taken across the board by the authorities was partially the result of a large public and political debate in the summer of 2000, following the disruption by a hundred skinheads of an address that the Federal Councillor Kaspar Villiger had delivered at the national holiday event at the Rütli (see below). Interviewed by the Swiss media right after the incident, Villiger claimed to know nothing of the political motivations of these Swiss extreme-right adherents.[235]

The Fronts: A Swiss Phenomenon

The fronts were only active from the mid 1980s to the early 1990s, but within the militant extreme right in Switzerland, they are considered a typical Swiss phenomenon. The fronts drew on the ideological and symbolic legacy of the Front Movement of the 1930s and were keen to present themselves as the true successors to this last and larger extreme-right movement in Switzerland. In fact, their ideology featured most of the characteristics of the fascist and National Socialist factions in the Front Movement of the 1930s. While classical racism, anti-Semitism, nationalism, anti-communism and authoritarianism were expressed through the groups' political program and propaganda, militaristic and violence-prone attitudes were manifest in the conduct of the group members. At the same time, the fronts sought to exploit patriotic symbols and references for radical nationalist and xenophobic purposes.

The first front group, the New National Front (*Neue Nationale Front –* NNF), was founded in the canton of Aargau in 1985. It had around forty members in 1987, most of whom were skinheads.[236] In December 1985, the NNF provoked public outrage when, under the leadership of National Action MP Eric Weber, several NFF members disturbed the sitting of the cantonal parliament of Basel City by throwing leaflets into the parliament hall bearing the slogan 'We don't want Turkish pigs'.[237] The adolescent NNF leaders, all between eighteen and twenty years old, made some effort to politicise their young followers and present the Front Movement of the 1930s as a historical model.[238] From 1985 to 1987, the NNF also released its own, simply made organ called *Der Wehrwolf* (The Wolf That Defends Itself), which mostly featured articles dealing with skinhead matters. After the NNF's failure to present a candidate list for the 1987 National Council elections, under the name of *Junges Aargau* (Young Aargau), the group paled into insignificance, although some leading figures did reappear in other extreme-right groups in the late 1980s.

More important was the Patriotic Front (*Patriotische Front* – PF), which was formed in 1988 and assumed a central role in the Small Springtime of Fronts in the late 1980s and early 1990s.[239] The PF is considered the most powerful organisation of the militant extreme right to date. Founding members had previously been active in a small racist group which called itself Ku Klux Klan (KKK) and was responsible for several violent acts in 1987. The PF established solid organisational structures featuring strong leadership and an elaborate internal communications network. It also set up a merchandising service, offering T-shirts, stickers and badges. According to its own information, the PF was able to count on four hundred members in 1989.[240] The PF espoused a racist ideology and made radical discriminatory claims on issues of migration and asylum policies. The political program had as its aim the 'predominance of the white race', the 'preservation of occidental culture', and the 'repulsion of influences foreign to the species'. It also demanded the abolition of the right to asylum, and the expulsion of Jews and 'all non-European immigrants'.[241] In public, however, the PF sought to disguise its extreme-right worldview and racist intentions by referring to patriotic symbolism and exploiting Swiss myths as emblematic sources of reference. The leading figure of the PF, Marcel Strebel (1950–2001), gained some public prominence by making appearances in the electronic and print media. For example, he took part in the renowned TV discussion round *Zischtigs-Club* (Tuesday-Club), where he overtly propagated his racist views.[242] The weekly magazine *Schweizer Illustrierte* published a seven-page cover story which presented the PF as being more like a group of devoted patriots than right-wing extremists.[243] Overall, the wide media coverage that the PF received in 1989 contributed to the group becoming disproportionately well known, despite its relatively small levels of membership.

The actions and demonstrations organised by the PF were usually meant to stir public attention. In late 1988, the group distributed flyers in several regions of central Switzerland that contained racist and xenophobic slogans such as 'invasion of niggers, Tamils and Turks' and 'fight the illegal immigration of Muslim bogus asylum seekers'.[244] In May 1989, the PF held a demonstration in front of an asylum seekers' accommodation in the canton of Zug, chanting the slogans 'Asylum seekers, go! Asylum seekers are criminals'.[245] PF members proved their propensity to use violent means of action, and were responsible for several attacks against asylum seekers and their lodgings. In November 1989, they attacked a home for asylum seekers in the canton of Zug. Since police forces responded hesitantly to the violent acts that were committed by the PF members, the public reacted with criticism and prompted the authorities to react in a more resolute fashion.[246] The legal actions that were eventually brought against leading members of the PF, and the erratic behaviour of the PF leader, Marcel Strebel, triggered the group's disintegration in the early 1990s. Nonetheless, Strebel participated in the 1991 National Council elections in the canton of Schwyz and his Party of the Future (*Partei der Zukunft*) gained 6.4 per cent of the overall vote and in fact they gained as much as around 10 per cent in some electoral districts.[247]

The New Front (*Neue Front* – NF) was another extreme-right group that emerged in the late 1980s.[248] It gained some degree of importance when it tried to unify the extreme right during the Small Springtime of Fronts by creating a rallying organisation. The attempt eventually failed because of squabbling among the leadership and the official foundation of the NF in September 1989 turned out to be a stillborn birth. Only twenty-five people showed up at the founding meeting, after the members of the Patriotic Front and the representatives from the different regional scenes had dissociated themselves from the attempt to create a rallying organisation. The significance of the NF lay in the endeavour to reach a certain degree of ideological sophistication among the young activists by introducing national-revolutionary ideas in the ideological realm of the Swiss extreme right. A further aspect of the NF was the effort to approach the left-wing scene in attempts to point to common ideological grounds, namely the shared anti-imperialistic and anti-capitalistic attitude, and the criticism of multinational corporations.[249] Under the guidance of Christian Scherrer (born 1970) and two former New National Front members, the NF developed the most elaborated ideological foundations so far seen in a combative extreme-right group from Switzerland. The eighteen-page political program declared that the NF sought to pursue a third way between liberalism/capitalism and communism, which rejected what they dubbed the 'cultural imperialism of Coca-Cola and Vodka'.[250] The program further stressed the importance of strengthening national and regional identities. In this respect, it referred explicitly to the concept of ethnopluralism which, it claimed, would 'prevent the self-alienation of peoples through egalitarian ideas' and allow for 'the diversity of cultures to be preserved'.[251]

After the attempt to establish an umbrella organisation had failed, the National-Revolutionary Party of Switzerland (*Nationalrevolutionäre Partei der Schweiz* – NRP) was founded in March 1989.[252] Based in the canton of Schaffhausen, the NRP numbered around twenty-five to thirty members, who were mostly young activists and members of the local skinhead scene. The group was able to establish firm organisational structures, including statutes, a political program, a magazine and training courses. Since the NRP sought to become known to the public, the party members took part in political meetings and pursued activities addressing a larger audience. Arthur Vogt, who later joined the faction of Swiss negationists, played an influential role in the elaboration of the NRP's political program. The program stated that the NRP saw itself as an opposition to capitalism, imperialism and marxism, and that the group would fight against any kind of internationalism and cultural imperialism because both would destroy the uniqueness of peoples and cultures.[253] According to an article published in the group's small publication *Nationale Opposition* (National Opposition), the politics of the future should give up on the outdated scheme of left and right and seek instead to find a 'healthy harmony between socialism and nationalism'.[254]

Despite these high-flown phrases, NRP members demonstrated a willingness to use violence in their actions. In 1989 and 1990, they were involved in a number of militant activities and acts of heavy violence.

After the NRP disappeared from the scene in 1990 and the afore-mentioned disintegration of the Patriotic Front, the Fronts lost their significance as organisational formations of the Swiss extreme right. However, as will be shown in the next section, extreme-right skinheads, who represented an important section of the activists engaged with the Fronts, continued to carry on the trends for militancy and violence in the Swiss extreme right scene.

Skinheads: Consolidation of a Racist Subculture

Of all the movements within the extreme right in Western Europe, it was the skinheads who experienced the greatest increase in membership and mobilisation throughout the 1990s. Extreme-right skinheads stand for one distinct current within the heterogeneous skinhead movement. Historically, the skinhead movement emerged in the U.K. in the late 1960s and featured a pronounced working-class image that found expression in clothing and outlook. It was meant to stand against the middle-class flower power or left-wing movements of the time.[255] In the late 1970s and 1980s, one part of the skinhead movement came under the influence of the British National Front. Consequently, the first groups of racist and extreme-right skinheads, so-called White Power Skins, came into being and gathered around the music label White Noise Records, the band Skrewdriver and its leader Ian Stuart, and the neo-fascist organisation Blood & Honour.[256] Since some skinheads opposed this shift towards racism and 'white supremacy', the skinhead movement became increasingly factionalised. One faction founded the Skinheads Against Racial Prejudices (SHARP) in New York in 1986, recalling the anti-racist origins of the movement.[257]

In the 1980s and 1990s, as skinheads spread all around Europe and North America, it was the racist and extreme-right faction that particularly appealed to young people, mostly young males under twenty years old. Consequently, the extreme-right skinhead subculture developed into one of the notable youth cultures of the 1990s.[258] It is a culture comprised of an array of small groups, loose networks and dispersed gangs, held together by cultural means such as music, parties, concerts, magazines and common dress codes.[259] Skinheads also use the Internet intensively and have thereby developed their own 'cyber community' which enjoys 'some sense of camaraderie without ever coming into face-to-face contact'.[260] Music is a key element of the skinhead counterculture and serves different purposes: it is used as a powerful propaganda tool that proliferates racist and neo-fascist messages or calls for violence.[261] But music also creates something like a collective identity for this subculture, or at least a common frame of cultural reference. As in other youth subcultures, music evocatively expresses the rejection of the normative order of mainstream society.[262] This youthful cultural rebellion of skinheads is also articulated in the glorification of the National Socialist period, most commonly expressed in skinhead magazines (called skinzines) and song lyrics, or through fascist salutes and birthday festivities for prominent figures of the National Socialist regime. Although the political ideas of extreme-right skinheads are hardly elaborate and often quite confused, they most commonly assemble ideological and symbolic references to National Socialism and fascism.[263]

As skinheads are persistently responsible for acts of violence and they express overtly racist and National Socialist views, they are considered to be the faction of the extreme right that is most prone to violence and the most offensive. As a result, they are at the centre of public concern and counter-reactions from state authorities and anti-fascist groups. Although skinheads generally refuse to create organised groups and are rather reluctant to engage in politics or espouse political doctrines, neo-fascist groups and leaders have regularly made attempts to politicise and organise parts of the skinhead movement.[264] There have also been indications in recent years that 'more or less racist youth movements are gradually developing into more "mature" political organisations and networks as their members grow older'.[265] As the example of France shows, there are links between skinheads and radical right-wing parties that go beyond the fact that young militants are usually attracted by charismatic political leaders.[266] Overall, however, one may agree with Walter Laqueur who argues that: 'The skinheads' political significance should not be overrated: Future historians will probably find them a fascinating footnote in the history of late-twenty-century [sic] customs and manners rather than politics'.[267]

In Switzerland, extreme-right skinheads were typically White Power Skins, the racist and militant current of the skinhead movement. There is still no comprehensive social science study of the Swiss skinhead movement. The existing accounts are rather impressionistic and provide little explanation for the mobilisation of extreme-right skinheads.[268] In Switzerland too, anti-racist skinheads existed in form of so-called red skins and the SHARP movement. As shown in a 1997 survey conducted among Swiss army recruits, 30 per cent of those who declared that they belonged to the skinhead movement (n = 295), affirmed that they were neither racists, nor prone to violence.[269] A few extreme-right skinheads had already been active in a neo-fascist group of the early 1980s, but they made their first public appearance in the mid 1980s, when they began to use various forms of violent acts. From that point on, skinheads have been considered, in the media and in public opinion, as the main actors of the militant extreme right. As in other European countries, skinzines, meetings and concerts became major attractions in the skinhead subculture and created a network of internal communication. The vast majority of Swiss skinheads were male and still very young. Female skinheads, called *Renees*, were highly under-represented. In terms of their socioeconomic situation, it appears that young skinheads were no more disadvantaged than other adolescents were. As the above-mentioned survey indicates, 74.3 per cent of those who admitted that they were members of the skinhead movement, racist or non-racist, had a stable job, compared to 62.6 per cent of the other recruits asked (n = 20,489).[270]

The development of the Swiss extreme-right skinhead movement in the period from the mid 1980s to the early 2000s can be divided into three phases. The first phase covers the second half of the 1980s, when skinheads were active in several regions and towns of Switzerland.[271] Since they carried out numerous racist-motivated offences and violent acts, this was the first time that the public was confronted with large-scale violence committed by the extreme right.[272] In 1985, according to the information of skinheads at the time, the movement numbered approximately two hundred followers, from all over the country. Although most skinheads were reluctant to organise themselves into structured groups, loosely organised *groupuscules* were initially created at the local level. For example, in 1986 and 1987, skinheads created several short-lived groups in the town of Schaffhausen, which later served as a recruitment base for the above-mentioned National-Revolutionary Party of Switzerland. During the Small Springtime of Fronts, skinheads were also found among the ranks of insurgent organisations, such as the New National Front, Patriotic Front, National-Revolutionary Party of Switzerland and Third Way/New Resistance. Skinheads belonged to the militant factions of these groups and contributed to the high level of aggressiveness and violence in their activities.

The second phase spans the first half of the 1990s and was characterised by a growing number of skinheads and the creation of larger skinhead organisations.[273] According to official figures, the number of extreme-right skinheads increased from two hundred in 1990 to five hundred in 1995.[274] Most continued to demonstrate an aggressive and racist attitude; many showed a propensity to commit violence and were eventually involved in a significant number of violent acts. The regional bastions were in the cantons of Aargau, Basel, Bern, Neuchâtel, Schaffhausen, Solothurn, Thurgau, Vaud and Zurich. Skinheads founded skinzines and regional-based groups which usually had some ten to fifty supporters. Of these groups, the Swiss and European Nationalist Party (*Parti nationaliste suisse et européen* – PNSE) appeared to be the best-organised (in terms of political program, formal membership, training courses and members' uniforms). It also had ties to counterparts in neighbouring countries, since the PNFE from France served as a model organisation and two key figures of the PNSE were also members of the PNFE.

The most significant skinhead group to date has been the Swiss Hammerskins (*Schweizerische Hammerskins* – SHS), which formed in Lucerne in 1990. Originally founded in the United States in the 1980s, the internationally active Hammerskins had followers in many European countries, and were perhaps the best example of what was called a 'global community of young neo-Nazi skinheads'.[275] According to the 2001 German Protection of the Constitution Report, 'the "Hammerskins" have a National Socialist and racist orientation and see themselves as an elite current within the scene'.[276] In the beginning, the Swiss Hammerskins had very little in the way of organisational structures and the group was primarily linked through regular gatherings. In addition, the release of skinzines ensured the possibility for communication within the group. To date, the SHS has been responsible for the publication of three series of skinzines: first *Totenkopf* (Death's Head) and *Berserker*, and since 1994, *Hammer*. It appears, however, that from the mid 1990s on, the SHS became more organised and eventually acted as an umbrella organisation for local and regional skinhead groups. To this end, the group founded the Swiss Organisation for the Development of Hammerskins (*Schweizerische Hammerskin-Aufbauorganisation* – SHS-AO) in 1994, which was responsible for recruiting and training new members.[277]

In the third phase – from the mid 1990s onwards – the development of the extreme-right skinhead movement in Switzerland has been characterised by seven distinct features. While some tendencies were already visible in the previous two phases and were now simply reinforced, others emerged only now and thereby gave the Swiss skinhead movement some new characteristics. First, the number of extreme-right skinheads increased significantly in the second half of the 1990s. According to estimates presented by the authorities, after a brief decline in 1996 and 1997 (to the level of 250 to 350 skinheads), the number of skinheads sharply increased in 1998 (to around five or six hundred) and reached a high of some 600 to 700 supporters in 2000.[278] Taking into account the difference in population size, such numbers are comparable to the estimates made for Germany, where authorities recorded 9,700 extreme-right activists in 2000, most of them skinheads.[279]

Second, the skinheads reinforced the efforts to implement organisational structures in the form of organised groups and skinzines. Despite the attempts to organise the movement, one must bear in mind that a large number of skinheads still preferred to act in a non-organised manner or to take advantage of selective organisational structures (e.g., skinzines, concerts, music CD distribution). In the second half of the 1990s, the SHS was still the largest skinhead organisation. The group was held together through the skinzine *Hammer,* an information bulletin, an internal information hotline and a clubroom named *Nibelungen,* which was established in 2000 in the small town of Malters (LU). Since the SHS claimed to be an elite organisation, the group made it difficult for new members to join.[280] Initially associated with the Hammerskins was the skinzine *Race et Nation* which had been published in the French-speaking part of Switzerland since 1998. Significantly, the magazine was keen to reveal the pagan and mystical foundations of fascism and National Socialism, and therefore featured long articles on Julius Evola and the German SS members Otto Rahn and Karl Maria Wiligut.[281]

Opposing such an elitist stance, Swiss skinheads created a new group in 1998 which took the name of Blood & Honour. Blood & Honour had originally been founded by Ian Stuart, in the U.K. in the 1980s, but the racist and neo-fascist group had since expanded into most European countries. In Switzerland, the group numbered around fifty skinheads from different regions and released two skinzines, *Blood & Honour Schweiz,* and *Blood & Honour Romandie,* which was written in French.[282] As well as the two main organisations, SHS and Blood & Honour, the Swiss skinhead movement has generated a number of small local or regional groups since the mid 1990s. Since most of these groups were short-lived and were continually changing their names, it appears that the skinhead movement was marked by a very high degree of organisational instability and fluctuation.[283]

Third, music culture took a dominant place in the subcultural activities of the skinheads. Such activities included the organisation of concerts and the distribution of music CDs. In addition, skinzines featured a great number of music-related articles, including interviews with band members and record reviews and they kept the audience informed about the international skinhead music scene.[284] The best-known of the Swiss skinhead bands to date was called Storm Troopers (*Sturmtruppen*), which was around in the early 1990s.[285] On a number of different occasions, the circulation of skin music provoked a reaction from the Swiss public.[286] Most significantly, the public was struck by the increased number of concerts drawing large audiences. In 1998, for example, a concert featuring well-known foreign bands attracted eight hundred skinheads, including many from France, Germany, Italy and Central Europe. The concert was organised by *Mjölnir Diffusion*, a Neuchâtel-based distributor that was associated with the SHS in the French-speaking regions of Switzerland.[287] A large number of concerts also took place in the German-speaking regions, where they were attended by up to a thousand people.

Fourth, skinheads continued to demonstrate a propensity to violence and were responsible for the majority of violent acts committed by the extreme right. While the targets in most cases were foreigners and often selected at random, there was also a growth in organised violent acts against groups of the left, in particular against anti-racist and left-libertarian groups. In November 1995, for example, the SHS-AO was responsible for an assault against the 'Festival of Friendship between Peoples' (*Festival der Völkerfreundschaft*), which was organised by anti-racist groups in the town of Hochdorf (LU).[288] As also happened in Germany, the summer of 2000 saw the first case in Switzerland of a skinhead posting the names and addresses of anti-racist activists on the Web.[289]

Fifth, internationalisation remained a central feature of the Swiss skinhead movement and this corresponded with the genuinely global character of skinhead subculture. The international linkage included the broad supply system of skin music and skinzines, as well as the use of the Internet as a tool for international networking. Skinheads also displayed a great deal of physical mobility. Skins from Germany, France, Austria and Italy have regularly attended concerts and gatherings organised in Switzerland. At the same time, Swiss skinheads have been regular visitors to concerts and meetings abroad.[290] Moreover, the dates of Hitler's birthday or the death of Rudolf Hess have been treated as nostalgic occasions that skinheads from different countries have used as an occasion to gather. The National Initiative of Switzerland (*Nationale Initiative Schweiz* – NIS) had particularly close ties to the German extreme right. NIS members took part in the large demonstration that was held in Munich in March of 1997, in protest against the historical exhibition 'The crimes of the *Wehrmacht*'.[291] In late 1999, the links to the German extreme right reached a new level, when the National-Democratic Party of Germany (*Nationaldemokratische Partei Deutschlands* – NPD) reportedly made plans to create a party section in Switzerland.[292] While the project turned out to be a failure, another party was founded in April 2001, under the name of the National Party of Switzerland (*Nationale Partei Schweiz* – NPS).[293] According to the 24-year old founder, David Mulas, the NPS sees itself as a 'sister party' of the German NPD.[294] Although the NPS issued its own paper, *Das nationale Blatt* (The National Paper), and asserted that the party would take part in elections, it appears that there has been very little party activity to date.

Sixth, skinheads deliberately set out to seek public attention, and in this respect they showed a fair amount of self-confidence and impertinence. For instance, on different occasions in April 1997, up to a hundred skinheads marched through the streets of Zurich's city centre, chanting Nazi slogans and harassing passers-by with racist insults.[295] In the same year, skinheads began to attend the August 1st celebration event on the Rütli, located in central Switzerland.[296] While it was still a small group of skinheads shouting National Socialist slogans and making Hitler salutes that year, the event was to become a major public appearance for skinheads in the years that followed. On 1 August 2000, more than one hundred skinheads attended the event on the Rütli and disrupted the address that was given by the Federal Councillor, Kaspar Villiger.[297] After this powerful public demonstration, Roger Wüthrich, founder of the Avalon circle (see below) and mouthpiece of the skinheads, presented a strategy paper to the public which proposed that the skinheads would give up the use of force if the authorities would stop targeting their meetings and their distribution of propaganda.[298] Although the authorities and senior party officials categorically rejected the skinhead's offer, Roger Wüthrich was received by the chief of the Swiss Federal Police.[299] Despite the public outrage in 2000, even more skinheads attended the August 1st commemorations that took place at the Rütli in the three years that followed.[300]

Seventh, there have been several attempts to increase levels of politicisation and ideological sophistication within the skinhead movement. To this end, lectures and seminars were proposed to skinheads and groups with party-like structures were created. In the late 1990s, the Avalon circle assumed a key role in the efforts to instruct skinheads on cultural, ideological and legal matters.[301] The circle was co-founded in 1990 by Andreas Gossweiler (born 1968), former member of the New National Front, and Roger Wüthrich (born 1961), former leader of the Viking Youth of Switzerland (*Wiking-Jugend Schweiz* – WJS). Created in 1987 and dissolved in 1991, the WJS was a section of the German Viking Youth.[302] The Avalon circle initially claimed to be interested in the premises of the French *Nouvelle droite* and in seeking to engage in cultural and intellectual activities. However, the circle's close links to the extreme right were clearly demonstrated as early as the first half of the 1990s, when it organised lectures with the best-known negationists from abroad. The broad range of non-public events was meant to target different audiences. The list of interested parties also included the skinheads, who were alleged to show particular interest in issues such as Celtic and Germanic legacy, the *Waffen SS* and National Socialism. Lately, Wüthrich has also acted as a legal adviser to skinheads, instructing them on their rights in cases of criminal proceedings, house searches and imprisonment.

The creation of party-like groups was another strategy designed to politicise the skinhead movement. 1996 saw the founding of the National Initiative of Switzerland which aimed to establish a party organisation and to stand in elections. Among its founders were Andreas Gossweiler and Mario Rigoni (born 1969). The latter had been a candidate for the Swiss Democrats in the 1995 National Council elections.[303] According to the political program of the NIS, the party demanded an 'immediate end to immigration and naturalisation', 'Swiss jobs for Swiss workers' and the 'support for Swiss-only classes in schools'.[304] The group numbered around thirty members, many of them skinheads, and held several meetings in the late 1990s, but ultimately, the NIS failed to establish itself as a political party.[305]

To date, the most significant example of a political party being launched was the Party of National Oriented Swiss (*Partei National Orientierter Schweizer* – PNOS).[306] Founded in 2000, the group was initiated by the 21-year old Sacha Kunz, former Blood & Honour member and owner of a skinhead merchandising store in the canton of Basel Country.[307] According to the group's English language self-portrait, posted on its professionally styled website, the 'PNOS is the party of modern nationalism, and is the only nationalist party in Switzerland which openly stands for those principles which assure the continued existence of Switzerland as the nation of the Swiss people'.[308] The negationist propagandist, Bernhard Schaub, sought to play an influential role in the partisan activities of the young activists. He held the position of executive party member and gave speeches at meetings and rallies organised by the PNOS.[309] The group set up organisational structures such as statutes, a political program and a magazine named *Zeitgeist*, as well as holding annual party assemblies.

Despite efforts to increase the level of politicisation and to implement organisational structures, the majority of the extreme-right skinhead movement in Switzerland maintained its rather non-political profile and its loosely organised character. One should not forget, however, that extreme right skinheads have often expressed their political attitude, marked by racist and radical nationalist beliefs, by committing violent acts directed in the main against foreigners or other marginalised groups. As the following sections show, because of their militant and violence-prone attitude, extreme-right skinheads were rather rarely in direct contact with political parties of the Swiss radical right. It was more common to see links between extreme-right ideologues and propagandists on the one hand, and radical right-wing populist parties on the other.

Between Distance and Proximity: Linkages with Political Parties

In recent years, the Swiss People's Party has come under public scrutiny for accepting adherents of the extreme right within its party ranks.[310] Another kind of criticism has argued that the provocative political campaigns of the SVP facilitate the spread of right-wing extremism.[311] Senior SVP officials have categorically rejected such allegations, however. For example, after the above-mentioned incident at the Rütli, in August 2000, SVP president Ueli Maurer firmly declared that 'the SVP dissociates itself from any kind of extremism'.[312] In an interview, Christoph Blocher rejected public criticism and argued that the SVP would in fact impede right-wing extremism by raising the kind of issues which were of great concern for many of the country's citizens. Conversely, he pointed out that those who did not combat the misuse of asylum would create favourable conditions for extremism. Moreover, Blocher voiced the view that 'exaggerated nationalist behaviour might also be a counter-reaction to the constant emphasis that the political class places on internationalism and to the self-abnegating, craven attitude shown towards other states and international organisations'.[313]

As was revealed by the affair over Christoph Blocher's acknowledgment of a book written by the Swiss negationist Jürgen Graf, the SVP leader, as Hans-Georg Betz puts it, 'had not always been careful to distance himself from the extreme right'.[314] In 1997, Christoph Blocher had written a letter in which he thanked a fellow CINS member for sending him Jürgen Graf's negationist book, *Vom Untergang der Schweizerischen Freiheit* (About the Decline of Swiss Freedom). Blocher expressed his agreement with Graf's premise, when writing that Graf 'is so right'.[315] Although information about this letter had been already published by a weekly paper in 1997, it was just one week before the 1999 National Council elections when Blocher's letter provoked the greatest public reaction.[316] Blocher claimed that he had only read the title of Graf's book and criticised the media for leading a smear campaign against him. According to some commentators, by cleverly playing the role of an underdog attacked by the media and the establishment, Blocher managed to benefit from this public outrage and the SVP eventually succeeded in attracting even more supporters in the subsequent elections.[317]

While the scope of the following examination of linkages is confined to radical right-wing populist parties, it is worth noting that there were also cases of other parties whose members were involved with the extreme right. For example, Walter Fischbacher, a member of the Liberal Democratic Party (FDP), was associated with the conspiracist current of the extreme right and had expressed racist and anti-Semitic views on a number of different occasions. It required increased public and internal party pressure for Fischbacher to resign from the FDP in January 1995.[318] Another example was the above-mentioned case of Ahmed Huber, a long-time member of the Social-Democratic Party.

Involvement with Radical Right-wing Populist Parties: Socialisation, Mobilisation, Endorsement

In order to examine the ways in which extreme-right actors have been involved with radical right-wing populist parties, it is first necessary to distinguish between three types of linkage. The first type refers to the political socialisation of extreme-right ideologues and activists. This implies that at some point of their political career, an extreme rightist has been involved in a radical right-wing populist party. In most of these cases, surprisingly enough, they have tended to start their political activity within a party and later moved to the realm of the extreme right, rather than the other way around.

For example, Arthur Vogt ran on a National Action ticket in the 1967 and 1975 National Council elections and published articles in the NA organ *Volk + Heimat*. In the 1971 National Council elections, Arthur Vogt was a candidate on a list called Country Sections of NA (*Landsektionen der NA*), which was not the official NA election list. In 1983, he ran on a ticket named Environment and Energy (*Umwelt und Energie*), which was associated with the SVP.[319] It was in the 1980s that Vogt then became increasingly involved with the Swiss extreme right. He attended meetings of National Coordination and wrote for Max Wahl's *Eidgenoss*; he also started to play an important role in Swiss negationism of the 1990s.[320] Also take the case of Max Wahl, a former member of the Swiss Republican Movement, co-founder of the Swiss Democratic Union (EDU) and the first president of the Zurich EDU section in 1975. After Wahl had been expelled from the EDU in 1981, because of his neo-Nazi and anti-Semitic attitude,[321] he started a new career as a prolific negationist propagandist.[322] Another prominent example was Roger Wüthrich, who joined the local NA section of Bern in 1982. He then moved to the extreme right, when he co-founded the Viking Youth in 1987 and attended meetings of National Coordination in the late 1980s. After the

Small Springtime of Fronts, he engaged in party politics once again and became a member of a local section of the Car Party of Switzerland (APS).[323] A final example of the same trend was the case of the National Initiative of Switzerland, founded in 1996. Three of the four founders had been affiliated with the Swiss Democrats before they created the NIS.[324]

The second category of linkage points to mobilisation events. This type of relationship identifies those moments when an extreme-right group joins radical right-wing populist parties in specific mobilisations and activities. For example, when the Swiss Republican Movement launched the federal initiative 'For the Limitation of the Reception of Asylum Seekers' in 1987, National Coordination actively supported the initiative and signature-sheets were enclosed in Amaudruz's *Courrier du Continent*.[325] The New National Front also helped the SRB to gather signatures for the initiative.[326] A further example was the SVP's first asylum initiative in 1992, which was endorsed by Amaudruz's *Courrier du Continent*, with the paper also enclosing a signature-sheet inside its edition.[327] Finally, Emil Rahm's paper *Memopress* included a signature-sheet in an issue published in 1992, in support of the federal initiative 'EC membership negotiations: Let the people decide!', which was launched by the Swiss Democrats and the *Lega dei Ticinesi*.[328]

Opposition to the anti-racism law in 1993–1994 is the most significant example to date of a mobilisation event involving actors from all factions of the Swiss radical right. While the referendum committee of the conspiracist ideologue Emil Rahm included members associated not just with the SVP, but also with the FDP and New Right groups, the committee of Herbert Meier was composed of New Right followers and high-ranking members of radical right-wing populist parties. In the *Courrier du Continent*, Gaston-Armand Amaudruz called on readers to support the signature collection and he also contributed his share to the signatures gathered in the French-speaking regions of Switzerland.[329] Ultimately, the call for a referendum on the anti-racism law was only made possible by the joint efforts of the different committees and groups which subsequently led a large public campaign in the run-up to the vote of September 1994.

Other examples of the type of linkage denoting mobilisation events were rallies and public meetings organised by radical right-wing populist parties and attended by extreme rightists. In the second half of the 1990s, skinheads were present at public events held by the Swiss People's Party. For instance, around forty skinheads marched in an anti-Europe rally of some ten thousand people that was co-organised by the Zurich cantonal party in September 1995, and they also got involved in violent attacks on the fringe of the demonstration.[330] In 1997, members of National Initiative of Switzerland were selling their magazine *Morgenstern* outside a meeting which had been organised by the Young SVP and featured an address delivered by Christoph Blocher.[331]

The third type of linkage refers to the concrete endorsements of radical right-wing populist parties and their leaders and policies. It indicates that the extreme right – in their publications and statements – directly refers to radical right-wing populist parties or adopts the rhetoric and demands put forward by these parties. Take the example of Amaudruz's *Courrier de continent:* in the section on domestic politics, the paper extensively covered the endeavours of radical right-wing populist parties. In the 1980s, the central focus was on the political activities of National Action and Vigilance, both of which the *Courrier du Continent* presented as the political representatives of like-minded people. In the early 1990s, the Swiss People's Party received increased attention in the paper's reports on Swiss politics. The *Courrier du Continent* was initially supportive of the SVP and its migration policy in particular, but the paper rapidly shifted to a less favourable stance because of Blocher's refusal to oppose the anti-racism law.[332] Eventually, Amaudruz took the view that Blocher had missed the chance 'to become the leader of a true national opposition'.[333] Another publication of the extreme right, the NIS magazine *Morgenstern*, was also an example of the interest the SVP received from the extreme right in the 1990s. In a 1997 issue, it acknowledged Christoph Blocher as the true advocate of Switzerland.[334] Moreover, the paper *Memopress* and its successor, *Prüfen + Handeln* supported with a fair amount of zeal campaigns of radical right-wing populist parties opposing European integration or the country's membership of the UN.[335]

The rather apolitical image of the skinheads contrasted to some extent with the fact that the skinzines also took a position on issues debated in Swiss politics. For example, the skinzine *Totenkopf* reported that signatures were collected at a skinhead party against Switzerland's membership of the EEA, and further wrote that approving the treaty would amount to treason.[336] Moreover, as was pointed out by the report on Swiss skinheads that was issued by the Swiss Federal Police in 2000, skinheads have referred in recent years to the rhetoric and arguments put forward by political organisations. The report notes that the rhetoric of skinheads is increasingly using the vocabulary of political organisations that stand to the right and that catchphrases such as 'homeland', 'Swissness', 'fight against overforeignization' and 'absolute independence of Switzerland from foreign influence' are being picked up by the skinheads and integrated into their racist and violent worldview.[337]

Involvement with the Extreme Right: Collaboration, Activity, Personal Network

Members of radical right-wing populist parties have been involved in organisations, publications and activities of the Swiss extreme right. The first type of involvement refers to organisational collaboration. It covers a range of significant party member activities, including the creation of extreme-right organisations or regular participation at meetings organised by extreme-right groups. In the 1970s and 1980s, there were examples of National Action members engaged in extreme-right organisations. In 1974, Rudolf Keller, who was president of the Young National Action (*Junge Nationale Aktion* – JNA) at the time, reportedly attended the foundation meeting of National Basis of Switzerland. The group's paper, *Visier*, also published two articles he had written under a pseudonym.[338] Keller has been party president of the National Action/Swiss Democrats since 1986. In the late 1980s, a number of NA members played an important role in the Small Springtime of Fronts.[339] Most prominently, Marcel Strebel was a member of National Action when he co-founded the Patriotic Front in 1988. As a matter of fact, the founders of the Patriotic Front initially intended to create a National Action section for central Switzerland.[340]

National Coordination (NK) was certainly the most significant example of links between NA and an extreme-right organisation. In the 1980s, a number of NA officials attended the meetings of the NK, headed by former NA member Elie Berset. The list of participants included Sylvain Collaud, member of the NA party executive in the canton of Vaud; Martine Boimond, member of the NA party executive in the canton of Geneva; and Mary Meissner, editor of the French-speaking NA paper *peuple + patrie*.[341] After the Federal Tribunal decision of 1987, the NA leadership was determined to apply a strategy of demarcation towards the extreme right and in 1988 it forced Martine Boimond to resign from the party because of her NK membership.[342] It is also worth noting that NK meetings were attended by Franz Baumgartner, successor to James Schwarzenbach as party president of the Republican Movement.[343]

In the 1990s, the SVP membership of Ernst Indlekofer and Emil Rahm provoked public stir. In 1989, along with Marcel Strebel and members of the National-Revolutionary Party of Switzerland and the Patriotic Front, Ernst Indlekofer – a member of the SVP section of Basel City – became a co-founder of the Patriotic People's Party (*Patriotische Volkspartei* – PVP), although the party was stillborn and never made any public appearance. In 1995, he launched the paper *Recht + Freiheit*, which became one of the main publications of Swiss negationism. When the SVP section of Basel City opened expulsion procedures against Indlekofer in 1996, he anticipated the party's decision and resigned from the SVP.[344] Emil Rahm, editor-in-chief of the conspiracist paper *Memopress*, has been a long-time member of the SVP section of Schaffhausen.[345] Although the SVP has regularly faced public criticism over Rahm's membership, the party executive has never taken any kind of action. In a 1999 interview, SVP president Ueli Maurer rejected such criticism and argued that Rahm 'has been embedded in the Schaffhausen party for years, both as a businessman and as a private person'.[346]

The second category of linkage points to the isolated activities of individual party members. It probably accounts for most of the endeavours undertaken by party members in the context of the Swiss extreme right. This type mainly includes the contributions made to publications and speeches given at meetings. As the examples of James Schwarzenbach and Valentin Oehen from the Movement against Overforeignization help to illustrate, prominent party leaders did not shrink from being involved with the groups and publications – domestic or foreign – that are associated with the extreme right. Before James Schwarzenbach began his career as a political leader in 1967, he was allegedly in contact with the Swiss neo-fascist Hans Oehler, who had been in charge of covering Switzerland for the German extreme-right paper *Nation Europa* since 1951, a periodical which also published texts written by Schwarzenbach.[347] At the high of his political career in 1970, Schwarzenbach agreed to collaborate with the monthly *Der Eckartbote* (The Eckart Messenger), organ of the extreme-right organisation Austrian Landsmannschaft.[348] In return, Schwarzenbach's paper *Der Republikaner* published articles taken from *Der Eckartbote*. When Schwarzenbach resigned as National Councillor in 1979, he gave an interview to the *Deutsche National-Zeitung* (German National Paper), Germany's largest extreme-right paper.[349]

Shortly after Valentin Oehen was elected to the NA presidency in April 1972, he gave a speech at an event organised by the Austrian National-Democratic Party (*Nationaldemokratische Partei* – NDP), a group led by the condemned extreme-right activist Norbert Burger.[350] Two years later, Heinz Manz, head of the neo-fascist Arminia fraternity, made contact with Oehen who then supplied the group with NA propaganda material.[351] In 1976, Oehen gave a talk at an Arminia meeting in Zurich and received the badge of honour from the group. After the public had learned about Oehen's involvement with Arminia, he gave it back.[352] Nonetheless, Oehen continued to acknowledge the group and wrote in a private letter from 1977 that 'Arminia is clearly nationally orientated and honours the idea of a European-federalist state. It is certainly not undemocratic – Hitlerist – anti-Semitic'.[353] Oehen also kept in touch with Emil Rahm, with whom he co-authored an article published in *Memopress* in 1991, which fiercely opposed Swiss membership of the European Community.[354] Most significantly, the case of Jean-Jacques Hegg, editor-in-chief of the NA organ *Volk + Heimat* from 1980 to 1990 and National Councillor in 1983–84, demonstrated the association between the NA paper and German extreme-right periodicals. While articles written by Hegg were reportedly published in *Nation Europa*,[355] *Volk + Heimat* included articles taken from *Nation Europa* and the racist periodical *Neue Anthropologie* (New Anthropology).[356] Moreover, the two leading members of the Geneva NA section, Martine Boimond and Mary Meissner, wrote contributions to Amaudruz's *Courrier du Continent* in 1987 and 1990.[357]

In the 1990s, several media reports on the involvement of SVP members with the extreme right provoked public reaction. The first case concerns Ernst Dünnenberger, member of an SVP local section in the canton of Zurich. He had previously been a Republican Movement representative in the local parliament of Winterthur, from 1974 to 1977. Dünnenberger had also taken part in the foundation of the Swiss Democratic Union in 1975, and twice ran for the party in National Council elections, in 1975 and 1979. Although he joined the SVP in the 1980s, Dünnenberger had attended events organised by the National-Revolutionary Party of Switzerland in the late 1980s and became the printer of Max Wahl's *Eidgenoss*. Only after increased public pressure was Dünnenberger expelled from the SVP in 1990. After 1992, he started to send negationist and inflammatory writings unsolicited to a select circle of addressees.[358] The second case was Roger Etter, an SVP MP in the canton of Ticino and candidate for the 1999 National Council elections. According to press reports, he participated in a Waffen-SS veterans' meeting in the autumn of 1999. Despite harsh public criticism, the Ticino SVP section refused to expel Etter from the party.[359] Finally, the young party secretary of a local SVP section in the canton of Uri was a part of the skinhead group which disrupted the above-mentioned celebration event on the Rütli, on 1st August 2000. The cantonal party executive forced the extreme activist to resign from the SVP.[360]

The most prominent example was Christoph Blocher who gave interviews to the two extreme-right papers in Germany, *Nation & Europa* and *Deutsche Wochen-Zeitung*, in 1996 and 1997.[361] In the *Nation & Europa* interview, he made a response to the criticism of being a populist and stated that 'populists are apparently people whose arguments are easily understood and realised'.[362] When the Swiss Sunday paper *SonntagsBlick* exposed Blocher's interviews in December 1999, he denied knowledge of the publications' extreme-right orientation.[363]

The third type of relationship refers to personal networks and mainly includes contact and collaboration between individuals. So far, little research has been done in this area, even so far as the historical figures of the postwar Swiss radical right are concerned. The biographical studies of Valentin Oehen and James Schwarzenbach are among the very few studies of leading Swiss radical right-wing populist figures that are based on private archives.[364] As the investigation of Schwarzenbach's correspondence revealed, the leader of the Movement against Overforeignization had contact with extreme-right actors, in particular with neo-fascist ideologues and propagandists. In the 1950s, before becoming a prominent politician, Schwarzenbach was in touch with the former SS-*Obersturmbannführer* Franz Riedweg, probably the most influential Swiss in the National Socialist regime.[365] After being private secretary to the former Federal Councillor, Jean-Marie Musy, in the 1930s, Riedweg later married the daughter of Field Marshal Werner von Blomberg and served as a member of Heinrich Himmler's staff. In 1947, a Swiss court sentenced Riedweg in absentia to sixteen years' imprisonment.[366] In the early 1970s, Schwarzenbach also corresponded with Gaston-Armand Amaudruz and eventually the two key figures of the Swiss radical right also met in person. At that time, Schwarzenbach was also in contact with James-Albert Mathez, the author of the anti-Semitic book, *Le passé, les temps présents et la question juive*, and contributor to Amaudruz's *Courrier du continent*.[367]

Although the investigation has confined itself to specific examples and does not claim that universal lessons can be drawn from an admittedly unrepresentative sample, it shows the variety of interactions and the key features of identified interactions that arise within the political family of the radical right. The described linkages also give evidence of the Swiss radical right as a collective actor which, beyond its commitment to common ideological references, was able to rely upon a network of collaboration between individuals, organisations and publications. Even though there were no large scale collaborations or coalitions between entire organisations, and while common activities were mainly pursued by a number of individuals, distinct mobilisation events had a unifying effect that crossed the existing organisational borders between extreme-right groups or publications and radical right-wing populist parties. In this way, the formally drawn and publicly affirmed line of demarcation between the two family members was regularly trespassed, and it was ideologues and propagandists from the extreme right that crossed this line more often than officials from the radical right-wing populist parties.

Conclusion

In this book I have shown how the history of the radical right in postwar Switzerland has been characterised by continuity in terms of ideology and by politics and persistence in terms of its organisations and activities. This has resulted in the enduring, though shifting, presence of a diverse radical right at various levels of the Swiss political and public arena. With the findings that emerged from my research, I have also tried to clear up some common misapprehensions about Swiss politics and the Swiss radical right in particular. In so doing, I have specifically challenged the long-standing notion that Switzerland represents an exceptional case in the history of the postwar radical right in Western Europe. Since focusing on structural contexts and socioeconomic processes in the case of Switzerland – as in most other countries – gives only limited explanations as to why the radical right has experienced variable success and portrayed differing degrees of organisational strength throughout the postwar period, I have applied an 'internalist perspective' in order to capture and explain this variation. Developing typologies based on organisational and ideological criteria helps to identify several subtypes of the Swiss radical right and to differentiate their respective intellectual legacies, political purpose and types of activities. The use of an actor-centred approach also echoes recent claims in the new literature on the radical right stating the need for more attention to be paid to agent and agency in order to comprehend the central role that political entrepreneurs, organisational formations and ideological suppliers assume in the development of radical-right politics as an effective vehicle for political and intellectual engagement.

The Process of Normalisation

In order to begin, it was necessary to revise a number of the arguments that are frequently used to press the claim that Switzerland is subject to a number of specific contextual and structural conditions that have the effect of impeding radical-right politics. In fact, a variety of opportunity structures exist in Switzerland which are ultimately favourable for the emergence and consolidation of a radical right. This gave evidence that there is little justification for holding to the notion of Swiss exceptionalism and for not applying the classifications and explanations that are relevant to the comparative literature on the radical right.

Taking an historical perspective, I have shown that while Switzerland had no fascist regime during the critical period of the 1930s and 1940s, exclusionist ideas, as well as authoritarian and anti-pluralist patterns of thought, were fairly widespread among intellectual and political elites and were also taken up later on by followers of the postwar radical right. As suggested, Swiss national identity is built not only on the idea of a state-nation based on political will and civic rights, but also on cultural categories and strong references to historical experience. Significantly, this conception of Swiss nationhood serves as a discursive and cultural framework in which the Swiss radical right presents its exclusionist migration agenda and its nationalist views on issues of foreign affairs. As I have also argued, while the country functions rather successfully as a multicultural state and thus fosters tolerant attitudes towards minorities or other cultures, the tolerance towards the 'other' only refers to 'native' minorities and the notion of a multicultural society draws on the conception of an exclusively 'indigenous multiculturalism'. It is of little surprise that opinion polls, some taken as early as the late 1960s, consistently provide empirical evidence suggesting that the intolerant attitudes towards immigrants that are found among the Swiss population are as widely spread as such attitudes are in other European societies. By looking at public opinion in this way, one can certainly say that the potential for a mobilisation of the radical-right exists in Switzerland as it does elsewhere.

The examination of a number of structural factors indicates that the radical right were able to take advantage of some of the political institutions that exist in Switzerland. As suggested, the system of direct democracy represents the most significant institutional opportunity structure for the radical right. It provides the radical right with the institutional means to mobilise constituencies, exert pressure on policy-making processes and other political parties, and to lead public campaigns in order to promote its agenda and ideas. This assessment contrasts with the view that limits itself to the institutionalised safety valve thesis and in so doing only explains the relative weakness of fringe radical right-wing populist parties in the parliamentarian arena. Swiss consociationalism, a constituent of the country's political culture which has grown historically and developed into a firm principle of Swiss politics throughout the postwar period, is also barely able to account for a structural factor that hinders the political fortune of the radical right. There are three reasons that allow us to say quite the opposite: First, consociational governance leaves itself open to the radical right's populist strategy of invoking resentments against the political establishment. Coming from the radical right, this type of attack goes some way to reinforcing the process of increasing dissatisfaction with political parties and mistrust towards political institutions which has been evident among the population in Switzerland and in other Western democracies since the 1980s. Second, the consociational system is a factor in determining the way that major left-wing and right-wing parties cluster around the centre, a context that eventually opens up the political space to more radical parties to the right. Third, the high capacity for integration that results from the consociational system made it possible for the SVP to stay in the federal government, granting the party acceptance and legitimacy in the political arena despite its radicalisation in the 1990s.

If we take into account other factors listed by the literature as success conditions for the radical right, such as an electoral system based on proportional representation, the post-materialist turn, the emergence of 'new politics' since the 1970s and 1980s and the growing political dealignment of voters, it has been shown that in Switzerland too there exists a rather promising environment for the radical right. Finally, there is a need to point to socioeconomic changes in Switzerland, despite the fact that the assumption that general economic conditions are factors in explaining the fortune of the radical right has been largely criticised in the literature and in many cases refuted by empirical research. In the case of Switzerland, the breakthrough of parties from the Movement against Overforeignization in the 1970s also demonstrates that the rise of the radical right did not necessarily have to correlate with times of economic crisis or recession. On the other hand, the forceful emergence of the new SVP occurred in the 1990s, while the Swiss economy was experiencing difficulties and rates of unemployment were rising, and the party was certainly successful in appealing to voters who were affected by these economic setbacks.

The Radical Right as a Collective Actor: Linkages and Collaborations

To conclude this investigation, it is important to summarize how these various organisations, parties and individual actors are connected and how these alliances have evolved over time. It is accurate to say that the degree of linkage and collaboration facilitated an enduring organisational consolidation of the radical right and contributed to its empowerment within Swiss politics and society. First, it has been shown that the Swiss radical right functions as a collective actor and that the various members of the radical right-wing political family are held together by a set of linkages and interactions. As I have demonstrated, the radical right in Switzerland, as in most West European countries, is characterised by a very high degree of organisational complexity, expressed by the variation in organisational formations, structural resources and means of action as well as by the different positions that distinct organisations take up in the political system and public space. At the same time, the network and collaboration that exists between organisations and individuals unites the radical right as a collective actor and the commitment to a common ideological core creates its collective identity. Since the Swiss radical right applies a broad action repertoire and is engaged in different forms of mobilisation, there is a wide-ranging division of labour that has allowed for various though often overlapping constituencies to be addressed, as well as different public and political arenas.

As this book's findings indicate, Switzerland belongs to the grouping of European countries, including France, Italy and Austria, where political parties play a dominant role in the radical right. In contrast to the new social movements of the 1970s and 1980s, where Swiss parties assumed a minor role in mobilisations and activities, political parties and their leaders have in more recent years acted as the true movement entrepreneurs and driving forces of the radical right. This became even more evident in the 1990s, when the SVP established a network of satellite organisations, associated interest groups and publications. Moreover, Swiss radical right-wing populist parties serve not only as electoral organisations that run for public office and advocate their policy agenda in the parliamentary arena, but also act as plebiscitary forces that make extensive use of the instruments of direct democracy as means of intervention in the policy-making processes. As a consequence, they have managed to produce a considerable record of direct democratic activities.

Following this perspective, I have made the point that direct democratic activities represent important mobilisation events that activate the personnel and the resources of various members of the Swiss radical right. Here, we also see how the significant role of parapolitical and extra-parliamentary organisations associated with the radical right comes into play. They either lend substantial support to political parties in direct democratic campaigns, or are themselves responsible for submitting initiatives and requesting referendums. Of the eighty-seven federal initiatives that came to the vote between 1970 and 2000, eleven were submitted by parties and groups of the Swiss radical right. The voters approved just one of these initiatives. This was above average, however, since a total of only four federal initiatives were accepted during this period. From the sixty-seven optional referendums that were held between 1970 and 2000, nine were initiated by parties and groups associated with the radical right. In four cases, the voters followed the radical right's rejection of policy change. This is higher than the overall approval rate seen in optional referendums, which stands at around one third. Calling for a referendum does not only express the rejection of a specific policy issue, but also often conveys a general disagreement with how the political elite pursues public policy. It therefore appears that the radical right is actually rather successful when it combines a populist anti-establishment strategy with a vetoing of policy changes.

Another important feature of the Swiss radical right is the wide-ranging network and the collaborations that exist between radical right-wing populist parties, the New Right and the extreme right. The most elaborated and the tightest relationship is the one that exists between the political parties and the New Right. This confirms the presumption that the New Right plays an important role as a supplier of ideology for the proponents of radical right-wing populism. In the German-speaking part of Switzerland in the 1960s and 1970s, New Right followers preferred to associate with the parties from the Movement against Overforeignization, while in the 1980s and 1990s, political partisanship shifted notably towards the new SVP. The neoconservative current acted as an important player in the political arena in the 1990s, as it maintained organisations and periodicals in close association with the SVP. The neo-nationalist current also established a close collaboration with radical right-wing populist parties, namely the SVP. Smaller though it was than its counterpart in the German-speaking part, one section of the New Right in the French-speaking part of Switzerland also made a strategic shift from culture to politics and was able to take front stage in party politics. While in the 1970s and 1980s, New Right followers preferred to associate themselves with the Vigilance party, in the 1990s they saw a new chance to increase their political influence in the partisanship that emerged for the new SVP. Overall, this gradual move towards being the dominant political party of the radical right in both linguistic regions was a factor not only in improving the ideological profile of the new SVP but also in strengthening the structural coherence of the radical right.

The linkage between the extreme right and other factions of the radical right is more difficult to capture. Radical right-wing populist parties and most members of the New Right consistently proclaim a strict policy of demarcation between themselves and extreme-right groups. Like the general public and the authorities, they denounce the extreme right as a pariah actor and support the police paying attention to and prosecuting incidents of racist propaganda and violent acts. Usually, the party leaderships react promptly in excluding extreme rightists once the media has exposed their party membership. Moreover, a large part of the extreme right is mistrustful of the party system and established politics and therefore rarely shows interest in participating or intervening directly in political processes, preferring instead to act autonomously.

Nonetheless, I have demonstrated that there exist a number of linkages and collaborations between the extreme right, in particular its ideologues and propagandists, and other members of the radical right-wing political family. So far as the Swiss New Right is concerned, it is especially in the French-speaking part of Switzerland where contacts and interactions exist at the level of personnel and organisations. Significantly, a section of the New Right in French-speaking Switzerland not only cultivates a relationship with domestic extreme-right groups, but also with the extreme right in France. In the German-speaking part, the New Right is generally more careful to distance itself from the extreme right. The association of extreme rightists with radical right-wing populist parties includes three different types of involvement: political socialisation within parties, distinct mobilisation events and the endorsement of radical right-wing populist policies. On the other hand, members of radical right-wing populist parties involve themselves with the extreme right by engaging in organisational collaboration and a number of different activities, as well as through personal networks.

The Radical Right as a Political Family: Ideology and Intellectual Agenda

The analysis presented in this book shows that, as members of the same political family, the various factions of the Swiss radical right espouse, in one way or another, the key ideological features, political views and sociocultural values that are characteristic of the radical-right worldview. They sometimes differ on specific political issues and are inspired by different intellectual traditions, or use different variations of arguments to translate their views into public and political discourse. This allows for a range of 'ideological specialisations' encompassing economically neoliberal, religiously fundamentalist and regionalist concerns among the political parties; ecologist, neo-nationalist and counter-revolutionary priorities among the currents of the New Right; and fascist, negationist and esoteric preferences among groupings of the extreme right. Moreover, while some take rather restrained and moderate views, others are more straightforward and express radical versions of an exclusionist ideology. Overall, however, convergence prevails over divergence and the ideological agreement between the organisational variants is particularly evident in the areas of exclusionism and identity politics, which represents the core of radical-right ideology and intellectual agenda.

The findings indicate that nationalism is a central ideological feature of all the parties, organisations and individuals associated with the Swiss radical right and it underpins their identity politics. From different elements of long-standing and widely accepted conceptions of Swiss national identity, the radical right distils a form of Helvetic nationalism and gives it a radical expression. In its nationalist thinking, the radical right refers to Switzerland as both a state-nation and as a culture-nation. It combines civic and cultural components in an exclusionist worldview in which nationhood and national identity are the main references in the perception of self and otherness. In a primordial and essentialist fashion, the radical right underscores the uniqueness of Swiss nationhood by pointing to distinct historical traditions, a particular mentality shared by the Swiss people, and the country's unique framework of political institutions. Since the linguistic, cultural and religious differences make it difficult to define specific and common characteristics of a Swiss identity, the radical right puts strong emphasis on both the rootedness and exclusiveness of Swiss nationhood. It produces an exalted version of the idea that Switzerland represents a special and exceptional case and thereby largely contributes to a reinforcement of the concept of 'Swissness' defined in terms of an historically developed and culturally determined 'essence' of the Swiss nation.

By presenting examples from various areas of public policy, I have provided evidence that the radical right exhibits a strong belief in the existence of external threats to the country, and in its concept of national identity, it emphasises a clear demarcation against the outside world. Drawing on a 'negative identity' of isolation, the radical right sees its mission in combating the country's international integration and its membership in supranational organisations. In the debate over the country's role in the Second World War, the persistence of the national myth of representing a special case has merged with a fierce rejection of the need to reexamine key foundations of the country's national identity, particularly when the request for reappraisal has come from abroad. This is of particular importance, since in nationalist thinking, history represents an especially powerful, almost sacred force for national integration and possesses, above all, a great symbolic value for the national community.

In my analysis, I have clearly shown that the exclusionary purpose of the Swiss radical right's nationalism becomes particularly visible in its agenda relating to migration, where nationalist thinking merges with other exclusionist ideologies and patterns of thought. Most commonly, the radical right promotes a vision of Switzerland that excludes non-members of the national community. While a sharp distinction is drawn between those who do belong and those who do not belong to the Swiss nation, the attitude towards groups perceived as 'foreign' or 'alien' is fuelled by xenophobic sentiments. By pointing to the alleged threat coming from immigrants and drawing on latent prejudices and stereotypes, the radical right continually expresses fear and hostility towards the 'other' and thereby keeps alive the discourse of 'overforeignization', a longstanding sociocultural code of exclusion in Switzerland's migration policy. In order to legitimise a xenophobic attitude, the radical right often dwells on the theoretical work of ethology research which claims that xenophobia and mistrustful views of 'strangers' represent natural characteristics inherent in human beings.

Large sections of the Swiss radical right have also followed their European counterparts in the shift that has been seen in the rhetoric of exclusion and which has been described by some as 'neoracism'. Adopting a neoracist argumentation, the Swiss radical right stresses the 'right to be different' and pretends to take an egalitarian view on the relation between cultures and ethnic groups, while they claim a presupposed incommensurability of different cultural identities. Cultural identity is thereby seen as a natural and deterministic category of differentiation. Universalism of Enlightenment is equated with cultural homogenisation and the destruction of cultural communities. Such cultural differentialist assumptions result in support for ethnopluralism and the accompanying call for segregation, and are expressed, for example, in discriminatory claims that immigrants from the so-called 'foreign cultural sphere' – meaning those who come from non-European countries and the Balkans – cannot integrate in Swiss society and should stay in the their own cultural environment.

Although classical racism drawing on biologically grounded conceptions of 'race differences' is discredited among most actors of the Swiss radical right, it did find some support from the fringe radical right-wing populist parties in the 1970s and 1980s and continues to be a significant point of reference in the ideological premises of most extreme-right groups. However, many radical right-wing actors continue to use racially marked language and repeatedly speak of 'races', albeit, in most cases, without approving a genetically based ranking of human beings. Moreover, while anti-Semitism based on hierarchical categorisation and pseudoscientific 'racial theories' is limited to extreme-right groups, namely neo-fascists and negationists, so-called secondary anti-Semitism has been promulgated by the Swiss radical right in the form of anti-Semitic prejudices and conspiracy theories, especially during the debates on 'unclaimed' Jewish assets that took place in the second half of the 1990s,.

Another important aspect of my findings is the fact that a vast majority of Swiss radical right-wing actors approve of democratic order and pluralist society so long as it does not include non-members of the national community. However, the radical right's ideology of inequality goes beyond the exclusionist claim of unequal chances for non-Swiss and the disapproval of a multicultural society that would also integrate new minorities. In fact, a number of members of the radical right, particularly some factions of the New Right, take a highly critical attitude towards the legacy of Enlightenment and the achievements of the French Revolution. In many cases, this results in the advocacy of a hierarchical and anti-egalitarian conception of society based on organically developed social structures and traditional values and ethics. Probably the most peculiar version of pre-democratic and anti-egalitarian types of society includes the revival of neo-paganism and Indo-European roots which is pursued by the *Nouvelle droite* and contrasts sharply with the support that Christianity and Christian values usually receive from the Swiss radical right.

The hierarchy-based views have an authoritarian tendency, namely when the radical right presents remedies for the alleged decay of social and moral order. This pattern of thought, however, does not draw on a fascist type of authoritarianism, since fascism and other authoritarian systems are categorically rejected by the Swiss radical right, except by some marginal factions of the extreme right. Instead, as many groups espouse pronounced social-conservative values and are critical of issues such as anti-authoritarian education, liberal drug policy, alternative ways of living together, homosexuality and abortion, they seek to reinforce beliefs in traditional authorities and social institutions and exalt the role of the family as the natural nucleus of society.

The rejection of egalitarian and emancipatory principles makes the radical right the most fervent opponent to the 'spirit of 1968'. As suggested, '1968' has a great significance for the Swiss radical right, having implications for its strategic choices and intellectual agenda: first, the radical right presents the 68-movement and its epigones as forces that firmly hold the discursive and cultural power in society, politics and public administration. In order to counter this alleged predominance from the left, the radical right sees it as its mission to promote a political and cultural counter-project based around anti-egalitarian, hierarchical and exclusionist ideas. By picturing '1968' as a 'revolution', the radical right emphasises its legitimate role to pursue a 'counter-revolution'. Second, the radical right is keen to make the 'spirit of 1968' responsible for supposed problems in many areas of society and politics, including education, welfare system, family policy, cultural affairs, etc. By doing so, the radical right succeeds to some extent in determining the historical picture of '1968' as well as the assessment of the impacts that '1968' has produced in contemporary society. Third, the radical right, in particular members of the New Right, take inspiration from the strategic choices made by some proponents of '1968', namely by pursuing a strategy of taboo breaks and non-conformist interventions and by emphasising the extraordinary significance that culture and ideas have for achieving changes in society and politics.

Finally, it is worth noting that the Swiss radical right's general belief in order and authority goes hand in hand with the quest for a strong state and the enforcement of law and order, when it comes to security issues, crime, the judicial system, illegal immigration and asylum policy. This contrasts with the anti-state and libertarian positions in economic policy and the fierce criticism of state bureaucracy and interventionism, prominently promoted in the neoliberal program of new radical right-wing populist parties and the neoconservative current of the New Right. However, since free-market ideology and an exaltation of individual achievements imply Social Darwinist conceptions of society and are combined with exclusionist welfare chauvinism, the advocacy of a neoliberal agenda continues to be in line with the anti-egalitarian premises of a radical-right ideology.

The 1990s and Beyond

In the course of the 1990s, the Swiss radical right underwent a process of fundamental transformation and enjoyed a significant rise in its electoral and public presence. Radical right-wing populist parties entered Swiss mainstream politics after being at the margins of the party system for almost thirty years. The sensational electoral advance of the new SVP not only altered the political balance between the four government parties but also resulted in Swiss politics becoming less consensual and more polarised. The New Right also experienced a boost in the 1990s that found expression in the founding of new circles, higher circulation numbers for periodicals and the increasing presence of New Right followers in public debates. The New Right was also satisfied with its rather successful efforts to increase intellectual influence over radical right-wing populist parties as well as public discussions in general. Finally, the Swiss extreme right managed to consolidate its role as a subculture by developing organisational structures and expanding its range of activities. It also exhibited a fair amount of confidence by way of a number of major public appearances.

As some argue, one main reason for the increased appeal and wider attraction of the radical right lies in the changing socioeconomic conditions that have been prevalent in Switzerland since the early 1990s, conditions marked by increased unemployment, a more precarious material situation and growing difficulties for the welfare state. For them, the general lack of confidence in the future has been reinforced by feelings of helplessness and impotence in the face of globalisation processes in the economy, culture and migration. In this context, the question of the country's role in the European integration process is seen as one of the most divisive issues in domestic political debates. It represents a conflict that some regard as the most important new cleavage in Swiss society, a cleavage that opposes those who are in favour of the country opening itself up towards the outside world and those who reveal an attitude of demarcation. Following this perspective, the new SVP is seen as the party that managed to gain the most from the emergence of this new cleavage, since the party found success in attracting a growing constituency as a result of addressing these uncertainties.

However, it is more important to stress that the new SVP was the chief engineer in the way this cleavage has been manufactured and structured in debates that mainly turned around themes of identity. By presenting issues such as European integration, immigration and asylum as serious threats to the country, the SVP consistently and forcefully pursued identity politics. In fact, the party had a vital interest in problematising and politicising these issues and in keeping them at the centre of Swiss political debates, since this tactic gave the party the opportunity to present itself as the only representative of the 'native people' and as the true defender of 'Swissness'. It is accurate to say, therefore, that the cleavage that emerged in the course of the 1990s was as much the product of the party's well-engineered political strategy and resourceful campaigning as the result of changing contextual conditions. In other words, the new SVP and with it an array of other groups from the radical right must be seen as the designers and builders of their own success. This assessment confirms the relevance of the actor-oriented perspective adopted in this book and sees the reason for the extraordinary 'success story' of the radical right in the 1990s in the substantial improvement of internal structures such as organisations, membership and leadership, as well as in the elaboration of an ideological profile that was inspired by the long-sustained intellectual work of the New Right.

The election of Christoph Blocher, a prominent representative of the new SVP, onto the Federal Council in December 2003 gave the radical right a seat in the federal government for the first time in post-war Switzerland. In the following years, a number of public policies proposed by the government, and particularly by Blocher's Federal Department of Justice and Police, showed clear evidence of the increased influence of the SVP, particularly those related to issues of migration and asylum policy. On the other hand, however, the polarised climate was carried into the government body and a number of conflicts between government members undermined the consensual principle of Swiss governance. As a consequence, in December 2007, a substantial faction of the two centre-right parties represented in the government gave up its strategy of integration towards the new SVP and helped to vote Christoph Blocher out of office by replacing him with Eveline Widmer-Schlumpf, who was known for her more consensual and moderate style of politics and was considered to be a representative of the old SVP.

These recent events forcefully revived the antagonism between the new, radical right-wing populist SVP and the old, right-wing, conservative SVP, resulting in the foundation of the Bourgeois Democratic Party, which included advocates of the old SVP, from the cantons of Graubünden and Bern in particular, as well as the two SVP representatives in the government. While the BDP's chances of success as a serious electoral force at the national level so far seem to be rather limited, the SVP itself regards the breakaway as beneficial for its own ideological and organisational consolidation. The future prospects for the SVP as a flagship of the Swiss radical right may depend less on the strength and performance of this new party than on the question of whether or not the SVP can continue to take advantage of its 'historical capital' and be recognised as a legitimate and reliable partner in Swiss consensual politics, despite the fact that the party pursues a populist, anti-establishment strategy and advocates an exclusionist agenda. In the event of the country opting for the kind of profound change that would abandon Swiss consociationalism and install an oppositional system in its place, this would not only reconfigure the position of the SVP in the Swiss party system, but also allow the other parties to choose a more straightforward strategy of demarcation towards the SVP.

Notes

Introduction

1. C.H. Church, *The Politics and Government of Switzerland*, Basingstoke, 2004, p. 3, italics in original.
2. Ibid.
3. J. Steinberg, *Why Switzerland?*, 2nd edn, Cambridge, 1996, p. xi.
4. The pre-parliamentarian consultation procedure represents one example of the way in which these institutional mechanisms of consociational arrangement and the way that policy-makers seek to find compromises that are acceptable to most of the important political and social groups. During the consultation phase of the law-making process, political parties, interest groups and cantons can comment on the legislation proposed by the federal government. Their responses are evaluated by the Federal Council which then tries to elaborate a bill that takes into account the different positions in order to reduce the risk of the law being rejected in a referendum.
5. *Threat Posed to Democracy by Extremist Parties and Movements in Europe*, Report of the Political Affairs Committee of the Council of Europe, Doc. 8607, 3 January 2000.
6. K. Armingeon, 'Der Schweizer Rechtsextremismus im internationalen Vergleich', *Swiss Political Science Review*, vol. 1, no. 4, 1995; L. Helms, 'Right-Wing Populist Parties in Austria and Switzerland: A Comparative Analysis of Electoral Support and Conditions of Success', *West European Politics*, vol. 20, no. 2, 1997; K. Armingeon, 'Fremdenfeindlichkeit in der Schweiz in international vergleichender Perspektive', in *Die Bedeutung des Ethnischen im Zeitalter der Globalisierung*, ed. R. Moser, Bern, 2000; C.T. Husbands, 'Switzerland: Right-Wing and Xenophobic Parties, from Margin to Mainstream?', *Parliamentary Affairs*, vol. 53, no. 3, 2000.
7. M.J. Goodwin, 'The Rise and Faults of the Internalist Perspective in Extreme Right Studies', *Representations*, vol. 42, no. 4, 2006.
8. R. Eatwell, 'Ten Theories of the Extreme Right', in *Right-Wing Extremism in the Twenty-First Century*, eds P.H. Merkl and L. Weinberg, 2nd rev. edn., London, 2000, p. 48.
9. E. Carter, *The Extreme Right in Western Europe*, Manchester, 2005, p. 3.
10. Goodwin, 'The Rise and Fault', p. 350. See also J.W.P. Veugelers, 'A Challenge for Political Sociology: The Rise of Far-Right Parties in Contemporary Western Europe', *Current Sociology*, vol. 47, no. 4, 1999; C. Mudde, *Populist Radical Right Parties in Europe*, Cambridge, 2007, chapter 11; H. Kitschelt, 'Growth and Persistence of the Radical Right in Postindustrial Democracies: Advances

and Challenges in Comparative Research', *West European Politics*, vol. 30, no. 5, 2007, pp. 1193–7, 1202.

11. M. Schain, A. Zolberg, and P. Hossay, 'The Development of Radical Right Parties in Western Europe', in *Shadows over Europe*, eds M. Schain, A. Zolberg, and P. Hossay, New York, 2002, pp. 3f.

12. M. Banks, and A. Gingrich, 'Introduction: Neo-nationalism in Europe and Beyond', in *Neo-nationalism in Europe and Beyond*, eds A. Gingrich, and M. Banks, New York, Oxford, 2006, p. 6.

13. L. Hunt ed., *The New Cultural History*, Berkeley, 1989; P. Burke, *What is Cultural History?*, Cambridge, 2005; U. Frevert and H.-G. Haupt, eds, *Neue Politikgeschichte*, Frankfurt/Main, 2005. See also the recent academic debate on fascism: R. Griffin, W. Loh, and A. Umland, eds, *Fascism Past and Present, West and East*, Stuttgart, 2006.

14. M. Swyngedouw and G. Ivaldi, 'The Extreme Right Utopia in Belgium and France: The Ideology of the Flemish Vlaams Blok and French Front National', *West European Politics*, vol. 24, no. 3, 2001.

15. J. Rydrgen, 'The Sociology of the Radical Right', *Annual Review of Sociology*, vol. 33, no. 1, 2007, p. 259.

1. The Concept of the Radical Right

1. For a discussion of the terminological diversity, see P. Ignazi, *Extreme Right Parties in Western Europe*, Oxford, 2003, pp. 28ff.; R. Eatwell, 'Introduction. The New Extreme Right Challenge', in *Western Democracies and the New Extreme Right Challenge*, eds R. Eatwell and C. Mudde, London, 2004, pp. 5–13; E. Carter, *The Extreme Right in Western Europe*, Manchester, 2005, pp. 20–23; P. Norris, *Radical Right*, Cambridge, 2005, pp. 44ff.

2. N. Bobbio, *Left and Right*, Chicago, 1996; see also P. Ignazi, *Extreme Right Parties*, pp. 4–19.

3. F. Decker, *Parteien unter Druck*, Opladen, 2000, pp. 67ff.

4. For historical examples, see Z. Sternhell, *Ni droite, ni gauche*, Brussels, 1987.

5. For instance, see H. Kitschelt, *The Radical Right in Western Europe*, Ann Arbor, 1995; P.H. Merkl and L. Weinberg, eds, *Right-Wing Extremism in the Twenty-First Century*, 2nd rev. edn., London, 2003.

6. See the classic article by E.K Scheuch, H.-D. Klingemann, 'Theorie des Rechtsradikalismus in westlichen Industriegesellschaften', *Hamburger Jahrbuch für Wirtschafts- und Gesellschaftspolitik*, vol. 12, 1967.

7. Carter, *The Extreme Right*, p. 22.

8. U. Backes, *Politischer Extremismus in demokratischen Verfassungsstaaten*, Opladen, 1989; A. Pfahl-Traughber, 'Der Extremismusbegriff in der politikwissenschaftlichen Diskussion – Definitionen, Kritik, Alternativen', in *Jahrbuch Extremismus & Demokratie*, eds U. Backes and E. Jesse, vol. 4, 1992; see also Carter, *The Extreme Right*, pp. 16–20.

9. For these critical assessments, see G.K. Roberts, 'Extremism in Germany: Sparrows or Avalanche?', *European Journal of Political Research*, vol. 25, no. 4,

1994; C. Kopke and L. Rensmann, 'Die Extremismus-Formel. Zur politischen Karriere einer wissenschaftlichen Ideologie', *Blätter für deutsche und internationale Politik*, vol. 44, no. 12, 2000.

10. For this understanding of 'extremism', see S.M. Lipset and E. Raab, *The Politics of Unreason*, New York, 1970.

11. D. Bell, ed., *The Radical Right*, Garden City, 1963. For recent examples, see Kitschelt, *The Radical Right*; Kaplan and Weinberg, *The Emergence of a Euro-American Radical Right*, New Brunswick, N.J., 1998; T.E. Givens, *Voting Radical Right in Western Europe*, New York, 2005; Norris, *Radical Right*.

12. Kaplan and Weinberg, *The Emergence*, p. 10.

13. Mudde, *Populist Radical Right Parties*, p. 26, italics in original.

14. H.-G. Betz, 'Introduction', in *The New Politics of the Right*, eds H.-G. Betz and S. Immerfall, New York, 1998, p. 3.

15. R. Williams, *Keywords*, New York, 1976, pp. 209ff.

16. See the overview by P. Wende, 'Radikalismus', in *Geschichtliche Grundbegriffe*, eds O. Brunner, W. Conze, and R. Koselleck, Stuttgart, 1984, pp. 113–33.

17. M. Fennema, 'Some Conceptual Issues and Problems in the Comparison of Anti-Immigrant Parties in Western Europe', *Party Politics*, vol. 3, no. 4, 1997, p. 486.

18. R. Eatwell,'The Dynamics of Right-wing Electoral Breakthrough', *Patterns of Prejudice*, vol. 32, no. 3, 1998, p. 3 note 1.

19. Betz, 'Introduction', p. 4.

20. For example, see M. Minkenberg, *Die neue radikale Rechte im Vergleich*, Opladen, 1998, p. 33; C. Mudde, *The Ideology of the Extreme Right*, Manchester, 2000, p. 16, 178; U. Backes, 'L'extrême droite: les multiples facettes d'une catégorie d'analyse', in *Les croisés de la société fermée*, ed. P. Perrineau, Paris, 2001, p. 15.

21. R. Eatwell, 'Ideologies: Approaches and Trends', in *Contemporary Political Ideologies*, eds R. Eatwell and A. Wright, London, 1993, pp. 9f.

22. R. Griffin, 'Afterword. Last Rights?', in *The Radical Right in Central and Eastern Europe since 1989*, ed. S. Ramet, University Park, 1999, p. 316.

23. M. Minkenberg, 'The Renewal of the Radical Right: Between Modernity and Anti-modernity', *Government and Opposition*, vol. 35, no. 2, 2000, pp. 171f; Mudde, *The Ideology*, pp. 10f.

24. C. Mudde, 'Right-Wing Extremism Analyzed. A Comparative Analysis of the Ideologies of Three Alleged Right-Wing Extremist Parties (NPD, NDP, CP'86)', *European Journal of Political Research*, vol. 27, no. 2, 1995; U. Druwe, '"Rechtsextremismus". Methodologische Bemerkungen zu einem politikwissenschaftlichen Begriff', in *Rechtsextremismus*, eds J.W. Falter, H.-G. Jaschke, and J.R. Winkler, Opladen, 1996.

25. Mudde, *The Ideology*, p. 11.

26. C.T. Husbands, 'The Other Face of 1992: The Extreme-right Explosion in Western Europe', *Parliamentary Affairs*, vol. 45, no. 3, 1992, p. 268; R. Griffin, 'Afterword', pp. 308–15.

27. M. Ebata, 'Right-Wing Extremism: In Search of a Definition', in *The Extreme Right*, eds A. Braun and S. Scheinberg, Boulder, 1997, p. 13.

28. Carter, *The Extreme Right*, p. 17.

29. See the classic studies by E. Gellner, *Nations and Nationalism*, Ithaca, 1983;

E.J. Hobsbawm, *Nations and Nationalism since 1780,* Cambridge, 1990; B. Anderson, *Imagined Communities,* London, 1991.

30. M. Finley, *The Use and Abuse of History,* New York, 1975; L. Greenfeld, *Nationalism,* Cambridge, 1992.

31. C. Calhoun, *Nationalism,* Minneapolis, 1997; A. Wimmer, *Nationalist Exclusion and Ethnic Conflict,* Cambridge, 2002.

32. M. Minkenberg, 'The Renewal', pp. 174f; R. Eatwell, 'The Rebirth of the "Extreme Right" in Western Europe?', *Parliamentary Affairs,* vol. 53, no. 3, 2000, p. 412.

33. Griffin, 'Afterword', p. 316.

34. For studies that distinguish between culture-nation and state-nation, for example, see A. Smith, *National Identity,* London, 1991; R. Brubaker, *Citizenship and Nationhood in France and Germany,* Cambridge, 1992.

35. R. Koopmans et al., *Contested Citizenship,* Minneapolis, 2005, chapter 5.

36. For a criticism of the definitional anti-thesis, see R. Brubaker, 'Myths and Misconceptions in the Study of Nationalism', in *The State of the Nation,* ed. J.A. Hall, Cambridge, 1998, pp. 298–301.

37. For example, see C.T. Husbands, *Racist Political Movements in Western Europe,* London, 1989; Fennema, 'Some Conceptual Issues', pp. 478ff.

38. See the historical studies by G.L. Mosse, *Toward the Final Solution,* New York, 1978, I. Hannaford, *Race,* Washington, 1996.

39. For these definitional approaches, see R. Miles, *Racism,* London, 1989; G.M. Fredrickson, *Racism,* Princeton, 2002.

40. M. Fennema, 'Legal Repression of Extreme-Right Parties and Racial Discrimination', in *Challenging Immigration and Ethnic Relations Politics,* eds R. Koopmans and P. Statham, Oxford, 2000.

41. M. Barker, *The New Racism,* London, 1981; P.-A. Taguieff, *La force du préjugé,* Paris, 1988; E. Balibar, 'Is There a "Neo-Racism"?', in *Race, Nation, Class,* E. Balibar and I. Wallerstein, London, 1991.

42. For example, see P.-A. Taguieff, *Sur la Nouvelle droite,* Paris, 1994, pp. 64–105; A.E. Ansell, *New Right, New Racism,* New York, 1997.

43. Taguieff, *La force,* p. 14.

44. D.R. Holmes, *Integral Europe,* Princeton, 2000, p. 7.

45. U. Altermatt and D. Skenderovic, 'Kontinuität und Wandel des Rassismus. Begriffe und Debatten', *Zeitschrift für Geschichtswissenschaft,* vol. 53, no. 9, 2005, pp. 780–90.

46. Mudde, *Populist Radical Right Parties,* p. 19.

47. J. Müller, 'From National Identity to National Interest: The Rise (and Fall) of Germany's New Right', *German Politics,* vol. 8, no. 3, 1999, p. 11; see also M. Terkessidis, *Kulturkampf,* Cologne, 1995, pp. 46–131.

48. For a definition of anti-Semitism, see H. Fein, 'Dimensions of Antisemitism: Attitudes, Collective Accusations, and Actions' in *The Persisting Question,* ed. H. Fein, Berlin, 1987, pp. 67–85; G.I. Langmuir, 'Toward a Definition of Antisemitism', in *Toward a Definition of Antisemitism,* G.I. Langmuir, Berkeley, 1990.

49. J. Katz, *From Prejudice to Destruction,* Cambridge, 1980; R.S., Wistrich, *Anti-Semitism,* London, 1991.

50. B. Marin, *Antisemitismus ohne Antisemiten*, Frankfurt/Main, 2000; W. Benz, *Was ist Antisemitismus?*, Munich, 2004.

51. For example, see L. Rensmann, *Demokratie und Judenbild*, Wiesbaden, 2004; C. Späti, *Die schweizerische Linke und Israel*, Essen, 2006, pp. 26–33.

52. For this approach to xenophobia, see I. Geiss, *Geschichte des Rassismus*, Frankfurt, 1988, p. 28; T. Bjørgo, 'Gewalt gegen ethnische und religiöse Minderheiten', in *Internationales Handbuch der Gewaltforschung*, eds W. Heitmeyer and J. Hagan, Wiesbaden, 2002, p. 982.

53. Langmuir, 'Toward a Definition', p. 329.

54. E. Cashmore, 'Xenophobia', in *Dictionary of Race and Ethnic Relations*, ed. E. Cashmore, 1st edn, London, 1984, p. 284.

55. M. Banton, 'Xenophobia', in *Dictionary of Race and Ethnic Relations*, ed. E. Cashmore, 4th edn, London, 1996, p. 382.

56. Ibid., italics in original.

57. G. Ford, *Fascist Europe*, London, 1992.

58. For example, see F. Halliday, '"Islamophobia" reconsidered', *Ethnic and Racial Studies*, vol. 22, no. 5, 1999; D. Skenderovic, 'Feindbild Muslime: Islamophobie in der radikalen Rechten', in *Der Islam in Europa*, eds U. Altermatt, M. Delgado, and G. Vergauwen, Munich, 2006.

59. M. Swyngedouw and G. Ivaldi, 'The Extreme Right Utopia in Belgium and France: The Ideology of the Flemish Vlaams Blok and French Front National', *West European Politics*, vol. 24, no. 3, 2001, p. 13.

60. Ibid., pp. 7f; Mudde, *The Ideology*, p. 175.

61. Mudde, 'Right-Wing Extremism', pp. 216ff.

62. P. Ignazi, 'The Silent Counter-Revolution. Hypotheses on the Emergence of Extreme Right-Wing Parties in Europe', *European Journal of Political Research*, vol. 22, no. 1/2, 1992.

63. On this important antagonistic relationship, see Kitschelt, *The Radical Right*, pp. 47–90; D. Skenderovic and C. Späti, eds. *1968 – Revolution und Gegenrevolution*, Basel, 2008.

64. L. Weinberg, 'Introduction', in *Encounters with the Contemporary Radical Right*, eds P. H. Merkl and L. Weinberg, Boulder, 1993, p. 7.

65. For example, see H.-G. Betz, *Radical Right-Wing Populism in Western Europe*, New York, 1994; Kitschelt, *The Radical Right*; H. Kriesi, 'Movements of the Left, Movements of the Right: Putting the Mobilization of Two New Types of Social Movements into Political Context', in *Continuity and Change in Contemporary Capitalism*, eds H. Kitschelt et al., Cambridge, 1999.

66. R. Heinisch, 'Success in Opposition – Failure in Government: Explaining the Performance of Right-Wing Populist Parties in Public Office', *West European Politics*, vol. 26, no. 3, 2003, p. 93.

67. H.-G. Betz, 'The New Politics of Resentment. Radical Right-Wing Populist Parties in Western Europe', *Comparative Politics*, vol. 25, no. 4, 1993, pp. 418f.

68. Ibid., pp. 419f.

69. Eatwell, 'The Rebirth', p. 413.

70. Minkenberg, 'The Renewal', p. 173.

71. For a recent study examining key features of the radical right's ideology, agenda and policies, see Swyngedouw and Ivaldi, 'The Extreme Right'.

72. M. Castells, *The Information Age, Vol. 2: The Power of Identity*, Malden, 1997, p. 2.

73. Holmes, *Integral Europe*, p. 5.

74. For accounts of the radical right's identity politics, see H.-G. Betz, 'Contre la mondialisation: xénophobie, politiques identitaires et populisme d'exclusion en Europe occidentale', *Politique et Sociétés*, vol. 21, no. 2, 2002; H.-G. Betz, *La droite populiste en Europe*, Paris, 2004.

75. Fennema, 'Some Conceptual Issues', p. 483.

76. H.-G. Betz and C. Johnson, 'Against the Current – Stemming the Tide: The Nostalgic Ideology of the Contemporary Radical Populist Right', *Journal of Political Ideologies*, vol. 9, no. 3, 2004, p. 318.

77. See several contributions in the edited volume by R. Koopmans and P. Statham, eds, *Challenging Immigration and Ethnic Relations Politics*, Oxford, 2000.

78. Brubaker, *Citizenship*, p. 182, italics in original.

79. For a discussion of recent debates on the welfare state, see J.D. Stephens and E. Huber, *Development and Crisis of the Welfare State*, Chicago, 2001.

80. H.G. Betz, 'Radikal rechtspopulistische Parteien in Westeuropa', *Aus Politik und Zeitgeschichte*, no. 44, 1991, p. 13; Kitschelt, *The Radical Right*, p. 22.

81. C. Fieschi, 'European Institutions: The Far-Right and Illiberal Politics in a Liberal Context', *Parliamentary Affairs*, vol. 53, no. 3, 2000.

82. Betz and Johnson, 'Against the Current', p. 321.

83. T. Todorov and A. Jacquet, *Guerre et paix sous l'Occupation*, Paris, 1996, p. 15; cited (and translated) by R.J. Golsan in 'Introduction', in *Fascism's Return*, ed. R.J. Golsan, Lincoln, 1998, p. 8.

84. For example, see R.J. Golsan, *Fascism's Return*, Lincoln, 1998; H.-G. Betz, 'Exclusionary Populism in Austria, Italy, and Switzerland', *International Journal*, vol. 56, no. 3, 2001, pp. 403f.

85. M. Fennema, 'Legal Repression', p. 139.

86. R. Koopmans and P. Statham, 'Introduction', in *Challenging Immigration and Ethnic Relations Politics*, eds R. Koopmans and P. Statham, Oxford 2000, p. 4.

87. H.G. Simmons, *The French National Front*, Boulder, 1996, pp. 223f.

88. Mudde, *The Ideology*; Carter, *The Extreme Right*; Norris, *Radical Right*.

89. P. Ignazi, 'The Extreme Right in Europe: A Survey', in *The Revival of Right-Wing Extremism in the Nineties*, eds P.H. Merkl and L. Weinberg, London, 1997, p. 48, italics in original.

90. M. Duverger, *Political Parties*, London, 1954, pp. 231f; M. Duverger, *The French Political System*, Chicago, 1958, pp. 84–111; D.-L. Seiler, *Partis et familles politiques*, Paris, 1980. For an overview of the use of the concept 'party family', see P. Mair and C. Mudde, 'The Party Family and its Study', *Annual Review of Political Science*, vol. 1, no. 1, 1998.

91. Minkenberg, *Die neue radikale Rechte*. p. 237.

92. P. Hainsworth, 'Introduction: The Extreme Right', in *The Politics of the Extreme Right*, ed. P. Hainsworth, London, 2000, pp. 4f; see also D. Skenderovic, *The Swiss Radical Right in Perspective*, Grenoble, 2001, pp. 9f.

93. Drawing on this approach, see the following studies: on France, by J.-Y. Camus and R. Monzat, *Les droites nationales et radicales en France*, Lyon, 1992; on Germany, by P. Dudek and H.-G Jaschke, *Entstehung und Entwicklung des Rech-*

tsextremismus in der Bundesrepublik, 2 vols, Opladen, 1984; and on Austria, by Stiftung Dokumentationsarchiv des österreichischen Widerstandes, ed., *Handbuch des österreichischen Rechtsextremismus,* 2nd edn, Vienna, 1993.

94. See also J.-Y. Camus, 'La structure du "camp national" en France: la périphérie militante et organisationnelle du Front national et du Mouvement national républicain', in *Les croisés de la société fermée,* ed. P. Perrineau, Paris, 2001, pp. 199ff.

95. Minkenberg, *Die neue radikale Rechte,* pp. 50–53; M. Minkenberg, 'The West European Radical Right as a Collective Actor: Modelling the Impact of Cultural and Structural Variables on Party Formation and Movement Mobilization', *Comparative European Politics,* vol. 1, no. 2, 2003.

96. On the concept of 'collective action', see the classic by S. Tarrow, *Power in Movement,* Cambridge, 1994.

97. W. Bergmann and R. Erb, '"In Treue zur Nation". Zur kollektiven Identität der rechtsextremen Bewegung', in *Paradigmen der Bewegungsforschung,* eds K.-U. Hellmann and R. Koopmans, Opladen, 1998; D. Rucht, *Modernisierung und neue soziale Bewegungen,* Frankfurt, 1994, pp. 79–82; Minkenberg, *Die neue radikale Rechte,* pp. 239f.

98. Rucht, *Modernisierung,* pp. 76f.

99. R. Koopmans and D. Rucht, 'Rechtsextremismus als soziale Bewegung?', in *Rechtsextremismus,* eds J.W. Falter, H.-G. Jaschke, and J.R. Winkler, Opladen, 1996, pp. 270f.

100. On the significance that this commitment has for the radical right, see Bergmann and Erb, '"In Treue zur Nation"'.

101. Tarrow, *Power in Movement,* pp. 4f.

102. Minkenberg, 'The West European Radical Right', p. 153.

103. Minkenberg, *Die neue radikale Rechte,* pp. 237–40.

104. For studies using the concept of 'radical right-wing populism', see Betz, 'The New Politics'; Betz, *Radical Right-Wing Populism;* J. Rydgren, ed., *Movements of Exclusion,* New York, 2004.

105. Mudde, 'The Populist Zeitgeist', *Government and Opposition,* vol. 39, no. 4, 2004, p. 543.

106. M. Freeden, 'Is Nationalism a Distinct Ideology?', *Political Studies,* vol. 46, no. 4, 1998, 744–63; see also Mudde, 'The Populist Zeitgeist', p. 544.

107. P.-A. Taguieff, *L'illusion populiste,* Paris, 2002.

108. M. Canovan, 'Trust the People! Populism and the Two Faces of Democracy', *Political Studies,* vol. 47, no. 1, 1999, p. 3.

109. M. Canovan, 'Taking Politics to the People: Populism as the Ideology of Democracy', in *Democracies and the Populist Challenge,* eds Y. Mény, Y. Surel, Basingstoke, 2002.

110. On these aspects, see Y. Mény and Y. Surel, *Par le peuple, pour le peuple,* Paris, 2000, pp. 270–83; Carter, *The Extreme Right,* chapter 3.

111. P. Taggart, 'New Populist Parties in Western Europe', *West European Politics,* vol. 18, no. 1, 1995, pp. 40f; Heinisch, 'Success in Opposition', p. 94.

112. Mény and Surel, *Par le peuple,* pp. 102–17; R. Eatwell, 'The Rebirth of Right-Wing Charisma? The Cases of Jean-Marie Le Pen and Vladimir Zhirinovsky', *Totalitarian Movements and Political Religions,* vol. 3, no. 3, 2002.

113. Mény and Surel, *Par le peuple*, pp. 117–27; Mudde, 'The Populist Zeitgeist', pp. 553f.

114. Canovan, 'Trust the People!', p. 6.

115. P. Taggart, *The New Populism and the New Politics*, Basingstoke, 1996, pp. 37f; A. Pedahzur and A. Brichta, 'The Institutionalization of Extreme Right-Wing Charismatic Parties: A Paradox?', *Party Politics*, vol. 8, no. 1, 2002, pp. 42f.

116. Simmons, *National Front*, p. 187. See also B. Klandermans and N. Mayer, 'Militer à l'extrême droite', in *Les croisés de la société fermée*, ed. P. Perrineau, Paris, 2001, p. 158.

117. For example, see Minkenberg, *Die neue radikale Rechte*, pp. 237–309.

118. Betz, *Radical Right-Wing Populism*, p. 108.

119. For a discussion of the New Right as a intellectual current and collective actor, see W. Gessenharter and H. Fröchling, 'Neue Rechte und Rechtsextremismus in Deutschland', in *Handbuch deutscher Rechtsextremismus*, ed. J. Mecklenburg, Berlin, 1996, pp. 555–61; Minkenberg, *Die neue radikale Rechte*, pp. 141f.

120. On the relationship between the New Right and radical right-wing populist parties, see M. Minkenberg, 'The New Right in France and Germany: *Nouvelle Droite, Neue Rechte*, and the New Right Radical Parties', in *The Revival of Right-Wing Extremism in the Nineties*, eds P.H. Merkl and L. Weinberg, London, 1997.

121. For accounts of the different currents of the New Right, see R. Levitas, ed., *The Ideology of the New Right*, Cambridge, 1986; Taguieff, *Nouvelle droite*; A. Brauner-Orthen, *Die Neue Rechte in Deutschland*, Opladen, 2001; T. Bar-On, *Where Have All the Fascists Gone?*, Aldershot, 2007.

122. Taguieff, *Nouvelle droite*, p. 65.

123. A.-M. Duranton-Crabol, *Visages de la Nouvelle droite*, Paris, 1988; W. Kowalsky, *Kulturevolution?*, Opladen, 1991.

124. P.-A. Taguieff, 'La stratégie culturelle de la "Nouvelle droite" en France (1968–1983)', in *Vous avez dit fascismes?*, ed. R. Badinter, Paris, 1984; Terkessidis, *Kulturkampf*.

125. For example, see E. Neaman, 'Ernst Jünger's Millenium: Bad Citizens for the New Century', in *Fascism's Return*, ed. R.J. Golsan, Lincoln, 1998, pp. 224–28; Müller, 'From National Identity', pp. 9–12.

126. K. von Beyme, 'Right-Wing Extremism in Post-War Europe', *West European Politics*, vol. 11, no. 2, 1988, p. 6; M. Feit, *Die "Neue Rechte" in der Bundesrepublik*, Frankfurt, 1987, pp. 144–49.

127. On the significance that the ethology research school has for the German New Right, see I. Weber, *Nation, Staat und Elite*, Cologne, 1997, pp. 26–29.

128. V. Stolcke, 'Talking Culture. New Boundaries, New Rhetorics of Exclusion in Europe', *Current Anthropology*, vol. 36, no. 1, 1995, p. 5.

129. M. Minkenberg, 'The New Right', p. 75.

130. W. Gessenharter, 'Neue radikale Rechte, intellektuelle Neue Rechte und Rechtsextremismus: Zur theoretischen und empirischen Neuvermessung eines politisch-ideologischen Raumes', in *Rechtsextremismus und Neue Rechte in Deutschland*, eds W. Gessenharter and H. Fröchling Opladen, 1998, pp. 47–54; R.J. Antonio, 'After Postmodernism: Reactionary Tribalism', *American Journal of Sociology*, vol. 106, no. 2, 2000.

131. P.-A. Taguieff, 'From Race to Culture: The New Right's View of European Identity', *Telos*, no. 98/99, 1993/94.

132. A central role in the revival of the Conservative Revolution was played by the Swiss Armin Mohler (1920–2003), who developed the concept *post festum* with his dissertation that was submitted to the University of Basel, where Herman Schmalenbach and Karl Jaspers were his thesis directors, and was published in 1950. Mohler was private secretary to Ernst Jünger from 1949 to 1953, before becoming a key intellectual of the German New Right. See T. Willms, *Armin Mohler*, Cologne, 2004.

133. For academic studies, see S. Breuer, *Anatomie der Konservativen Revolution*, Darmstadt, 1993; R. Woods, *The Conservative Revolution in the Weimar Republic*, Basingstoke, 1996.

134. R. Woods, 'The Radical Right: The "Conservative Revolutionaries" in Germany', in *The Nature of the Right*, eds R. Eatwell and N. O'Sullivan, Boston, 1989, p. 127.

135. A. Pfahl-Traughber, *"Konservative Revolution" und "Neue Rechte"*, Opladen, 1998, pp. 188–201.

136. K. Lenk, G. Meuter, and H.-R. Otten, *Vordenker der Neuen Rechten*, Frankfurt, 1997, pp. 83–108; Antonio, 'After Postmodernism', pp. 59ff.

137. W. Laqueur, *Fascism*, New York, 1997, p. 99.

138. For the conceptualisation of the extreme right as 'micro-mobilisation', see W. Bergmann, 'Ein Versuch, die extreme Rechte als soziale Bewegung zu beschreiben', in *Neonazismus und rechte Subkultur*, eds W. Bergmann and R. Erb, Berlin, 1994, pp. 190ff.

139. On the violence aspect of the extreme right, see T. Bjørgo and R. Witte, eds, *Racist Violence in Europe*, New York, 1993; T. Bjørgo, ed., *Terror from the Extreme Right*, London, 1995.

140. L. Weinberg, 'An Overview of Right-Wing Extremism in Western World: A Study of Convergence, Linkage, and Identity', in *Nation and Race*, eds J. Kaplan and T. Bjørgo, Boston, 1998; Kaplan and Weinberg, *The Emergence*.

141. Minkenberg, *Die neue radikale Rechte*, pp. 237–309.

142. R. Hofstadter, *The Paranoid Style in American Politics and Other Essays*, New York, 1965; M. Barkun, *A Culture of Conspiracy*, Berkeley, 2003.

143. For recent studies that include accounts of the extreme-right subculture, see Laqueur, *Fascism*; Kaplan and Weinberg, *The Emergence*, J. Kaplan and T. Bjørgo, eds, *Nation and Race*, Boston, 1998.

144. Klandermans and Mayer, 'Militer'.

2. Success Conditions and Organisational Variation in Switzerland

1. For example, see D. Prowe, '"Classic" Fascism and the New Radical Right in Western Europe: Comparisons and Contrasts', *Contemporary European History*, vol. 3, no. 3, 1994.

2. R. Karapin, 'Radical-Right and Neo-Fascist Political Parties in Western Europe', *Comparative Politics*, vol. 30, no. 2, 1998, pp. 225ff.; R. Eatwell, 'Ten Theo-

ries of the Extreme Right', in *Right-Wing Extremism in the Twenty-First Century*, eds P.H. Merkl and L. Weinberg, 2nd rev. edn, London, 2003, pp. 62f.

3. A striking fact in Swiss historical research is that that the most comprehensive studies on the interwar radical right date from the 1960s and 1970s; see P. Gilg and E. Gruner, 'Nationale Erneuerungsbewegungen in der Schweiz 1925–1940', *Vierteljahrshefte für Zeitgeschichte*, vol. 14, no. 1, 1966; B. Glaus, *Die Nationale Front*, Zurich, 1969; W. Wolf, *Faschismus in der Schweiz*, Zurich, 1969; R. Joseph, *L'Union nationale, 1932–1939*, Neuchâtel, 1975.

4. B. Glaus, 'The National Front in Switzerland', in *Who Were the Fascists?*, eds S.U. Larsen, B. Hagtvet and J.P. Myklebust, Bergen, 1980.

5. S. Zala, 'Governmental Malaise with History: From the White Paper to the Bonjour Report', in *Switzerland and the Second World War*, ed. G. Kreis, London, 2000, p. 313; see also H.J. Jost, *Politik und Wirtschaft im Krieg*, Zurich, 1998, pp. 214f.

6. *Bundesblatt*, vol. I, no. 1, 1946, pp. 1–143; vol. II, no. 11, 1946, pp. 173–211.

7. For example, see J. Picard, *Die Schweiz und die Juden 1933–1945*, Zurich, 1994; U. Altermatt, *Katholizismus und Antisemitismus*, Frauenfeld, 1999; Independent Commission of Experts Switzerland – Second World War, *Switzerland, National Socialism and the Second World War*, Zurich, 2002.

8. On these general changes in Swiss society, see König et al., eds, *Dynamisierung und Umbau*, Zurich, 1998; M. Eisner, 'Sozialer Wandel und neue Integrationsprobleme seit den Siebzigerjahren', in *Sozialbericht 2000*, ed. C. Suter, Zurich, 2000; S. Hug and P. Sciarini, eds, *Changements de valeurs et nouveaux clivages politiques en Suisse*, Paris, 2002; H. Kriesi et al., eds, *Contemporary Switzerland*, Basingstoke, 2005.

9. For example, see E.K. Scheuch and H.-D. Klingemann, 'Theorie des Rechtsradikalismus in westlichen Industriegesellschaften', *Hamburger Jahrbuch für Wirtschafts- und Gesellschaftspolitik*, vol. 12, 1967; Betz, *Radical Right-Wing Populism*; Minkenberg, *Die neue radikale Rechte*.

10. Kriesi, 'Movements of the Left', p. 406.

11. Kitschelt, *The Radical Right*, p. 275; R.W. Jackman and K. Volpert, 'Conditions Favouring Parties of the Extreme Right in Western Europe', *British Journal of Political Science*, vol. 26, no. 4, 1996, p. 517.

12. *Statistisches Jahrbuch der Schweiz 2002*, published by the Federal Statistical Office, vol. 109, Zurich, 2002, pp. 169f; *Schweizerische Nationalbank*, 89th Annual Report 1996, p. 8; 93rd Annual Report 2000, p. 10; 95th Annual Report 2002, p. 10.

13. Givens, *Voting Radical Right*, pp. 68–89.

14. M. Küchler, 'Xenophobie im internationalen Vergleich', in *Rechtsextremismus*, eds J.W. Falter, H.-G. Jaschke, and J.R. Winkler, Opladen, 1996; C. Mudde, 'The Single-Issue Party Thesis: Extreme Right Parties and the Immigration Issue', *West European Politics*, vol. 22, no. 3, 1999.

15. Betz, *Radical Right-Wing Populism*, pp. 85–90; M. Golder, 'Explaining Variation in the Success of Extreme Right Parties in Western Europe', *Comparative Political Studies*, vol. 36, no. 4, 2003.

16. K. Armingeon, 'Fremdenfeindlichkeit in der Schweiz in international

vergleichender Perspektive', in *Die Bedeutung des Ethnischen im Zeitalter der Globalisierung*, ed. R. Moser, Bern, 2000, p. 222.

17. Ibid., pp. 224ff.

18. Betz, *Radical Right-Wing Populism*, pp. 37–67; P. Knigge, 'The Ecological Correlates of Right-Wing Extremism in Western Europe', *European Journal of Political Research*, vol. 34, no. 2, 1998.

19. R. Nabholz, 'Das Wählerverhalten in der Schweiz: Stabilität oder Wandel? Eine Trendanalyse von 1971–1995', in *Schweizer Wahlen 1995*, eds H. Kriesi, W. Linder, and U. Klöti, Bern, 1998, p. 34; C. Suter, ed., *Sozialbericht 2000*, Zurich, 2000, p. 191.

20. S. Kobi, *Des citoyens suisses contre l'élite politique*, Paris, 2000, pp. 75ff.; M. Bühlmann, M. Freitag, and A. Vatter, 'Die schweigende Mehrheit: Eine Typologie der Schweizer Nichtwählerschaft', in *Schweizer Wahlen 1999*, eds P. Sciarini, S. Harmeier, and A. Vatter, Bern, 2003, pp. 27f.

21. Ignazi, 'The Silent Counter-Revolution'; Kitschelt, *The Radical Right*, pp. 47–90; P. Taggart, *The New Populism and the New Politics*, Basingstoke, 1996; Minkenberg, *Die neue radikale Rechte*, pp. 206–36.

22. R. Karapin, 'Radical-Right and Neo-Fascist Political Parties in Western Europe', p. 228f; R. Eatwell, 'Ten Theories of the Extreme Right', pp. 54ff.

23. H. Kriesi et al., *New Social Movements in Western Europe*, Minneapolis, 1995; M. Giugni and F. Passy, *Histoires de mobilisation politique en Suisse*, Paris, 1997.

24. S. Sacchi, 'Postmaterialismus in der Schweiz von 1972 bis 1990', *Schweizerische Zeitschrift für Soziologie*, vol. 18, no. 1, 1992; M. Finger and P. Sciarini, 'Integrating "New Politics" into "Old Politics": The Swiss Party Elite', *West European Politics*, vol. 14, no.1, 1991.

25. Hug and Sciarini, *Changements de valeurs*.

26. For example, see Kitschelt, *Radical Right*, pp. 14–19; Minkenberg, *Die neue radikale Rechte*, pp. 62–67; R. Eatwell, 'Ethnocentric Party Mobilization in Europe: the Importance of the Three-Dimensional Approach', in *Challenging Immigration and Ethnic Relations Politics*, eds R. Koopmans and P. Statham, Oxford, 2000, pp. 356–63.

27. K.W. Kobach, *The Referendum*, Aldershot, 1993, W. Linder, *Swiss Democracy*, 2nd edn, London, 1998; C.H. Church, *The Politics and Government of Switzerland*, Basingstoke, 2004, pp. 143–53.

28. L. Helms, 'Right-Wing Populist Parties in Austria and Switzerland: A Comparative Analysis of Electoral Support and Conditions of Success', *West European Politics*, vol. 20, no. 2, 1997, p. 47; D. Skenderovic, 'Immigration and the Radical Right in Switzerland: Ideology, Discourse and Opportunities', *Patterns of Prejudice*, vol. 41, no. 2, 2007, pp. 171–174.

29. For a discussion of the significance that Swiss direct democratic institutions have for small parties, see Y. Papadopoulos, 'Quel rôle pour les petits partis dans la démocratie directe?', *Schweizerisches Jahrbuch für Politische Wissenschaft*, no. 31, 1991.

30. K.W. Kobach, 'Spurn Thy Neighbour: Direct Democracy and Swiss Isolationism', *West European Politics*, vol. 20, no. 3, 1997, p. 207; see also Kobi, *Des citoyens suisses*.

31. On different aspects of the Swiss party system, see H.H. Kerr, 'The Swiss

Party System: Steadfast and Changing', in *Party Systems in Denmark, Austria, Switzerland, the Netherlands, and Belgium,* ed. H. Daalder, London, 1987; A. Ladner, 'The Political Parties and the Party System', in *Handbook of Swiss Politics,* eds U. Klöti et al., Zurich, 2004.

32. On the significance that the regional level has for anti-immigration parties, see T. Perlmutter, 'Bringing Parties Back In: Comments on "Modes of Immigration Politics in Liberal Democratic Societies"', *International Migration Review,* vol. 30, no. 1, 1996, p. 382; R. Karapin, 'The Politics of Immigration Control in Britain and Germany. Subnational Politicians and Social Movements', *Comparative Politics,* vol. 31, no. 4, 1999, pp. 425f.

33. Jackman and Volpert, 'Conditions Favouring Parties', pp. 506f; Golder, 'Explaining Variation'; Carter, *The Extreme Right,* pp. 147–62.

34. H. Kriesi, *Le système politique suisse,* Paris, 1995, pp. 141–48; Linder, *Swiss Democracy,* pp. 44ff.; Church, *The Politics,* pp.133–42.

35. Eatwell, 'Ethnocentric Party Mobilization', pp. 357f; Kitschelt, *Radical Right,* p. vii; Carter, *The Extreme Right,* chapter 4.

36. A. Lijphart, *Democracies,* New Haven, 1984. For a recent account of different aspects of Switzerland's consociational governance, see U. Klöti, 'Consensual Government in a Heterogeneous Polity', in *The Swiss Labyrinth,* ed. J.-E. Lane, London, 2001.

37. When the Federal State was founded in 1848, the government was composed of seven representatives of what is called the *freisinnige Grossfamilie* (extended liberal family). With the introduction of the optional referendum in 1874 and the federal initiative in 1891, the Catholic-Conservatives, the precursors of today's CVP, received the opportunity to obstruct policy-making processes by using the means of direct democracy. In the face of this risk of referendums, the Liberals complied with the proposal that one member of the Catholic-Conservatives should be elected into the government. Once proportional representation had been introduced in the National Council elections of 1919 and the Liberals suffered major vote losses, the Catholic-Conservatives received a second seat in the Federal Council. In 1929, it was the turn of the Farmers, Artisans and Citizens Party (*Bauern-, Gewerbe- und Bürgerpartei* – BGB), precursors of the SVP, to enter government, as one of its members came into office. Only in 1943, during the Second World War, was a representative of Social Democrats temporarily elected to the government. In 1959, this long process of integration resulted in the 'magic formula', instituting a system of power-sharing between the four major political parties.

38. O. Mazzoleni and D. Skenderovic, 'The Rise and Impact of the Swiss People's Party: Challenging the Rules of Governance in Switzerland', in *Extrême droite et pouvoir en Europe – The extreme right parties and power in Europe,* eds P. Delwit, and P. Poirier, Brussels, 2007.

39. Q. Skinner, 'Some Problems in the Analysis of Political Thought and Action', in *Meaning and Context: Quentin Skinner and His Critics,* ed. J. Tully, Princeton, 1988, pp. 97–118.

40. R. Koopmans and P. Statham, 'Ethnic and Civic Conceptions of Nationhood and the Differential Success of the Extreme Right in Germany and Italy', in *How Social Movements Matter,* eds M. Giugni et al., Minneapolis, 1999, p. 229.

41. H. Kohn, *Nationalism and Liberty*, London, 1956; K.W. Deutsch, *Die Schweiz als ein paradigmatischer Fall politischer Integration*, Bern, 1976; Anderson, *Imagined Communities*, pp. 135–39.

42. P. Sciarini, S. Hug, and C. Dupont, *Example, Exception or Both?*, San Domenico, 1997.

43. J.-B. Racine and C. Raffestin, eds, *Nouvelle géographie de la Suisse et des Suisses*, 2 vols, Lausanne, 1990; G.P. Marchal and A. Mattioli, eds, *Erfundene Schweiz*, Zurich, 1992; O. Zimmer, *A Contested Nation*, Cambridge, 2003.

44. D. Froidevaux, 'Construction de la nation et pluralisme suisses: idéologie et pratiques', *Swiss Political Science Review*, vol. 3, no. 4, 1997, p. 58.

45. Koopmans et al., *Contested Citizenship*. On the historical development and the specificities of citizenship policies in Switzerland, see B. Studer, G. Arlettaz, and R. Argast, *Das Schweizer Bürgerrecht*, Zurich, 2008

46. R. Koopmans and H. Kriesi, 'Citoyenneté, identité nationale et mobilisation de l'extrême droite. Une comparaison entre la France, l'Allemagne, les Pays-Bas et la Suisse', in *Sociologie des nationalismes*, ed. P. Birnbaum, Paris, 1997.

47. Zimmer, *A Contested Nation*, pp. 240ff.

48. Kriesi, *Le système politique*, pp. 12–21.

49. On these changes in Swiss foreign policy, see C. Dupont and P. Sciarini, 'Switzerland and the European Integration Process: Engagement without Marriage', in *The Swiss Labyrinth*, ed. J.-E. Lane, London, 2001; L. Goetschel, M. Bernath, and D. Schwarz, *Swiss Foreign Policy*, London, 2005.

50. For the overview of the postwar historical research, see G. Kreis, 'Introduction: Four Debates and Little Dissent', in *Switzerland and the Second World War*, ed. G. Kreis, London, 2000.

51. T. Maissen, *Verweigerte Erinnerung*, Zurich, 2005.

52. P. Kury, *Über Fremde reden*, Zurich, 2003; D. Skenderovic, 'Constructing Boundaries in a Multicultural Nation: The Discourse of "Overforeignization" in Switzerland', in *European Encounters*, eds R. Ohliger, K. Schönwälder, and T. Triadafilopoulos, Aldershot, 2003.

53. R. Misteli and A. Gisler, 'Überfremdung. Karriere und Diffusion eines fremdenfeindlichen Deutungsmusters', in *Vom kalten Krieg zur Kulturrevolution*, eds K. Imhof, H. Kleger, and G. Romano, Zurich, 1999; G. Romano, 'Vom Sonderfall zur Überfremdung. Zur Erfolgsgeschichte gemeinschaftsideologischen Denkens im öffentlichen politischen Diskurs der späten fünfziger und der sechziger Jahre', *Vom kalten Krieg zur Kulturrevolution*, eds K. Imhof, H. Kleger, and G. Romano, Zurich, 1999.

54. H. Fröhlich and B. Müller, *Überfremdungsdiskurse und die Virulenz von Fremdenfeindlichkeit vor dem Hintergrund internationaler Migrationsbewegungen*, Zurich, 1995.

55. J. Stolz, 'Einstellungen zu Ausländern und Ausländerinnen 1969 und 1995: eine Replikationsstudie', in *Das Fremde in der Schweiz*, ed. H.-J. Hoffmann-Nowotny, Zurich, 2001.

56. Armingeon, 'Fremdenfeindlichkeit', p. 222.

57. D. Schloeth, *Analyse der eidgenössischen Abstimmungen vom 25. September 1994*, Adliswil, 1994, p. 17.

58. G. Kreis, 'Antisemitismus in der Schweiz nach 1945', in *Neuer Antisemitismus – alte Vorurteile?*, ed. C. Tuor-Kurth, Stuttgart, 2001; C. Späti, 'Kontinuität und Wandel des Antisemitismus und dessen Beurteilung in der Schweiz nach 1945', *Schweizerische Zeitschrift für Geschichte*, vol. 55, no. 4, 2005.

59. B.R. Erdle, and D. Wildmann, 'Die Macht, das Geld und die Juden. Essay zum öffentlichen Umgang mit Antisemitismus in der Schweiz', *traverse. Zeitschrift für Geschichte – Revue de l'histoire*, vol. 5, no. 1, 1998; W. Benz, 'Antisemitismus in der Schweiz', *Judaica. Beiträge zum Verstehen des Judentums*, vol. 56, no. 1, 2000; C. Späti, 'Enttabuisierung eines Vorurteils: Antisemitismus in der Schweiz', in *Feindbild Judentum*, eds. L. Rensmann and J.H. Schoeps, Berlin 2008, pp. 190–193.

60. C. Longchamp, J. Dumont and P. Leuenberger, *Einstellungen der SchweizerInnen gegenüber Jüdinnen und Juden und dem Holocaust*, Bern, 2000, pp. 17, 49f.

61. M. Schain, A. Zolberg and P. Hossay, 'The Development of Radical Right Parties in Western Europe', in *Shadows over Europe*, eds M. Schain, A. Zolberg and P. Hossay, New York, 2002.

62. M. Schain, 'The Comparative Study of Immigration in Britain, France and the United States', Portsmouth, 2001; Skenderovic, 'Constructing Boundaries'.

63. E. Hennig, 'Politische Unzufriedenheit – ein Resonanzboden für Rechtsextremismus?', in *Rechtsextremismus*, eds W. Kowalsky and W. Schroeder, Wolfgang, Opladen, 1994.

64. For example, see Minkenberg, *Die neue radikale Rechte*, pp. 237–45.

65. Betz, *Radical Right-Wing Populism*, p. 108.

3. An Early Precursor: The Movement against Overforeignization in the 1960s and 1970s

1. On the Poujadist movement, see the classic volume by S. Hoffmann, ed., *Le mouvement Poujade*, Paris, 1956.

2. On the history of NA, see K.J. Pitterle, *The Limits of Interdependence*, Ann Arbor, 1981; U. Altermatt, 'Xenophobie und Superpatriotismus. Die populistische Anti-Überfremdungsbewegung in der Schweiz der sechziger und siebziger Jahre', *Faschismus in Österreich und international. Jahrbuch für Zeitgeschichte 1980/1981*, Vienna, 1982; Buomberger, *Kampf gegen unerwünschte Fremde*, Zurich, 2004; D. Skenderovic and G. D'Amato, *Mit dem Fremden politisieren*, Zurich, 2008.

3. For biographical accounts of Schwarzenbach, see Buomberger, *Kampf gegen*, pp. 97–132; I. Drews, *"Schweizer erwache!" Der Rechtspopulist James Schwarzenbach (1967–1978)*, Frauenfeld, 2005.

4. G. Romano, 'Die Überfremdungsbewegung als "Neue soziale Bewegung". Zur Kommerzialisierung, Oralisierung und Personalisierung massenmedialer Kommunikation in den 60er Jahren', in *Dynamisierung und Umbau*, eds M. König et al., Zurich, 1998, p. 146.

5. Buomberger, *Kampf gegen*, p. 176; Drews, *"Schweizer erwache!"*, pp. 122–38.

6. 'Politische Richtlinien der schweizerischen Republikaner', *Der Republikaner*, no. 1, 16 November 1970, p. 1.

7. The SRB deputies came from the cantons of Zurich (4), Bern (1), Aargau (1) and Thurgau (1). NA won one seat each in the cantons of Zurich, Bern, Basel City and Vaud. For a full account of the 1971 national elections, see Pitterle, *Interdependence*, pp. 600–30.

8. Altermatt, 'Xenophobie und Superpatriotismus', pp. 172f.

9. J. Frischknecht, *"Schweiz wir kommen"*, 2nd edn, Zurich, 1991, pp. 40f.

10. For accounts of the 1971 elections, see P. Gilg 'Der Erfolg der neuen Rechtsgruppen in den Nationalratswahlen von 1971', *Schweizerische Zeitschrift für Volkswirtschaft und Statistik*, vol. 108, no. 4, 1972; Pitterle, *Interdependence*, pp. 636–42; Altermatt, 'Xenophobie und Superpatriotismus', p. 179.

11. In the 1975 National Council elections, NA lost two of its four seats and the parliamentary representation of the SRB was reduced from seven to three seats. While NA had one deputy each from the cantons of Zurich and Bern, the SRB MPs came from the cantons of Zurich (2) and Aargau (1).

12. Buomberger, *Kampf gegen*, pp. 218f; Drews, *"Schweizer erwache!"*, p. 134.

13. H. Mahnig and E. Piguet, 'Die Immigrationspolitik der Schweiz von 1948 bis 1998: Entwicklung und Auswirkungen', in *Migration und die Schweiz*, eds. H.-R. Wicker, R. Fibbi, and W. Haug, Zurich, 2003, pp. 76–88.

14. B. Schmitter Heisler, 'From Conflict to Accommodation: The "Foreigners Question" in Switzerland', *European Journal of Political Research*, vol. 16, 1988, p. 692; E. Piguet, *L'immigration en Suisse depuis 1948*, Zurich, 2005, pp. 70–76.

15. For example, see P.J. Katzenstein, *Corporatism and Change*, Ithaca, 1984, p. 150; P.R. Ireland, *The Policy Challenge of Ethnic Diversity*, Cambridge, 1994, p. 166; Mahnig and Piguet, 'Immigrationspolitik', p. 85.

16. P. Fankhauser, *"Hört auf, die Erde zu ermorden!" Valentin Oehen, 1970-1980* (M.A. thesis, University of Bern, 1995), pp. 55–60; Buomberger, *Kampf gegen*, pp. 174ff.; Drews, *"Schweizer erwache!"*, pp. 130–33.

17. In the National Council elections held between 1967 and 1991, Vigilance regularly received a considerable share of the vote in the canton of Geneva: 4.8 per cent (1967), 5.4 per cent (1971), 6.9 per cent (1975), 6.6 per cent (1979), 12.2 per cent (1983), 6.9 per cent (1987) and 2.0 per cent (1991).

18. On the political career of Mario Soldini, see *Année politique suisse 1967*, Bern 1968, p. 23; *Die Weltwoche*, 6 October 1983; C. Cantini, *Les ultras*, Lausanne, 1992, p. 130; P. Niggli and J. Frischknecht, *Rechte Seilschaften*, Zurich, 1998, p. 145.

19. On the beginnings of Vigilance, see Pitterle, *Interdependence*, pp. 28–50; F. Saint-Quen, 'Vers une remontée du national-populisme en Suisse? Le cas des vigilants genevois', *Schweizerisches Jahrbuch für Politische Wissenschaft*, vol. 26, 1986, p. 216.

20. *Journal de Genève*, 25 October 1965.

21. J.-P. Chenaux, *La presse d'opinion en Suisse Romande ou La bataille des idées*, Lausanne, n.d. [1986], p. 55.

22. *Vigilance*, no. 7, October 1965, p. 3.

23. Saint-Quen, 'Vers une remontée', pp. 217ff.

24. C.T. Husbands, 'The Other Face of 1992: The Extreme-right Explosion in Western Europe', *Parliamentary Affairs*, vol. 45, no. 3, 1992, p. 281.

25. For accounts of these cantonal elections, see Cantini, *Les ultras*, pp. 119f;

Année politique suisse 1984, Bern, 1985, pp. 38f; *Année politique suisse 1985*, Bern, 1986, pp. 36f; *Année politique suisse 1986*, Bern, 1987, pp. 38f.

26. W. Linder, 'Migrationswirkungen, institutionelle Politik und politische Öffentlichkeit', in *Migrationen aus der Dritten Welt*, eds W. Kälin and R. Moser, Bern, 1989, pp. 146f; L. Parini and M. Gianni, 'Enjeux et modifications de la politique d'asile en Suisse de 1956 à nos jours', in *Histoire de la politique de migration, d'asile et d'intégration en Suisse depuis 1948*, ed. H. Mahnig, Zurich, 2005, pp. 211–14.

27. Husbands, 'The Other Face', p. 281.

28. For a biographical account of Valentin Oehen, see P. Fankhauser, *"Hört auf, die Erde zu ermorden!"*.

29. Young Bern had been founded in 1955 by students who sought to present an alternative political force to the traditional parties in Bern.

30. For this assessment, see E. Gruner, *Die Parteien in der Schweiz*, revised and expanded edn, Bern, 1977, p. 296; Frischknecht, *"Schweiz wir kommen"*, pp. 102–5; H. Fröhlich and B. Müller, *Überfremdungsdiskurse und die Virulenz von Fremdenfeindlichkeit vor dem Hintergrund internationaler Migrationsbewegungen*, Zurich, 1995, pp. 76f, 88ff.

31. Excerpts from Markus Ruf's address to the National Front assembly were published by *peuple + patrie*, no. 9, December 1985, p. 2.

32. Quoted in: Frischknecht, *"Schweiz wir kommen"*, p. 101, my translation.

33. Ibid., p. 102.

34. C.T. Husbands, 'Switzerland: Right-Wing and Xenophobic Parties, from Margin to Mainstream?', *Parliamentary Affairs*, vol. 53, no. 3, 2000, p. 506.

35. *Neue Zürcher Zeitung*, 7 March 1988.

36. *La Suisse*, 8 September 1990.

37. W. Seitz, *Nationalratswahlen 1995*, Bern, 1995, p. 70.

38. See the official website of the cantonal SVP party in Genva: http://www.udc-geneve.ch, retrieved 15 January 2003.

39. Ireland, *Policy Challenge*, p. 165; see also H.-J. Hoffmann-Nowotny, 'Switzerland', in *European Immigration Policy*, ed. T. Hammar, Cambridge, 1985, p. 231.

40. H. Mahnig, 'Between Economic Demands and Popular Xenophobia: The Swiss System of Immigration Regulation', in *Regulation of Migration*, eds A. Böcker, Amsterdam, 1998, pp. 177ff.; Mahnig and Piguet, 'Immigrationspolitik', pp. 76–80, 102.

41. Husbands, 'Switzerland', p. 509; Buomberger, *Kampf gegen*, pp. 131–60.

42. Altermatt, 'Xenophobie und Superpatriotismus', p. 172.

43. The description of the voter profile draws on polls and analyses taken from: *Neue Zürcher Zeitung*, morning issue, 9 June 1970; *Der Bund*, 21 June 1970; *Année politique suisse 1970*, Bern 1972, pp. 131f; V. Gawronski, 'Motive der Befürworter des Volksbegehrens gegen die Überfremdung. Ergebnisse einer Umfrage', *Mitteilungsblatt des Delegierten für Konjunkturfragen*, vol. 26, no. 4, 1970; Altermatt, 'Xenophobie und Superpatriotismus', p. 172; Buomberger, *Kampf gegen*, pp. 161f.

44. Schmitter Heisler, 'Conflict to Accommodation', p. 698 note 26.

45. Hoffmann-Nowotny, 'Switzerland', p. 230.

46. Mahnig and Piguet, 'Immigrationspolitik', pp. 76ff.; Buomberger, *Kampf gegen*, pp. 142f; H. Mahnig, 'La politique migratoire de 1970 au milieu des années 1980', in *Histoire de la politique de migration, d'asile et d'intégration en Suisse depuis 1948*, ed. H. Mahnig, Zurich, 2005, pp. 135–43.

47. *Der Republikaner*, no. 6, 29 April 1971, p. 1, my translation.

48. R. Misteli and A. Gisler, 'Überfremdung. Karriere und Diffusion eines fremdenfeindlichen Deutungsmusters', in *Vom kalten Krieg zur Kulturrevolution*, eds K. Imhof, H. Kleger, and G. Romano, Zurich, 1999, pp. 109f; Mahnig, 'politique migratoire', pp. 156–59.

49. Hoffmann-Nowotny, 'Switzerland', p. 230.

50. Romano, 'Überfremdungsbewegung', p. 150; Mahnig and Piguet, 'Immigrationspolitik', pp. 85ff.

51. Pitterle, *Interdependence*, pp. 1267–75.

52. 'Botschaft zur Genehmigung des Abkommens über den Europäischen Wirtschaftsraum', *Bundesblatt*, vol. VII, no. 33, 1991, pp. 1–667, here pp. 538–42.

53. Pitterle, *Interdependence*, pp. 1204–22.

54. Quoted in: Drews, "*Schweizer erwache!*", p. 82.

55. Pitterle, *Interdependence*, p. 1210.

56. K.W. Kobach, *The Referendum*, Aldershot, 1993, p. 190.

57. W. Linder, *Swiss Democracy*, 2nd edn, London, 1998, p. 68.

58. *Analyse der eidgenössischen Abstimmung vom 20. Mai 1984*, August 1984, pp. 22f.

59. On the 'Togetherness Initiative', see Ireland, *Policy Challenge*, pp. 180–83; B. Gerber, *Die antirassistische Bewegung in der Schweiz*, Zurich, 2003, pp. 103–12; J.M. Niederberger, *Ausgrenzen, Assimilieren, Integrieren*, Zurich 2004, pp. 106–16.

60. For this assessment, see Niederberger, *Ausgrenzen*, pp. 114f.

61. Ireland, *Policy Challenge*, p. 183.

62. *Volk + Heimat*, no. 9, June/July 1982, p. 2, my translation.

63. *Analyse der eidgenössischen Abstimmung vom 6. Juni 1982*, August 1982, pp. 14ff.

64. *Bundesblatt*, vol. I, no. 8, 1988, p. 592.

65. *Analyse der eidgenössischen Abstimmung vom 4. Dezember 1988*, April 1989, p. 28.

66. *Bundesblatt*, vol. I, no. 1, 1986, pp. 99ff.

67. *Bundesblatt*, vol. II, no. 21, 1987, pp. 758ff.

68. U. Fischer, *Gaston-Armand Amaudruz* (M.A. thesis, University of Fribourg, 1999), pp. 175ff.

69. Altermatt, 'Xenophobie und Superpatriotismus', p. 185.

70. *Der Republikaner*, no. 11, 17 August 1973, p. 1, my translation.

71. Pitterle, *Interdependence*, pp. 582ff., 1623; Drews, "*Schweizer erwache!*", p. 79.

72. Pitterle, *Interdependence*, p. 639.

73. Altermatt, 'Xenophobie und Superpatriotismus', pp. 183f; Misteli and Gisler, 'Überfremdung', p. 105, my translation.

74. See also the analysis of the NA paper *Volk + Heimat* by M. Eisenegger and H. Karl, *Die Differenzsemantiken der schweizerischen "Neuen Rechten" und des politischen Konservatismus* (M.A. thesis, University of Zurich, 1995).

75. Drews, *"Schweizer erwache!"*, pp.189f.

76. *Volk + Heimat*, no. 7, July 1968, p. 3, my translation.

77. A. Wimmer, *Nationalist Exclusion and Ethnic Conflict*, Cambridge, 2002, p. 201.

78. *Politisches Schwerpunktsprogramm der National Aktion für Volk und Heimat*, 31 March 1973; *Nationale Aktion für Volk und Heimat. Die nationale Marktwirtschaft – das Wirtschaftsprogramm der Nationalen Aktion*, Killwangen 1977.

79. Romano, 'Überfremdungsbewegung', pp. 147f; see also Misteli and Gisler, 'Überfremdung', p. 102.

80. Niederberger, *Ausgrenzen*, pp. 68–75.

81. For an example, see *Nationale Aktion*, no. 7, July 1967, p. 1.

82. For examples, see *Volk + Heimat*, no. 7, July 1968, p. 3; no. 12, December 1969, p. 6.

83. D. Skenderovic, 'Constructing Boundaries in a Multicultural Nation: The Discourse of "Overforeignization" in Switzerland', in *European Encounters*, eds. R. Ohliger, K. Schönwälder, and T. Triadafilopoulos, Aldershot, 2003, pp. 192f.

84. *Nationale Aktion. Politisches Programm für die Legislaturperiode 1979–1983*, n.d. [1979], my translation.

85. Fröhlich and Müller, *Überfremdungsdiskurse*, pp. 84ff., 107–18.

86. *Amtliches Bulletin der Bundesversammlung. Nationalrat*, 1985, p. 1473, my translation.

87. For examples, see *Volk + Heimat*, no. 17, September 1979, p. 2; no. 5, April 1981, p. 4; *peuple + patrie*, no. 6, July 1981, p. 2; no. 10, December 1982, p. 1.

88. *Amtliches Bulletin der Bundesversammlung. Nationalrat*, 1985, p. 1468.

89. Pitterle, *Interdependence*, pp. 1452ff. For an example of a statement based on classical racism, see *Volk + Heimat*, no. 2, February 1968, p. 1.

90. For examples, see *Volk + Heimat*, no. 2, February 1983, pp. 3f; no. 9, July/August 1983, p. 2; no. 15, November/December 1983, pp. 2ff.; no. 5, April 1984, p. 6; no. 11, August/September 1985, p. 2. See also the account by Fröhlich and Müller, *Überfremdungsdiskurse*, pp. 156f.

91. For information on Jean-Jacques Hegg, see *Tages Anzeiger*, 14 November 1983; 21 January 1985; J. Frischknecht et al., *Die unheimlichen Patrioten*, 6th edn, Zurich 1987, pp. 745, 748–51; Frischknecht, *"Schweiz wir kommen"*, pp. 102–5.

92. *Neue Zürcher Zeitung*, 18 August 1974.

93. For examples, see *Volk + Heimat*, no. 14, October 1981, p. 2; no. 2, February 1988, p. 2; no. 13, October/November 1989, p. 3.

94. For analyses of the parties' nationalist discourse, see Eisenegger and Karl, *Die Differenzsemantiken;* G. Romano, 'Vom Sonderfall zur Überfremdung. Zur Erfolgsgeschichte gemeinschaftsideologischen Denkens im öffentlichen politischen Diskurs der späten fünfziger und der sechziger Jahre', in *Vom kalten Krieg zur Kulturrevolution*, eds K. Imhof, H. Kleger, G. Romano, Zurich, 1999, pp. 74–90; D. Skenderovic, 'Nation, Nationalismus und politische Parteien: Die Schweiz – keine Insel in Europa', in *On European Identity*, ed. C. Szaló, Brno, 1998, pp. 172ff.; Skenderovic, 'Constructing Boundaries', pp. 198ff.; Drews, *"Schweizer erwache!";* pp. 195–203.

95. For example, see various sections in the books by James Schwarzenbach, *Die Überfremdung der Schweiz – wie ich sie sehe*, Zurich: Verlag der Republikaner, 1974; *Im Rücken das Volk*, Zurich: Thomas-Verlag, 1980.

96. *Volk + Heimat*, no. 10, October 1972, p. 10.
97. *Volk + Heimat*, no. 10, August 1988, p. 1.

4. Outsiders in the Party System: Fringe Parties in the 1980s and 1990s

1. For this assessment, see A. Ladner, 'The Political Parties and the Party System', in *Handbook of Swiss Politics*, eds U. Klöti et al., Zurich, 2004, p. 220.
2. *Volk + Heimat*, no. 8, June 1990, p. 4.
3. For this assessment, see *Tages Anzeiger*, 11 June 1990; J. Frischknecht, *"Schweiz wir kommen"*, 2nd edn, Zurich, 1991, p. 114.
4. P. Ignazi, 'The Silent Counter-Revolution. Hypotheses on the Emergence of Extreme Right-Wing Parties in Europe', *European Journal of Political Research*, vol. 22, no. 1/2, 1992; H. Kitschelt, *The Radical Right in Western Europe*, Ann Arbor, 1995; D. Skenderovic, 'Nation, Nationalismus und politische Parteien: Die Schweiz – keine Insel in Europa', in *On European Identity*, ed. C. Szaló, Brno, 1998.
5. *Schweizer Demokrat*, no. 12, December 1991, p. 4; see also *Der Bund*, 6 August 1991.
6. *Der Bund*, 6 August 1991.
7. W. Seitz, *Nationalratswahlen 1995*, Bern, 1995, p. 10.
8. *Schweizer Demokraten: Politisches Programm für die Legislaturperiode 1995–1999*, n.d. [1995]; *Schweizer Demokrat*, no. 10, October 1995, pp. 1–4; no. 11, November 1995, pp. 1ff.
9. W. Seitz, *Nationalratswahlen 1999*, Neuchâtel, 1999, p. 7
10. *SD-Programm 2000: Mit den Schweizer Demokraten ins neue Jahrtausend!*, approved by the central committee on 31 January 1998, p. 1, my translation.
11. For a critical evaluation of the electoral study of fringe parties of the Swiss radical right, see C.T. Husbands, 'Switzerland: Right-Wing and Xenophobic Parties, from Margin to Mainstream?', *Parliamentary Affairs*, vol. 53, no. 3, 2000, p. 513.
12. P. Gentile and H. Kriesi, 'Contemporary Radical-Right Parties in Switzerland: History of a Divided Family', in *The New Politics of the Right*, eds. H.-G. Betz and S. Immerfall, New York, 1998, pp. 135f, 139 note 16. Unfortunately, the two authors omit to indicate the source of the data they used.
13. M. Brändle, 'Strukturen der Parteiorganisationen', in *Die Schweizer Parteien im Wandel*, eds A. Ladner and M. Brändle, Zurich, 2001, p. 52.
14. For this figure, see the party's official website http://www.schweizerdemokraten.ch, retrieved 15 September 2002.
15. A. Ladner, 'Mitgliederzahlen der Kantonalparteien und ihre Entwicklung in den letzten Jahren', in *Die Schweizer Parteien im Wandel*, eds A. Ladner and M. Brändle, Zurich, 2001, p. 134.
16. *Tages Anzeiger*, 8 June 1991.
17. *Tages Anzeiger*, 5 November 1998; *Neue Zürcher Zeitung*, 19 December 1998.
18. *Neue Zürcher Zeitung*, 30 October 1991; *Basler Zeitung*, 16 April 1992; Seitz, *Nationalratswahlen 1995*, p. 44.

19. *Schweizer Demokrat*, no. 4, April 1998, p. 13.
20. *Schweizer Demokrat*, no. 11, September 1990, p. 1.
21. N. Känel and H. Bigler, *Wenn Extreme Alltag werden*, Bern, 2000, p. 20. Since July 1999, the issues of *Schweizer Demokrat* are posted on the party's official website http://www.schweizer-demokraten.ch, accessed 31 August 2008.
22. See the announcement in: *Schweizer Demokrat*, no. 1, January 1991, p. 4.
23. For example, see *Schweizer Demokrat*, no. 11, November 1996, pp. 1f.
24. *Neue Zürcher Zeitung*, 16 January 1990; *Bundesblatt*, vol. III, no. 34, 1991, p. 1227.
25. *Signature-sheet, 'Eidgenössische Volksinitiative "Für eine vernünftige Asylpolitik"'*, n.d. [1991].
26. *Bundesblatt*, vol. III, no. 38, 1994, pp. 1492–1500.
27. *Schweizer Demokrat*, no. 4, April 1997, p. 1.
28. *Neue Zürcher Zeitung*, 10 June 1996.
29. K.W. Kobach, 'Spurn Thy Neighbour: Direct Democracy and Swiss Isolationism', *West European Politics*, vol. 20, no. 3, 1997, p. 198.
30. *Schweizer Demokrat*, no. 8/9, August/September 1995, p. 1.
31. U. Serdült, *Analyse der eidgenössischen Abstimmungen vom 25. Juni 1995*, Adliswil, 1995, p. 28.
32. *Volk + Heimat*, no. 9, July 1989, p. 2.
33. *Bundesblatt*, vol. III, no. 25, 1992, pp. 889–907.
34. *Tages Anzeiger*, 9 September 1993.
35. B. Wernli, S. Wälti, and D. Caramani, *Analyse der eidgenössischen Abstimmung vom 26. September 1993*, Adliswil, 1993, p. 23.
36. *Schweizer Demokrat*, no. 8, August 1993, p. 4.
37. Kobach, 'Spurn Thy Neighbour', p. 198.
38. B. Wernli, P. Sciarini, and J. Barranco, *Analyse der eidgenössischen Abstimmungen vom 12. Juni 1994*, Adliswil, 1994, p. 11.
39. *Schweizer Demokrat*, no. 11, November 1992, p. 1.
40. After the European Community changed its name to the European Union in 1993, the initiative was called 'EU membership negotiations: Let the people decide!'.
41. *Schweizer Demokrat*, no. 8, August 1992, pp. 1ff.; *Signature-sheet, 'Eidgenössische Volksinitiative "EG-Beitrittsverhandlungen vors Volk!"'*, n.d. [1992].
42. M. Delgrande and W. Linder, *Analyse der eidgenössischen Abstimmungen vom 8. Juni 1997*, Bern, 1997, pp. 11–15.
43. S. Hardmeier 'Switzerland', *European Journal of Political Research*, vol. 34, no. 3/4, 1998, p. 534.
44. C. Dupont and P. Sciarini, 'Switzerland and the European Integration Process: Engagement without Marriage', in *The Swiss Labyrinth*, ed. J.-E. Lane, London, 2001, pp. 224ff.
45. On the various groups that supported the collection of signatures, see the accounts in: *Tages Anzeiger*, 3 February 2000; *Neue Zürcher Zeitung*, 4 February 2000.
46. *Schweizer Demokrat*, no. 10, October 1999, p. 10. See also the article by Flavio Maspoli, the leader of the *Lega di Ticinesi*, in *Neue Zürcher Zeitung*, 5 May 2000.

47. *Schweizer Demokrat,* no. 3, March/April 2000.
48. H. Hirter and W. Linder *Analyse der eidgenössischen Abstimmungen vom 21. Mai 2000,* Bern, 2000.
49. *Neue Zürcher Zeitung,* 22 May 2000.
50. *Schweizer Demokrat,* no. 10, October 1999, p. 1, my translation. The term '*Asylanten*' has a derogatory meaning in German language, since it connotes with words such as '*Querulanten*' (whinger), '*Simulanten*' (malingerer) and '*Spekulanten*' (speculators). Therefore, the term '*Asyl Suchende*' became more common in the political and media language of the 1990s. In contrast, the radical right continued to use the term in order to underline its hostile attitude towards asylum seekers.
51. For example, see *Schweizer Demokrat,* no. 11, November 1992, p. 3, my translation.
52. *Schweizer Demokrat,* no. 10, October 1996, p. 6.
53. *Schweizer Demokraten: Politisches Programm für die Legislaturperiode 1995–1999,* published by the SD central office, Bern, n.d. [1995], p. 2.
54. *Schweizer Demokraten: Politisches Programm für die Legislaturperiode 1999–2003,* published by the SD central office, Bern, n.d. [1999], p. 2.
55. Ibid.
56. *Schweizer Demokrat,* no. 10, October 1998, p. 11, my translation.
57. Statement: *Schweizer Demokraten, 'Erläuterungen zur stadtzürcherischen Volksinitiative "Die Schweizer/innen zuerst!"',* n.d. [1998], http://www.schweizer-demokraten.ch/initzh.htm, retrieved 15 July 1998, my translation.
58. Federal Tribunal decision 1P.27/2003, 21 November 2003, in *BGE* 129 I, pp. 392–401.
59. For examples, see *Schweizer Demokrat,* no. 5, May 1995, p. 8; no. 11, November 1997, pp. 1f; no. 1, January 1998, p. 15.
60. P. Niggli and J. Frischknecht, *Rechte Seilschaften,* Zurich, 1998, pp. 269f. See also Bäschlin's particularly radical version of Islamophobic propaganda: *Der Islam wird uns fressen! Der islamische Ansturm auf Europa und die europäischen Komplizen dieser Invasion,* 4th edn, Tegna: Selvpiana, 1992.
61. *Volk + Heimat,* no. 8, June 1990, p. 3, my translation.
62. For an example, see *Schweizer Demokrat,* no. 5, May 2002, p. 2.
63. *Volk + Heimat,* no. 8, June 1990, p. 1, my translation.
64. Ibid., p. 2, my translation.
65. For example, see *Schweizer Demokrat,* no. 6, June 1997, p. 1.
66. *Schweizer Demokrat,* no. 5, May 2002, p. 7, my translation.
67. *Schweizer Demokraten: Politisches Programm für die Legislaturperiode 1995–1999,* p. 5, my translation.
68. *Schweizer Demokrat,* no. 7, July 1992, p. 2, my translation.
69. *Schweizer Demokraten: Politisches Programm für die Legislaturperiode 1995–1999,* p. 15.
70. *Schweizer Demokrat,* no. 4, April 2002, p. 1.
71. *Schweizer Demokrat,* no. 4, April, 1997, p. 1, my translation.
72. Press release: Schweizer Demokraten, '*SD-Aufruf zum Amerika-Boykott*', 3 July 1998, http://www.schweizer-demokraten.ch/pressech.htm, retrieved 15 July 1998, my translation.

73. *Neue Zürcher Zeitung,* 13 March 1999; see also *Schweizer Demokrat,* no. 7, July 1999, p. 1.

74. *SD-Programm 2000: Mit den Schweizer Demokraten ins neue Jahrtausend!,* approved by the central committee on 31 January 1998, p. 1.

75. *Schweizer Demokraten: Politisches Programm für die Legislaturperiode 1995–1999,* p. 2.

76. For examples, see *Schweizer Demokrat,* no. 3, March 1998, pp. 1f; *SD-Programm 2000,* p. 2.

77. Gentile and Kriesi, 'Contemporary Radical-Right Parties', p. 126.

78. On the New Christian Right in the U.S., for example, see J. Watson *The Christian Coalition,* New York, 1997; M. Durham, *The Christian Right, the Far Right and the Boundaries of American Conservatism,* Manchester, 2000; J.C. Green, M.J. Rozell, C. Wilcox, eds, *The Christian Right in American Politics,* Washington, 2003.

79. *KVP Parteiprogramm 2002,* http://www.kvp.ch, retrieved 4 December 2002.

80. Niggli and Frischknecht, *Rechte Seilschaften,* pp. 584ff.

81. On the foundation of the EDU, see K.J. Pitterle, *The Limits of Interdependence,* Ann Arbor, 1981, pp. 1096ff.; R. Strasser, *Protestantische Parteien und evangelisch-konservative Christen,* n.d. [1996, 2001]; Ladner, 'Political Parties', p. 222.

82. *Neue Zürcher Zeitung,* 24 September 1975, my translation.

83. *Rückblick – Aufblick – Ausblick,* p. 6, my translation.

84. Strasser, *Protestantische Parteien.*

85. On the EVP, see E. Gruner and K.J. Pitterle, 'Switzerland's Political Parties', in *Switzerland at the Polls,* ed. H.R. Penniman, Washington, 1983, p. 51; Ladner, 'Political Parties', p. 219.

86. *EDU-Standpunkt: Christlich-politische Monatszeitung. Offizielles Organ der Eidgenössisch-Demokratischen Union EDU,* no. 10, October 1995, p. 7.

87. Another example of a shift towards the extreme right was Ernst Dünnenberger, a former member of the Republican Movement. In 1975 and 1979, he ran on an EDU ticket in the National Council elections in the canton of Zurich. In the 1980s, Dünnenberger became a notorious figure of the Swiss extreme right. See J. Frischknecht et al., *Die unheimlichen Patrioten,* 6th edn, Zurich, 1987, pp. 653–56; U. Altermatt and D. Skenderovic, 'Die extreme Rechte: Organisationen, Personen und Entwicklungen in den achtziger und neunziger Jahren', in *Rechtsextremismus in der Schweiz,* eds U. Altermatt and H. Kriesi, Zurich, 1995, pp. 64, 72.

88. Altermatt and Skenderovic, 'Die extreme Rechte', pp. 70f.

89. *EDU-Standpunkt,* no. 1, September 1981.

90. Rüst Peter, *EDU und christliches Gedankengut: Eine persönliche weltanschauliche Betrachtung zum Grundsatzprogramm der Eidgenössisch-Demokratischen Union (EDU),* 2nd edn, Bern, 1982.

91. Frischknecht et al., *Patrioten,* pp. 367f; Ladner, 'Political Parties', p. 222.

92. For example, in 1988, the EDU collected over thirty-four thousand signatures for a petition calling for a screening to be stopped of Martin Scorsese's movie The Last Temptation of Christ; see *Rückblick – Aufblick – Ausblick: 25 Jahre EDU-UDF,* published by EDU Switzerland, Thun, 2000, p. 4.

93. *Rückblick – Aufblick – Ausblick,* p. 14.

94. Seitz, *Nationalratswahlen 1999*, p. 52.

95. *EDU-Standpunkt*, no. 7, July 1991, p. 1.

96. *EDU-Standpunkt*, no. 1, January 1999, pp. 7f; no. 3, March 1999, p. 3; no. 5, May 1999, p. 7; see also *Neue Zürcher Zeitung*, 26 October 1998.

97. *EDU-Standpunkt*, no. 10, October 1995, p. 3.

98. See the party's official Website: http://www.edu-udf.ch, retrieved 1 December 2003.

99. A. Ladner 'Die Basis der Parteien', in *Die Schweizer Parteien im Wandel*, eds A. Ladner and M. Brändle, Zurich, 2001, p. 95.

100. For example, see *EDU-Standpunkt*, no. 10, October 1995.

101. On this campaign, see *EDU-Standpunkt*, no. 8, August 1994, p. 6; *Rückblick – Aufblick – Ausblick*, p. 5.

102. On the history and ideology of revolutionary nationalism, see P. Moreau, *Nationalsozialismus von links*, Stuttgart, 1985; M. Feit, *Die "Neue Rechte" in der Bundesrepublik*, Frankfurt, 1987, pp. 48–62.

103. *EDU Grundsatzprogramm: Solidarität, Souveränität, Legalität*, Zurich, n.d. [1975], p. 12, my translation.

104. Ibid., p. 6, my translation.

105. Ibid., p. 3.

106. *EDU-Standpunkt*, no. 1, September 1981, p. 1, my translation.

107. For example, see *EDU-Standpunkt*, no. 5, May 1990, p. 5.

108. *Rückblick – Aufblick – Ausblick*, p. 7.

109. *EDU-UDF Aktionsprogramm 1999–2003*, approved by the delegates' assembly on March 13, 1999, p. 3.

110. *EDU-Standpunkt*, no. 10, October 1995, p. 1.

111. *EDU-UDF Aktionsprogramm 1999–2003*, p. 4.

112. For example, see *EDU-Standpunkt*, no. 10, October 1996, p. 2.

113. *EDU-Standpunkt*, no. 7, July 1991, p. 1, my translation.

114. *EDU-Standpunkt*, no. 4, April 1990, p. 1. The EDU liked to refer to the Swiss German term *'Päckli'* (which literally means 'small parcel') in relation to politics, probably suggesting that the political parties were giving small presents to each other.

115. For example, see *EDU-Standpunkt*, no. 7, July 1991, p. 1

116. *EDU-Standpunkt*, no. 6, June 1993, p. 6. For his study of anti-Semitism in Switzerland, see F. Külling, *Antisemitismus: Bei uns wie überall?*, Zurich, n.d. [1977].

117. For example, see *EDU-Standpunkt*, no. 11, November 1995, p. 3.

118. For an account of the campaign for this initiative, see Niggli and Frischknecht, *Rechte Seilschaften*, pp. 245–51.

119. *EDU-Standpunkt*, no. 10, October 1994, p. 2, my translation.

120. For example, see *EDU-Standpunkt*, no. 7, February 1991, p. 8; no. 12, December 1991, p. 5.

121. *EDU-Standpunkt*, no. 4, April 2002, p. 5.

122. *EDU-Standpunkt*, no. 9, September 2000, p. 8, my translation.

123. Ibid., my translation.

124. On Scherrer's presidency, see Strasser, *Protestantische Parteien*. The EDU program included a paragraph on Israel stating that the party commits itself to

the fact that Switzerland is also looking after the interest of the state Israel and of the Jewish people; see *EDU-UDF Aktionsprogramm 1999–2003*, p. 7.

125. *EDU-Standpunkt*, no. 3, March 1991, p. 5; no. 4, April 1994, p. 5.

126. *EDU-Standpunkt*, no. 8, August 1998, p. 1.

127. *EDU-Standpunkt*, no. 11, November 1992, p. 5.

128. *EDU-Standpunkt*, no. 12, December 1992, p. 1, my translation.

129. For example, see F. Decker, *Der neue Rechtspopulismus*, 2nd rev. edn, Opladen, 2004, pp. 87f.

130. For example, see H.-G. Betz, *Radical Right-Wing Populism in Western Europe*, New York, 1994, pp. 114f.

131. Betz, *Radical Right-Wing Populism*; Kitschelt, *Radical Right*; L. Helms, 'Right-Wing Populist Parties in Austria and Switzerland: A Comparative Analysis of Electoral Support and Conditions of Success', *West European Politics*, vol. 20, no. 2, 1997; Skenderovic, 'Nation, Nationalismus'.

132. Frischknecht et al., *Patrioten*, p. 531. For a collection of adverts released by the Citizens' Action Group, see M.E. Dreher., B. Bär, and T. Ebeling-Stiefelmeier, eds, *5 Jahre Bürgeraktion: "Werkkatalog"*, n.d. [1986].

133. Dreher, Bär, and Ebeling-Stiefelmeier, *5 Jahre Bürgeraktion*, p. 36, my translation.

134. Decker, *Rechtspopulismus*, pp. 236f.

135. H. Gschwend, 'Die Umweltbewegung verändert die Parteienlandschaft - oder umgekehrt', *Schweizerisches Jahrbuch für Politische Wissenschaft*, vol. 26, 1986.

136. Quoted in: G. Schiesser, 'Die Schweizer Auto-Partei', *Die Neue Gesellschaft/Frankfurter Hefte*, vol. 39, no. 4, 1992, p. 331.

137. For this view, see C. Longchamp, '"Linke und Grüne an die Wand nageln und mit dem Flammenwerfer drüber!"', 1988, p. 20; Schiesser, 'Schweizer Auto-Partei', p. 334; U. Altermatt and M. Furrer, 'Die Autopartei: Protest für Freiheit, Wohlstand und das Auto', in *Rechte und linke Fundamentalopposition*, U. Altermatt et al., Basel, 1994, p. 149.

138. Quoted in: *Die WochenZeitung*, 7 April 1995. For APS statements directed against NA, see *Tacho*, no. 13, 1987, p. 12; no. 23, 1988, p. 9.

139. *Tacho*, no. 16, 1987, p. 9.

140. *Journal de Genève*, 26 July 1989.

141. For this assessment, see Ladner, 'Political Parties', p. 221.

142. *Neue Zürcher Zeitung*, 14 March 1989; 21 January 1992.

143. Niggli and Frischknecht, *Rechte Seilschaften*, p. 507.

144. *Tacho*, no. 17/18, 1987, p. 3.

145. For example, see *Neue Zürcher Zeitung*, 22 October 1991.

146. *Tacho*, no. 43, 1991; no. 45, 1991; see also *Neue Zürcher Zeitung*, 18 September 1991.

147. *Tacho*, no. 45, 1991, p. 13.

148. C. Longchamp and S. Hardmeier, *Analyse der Nationalratswahlen 1991*, Adliswil, 1992, p. 23.

149. C. Longchamp et al., *Hin zur Tripolarität im Parteiensystem der Schweiz*, Bern, 1995, p. 48; D. Caramani, 'The Swiss Parliamentary Election of 1995', *Electoral Studies*, vol. 15, no. 1, 1996, p. 135.

150. For example, see *Tacho*, no. 83, 1995, p. 14; see also the FPS election campaign ad in *Tages Anzeiger*, 11 October 1995.

151. C.H. Church, 'The Swiss Elections of October 1999: Learning to Live in More Interesting Times', *West European Politics*, vol. 23, no. 3, 2000, p. 216; W. Linder and G. Lutz, 'The Parliamentary Elections in Switzerland, October 1999', *Electoral Studies*, vol. 21, no. 1, 2002, p. 130.

152. *FPS-Wahlplattform 1999*, approved by the twenty-sixth presidents' conference on 30 April 1999.

153. For example, see Betz, *Radical Right-Wing Populism*, pp. 157ff.

154. Longchamp and Hardmeier, *Nationalratswahlen 1991*, pp. 21ff.

155. Gentile and Kriesi, 'Contemporary Radical-Right Parties', p. 136.

156. For a criticism of the significance of the left–right self-placement, see Kitschelt, *Radical Right*, pp. 135f.

157. H.-G. Betz, 'Radikal rechtspopulistische Parteien in Westeuropa', *Aus Politik und Zeitgeschichte*, no. 44, 1991, p. 6.

158. Brändle, 'Strukturen', p. 52; A. Ladner, 'Mitgliederzahlen der Kantonalparteien und ihre Entwicklung in den letzten Jahren', in *Die Schweizer Parteien im Wandel*, eds A. Ladner and M. Brändle, Zurich, 2001, p.130.

159. Altermatt and Furrer, 'Die Autopartei', p. 139.

160. Ladner, 'Mitgliederzahlen', pp. 131, 134

161. A. Ladner, 'Swiss Political Parties: Between Persistence and Change', in *The Swiss Labyrinth*, ed. J.-E. Lane, London, 2001, p. 131.

162. *Tacho*, no. 43, 1991, pp. 12f; see also folding brochure: *Freiheit – Wohlstand – Lebensfreude! Unsere 10 politischen Leitlinien*, published by the APS, n.d.

163. *Parteiprogramm der APS für die Legislaturperiode 1991–1995*, adopted by the Swiss delegates' assembly on 20 April 1991.

164. *Parteiprogramm der Freiheits-Partei der Schweiz*, adopted by the thirteenth presidents' conference on 20 May, 1995; *Parteiprogramm der Freiheits-Partei der Schweiz FPS – Die Auto-Partei*, adopted by the Swiss delegates' assembly on 8 May 1999.

165. Another means of communication was the party's website, which was set up in May 1998. This was quite late in comparison with other Swiss parties; see http://www.freiheits-partei.ch, accessed 20 December 2002.

166. *Tacho*, no. 1, 1986; see also Altermatt and Furrer, 'Die Autopartei', p. 140.

167. Decker, *Rechtspopulismus*, p. 87. Significantly, the first issue of *Tacho* published an extensive interview with Peter Uebersax, who was editor-in-chief at the time of the leading Swiss tabloid daily paper *Blick*; see *Tacho*, no. 1, 1986, p. 2.

168. *Tacho*, no. 45, 1991, p. 9; no. 46, 1991, p. 7; no. 56, 1992, p. 11.

169. For this assessment, see *Neue Zürcher Zeitung*, 28 August 1995.

170. For examples of these disputes, see *Année politique suisse 1989*, Bern 1990, p. 323; *Le Nouveau Quotidien*, 10 November, 1992.

171. For example, see *Neue Zürcher Zeitung*, 5 May 1997.

172. See the interview with Ulrich Giezendanner in: *SVP Aktuell: Schweizerische Volkspartei des Kantons Aargau*, no. 3, August 1996, pp. 13f.

173. *NZZ am Sonntag*, 21 April 2002.

174. For examples, see the accounts in: *Année politique suisse 1996*, Bern 1997,

p. 366; *Année politique suisse 1999*, Bern 2000, p. 394; *Neue Zürcher Zeitung*, 12 July 2000.
  175. *Bundesblatt*, vol. I, no. 8, 1993, p. 641.
  176. *Bundesblatt*, vol. I, no. 18, 1993, p. 1589; D. Schloeth and U. Klöti, *Analyse der eidgenössischen Abstimmungen vom 7. März 1993*, Bern, 1993.
  177. *Tacho*, no. 24, 1988, p. 21.
  178. *Année politique suisse 1995*, Bern 1996, p. 349.
  179. *FPS-Medieninformation*, no. 58, 14 January 1998, my translation.
  180. For instance, see *Tacho*, no. 40, 1990, p. 3.
  181. *Tacho*, no. 106, 1998, p. 6, my translation.
  182. See the accounts in: *Neue Zürcher Zeitung*, 18 March 1988; Longchamp, '"Linke und Grüne"', pp. 3f.
  183. Quoted in: *Der Bund*, 20 March 1996, my translation. The cantonal president and a cantonal MP, both responsible for editing the brochure, were accused of breaking the anti-racism law over this statement. While the court initially found them guilty, the appeal court later acquitted them of the charge. On these legal proceedings, see the press reports in: *Journal de Genève*, 20 March 1996; *Tages Anzeiger*, 17 June 1997.
  184. Betz, *Radical Right-Wing Populism*, p. 121.
  185. *Parteiprogramm der Freiheits-Partei der Schweiz FPS*, n.d. [1999], pp. 12f; see also Altermatt and Furrer, 'Die Autopartei', pp. 146f.
  186. *Tacho*, no. 57, 1993, p. 7.
  187. *Freiheits-Partei der Schweiz (FPS), Die politischen Schwerpunkte*, n.d. [2001], http://www.freiheits-partei.ch, retrieved 20 December 2002, my translation.
  188. Ibid.
  189. *Tacho*, no. 13, 1987, p. 3, my translation.
  190. *Tacho*, no. 78, 1995, p. 17.
  191. *Tages Anzeiger*, 15 September 1994, my translation.
  192. *Parteiprogramm der Freiheits-Partei der Schweiz*, n.d. [1995]; *Für Ruhe, Ordnung und Sicherheit: Resolution zu handen des Schweizerischen Bundesrates*, adopted by the FPS delegates' assembly on 12 May 2001, and published in *FPS-Medieninformation*, 12 May 2001.
  193. *Freiheits-Partei der Schweiz (FPS), Die politischen Schwerpunkte*, n.d. [2001].
  194. *Neue Zürcher Zeitung*, 9 November 1992; *Basler Zeitung*, 20 August 1994.
  195. *Standpunktpapier 'Ruhe, Ordnung, Sicherheit'*, adopted by the delegates' assembly on 14 February 1998; *Tacho*, no. 106, 1998; see also *Neue Zürcher Zeitung*, 16 February 1998; *Tages Anzeiger*, 16 February 1998.
  196. For a still somewhat moderate statement by the APS parliamentary group on the European Economic Area and European Community, see *Tacho*, no. 53, 1992, p. 19.
  197. *Tacho*, no. 95, 1996, p. 14, my translation.
  198. The signature-sheet for the petition demanding a referendum was enclosed in *Tacho*, no. 63/64, 1993, p. 13.
  199. *Tacho*, no. 100, 1997, p. 17.
  200. *FPS Fraktion: Information der Nationalratsfraktion*, supplement to *Tacho*, no. 97/98, 1997, p. 1.

201. *FPS-Medieninformation*, no. 87, 13 August 1998.
202. *Parteiprogramm der APS für die Legislaturperiode 1991–1995*, p. 19.
203. Betz, *Radical Right-Wing Populism*, p. 115.
204. *Parteiprogramm der APS für die Legislaturperiode 1991–1995*, p. 2; *Parteiprogramm der Freiheits-Partei der Schweiz FPS*, n.d. [1999], p. 20.
205. I would like to thank Catrina Demund for helping me with the translation of the Italian-language primary sources.
206. For example, see G. Rusconi, 'La Lega dei Ticinesi: Gegen die Tessiner "Partitokratie"', in *Rechte und linke Fundamentalopposition*, U. Altermatt et al., Basel, 1994; O. Mazzoleni, 'La Lega dei Ticinesi: Vers l'intégration?', *Swiss Political Science Review*, vol. 5, no. 3, 1999.
207. P. Taggart, *Populism*, Buckingham, 2000, p. 83.
208. Betz, *Radical Right-Wing Populism*, p. 22; O. Mazzoleni, 'Unité et diversité des "national-populismes" suisses: l'Union démocratique du centre et la Lega dei Ticinesi', in *La tentation populiste au coeur de l'Europe*, eds O. Ihl et al., Paris, 2003.
209. O. Mazzoleni, 'Multi-Level Populism and Centre–Periphery Cleavage in Switzerland. The Case of the *Lega dei Ticinesi*', in *Challenges to Consensual Politics*, eds D. Caramani and Y. Mény, Brussels, 2005, p. 212.
210. Betz, *Radical Right-Wing Populism*, p. 22; Rusconi, 'La Lega dei Ticinesi', pp. 166f.
211. Mazzoleni, 'La Lega dei Ticinesi', p. 81.
212. R. Knüsel and J. Hottinger, *Regionalist Movements and Parties in Switzerland*, Lausanne, 1994, p. 11.
213. Rusconi, 'La Lega dei Ticinesi', pp. 160f.
214. Mazzoleni, 'La Lega dei Ticinesi', p. 82.
215. For this assessment, see *Die Weltwoche*, 25 January 1996.
216. For this assessment, see *Neue Zürcher Zeitung*, 26 October 1999.
217. Knüsel and Hottinger, *Regionalist Movements*, pp. 21f.
218. O. Mazzoleni and B. Wernli, *Cittadini e politica*, Bellinzona, 2002, pp. 126f.
219. Ibid., p. 97.
220. For the paper's first issue, see *Il Mattino della domenica*, 18 March 1990.
221. *Il Mattino della domenica*, 17 October 1991; see also Rusconi, 'La Lega dei Ticinesi', p. 165.
222. Taggart, *Populism*, p. 83.
223. *Die Weltwoche*, 13 January 2000.
224. For example, see *Tages Anzeiger*, 29 January 1993.
225. For an overview of this type of activities, see Rusconi, 'La Lega dei Ticinesi', pp. 161ff.
226. Ibid., p. 161.
227. For example, one cantonal initiative submitted by the party demanded the abolition of inheritance tax; another requested tax reductions for corporations and well-to-do individuals. Both initiatives were accepted in a popular vote in February 2000. See the account of these initiatives in: *Basler Zeitung*, 7 February 2000.
228. Mazzoleni, 'La Lega dei Ticinesi'; Mazzoleni, 'Unité et diversité', p. 192.
229. Kitschelt, *Radical Right*, p. 161.

230. *Schweizer Demokrat*, no. 12, December 1991, p. 4; no. 1, January 1997, p. 16.
231. Rusconi, 'La Lega dei Ticinesi', p. 162.
232. See the reproduced agreement in: M. de Lauretis and B. Giussani, *La Lega dei ticinesi*, Locarno, 1992, p. 258.
233. *Il Mattino della domenica*, 11 June 1995, p. 3.
234. See the interview with SD president Rudolf Keller in *Il Mattino della domenica*, 7 June 1992, p. 35.
235. L. De Winter, 'Conclusion. A Comparative Analysis of the Electoral, Office and Policy Success of Ethnoregionalist Parties', in *Regionalist Parties in Western Europe*, eds. L. De Winter and H. Türsan, London, 1998, p. 205; Knüsel and Hottinger, *Regionalist Movements*, pp. 28–31.
236. Mazzoleni, 'Multi-Level Populism'.
237. De Winter, 'Conclusion', p. 204.
238. H. Türsan 'Introduction. Ethnoregionalist Parties as Ethnic Entrepreneurs', in *Regionalist Parties in Western Europe*, eds L. De Winter and H. Türsan, London, 1998, p. 5.
239. *Il Mattino della domenica*, 7 August 1994, p. 1, my translation.
240. *Il Mattino della domenica*, 8 December 1996, p. 6.
241. Rusconi 1994, pp. 165f.
242. Mazzoleni, 'Multi-Level Populism', pp. 216ff.
243. 'del programma della Lega per la legislatura '95–'99', in *Il Mattino della domenica*, 26 February 1995, pp. 19, 21–23, here p. 19, my translation.
244. *Il Mattino della domenica*, 8 August 1993, p. 3, my translation.
245. For example, see *Il Mattino della domenica*, 6 December 1998, p. 3.
246. *Il Mattino della domenica*, 29 July 1990, p. 3, my translation.
247. *Il Mattino della domenica*, 5 September 1993, p. 3.
248. 'il programma della Lega', p. 2.
249. For example, see *Il Mattino della domenica*, 4 April 1999, p. 24.
250. *Il Mattino della domenica*, 10 September 2000, p. 7.
251. See the reports in: *Neue Zürcher Zeitung*, 15 July 1998; *Die WochenZeitung*, 23 July 1998.
252. The Volcker Commission, named after its director Paul Volcker, was assigned to investigate the 'unclaimed' Jewish assets in Swiss banks.
253. *Il Mattino della domenica*, 14 June 1998, p. 23, my translation.
254. *Année politique suisse 1998*, Bern 1999, p. 381.
255. 'del programma della Lega per la legislatura '95–'99', p. 21.
256. Ibid.
257. 'il programma della Lega', pp. 2f; 'programma per la legislatura '99–'03', p. 13.

5. Entering the Mainstream: The Emergence of the New SVP in the 1990s

1. O. Mazzoleni, *Nationalisme et populisme en Suisse*, Lausanne, 2003.
2. H.-G. Betz, *La droite populiste en Europe*, Paris, 2004; F. Decker, *Der neue*

Rechtspopulismus, 2nd rev. edn, Opladen, 2004; P. Norris, *Radical Right*, Cambridge, 2005.

3. H.G. Betz, 'Exclusionary Populism in Austria, Italy, and Switzerland', *International Journal*, vol. 56, no. 3, 2001, p. 397.

4. Norris, *Radical Right*, p. 210.

5. J.-Y. Camus, 'Die radikale Rechte in Westeuropa. Vom nostalgischen Aktionismus zum fremdenfeindlichen Populismus', in *Rechtspopulismus – Österreichische Krankheit oder europäische Normalität?*, ed. W. Eismann, Vienna, 2002, p. 44.

6. Mazzoleni, *Nationalisme*; M. Girod, 'L'Union démocratique du centre: les raisons d'un succès', in *Extrême droite et national-populisme en Europe de l'Ouest*, eds P. Blaise and P. Moreau, Brussels, 2004; D. Skenderovic, 'Das rechtspopulistische Parteienlager in der Schweiz. Von den Splitterparteien zur Volkspartei', *traverse. Zeitschrift für Geschichte – Revue de l'histoire*, vol. 14, no. 1, 2007; D. Skenderovic and G. D'Amato, *Mit dem Fremden politisieren*, Zurich, 2008.

7. H. Kitschelt and A.J. McGann, 'Die Dynamik der schweizerischen Neuen Rechten in komparativer Perspektive: Die Alpenrepubliken', in *Schweizer Wahlen 1999*, eds P. Sciarini, S. Harmeier, and A. Vatter, Bern, 2003.

8. For example, see C. Longchamp, 'Die nationalkonservative Revolte in der Gestalt der SVP. Eine Analyse der Nationalratswahlen 1999 in der Schweiz', in *Das österreichische Wahlverhalten*, eds F. Plasser, P.A. Ulram, and F. Sommer, Vienna, 2000; W. Linder and G. Lutz, 'The Parliamentary Elections in Switzerland, October 1999', *Electoral Studies*, vol. 21, no. 1, 2002. For an overview of terms used to define the new SVP, see O. Mazzoleni, 'Définir le parti: un enjeu scientifique et politique', in *L'Union démocratique du centre*, eds O. Mazzoleni, P. Gottraux, and C. Péchu, Lausanne, 2007.

9. Longchamp, 'Nationalkonservative Revolte', p. 403.

10. For example, see U. Altermatt, *Das Fanal von Sarajevo*, Zurich 1996, pp. 184f.

11. H. Kriesi et al., eds, *Der Aufstieg der SVP*, Zurich, 2005.

12. On the beginnngs of the SVP, see E. Gruner, *Die Parteien in der Schweiz*, revised and expanded edn, Bern, 1977, pp. 150–58; E. Gruner and K.J. Pitterle, 'Switzerland's Political Parties', in *Switzerland at the Polls*, ed. H.R. Penniman, Washington, 1983, pp. 47ff.

13. E. Wigger, *Krieg und Krise in der politischen Kommunikation*, Zurich, 1997, pp. 96–99.

14. B. Junker, *Die Bauern auf dem Wege zur Politik*, Bern, 1968.

15. Gruner and Pitterle, 'Political Parties', p. 47.

16. Gruner, *Die Parteien in der Schweiz*, pp. 154f.

17. W. Baumann and P. Moser, *Bauern im Industriestaat*, Zurich, 1999, p. 27.

18. W. Baumann, 'Von der Krise zur Konkordanz. Die Rolle der Bauern', in *Krisen und Stabilisierung*, eds S. Guex, Zurich, 1998, pp. 102–7; Baumann and Moser, *Bauern*, pp. 238–49.

19. *Markus Feldmann: Tagebuch 1923–1939*, vol. XIII/1, ed. P. Moser, published by the Swiss Society for History, Basel, 2001.

20. E. Dreifuss, *Die Schweiz und das Dritte Reich*, Frauenfeld, 1971, pp. 192f; K. Zollinger, *Frischer Wind oder faschistische Reaktion?*, Zurich, 1991, pp. 258–65.

21. Baumann and Moser, *Bauern*, p. 243, my translation.
22. P. Gilg and E. Gruner, 'Nationale Erneuerungsbewegungen in der Schweiz 1925–1940', *Vierteljahrshefte für Zeitgeschichte*, vol. 14, no. 1, 1966, p. 18; Baumann and Moser, *Bauern*, pp. 206–9, 234ff., 247ff.
23. S. Süess, "*Unsere wunde Welt braucht tapfere Herzen*" (M.A. thesis, University of Bern, 1997), p. 66.
24. Baumann and Moser, *Bauern*, pp. 244f.
25. J. Mooser, '"Spiritual National Defence" in the 1930s: Swiss Political Culture between the Wars', in *Switzerland and the Second World War*, ed. G. Kreis, London, 2000, p. 244.
26. Independent Commission of Experts Switzerland – Second World War, *Switzerland, National Socialism and the Second World War*, Zurich, 2002, p. 128, 172 note 69.
27. M. Brändle, 'Konkordanz gleich Konvergenz? Die Links-rechts-Positionierung der Schweizer Bundesratsparteien, 1947–1995', *Swiss Political Science Review*, vol. 5, no. 1, 1999.
28. Gruner, *Parteien in der Schweiz*, p. 158.
29. For the results in National Council elections, see http://www.parlament.ch/wa-nr-nationalratswahlen-waehlerstimmen-1919.xls, retrieved 31 August 2008.
30. F. Jacobs, 'Switzerland', in *Western European Political Parties*, ed. F. Jacobs, Harlow, 1989, p. 653.
31. M. König, 'Auf dem Weg in die Gegenwart – Der Kanton Zürich seit 1945', in *Geschichte des Kantons Zürich*, eds N. Flüeler and M. Flüeler-Grauwiler, 3 vols, Zurich, 1994, vol. 3, pp. 449–54.
32. H. Hartmann and F. Horvath, *Zivilgesellschaft von rechts*, Zurich, 1995, p. 13.
33. Ibid., pp. 29–33.
34. E. Gruner, *Parteien in der Schweiz*, p. 304; A. Ladner, 'Swiss Political Parties: Between Persistence and Change', in *The Swiss Labyrinth*, ed. J.-E. Lane, London, 2001, p. 130.
35. C. Gruber, *Die politischen Parteien der Schweiz im Zweiten Weltkrieg*, Vienna, 1966, pp. 139–58; Gruner, *Parteien in der Schweiz*, pp. 99ff.
36. Hartmann and Horvath, *Zivilgesellschaft*, pp. 40ff.
37. A. Ladner, 'The Political Parties and the Party System', in *Handbook of Swiss Politics*, eds U. Klöti et al., Zurich, 2004, p. 216.
38. Hartmann and Horvath, *Zivilgesellschaft*, pp. 52–59; Ladner, 'Political Parties', p. 233.
39. L. Zollinger, *Der Mittelstand am Rande*. Bern, 2004, pp. 33–37.
40. As shown by figures from 1998, the Bern party was by far the strongest cantonal section with 27,000 members; the Zurich party held second place with 11,800 members, followed by the Aargau section with less than 5,000 members; see A. Ladner, 'Mitgliederzahlen der Kantonalparteien und ihre Entwicklung in den letzten Jahren', in *Die Schweizer Parteien im Wandel*, eds A. Ladner and M. Brändle, Zurich, 2001, pp. 109–14.
41. C.H. Church, 'The Swiss Elections of October 1999: Learning to Live in More Interesting Times', *West European Politics*, vol. 23, no. 3, 2000, p. 217.

42. U. Klöti, 'Kantonale Parteiensysteme. Bedeutung des kantonalen Kontexts für die Positionierung der Parteien', in *Schweizer Wahlen 1995*, eds H. Kriesi, W. Linder, and U. Klöti, Bern, 1998; Kriesi et al., *Aufstieg der SVP.*
43. On the developments of the cantonal SVP party of Zurich in the 1970s and 1980s, see Hartmann and Horvath, *Zivilgesellschaft.*
44. On the JSVP's goal of countering the New Left, see *Schweizerzeit*, no. 1, 24 January 1980, p. 3.
45. C. Moos, *Ja zum Völkerbund – Nein zur UNO*, Zurich, 2001, pp. 117–36.
46. K.J. Pitterle, *The Limits of Interdependence*, Ann Arbor, 1981, pp. 1362ff.
47. *Année politique suisse 1978*, Bern 1979, p. 174.
48. *Schweizerzeit*, no. 1, 1 March 1979.
49. Ladner, 'Political Parties'.
50. M. Brändle, 'Die finanziellen Mittel der Parteien', in *Die Schweizer Parteien im Wandel*, eds. A. Ladner and M. Brändle, Zurich, 2001, p. 156.
51. For these figures, see *Neue Zürcher Zeitung*, 22 March 2000.
52. L. Neidhart, '"Tue Gutes und sprich darüber". Die SVP im Kampf um politischen Einfluss in der Stadt Zürich', *Neue Zürcher Zeitung*, 9 March 1998, p 37.
53. New cantonal sections were founded in the cantons of Zug (1991), Basel City (1991), Solothurn (1991), Lucerne (1992), St. Gallen (1992), Appenzell Outer Rhodes (1993), Appenzell Inner Rhodes (1996), Uri (1998), Valais (1999), Nidwald (1999), Obwald (1999) and Neuchâtel (2001).
54. *Statuten der Schweizerischen Volkspartei*, January 2002, articles 13 to 16.
55. *Neue Zürcher Zeitung*, 21 August 2000; *Der Bund*, 21 August 2000; *Tages Anzeiger*, 22 August 2000.
56. *Année politique suisse 1988*, Bern 1989, p. 321.
57. For this view, see *Neue Zürcher Zeitung*, 11 January 1996; 29 January 1996; *Tages Anzeiger*, 29 January 1996.
58. Kitschelt and McGann, 'Dynamik', pp. 209f.
59. *SVPja*, no. 10, 11 October 1990, pp. 8f; *Parteiprogramm '91 der Schweizerischen Volkspartei (SVP)*, adopted by the delegates' assembly on 16 February 1991, Bern 1991, pp. 12f; *Europapolitik der SVP. Schrift 1992*, adopted by the program commission of SVP Switzerland on 10 August 1992, Bern 1992.
60. See the interview with Christoph Blocher in: *Der Zürcher Bauer*, no. 45, 8. November 1991, pp. 1, 6.
61. H. Kriesi et al., *Analyse der eidgenössischen Abstimmung vom 6. Dezember 1992*, Adliswil, 1993, p. 35.
62. *SVPja*, no. 8, 12 December 1997, p. 6.
63. P. Niggli and J. Frischknecht, *Rechte Seilschaften*, Zurich, 1998, pp. 183f.
64. *SVPja*, no. 12, 13 December 1990, p. 19; no. 3, 14 March 1991, p. 24; *Der Zürcher Bauer*, no. 4, 24 January 1992, p. 5.
65. As a consequence of this manoeuvre by the cantonal party of Zurich, an internal working group was appointed in 1993 to examine the relationship between the national party and the cantonal sections. Based on its report of 1994, a new statute article was introduced decreeing that the launch of a federal initiative and the request for a referendum require the approval of both the central committee and the delegates' assembly. See *Statuten der Schweizerischen*

Volkspartei, January 2002, article 13, paragraph 6; on the change of the statutes, see *Tages Anzeiger*, 4 February 1998.

66. *Bundesblatt*, vol. III, no. 38, 1994, pp. 1490ff., 1501–9, 1514–20.

67. S. Hardmeier, *Analyse der eidgenössischen Abstimmungen vom 1. Dezember 1996*, Zurich, 1997, pp. 8–11.

68. Niggli and Frischknecht, *Rechte Seilschaften*, pp. 210–13; see also *Schweizerzeit*, no. 7, 20 March 1998, p. 3, and the press reports in *Neue Zürcher Zeitung*, 14/15 March 1998; *Tages Anzeiger*, 28 August 1998.

69. *Bundesblatt*, vol. III, no. 38, 2000, pp. 3424–28.

70. *NZZ am Sonntag*, 24 November 2002; *Le Temps*, 25 November 2002.

71. H. Hirter and W. Linder, *Analyse der eidgenössischen Abstimmungen vom 24. November 2002*, Bern, 2002.

72. C. Blocher, *Die Schweiz im Jubiläumsjahr 1998*, Albisgüetli Speech 1998, n.d. [1998], pp. 13f.

73. T. Maissen, *Verweigerte Erinnerung*, Zurich 2005, pp. 305–13.

74. *Neue Zürcher Zeitung*, 30 August, 2002; *Der Bund*, 31 August, 2002. Christoph Blocher was able to draw on a discourse that had been also supported by Jean-Pascal Delamuraz, Federal Councilor (1984-1998) and FDP member, who used a 1996 newspaper interview to equate the claims of Jewish organizations for a compensation fund to benefit Shoah victims with blackmail; *24 heures*, 31 December 1996. See also C. Späti, 'Enttabuisierung eines Vorurteils: Antisemitismus in der Schweiz', in *Feindbild Judentum*, eds. L. Rensmann and J.H. Schoeps, Berlin 2008, pp. 191ff.

75. F. Mahnig and T. Milic, *Analyse der eidgenössischen Abstimmungen vom 22. Sept. 2002*, Bern, 2002.

76. An article in the German weekly *Die Zeit* (26 September 1997) on Europe's right-wing populist leaders portrayed Christoph Blocher, along with Umberto Bossi, Carl I. Hagen and Bruno Mégret.

77. Kriesi et al., *Aufstieg der SVP*.

78. P. Taggart, 'New Populist Parties in Western Europe', *West European Politics*, vol. 18, no. 1, 1995, p. 1.

79. For biographical accounts of Christoph Blocher, see C. Schilling, *Blocher*, Zurich, 1994; F. Gsteiger, *Blocher*, Basel, 2002.

80. On the combination of fortune and politics in Blocher's career, see the article 'A Billionaire Leads the Campaign to Keep Switzerland Apart', *The New York Times*, 24 February 2002.

81. Hartmann and Horvath, *Zivilgesellschaft*, p. 43.

82. Church, 'Swiss Elections of October 1999', p. 217.

83. http://www.blocher.ch, accessed 31 August 2008. During his time in government, the website was no longer updated.

84. On the significance of the *Albisgüetli* meetings, see Girod, 'L'Union démocratique', p. 423.

85. Gsteiger, *Blocher*, p. 109.

86. M. Canovan, 'Trust the People! Populism and the Two Faces of Democracy', *Political Studies*, vol. 47, no. 1, 1999, pp. 5f.

87. R. Eatwell, 'The Rebirth of Right-Wing Charisma? The Cases of Jean-Marie Le Pen and Vladimir Zhirinovsky', *Totalitarian Movements and Political Religions*, vol. 3, no. 3, 2002.

88. R. Harmel and L. Svåsand, 'Party Leadership and Party Institutionalization: Three Phases of Development', *West European Politics*, vol. 16, no. 2, 1993.

89. A. Pedahzur and A. Brichta, 'The Institutionalization of Extreme Right-Wing Charismatic Parties: A Paradox?', *Party Politics*, vol. 8, no. 1, 2002, p. 36.

90. For this assessment, see *Neue Zürcher Zeitung*, 8 March 2000; 22 March 2000.

91. H.-G. Betz, 'Introduction', in *The New Politics of the Right*, eds H.-G. Betz and S. Immerfall, New York, 1998, p. 9.

92. Gsteiger, *Blocher*, pp. 193–96.

93. Ibid., pp. 196–99.

94. Ladner, 'Swiss Political Parties', pp.134f.

95. H. Kriesi, 'The Federal Parliament: The Limits of Institutional Reform', in *The Swiss Labyrinth*, ed. J.-E. Lane, London, 2001, p. 60.

96. S. Hardmeier, 'Amerikanisierung der Wahlkampfkommunikation? Einem Schlagwort auf der Spur', in *Schweizer Wahlen 1999*, eds P. Sciarini, S. Hardmeier, and A. Vatter, Bern, 2003; Kriesi et al., *Aufstieg der SVP*.

97. For these figures, see *Neue Zürcher Zeitung*, 22 March 2000.

98. Gsteiger, *Blocher*, pp. 160–67.

99. *Berner Zeitung*, 11 October 1996.

100. On the launching of *Le Pays Romand*, see *SVPja*, no. 8, 20 December 1996, p. 13; *Le Pays Romand*, no. 1, 23 January 1997. See the statement in the last issue: *Le Pays Romand*, no. 11, 18 December 1997, p. 1.

101. Hartmann and Horvath, *Zivilgesellschaft*, pp. 13–16; Mazzoleni, *Nationalisme*, p. 83; see also *Neue Zürcher Zeitung*, 14 September 1999.

102. S. Hardmeier and A. Vatter, 'Synthese – Die Ursachen des SVP-Wahlerfolgs', in *Schweizer Wahlen 1999*, eds P. Sciarini, S. Hardmeier, and A. Vatter, Bern, 2003, p. 456.

103. Canovan, 'Trust the People!', p. 6.

104. For an account of these events, see *Neue Zürcher Zeitung*, 9 March 1998.

105. See the classical study by L. Neidhart, *Plebiszit and pluralitäre Demokratie*, Bern, 1970.

106. Niggli and Frischknecht, *Seilschaften*, pp. 417f; see also *Spectrum: Junge europäische Schüler- und Studenteninitiative der Schweiz*, no. 2, March/April 1996, pp. 1f.

107. *Neue Zürcher Zeitung*, 6 March 2000.

108. *Tages Anzeiger*, 2 May 2000; *Neue Zürcher Zeitung*, 22 May 2000; *SonntagsZeitung*, 28 May 2000.

109. *Neue Zürcher Zeitung*, 13 August 2002; *Tages Anzeiger*, 23 September 2002.

110. *Schweizerzeit*, no. 1, 7 January 2000, p. 3, my translation.

111. Ladner, 'Swiss Political Parties', p. 129.

112. H. Kriesi, 'Wahlentscheide bei Ständeratswahlen', in *Schweizer Wahlen 1999*, eds P. Sciarini, S. Hardmeier, and A. Vatter, Bern, 2003.

113. C.H. Church, 'The Swiss Election of 1991: Stability, not Stasis', *West European Politics*, vol. 15, no. 4, 1992, p. 187; C. Longchamp and S. Hardmeier, *Analyse der Nationalratswahlen 1991*, Adliswil, 1992, pp. 2–5.

114. W. Seitz, *Nationalratswahlen 1995*, Bern. 1995, p. 63.

115. On the debates over establishing electoral alliances with the APS, see *Tages Anzeiger*, 12 July 1991; *Journal de Genève*, 11 September 1991; 11 October 1991.

116. Longchamp and Hardmeier, *Nationalratswahlen 1991*, p. 21.
117. Seitz, *Nationalratswahlen 1995*, p. 6; A. Ladner, 'Switzerland', *European Journal of Political Research*, vol. 30, no. 2, 1996, p. 474.
118. C. Longchamp et al., *Hin zur Tripolarität im Parteiensystem der Schweiz*, Bern, 1995, p. 3; C.H. Church, 'The Swiss Elections of 1995: Real Victors and Real Losers at Last?', *West European Politics*, vol. 19, no. 3, 1996, pp. 646f.
119. D. Caramani, 'The Swiss Parliamentary Election of 1995', *Electoral Studies*, vol. 15, no. 1, 1996, p. 128.
120. For this conclusion, see also the statement by Hans Uhlmann, party president and partisan of the moderate faction within the SVP, in: *Der Zürcher Bauer*, 22 December, 1995, p. 3.
121. Caramani, 'Swiss Parliamentary Election', pp. 132f; Ladner, 'Switzerland', p. 474.
122. *Schwerpunktprogramm '95 der Schweizerischen Volkspartei (SVP)*, adopted by the delegates' assembly on 21 January 1995, p. 20.
123. *Der Zürcher Bote*, Special Issue, 6 October 1995, pp. 1ff.; *SVPja*, no. 6, 13 October 1995, p. 17; see press reports in *SonntagsZeitung*, 24 September 1995; *Neue Zürcher Zeitung*, 25 September 1995.
124. Seitz, *Nationalratswahlen 1995*, pp. 74–80; Caramani, 'Swiss Parliamentary Election', p. 130.
125. For reactions from the international press, see *The New York Times*, 25 October 1999; *The Guardian*, 25 October 1999; *Le Monde*, 26 October 1999.
126. W. Seitz, *Nationalratswahlen 1999*, Neuchâtel, 1999, p. 6. To be precise, the SVP received 22.54 per cent of the vote, while the SPS scored 22.47 per cent.
127. Church, 'Swiss Elections of October 1999', p. 216; W. Linder and G. Lutz, 'The Parliamentary Elections in Switzerland, October 1999', *Electoral Studies*, vol. 21, no. 1, 2002, pp. 130f.
128. *SVP Parteiprogramm 1999–2003*, n.d. [1999], p. 9, http://www.svp.ch/file/Parteiprogramm99_-_03.doc, retrieved 31 August 2008; *SVPja*, no. 1, 12 February 1999, pp. 1–5; see also the press reports in *Neue Zürcher Zeitung*, 29 December 1998; 25 January 1999.
129. Longchamp, 'Nationalkonservative Revolte', pp. 409–12; P. Sciarini and H. Kriesi, 'Stabilité et changement d'opinion durant la campagne électorale', in *Schweizer Wahlen 1999*, eds P. Sciarini, S. Hardmeier, and A. Vatter, Bern, 2003, pp. 366ff.
130. Longchamp, 'Nationalkonservative Revolte', p. 411.
131. Kriesi et al., *Aufstieg der SVP*.
132. For these figures, see Niggli and Frischknecht, *Seilschaften*, p. 507; see also *Neue Zürcher Zeitung*, 9 April 2003.
133. For these figures, see *Neue Zürcher Zeitung*, 19 October 2001; 9 April 2003.
134. For this assessment, see *Neue Zürcher Zeitung*, 19 October 2001.
135. For the results in cantonal elections, see the issues of *Année politique suisse* from 1990 to 2003.
136. *Neue Zürcher Zeitung*, 19 April 1999.
137. See also Kitschelt and McGann, 'Dynamik', pp. 197f; Mazzoleni, *Nationalisme*, pp. 90f.

138. Kitschelt and McGann, 'Dynamik', p. 200.
139. Longchamp, 'Nationalkonservative Revolte', pp. 406ff.
140. P. Gentile and H. Kriesi, 'Contemporary Radical-Right Parties in Switzerland: History of a Divided Family', in *The New Politics of the Right*, eds H.-G. Betz and S. Immerfall, New York, 1998, p. 135.
141. Longchamp and Hardmeier, *Nationalratswahlen 1991*, p. 20; P. Farago, *Wahlen 95*, Bern, 1996, p. 20; H. Hirter, *Wahlen 1999*, Bern, 2000, pp. 18, 21.
142. Hirter, *Wahlen 1999*, p. 21.
143. Ibid., pp. 18–21.
144. Kriesi et al., *Aufstieg der SVP*.
145. Mazzoleni, *Nationalisme*, pp. 96ff.
146. Ibid., p. 92.
147. Longchamp, 'Nationalkonservative Revolte'.
148. Kitschelt and McGann, 'Dynamik'; W. Seitz, *Les élections au Conseil national de 1999*, Neuchâtel 2003.
149. Ladner, 'Swiss Political Parties', p. 141.
150. Kitschelt and McGann, 'Dynamik', pp. 196–99. The authors emphasise that the SVP was underrepresented among employees in higher positions and managerial roles in 1999, but fail to notice the considerable increase in electoral support that the SVP received in the 1990s among people with fairly high income and better education.
151. F. Plasser and P.A. Ulram, 'Rechtspopulistische Resonanzen: Die Wählerschaft der FPÖ', in *Das österreichische Wahlverhalten*, eds F. Plasser, P.A. Ulram, and F. Sommer, Vienna, 2000, pp. 230–34; A. Widfeldt, 'Scandinavia: Mixed Success for the Populist Right', in *Parliamentary Affairs*, vol. 53, no. 3, 2000, pp. 497f.
152. D. Schloeth, *Vor die Wahl gestellt*, Bern, 1998, pp. 177–95; Kitschelt and McGann, 'Dynamik', p. 203.
153. See also H. Kriesi, 'Zusammenfassung und Schlussfolgerung', in *Der Aufstieg der SVP*, eds H. Kriesi et al., Zurich, 2005, pp. 258ff.
154. Kitschelt and McGann, 'Dynamik', p. 203; see also Mazzoleni, *Nationalisme*, p. 94.
155. O. Mazzoleni, 'La dimension gauche–droite et le choix partisan. Une perspective comparée', in *Schweizer Wahlen 1999*, eds P. Sciarini, S. Hardmeier, and A. Vatter, Bern, 2003, pp. 142, 144.
156. Hirter, *Wahlen 1999*, p. 23. Fifty-nine per cent of FDP voters and sixty-three per cent of CVP voters placed themselves at the centre of the left–right continuum.
157. Plasser and Ulram, 'Rechtspopulistische Resonanzen', p. 235; Kitschelt and McGann, 'Dynamik', p. 207.
158. See also O. Mazzoleni and B. Wernli, *Cittadini e politica*, Bellinzona, 2002, p. 97.
159. Schloeth, *Vor die Wahl*, pp. 208f.
160. G. Lutz, 'Mobilisierung als Schlüsselfaktor für den Wahlerfolg?', in *Schweizer Wahlen 1999*, eds P. Sciarini, S. Hardmeier, and A. Vatter, Bern, 2003, pp. 76–79; see also Longchamp, 'Nationalkonservative Revolte', p. 409.
161. Kriesi, 'Zusammenfassung', pp. 260–64.

162. H.-G. Betz, 'The New Politics of Resentment. Radical Right-Wing Populist Parties in Western Europe', *Comparative Politics*, vol. 25, no. 4, 1993, p. 419.

163. W. van der Brug, M. Fennema, and J. Tillie, 'Anti-Immigrant Parties in Europe: Ideological or Protest Vote?', *European Journal of Political Research*, vol. 37, no. 1, 2000; E. Carter, *The Extreme Right in Western Europe*, Manchester, 2005, pp. 54–63.

164. See also H.-G. Betz, 'Conditions Favouring the Success and Failure of Radical Right-Wing Populist Parties in Contemporary Democracies', in *Democracies and the Populist Challenge*, eds Y. Mény and Y. Surel, Basingstoke, 2002, pp. 199–205; Betz, *La droite populiste*, pp. 114ff.

165. Quoted in: *NZZ am Sonntag*, 30 June 2002, my translation.

166. R. Heinisch, 'Success in Opposition – Failure in Government: Explaining the Performance of Right-Wing Populist Parties in Public Office", *West European Politics*, vol. 26, no. 3, 2003, p. 94.

167. *Neue Zürcher Zeitung*, 16 June 2001, my translation; see also Schilling, *Blocher*, pp. 117–27.

168. Canovan, 'Trust the People!', p. 2.

169. *Der Zürcher Bauer*, no. 24, June 1994, p. 1, my translation.

170. *Schweizer Qualität – SVP: Wahlplattform 2003 bis 2007*, published by the SVP general office, Bern, n.d. [2003], pp. 6f.

171. C. Blocher, *Die Schweiz im Jubiläumsjahr 1998*, Albisgüetli Speech 1998, n.d. [1998], p. 8, my translation.

172. C. Longchamp 'Den Pelz waschen, ohne ihn nass zu machen. Eine sozialwissenschaftliche Analyse der Entscheidung der Schweiz über den Beitritt zum Europäischen Wirtschaftsraum vom 6. Dezember 1992', in *Europa-Kampagnen*, ed. H. Rust, Vienna, 1993, p. 42.

173. C. Blocher, *Anpassung und Widerstand: Eine politische Standortbestimmung*, presented at the Albisgüetli meeting of the SVP cantonal party of Zurich on 24 January 1992, Schweizerzeit publication series no. 11, 1992, p. 6, my translation.

174. Longchamp, 'Den Pelz waschen', p. 43.

175. For advertisements incorporating the slogan, see *Neue Zürcher Zeitung*, 15 August 1995; 2 October 1995; *Tages Anzeiger*, 26 September 1995, my translation.

176. Originally published in 1997 in France, the book describes the crimes and atrocities committed by communist regimes and argues that the policies of extermination applied by these regimes were not really so different from those used by the National Socialist regime and that, in fact, the number of victims was much higher under communism; see S. Courtois et al., *The Black Book of Communism: Crimes, Terror, Repression*, Cambridge, MA: Harvard University Press, 1999.

177. C. Blocher, *Freedom not Socialism: A Call Addressed to Socialists in All Parties*, English translation, April 2000, p. 4, http://www.blocher.ch/en/artikel/000400socialism.pdf, retrieved 31 August 2008.

178. Ibid., p. 9. In the German language, 'brown' is a commonly used as shorthand for National Socialists.

179. *Der Zürcher Bauer*, no. 45, 12 November 1993, p. 8.

180. C. Blocher, *Switzerland and the Second World War: A Clarification*, speech given on 1 March 1997, English translation, n.d. [1997], p. 10, http://www.blocher.ch/en/artikel/970301worldwar2.pdf, retrieved 31 August 2008.

181. C. Blocher, *Switzerland and the Eizenstat Report*, speech given on 21 June 1997 in Bern, English Translation, n.d. [1997], pp. 21, 26, http://www.blocher.ch/en/artikel/970621eizenstat.pdf, retrieved 31 August 2008.

182. Blocher, *Switzerland and the Second World War*, p. 15.

183. *Der Bund*, 6 September 2000; *Neue Zürcher Zeitung*, 7 September 2000; 3 July 2001; 12 December 2001; see also Maissen, *Verweigerte Erinnerung*, pp. 302f.

184. *Amtliches Bulletin der Bundesversammlung. Ständerat*, 2001, pp. 954ff.; *Amtliches Bulletin der Bundesversammlung. Nationalrat*, 2001, pp. 1093–96.

185. *Neue Zürcher Zeitung*, 18 August 1998.

186. *Schweizer Qualität – SVP*, pp. 35, 45.

187. *Die SVP fordert neue Sicherheitspolitik für die Stadt Zürich*, published by the Swiss People's Party of the city of Zurich, 2nd edn, 1994; see also Hartmann and Horvath, *Zivilgesellschaft*, pp. 155–59.

188. *Schweizer Qualität – SVP*, p. 12.

189. H.-R. Wicker, 'Einleitung: Migration, Migrationspolitik und Migrationsforschung', in *Migration und die Schweiz*, eds H.-R. Wicker, R. Fibbi, and W. Haug, Zurich, 2003, pp. 32–35.

190. *Aktionsprogramm '87 der Schweizerischen Volkspartei*, adopted by the central committee on 20 March 1987, Bern, April 1987, p. 26.

191. See also D. Skenderovic, 'Constructing Boundaries in a Multicultural Nation: The Discourse of "Overforeignization" in Switzerland', in *European Encounters*, eds R. Ohliger, K. Schönwälder, and T. Triadafilopoulos, Aldershot, 2003, pp. 192ff.; Skenderovic and D'Amato, *Mit dem Fremden politisieren*.

192. *SVPja*, no. 7, 31 October 1997, p. 5, my translation.

193. *Neue Zürcher Zeitung*, 22 June 1995.

194. For example, see C. Blocher, *The Seven Secrets of the SVP (strictly confidential)*, Albisgüetli Speech 2000, English translation, n.d. [2000], p. 10.

195. *Konzept für eine Zürcher Ausländerpolitik*, published by the Swiss People's Party of the city of Zurich, 1st edn, 1999, p. 24.

196. For the SVP, see also Girod, 'L'Union démocratique', pp. 426ff.

197. For example, see *Schweizerzeit*, no. 6, 3 March 2000, pp. 5f.

198. *Vernehmlassung der SVP der Stadt Zürich zum Entwurf für eine "Leitbild zur Integrationspolitik der Stadt Zürich"*, Zurich, 28 August 1998, p. 3.

199. Ibid., p. 4, my translation. See also the position paper on migration policy from 1998, the most comprehensive programmatic writing from the SVP regarding this issue in the 1990s: *Migrationspolitik: Glaubwürdig und zukunftsorientiert*, position paper of the SVP Switzerland, March 1998.

200. Ibid., p. 15, my translation.

201. *Vernehmlassung der Schweizerischen SVP zur Verordnung über die soziale Integration der Ausländerinnen und Ausländer (VIA)*, Bern, 20 June 2000.

202. M.A. Niggli, 'Diskriminierung durch Plakataushang', in *Rassendiskriminierung: Gerichtspraxis zu Art. 261bis StGB*, Zurich, 1999, pp. 265–81; see also *Neue Zürcher Zeitung*, 19 December 2002.

203. *Parteiprogramm '91 der Schweizerischen Volkspartei (SVP)*, adopted by the

delegates' assembly on 16 February 1991, Bern 1991, p. 51; see also *SVPja*, no. 9, 5 September, 1990.

204. *SVP Parteiprogramm 1999–2003*, p. 9; *Schweizer Qualität – SVP*, p. 13; *Migrationspolitik*, p. 21.

205. *Schweizer Qualität – SVP*, p. 13.

206. *Sorge tragen zum Schweizer Bürgerrecht*, position paper of the SVP Switzerland on naturalisation policy, July 2001, pp. 18f.

207. See the reports in: *Neue Zürcher Zeitung*, 22 November 2002; 17 March 2003; 10 July 2003; 25 July 2003.

208. For example, see *Aktionsprogramm '87 der Schweizerischen Volkspartei*, p. 25.

209. L. Parini and M. Gianni, 'Enjeux et modifications de la politique d'asile en Suisse de 1956 à nos jours', in *Histoire de la politique de migration, d'asile et d'intégration en Suisse depuis 1948*, ed. H. Mahnig, Zurich, 2005, p. 213.

210. Schilling, *Blocher*, p. 112.

211. *Schweizerzeit*, no. 22, 13 December 1985, p. 2.

212. *SVPja*, no. 12, 13 December 1990, pp. 1f; no. 2, 7 February 1991, p. 19; no. 5, 10 May 1991, pp. 10f; no. 9, 5 September 1991, p. 24; no. 11/12, 21 November 1991, p. 7.

213. *Le pays romand*, no. 11, 18 December 1997, p. 10; *SVPja*, no. 9, 2002, pp. 5–9; see also Girod, 'L'Union démocratique', pp. 428–31.

214. *SVP Parteiprogramm 1999–2003*, p. 8.

215. Ibid., p. 4.

216. *Einstehen für die Schweiz: Parteiprogramm 2003–2007 der SVP des Kantons Zürich*, October 2002, p. 13, my translation.

217. Blocher, *The Seven Secrets of the SVP*, pp. 11–16.

218. H. Kriesi, *Le système politique suisse*, Paris, 1995, pp. 12–21.

219. See also D. Skenderovic, 'Nation, Nationalismus und politische Parteien: Die Schweiz – keine Insel in Europa', in *On European Identity*, ed. C. Szaló Brno, 1998, p. 172.

220. *SVPja*, no. 1, 2002, p. 3, my translation.

221. Blocher, *The Seven Secrets of the SVP*, p. 15.

222. C. Mörgeli, 'Gedanken zum schweizerischen Nein', *Der Zürcher Bauer*, no. 48, 27 November 1998, p. 1; C. Mörgeli, *Der Kleinstaat und die Ideologie des Grossräumigen*, Schweizerzeit publication series no. 37, Flaach, 2001.

223. K.W. Kobach, 'Spurn Thy Neighbour: Direct Democracy and Swiss Isolationism', *West European Politics*, vol. 20, no. 3, 1997, pp. 197f. As noted by a post-vote survey, the SVP supporters endorsed the party's call to reject the provision of UN peacekeeping troops by a large majority of eighty-two per cent and they were joined by supporters of the SD and the *Lega dei Ticinesi*, who rejected the proposal with eighty-seven per cent; see B. Wernli, P. Sciarini, and J. Barranco, *Analyse der eidgenössischen Abstimmungen vom 12. Juni 1994*, Adliswil, 1994, p. 11.

224. Blocher, *Switzerland and the Second World War*, p. 8; see also *SVPja*, no. 2, 28 March 1997, pp. 8f.

225. Press release: SVP, 'Veröffentlichung des Schlussberichts der UEK', 22 March, 2002, my translation.

226. A. Gamble, 'The Political Economy of Freedom', in *The Ideology of the New Right*, ed. R. Levitas, Cambridge, 1986.

227. On the influence of Mont Pèlerin Society on the neoliberal current of the New Right, see B. Walpen, *Die offenen Feinde und ihre Gesellschaft*, Hamburg, 2004.

228. *Der Weg der SVP in die schwarzen Zahlen*, position paper of the SVP on federal finances, Bern, 1996; see also the press report in *Neue Zürcher Zeitung*, 26 March, 1996.

229. *Einstehen für die Schweiz*, p. 29, my translation.

230. *SVP Parteiprogramm 1999–2003*, 4, pp. 36f.

231. *Einstehen für die Schweiz*, p. 19.

232. Betz, 'New Politics of Resentment', p. 418.

233. *SVP Parteiprogramm 1999–2003*, p. 31.

234. *SVPja*, no. 3, 28 May 1994, p. 10.

235. On this cleavage, see S. Hug and P. Sciarini, eds, *Changements de valeurs et nouveaux clivages politiques en Suisse*, Paris, 2002.

236. A.J. McGann and H. Kitschelt, 'The Radical Right in the Alps. Evolution of Support for the Swiss SVP and Austrian FPÖ', *Party Politics*, vol. 11, no. 2, 2005.

6. A Supplier of Ideology: The New Right in the German-speaking Part of Switzerland

1. H.U. Jost, *Die reaktionäre Avantgarde*, Zurich, 1992; A. Mattioli, ed., *Intellektuelle von rechts*, Zurich, 1995.

2. J. Mooser, '"Spiritual National Defence" in the 1930s: Swiss Political Culture between the Wars', in *Switzerland and the Second World War*, ed. G. Kreis, London, 2000, pp. 240–46.

3. H.U. Jost, 'Bedrohung und Enge (1919–1945)', in *Geschichte der Schweiz und Schweizer*, eds B. Messmer, Basel, 1986, pp. 804f; D. Skenderovic, 'Constructing Boundaries in a Multicultural Nation: The Discourse of "Overforeignization" in Switzerland', in *European Encounters*, eds R. Ohliger, K. Schönwälder, and T. Triadafilopoulos, Aldershot, 2003, p. 188; D. Skenderovic, 'Fremdenfeindlichkeit', in *Historisches Lexikon der Schweiz*, Basel, 2005, vol. 4, p. 797.

4. J. Mooser, '"Spiritual National Defence"', pp. 246–51.

5. A. Mattioli, *Zwischen Demokratie und totalitärer Diktatur*, Zurich, 1994; G. Kreis, 'Philipp Etter – "voll auf eidgenössischem Boden"', in *Intellektuelle von rechts*, ed. A. Mattioli, Zurich, 1995.

6. C. Siegrist, 'Der zerrissene Jakob Schaffner: überzeugter Nationalsozialist und Schweizer Patriot', in *Intellektuelle von rechts*, ed. A. Mattioli, Zurich, 1995.

7. B. Glaus, *Die Nationale Front*, Zurich, 1969.

8. L. van Dongen, 'Swiss Memory of the Second World War in the Immediate Post-War Period, 1945–1948', in *Switzerland and the Second World War*, ed. G. Kreis, London, 2000, pp. 272f.

9. M. Furrer, 'Die Apotheose der Nation. Konkordanz und Konsens in den 1950er Jahren', in *Die Konstruktion einer Nation*, eds U. Altermatt, C. Bosshart-

Pfluger, and A. Tanner, Zurich, 1998; M. König, 'Rasanter Stillstand und zähe Bewegung. Schweizerische Innenpolitik im Kalten Krieg – und darüber hinaus', in *"Goldene Jahre"*, eds W. Leimgruber and W. Fischer, Zurich, 1999.

10. J. Frischknecht et al., *Die unheimlichen Patrioten*, 6th edn, Zurich, 1987,

11. K. Imhof, 'Wiedergeburt der geistigen Landesverteidigung: Kalter Krieg in der Schweiz', in *Konkordanz und Kalter Krieg*, eds K. Imhof, H. Kleger, and G. Romano, Zurich, 1996; B. Studer, 'Antikommunismus', in *Historisches Lexikon der Schweiz*, Basel, 2002, vol.1.

12. I. Drews, *"Schweizer erwache!" Der Rechtspopulist James Schwarzenbach (1967–1978)*, Frauenfeld, 2005.

13. U. Altermatt, 'Conservatism in Switzerland: A Study in Antimodernism', *Journal of Contemporary History*, vol. 14, no. 4, 1979, p. 584.

14. R.J. Antonio, 'After Postmodernism: Reactionary Tribalism', *American Journal of Sociology*, vol. 106, no. 2, 2000, p. 51.

15. W. Gessenharter, *Kippt die Republik?*, Munich, 1994, p. 123.

16. I. Fetscher, ed., *Neokonservative und "Neue Rechte"*, Munich, 1983; W.H. Lorig, *Neokonservatives Denken in der Bundesrepublik Deutschland und in den Vereinigten Staaten von Amerika*, Opladen, 1988.

17. P. Steinfels, *The Neoconservatives*, New York, 1979; G. Peele, *Revival and Reaction*, reprinted edn, Oxford, 1987; T.J. Lowi, *The End of the Republican Era*, Norman, 1995.

18. M. Minkenberg, *Die neue radikale Rechte im Vergleich*, Opladen, 1998, p. 157. Among these intellectuals, Hermann Lübbe, a former professor (1971–1991) and current honorary professor of philosophy and political theory at the University of Zurich, was perhaps the most influential representative of the neoconservative current in both Germany and Switzerland; see N. Hilger, *Deutscher Neokonservatismus – das Beispiel Herman Lübbes*, Baden-Baden, 1995.

19. J. Müller, 'From National Identity to National Interest: The Rise (and Fall) of Germany's New Right', *German Politics*, vol. 8, no. 3, 1999, p. 10.

20. M. Venner, *Nationale Identität*, Cologne, 1994, pp. 48–55; Minkenberg, *Die neue radikale Rechte*, pp. 156–64.

21. K. Schönekäs, 'Bundesrepublik Deutschland', in *Neue Rechte und Rechtsextremismus in Europa*, eds F. Gress, H.-G. Jaschke, and K. Schönekäs, Opladen, 1990, pp. 287–90.

22. C. Leggewie, *Der Geist steht rechts*, 2nd edn, Berlin, 1987, pp. 49–54; J. Mecklenburg, ed., *Handbuch deutscher Rechtsextremismus*, Berlin, 1996, pp. 207ff.

23. Leggewie, *Geist steht recht*, pp. 185f, 209ff.; M. Minkenberg, 'The New Right in France and Germany: *Nouvelle Droite, Neue Rechte*, and the New Right Radical Parties', in *The Revival of Right-Wing Extremism in the Nineties*, eds P.H. Merkl and L. Weinberg, London, 1997, pp. 73f.

24. On Herbert Meier's various activities, see J. Frischknecht et al., *Die unheimlichen Patrioten*, 6th edn, Zurich, 1987, pp. 313–98, 689–719; P. Niggli and J. Frischknecht, *Rechte Seilschaften*, Zurich, 1998, pp. 567–91.

25. Frischknecht et al., *Die unheimlichen Patrioten*, pp. 406f.

26. On the Mont Pèlerin Society, see B. Walpen, *Die offenen Feinde und ihre Gesellschaft*, Hamburg, 2004.

27. G.K. Kaltenbrunner, ed., *Die Herausforderung der Konservativen: Absage an Illusionen*, Munich: Herder, 1974.
28. Niggli and Frischknecht, *Rechte Seilschaften*, p. 573.
29. *Abendland*, no. 178, September 1987, p. 1; see also U. Altermatt and D. Skenderovic, 'Die extreme Rechte: Organisationen, Personen und Entwicklungen in den achtziger und neunziger Jahren', in *Rechtsextremismus in der Schweiz*, eds U. Altermatt and H. Kriesi, Zurich, 1995, p. 49.
30. *Gegner des Antirassismus-Gesetzes*, press documentation, published by the Swiss Committee 'Yes to the Anti-Racism Law', 2 vols, Zurich, August 1994, vol. 2; Niggli and Frischknecht, *Rechte Seilschaften*, p. 302.
31. See the signature-sheet by the KFRD for the petition requesting a referendum, enclosed in *Abendland*, no. 204, September 1993.
32. Frischknecht et al., *Die unheimlichen Patrioten*, pp. 357f.
33. *Abendland*, no. 206, March 1994.
34. For example, see L. Stamm, *Wer hat die Macht in Bern? Ist tatsächlich das Parlament für das Versagen der Politik in den 90er Jahren verantwortlich?*, Zofingen: Zofinger Tagblatt, 2000; *Die gezielte Zerstörung unserer direkten Demokratie und unseres Wohlstands*, Aarau: KDA-Verlag, 2003.
35. Frischknecht et al., *Die unheimlichen Patrioten*, pp. 695–99; K. Zellhofer and M.A. Gassner, 'SS und Rosenkranz – Völkischer Katholizismus', in *Die Ordnung, die sie meinen*, ed. W. Purtscheller, Vienna, 1994, p. 119.
36. *Abendland*, no. 203, March 1993, p. 8.
37. *Criticón*, no. 37, September/October 1976, p. 252.
38. *Abendland*, no. 179, October 1987, p. 1, my translation.
39. For example, see *Abendland*, no. 41, 31 July 1968, pp. 2–11; no. 59, January 1973, pp. 7f; no. 63, March 1974, p. 3; no. 65, September 1974, pp. 5ff.
40. *Abendland*, no. 40, 20 June 1968, p. 6.
41. Ibid., pp. 11f, my translation.
42. *Abendland*, no. 10, 23 October 1965, p. 6, my translation.
43. *Abendland*, no. 1, 15 August 1964, p. 1.
44. Frischknecht et al., *Die unheimlichen Patrioten*, pp. 403–13.
45. *Abendland*, no. 213, December 1995, p. 1.
46. *Abendland*, no. 217, December 1996, p. 1.
47. See the endorsement of James Schwarzenbach for the 1967 National Council elections in: *Abendland*, no. 35, 25 October 1967, p. 3.
48. *Abendland*, no. 54, 10 August 1970, p. 4.
49. *Abendland*, no. 62, November 1973, p. 2, my translation. See also T. Buomberger, *Kampf gegen unerwünschte Fremde*, Zurich, 2004, p. 176.
50. In 1986, *Abendland* had already rejected UN membership for Switzerland; see *Abendland*, no. 169, March 1986, pp. 1f.
51. *Abendland*, no. 203, March 1993, p. 2, my translation.
52. For example, see *Abendland*, no. 218, March 1997, p. 1.
53. *Abendland*, no. 161, January 1985, p. 3.
54. *Abendland*, no. 206, March 1994, p. 3, my translation.
55. *Abendland*, no. 221, June 1995, p. 8.
56. *Abendland*, no. 227, July 1999, p. 2, my translation.
57. *Neue Zürcher Zeitung*, 25 March 1982.

58. According to Jenny's own statement, he was a member of the National Front until 1938; see *Die WochenZeitung*, 12 April 1985.

59. H. Jenny, *Balkanreise im Krieg: Aus dem Tagebuch eines Journalisten*, Zurich: own publishing venture, 1942; *Der europäische Südosten*, Zurich: Verlag Nationale Hefte, 1943.

60. For a biographical note, see E. Stäuble, *Die Schweiz und die geistige Situation der Gegenwart*, STAB publication series no. 35, Zurich, 1999, p. 4.

61. E. Stäuble, *Stromaufwärts: Ein Kulturauftrag*, 25 years of the Foundation for Occidental Consciousness, an account, Zurich: Arborea Verlag, 1993, p. 129.

62. For a selected presentation of prize winners and their essays, see ibid., pp. 25–108.

63. For a list of associations funded by the STAB, see ibid., pp. 129f.

64. H. Jenny, 'Der Weg zu den Quellen', in Stäuble, *Stromaufwärts*, pp. 5ff.

65. An excerpt from the foundation document is reprinted in 'Die Stiftung für abendländische Besinnung (STAB). Entstehung und Grundgedanken', in H. Jenny, *Abendländische Gedanken*, Stäfa: Th. Gut + Co, 1977, pp. 139f.

66. Stäuble, *Stromaufwärts*, 11, italics in original, my translation.

67. Jenny, 'Der Weg zu den Quellen', pp. 7ff.

68. The basic principles are reprinted in: 'Die Stiftung für abendländische Besinnung (STAB)', pp. 140–50 (reference here to pp. 149f., quote from p. 150, my translation).

69. *Rundbrief Nr. 11 an die Freunde der Stiftung für abendländische Besinnung (STAB)*, Zollikon, 27 June 1973, p. 5.

70. *Vom Mut zu guter Erziehung*, STAB-Prize 1995 awarded to Christa Meves and Wolfgang Brezinka, STAB publication series no. 29, Zurich: Arborea Verlag, 1995, pp. 19–33. Meves' award address was also published by *Schweizerzeit*, no. 18, 27 October 1995, pp. 1f; see also the report by *Abendland*, no. 213, December 1995, p. 3.

71. *Neue Zürcher Zeitung*, 16 October 1995.

72. For critical accounts of Eibl-Eibesfeldt's work, see F. Seifert, 'Das Argument der menschlichen Natur in der Einwanderungsdebatte veranschaulicht am Beispiel Irenäus Eibl-Eibesfeldt', *Österreichische Zeitschrift für Politikwissenschaft*, vol. 25, no. 2, 1996; I. Weber, *Nation, Staat und Elite*, Cologne, 1997, pp. 25–31.

73. *Die Konkurrenzfalle – Sind wir fähig, unsere Zukunft zu gestalten?* STAB-Prize 1997 awarded to Prof. Dr. Dr. h.c. Irenäus Eibl-Eibesfeldt, published by the Foundation for Occidental Consciousness, Zurich, 1997, p. 11.

74. Ibid., p. 34, my translation. A revised version of Eibl-Eibesfeldt's address was published by *Abendland*, no. 222, March/April 1998, pp. 5f.

75. *Die Konkurrenzfalle*, p. 36, my translation.

76. Jenny, *Um was es geht*, p. 50.

77. Ibid., p. 87, my translation.

78. On the paper *Schweizerzeit*, see also Altermatt and Skenderovic, 'Die extreme Rechte', p. 50.

79. On Urich Schlüer, see Buomberger, *Kampf gegen*, pp. 218f; Frischknecht et al., *Die unheimlichen Patrioten*, pp. 515–19.

80. *Schweizerzeit*, no. 12, 4 October 1979, p. 1.

81. *Schweizerzeit*, no. 20, 11 November 1994, p. 3.
82. Niggli and Frischknecht, *Rechte Seilschaften*, p. 522. For the latest figures, see the official website of *Schweizerzeit:* http://www.schweizerzeit.ch/frame_impressum.htm, accessed 31 August 2008.
83. See the on-line mail order service of *Schweizerzeit:* http://www.schweizerzeit.ch/ frame_buecher2.htm, retrieved 30 October 2003. On de Benoist's book and the two German publishing houses, see *Verfassungsschutzbericht 2001*, published by the Federal Ministry of Interior, press version, Bonn, Berlin 2001, pp. 128f.
84. *Schweizerzeit*, no. 21, 26 November 1993, p. 3.
85. Frischknecht et al., *Die unheimlichen Patrioten*, p. 516.
86. For their contributions to periodicals of the German New Right, see A. Lange, *Was die Rechten lesen*, Munich, 1993; H. Kellershohn, ed., *Das Plagiat*, Duisburg, 1994.
87. *Schweizerzeit*, no. 23, 28 November 1997, p. 5.
88. *Schweizerzeit*, no. 11, 11 June 1993, p. 5.
89. Kellershohn, *Plagiat*, pp. 71–77; Mecklenburg *Handbuch*, pp. 481f.
90. *Schweizerzeit*, no. 12, 24 June 1994, pp. 1f.
91. *Junge Freiheit*, no. 6, 9 February 1996, p. 3.
92. See the official website of *Junge Freiheit:* http://www.jungefreiheit.de/Autoren.52.0.html, retrieved 31 August 2008.
93. Niggli and Frischknecht, *Rechte Seilschaften*, p. 479.
94. On the publishing activities of Herbert Fleissner, see H. Sarkowicz, *Rechte Geschäfte*, Frankfurt, 1994.
95. *Schweizerzeit*, no. 5, 11 March 1988, p. 2. It was a review of H. Schoeck, *Das Recht auf Ungleichheit*, 3rd edn, Munich: Herbig, 1988. The first edition was already reviewed by *Schweizerzeit*, no. 5, 20 March 1980, p. 6.
96. *Schweizerzeit*, no. 8, 29 April 1994, pp. 1f, my translation. It was the heading of a front-page review of G. Pfreundschuh, *Die kulturelle Umweltzerstörung in Politik und Wirtschaft*, Munich: v. Hase & Koehler, 1994.
97. *Schweizerzeit*, no. 9, 8 May 1987, p. 1.
98. *Schweizerzeit*, no. 12, 24 June 1994, p. 2.
99. *Schweizerzeit*, no. 5, 17 March 1995, pp. 1f.
100. *Schweizerzeit*, no. 1, 1 March 1979, pp. 1f.
101. Ibid., p. 1.
102. See also M. Eisenegger and H. Karl, *Die Differenzsemantiken der schweizerischen "Neuen Rechten" und des politischen Konservatismus* (M.A. thesis, University of Zurich, 1995), pp. 196–219.
103. *Schweizerzeit*, no. 8, 14 June 1979, p. 4.
104. *Schweizerzeit*, no. 10, 16 August 1979, p. 4.
105. *Schweizerzeit*, no. 16, 29 September 1995, p. 3.
106. *Schweizerzeit*, no. 23, 28 November 1997, p. 2, my translation. It was a posthumous published excerpt from: W. von Wartburg, *Die europäische Dimension der Schweiz*, Schaffhausen: Novalis, 1996.
107. *Schweizerzeit*, no. 18, 16 October 1992, p. 1, italics in original, my translation.
108. Taken from Ulrich Schlüer's preface in a book compiling articles and

commentaries on the historical debate published in *Schweizerzeit* from 1996 to 1998; see U. Schlüer, *Schweizerische Selbstbehauptung während des Zweiten Weltkriegs: Die militärischen, kriegswirtschaftlichen und humanitären Pfeiler schweizerischer Neutralitätspolitik in der Zeit schwerer Bedrohung*, Schweizerzeit publication series no. 29, Flaach: Schweizerzeit Verlag, 1998, p. 5, my translation.

109. *Schweizerzeit*, no. 5, 16 March 1990, pp. 1f.

110. For an account of the acknowledgment that Graf received in the early 1990s as an alleged expert on asylum, see *Neue Zürcher Zeitung*, 30 December 1999.

111. *Schweizerzeit*, no. 18, 25 October 1996.

112. For example, see *Schweizerzeit*, no. 15, 2 September 1994, p. 6; no. 15, 15 September 1995, p. 1; no. 8, 24 March 2000, p. 6.

113. *Schweizerzeit*, no. 20, 24 November 1995, p. 7, my translation.

114. *Schweizerzeit*, no. 2, 27 January 1995, p. 7.

115. *Schweizerzeit*, 19 August 1994, p. 1, my translation.

116. *Schweizerzeit*, no. 6, 3 March 2000, pp. 5f.

117. Ibid., p. 5, my translation.

118. *Spectrum*, Special Issue 1995, p. 1.

119. *Junge Europäische Schüler- und Studenteninitiative der Schweiz*, published by the Young European Pupils and Students Initiative of Switzerland, 3rd edn (1st edn 1982), Zurich, 1986, p. 11.

120. Zellhofer and Gassner, 'SS und Rosenkranz'.

121. *Criticón*, no. 77, May/June 1983, p. 137.

122. Frischknecht et al., *Die unheimlichen Patrioten*, pp. 692f.

123. For example, see *Allgemeine Schweizerische Militärzeitschrift*, published by the Swiss Officers' Association, no. 12, December 1995.

124. *Junge Europäische Schüler- und Studenteninitiative der Schweiz*, pp. 3ff.

125. Ibid., pp. 17–20.

126. *Spectrum*, no. 6, November 1994, p. 4.

127. For example, see *Spectrum*, no. 5, September/October 1991, pp. 1–4.

128. *Islam im Vormarsch: Gefahr für das Abendland?*, published by the Young European Pupils and Students Initiative of Switzerland, Zurich, n.d. [1996].

129. Niggli and Frischknecht, *Rechte Seilschaften*, p. 367.

130. E. Schreyger, 'Islam im Vormarsch', in *Islam im Vormarsch*, pp. 2f.

131. Rudin Robert, 'Stellt der Islam für das demokratische Zusammenleben eine Gefahr dar?', in *Islam im Vormarsch*, p. 24, my translations.

132. *Einwanderungsland Schweiz – wohin?*, published by the Young European Pupils and Students Initiative of Switzerland, Zurich, n.d. [1995].

133. *20 Jahre Vereinigung Pro Libertate: Rückschau – Ausschau*, Bern, n.d. [1976], p. 1.

134. For this figure, see *Zeit-Fragen*, no. 18, 5 June 2000, p. 3. Other reports talked about 1,200 members and 1,500 sympathizers in 1998; see Niggli and Frischknecht, *Rechte Seilschaften*, p. 527.

135. Frischknecht et al., *Die unheimlichen Patrioten*.

136. For example, see *Volk + Heimat*, no. 17, December 1981, p. 3.

137. *Pro Libertate Mitteilungen*, no. 5, November 1993, p. 3, my translation.

138. *Mitteilungen Pro Libertate*, no. 4, December 1999, p. 5.

139. *Mitteilungen Pro Libertate,* May 1991, p. 7, my translation.
140. *Mitteilungen Pro Libertate,* December 1991, p. 5, my translation.
141. *Mitteilungen Pro Libertate,* no. 3, August 1994, pp. 7f.
142. Frischknecht et al., *Die unheimlichen Patrioten,* pp. 567ff., 574–81; Niggli and Frischknecht, *Rechte Seilschaften,* pp. 555ff., 563ff.
143. T. Kröter, 'Political Correctness: Vom linken Wahn zur rechten Wirklichkeit', *Blätter für deutsche und internationale Politik,* vol. 40, no. 11, 1995; A. Brauner-Orthen, *Die Neue Rechte in Deutschland,* Opladen, 2001, pp. 131–43.
144. P. Ehinger, *Herrschaft durch Sprache: Political Correctness – auch in der Schweiz,* published by Association Media Curiosities and Association Pro Libertate, Pro Libertate publication series no. 3, Zofingen, 1996.
145. *Schweizerzeit,* no. 2, 24 January 1997, p. 4; *Memopress,* vol. 30, no. 4, 1996; supplement, vol. 31, no. 1, 1997, p. 9.
146. *Verfassungsschutzbericht 2001,* published by the Federal Ministry of the Interior, press version, Bonn, Berlin 2001, p. 129.
147. H.-H. Knütter, *Die Faschismus-Keule: Das letzte Aufgebot der deutschen Linken,* Frankfurt, Berlin: Ullstein, 1993.
148. On Jürgen Hatzenbichler, see W. Purtscheller, ed., *Die Ordnung, die sie meinen,* Vienna, 1994; A. Pfahl-Traughber, *"Konservative Revolution" und "Neue Rechte",* Opladen, 1998, pp. 179–84. On Hans-Helmuth Knütter, see S. Salzborn, 'Unterwegs in deutscher Mission. Randnotizen zum Wirken eines rechten Emeritus', in *Alte und Neue Rechte an den Hochschulen,* eds C. Butterwegge and G. Hentges, Münster, 1999; 'Hans-Helmuth Knütter', in *Lexikon des Informationsdienstes gegen Rechtsextremismus (IDGR),* http://lexikon.idgr.de/k/k_n/knuetter-hans-helmuth/knuetter-hans-helmuth.php, retrieved 16 August 2006.
149. Ehinger, *Herrschaft durch Sprache,* p. 6, my translation.
150. Ibid., p. 21, my translation.
151. E. Stäuble, *"… so dass keiner mehr die Sprache des anderen versteht": Politik mit verfälschten Begriffen,* published by Association Media Curiosities, Association Pro Libertate, and Church – Where Now?, Pro Libertate publication series no. 6, n.p. [Bern], 1997.
152. *Neue Zürcher Zeitung,* 12 June 1999, p. 94.
153. 'Claus Nordbruch', in *Lexikon des Informationsdienstes gegen Rechtsextremismus (IDGR),* http://lexikon.idgr.de/n/n_o/nordbruch-claus/nordbruch-claus.php, retrieved 16 August 2006.
154. *The Journal of Historical Review,* no. 4, 1999.
155. *Neue Zürcher Zeitung,* 12 June 1999, p. 94.
156. C. Nordbruch, *Sind Gedanken noch frei? Zensur in Deutschland,* with a afterword by K. Hornung, Munich: Universitas, 1998.
157. *Federal Office for the Protection of the Constitution: Annual Report 1998,* published by the Federal Ministry of the Interior, English version, n.d. [1998], p. 56.
158. I. Efler, 'Bündnispolitik. Der VPM und die "Konservative Revolution"', in *VPM – Die Psychosekte,* eds I. Efler and H. Reile, Reinbek, 1995, p. 94.
159. Press release: VPM, *Der VPM löst sich auf,* 3 March 2002.
160. *Neue Zürcher Zeitung,* 5 March 2002; *St. Galler Tagblatt,* 5 March 2002.
161. *Neue Zürcher Zeitung,* 21 June 2002; *NZZ am Sonntag,* 26 January 2003.

162. H. Stamm, 'Der VPM in der Schweiz. Strammer Marsch an den rechten Flügel', in *VPM – Die Psychosekte*, eds I. Efler and H. Reile, Reinbek, 1995, p. 148.

163. *Positionsbestimmung des VPM*, Zurich, May 1994.

164. *Gestatten....VPM*, published by the Society for Advancing the Psychological Knowledge of Human Nature, Zurich, 1993; see also Efler, 'Bündnispolitik'.

165. Niggli and Frischknecht, *Rechte Seilschaften*, p. 340.

166. I. Efler and H. Reile, eds, *VPM – Die Psychosekte*, Reinbek, 1995.

167. Quoted in: *Tages Anzeiger*, 30 June 1992, my translation.

168. Niggli and Frischknecht, *Rechte Seilschaften*, p. 341.

169. See the 1997 list of publications posted on VPM's official website: http://www.vpm.ch, retrieved 10 December 2000.

170. Niggli and Frischknecht, *Rechte Seilschaften*, p. 342.

171. Ibid., p. 355.

172. For example, see *Die WochenZeitung*, 8 March 1991; *Tages Anzeiger*, 3 March 2000.

173. Stamm, 'Der VPM in der Schweiz', pp. 149–54.

174. Niggli and Frischknecht, *Rechte Seilschaften*, pp. 343–52.

175. The initiative was also supported by some of Switzerland's best-known sportsmen and women. For the list of committee members, see Niggli and Frischknecht, *Rechte Seilschaften*, p. 345.

176. D. Wisler, L. Marquis, and M. Bergman, *Analyse der eidgenössischen Abstimmungen vom 28. September 1997*, Zurich, 1997, p. 25.

177. See the official website of the Berlin section: http://www.gfpm-berlin.de/index.html, retrieved 1 December 2003.

178. Efler, 'Bündnispolitik', pp. 93f.

179. Ibid., pp. 102, 121f.

180. E. Awadalla, '"Sage mir, mit wem du umgehst, und ich sage dir, wer du bist!". Das "Institut zur Förderung der psychologischen Menschenkenntnis"', in *Die Ordnung, die sie meinen*, ed. W. Purtscheller, Vienna, 1994, p. 188; E. Awadalla, 'Eine Seuche, die speziell Lehrer befällt', in *Die Rechte in Bewegung*, ed. W. Purtscheller, Vienna, 1995, p. 162.

181. Awadalla, 'Eine Seuche', pp. 170–76; Niggli and Frischknecht, *Rechte Seilschaften*, pp. 368f.

182. Apart from Peter Lutz, the editor-in-chief until Feburary 2000, the publisher's imprint did not list the members of the editorial staff.

183. *Zeit-Fragen*, no. 4, April 1998, p. 4. The article by Silvio Borner was published with permission of the author as a reprint from *Aargauer Zeitung*, 14 February 1998.

184. The circulation was listed on the paper's front-page. In a large promotional campaign during its first year, free copies of *Zeit-Fragen* were sent unsolicited to professors and public figures in Switzerland.

185. See the official website of *Zeit-Fragen*: http://www.zeit-fragen.ch, accessed 31 August 2008.

186. See the official website of Current Concerns: http://currentconcerns.ch, accessed 31 August 2008.

187. See the official website of *Horizons et débats*: http://www.horizons-et-debats.ch, accessed 31 August 2008.

188. *Zeit-Fragen*, no. 11-12, November/December 1999, p. 11.

189. W. v. Wartburg, *Die europäische Dimension der Schweiz: Zur Geschichte der Schweiz und ihrer Stellung in Europa*, Schaffhausen: Novalis, 1996.

190. *Zeit-Fragen*, no. 19, 13 June 2000, p. 1.

191. For example, see Löwenthal's article of principle in: *Zeit-Fragen*, no. 9, September 1998, p. 3.

192. For example, see *Zeit-Fragen*, no. 9, July/August 1994, p. 11; no. 18, June 1995, p. 9.

193. *Zeit-Fragen*, no. 18, June 1995, pp. 9f.

194. B. Strauss, 'Anschwellender Bockgesang', in *Die selbstbewusste Nation*, eds H. Schwilk and U. Schacht, 3rd edn, Frankfurt: Ullstein, 1996, pp. 10–40.

195. Müller, 'National Identity', p. 1.

196. *Zeit-Fragen*, no. 8, June 1994, p. 8.

197. G. Seidel, 'Culture, Nation and "Race" in the British and French New Right', in *The Ideology of the New Right*, ed. R. Levitas, Cambridge, 1986.

198. *Zeit-Fragen*, no. 1, January 1997, p. 9; no. 2, February 1997, p. 13; no. 3, March 1997, p. 14.

199. After a first conference in Bregenz, Germany, in 1993, subsequent conferences took place in Feldkirch, Austria. Both cities are near the Swiss border.

200. Efler, 'Bündnispolitik', p. 102. For the conference volume, see *Mut zur Erziehung*, Stuttgart: Klett-Cotta, 1979.

201. Member organisations were from Switzerland, Germany, Austria, France, Great Britain, USA, Czech Republic, Hungary and Italy. For the list of member organisations, see the official website of the conference: http://www.mut-zur-ethik.ch, accessed 1 December 2003.

202. See the organiser's note for the 2000 conference, posted on the official website of the conference: http://www.mut-zur-ethik.ch/fdefmze.htm, retrieved 23 August 2000.

203. See the organiser's note on the official website of the conference: http://www.mut-zur-ethik.ch, retrieved 1 December 2003.

204. Efler, 'Bündnispolitik', p. 102.

205. Salzborn, 'Unterwegs in deutscher Mission', p. 215.

206. See also Niggli and Frischknecht, *Rechte Seilschaften*, pp. 371ff.

207. O. Geden, *Rechte Ökologie*, Berlin, 1996; J. Olsen, *Nature and Nationalism*, New York, 1999.

208. T. Jahn and P. Wehling, *Ökologie von rechts*, Frankfurt, 1991, pp. 33ff.

209. H.-G. Betz, *Postmodern Politics in Germany*, New York, 1991, pp. 94f.

210. S. Heim and U. Schaz, *Berechnung und Beschwörung*, Berlin, 1996.

211. M. Feit, *Die "Neue Rechte" in der Bundesrepublik*, Frankfurt, 1987, pp. 151–56.

212. H. Gruhl, *Ein Planet wird geplündert: Die Schreckensbilanz unserer Politik*, Frankfurt: S. Fischer, 1975.

213. Geden, *Rechte Ökologie*, pp. 83–94.

214. E. Gugenberger and R. Schweidlenka, *Mutter Erde, Magie und Politik*, Vienna, 1987, pp. 163ff.; Jahn and Wehling, *Ökologie von rechts*, pp. 29f.

215. V. Wölk, *Natur und Mythos*, Duisburg, 1992, pp. 6–43; Geden, *Rechte Ökologie*, pp. 105–17.

216. K.J. Pitterle, *The Limits of Interdependence*, Ann Arbor, 1981, pp. 1450f.

217. F. Meier, *Grundsätze der Nationalen Aktion gegen Überfremdung von Volk und Heimat*, Winterthur, 1963, reprinted in: M. Ebel and P. Fiala, *Sous le consensus, la xénophobie*, Lausanne, 1983, p. 47.

218. For example, see *Schweizer Naturschutz: Zeitschrift des Schweizerischen Bundes für Naturschutz*, no. 5, April 1969, pp. 27ff.; *Natur und Mensch: Schweizerische Blätter für Natur- und Heimatschutz*, no. 4, July 1970, pp. 145f.

219. F. Walter, *Les Suisses et l'environnement*, Geneva, 1990, pp. 114–44; D. Skenderovic, 'Die Umweltschutzbewegung im Spannungsfeld der 50er Jahre', in *achtung: die 50er Jahre!*, eds J.-D. Blanc and C. Luchsinger, Zurich, 1994.

220. *Schweizer Naturschutz*, no. 5, October 1962, p. 122, my translation.

221. *Schweizer Naturschutz*, no. 4, August 1969, p. 85.

222. S. Süess, "Unsere wunde Welt braucht tapfere Herzen" (M.A. thesis, University of Bern, 1997), pp. 55f.

223. Ibid., pp. 59–62.

224. For example, see *Der Republikaner*, no. 5, 30 March 1972, p. 7.

225. D. Skenderovic, 'Nation, Nationalismus und politische Parteien: Die Schweiz – keine Insel in Europa', in *On European Identity*, ed. C. Szaló, Brno, 1998, p. 163.

226. *Politisches Schwerpunktsprogramm der National Aktion für Volk und Heimat*, March 31, 1973; *Nationale Aktion für Volk und Heimat: Die nationale Marktwirtschaft – das Wirtschaftsprogramm der Nationalen Aktion*, Killwangen, 1977.

227. *Manifest der Schweizerischen Republikanischen Bewegung*, Zurich, n.d. [1971], my translation.

228. P. Fankhauser, "Hört auf, die Erde zu ermorden!" *Valentin Oehen 1970–1980* (M.A. thesis, University of Bern, 1995), pp. 48–55.

229. *Gründungserklärung der Nationalen Aktion*, 27 March, 1971, quoted in: Fankhauser, "Hört auf, die Erde zu ermorden!", p. 49.

230. Fankhauser, "Hört auf, die Erde zu ermorden!", pp. 90–99.

231. *Volk + Heimat*, no. 12, September 1982, pp. 5f, see also Fankhauser, "Hört auf, die Erde zu ermorden!", p. 99.

232. Fankhauser, "Hört auf, die Erde zu ermorden!", p. 62.

233. D. Skenderovic, 'Die Umweltschutzbewegung im Zeichen des Wertewandels', in *Rechte und linke Fundamentalopposition*, U. Altermatt et al., Basel, 1994, p. 43.

234. *Leitlinien der Oekologischen Freiheitlichen Partei der Schweiz (ÖFP)*, adopted by the executive committee on 13 December 1986.

235. *Volk + Heimat*, no. 15, November 1982, p. 4.

236. Jahn and Wehling, *Ökologie von rechts*, p. 35; Eisenegger and Karl, *Differenzsemantiken*, p. 9.

237. Schönekäs, 'Bundesrepublik Deutschland', pp. 329f note 52.

238. Betz, *Postmodern Politics*, pp. 94–97.

239. *Volk + Heimat*, no. 15, November 1982, p. 4, my translation.

240. For example, see *Volk + Heimat*, no. 11, August/September 1985, p. 2.

241. *Volk + Heimat*, no. 17, December 1982, p. 2.

242. *Schweizer Demokrat*, no. 8/9, August/September 1995, pp. 1ff.

243. *Schweizer Demokrat*, no. 2, February 1994, p. 7.

244. Fankhauser, "*Hört auf, die Erde zu ermorden!*", p. 10; *25 Jahre ECOPOP: Für eine ökologisch orientierte Bevölkerungspolitik in der Schweiz*, 2nd rev. edn, Bern, 1996, p. 4.

245. *ECOPOP-Bulletin*, no. 32, February 2001, p. 4.

246. *ECOPOP-Bulletin*, no. 4, October 1991, p. 2; *Der Bund*, 12 June 1982.

247. *Volk + Heimat*, no. 9, November 1971, p. 14.

248. For the membership list of the support committee, see the official website of ECOPOP: http://www.ecopop.ch/index.php?option=com_content&task=view&id=60&Itemid=109, retrieved 31 August 2008.

249. Fankhauser, "*Hört auf, die Erde zu ermorden!*", p. 49.

250. Ibid., pp. 10, 62f.

251. Ibid., p. 92.

252. *Die WochenZeitung*, 26 July 1996; 27 September 1996.

253. See the overview of activities since 1970, posted on the official website of ECOPOP: http://www.ecopop.ch/index.php?option=com_content&task=view&id=62&Itemid=111, retrieved 31 August 2008.

254. For example, see *Neue Zürcher Zeitung*, 2 October 1998.

255. *25 Jahre ECOPOP*.

256. See excerpts from the ECOPOP statutes, posted on the group's official website: http:// http://www.ecopop.ch/index.php?option=com_content&task=view&id=64&Itemid=113, retrieved 31 August 2008.

257. For this line of reasoning, see *20 Jahre ECOPOP: 20 Jahre Misserfolg der Bevölkerungspolitik in der Schweiz*, Bern, 1991; *Wir sind zu viele: Fakten und Argumente zur Überbevölkerung*, published by ECOPOP, Zollikofen, 1996.

258. *20 Jahre ECOPOP*, pp. 6f.

259. For example, see *ECOPOP-Bulletin*, no. 2, January 1991, p. 1; see also ECOPOP's account of a critical article from an opposing point of view in: *Die WochenZeitung*, 27 September 1996.

260. *Thesen zur schweizerischen Migrationspolitik*, published by ECOPOP, Bern, 1992, p. 10, my translation. The brochure was published in a circulation of one thousand.

261. *ECOPOP-Bulletin*, no. 21, June 1997, p. 2.

262. *Thesen zur schweizerischen Migrationspolitik*, p. 16.

263. *20 Jahre ECOPOP*, pp. 15ff.

264. *ECOPOP-Bulletin*, no. 6, June 1992, p. 2.

265. *Wir sind zu viele: Fakten und Argumente zur Überbevölkerung*, p. 24.

266. *ECOPOP-Bulletin*, no. 8, January 1993, p. 1.

267. M. Banks, and A. Gingrich, 'Introduction: Neo-nationalism in Europe and Beyond', in *Neo-nationalism in Europe and Beyond*, eds A. Gingrich, and M. Banks, New York, Oxford, 2006, p. 2.

268. On the neo-nationalism of the New Right in Germany, see Betz, *Postmodern Politics*, pp. 97–106; Venner, *Nationale Identität*.

269. For a general discussion of the concepts and theories of nationalism, see chapter 1.

270. While in German the group calls itself *Aktion für eine unabhängige und neutrale Schweiz* (AUNS), the French name is *Action pour une Suisse indépendante et neutre* (ASIN).

271. K.W. Kobach, *The Referendum*, Aldershot, 1993, pp. 194ff.; Niggli and Frischknecht, *Rechte Seilschaften*, pp. 142–53; C. Moos, *Ja zum Völkerbund – Nein zur UNO*, Zurich, 2001, pp. 117–21.

272. M. Wiget, *Der rasche Aufstieg der rechten Blocker* (M.A. thesis, University of Bern, 2002), pp. 33ff.

273. *AUNS Geschäftsbericht 2003*, published by the CINS office, Bern, n.d. [2004], p. 27.

274. *La Lettre verte*, no. 1, April 1999.

275. Wiget, *Der rasche Aufstieg*, pp. 37f.

276. For these figures, see *AUNS Geschäftsbericht 1997*, published by the CINS office, Bern, n.d. [1998], p. 10; *AUNS Geschäftsbericht 2001*, published by the CINS office, Bern, n.d. [2002], p. 16.

277. See the official website of the CINS: http://www.auns.ch, accessed 31 August 2008.

278. For example, C. Blocher, *Zum Kampf gegen den EWR/EG-Beitritt: Was tun in der Europa-Politik?*, published by the CINS office, Bern, n.d. [1994]; C. Blocher, *Kampf für die schweizerische Unabhängigkeit und Neutralität*, published by the CINS office, Bern, n.d. [1994].

279. C. Blocher, *Die Schweiz und Europa: 5 Jahre nach dem EWR-Nein*, Bern, n.d. [1997].

280. See the interview with Christoph Blocher in: *Facts*, 12 February 1998.

281. For the list of executive committee members between 1986 and 1991, see Niggli and Frischknecht, *Rechte Seilschaften*, p. 146.

282. For a brochure containing endorsements for lists of parties and candidates, see *Eidgenössische Wahlen 1995: Wer tritt für die Unabhängigkeit und Neutralität der Schweiz ein?*, released by the CINS and signed by CINS president Christoph Blocher, Bern, n.d. [1995].

283. Wiget, *Der rasche Aufstieg*, pp. 41–48.

284. See chapter 8 on the CINS membership of Mariette Paschoud, who was involved in negationist activities in the French-speaking part of Switzerland and served as an editor of the counter-revolutionary paper *Le Pamphlet*.

285. *Nouveau Quotidien*, 9 May 1995; *La Liberté*, 15 May 1995.

286. For example, see *Grauer Brief*, no. 35, December 1992, p. 3; *AUNS Geschäftsbericht 1995*, published by the CINS office, Bern, n.d. [1996], pp. 5ff.; *AUNS Geschäftsbericht 1996*, published by the CINS office, Bern, n.d. [1997], pp. 5ff.

287. *AUNS Statuten*, 19 June 1986, revised on 16 June 1987, Art. 2c, my translation.

288. H. Kriesi et al., *Analyse der eidgenössischen Abstimmung vom 6. Dezember 1992*, Adliswil, 1993, pp. 13–22; P. Sciarini and O. Listhaug, *Single Cases or a Unique Pair?*, San Domenico, 1997, p. 14.

289. Moos, *Ja zum Völkerbund*, pp. 121–36.

290. *Grauer Brief*, no. 34, October 1992, p. 1. The term also referred to the conception of 'satellite states' that was used during the Cold War to label countries which were dependent on the Soviet Union.

291. Wiget, *Der rasche Aufstieg*, p. 97.

292. P. Stadler, *Schweizerische Neutralität – eine geschichtliche Würdigung*, published by the CINS office, Bern, n.d. [1996], p. 17.

293. For instance, see Christoph Mörgeli's address to the general meeting on 8 May 1999, translated into English under the title 'The essence of Swiss Neutrality' and posted on CINS's official website: http://www.auns.ch/en/meldungen/990508essence.htm, retrieved 31 August 2008.
294. *Grauer Brief*, no. 25, April 1991, p. 10, my translation.
295. *Grauer Brief*, no. 5, July 1987, p. 5.
296. *Grauer Brief*, no. 5, July 1987, p. 6, my translation.
297. *AUNS Geschäftsbericht 1994*, published by the CINS office, Bern, n.d. [1995], p. 7, my translation.
298. *Grauer Brief*, no. 23, November 1990, p. 7, my translation.
299. *Grauer Brief*, no. 21, July 1990, p. 5, my translation.
300. For a CINS advertisement, see *Neue Zürcher Zeitung*, 31 October/1 November 1992.
301. His publication list includes a widely acknowledged study of Swiss Catholicism in the late nineteenth century and biographies of Johann Heinrich Pestalozzi and the Italian statesman Cavour.
302. P. Stadler, 'Die Schweiz als Exilland', in *In Europas Mitte: Deutschland und seine Nachbarn*, ed. H. Duchhardt, Bonn: Europa Union Verlag, 1988, pp. 101–7.
303. *Schweizerzeit*, no. 4, 6 March 1992, pp. 1f. The long version drew on a speech that Stadler had given on the national holiday, on 1 August 1991, see P. Stadler, 'Eine Schweiz zwischen Mythenjagd, Identitätskrise und Verfremdung', *Schweizer Monatshefte*, no. 9, 1991, pp. 701–14.
304. P. Stadler, *Nachdenken über die Schweiz: Geschehene und geschehende Geschichte. Studien und Stellungnahmen*, Schaffhausen: Novalis, 2001, pp. 226–42.
305. *Schweizerzeit*, no. 4, 6 March 1992, p. 1, italics in original, my translation.
306. P. Stadler, *Schweizerische Neutralität – eine geschichtliche Würdigung*, published by the CINS office, Bern, n.d. [1996], p. 14 note 18.
307. P. Stadler, 'Geschichte, Heimat und Gesellschaft', *Freiburger Geschichtsblätter*, vol. 71, 1994, pp. 7–22, here p. 17, my translation. The article was reissued in his collection of essays: Stadler, *Nachdenken über die Schweiz*, pp. 248–63.
308. O. Spengler, *Jahre der Entscheidung: Erster Teil. Deutschland und die weltgeschichtliche Entwicklung*, Munich: C. H. Beck, 1933. On Oswald Spengler, see S. Breuer, *Anatomie der Konservativen Revolution*, Darmstadt, 1993; K. Lenk, G. Meuter, and H.R. Otten, *Vordenker der Neuen Rechten*, Frankfurt, 1997, pp. 39–58.
309. Pfahl-Traughber, *"Konservative Revolution"*, p. 62.
310. Stadler, 'Geschichte, Heimat', p. 19, my translation.
311. P. Stadler, 'Eigenständige Nation oder Einwanderungsgesellschaft?', *Schweizer Monatshefte*, no. 10, 1992, pp. 781–90; P. Stadler, 'Eigenständige Nation oder Einwanderungsgesellschaft?', in *Einwanderungsland Schweiz – wohin?*, published by the Young European Pupils and Students Initiative of Switzerland, Zurich, n.d. [1995], pp. 19–32.
312. *Der Zürcher Bauer*, 31 July 1992, p. 1, 4; *Schweizerzeit*, no. 4, 3 March 1995, pp. 1f.
313. Stadler, 'Eigenständige Nation', p. 21.
314. Ibid., pp. 26f, my translations.

315. Ibid., p. 29, my translation.

316. For reactions, see *SonntagsZeitung*, 12 May 1996; *Der Bund*, 13 May 1996; *Le Nouveau Quotidien*, May 13 1996. See also the reader's letter by two editorial board members of the Swiss history journal *traverse* and Peter Stadler's reply in: *Neue Zürcher Zeitung*, 31 May 1996; 11 June 1996. A short version of Stadler's essay was published in: *Schweizerzeit*, no. 10, 24 May 1996, pp. 7f.

317. Stadler, *Schweizerische Neutralität*, pp. 14f, my translations.

318. *Neue Zürcher Zeitung*, 4 March 2000, p. 83. The article was reissued in: Stadler, *Nachdenken über die Schweiz*, pp. 157–66.

319. *Neue Zürcher Zeitung*, 4 March 2000, p. 83, my translation.

320. For the list of publications, see the official website of ICE: http://www.uek.ch, accessed 31 August 2008.

321. *Anti-Semitism in Switzerland: A Report on Historical and Current Manifestations with Recommendations for Counter-Measures*, published by the Federal Commission against Racism, Bern, 1998, p. 38.

322. See interview with Jean-Pascal Delamuraz in: *24 heures*, 31 December 1996.

323. *Spectrum*, no. 2, March/April 1997, p. 3.

324. *Mitteilungen Pro Libertate*, no. 1, February 2000, p. 5, my translation.

325. See the critical assessment by G. Kreis, 'Zurück in die Zeit des Zweiten Weltkrieges (Teil II). Zur Bedeutung der 1990er Jahre für den Ausbau der schweizerischen Zeitgeschichte', *Schweizerische Zeitschrift für Geschichte*, vol. 52, no. 4, 2002, p. 510.

326. On these various groups, see Niggli and Frischknecht, *Rechte Seilschaften*, pp. 458–61.

327. For the statutes and goals of the AGG, see the group's official website: http://www.gelebte-geschichte.ch, retrieved 31 August 2008.

328. On Hans-Georg Bandi, see Frischknecht et al., *Die unheimlichen Patrioten*, p. 516.

329. For an example, see *Zeit-Fragen*, no. 45, 18 December 2000, p. 6.

330. *Neue Zürcher Zeitung*, 7 July 2000. Sigmund Widmer also portrayed the IG in an article published by *Pro Libertate Mitteilungen*, no. 3, 2001, p. 2.

331. *Erpresste Schweiz: Zur Auseinandersetzung um die Haltung der Schweiz im Zweiten Weltkrieg und um die Berichte der Bergier-Kommission. Eindrücke und Wertungen von Zeitzeugen*, a joint work of the Study Circle of Lived History (AGG), Stäfa: Th. Gut Verlag, 2002. See also the two-page summary in: *Abendland*, no. 236, March 2002, pp. 3f.

332. *Erpresste Schweiz*, pp. 13, 24, 113.

333. Ibid., p. 25. The letter from the AGG was also published in: *Abendland*, no. 224, October 1998, pp. 1f.

334. Quoted in: *Erpresste Schweiz*, p. 147.

335. *Neue Zürcher Zeitung*, 13 March 2002.

336. E. Leisi, *Freispruch für die Schweiz: Erinnerungen und Dokumente entlasten die Kriegsgeneration*, 3rd edn, Frauenfeld: Huber Verlag, 1997; L. Stamm, *Der Kniefall der Schweiz*, Zofingen: Verlag Zofinger Tagblatt, 1998.

337. For example, see *Abendland*, no. 218, March 1997, pp. 1f. *Tacho*, no. 112, 1998, p. 8.

338. P. Rothenhäusler, ed., *Nun lügen sie wieder,* 2nd edn (1st edn 1999), Stäfa: Rothenhäusler Verlag, 2000.
339. N. Finkelstein, *The Holocaust Industry: Reflections on the Exploitation of Jewish Suffering,* New York: Verso, 2000.
340. Ibid., p. 2, my translation.

7. An Intellectual Elite: The New Right in the French-speaking Part of Switzerland

1. For a study of right-wing intellectuals in the French-speaking part of Switzerland at the turn of the twentieth century, see A. Clavien, *Les helvétistes,* Lausanne, 1994.
2. A. Mattioli, ed., *Intellektuelle von rechts,* Zurich, 1995.
3. A. Clavien, 'Georges Oltramare. Von der Theaterbühne auf die politische Bühne', in *Intellektuelle von rechts,* ed. A. Mattioli, Zurich, 1995. In 1947, the Federal Tribunal sentenced George Oltramare to three years' imprisonment for acts committed against the sovereignty of Switzerland.
4. R. Butikofer, 'Marcel Regamey – eine traditionalistische Sicht des eidgenössischen Bundes', in *Intellektuelle von rechts,* ed. A. Mattioli, Zurich, 1995
5. A. Mattioli, *Zwischen Demokratie und totalitärer Diktatur,* Zurich, 1994.
6. For France, see T. Judt, *Past Imperfect,* Berkeley, 1992.
7. J. Frischknecht et al., *Die unheimlichen Patrioten,* 6th edn, Zurich, 1987, pp. 605–8; C. Cantini, *Les ultras,* Lausanne, 1992, pp. 106ff.
8. J. Kaplan and L. Weinberg, *The Emergence of a Euro-American Radical Right,* New Brunswick, 1998, p. 41; see also S. Anderson and J.L. Anderson, *Inside the League,* New York, 1986.
9. P.-A. Taguieff, *Sur la Nouvelle droite,* Paris, 1994.
10. A. Chebel d'Appollonia, *L'extrême droite en France,* Brussels, 1988, pp. 20–23; M. Winock, 'L'héritage contre-révolutionnaire', in *Histoire de l'extrême droite en France,* ed. M. Winock, Paris, 1993.
11. J.S. McClelland, 'The Reactionary Right: The French Revolution, Charles Maurras and the Action Française', in *The Nature of the Right,* eds R. Eatwell and N. O'Sullivan, Boston, 1989, p. 79.
12. E. Weber, *L'Action française,* Paris, 1985; M. Sutton, *Nationalism, Positivism and Catholicism,* Cambridge, 2002.
13. Chebel d'Appollonia, *L'extrême droite;* H.G. Simmons, *The French National Front,* Boulder 1996, pp. 19f.
14. J.-P. Rioux, 'Des clandestins aux activistes (1945–1965)', in *Histoire de l'extrême droite en France,* ed. M. Winock, Paris, pp. 219f; Simmons, *National Front,* p. 197.
15. On the history of the Vaud League up until the end of the Second World War, see the study by R. Butikofer, *Le refus de la modernité,* Lausanne, 1996.
16. P. Milza, *Les fascismes,* Paris, 1991, p. 370.
17. The 'Petition of the 200' was submitted to the Swiss government in 1940 and demanded, among other things, that the authorities should control and

eventually suppress the criticism of the press which had risen against the regimes of neighbouring countries; see Independent Commission of Experts Switzerland – Second World War, *Switzerland, National Socialism and the Second World War,* Zurich, 2002, p. 80.

18. H.J. Jost, *Die reaktionäre Avantgarde,* Zurich, 1992, pp. 139f.
19. Butikofer, *Le refus,* pp, 130ff., 135f note 47.
20. P. Gilg and E. Gruner, 'Nationale Erneuerungsbewegungen in der Schweiz 1925–1940', *Vierteljahrshefte für Zeitgeschichte,* vol. 14, no. 1, 1966, p. 15.
21. Butikofer, *Le refus,* pp. 457f.
22. For example, see *La Nation,* no. 1423, 11 July 1992, pp. 1f; P. Bolomey and O. Delacrétaz, *EEE: la nébuleuse,* Cahiers de la Renaissance vaudoise no. 124, Lausanne, 1992.
23. J.P. Chenaux, *La presse d'opinion en Suisse Romande ou La bataille des idées,* Lausanne, n.d. [1986], p. 55.
24. The volume was also very positively reviewed by Mariette Paschoud (see next section) in: *Le Pamphlet,* no. 97, September 1980, p. 2.
25. *La Nation,* no. 1468, 31 March 1994, p. 1.
26. *La Nation,* no. 1551, 6 June 1997, p. 1.
27. *La Nation,* no. 1556, 15 August 1997, p. 1.
28. *La Nation,* no. 1694, 29 November 2002, p. 1.
29. O. Delacrétaz, *L'universel enraciné: Remarques sur le racisme et l'antiracisme,* Cahiers de la Renaissance vaudoise no. 125, Lausanne, 1993. See also the enthusiastic endorsement of Delacrétaz's booklet by Mariette Paschoud (see next section) in: *Le Pamphlet,* no. 225, May/June 1993, p. 4.
30. *Bundesblatt,* vol. IV, no. 50, 1993, p. 445.
31. Delacrétaz, *L'universel enraciné,* pp. 11f.
32. Ibid., pp. 8ff.
33. Ibid., pp. 21f.
34. Ibid., p. 34.
35. Ibid., pp. 17f, 23.
36. Ibid., p. 35.
37. Ibid., p. 40.
38. Ibid., pp. 61f, 92. Delacrétaz quoted from a speech that Windisch had delivered in May 1990 and which was eventually translated and published in German as: 'Die Angst vor dem Fremden. Was können wir tun?' in *Die Angst vor dem Fremden: Fremdenangst, Fremdenhass. Hintergründe der Xenophobie – können wir etwas dagegen tun,* SKAF general meeting, 30 May 1990, SKAF Documentation no. 2, July 1990, pp. 32–56.
39. For example, see *La Nation,* no. 1636, 8 September 2000, p. 1.
40. *La Nation,* no. 1631, 30 June 2000, p. 4.
41. For example, see *Contre-poisons,* Cahiers de la Renaissance vaudoise no. 106, Lausanne, 1984, pp. 50ff.
42. Chenaux, *La presse d'opinion,* p. 47; C. Cantini, *Les ultras,* Lausanne, 1992, p. 126. Claude Paschoud and Mariette Pache were married in 1973, and Mariette used the surname of her spouse from that point on.
43. Chenaux, *La presse d'opinion,* p. 55.
44. *Le Pamphlet: Périodique indépendant,* no. 260, December 1996, p. 1.

45. http://www.pradoz.com/pamphlet/index.html, accessed 31 August 2008.
46. *Le Pamphlet,* no. 1, 30 November 1970, p. 1. See also the interview with Mariette Paschoud in: *Die WochenZeitung,* 22 August 1986.
47. See also U. Altermatt and D. Skenderovic, 'Die extreme Rechte: Organisationen, Personen und Entwicklungen in den achtziger und neunziger Jahren', in *Rechtsextremismus in der Schweiz,* eds. U. Altermatt and H. Kriesi, Zurich, 1995, p. 69; J. Tschirren, *Negationistische Propaganda in der Schweiz 1946–1994* (M.A. thesis, University of Fribourg, 1999), pp. 107–14.
48. *Bulletin de l'Association des amis de Robert Brasillach,* no. 63, 5 December 1973, p. 8.
49. Altermatt and Skenderovic, 'Die extreme Rechte', p. 68.
50. *La Liberté,* 2/3 July 1988; *Le Matin,* 3 July 1988; *Tages Anzeiger,* 5 July 1988; *L'Hebdo,* 7 July 1988.
51. Tschirren, *Negationistische Propaganda,* pp. 112f.
52. Altermatt and Skenderovic, 'Die extreme Rechte', p. 68; Tschirren, *Negationistische Propaganda,* pp. 109–12.
53. Federal Tribunal decision, 6S.199/194, 17 February 1995, in: *Neue Zürcher Zeitung,* 18 May 1995.
54. M. de Preux, *Une Suisse totalitaire,* Lausanne: L'Age d'Homme, 1984. The postscript was written by Eric Werner.
55. For Mayor's editorial, see *Nouvelle Revue de Lausanne,* 12 February 1981; see also Tschirren, *Negationistische Propaganda,* p. 113.
56. Cantini, *Les ultras,* p. 81; U. Fischer, *Gaston-Armand Amaudruz* (M.A. thesis, University of Fribourg, 1999), p. 37.
57. E. Werner and J.-P. Chenaux, *Coupable d'être soupçonné: Claude Paschoud devant ses "juges",* Lausanne: Les Dossiers de la communication, 1988.
58. *Le Pamphlet,* no. 200, December 1990, p. 4.
59. *Le Pamphlet,* no. 240, December 1994, p. 4, my translation.
60. *Le Pamphlet,* no. 258, October 1996, p. 3.
61. *Le Pamphlet,* no. 214, April 1992, p. 1; no. 271, January 1998, p. 3.
62. For example, see *Le Pamphlet,* no. 167, September 1987, pp. 1, 3.
63. *Le Pamphlet,* no. 151, January 1986, p. 1, my translation.
64. *Le Pamphlet,* no. 266, June 1997, p. 3.
65. *Le Pamphlet,* no. 183, March 1989, p. 4.
66. *Le Pamphlet,* no. 204, April 1991, p. 3.
67. For example, see *Le Pamphlet,* no. 180, December 1988, p. 2; no. 246, August 1995, p. 3; no. 282, February 1999, p. 2.
68. *Le Pamphlet,* no. 162, March 1987, p. 4, my translation.
69. *Le Pamphlet,* no. 180, December 1988, p. 2.
70. *Le Pamphlet,* no. 208, October 1991, p. 3.
71. *Le Pamphlet,* no. 103, March 1981, p. 4, my translation.
72. *Le Pamphlet,* no. 260, December 1996, pp. 3f.
73. *Le Pamphlet,* no. 113, March 1982, p. 2, my translation.
74. *Le Pamphlet,* no. 262, February 1997, p. 4, my translation.
75. For example, see *Le Pamphlet,* no. 122, February 1983, p. 1; no. 175, May 1988, p. 1; no. 240, December 1994, p. 4.
76. *Le Pamphlet,* no. 277, September 1998, p. 4.

77. *Le Pamphlet*, no. 163, April 1987, p. 2, my translation. In an editorial, the paper dissociated itself from de Preux's statements; see *Le Pamphlet*, no. 164, May 1987, p. 1.

78. *Le Pamphlet*, no. 245, May/June/July, 1995, p. 3; no. 246, August 1995, p. 3.

79. *Le Pamphlet*, no. 256, June 1996, p. 3.

80. *Le Pamphlet*, no. 110, December 1981, p. 4. On Gustave Thibon, see J.-Y. Camus and R. Monzat, *Les droites nationales et radicales en France*, Lyon, 1992, p. 159.

81. *Le Pamphlet*, no. 149, November 1985, p. 1.

82. *Le Pamphlet*, no. 237, September 1994, pp. 1, 4

83. *Le Pamphlet*, no. 70, December 1977, p. 1.

84. *Le Pamphlet*, no. 211, January 1992, p. 4.

85. *Le Pamphlet*, no. 248 October 1995, pp. 1f.

86. Since the present study focuses on political and ideological aspects, limited treatment will be given to the theological, canonical and ecclesiastic questions of integrism.

87. E. Poulat, *Intégrisme et catholicisme intégral*, Tournai, 1969, p. 9.

88. X. Ternisien, *L'extrême droite et l'église*, Paris, 1997.

89. Winock, 'L'héritage', p. 47; Ternisien, *L'extrême droite*, p. 164.

90. E. Borne, 'Le catholicisme', in *Forces religieuses et attitudes politiques dans la France contemporaine*, ed. R. Rémond, Paris, 1965, p. 14; cited (and translated) by by Simmons, *National Front*, p. 200.

91. Poulat, *Intégrisme*.

92. Winock,'L'héritage', pp. 143f.

93. Camus and Monzat, *Les droites nationales*, pp. 64ff., 192–95; Rioux, 'Des clandestins'.

94. J.-Y. Camus, 'Intégrisme catholique et extrême droite en France. Le parti de la contre-révolution (1945–1988)', *Lignes*, no. 4, 1988, p. 76; Camus and Monzat, *Les droites nationales*, pp. 12f.

95. Camus, 'Intégrisme catholique'.

96. On Bernard Antony, see Camus and Monzat, *Les droites nationales*, pp. 63f, 476f; J.-Y. Camus, 'La structure du "camp national" en France: la périphérie militante et organisationnelle du Front national et du Mouvement national républicain', in *Les croisés de la société fermée*, ed. P. Perrineau, Paris, 2001, p. 204. In an article published by *Le Pamphlet*, Michel de Preux referred to Antony as his friend from the political bureau of the National Front; see *Le Pamphlet*, no. 263, March 1997, p. 3.

97. Camus, 'Intégrisme catholique', p. 82; M. Minkenberg, *Die neue radikale Rechte im Vergleich*, Opladen, 1998, p. 283.

98. On the history of the SSPX, see also A. Schifferle, *Was will Lefebvre eigentlich?*, Fribourg, 1989.

99. For Lefebvre's biography, see A. Schifferle, *Marcel Lefebvre – Ärgernis und Besinnung*, Kevelaer, 1983.

100. See the official website of the Priestly Society of Saint Pius X: http://www.fsspx.org, retrieved 15 October 2003.

101. For these figures, see Chebel d'Appollonia, *L'extrême droite*, p. 359; E. D'Alessio, 'Switzerland', in *Extremism in Europe*, ed. J.-Y. Camus, Paris, 1997, p. 349; Minkenberg, *Die neue radikale Rechte*, p. 283.

102. Declaration of Principles, posted on the official English website of the SSPX, http://www.fsspx.org/eng/ index.html, retrieved 15 October 2003.

103. I. Raboud, *Temps nouveaux, vents contraires*, Sierre, 1992, pp. 121f.

104. Camus, 'La structure', pp. 208f.

105. Simmons, *National Front*, p. 200.

106. See the report by the integrist periodical *Journal Controverses*, no. 20, July 1990, pp. 1, 7.

107. Quoted in: Ternisien, *L'extrême droite*, pp. 188f, my translation; see also Camus, 'La structure', p. 205.

108. Quoted in: Ternisien, *L'extrême droite*, p. 189, my translation.

109. Camus, 'Intégrisme catholique', p. 82; Raboud, *Temps nouveaux*, pp. 121f; D'Alessio, 'Switzerland', p. 349.

110. *Das Magazin*, no. 43, 30 October 1993, pp. 18–22.

111. On this support from prominent political figures, see Frischknecht et al., *Die unheimlichen Patrioten*, pp. 324f; Raboud, *Temps nouveaux*; D'Alessio, 'Switzerland', pp. 348ff., 352f note 17.

112. *Le Pamphlet*, no. 154, April 1986, p. 2. See also the obituary for Lovey in: *Journal Controverses*, no. 10, September 1989, p. 5.

113. Raboud, *Temps nouveaux*, p. 217.

114. Cantini, *Les ultras*, pp. 116f; Raboud, *Temps nouveaux*, p. 221.

115. Raboud, *Temps nouveaux*, pp. 222–25.

116. *Le Nouvelliste et Feuille d'Avis du Valais*, 28 January 1985, pp. 13ff.

117. Raboud, *Temps nouveaux*, pp. 197–202.

118. *Le Nouvelliste et Feuille d'Avis du Valais*, 28 January 1985, p. 13.

119. D'Alessio, 'Switzerland', pp. 352f note 17; Raboud, *Temps nouveaux*, p. 217.

120. Raboud, *Temps nouveaux*, p. 218.

121. Cantini, *Les ultras*, p. 117.

122. D'Alessio, 'Switzerland', p. 349.

123. For membership numbers, see *Neue Zürcher Zeitung*, 25 November 1997.

124. See Germanier's letter to the editor in: *Le Nouvelliste et Feuille d'Avis du Valais*, 12/13 April 1997.

125. *Statuts du Mouvement chrétien-conservateur valaisan*, 15 November 1995, article 1.

126. *Axes de son engagement politique*, program of the Valais Christian Conservative Movement, October 1997.

127. *Tages Anzeiger*, 25 November 1997; *Neue Zürcher Zeitung*, 25 November 1997; 12 May 1998; Niggli and Frischknecht, *Rechte Seilschaften*, p. 591.

128. *Neue Zürcher Zeitung*, 12 May 1998; 8 October 1999.

129. On the journal's unconditional support for Lefebvre and the Priestly Society of Saint Pius X, see the editorial in the first issue: *Journal Controverses*, no. 0, September 1988, p. 1.

130. On the subject of Bertinat's admiration for Marcel Lefebvre, see M. Simoulin and E. Bertinat, *In memoriam: Monseigneur Marcel Lefebvre (30 juin 1988 – 25 mars 1991 – 2 avril 1991)*, Les cahiers du journal Controverses, no. 1, September 1991.

131. See the personal website of Eric Bertinat: http://www.ericbertinat.ch, retrieved 31 August 2008; see also *Dimanche.ch*, 13 February 2000; *Die Wochen-Zeitung*, 17 February 2000.

132. For example, see the full-page advertisement in: *Journal Controverses*, no. 23, October 1990, p. 12.

133. Simmons, *National Front*, p. 125; R. Eatwell, *Fascism*, New York, 1997, pp. 315–18.

134. *Journal Controverses*, no. 8, May/June 1989, p. 10.

135. See also Camus and Monzat, *Les droites nationales*, p. 171.

136. On Suzanne Labin, see also Frischknecht et al., *Die unheimlichen Patrioten*, pp. 126–29; Cantini, *Les ultras*, p. 107.

137. Y. Chiron, *La vie de Charles Maurras*, Paris: Perrin, 1991. Chiron's book was very favourably reviewed by Anne Bernet in: *Journal Controverses*, no. 34, July 1991, p. 6.

138. For examples, see *Journal Controverses*, no. 96, February 1996, p. 4; no. 99, May 1996, p. 4.

139. *Journal Controverses*, no. 33, June 1991, p. 5; no. 33, June 1991, p. 2.

140. *Journal Controverses*, no. 14, June 1990, p. 1.

141. *Journal Controverses*, no. 34, July 1991, p. 6, my translation.

142. *Journal Controverses*, no. 72, March 1994, p. 3.

143. *Journal Controverses*, no. 4, June 1989, p. 1, my translation. On the monthly paper *L'Anti-89*, see Winock, 'L'héritage', pp. 17f.

144. *Journal Controverses*, no. 36, September, 1991, pp. 2f, quote from p. 3, my translation.

145. *Journal Controverses*, no. 16, March 1990, p. 6.

146. *Journal Controverses*, no. 50, September 1992, p. 1.

147. *Journal Controverses*, no. 43, March 1992, p. 7, my translation.

148. *Journal Controverses*, no. 80, September 1994, p. 5.

149. A.-M. Duranton-Crabol, *Visages de la Nouvelle droite*, Paris, 1988; Taguieff, *Nouvelle droite*.

150. P.-A. Taguieff, 'From Race to Culture: The New Right's View of European Identity', *Telos*, no. 98/99, 1993/94, pp. 104–10.

151. M. Olender, 'Georges Dumézil et les usages "politiques" de la préhistoire indo-européenne', in *Les Grecs, les Romains et nous*, ed. R.-P. Droit, Paris, 1991; Taguieff, *Nouvelle droite*, pp. 174–78.

152. T. Sheehan, 'Myth and Violence: The Fascism of Julius Evola and Alain de Benoist', *Social Research*, vol. 48, no. 1, 1981.

153. Quoted in: ibid., p. 47.

154. Eatwell, *Fascism*, p. 254. See J. Evola, *Sintesi di dottrina della razza*, Milan: Hoepli, 1941.

155. Sheehan, 'Myth and Violence', p. 51.

156. Eatwell, *Fascism*, pp. 314f; A. Pfahl-Traughber, *"Konservative Revolution" und "Neue Rechte"*, Opladen, 1998, pp. 117–22.

157. P.-A. Taguieff, *La force du préjugé*, Paris, 1988.
158. R. Wolin, 'Designer Fascism', in *Fascism's Return*, ed. R.J. Golsan, Lincoln, 1998, p. 55.
159. M. Christadler, 'Die "Nouvelle Droite" in Frankreich', in *Neokonservative und "Neue Rechte"*, ed. I. Fetscher, Munich, 1983; Duranton-Crabol, *Visages;* Taguieff, *Nouvelle droite*.
160. On the periodicals of GRECE, see O. Corpet, 'La revue', in *Histoires des droites en France*, ed. J.-F. Sirinelli, 3 vols, Paris, 1992, vol. 2, pp. 201–12.
161. Duranton-Crabol, *Visages*, pp. 186–97; W. Kowalsky, *Kulturevolution?*, Opladen, 1991, pp. 123ff.
162. A. de Benoist, *Vu de droite: Anthologie critique des idées contemporaines*, Paris: Copernic, 1977.
163. Taguieff, *Nouvelle droite*, pp. 109–336.
164. See also Altermatt and Skenderovic, 'Die extreme Rechte', pp. 34–46; U. Altermatt and D. Skenderovic, 'Die Nouvelle droite in Frankreich und der Westschweiz', *Universitas Friburgensis*, no. 2, 1996.
165. Altermatt and Skenderovic, 'Die extreme Rechte', p. 36.
166. According to the circle's requirements, an active member was supposed to pay a membership fee equal to five per cent of his or her annual income; see *Membership form Forces nouvelles*, n.d. [1979].
167. On this early activity of Pascal Junod, see the interview with Daniel Cologne in: *Vox NR com*, 12 July 2002, http://www.voxnr.com/cogit_content/documents/Lesnon-conformistesdesanne.shtml, retrieved 30 September 2003.
168. Chenaux, *La presse d'opinion*, p. 54; Altermatt and Skenderovic, 'Die extreme Rechte', p. 39.
169. *Elemente: Die Zeitschrift der Neuen Kultur*, no. 1, winter 1985/86, advertising brochure, n.d. [1985].
170. *Orientations: Revue culturelle pluridisciplinaire*, no. 8, November/December 1986.
171. On Pascal Junod's involvement with the SVP, see *Tages Anzeiger*, 2 September 1999; 13 September 1999; *Le Temps*, 3 September 1999; 13 September 1999; *Neue Zürcher Zeitung*, 13 September 1999; 1 October 1999; 24 December 1999.
172. *Manifeste des Forces nouvelles*, Geneva, n.d. [1979]; *Principes politiques des Forces nouvelles*, n.d. [1979].
173. *Manifeste des Forces nouvelles*, p. 2, my translation.
174. Ibid., p. 7, my translations.
175. Ibid., p. 3, my translation.
176. Ibid., p. 6.
177. Ibid., 5, my translation.
178. On the Thule Circle, see also Altermatt and Skenderovic, 'Die extreme Rechte', pp. 37–40.
179. R. Fromm and B. Kernbach, *... und morgen die ganze Welt?*, Marburg, 1994, p. 315.
180. M. Feit, *Die "Neue Rechte" in der Bundesrepublik*, Frankfurt, 1987, pp. 77–82; I. Weber, *Nation, Staat und Elite*, Cologne, 1997, pp. 35ff.
181. R. Sünner, *Schwarze Sonne*, Freiburg, 1999, pp. 28–32.
182. Cantini, *Les ultras*, p. 115. For information on Jean-François Mayer, see

Camus and Monzat, *Les droites nationales*, pp. 360f; *Carrefour*, December 1997; *Tages Anzeiger*, 4 February 1997.

183. R. Monzat, *Enquêtes sur la droite extrême*, Paris, 1992, p. 171.

184. See the statement from a promotion letter released by the magazine *Elemente* and quoted in: A. Lange, *Was die Rechten lesen*, Munich 1993, p. 91.

185. Until the late 1980s, the mail order bulletin operated under the name of *Thulé. Centre national de la pensée européenne*. Thereafter, the bulletin carried the name *Diffusion Thulé*.

186. This selection of authors and publications is based on a survey of ten issues of the Thule Circle's mail order bulletin released between January 1988 and September 1998. Some of the publications that were offered were presented with a short comment or table of contents.

187. Altermatt and Skenderovic, 'Die extreme Rechte', pp. 39f.

188. Monzat, *Enquêtes*, pp. 222f.

189. Program brochure: '*Lugnasad 1988, 2e Fête Communautaire Grande-Europe'*, organised by the Thule Circle on 29–31 July 1988. The four-page (A5 format) program was published in four languages, French, German, English and Italian.

190. *24 heures*, 5 August 1988; *La Suisse*, 6 August 1988; *Jüdische Rundschau*, 11 August 1988.

191. Invitation flyer: '*Conférence. Jean-Marc Vivenza: Futurisme et Fascisme'*, organised by the Thule Circle in Geneva on 5 October 1996.

192. On the Proudhon Circle, see also Altermatt and Skenderovic, 'Die extreme Rechte', pp. 40ff.

193. For this figure, see *Die WochenZeitung*, 13 January 1989.

194. Altermatt and Skenderovic, 'Die extreme Rechte', p. 40.

195. Z. Sternhell, *Ni droite, ni gauche*, new edn, Brussels, 1987, p. 39; Milza, *Les fascismes*, pp. 255f.

196. The programmatic text was part of the membership form '*Pourquoi un Cercle Proudhon circle?'*, issued by the Proudhon Circle, Geneva, n.d.

197. Advertising flyer: '*1er Colloque Européen pour la Nouvelle Culture. Europe: Le droit à l'identité'*, organised by the Proudhon Circle in Geneva on 3 March 1985.

198. For a brief report on the conference, see *Le Pamphlet*, no. 149, November 1985, p. 1.

199. *Die WochenZeitung*, January 13, 1989; see also Altermatt and Skenderovic, 'Die extreme Rechte', p. 42.

200. M. Olender, 'Indogermanische Urgeschichte und "Nouvelle Droite"', in *Rechtsextremismus*, eds R. Faber, H. Funke, and G. Schoenberner, Berlin, 1995.

201. *Die WochenZeitung*, 13 January 1989; *Le Courrier*, 17 January 1990.

202. Invitation flyer: '*Conférence-débat. Bernard Notin: Police de la pensée. Le retour de l'intolérance!'*, organised by the Proudhon Circle in Geneva on 22 February 1997.

203. *Le Monde*, 28/29 January 1990; 18/19 February 1990; see also V. Igounet, *Histoire du négationnisme en France*, Paris, 2000, pp. 428–34.

204. Invitation flyer: '*Conférence-débat. Pierre Vial: France: où va la droite nationale?'*, organised by the Proudhon Circle on 12 February 1999.

205. *Le Monde*, 3/4 May 1998.
206. R. Garaudy, *Mythes fondateurs de la politique israélienne*, Paris: La Vieille Taupe, 1995. See Invitation flyer: *'Dîner-conférence. Roger Garaudy: O.T.A.N.: 50 ans de crimes. Serbie, une guerre américaine en Europe!'*, organised by the Proudhon Circle on 28 May 1999.
207. The Swiss address of European Synergies indicated the same P.O. Box as for Proudhon Circle; see Membership bulletin, *Hommes et femmes d'Europe! Rejoignez Synergies Européennes*, n.d.
208. Pfahl-Traughber, "*Konservative Revolution*", pp. 150ff.
209. Program brochure: *'Colloque. Julius Evola 1898–1998: Éveil, destin et expériences de terres spirituelles'*, organised in Geneva on 14 November 1998, by European Synergies, in collaboration with the publisher L'Age d'Homme and the bookstores Delphica (Geneva) and La Librairie de la Cathédrale (Amneville, France).
210 J. Evola, *Révolte contre le monde moderne*, Lausanne: L'Age d'Homme, 1991. For the original edition, see J. Evola, *Rivolta contro il mondo moderno*, Milan: Hoepli, 1934.
211. Evola, *Révolte*, pp. 431–55.
212. J. Evola, *Masques et visages du spiritualisme contemporain*, Puiseaux: Éditions Pardès, 1991, pp. 239–67.
213. *Le Courrier*, 17 January 1990. The Hagal Cultural Circle was closely associated with the Association of the Friends of Robert Brasillach, see *Bulletin de l'Association des amis de Robert Brasillach*, no. 101, March 1993, p. 2.
214. Invitation flyer: *'Cocktail d'inauguration du Centre librairie Excalibur'*, organised by the Hagal Cultural Circle and the Association of the Friends of Robert Brasillach in Geneva on 18 December 1993.
215. Camus and Monzat, *Les droites nationales*, p. 255.
216. Altermatt and Skenderovic, 'Die extreme Rechte', p. 43.
217. *Program Excalibur: Mars 1994*, Geneva, n.d. [1994].
218. *Le Nouveau Quotidien*, 8 April 1994; 9/10 April 1994; *Tribune de Genève*, 9/10 April 1994; *Libération*, 14 April 1994.
219. See Junod's two letters to the editor in: *Le Nouveau Quotidien*, 13 April 1994; *Tribune de Genève*, 14 April 1994.
220. *Bulletin de l'Association des amis de Robert Brasillach*, no. 104, Spring 1995, p. 15, my translation.
221. *24 heures*, 14 June 1996; *Le Nouveau Quotidien*, 17 June 1996.
222. U. Altermatt and D. Skenderovic, 'Switzerland', in *Extremism in Europe, 1998 Survey*, ed. J.-Y. Camus, Paris, 1998, p. 345; Tschirren, *Negationistische Propaganda*, pp. 90–95.
223. Federal Tribunal decision 6S.810-813/1999, 10 August 1999, in *BGE* 125 IV, pp. 206–12; see also *Le Temps*, 8 February 2000.
224. *Le Temps*, 3 February 2000.
225. On Vladimir Dimitrijević, see his autobiography in the form of an interview: V. Dimitrijević, *Personne déplacé: Entretiens avec Jean-Louis Kuffer*, Lausanne: Édition Pierre-Marcel Favre, 1986.
226. See the official website of L'Age d'Homme: http://www.agedhomme.com, accessed 31 August 2008.

227. Y. Laplace, *L'âge d'homme en Bosnie*, Lausanne, 1997.

228. See the website of the Society of Friends of Pierre Gripari: http://www.gripari.net, retrieved 31 April 2003.

229. Camus and Monzat, *Les droites nationales*, p. 395.

230. Ibid., p. 159.

231. See the program of the 35th GRECE colloquium, posted on GRECE's official website: http://www.grece-fr.net/activites/colloque2002.htm, retrieved 30 September 2003.

232. On the journal *Politica Hermetica*, see also Camus and Monzat, *Les droites nationales*, pp. 360f. The Association Politica Hermetica had already been founded in 1984.

233. This is noted, for example, in the following issue: *René Guénon, lectures et enjeux*, Politica Hermetica, no. 16, Paris: Éditions L'Age d'Homme, 2002.

234. For the declaration, see *Métaphysique et politique, Guénon et Evola*, Politica Hermetica, no. 1, Paris: Éditions L'Age d'Homme, 1987, pp. 3f.

235. Ibid., pp. 119–28.

236. *Les contrées secrètes*, Politica Hermetica, no. 12, Paris: L'Age d'Homme, 1998, pp. 271–78.

237. Ibid., pp. 261–70.

238. T. Molnar, *L'Américanologie: Triomphe d'un modèle planétaire?*, Lausanne: L'Age d'Homme, 1991.

239. Duranton-Crabol, *Visages*, pp. 124, 165, 167; Camus and Monzat, *Les droites nationales*, pp. 41, 469

240. A. de Benoist, *Dernière année: Notes pour conclure le siècle*, Lausanne: L'Age d'Homme, 2001; A. de Benoist, *Critiques – Théoriques*, Lausanne: L'Age d'Homme, 2003.

241. A. Guyot-Jeannin, ed., *Aux sources de la droite: Pour en finir avec les clichés*, Lausanne: L'Age d'Homme, 2000.

242. A. Guyot-Jeannin, ed, *Julius Evola*, Lausanne: L'Age d'Homme, 1997.

243. Guyot-Jeannin, *Aux sources*, p. 16.

244. Chenaux, *La presse d'opinion*, pp. 54f.

245. Eric Werner's first book, *De la Violence au totalitarisme* (From Violence to Totalitarianism), was published in 1972 by the renowned French publisher Éditions Calmann-Lévy.

246. E. Werner, *De l'extermination*, Lausanne: Éditions Thael, 1993.

247. E. Werner, *L'avant-guerre civile*, Lausanne: L'Age d'Homme, 1998, pp. 59–64. See also Werner's brochure *L'immigration en face* (Facing Immigration; 1987), which was fuelled by xenophobic sentiments.

248. *Le Vigilant*, no. 203, July/August 1985, p. 3; no. 225, October 1987, p. 8.

249. E. Werner *Ne dites surtout pas que je doute, on finirait par le croire… A propos de l'"affaire Paschoud"*, Lausanne: Éditions Thael, 1988, pp. 85f. On Werner's links with negationism in the French-speaking regions of Switzerland, see Tschirren, *Negationistische Propaganda*, pp. 113f.

250. See the publisher's note in: R. Berthod, *Rembarre: Billets 1978–1990*, Lausanne: L'Age d'Homme, 1992, p. 8.

251. Ibid., p. 30.

252. On the Association of the Friends of Robert Brasillach, see also Altermatt and Skenderovic, 'Die extreme Rechte', pp. 43–46, 93. In 1992, the ARB had moved its address from Lausanne to Geneva; see *Bulletin de l'Association des amis de Robert Brasillach,* no. 101, March 1993, p. 1.

253. *Bulletin de l'Association des amis de Robert Brasillach,* no. 104, Spring 1995, p. 19.

254. A. Kaplan, *The Collaborator,* Chicago, 2001, p. 233.

255. Judt, *Past Imperfect,* p. 65.

256. Kaplan, *The Collaborator,* p. 13.

257. Ibid., p. x. On the newspaper *Je suis partout,* see also J.-P. Azéma, 'Vichy', *Histoire de l'extrême droite en France,* ed. M. Winock, Paris, 1993, p. 207.

258. Kaplan, *The Collaborator,* p. 27. See R. Brasillach, *Les sept couleurs,* Paris: Plon, 1939.

259. Interestingly enough, in interviews with two mainstream French-language newspapers of Switzerland in 1974, Jacques Isorni publicly demanded a retrial of Pétain; see *La Suisse,* 6 October 1974; *Construire,* 30 October 1974.

260. For a detailed historical reconstruction of Brasillach's court trial in January 1945, see Kaplan, *The Collaborator,* pp. 143–88.

261. Ibid., p. xiv.

262. I.R. Barnes, 'Antisemitic Europe and the "Third Way": The Ideas of Maurice Bardèche', *Patterns of Prejudice,* vol. 34, no. 2, 2000, p. 60.

263. M. Bardèche and R. Brasillach, *Histoire du cinema,* Paris: Denoël, 1935; *Histoire de la guerre d'Espagne,* Paris: Plon, 1939.

264. Barnes, 'Antisemitic Europe', p. 59.

265. M. Abramowicz, *Extrême-droite et antisémitisme en Belgique de 1945 à nos jours,* Brussels, 1993, p. 125; Fromm and Kernbach, *... und morgen die ganze Welt?,* p. 274. As a recent historical study has revealed, Switzerland served in the immediate postwar years as a safe haven for a number of former fascists, Nazis and collaborators; L. van Dongen, *Un purgatoire très discret,* Paris, 2008.

266. The ARB has never issued official membership figures. For the year 1985, the Belgian journalist Manuel Abramowicz mentioned seven hundred and fifty members. In his report on the ARB annual meeting in 1988, Roger Pache, an ARB member and journalist with the Swiss paper *Journal de Payerne,* wrote that the circle had more than seven hundred members; see Abramowicz, *Extrême-droite,* p. 125; *Journal de Payerne,* 10 May 1988.

267. *A propos de Robert Brasillach,* report issued by the press office of the Swiss Federation of Jewish Communities (JUNA) on 27 November 1957.

268. M. Syfrig and C. Defaye, *L'extrême-droite en Suisse,* Lausanne, 1967, p. 10; S. Niklaus, *Wir nicht?,* Basel, 1969, p. 17.

269. *Bulletin de l'Association des amis de Robert Brasillach,* no. 98, March 1990, p. 2.

270. Camus and Monzat, *Les droites nationales,* p. 397.

271. Cantini, *Les ultras,* p. 111; Butikofer, *Le refus,* p. 248.

272. Altermatt and Skenderovic, 'Die extreme Rechte', p. 45. See M. Bardèche, *Nuremberg – ou la Terre promise,* Paris: Les Sept Couleurs, 1948; F. Duprat, *L'Ascension du M.S.I. (Movimento sociale italiano),* Paris: Les Sept Couleurs, 1972.

273. *Bulletin de l'Association des amis de Robert Brasillach*, no. 98, March 1990, pp. 1ff.
274. *Bulletin de l'Association des amis de Robert Brasillach*, no. 101, March 1993, p. 1, my translation.
275. Cantini, *Les ultras*, p. 111.
276. Altermatt and Skenderovic, 'Die extreme Rechte', p. 45.
277. *A propos de Robert Brasillach*, report issued by the press office of the Swiss Federation of Jewish Communities (JUNA) on 27 November 1957, p. 2.
278. *Bulletin de l'Association des amis de Robert Brasillach*, no. 59, 1 October 1972, p. 6.
279. *Hommages à Robert Brasillach*, Cahiers des amis de Robert Brasillach, no. 11/12, 6 February 1965, Lausanne.
280. *Cahiers des amis de Robert Brasillach*, no. 40, 1995, pp. 7–12.
281. *Cahiers des amis de Robert Brasillach*, no. 44/45, 1999/2000, 334–366.
282. Kaplan, *The Collaborator*, p. xiv. See R. Brasillach, *Œuvres complètes*, ed. M. Bardèche, 12 vol., Paris: Club de l'Honnête homme, 1963-66.
283. For example, see ibid., pp. 37–40.
284. *Bulletin de l'Association des amis de Robert Brasillach*, no. 2, 15 October 1958, p. 1.
285. *Bulletin de l'Association des amis de Robert Brasillach*, no. 58, 20 June 1972, p. 4.
286. *Bulletin de l'Association des amis de Robert Brasillach*, no. 63, 5 December 1973, p. 6.
287. For example, see *Bulletin de l'Association des amis de Robert Brasillach*, no. 103, autumn 1994, p. 6.
288. Altermatt and Skenderovic, 'Die extreme Rechte', p. 45.
289. http://www.brasillach.org/soutiens.htm, retrieved 31 August 2008.
290. For information on Swiss members of the ARB, see also Cantini, *Les ultras*, p. 111; Niklaus, *Wir nicht?*, p. 17.
291. *Bulletin de l'Association des amis de Robert Brasillach*, no. 67, 6 February 1975, p. 15.
292. For examples, see *Journal de Payerne*, 10 May 1988; 9 June 1989.
293. R. Pache, *Rencontres et Souvenirs*, Volumes 1, 2, Payerne: Éditions du Comte-Verte, 1985, 1993.
294. Fischer, *Gaston-Armand Amaudruz*, p. 158 note 761.

8. At the Margins of Society and Politics: The Subculture of the Extreme Right

1. On the concept of groupuscule, see R. Griffin, 'From Slim Mould to Rhizome: An Introduction to the Groupuscular Right', *Patterns of Prejudice*, vol. 37, no. 1, 2003.
2. J. Kaplan and L. Weinberg, *The Emergence of a Euro-American Radical Right*, New Brunswick, 1998, p. 53. The figures are based on estimates provided by the European Centre for Research and Action on Racism and Antisemitism (*Centre européen de recherche et d'action sur le racisme et l'antisémitisme* – CERA) in Paris.

3. W. Laqueur, *Fascism*, New York, 1997, p. 121.

4. M. Ebata, 'The Internationalization of the Extreme Right', in *The Extreme Right. Freedom and Security at Risk*, eds A. Braun and S. Scheinberg, Boulder, 1997, pp. 220–28; L. Weinberg, 'An Overview of Right-Wing Extremism in the Western World: A Study of Convergence, Linkage, and Identity', in *Nation and Race*, eds J. Kaplan and T. Bjørgo, Boston, 1998, pp. 24–28.

5. L. Back, M. Keith, and J. Solomos, 'Racism on the Internet: Mapping Neo-Fascist Subcultures in Cyberspace', in *Nation and Race*, eds J. Kaplan and T. Bjørgo, Boston, 1998, p. 98.

6. Weinberg, 'An Overview', p. 15.

7. T. Bjørgo and R. Witte, eds, *Racist Violence in Europe*, New York, 1993.

8. See also U. Altermatt and D. Skenderovic, 'Die extreme Rechte: Organisationen, Personen und Entwicklungen in den achtziger und neunziger Jahren', in *Rechtsextremismus in der Schweiz*, eds U. Altermatt and H. Kriesi, Zurich, 1995.

9. R. Griffin, 'Interregnum or Endgame? The Radical Right in the "Post-Fascist" Era', *Journal of Political Ideologies*, vol. 5, no. 2, 2000, p. 169.

10. For historical overviews, see K.P. Tauber, *Beyond Eagle and Swastika*, 2 vols, Middletown, 1967; J. Algazy, *La tentation néo-fasciste en France, 1944–1965*, Paris, 1984; P. Dudek and H.-G. Jaschke, *Entstehung und Entwicklung des Rechtsextremismus in der Bundesrepublik*, Opladen, 1984.

11. R. Eatwell, *Fascism*, New York, 1997, p. 305; see also P. Milza, *Les fascismes*, Paris, 1991. pp. 470ff.

12. Griffin, 'Interregnum', p. 166.

13. Kaplan and Weinberg, pp. 39–43.

14. A.-M. Duranton-Crabol, *L'Europe de l'extrême droite*, Brussels, 1991, pp. 159–71.

15. Ibid., pp. 173–76; A. Pfahl-Traughber, 'Der organisierte Rechtsextremismus in Deutschland nach 1945. Zur Entwicklung auf den Handlungsfeldern "Aktion" – "Gewalt" – "Kultur" – "Politik"', in *Rechtsextremismus in der Bundesrepublik Deutschland*, eds W. Schubarth and R. Stöss, Opladen, 2001, pp. 83ff.

16. J.-Y. Camus, 'La structure du "camp national" en France: la périphérie militante et organisationnelle du Front national et du Mouvement national républicain', in *Les croisés de la société fermée*, ed. P. Perrineau, Paris, 2001, pp. 205f.

17. For Germany, see P. Moreau and U. Backes, 'Federal Republic of Germany', in *Extremism in Europe, 1998 Survey*, ed. J.-Y. Camus Paris, 1998, pp. 160f.

18. On the VPS, see Frischknecht et al., *Die unheimlichen Patrioten*, 6th edn, Zurich, 1987, pp. 470ff.; U. Fischer, *Gaston-Armand Amaudruz* (M.A. thesis, University of Fribourg, 1999), pp. 75–89.

19. Quoted in: Fischer, *Gaston-Armand Amaudruz*, p. 83.

20. On the European Social Movement, see Milza, *Les fascismes*, pp. 471f; Kaplan and L. Weinberg, *The Emergence*, pp. 39f.

21. M. Syfrig and C. Defaye, *L'extrême-droite en Suisse*, Lausanne, 1967; M. Syfrig and C. Defaye, *Les nazis parmi nous*, Lausanne, 1967; S. Niklaus, *Wir nicht?*, Basel, 1969; Frischknecht et al., *Die unheimlichen Patrioten*, pp. 445–85; Fischer, *Gaston-Armand Amaudruz*, pp. 52–89.

22. Fischer, *Gaston-Armand Amaudruz*.
23. On the NOE, see Duranton Crabol, *L'Europe*, pp. 165f; Milza, *Les fascismes*, p. 472; J.-Y. Camus and R. Monzat, *Les droites nationales et radicales en France*, Lyon, 1992, pp. 252ff.; Altermatt and Skenderovic, 'Die extreme Rechte', pp. 25–28; Fischer, *Gaston-Armand Amaudruz*, pp. 90–137.
24. P.-A. Taguieff, *Sur la Nouvelle droite*, Paris, 1994, pp. 237f.
25. Fischer, *Gaston-Armand Amaudruz*, pp. 38f.
26. *Le Mois suisse*, no. 73, April 1945, pp. 75–89.
27. Altermatt and Skenderovic, 'Die extreme Rechte', p. 28.
28. U. Altermatt and D. Skenderovic, 'Switzerland', in *Extremism in Europe, 1998 Survey*, ed. J.-Y. Camus, Paris, 1998, p. 348.
29. Fischer, *Gaston-Armand Amaudruz*, pp. 185–89.
30. In reference to the 'Springtime of Fronts' in 1933, the term 'Small Springtime of Fronts' was coined in 1989 by the Swiss journalist Jürg Frischknecht, who has extensively covered the extreme right in Switzerland; see Niggli and Frischknecht, *Rechte Seilschaften*, Zurich, 1998, p. 599.
31. J. Frischknecht, *"Schweiz wir kommen"*, 2nd edn, Zurich, 1991, pp. 170f; Fischer, *Gaston-Armand Amaudruz*, pp. 159–63.
32. On the NK, see Frischknecht, *"Schweiz wir kommen"*, pp. 166–71; Altermatt and Skenderovic, 'Die extreme Rechte', p. 54; Fischer, *Gaston-Armand Amaudruz*, pp. 146–56.
33. For example, see *Volk + Heimat*, no. 1, January 1985, p. 5; *Der Republikaner*, no. 11, June 1987, p. 2.
34. P. Niggli and J. Frischknecht, *Rechte Seilschaften*, p. 614.
35. R. Tobler, 'Die Internationale Konvention zur Beseitigung jeder Form von Rassendiskriminierung und die Schweiz', 1994, p. 15; Niggli and Frischknecht, *Rechte Seilschaften*, p. 285.
36. *Gegner des Antirassismus-Gesetzes*, press documentation, published by the Federal Committee 'Yes to the Antiracism Law', 2 vols, Zurich, August 1994, vol. 2.
37. Duranton-Crabol, *L'Europe*, p. 167.
38. Frischknecht, *"Schweiz wir kommen"*, pp. 123f; K. Laske, *Ein Leben zwischen Hitler und Carlos: François Genoud*, Zurich, 1996; P. Péan, *L'extrémiste*, Paris, 1996.
39. Frischknecht et al., *Die unheimlichen Patrioten*, pp. 446–55, 732ff.; C. Cantini, *Les ultras*, Lausanne, 1992, pp. 141f.
40. Frischknecht et al., *Die unheimlichen Patrioten*, pp. 456–67, 735f; Frischknecht, *"Schweiz wir kommen"*, p. 65; Cantini, *Les ultras*, pp. 143f.
41. Frischknecht et al., *Die unheimlichen Patrioten*, pp. 483ff.; Cantini, *Les ultras*, pp. 161f.
42. Frischknecht, *"Schweiz wir kommen"*, pp. 73–82; Niggli and Frischknecht, *Rechte Seilschaften*, p. 623.
43. D.E. Lipstadt, *Denying the Holocaust*, New York, 1993, p. 23.
44. B. Bailer-Galanda, '"Revisionismus" – pseudowissenschaftliche Propaganda des Rechtsextremismus', in *Wahrheit und "Auschwitzlüge"*, eds B. Bailer-Galanda, W. Benz, and W. Neugebauer, Vienna, 1995; W. Benz, *Legenden, Lügen, Vorurteile*, Munich, 1998.

45. Lipstadt, *Denying*; M. Shermer and A. Grobman, *Denying History*, Berkeley, 2000.

46. Shermer and Grobman, *Denying History*, pp. xv–xvi; see also P. Milza, 'Le négationnisme en France', *Relations internationales*, no. 65, 1991, p. 9; Lipstadt, *Denying*, pp. 20f.

47. Shermer and Grobman, *Denying History*, p. xvi, italics in original.

48. Altermatt and Skenderovic, 'Die extreme Rechte', p. 66; V. Igounet, *Histoire du négationnisme en France*, Paris, 2000, pp. 15f.

49. See also Altermatt and Skenderovic, 'Die extreme Rechte', pp. 66f.

50. H. Rousso, *Le syndrome de Vichy*, Paris, 1987, pp. 166–72; see also Igounet, *Histoire du négationnisme*, p. 14.

51. A. Kaspi, 'Introduction. Le génocide des Juifs: le négationnisme est-il une entreprise transnationale?', *Relations internationales*, no. 65, 1991; A. Bihr et al., *Négationnistes: les chiffonniers de l'histoire*, Villeurbanne, 1997; Igounet, *Histoire du négationnisme*.

52. Bailer-Galanda, '"Revisionismus"', p. 23; Shermer and Grobman, *Denying History*, p. xv.

53. On this distinction between methods, see P. Vidal-Naquet, *Assassins of Memory*, New York, 1992, pp. 21ff.; Altermatt and Skenderovic, 'Die extreme Rechte', p. 67.

54. Shermer and Grobman, *Denying History*, p. 34.

55. G. Desbuissons, 'Maurice Bardèche: un précurseur du "révisionnisme"', in *Relations internationales*, no. 65, 1991; F. Brayard, *Comment l'idée vint à M. Rassinier*, Paris, 1996.

56. Shermer and Grobman, *Denying History*, p. 41.

57. For example, Maurice Bardèche's 1948 book *Nuremberg – ou la Terre promise* (Nuremberg – or the Promised Land) was published in a run of twenty-five thousand copies. Although Bardèche was sentenced in 1952 for publishing this book, negationist literature continued to be produced and to circulate in France; see Igounet, *Histoire du négationnisme*, p. 45; A. Kaplan, *The Collaborator*, Chicago, 2001, pp. 219f.

58. Lipstadt, *Denying*, pp. 157–82.

59. P.-A. Taguieff 'L'abbé Pierre et Roger Garaudy. Négationisme, antijudaïsme, antisionisme', *Esprit*, no. 224, 1996; Igounet, *Histoire du négationnisme*, pp. 231–488.

60. Kaspi, 'Introduction', Igounet, *Histoire du négationnisme*, pp. 574ff.

61. On the IHR, see the excellent study by Shermer and Grobman, *Denying History*.

62. Shermer and Grobman, *Denying History*, pp. 9–18; M. Fennema, 'Legal Repression of Extreme-Right Parties and Racial Discrimination', in *Challenging Immigration and Ethnic Relations Politics*, eds R. Koopmans and P. Statham, Oxford, 2000, pp. 134–38.

63. Back, Keith and Solomos, 'Racism', pp. 95ff.

64. On the history of Swiss negationism, see also J. Tschirren, *Negationistische Propaganda in der Schweiz 1946–1994* (M.A. thesis, University of Fribourg, 1999).

65. Taguieff, *Nouvelle droite*, p. 237.

66. For the book, see G.-A. Amaudruz, *Ubu justicier au premier procès de Nuremberg*, Paris: Aux Actes des Apôtres, 1949; for the article, see G.-A. Amaudruz, 'Le procès de Nuremberg', *Courrier du Continent*, no. 3, October 1946, pp. 31–46.

67. See also J. Tschirren, *Negationistische Propaganda*, pp. 34f.

68. Tauber, *Beyond Eagle*, p. 1267 note 40; Niklaus, *Wir nicht?*, pp. 10f; Tschirren, *Negationistische Propaganda*, p. 102.

69. Frischknecht, *"Schweiz wir kommen"*, pp. 45–48; Fischer, *Gaston-Armand Amaudruz*, pp. 47–51.

70. For example, see *Turmwart*, no. 12, December 1947, p. 421. See also Tschirren, *Negationistische Propaganda*, pp. 102–7.

71. Tschirren, *Negationistische Propaganda*, pp. 38–49.

72. *Courrier du Continent. L'appel du peuple*, no. 13, February, 1953, pp. 6f; no. 19, August 1953, pp. 6f; no. 21, November 1953, p. 3.

73. Altermatt and Skenderovic, 'Switzerland', p. 348.

74. J.-A. Mathez, *Le passé, les temps présents et la question juive*, Vevey: private publishing venture, n.d. [1965].

75. Tschirren, *Negationistische Propaganda*, pp. 36ff.

76. *Courrier du Continent/Europe réelle*, Special Issue, January 1966.

77. Tschirren, *Negationistische Propaganda*, pp. 52ff.

78. Frischknecht, *"Schweiz wir kommen"*, pp. 121ff.; Altermatt and Skenderovic, 'Die extreme Rechte', pp. 70f.

79. *Eidgenoss*, no. 3, 24 March 1992, p. 1, my translation.

80. *Verfassungsschutzbericht 1992*, published by the Federal Ministry of Interior, Bonn, 1993, p. 128.

81. Altermatt and Skenderovic, 'Switzerland', p. 346.

82. Altermatt and Skenderovic, 'Die extreme Rechte', pp. 68ff.; Tschirren, *Negationistische Propaganda*, pp. 115–18.

83. Igounet, *Histoire du négationnisme*, pp. 181–98.

84. *24 heures*, 11 August 1986.

85. *Le Pamphlet*, no. 151, January 1986, p. 2. On the 'Roques affaire', see Igounet, *Histoire du négationnisme*, pp. 407–21.

86. Camus and Monzat, *Les droites nationales*, p. 96. It is worth noting, however, that as early as September 1985, Max Wahl had written in *Eidgenoss* that Roques' study demonstrated how there should be serious doubts about the figure of six millions Jews killed; see *Eidgenoss*, no. 7–9, 27 September 1985, p. 4.

87. *Neue Zürcher Zeitung*, 14 August 1986; 24 December 1987; *Jüdische Rundschau*, 26 February 1987; 19 March 1987.

88. *Journal de Nyon*, 15 Octobre 1986.

89. *Tribune de Genève*, 7 November 1986.

90. For example, see E. Werner *L'expression sanctionnée*, Lausanne: private publishing venture, n.d. [1986]; E. Werner, *Ne dites surtout pas que je doute, on finirait par le croire ... A propos de l'"affaire Paschoud"*, Lausanne: Éditions Thael, 1988.

91. Altermatt and Skenderovic, 'Die extreme Rechte', p. 69; Tschirren, *Negationistische Propaganda*, pp. 118–22.

92. Jürgen Graf, Bernhard Schaub and Andres J.W. Studer worked as teachers and were, at some point of their negationist activities, discharged by the

schools at which they were employed. It is worth noting that Gaston-Armand Amaudruz, Mariette Paschoud and Arthur Vogt (see below) had also been working as teachers.

93. Altermatt and Skenderovic, 'Die extreme Rechte', pp. 72–75; Niggli and Frischknecht, *Rechte Seilschaften*, pp. 653–701; Tschirren, *Negationistische Propaganda*, pp. 69–89.

94. For the German original, see Jürgen Graf, *Riese auf tönernen Füssen. Raul Hilberg und sein Standardwerk über den "Holocaust"*, Hastings, UK: Castle Hull Publishers, 1999.

95. See also Tschirren, *Negationistische Propaganda*, pp. 82–86.

96. See the annotated bibliography in: B. Schaub, *Adler und Rose: Wesen und Schicksal des deutschsprachigen Raumes*, Brugg: Konradin Verlag, 1992, pp. 101–4.

97. In the following year, the name was changed to Working Group for the Research on Contemporary History (*Arbeitsgemeinschaft zur Erforschung der Zeitgeschichte*).

98. *Statuten der Arbeitsgemeinschaft zur Enttabuisierung der Zeitgeschichte*, 30 March 1994, article 3, my translation.

99. W. Lasek, '"Revisionistische" Autoren und ihre Publikationen', in *Wahrheit und "Auschwitzlüge"*, eds B. Bailer-Galanda, W. Benz, and W. Neugebauer, Vienna, 1995, p. 288.

100. 'Switzerland', in *Antisemitism Worldwide 2000/1*, published by the Stephen Roth Institute for the Study of Contemporary Anti-Semitism and Racism at Tel Aviv University, Tel Aviv, 2001, http://www.tau.ac.il/Anti-Semitism/asw2001-2/switzerland.htm, retrieved 31 August 2008.

101. *Bericht Innere Sicherheit der Schweiz 2002*, published by the Federal Office of Police, Federal Department of Justice and Police, preprint, June 2003, p. 14.

102. Altermatt and Skenderovic, 'Switzerland', p. 347; Niggli and Frischknecht, *Rechte Seilschaften*, pp. 676–80.

103. For example, see *Recht + Freiheit*, no. 6, November 1995, p. 3; no. 4, June 1996, pp. 1f.

104. Niggli and Frischknecht, *Rechte Seilschaften*, pp. 680–84; Tschirren, *Negationistische Propaganda*, pp. 71f.

105. C. Longchamp, J. Dumont and P. Leuenberger, *Einstellungen der SchweizerInnen gegenüber Jüdinnen und Juden und dem Holocaust*, Bern, 2000, pp. 26–29.

106. *Die Weltwoche*, 8 April 1993.

107. U. Altermatt, and D. Skenderovic, 'Die rechtsextreme Landschaft in der Schweiz: Typologie und aktuelle Entwicklungen', *Österreichische Zeitschrift für Politikwissenschaft*, vol. 28, no. 1, 1999, p. 106.

108. Fennema, 'Legal Repression', p. 136.

109. P. Liatowitsch, 'Holocaust-Leugnung in der Schweiz und Art. 261[bist] StGB', in *Neuer Antisemitismus – alte Vorurteile?*, ed. C. Tuor-Kurth, Stuttgart, 2001, pp. 145ff.

110. For example, see *Die Weltwoche*, 9 July 1998; *Neue Zürcher Zeitung*, 17 July 1998; 22 July 1998; *Tages Anzeiger*, 22 September 1998.

111. M.A. Niggli, *Rassendiskriminierung*, 2nd rev. edn, Zurich, 2007.

112. For example, see Federal Tribunal decision 5C.155/2002, 13 November 2002, in *BGE* 129 III, p. 52.

113. On the significance of the Internet for international negationism, see Back, Keith and Solomos, 'Racism', pp. 91–97.

114. *Staatsschutzbericht 1998*, published by the Federal Department of Justice and Police, Bern, 1999, p. 45; Federal Tribunal decision 6S.719/1999, 22 March 2000 (non-published), in *Neue Zürcher Zeitung*, 27 April 2000; Liatowitsch, 'Holocaust-Leugnung', pp. 150–53.

115. *Neue Zürcher Zeitung*, December 1, 2000; 'Switzerland', in *Antisemitism Worldwide 2000/1*; 'Jürgen Graf', in *Lexikon des Informationsdienstes gegen Rechtsextremismus (IDGR)*, http://lexikon.idgr.de/g/g_r/graf-juergen/graf-juergen.php, retrieved 15 August 2006.

116. *Neue Zürcher Zeitung*, 11 April 2000; 21 November 2000; 3/4 November 2001; Federal Tribunal decision 6S.399/2001, 16 October 2001, in *BGE* 127 IV, pp. 203–9; 'Gaston-Armand Amaudruz', in *Lexikon des Informationsdienstes gegen Rechtsextremismus (IDGR)*, http://lexikon.idgr.de/a/a_m/amaudruz-gaston/amaudruz-gaston-armand.php, retrieved 15 August 2006.

117. Altermatt and Skenderovic, 'Die extreme Rechte', p. 48.

118. Niggli and Frischknecht, *Rechte Seilschaften*, p. 668; 'Avalon', in *Lexikon des Informationsdienstes gegen Rechtsextremismus (IDGR)*, http://lexikon.idgr.de/a/a_v/avalon/avalon.php, retrieved 15 August 2006.

119. Niggli and Frischknecht, *Rechte Seilschaften*, p. 661; 'Bernhard Schaub', in *Lexikon des Informationsdienstes gegen Rechtsextremismus (IDGR)*, http://lexikon.idgr.de/s/s_c/schaub-bernhard/schaub-bernhard.php, retrieved 15 August 2006.

120. For a list of articles, see the JHR website: http://www.ihr.org/journal/jhrfulllist.shtml#g, retrieved 31 August 2008.

121. For a list of articles, see the journal's website: http://vho.org/VffG/, retrieved 31 August 2008. On the VHO, see 'Vrij Historisch Onderzoek (VHO)', in *Lexikon des Informationsdienstes gegen Rechtsextremismus (IDGR)*, http://lexikon.idgr.de/v/v_r/vrij-historisch-onderzoek/vho.php, retrieved 15 August 2006.

122. Altermatt and Skenderovic, 'Switzerland', p. 346.

123. U. Altermatt and D. Skenderovic, 'Extreme Rechte, Rassismus und Antisemitismus in der Schweiz. Überblick und Typologie', *Forschungsjournal Neue Soziale Bewegungen*, vol. 12, no. 1, 1999, p. 87.

124. See the website of the VHO: http://www.vho.org, retrieved 31 August 2008.

125. For the mirrored website of *Wilhelm Tell*, see http://www.ety.com/tell/index.htm, retrieved 15 August 2006. See also R. Fromm and B. Kernbach, *Rechtsextremismus auf dem Internet*, Munich, 2001, pp. 269ff.

126. Igounet, *Histoire du négationnisme*, pp. 479–83; G. Nordbruch, 'Leugnungen des Holocaust in arabischen Medien. Reaktionen auf "Die Gründungsmythen der israelischen Politik" von Roger Garaudy', in *Jahrbuch für Antisemitismusforschung*, vol. 10, ed. W. Benz, Frankfurt, 2001.

127. *Jüdische Rundschau*, 15 March 2001; *Neue Zürcher Zeitung*, 20 March 2001; *Jungle World*, 4 April 2001; see also *Verfassungsschutzbericht 2001*, published by the Federal Ministry of Interior, press version, Bonn, Berlin, 2001, p. 122.

128. 'Ahmed Huber', in *Lexikon des Informationsdienstes gegen Rechtsextremismus (IDGR)*, http://lexikon.idgr.de/h/h_u/huber-ahmed/huber-ahmed.php, retrieved 15 August 2006.

129. K. Coogan, 'The Mysterious Achmed Huber: Friend to Hitler, Allah and ... Ibn Ladin?', *Hitlist*, April/May 2002, pp. 120–25.

130. C. Späti, *Die schweizerische Linke und Israel*, Essen, 2006, pp. 129–32.

131. C.F. Graumann and S. Moscovici, eds, *Changing Conceptions of Conspiracy*, New York, 1987; E. Gugenberger, F. Petri, and R. Schweidlenka, *Weltverschwörungstheorien*, Vienna, 1998; M. Barkun, *A Culture of Conspiracy*, Berkeley, 2003.

132. M. Barkun, 'Conspiracy Theories as Stigmatized Knowledge: The Basis for a New Age Racism?', in *Nation and Race*, eds J. Kaplan and T. Bjørgo, Boston, 1998, p. 62.

133. M. Billig, 'The Extreme Right: Continuities in Anti-Semitic Conspiracy Theory in Post-War Europe', in *The Nature of the Right*, eds R. Eatwell and N. O'Sullivan, Boston, 1989.

134. Ibid., p. 155.

135. On *Memopress*, see Frischknecht et al., *Die unheimlichen Patrioten*, pp. 414–18; Altermatt and Skenderovic, 'Die extreme Rechte', pp. 48f; Niggli and Frischknecht, *Rechte Seilschaften*, pp. 721–26.

136. *Freie Meinungsäusserung. Gegen UNO-Bevormundung*, no. 1, 1993, p. 1; see also the reports in: *Die WochenZeitung*, 16 July 1993; *Gegner des Antirassismus-Gesetzes*, press documentation, published by the Federal Committee 'Yes to the Antiracism Law', 2 vols, Zurich, July 1994, vol. 1.

137. *Basler Zeitung*, 24 August 1994; *Aargauer Tagblatt*, 26 August 1994.

138. Leaflet: '*Aktion für freie Meinungsäusserung – Gegen UNO-Bevormundung*', 3 June 1993, my translation.

139. *Memopress*, no. 1, 1976, p. 1.

140. Barkun, 'Conspiracy Theories'; Barkun, *Culture of Conspiracy*.

141. http://www.klettgau.ch/memopress/1.htm, retrieved 30 August 2003, my translation.

142. K. Urner, 'Emil Rahm und der Antisemitismus. Stossrichtung und Methoden der "Memopress"', *Neue Zürcher Zeitung*, 17/18 September 1994.

143. *Verfassungsschutzbericht 1992*, published by the Federal Ministry of Interior, Bonn, 1993, p. 125; Fromm and Kernbach, *... und morgen die ganze Welt?*, pp. 140–43; 'CODE', in *Lexikon des Informationsdienstes gegen Rechtsextremismus (IGDR)*, http://lexikon.idgr.de/c/c_o/code/code.php, retrieved 15 August 2006.

144. *Memopress*, no. 2, 1983, p. 3, my translation.

145. *Memopress*, no. 3, 1993, pp. 1–4, here p. 1, my translation.

146. *Volk + Heimat*, no. 11, September 1984, p. 4; no. 11, August/September 1985, p. 2. On the public reactions of the 1990s, see Altermatt and Skenderovic, 'Die extreme Rechte', p. 49.

147. Niggli and Frischknecht, *Rechte Seilschaften*, p. 296; *Neue Zürcher Zeitung*, 18 April 1997.

148. *Recht + Freiheit*, no. 3, supplement, June 1998, pp. 33–36.

149. H. Scholl, *Von der Wallstreet gekauft: Die Finanzierung Hitlers durch ausländische Finanzmächte. Eine Dokumentation*, Vaduz: Contempora, 1981.

150. Urner, 'Emil Rahm', pp. 99f.

151. *Memopress*, no. 2, 1978, pp. 1ff.; no. 1, 1993, p. 4.

152. On Des Griffin, see 'Des Griffin', in *Lexikon des Informationsdienstes gegen Rechtsextremismus (IGDR)*, http://lexikon.idgr.de/g/g_r/griffin-des/griffin-des. php, retrieved 15 August 2006.
153. Niggli and Frischknecht, *Rechte Seilschaften*, p. 717.
154. Barkun, *Culture of Conspiracy*, p. 142; see also N. Cohn, *Warrant for Genocide*, new edn, London, 1996.
155. U. Lüthi, *Der Mythos von der Weltverschwörung*, Basel, 1992.
156. *Memopress*, no. 2, 1996, p. 4.
157. Niggli and Frischknecht, *Rechte Seilschaften*, p. 706.
158. Ibid., p. 705. In 1996, Jan van Helsing also supplied a third volume named *Buch 3 - der Dritte Weltkrieg* (Book 3 – the Third World War).
159. H. Stamm, *Im Bann der Apokalypse*, Zurich,1998, pp. 89–105; F.P. Heller and A. Maegerle, *Die Sprache des Hasses*, Stuttgart, 2001, pp. 125–64.
160. In summer 2006, these publications of van Helsing could still be downloaded from the Internet, mainly from websites with U.S. providers. More recent writings by van Helsing were also available at http://www.amazon.de, accessed 31 August 2008.
161. Gugenberger, Petri, and Schweidlenka, *Weltverschwörungstheorien*, pp. 205–26; Heller and Maegerle *Sprache des Hasses*, pp. 164–66.
162. Barkun, 'Conspiracy Theories', p. 68.
163. H. Stutz, 'Mäandern im esoterischen Sumpf', *Tangram. Bulletin der Eidgenössischen Kommission gegen Rassismus*, no. 6, 1999.
164. On the UK, see also H. Gasper, J. Müller, and F. Valentin, *Lexikon der Sekten, Sondergruppen und Weltanschauungen*, Freiburg, 1997, pp. 1056–60; Stamm, *Im Bann*, pp. 62f.
165. Niggli and Frischknecht, *Rechte Seilschaften*, pp. 709–16; Altermatt and Skenderovic, 'Switzerland', p. 347; Stamm, *Im Bann*, pp. 108–10.
166. Quoted in: Stamm, *Im Bann*, p. 108; Niggli and Frischknecht, *Rechte Seilschaften*, p. 714, my translation.
167. Quoted in: *Neue Zürcher Zeitung*, 12 July 1996, my translation. The statement was allegedly a citation from a speech by a well-known Polish priest which had been quoted in *TIME Magazine International* of 3 July 1995. For this alleged reference, see *ZeitenSchrift*, Special Issue, no. 13, 1997, pp. 10ff.
168. Niggli and Frischknecht, *Rechte Seilschaften*, p. 716.
169. Stamm, *Im Bann*, pp. 108f.
170. Federal Tribunal decision 6S.331/1997, 5 December 1997, in *BGE* 123 IV, pp. 202–10.
171. On *ZeitenSchrift*, see Gugenberger, Petri, and Schweidlenka, *Weltverschwörungstheorien*, pp. 227–38; Stamm, *Im Bann*, pp. 110f.
172. Gugenberger, Petri, Schweidlenka, *Weltverschwörungstheorien*, p. 227.
173. *ZeitenSchrift*, Special Issue, no. 13, 1997, p. 12.
174. On the VgT and Erwin Kessler, see Altermatt and Skenderovic, 'Switzerland', p. 347. 'Erwin Kessler', in *Lexikon des Informationsdienstes gegen Rechtsextremismus (IGDR)*, http://lexikon.idgr.de/k/k_e/kessler-erwin/kessler-erwin. php, retrieved 15 August 2006.
175. See the official website of the VgT: http://www.vgt.ch/about/index.htm, retrieved 30 August 2003.

176. *Tierschutz-Nachrichten*, no.1/2, January/February 1995, p. 1; *VgT-Nachrichten*, no. 5, September/October 1996, p. 1; no. 2, March/April 1999, p. 1.
177. For this assessment, see the study by P. Krauthammer, *Das Schächtverbot in der Schweiz 1854–2000*, Zurich, 2000, pp. 249–62.
178. *Tierschutz-Nachrichten*, no. 7, August 1995, p. 4, my translation.
179. For example, see *VgT-Nachrichten*, no. 1, January/February 1997, p. 10; no. 1, January/February 1999, p. 11.
180. *VgT-Nachrichten*, no. 2, March/April 1998, p. 11, my translation.
181. *VgT-Nachrichten*, no. 6, November/December 1996, 11, my translation.
182. *VgT-Nachrichten*, no. 4, July/August 1997, p. 23, my translation.
183. *Recht + Freiheit*, no. 4, 24 June 1996, p. 4; *Recht + Freiheit*, no. 4, 30 September 1998, p. 3.
184. Niggli and Frischknecht, *Rechte Seilschaften*, p. 315; see also *Jüdische Rundschau*, 10 July 1997; *Tachles*, 6 June 2003.
185. Federal Tribunal decision 6S.367/1998, 26 September 2000.
186. Federal Tribunal decision 5C.155/2002, 13 November 2002, in *BGE* 129 III, p. 54. Orig.: 'im konkreten Zusammenhang mit der antisemitisch motivierten Polemik um das Schächtverbot ... Kontakte zur Neonazi- und Revisionistenszene'; my translation.
187. On the historical origins of national-revolutionaries, see P. Moreau, *Nationalsozialismus von links*, Stuttgart, 1985.
188. M. Feit, *Die "Neue Rechte" in der Bundesrepublik*, Frankfurt, 1987, pp. 111–16; R. Griffin, 'Interregnum or Endgame? The Radical Right in the "Post-Fascist" Era', *Journal of Political Ideologies*, vol. 5, no. 2, 2000, p. 168.
189. P.-A. Taguieff, 'Les droites radicales en France: nationalisme révolutionnaire et national-libéralisme', *Les Temps modernes*, no. 465, 1985.
190. Camus and Monzat, *Les droites nationales*, pp. 89f.
191. On the often confusing organisational development of the national-revolutionary movement in France, see *France Politique. Dossier extrême droite radicale*, http://francepolitique.free.fr/PUR4.htm, retrieved 31 August 2008; 'Unité Radicale', in *Lexikon des Informationsdienstes gegen Rechtsextremismus (IGDR)*, http://lexikon.idgr.de/u/u_n/unite-radicale/unite-radicale.php, retrieved 16 August 2006.
192. On the NOS, see Cantini, *Les Ultras*, p. 152; Altermatt and Skenderovic, 'Die extreme Rechte', pp. 34f.
193. See also Fischer, *Gaston-Armand Amaudruz*, pp. 138f.
194. See the interview with Daniel Cologne, in which he gives a revealing picture of the Swiss national-revolutionaries during the 1970s and which was republished in 2002 by the national-revolutionary web magazine *Vox NR com* under the title 'Les non-conformistes des années 70' (The Non-Conformists of the 1970s): *Vox NR com*, 12 July 2002, http://www.voxnr.com/cogit_content/documents/Lesnon-conformistesdesanne.shtml, retrieved 30 September 2003.
195. *Le Courrier*, 17 December 1976; *Voix ouvrière*, 17 December 1976. On the Culture and Liberty Circle, see P. Chairoff, *Dossier néo-nazisme*, Paris, 1977, p. 247.
196. For example, the group published the brochure *Giorgio Freda, "nazimaoïste" ou révolutionnaire inclassable?* (Giorgio Freda, "Nazi-Maoist" or Un-

classifiable Revolutionary?) in 1976, which circulated widely among the European extreme right; see R. Monzat, *Enquêtes sur la droite extrême,* Paris, 1992, p. 91.

197. *Bulletin de l'Association des amis de Robert Brasillach,* no. 63, 5 December 1973, p. 6.

198. *Renaissance,* no. 1, May 1972, p. 9

199. *Renaissance,* no. 3, July 1973, pp. 2–5.

200. *Avant-Garde,* no. 4, July/August 1977, p. 6.

201. For example, see *Avant-Garde,* no. 6, November/December 1977, p. 16; no. 5, September/October 1977, pp. 6f.

202. On the *Le Rat noir,* see also Altermatt and Skenderovic, 'Die extreme Rechte', p. 36.

203. *Le Rat noir: Journal différent,* no. 16, August 1984, p. 2.

204. *Le Rat noir: Journal Différent,* no. 14, n.d. [1984], pp. 2–5.

205. Altermatt and Skenderovic, 'Die extreme Rechte', pp. 34ff.

206. *Le Rat noir: Bulletin de liaison et d'information NR de suisse,* no. 1, January 1979, p. 1.

207. Altermatt and Skenderovic, 'Die extreme Rechte', p. 37.

208. *Le Matin,* 4 May 1985.

209. Advertising leaflet: '*Le Rat noir. Un offre unique. Top prix et qualité*', Bernex, n.d. [1987]. The offer was made by a mail order service named Ares Diffusion; see Advertising note: '*Ares Diffusion*', n.d. [1987]. On the promotion campaign, see also *Genève home informations,* 8 January 1987.

210. On the Third Way and the involvement of Pascal Junod, see Altermatt and Skenderovic, 'Die extreme Rechte', pp. 57ff. The postal account number of *Le Rat noir* was written on membership forms, meeting invitations and propaganda posters released by the group Third Way.

211. The information on membership is taken from: F. Arévalo, *L'application du modèle de la Troisième voie en Suisse romande* (Seminar Thesis in Political Science, University of Geneva, 1994), p. 13.

212. Invitation flyer: '*Mouvement 3e Voie*', meeting organized by Third Way on 6 October 1990.

213. Fromm and Kernbach, *… und morgen die ganze Welt?,* pp. 274f.

214. Cantini, *Les ultras,* p. 158.

215. There are no reliable figures or detailed documentation concerning the combative and violent actions of the Swiss extreme right in the period before the mid-1980s.

216. Frischknecht, *"Schweiz wir kommen",* pp. 128f.

217. U. Altermatt, 'Rechtsextremismus in der Schweiz: Randphänomen oder Pathologie des normalen Alltags?', *Civitas,* vol. 41, no. 3, 1986.

218. P. Gentile et al., 'Die rechtsradikale Radikalisierung: eine Fallstudie', in *Rechtsextremismus in der Schweiz,* eds. U. Altermatt and H. Kriesi, Zurich, 1995, p. 166.

219. R. Koopmans, 'Explaining the Rise of Racist and Extreme Right Violence in Western Europe: Grievances or Opportunities?', *European Journal of Political Research,* vol. 30, no. 6, 1996, p. 193.

220. Gentile et al., 'Die rechtsradikale Radikalisierung', pp. 166–169.

221. P. Gentile, 'Radical Right Protest in Switzerland', in *Acts of Dissent*, eds. D. Rucht, R. Koopmans, and F. Neidhardt, Lanham, 1999, p. 243.

222. The chronology has been published since 1991. It was first compiled by Regula Bähler (1991–1994), and then since 1995, by Hans Stutz. The regularly updated version of the chronology can be found on the Internet at: http://chrono.gra.ch/chron/chron_index.asp, accessed 31 August 2008.

223. For an example, see *Staatsschutzbericht 2000*, published by the Federal Department of Justice and Police, Bern, 2001, pp. 27–33, 37.

224. H. Willems et al., *Fremdenfeindliche Gewalt*, Opladen, 1993; T. Bjørgo and R. Witte, eds, *Racist Violence in Europe*, New York, 1993; W. Heitmeyer, 'Rechtsextremistische Gewalt', in *Internationales Handbuch der Gewaltforschung*, eds. W. Heitmeyer and J. Hagan, Wiesbaden, 2002.

225. Gentile et al., 'Die rechtsradikale Radikalisierung', p. 174.

226. Since there is no comprehensive analysis of extreme-right violence since1994, this assessment remains rather impressionistic.

227. For example, see T. Bjørgo, *Racist and Right-Wing Violence in Scandinavia*, Oslo, 1997.

228. Altermatt and Skenderovic, 'Die extreme Rechte', pp. 107f.

229. T. Bjørgo, 'Xenophobic Violence and Ethnic Conflict at the Local Level: Lessons from the Scandinavian Experience', in *Challenging Immigration and Ethnic Relations Politics*, eds. R. Koopmans and P. Statham, Oxford, 2000, pp. 380ff.

230. As was revealed by a parliamentary investigations committee, the state protection services and the Swiss Federal Police, in particular, maintained substantial records on left-wing groups, intellectuals and activists throughout the postwar era right up until the late 1980s. These records were kept on a large scale and were essentially maintained without the supervision of parliament or other political authorities. For a historical account of the Swiss state protection services, see G. Kreis, ed., *Staatsschutz in der Schweiz*, Bern, 1993.

231. For examples of a reserved attitude adopted by cantonal and federal police forces, see Altermatt and Skenderovic, 'Die extreme Rechte', pp. 110f; Gentile et al., 'Die rechtsradikale Radikalisierung', pp. 240ff.; Niggli and Frischknecht, *Rechte Seilschaften*, pp. 614–618.

232. *Extremismus in der Schweiz*, report by the Federal Council on extremism in Switzerland, 16 March 1992; *Staatsschutzbericht 1993/1994*, published by the Federal Department of Justice and Police, Bern, Zurich, 1995; U. Altermatt and H. Kriesi, eds, *Rechtsextremismus in der Schweiz*, Zurich, 1995.

233. *Skinheads in der Schweiz: Eine Dokumentation*, published by the Swiss Federal Police, Bern, 1996.

234. In May 2002, the Swiss National Science Foundation launched the National Research Program 40+ 'Right-wing Extremism – Causes and Countermeasures'. For information, see the program's officiall website: http://www.nfp40plus.ch, accessed 31 August 2008.

235. *Tages Anzeiger*, 5 August 2000.

236. On the NNF, see also Frischknecht, *"Schweiz wir kommen"*, pp. 92–98; Altermatt and Skenderovic, 'Die extreme Rechte', pp. 60f.

237. *Basler Zeitung*, 20 December 1985; 21 December 1985. After Eric Weber had left NA, he was re-elected to the cantonal parliament of Basel City in 1988

on the list of his one-man party, People's Campaign against too Many Foreigners and Asylum Seekers (*Volksaktion gegen zu viele Ausländer und Asylanten*); see Frischknecht, "*Schweiz wir kommen*", pp. 115f.

238. See the following brochure: NNF, *Haraus: Der Kampf der (Neuen) Nationalen Front von damals bis heute!*, 1986.

239. On the PF, see also Frischknecht, '*Schweiz wir kommen*', pp. 137–148; Altermatt and Skenderovic, 'Die extreme Rechte', pp. 62–66, 109.

240. For this figure, see *Extremismus in der Schweiz*, p. 7.

241. *Grundsatzprogramm der Patriotischen Front*, n.d. [1989], my translation.

242. *Neue Zürcher Zeitung*, 24 August 1989; *Tages Anzeiger*, 1 September 1989.

243. *Schweizer Illustrierte*, 5 June 1989.

244. Various flyers by Patriotische Front, n.d., my translation.

245. Altermatt and Skenderovic, 'Die extreme Rechte', p. 65.

246. *Tages Anzeiger*, 6 November 1989; *Berner Zeitung*, 6 November 1989; *Der Bund*, 7 November 1989; *Jüdische Rundschau*, 9 November 1989.

247. See the press report in: *Tages Anzeiger*, 26 October 1991.

248. On the NF, see also Frischknecht, "*Schweiz wir kommen*", pp. 148–152, 157–160; Altermatt and Skenderovic, 'Die extreme Rechte', pp. 51ff.

249. Such arguments were made in readers' letters written by NF supporters and published in the leading left-wing weekly paper *Die WochenZeitung*; see Niggli and Frischknecht, *Rechte Seilschaften*, p. 609.

250. *Basisprogramm der Neuen Front*, Winterthur, 1989, p. 13, my translation.

251. Ibid, pp. 13f., my translation.

252. On the NRP, see also Frischknecht, "*Schweiz wir kommen*", pp. 152–156; Altermatt and Skenderovic, 'Die extreme Rechte', pp. 54–57.

253. *Grundsatzprogramm der Nationalrevolutionären Partei (Schweiz)*, Neuhausen, n.d. [1989].

254. *Nationale Opposition: Stimme der Nationalrevolutionären Partei (Schweiz)*, no. 1, 1989, p. 2, my translation.

255. A. Nevill, 'The Good, the Bad, and the Skins. Die Geschichte der Skinhead-Bewegung in England', in *Neue Soundtracks für den Volksempfänger*, eds M. Annas and R. Christoph, 2nd edn, Berlin, 1993; G. Marshall, *Spirit of '69*, 2nd edn, Dunoon, 1994.

256. Kaplan and Weinberg, *The Emergence*, p. 19.

257. Marshall, *Spirit of '69*, pp. 148–51; K. Farin and E. Seidel-Pielen, *Skinheads*, 3rd edn, Munich, 1995, pp. 118–36.

258. D. Diederichsen, *Freiheit macht arm*, Cologne, 1993, pp. 253–83.

259. Laqueur, *Fascism*, pp. 125–31.

260. Kaplan and Weinberg, *The Emergence*, p. 21.

261. E. Sprinzak, 'Right-wing Terrorism in a Comparative Perspective: The Case of Split Delegitimization', in *Terror from the Extreme Right*, ed. T. Bjørgo, London, 1995, p. 35.

262. M. Annas and R. Christoph, eds, *Neue Soundtracks für den Volksempfänger*, 2nd edn, Berlin, 1993.

263. P.H. Merkl, 'Why Are They So Strong Now? Comparative Reflections on the Revival of the Radical Right in Europe', in *The Revival of Right-Wing Extremism in the Nineties*, eds P.H. Merkl and L. Weinberg, London, 1997, p. 23.

264. Sprinzak, 'Right-wing Terrorism', pp. 36f; Pfahl-Traughber, 'Der organisierte Rechtsextremismus', p. 88.
265. T. Bjørgo, 'Introduction', *Terror from the Extreme Right*, ed. T. Bjørgo, London, 1995, p. 11.
266. M. Minkenberg, 'Context and Consequence. The Impact of the New Radical Right on the Political Process in France and Germany', *German Politics and Society*, vol. 16, no. 3, 1998, pp. 8f; B. Klandermans and N. Mayer, 'Militer à l'extrême droite', in *Les croisés de la société fermée*, ed. P. Perrineau, Paris, 2001, p. 156.
267. Laqueur, *Fascism*, p. 131.
268. Altermatt and Skenderovic, 'Die extreme Rechte', pp. 75–87; Gentile et al., 'Die rechtsradikale Radikalisierung'; Niggli and Frischknecht, *Rechte Seilschaften*, pp. 622–52.
269. R. Vignando and H. Haas, 'Le mouvement skinhead: Une étude empirique', *Crimiscope*, no. 15, 2001, p. 4.
270. Ibid., p. 4.
271. On this first phase, see also Altermatt and Skenderovic, 'Die extreme Rechte', pp. 78f.
272. Altermatt, 'Rechtsextremismus'.
273. On this second phase, see also Altermatt and Skenderovic, 'Die extreme Rechte', pp. 80–87; Niggli and Frischknecht, *Rechte Seilschaften*, pp. 622–52.
274. *Skinheads in der Schweiz*, published by the Swiss Federal Police, 2nd updated version, Bern, 2000, p. 8.
275. S. Talty, 'The Method of a Neo-Nazi Mogul', *The New York Times Magazine*, 25 February 1996, p. 40.
276. *Verfassungsschutzbericht 2001*, p. 47, my translation.
277. Altermatt and Skenderovic, 'Switzerland', p. 343.
278. *Skinheads in der Schweiz*, 2nd updated version, p. 8; *Staatsschutzbericht 2000*, p. 13.
279. *Verfassungsschutzbericht 2001*, p. 31.
280. *Skinheads in der Schweiz*, 2nd updated version, pp. 56f.
281. *Race et Nation: Une publication Hammerskin*, no. 2, n.d. [1998]; *Race et Nation: Une publication racialiste et traditionaliste*, no. 3, n.d. [1999].
282. *Skinheads in der Schweiz*, 2nd updated version, pp. 56f; H. Stutz, *Rassistische Vorfälle in der Schweiz*, Zurich, 2000, pp. 38f.
283. *Skinheads in der Schweiz*, 2nd updated version, pp. 9, 57ff.
284. Ibid., pp. 15–25; see also Niggli and Frischknecht, *Rechte Seilschaften*, pp. 630ff.
285. Altermatt and Skenderovic, 'Die extreme Rechte', p. 79.
286. For example, see *SonntagsZeitung*, 3 August 1997; *Israelitisches Wochenblatt*, 8 August 1997.
287. *Staatsschutzbericht 1998*, published by the Federal Department of Justice and Police, Bern, 1999, p. 28.
288. Altermatt and Skenderovic, 'Switzerland', p. 343.
289. Stutz, *Rassistische Vorfälle*, 2000, p. 28.
290. *Skinheads in der Schweiz*, 2nd updated version, pp. 23ff.
291. Niggli and Frischknecht, *Rechte Seilschaften*, pp. 649f.

292. *Staatsschutzbericht 2000*, p. 15.
293. *Der Bund*, 26 April 2000; *Neue Zürcher Zeitung*, 27 April 2000; *Le Temps*, 18 August 2000; see also *Staatsschutzbericht 2000*, pp. 15f.
294. Quoted in: *Neue Zürcher Zeitung*, 27 April 2000, my translation.
295. *Tages Anzeiger*, 7 March 1997; *Die WochenZeitung*, 11 April 1997; *Neue Zürcher Zeitung*, 23 April 1997.
296. *Switzerland*, Report published by the Institute for Jewish Policy Research and the American Jewish Committee, 1999, http://www.axt.org.uk/antisem/archive/archive2/switzerland/index.html, retrieved 31 August 2008.
297. *Frankfurter Rundschau*, 10 August 2000; *Neue Zürcher Zeitung*, 10 August 2000; *Tages Anzeiger*, 10 August, 2000.
298. *SonntagsZeitung*, 27 August 2000; *Die WochenZeitung*, 31 August 2000; see also *Skinheads in der Schweiz*, 2nd updated version, pp. 11f, 33.
299. *Le Temps*, 14 September 2000; 16 September 2000.
300. Up to three hundred skinheads came to the event at the Rütli in 2001 and 2002; see *Neue Zürcher Zeitung*, 2 August 2003. On 1 August 2003, 450 skinheads were among the 1,400 persons attending the commemoration; see *Neue Zürcher Zeitung*, 2 August 2003; *NZZ am Sonntag*, 3 August 2003.
301. On the Avalon circle, see Altermatt and Skenderovic, 'Die extreme Rechte', pp. 47f; Niggli and Frischknecht, *Rechte Seilschaften*, pp. 685–95; *Skinheads in der Schweiz*, 2nd updated version, pp. 33, 38; 'Avalon', in *Lexikon des Informationsdienstes gegen Rechtsextremismus (IDGR)*, http://lexikon.idgr.de/a/a_v/avalon/avalon.php, retrieved 15 August 2006.
302. Frischknecht, *"Schweiz wir kommen"*, pp. 160–64.
303. *Facts*, 22 May 1997; *Die WochenZeitung*, 31 October 1997; see also Altermatt and Skenderovic, 'Switzerland', pp. 344f; *Staatsschutzbericht 1997*, p. 15; *Staatsschutzbericht 2000*, p. 17.
304. Quoted in: Niggli and Frischknecht, *Rechte Seilschaften*, p. 650, my translation.
305. Under the anti-racism law, legal proceedings were opened against leading NIS members; see *Staatsschutzbericht 1997*, p. 15.
306. On the PNOS, see *Staatsschutzbericht 2000*, p. 18; *Bericht Innere Sicherheit der Schweiz 2002*, published by the Federal Office of Police, Federal Department of Justice and Police, preprint, June 2003, pp. 13f; see also *Aktion Kinder des Holocaust*, http://www.akdh.ch/pnos.htm, retrieved 31 August 2008.
307. *SonntagsZeitung*, 18 November 2001; H. Stutz, *Rassistische Vorfälle in der Schweiz*, Zurich, 2002, p. 45.
308. PNOS portrait: 'Who we are and where we stand', posted on the official website of the PNOS: http://www.pnos.ch/e/portrat.html, retrieved 1 September 2003.
309. In March 2003, for example, Bernhard Schaub reportedly gave a speech at a public demonstration against the U.S. bombing of Iraq. Organized by the PNOS in the town of Zofingen (AG), the rally was attended by one hundred and twenty people. On the rally, see *Zofinger Tagblatt*, 23 March 2003; 24 March 2003.
310. For example, see *SonntagsZeitung*, 17 September 2000; *Le Temps*, 28 September 2000; *Tages Anzeiger*, 28 September 2000.

311. *Neue Zürcher Zeitung*, 28 September 2000.
312. Quoted in: *Neue Zürcher Zeitung*, 28 September 2000, my translation.
313. Interview with Christoph Blocher in: *Neue Zürcher Zeitung*, 28 September 2000, my translation.
314. H.G. Betz, 'Exclusionary Populism in Austria, Italy, and Switzerland', *International Journal*, vol. 56, no. 3, 2001, p. 405.
315. Quoted in: *Neue Zürcher Zeitung*, 18 October 1999, my translation.
316. *Die WochenZeitung*, 17 October 1997.
317. For press reports and commentaries on the so-called 'letter affair,' see *SonntagsBlick*, 17 October 1999; *Der Bund*, 18 October 1999; *Tages Anzeiger*, 18 October 1999; 21 October 1999; *Le Temps*, 18 October 1999; *Neue Zürcher Zeitung*, 20 October 1999; 21 October 1999; 29 October 1999.
318. Altermatt and Skenderovic, 'Die extreme Rechte', p. 49; see also *Neue Zürcher Zeitung*, 10 January 1995; 19 January 1995.
319. Niggli and Frischknecht, *Rechte Seilschaften*, p. 659.
320. Altermatt and Skenderovic, 'Die extreme Rechte', pp. 71f.
321. *EDU-Standpunkt*, no. 6, November 1986, p. 8.
322. Altermatt and Skenderovic, 'Die extreme Rechte', pp. 70f.
323. Niggli and Frischknecht, *Rechte Seilschaften*, pp. 601, 606, 620.
324. Ibid., pp. 648f.
325. Fischer, *Gaston-Armand Amaudruz*, p. 176.
326. Frischknecht, *"Schweiz wir kommen"*, p. 96.
327. *Courrier du Continent*, no. 337, June 1992, p. 2; see also Fischer, *Gaston-Armand Amaudruz*, p. 181.
328. *Memopress*, edition K, no. 3, 1992.
329. For the call to support the signature collection, see *Courrier du Continent*, no. 348, June 1993, p. 2; no. 350, August 1993, p. 12; no. 351, September 1993, p. 12.
330. *Neue Zürcher Zeitung*, 25 September 1995; see also *Staatschutzbericht 1995/96*, published by the Federal Department of Justice and Police, Bern, 1997, p. 30; Altermatt and Skenderovic, 'Switzerland', p. 343.
331. Niggli and Frischknecht, *Rechte Seilschaften*, p. 651.
332. Fischer, *Gaston-Armand Amaudruz*, pp. 172–84.
333. *Courrier du Continent*, no. 363, October 1994, p. 2, my translation.
334. Niggli and Frischknecht, *Rechte Seilschaften*, pp. 651f.
335. *Memopress*, edition D, no. 3, 1992, p. 2; *Memopress*, Special Issue, no. 3, 1995; *Prüfen + Handeln*, no. 4, 1999; *Prüfen + Handeln*, 1 December 2001.
336. *Totenkopf*, no. 5, 1992. Third Way was another example of a combative extreme-right group which urged its members to oppose Switzerland's EEA membership, see Membership form: 'Mouvement 3 voie/Nouvelle résistance', Bernex, 22 November 1992.
337. *Skinheads in der Schweiz*, 2nd updated version, p. 33, my translations.
338. Frischknecht, *"Schweiz wir kommen"*, p. 65.
339. Frischknecht, *"Schweiz wir kommen"*, pp. 96, 113, 168ff ; Fischer, *Gaston-Armand Amaudruz*, pp. 146–57.
340. Altermatt and Skenderovic, 'Die extreme Rechte', p. 62.

341. Frischknecht, *"Schweiz wir kommen"*, pp. 169f; Fischer, *Gaston-Armand Amaudruz*, p. 150.
342. Fischer, *Gaston-Armand Amaudruz*, p. 172.
343. Frischknecht, *"Schweiz wir kommen"*, pp. 168f.
344. Altermatt and Skenderovic, 'Die extreme Rechte', p. 64; Niggli and Frischknecht, *Rechte Seilschaften*, pp. 676f.
345. Altermatt and Skenderovic, 'Die extreme Rechte', p. 48.
346. Interview with Ueli Maurer in: *SonntagsZeitung*, 19 September 1999, my translation.
347. Frischknecht et al., *Die unheimlichen Patrioten*, p. 453; Drews, *"Schweizer erwache!"*, pp. 108ff.
348. Drews, *"Schweizer erwache!"*, p. 113. On the Austrian Landsmannschaft, see Stiftung Dokumentationsarchiv des österreichischen Widerstandes, ed., *Handbuch des österreichischen Rechtsextremismus*, 2nd edn, Vienna, 1993, pp. 176–83.
349. Frischknecht, *"Schweiz wir kommen"*, p. 453; On the *Deutsche National-Zeitung*, see A. Lange, *Was die Rechten lesen*, Munich, 1993, pp. 73f.
350. P. Fankhauser, *"Hört auf, die Erde zu ermorden!" Valentin Oehen 1970–1980* (M.A. thesis, University of Bern, 1995), p. 67; On Norbert Burger who played a key role in Austria's postwar extreme right, see Stiftung Dokumentationsarchiv des österreichischen Widerstandes, *Handbuch*, p. 291.
351. Fankhauser, *"Hört auf, die Erde zu ermorden!"*, pp. 68f; Frischknecht, *"Schweiz wir kommen"*, p. 60.
352. Frischknecht, *"Schweiz wir kommen"*, p. 60.
353. Quoted in: Fankhauser, *"Hört auf, die Erde zu ermorden!"*, p. 69, my translation.
354. *Memopress*, edition K, no. 4, 1991, p. 1; see also Fankhauser, *"Hört auf, die Erde zu ermorden!"*, p. 70.
355. Frischknecht, *"Schweiz wir kommen"*, pp. 103ff.
356. *Volk + Heimat*, no. 5, April 1981, p. 4; no. 2, February 1983, pp. 3f. On *Neue Anthropologie*, see Lange, *Was die Rechten lesen*, pp. 117–20; S. Kühl, *Die Internationale der Rassisten*, Frankfurt 1997, pp. 229f.
357. *Courrier du Continent*, no. 279, January 1987, p. 9; no. 317, September 1990, p. 9.
358. Frischknecht, *"Schweiz wir kommen"*, p. 267; Altermatt and Skenderovic, 'Die extreme Rechte', p. 72; Niggli and Frischknecht, *Rechte Seilschaften*, pp. 289f.
359. *SonntagsBlick*, 26 September 1999; *Tages Anzeiger*, 28 September 1999; *Neue Zürcher Zeitung*, 2 October 1999.
360. *SonntagsZeitung*, 17 September 2000; *Neue Zürcher Zeitung*, 18 September 2000; *Tages Anzeiger*, 18 September 2000.
361. See the interviews with Christoph Blocher in: *Nation & Europa*, October 1996, pp. 28–31; *Deutsche Wochen-Zeitung*, no. 51, December 1997, p. 7. For assessments made by the German authorities regarding the two extreme-right papers, see *Verfassungsschutzbericht 2001*, pp. 91, 129.
362. *Nation & Europa*, October 1996, p. 30, my translation.

363. *SonntagsBlick,* 19 December 1999; *Neue Zürcher Zeitung,* 20 December 1999. In the press reports, Blocher's interview in the *Deutsche Wochen-Zeitung* was mistakenly attributed to the *National-Zeitung,* another German extreme-right paper closely affiliated with *Deutsche Wochen-Zeitung.* Blocher also posted the two interviews and the subsequent controversy on his personal website: http://www.blocher.ch/de/index.php?item=aktuell, retrieved 31 August 2008.

364. Fankhauser, *"Hört auf, die Erde zu ermorden!";* Drews, *"Schweizer erwache!".*

365. Drews, *"Schweizer erwache!",* pp. 105–10.

366. N. Meienberg, *Die Welt als Wille & Wahn,* Zurich, 1987, pp. 136f; L. Reichlin, *Kriegsverbrecher Wipf, Eugen,* Zurich, 1994.

367. Drews, *"Schweizer erwache!",* pp. 105f

References

The following list of references contains only academic literature on the issues treated in this book. Short articles that were published in newspapers or posted on the Internet, and reports by state authorities and non-governmental organisations are referenced in the endnotes, as are all the primary sources on which I have drawn my empirical research.

Abramowicz, M. *Extrême-droite et antisémitisme en Belgique de 1945 à nos jours*. Brussels, 1993.
Algazy, J. *La tentation néo-fasciste en France, 1944–1965*. Paris, 1984.
Altermatt, U. 'Conservatism in Switzerland: A Study in Antimodernism', *Journal of Contemporary History* vol. 14, no. 4 (1979), 581–610.
——— 'Xenophobie und Superpatriotismus: Die populistische Anti-Überfremdungsbewegung in der Schweiz der sechziger und siebziger Jahre', *Faschismus in Österreich und international. Jahrbuch für Zeitgeschichte 1980/1981*, Vienna, 1982, pp. 167–93.
——— 'Rechtsextremismus in der Schweiz: Randphänomen oder Pathologie des normalen Alltags?' *Civitas* vol. 41, no. 3 (1986), 85–93.
——— *Das Fanal von Sarajevo: Ethnonationalismus in Europa*. Zurich, 1996.
——— *Katholizismus und Antisemitismus: Mentalitäten, Kontinuitäten, Ambivalenzen. Zur Kulturgeschichte der Schweiz 1918–1945*. Frauenfeld, Stuttgart, Vienna, 1999.
Altermatt, U. and M. Furrer. 'Die Autopartei: Protest für Freiheit, Wohlstand und das Auto', in *Rechte und linke Fundamentalopposition: Studien zur Schweizer Politik 1965–1990*, U. Altermatt et al., Basel, 1994, pp. 135–53.
Altermatt, U. and H. Kriesi, eds. *Rechtsextremismus in der Schweiz: Organisationen und Radikalisierung in den 1980er und 1990er Jahren*. Zurich, 1995.
Altermatt, U. and D. Skenderovic. 'Die extreme Rechte: Organisationen, Personen und Entwicklungen in den achtziger und neunziger Jahren', in *Rechtsextremismus in der Schweiz: Organisationen und Radikalisierung in den 1980er und 1990er Jahren*, eds U. Altermatt, and H. Kriesi. Zurich, 1995, pp. 11–155.
——— 'Die Nouvelle droite in Frankreich und der Westschweiz', *Universitas Friburgensis* no. 2 (1996), 37–39.
——— 'Switzerland', in *Extremism in Europe, 1998 Survey*, ed. J.-Y. Camus. Paris, 1998, pp. 340–52.
——— 'Die rechtsextreme Landschaft in der Schweiz: Typologie und aktuelle Entwicklungen', *Österreichische Zeitschrift für Politikwissenschaft* vol. 28, no. 1 (1999), 101–9.

―――― 'Extreme Rechte, Rassismus und Antisemitismus in der Schweiz. Überblick und Typologie', *Forschungsjournal Neue Soziale Bewegungen* vol. 12, no. 1 (1999), 83–89.

―――― 'Kontinuität und Wandel des Rassismus. Begriffe und Debatten', *Zeitschrift für Geschichtswissenschaft* vol. 53, no. 9 (2005), 773–90.

Anderson, B. *Imagined Communities: Reflections on the Origin and Spread of Nationalism*, rev. edn. London, New York, 1991.

Anderson, S. and J.L. Anderson. *Inside the League: The Shocking Exposé of How Terrorists, Nazis, and Latin American Death Squads Have Infiltrated the World Anti-Communist League.* New York, 1986.

Annas, M. and R. Christoph, eds. *Neue Soundtracks für den Volksempfänger: Nazirock, Jugendkultur und rechter Mainstream,* 2nd edn. Berlin, 1993.

Ansell, A.E. *New Right, New Racism: Race and Reaction in the United States and Britain.* New York, 1997.

Antonio, R.J. 'After Postmodernism: Reactionary Tribalism', *American Journal of Sociology* vol. 106, no. 2 (2000), 40–87.

Arévalo, F. *L'application du modèle de la Troisième voie en Suisse romande,* Seminar Thesis in Political Science, University of Geneva, 1994.

Armingeon, K. 'Der Schweizer Rechtsextremismus im internationalen Vergleich', *Swiss Political Science Review* vol. 1, no. 4 (1995), 41–64.

―――― 'Rechtsextremismus: Die Schweiz im internationalen Vergleich', in *Nationalismus, Multikulturalismus und Ethnizität: Beiträge zur Deutung von sozialer und politischer Einbindung und Ausgrenzung,* ed. H.-R. Wicker. Bern, Stuttgart, Vienna, 1998, 79–99.

―――― 'Fremdenfeindlichkeit in der Schweiz in international vergleichender Perspektive', in *Die Bedeutung des Ethnischen im Zeitalter der Globalisierung: Einbindungen – Ausgrenzungen – Säuberungen,* ed. R. Moser. Bern, Stuttgart, Vienna, 2000, pp. 219–37.

Awadalla, E. '"Sage mir, mit wem du umgehst, und ich sage dir, wer du bist!" Das "Institut zur Förderung der psychologischen Menschenkenntnis"', in *Die Ordnung, die sie meinen: "Neue Rechte" in Österreich,* ed. W. Purtscheller. Vienna, 1994, pp. 188–203.

―――― 'Eine Seuche, die speziell Lehrer befällt', in *Die Rechte in Bewegung: Seilschaften und Vernetzungen der "Neuen Rechten",* ed. W. Purtscheller. Vienna, 1995, pp. 160–93.

Azéma, J.-P. 'Vichy', in *Histoire de l'extrême droite en France,* ed. M. Winock. Paris, 1993, pp. 191–214.

Back, L., M. Keith and J. Solomos. 'Racism on the Internet: Mapping Neo-Fascist Subcultures in Cyberspace', in *Nation and Race: The Developing Euro-American Racist Subculture,* eds J. Kaplan and T. Bjørgo. Boston, MA, 1998, pp. 73–101.

Backes, U. *Politischer Extremismus in demokratischen Verfassungsstaaten: Elemente einer normativen Rahmentheorie.* Opladen, 1989.

―――― 'L'extrême droite: les multiples facettes d'une catégorie d'analyse', in *Les croisés de la société fermée: L'Europe des extrêmes droites,* ed. P. Perrineau. Paris, 2001, pp. 13–29.

Bailer-Galanda, B. '"Revisionismus" – pseudowissenschaftliche Propaganda des Rechtsextremismus', in *Wahrheit und "Auschwitzlüge": Zur Bekämpfung "revisionistischer" Propaganda*, eds B. Bailer-Galanda, W. Benz and W. Neugebauer. Vienna, 1995, pp. 16–32.

Balibar, E. 'Is There a "Neo-Racism"?', in *Race, Nation, Class: Ambiguous Identities*, E. Balibar and I. Wallerstein. London, 1991, pp. 17–28.

Banks, M. and A. Gingrich. 'Introduction: Neo-nationalism in Europe and Beyond', in *Neo-nationalism in Europe and Beyond: Perspectives from Social Anthropology*, eds A. Gingrich and M. Banks. New York, Oxford, 2006, pp. 1–26.

Banton, M. 'Xenophobia', in *Dictionary of Race and Ethnic Relations*, ed. E. Cashmore, 4th edn. London, New York, 1996, pp. 382–83.

Barker, M. *The New Racism: Conservatives and the Ideology of the Tribe*. London, 1981.

Barkun, M. 'Conspiracy Theories as Stigmatized Knowledge: The Basis for a New Age Racism?' in *Nation and Race: The Developing Euro-American Racist Subculture*, eds J. Kaplan and T. Bjørgo. Boston, MA, 1998, pp. 58–72.

——— *A Culture of Conspiracy: Apocalyptic Visions in Contemporary America*. Berkeley, CA, Los Angeles, London, 2003.

Barnes, I.R. 'Antisemitic Europe and the "Third Way": The Ideas of Maurice Bardèche', *Patterns of Prejudice* vol. 34, no. 2 (2000), 57–73.

Bar-On, T. *Where Have All the Fascists Gone?* Aldershot, 2007.

Baumann, W. 'Von der Krise zur Konkordanz. Die Rolle der Bauern', in *Krisen und Stabilisierung: Die Schweiz in der Zwischenkriegszeit*, eds S. Guex et al. Zurich, 1998, pp. 97–113.

Baumann, W. and P. Moser. *Bauern im Industriestaat: Agrarpolitische Konzeptionen und bäuerliche Bewegungen in der Schweiz 1918–1968*. Zurich, 1999.

Bell, D. ed. *The Radical Right: The New American Right, Expanded and Updated*. Garden City, NY, 1963.

Benz, W. *Legenden, Lügen, Vorurteile: Ein Wörterbuch zur Zeitgeschichte*. Munich, 1998.

——— 'Antisemitismus in der Schweiz', *Judaica: Beiträge zum Verstehen des Judentums* vol. 56, no. 1 (2000), 4–18.

——— *Was ist Antisemitismus?* Munich, 2004.

Bergmann, W. 'Ein Versuch, die extreme Rechte als soziale Bewegung zu beschreiben', in *Neonazismus und rechte Subkultur*, eds W. Bergmann and R. Erb. Berlin, 1994, pp. 183–207.

Bergmann, W. and R. Erb. '"In Treue zur Nation". Zur kollektiven Identität der rechtsextremen Bewegung', in *Paradigmen der Bewegungsforschung: Entstehung und Entwicklung von Neuen sozialen Bewegungen und Rechtsextremismus*, eds K.-U. Hellmann and R. Koopmans. Opladen, 1998, pp. 149–65.

Betz, H.-G. *Postmodern Politics in Germany: The Politics of Resentment*. New York, 1991.

——— 'Radikal rechtspopulistische Parteien in Westeuropa', *Aus Politik und Zeitgeschichte* no. 44 (1991), 3–14.

——— 'The New Politics of Resentment. Radical Right-Wing Populist Parties in Western Europe', *Comparative Politics* vol. 25, no. 4 (1993), 413–27.

——— *Radical Right-Wing Populism in Western Europe*. New York, 1994.

―――― 'Introduction', in *The New Politics of the Right: Neo-Populist Parties and Movements in Established Democracies*, eds H.-G. Betz and S. Immerfall. New York, 1998, pp. 1–10.

―――― 'Exclusionary Populism in Austria, Italy, and Switzerland', *International Journal* vol. 56, no. 3 (2001), 393–420.

―――― 'Conditions Favouring the Success and Failure of Radical Right-Wing Populist Parties in Contemporary Democracies', in *Democracies and the Populist Challenge*, eds Y. Mény and Y. Surel. Basingstoke, New York, 2002, pp. 197–213.

―――― 'Contre la mondialisation: xénophobie, politiques identitaires et populisme d'exclusion en Europe occidentale', *Politique et Sociétés* vol. 21, no. 2 (2002), 9–28.

―――― *La droite populiste en Europe: Extrême et démocrate?* Paris, 2004.

Betz, H.-G. and C. Johnson. 'Against the Current – Stemming the Tide: The Nostalgic Ideology of the Contemporary Radical Populist Right', *Journal of Political Ideologies* vol. 9, no. 3 (2004), 311–27.

Beyme, K. von. 'Right-Wing Extremism in Post-War Europe', *West European Politics* vol. 11, no. 2 (1988), 1–18.

Bihr, A. et al. *Négationnistes: les chiffonniers de l'histoire*. Villeurbanne, Paris 1997.

Billig, M. 'The Extreme Right: Continuities in Anti-Semitic Conspiracy Theory in Post-War Europe', in *The Nature of the Right: American and European Politics and Political Thought since 1789*, eds R. Eatwell and N. O'Sullivan. Boston, MA, 1989, pp. 146–66.

Bjørgo, T. 'Introduction', in *Terror from the Extreme Right*, ed. T. Bjørgo. London, 1995, pp. 1–16.

―――― *Racist and Right-Wing Violence in Scandinavia: Patterns, Perpetrators and Responses*. Oslo, 1997.

―――― 'Xenophobic Violence and Ethnic Conflict at the Local Level: Lessons from the Scandinavian Experience', in *Challenging Immigration and Ethnic Relations Politics*, eds R. Koopmans and P. Statham, Oxford, 2000, pp. 368–385.

―――― 'Gewalt gegen ethnische und religiöse Minderheiten', in *Internationales Handbuch der Gewaltforschung*, eds W. Heitmeyer and J. Hagan. Wiesbaden, 2002, pp. 981–99.

Bjørgo, T., ed. *Terror from the Extreme Right*. London, 1995.

Bjørgo, T. and R. Witte, eds. *Racist Violence in Europe*. New York, 1993.

Bobbio, N. *Left and Right: The Significance of a Political Distinction*. Chicago, 1996.

Borne, E. 'Le catholicisme', in *Forces religieuses et attitudes politiques dans la France contemporaine*, ed. R. Rémond. Paris, 1965, pp. 9–25.

Brändle, M. 'Konkordanz gleich Konvergenz? Die Links-rechts-Positionierung der Schweizer Bundesratsparteien, 1947–1995', *Swiss Political Science Review* vol. 5, no. 1 (1999), 11–29.

―――― 'Die finanziellen Mittel der Parteien', in *Die Schweizer Parteien im Wandel: Von Mitgliederparteien zu professionalisierten Wählerorganisationen?* A. Ladner and M. Brändle. Zurich, 2001, pp. 149–92.

――― 'Strukturen der Parteiorganisationen', in *Die Schweizer Parteien im Wandel: Von Mitgliederparteien zu professionalisierten Wählerorganisationen?* A. Ladner and M. Brändle. Zurich, 2001, pp. 45–72.

Brauner-Orthen, A. *Die Neue Rechte in Deutschland: Antidemokratische und rassistische Tendenzen.* Opladen, 2001.

Brayard, F. *Comment l'idée vint à M. Rassinier: Naissance du révisionnisme.* Paris, 1996.

Breuer, S. *Anatomie der Konservativen Revolution.* Darmstadt, 1993.

Brubaker, R. *Citizenship and Nationhood in France and Germany.* Cambridge, MA, London, 1992.

――― 'Myths and Misconceptions in the Study of Nationalism', in *The State of the Nation: Ernest Gellner and the Theory of Nationalism*, ed. J.A. Hall. Cambridge, 1998, pp. 272–306.

Brug, W. van der, M. Fennema and J. Tillie. 'Anti-Immigrant Parties in Europe: Ideological or Protest Vote?' *European Journal of Political Research* vol. 37, no. 1 (2000), 77–102.

Bühlmann, M., M. Freitag and A. Vatter. 'Die schweigende Mehrheit: Eine Typologie der Schweizer Nichtwählerschaft', in *Schweizer Wahlen 1999*, eds P. Sciarini, S. Hardmeier and A. Vatter. Bern, Stuttgart, Vienna, 2003, pp. 27–58.

Buomberger, T. *Kampf gegen unerwünschte Fremde: Von James Schwarzenbach bis Christoph Blocher.* Zurich, 2004.

Burke, P. *What is Cultural History?* Cambridge, 2005.

Butikofer, R. 'Marcel Regamey – eine traditionalistische Sicht des eidgenössischen Bundes', in *Intellektuelle von rechts: Ideologie und Politik in der Schweiz 1918–1939*, ed. A. Mattioli. Zurich, 1995, pp. 171–83.

――― *Le refus de la modernité. La Ligue vaudoise: une extrême droite et la Suisse (1919–1945).* Lausanne, 1996.

Calhoun, C. *Nationalism.* Minneapolis, MN, 1997.

Camus, J.-Y. 'Intégrisme catholique et extrême droite en France. Le parti de la contre-révolution (1945–1988)', *Lignes* no. 4 (1988), 76–89.

――― 'La structure du "camp national" en France: la périphérie militante et organisationnelle du Front national et du Mouvement national républicain', in *Les croisés de la société fermée: L'Europe des extrêmes droites*, ed. P. Perrineau. Paris, 2001, pp. 199–223.

――― 'Die radikale Rechte in Westeuropa. Vom nostalgischen Aktionismus zum fremdenfeindlichen Populismus', in *Rechtspopulismus – Österreichische Krankheit oder europäische Normalität?* ed. W. Eismann. Vienna, 2002, pp. 40–55.

Camus, J.-Y. and R. Monzat. *Les droites nationales et radicales en France: Répertoire critique.* Lyon, 1992.

Canovan, M. 'Trust the People! Populism and the Two Faces of Democracy', *Political Studies* vol. 47, no. 1 (1999), 2–16.

――― 'Taking Politics to the People: Populism as the Ideology of Democracy', in *Democracies and the Populist Challenge*, eds Y. Mény and Y. Surel, Basingstoke, New York, 2002, pp. 25–44.

Cantini, C. *Les ultras. Extrême droite et droite extrême en Suisse: les mouvements et la presse de 1921 à 1991.* Lausanne, 1992.

Caramani, D. 'The Swiss Parliamentary Election of 1995', *Electoral Studies* vol. 15, no. 1 (1996), 128–38.
Carter, E. *The Extreme Right in Western Europe: Success or Failure?* Manchester, New York, 2005.
Cashmore, E. 'Xenophobia', in *Dictionary of Race and Ethnic Relations*, ed. E. Cashmore, 1st edn. London, 1984, p. 284.
Castells, M. *The Information Age, Vol. 2: The Power of Identity*. Malden, MA, Oxford, 1997.
Chairoff, P. *Dossier néo-nazisme*. Paris, 1977.
Chebel d'Appollonia, A. *L'extrême droite en France: De Maurras à Le Pen*. Brussels, 1988.
Chenaux, J.-P. *La presse d'opinion en Suisse Romande ou La bataille des idées*. Lausanne, Geneva, n.d. [1986].
Christadler, M. 'Die "Nouvelle Droite" in Frankreich', in *Neokonservative und "Neue Rechte": Der Angriff gegen Sozialstaat und liberale Demokratie in den Vereinigten Staaten, Westeuropa und der Bundesrepublik*, ed. I. Fetscher. Munich, 1983, pp. 163–215.
Church, C.H. 'The Swiss Election of 1991: Stability, not Stasis', *West European Politics* vol. 15, no. 4 (1992), 184–88.
——— 'The Swiss Elections of 1995: Real Victors and Real Losers at Last?', *West European Politics* vol. 19, no. 3 (1996), 641–48.
——— 'The Swiss Elections of October 1999: Learning to Live in More Interesting Times', in *West European Politics* vol. 23, no. 3 (2000), 215–30.
——— *The Politics and Government of Switzerland*. Basingstoke, New York, 2004.
Clavien, A. *Les helvétistes: Intellectuels et politique en Suisse romande au début du siècle*. Lausanne, 1994.
——— 'Georges Oltramare. Von der Theaterbühne auf die politische Bühne', in *Intellektuelle von rechts: Ideologie und Politik in der Schweiz 1918–1939*, ed. A. Mattioli. Zurich, 1995, pp. 157–70.
Cohn, N. *Warrant for Genocide: The Myth of the Jewish World Conspiracy and the Protocols of the Elders of Zion*, new edn. London, 1996.
Corpet, O. 'La revue', in *Histoires des droites en France*, 3 vols, ed. J.-F. Sirinelli. Paris, 1992, vol. 2, pp. 161–212.
D'Alessio, E. 'Switzerland', in *Extremism in Europe*, ed. J.-Y. Camus. Paris, 1997, pp. 344–53.
Decker, F. *Parteien unter Druck: Der neue Rechtspopulismus in den westlichen Demokratien*. Opladen, 2000.
——— *Der neue Rechtspopulismus*, 2nd rev. edn. Opladen, 2004.
Delgrande, M. and W. Linder. *Analyse der eidgenössischen Abstimmungen vom 8. Juni 1997*, VOX no. 61, Bern, 1997.
Desbuissons, G. 'Maurice Bardèche: un précurseur du "révisionnisme"', *Relations internationales* no. 65 (1991), 23–37.
Deutsch, K.W. *Die Schweiz als ein paradigmatischer Fall politischer Integration*. Bern, 1976.
De Winter, L. 'Conclusion: A Comparative Analysis of the Electoral, Office and Policy Success of Ethnoregionalist Parties', in *Regionalist Parties in West-*

ern Europe, eds L. De Winter and H. Türsan, London, New York, 1998, pp. 204–47.
Diederichsen, D. *Freiheit macht arm: Das Leben nach Rock'n'Roll 1990–93*. Cologne, 1993.
Dongen, L. van. 'Swiss Memory of the Second World War in the Immediate Post-War Period, 1945–1948', in *Switzerland and the Second World War*, ed. G. Kreis. London, Portland, OR, 2000, 261–81.
—— *Un purgatoire très discret: La transition "helvétique" d'anciens nazis, fascistes et collaborateurs*. Paris, 2008.
Dreifuss, E. *Die Schweiz und das Dritte Reich: Vier deutschschweizerische Zeitungen im Zeitalter des Faschismus 1933–1939*. Frauenfeld, Stuttgart, 1971.
Drews, I. *"Schweizer erwache!" Der Rechtspopulist James Schwarzenbach (1967–1978)*. Frauenfeld, Stuttgart, Vienna, 2005.
Druwe, U. (in collaboration with S. Mantino). '"Rechtsextremismus". Methodologische Bemerkungen zu einem politikwissenschaftlichen Begriff', in *Rechtsextremismus: Ergebnisse und Perspektiven der Forschung*, Special Issue of *Politische Vierteljahresschrift*, vol. 27, eds J.W. Falter, H.-G. Jaschke and J.R. Winkler. Opladen, 1996, pp. 66–80.
Dudek, P. and H.-G. Jaschke. *Entstehung und Entwicklung des Rechtsextremismus in der Bundesrepublik: Zur Tradition einer besonderen politischen Kultur*, 2 vols. Opladen, 1984.
Dupont, C. and P. Sciarini. 'Switzerland and the European Integration Process: Engagement without Marriage', in *The Swiss Labyrinth: Institutions, Outcomes and Redesign*, Special Issue of *West European Politics*, vol. 24, no. 2, ed. J.-E. Lane. London, 2001, pp. 211–32.
Duranton-Crabol, A.-M. *Visages de la Nouvelle droite: Le GRECE et son histoire*. Paris, 1988.
—— *L'Europe de l'extrême droite: De 1945 à nos jours*. Brussels, 1991.
Durham, M. *The Christian Right, the Far Right and the Boundaries of American Conservatism*. Manchester, New York, 2000.
Duverger, M. *Political Parties: Their Organization and Activity in the Modern State*. London, New York, 1954.
—— *The French Political System*. Chicago, 1958.
Eatwell, R. 'Ideologies: Approaches and Trends', in *Contemporary Political Ideologies*, eds R. Eatwell and A. Wright. London, New York, 1993, pp. 1–22.
—— *Fascism: A History*. New York, 1997.
—— 'The Dynamics of Right-wing Electoral Breakthrough', *Patterns of Prejudice* vol. 32, no. 3 (1998), 3–31.
—— 'Ethnocentric Party Mobilization in Europe: The Importance of the Three-Dimensional Approach', in *Challenging Immigration and Ethnic Relations Politics: Comparative European Perspectives*, eds R. Koopmans and P. Statham. Oxford, New York, 2000, pp. 348–67.
—— 'The Rebirth of the "Extreme Right" in Western Europe?' *Parliamentary Affairs* vol. 53, no. 3 (2000) 407–25.
—— 'The Rebirth of Right-Wing Charisma? The Cases of Jean-Marie Le Pen and Vladimir Zhirinovsky', *Totalitarian Movements and Political Religions* vol. 3, no. 3 (2002), 1–24.

——— 'Ten Theories of the Extreme Right', in *Right-Wing Extremism in the Twenty-First Century*, 2nd rev. edn, eds P.H. Merkl and L. Weinberg. London, Portland, OR, 2003, pp. 47–73.

——— 'Introduction. The New Extreme Right Challenge', in *Western Democracies and the New Extreme Right Challenge*, eds R. Eatwell and C. Mudde. London, 2004, pp. 1–16.

Ebata, M. 'Right-Wing Extremism: In Search of a Definition', in *The Extreme Right: Freedom and Security at Risk*, eds A. Braun and S. Scheinberg. Boulder, CO, 1997, pp. 12–35.

——— 'The Internationalization of the Extreme Right', in *The Extreme Right: Freedom and Security at Risk*, eds A. Braun and S. Scheinberg. Boulder, CO, Oxford, 1997, pp. 220–49.

Ebel, M. and P. Fiala. *Sous le consensus, la xénophobie: Paroles, arguments, contextes (1961–1981)*. Lausanne, 1983.

Efler, I. 'Bündnispolitik. Der VPM und die "Konservative Revolution"', in *VPM – Die Psychosekte*, eds I. Efler and H. Reile. Reinbek, 1995, pp. 93–142.

Efler, I. and H. Reile, eds. *VPM – Die Psychosekte*. Reinbek, 1995.

Eisenegger, M. and H. Karl. *Die Differenzsemantiken der schweizerischen "Neuen Rechten" und des politischen Konservatismus: Zur ideologischen Konstruktion von "Eigen" und "Fremd" im massenmedialen Diskurs. Eine vergleichende, inhaltsanalytische Studie der Presseorgane "Volk+Heimat" und "Schweizerzeit"*, Master's dissertation, University of Zurich, 1995.

Eisner, M. 'Sozialer Wandel und neue Integrationsprobleme seit den Siebzigerjahren', in *Sozialbericht 2000*, ed. C. Suter. Zurich, 2000, pp. 164–81.

Erdle B.R. and D. Wildmann. 'Die Macht, das Geld und die Juden. Essay zum öffentlichen Umgang mit Antisemitismus in der Schweiz', *traverse: Zeitschrift für Geschichte – Revue de l'histoire* vol. 5, no. 1 (1998), 150–56.

Fankhauser, P. *"Hört auf, die Erde zu ermorden!" Valentin Oehen, 1970–1980: Ein Beitrag zur biographischen Geschichtsschreibung*, Master's dissertation, University of Bern, 1995.

Farago, P. *Wahlen 95: Zusammensetzung und politische Orientierungen der Wählerschaft an den eidgenössischen Wahlen 1995*. Bern, Geneva, Zurich, 1996.

Farin, K. and E. Seidel-Pielen. *Skinheads*, 3rd edn. Munich, 1995.

Fein, H. 'Dimensions of Antisemitism: Attitudes, Collective Accusations, and Actions' in *The Persisting Question: Sociological Perspectives and Social Contexts of Modern Antisemitism*, ed. H. Fein. Berlin, New York, 1987, pp. 67–85.

Feit, M. *Die "Neue Rechte" in der Bundesrepublik: Organisation – Ideologie – Strategie*. Frankfurt, New York, 1987.

Fennema, M. 'Some Conceptual Issues and Problems in the Comparison of Anti-Immigrant Parties in Western Europe', *Party Politics* vol. 3, no. 4 (1997), 473–92.

——— 'Legal Repression of Extreme-Right Parties and Racial Discrimination', in *Challenging Immigration and Ethnic Relations Politics: Comparative European Perspectives*, eds R. Koopmans and P. Statham. Oxford, New York, 2000, pp. 119–44.

Fetscher, I., ed. *Neokonservative und "Neue Rechte": Der Angriff gegen den Sozialstaat und liberale Demokratie in den Vereinigten Staaten, Westeuropa und der Bundesrepublik*. Munich, 1983.

Fieschi, C. 'European Institutions: The Far-Right and Illiberal Politics in a Liberal Context', *Parliamentary Affairs* vol. 53, no. 3 (2000), 517–31.
Finger, M. and P. Sciarini. 'Integrating "New Politics" into "Old Politics": The Swiss Party Elite', *West European Politics* vol. 14, no. 1 (1991), 98–112.
Finley, M. *The Use and Abuse of History.* New York, 1975.
Fischer, U. *Gaston-Armand Amaudruz: Ein Schweizer im Beziehungsnetz des europäischen Rechtsextremismus,* Master's dissertation, University of Fribourg, 1999.
Ford, G. *Fascist Europe: The Rise of Racism and Xenophobia.* London, Concord, MA, 1992.
Freeden, M. 'Is Nationalism a Distinct Ideology?' *Political Studies* vol. 46, no. 4 (1998), 744–63.
Fredrickson, G.M. *Racism: A Short History.* Princeton, NJ, 2002.
Frevert U. and H.-G. Haupt, eds. *Neue Politikgeschichte: Perspektiven einer historischen Politikforschung.* Frankfurt, New York, 2005.
Frischknecht, J. *"Schweiz wir kommen": Die neuen Fröntler und Rassisten,* 2nd edn. Zurich, 1991.
Frischknecht, J. et al. *Die unheimlichen Patrioten: Politische Reaktion in der Schweiz. Ein aktuelles Handbuch mit Nachtrag 1979–1984,* 6th edn. Zurich, 1987.
Fröhlich, H. and B. Müller. *Überfremdungsdiskurse und die Virulenz von Fremdenfeindlichkeit vor dem Hintergrund internationaler Migrationsbewegungen.* Zurich, 1995.
Froidevaux, D. 'Construction de la nation et pluralisme suisses: idéologie et pratiques', *Swiss Political Science Review* vol. 3, no. 4 (1997), 29–58.
Fromm, R. and B. Kernbach. *... und morgen die ganze Welt? Rechtsextreme Publizistik in Westeuropa.* Marburg, Berlin, 1994.
——— *Rechtsextremismus auf dem Internet: Die neue Gefahr.* Munich, 2001.
Furrer, M. 'Die Apotheose der Nation. Konkordanz und Konsens in den 1950er Jahren', in *Die Konstruktion einer Nation: Nation und Nationalisierung in der Schweiz, 18.-20. Jahrhundert,* eds U. Altermatt, C. Bosshart-Pfluger and A. Tanner. Zurich, 1998, pp. 101–18.
Gamble, A. 'The Political Economy of Freedom', in *The Ideology of the New Right,* ed. R. Levitas. Cambridge, 1986, pp. 25–54.
Gasper, H., J. Müller and F. Valentin. *Lexikon der Sekten, Sondergruppen und Weltanschauungen: Fakten, Hintergründe, Klärungen.* Freiburg, Basel, Vienna, 1997.
Gawronski, V. 'Motive der Befürworter des Volksbegehren gegen die Überfremdung. Ergebnisse einer Umfrage', *Mitteilungsblatt des Delegierten für Konjunkturfragen* vol. 26, no. 4 (1970), 56–64.
Geden, O. *Rechte Ökologie: Umweltschutz zwischen Emanzipation und Faschismus.* Berlin, 1996.
Geiss, I. *Geschichte des Rassismus.* Frankfurt, 1988.
Gellner, E. *Nations and Nationalism.* Ithaca, NY, 1983.
Gentile, P. 'Radical Right Protest in Switzerland', in *Acts of Dissent: New Developments in the Study of Protest,* eds D. Rucht, R. Koopmans and F. Neidhardt. Lanham, MD, 1999, pp. 227–52.
Gentile, P. and H. Kriesi. 'Contemporary Radical-Right Parties in Switzerland: History of a Divided Family', in *The New Politics of the Right: Neo-Populist Parties and Movements in Established Democracies,* eds H.-G. Betz and S. Immerfall. New York, 1998, pp. 125–41.

Gentile, P. et al. 'Die rechtsradikale Radikalisierung: eine Fallstudie', in *Rechtsextremismus in der Schweiz: Organisationen und Radikalisierung in den 1980er und 1990er Jahren*, eds U. Altermatt and H. Kriesi. Zurich, 1995, pp. 157–263.

Gerber, B. *Die antirassistische Bewegung in der Schweiz: Organisationen, Netzwerke und Aktionen*. Zurich, 2003.

Gessenharter, W. *Kippt die Republik? Die Neue Rechte und ihre Unterstützung durch Politik und Medien*. Munich, 1994.

——— 'Neue radikale Rechte, intellektuelle Neue Rechte und Rechtsextremismus: Zur theoretischen und empirischen Neuvermessung eines politisch-ideologischen Raumes', in *Rechtsextremismus und Neue Rechte in Deutschland: Neuvermessung eines politisch-ideologischen Raumes?* eds W. Gessenharter and H. Fröchling. Opladen, 1998, pp. 25–66.

Gessenharter, W. and H. Fröchling. 'Neue Rechte und Rechtsextremismus in Deutschland', in *Handbuch deutscher Rechtsextremismus*, ed. J. Mecklenburg. Berlin, 1996, pp. 550–71.

Gilg, P. 'Der Erfolg der neuen Rechtsgruppen in den Nationalratswahlen von 1971', *Schweizerische Zeitschrift für Volkswirtschaft und Statistik* vol. 108, no. 4 (1972), 591–622.

Gilg, P., and Gruner, E. 'Nationale Erneuerungsbewegungen in der Schweiz 1925–1940', *Vierteljahrshefte für Zeitgeschichte* vol. 14, no. 1 (1966), 1–25.

Girod, M. 'L'Union démocratique du centre: les raisons d'un succès', in *Extrême droite et national-populisme en Europe de l'Ouest*, eds P. Blaise and P. Moreau, Brussels, 2004, pp. 413-442.

Giugni, M. and F. Passy. *Histoires de mobilisation politique en Suisse: De la contestation à l'intégration*. Paris, Montreal, 1997.

Givens, T.E. *Voting Radical Right in Western Europe*. New York, 2005.

Glaus, B. *Die Nationale Front: Eine Schweizer faschistische Bewegung 1930–1940*. Zurich, 1969.

——— 'The National Front in Switzerland', in *Who Were the Fascists? Social Roots of European Fascism*, eds S.U. Larsen, B. Hagtvet and J.P. Myklebust. Bergen, Oslo, Tromsø, 1980, pp. 467–78.

Goetschel, L., M. Bernath and D. Schwarz. *Swiss Foreign Policy: Foundations and Possibilities*. London, New York, 2005.

Golder, M. 'Explaining Variation in the Success of Extreme Right Parties in Western Europe', *Comparative Political Studies* vol. 36, no. 4 (2003), 432–66.

Golsan, R.J. 'Introduction', in *Fascism's Return: Scandal, Revision, and Ideology since 1980*, ed. R.J. Golsan. Lincoln, NK, London, 1998, pp. 1–18.

Golsan, R.J., ed. *Fascism's Return: Scandal, Revision, and Ideology since 1980*. Lincoln, NK, London, 1998.

Goodwin, M.J. 'The Rise and Faults of the Internalist Perspective in Extreme Right Studies', *Representations* vol. 42, no. 4 (2006), 347–64.

Graumann, C.F. and S. Moscovici, eds. *Changing Conceptions of Conspiracy*. New York, 1987.

Green, J.C., M.J. Rozell and C. Wilcox, eds. *The Christian Right in American Politics: Marching to the Millennium*. Washington, DC, 2003.

Greenfeld, L. *Nationalism: Five Roads to Modernity*. Cambridge, MA, London, 1992.

Griffin, R. 'Afterword. Last Rights?' in *The Radical Right in Central and Eastern Europe since 1989*, ed. S.P. Ramet. University Park, PA, 1999, pp. 297–321.

―――― 'Interregnum or Endgame? The Radical Right in the "Post-Fascist" Era', *Journal of Political Ideologies* vol. 5, no. 2 (2000), 163–78.

―――― 'From Slim Mould to Rhizome: An Introduction to the Groupuscular Right', *Patterns of Prejudice* vol. 37, no. 1 (2003), 27–50.

Griffin, R., W. Loh and A. Umland, eds. *Fascism Past and Present, West and East: An International Debate on Concepts and Cases in the Comparative Study of the Extreme Right*, Special Issue of *Soviet and Post-Soviet Politics and Society*, vol. 35, Stuttgart, 2006

Gruber, C. *Die politischen Parteien der Schweiz im Zweiten Weltkrieg*. Vienna, Zurich, Frankfurt, 1966.

Gruner, E. *Die Parteien in der Schweiz*, rev. edn. Bern, 1977.

Gruner, E. and K.J. Pitterle. 'Switzerland's Political Parties', in *Switzerland at the Polls: The National Elections of 1979*, ed. H.R. Penniman. Washington, London, 1983, pp. 30–59.

Gschwend, H. 'Die Umweltbewegung verändert die Parteienlandschaft – oder umgekehrt', *Schweizerisches Jahrbuch für Politische Wissenschaft* vol. 26 (1986), 243–56.

Gsteiger, F. *Blocher: Ein unschweizerisches Phänomen*. Basel, 2002.

Gugenberger, E., F. Petri and R. Schweidlenka. *Weltverschwörungstheorien: Die neue Gefahr von rechts*. Vienna, Munich, 1998.

Gugenberger, E. and R. Schweidlenka. *Mutter Erde, Magie und Politik: Zwischen Faschismus und neuer Gesellschaft*. Vienna, 1987.

Hainsworth, P. 'Introduction: The Extreme Right', in *The Politics of the Extreme Right: From the Margins to the Mainstream*, ed. P. Hainsworth. London, New York, 2000, pp. 1–17.

Halliday, F. '"Islamophobia" reconsidered', *Ethnic and Racial Studies* vol. 22, no. 5 (1999), 892–902.

Hannaford, I. *Race: The History of an Idea in the West*. Washington, Baltimore, MD, 1996.

Hardmeier, S. *Analyse der eidgenössischen Abstimmungen vom 1. Dezember 1996*, VOX no. 60, Zurich, 1997.

―――― 'Switzerland', *European Journal of Political Research* vol. 34, no. 3/4 (1998), 531–38.

―――― (in collaboration with S. Brunner and S. Libsig). 'Amerikanisierung der Wahlkampfkommunikation? Einem Schlagwort auf der Spur', in *Schweizer Wahlen 1999*, eds P. Sciarini, S. Hardmeier and A. Vatter. Bern, Stuttgart, Vienna, 2003, pp. 219–55.

Hardmeier, S. and A. Vatter. 'Synthese – Die Ursachen des SVP-Wahlerfolgs', in *Schweizer Wahlen 1999*, eds P. Sciarini, S. Hardmeier and A. Vatter, Bern, Stuttgart, Vienna, 2003, pp. 427–56.

Harmel, R. and L. Svåsand. 'Party Leadership and Party Institutionalization: Three Phases of Development', *West European Politics* vol. 16, no. 2 (1993), 67–88.

Hartmann, H. and F. Horvath. *Zivilgesellschaft von rechts: Die Erfolgsstory der Zürcher SVP*. Zurich, 1995.

Heilbrunn, J. 'Germany's New Right', *Foreign Affairs* vol. 75, no. 6 (1996), 80–98.
Heim, S. and U. Schaz. *Berechnung und Beschwörung: Übervölkerung – Kritik einer Debatte*. Berlin, 1996.
Heinisch, R. 'Success in Opposition – Failure in Government: Explaining the Performance of Right-Wing Populist Parties in Public Office', *West European Politics* vol. 26, no. 3 (2003), 91–130.
Heitmeyer, W. 'Rechtsextremistische Gewalt', in *Internationales Handbuch der Gewaltforschung*, eds W. Heitmeyer and J. Hagan. Wiesbaden, 2002, pp. 501–46.
Heller, F.P. and A. Maegerle. *Die Sprache des Hasses: Rechtsextremismus und völkische Esoterik – Jan van Helsing, Horst Mahler* ... Stuttgart, 2001.
Helms, L. 'Right-Wing Populist Parties in Austria and Switzerland: A Comparative Analysis of Electoral Support and Conditions of Success', *West European Politics* vol. 20, no. 2 (1997), 37–52.
Hennig, E. 'Politische Unzufriedenheit – ein Resonanzboden für Rechtsextremismus?' in *Rechtsextremismus: Einführung und Forschungsbilanz*, eds W. Kowalsky and W. Schroeder. Opladen, 1994, pp. 339–80.
Hilger, N. *Deutscher Neokonservatismus – das Beispiel Hermann Lübbes*. Baden-Baden, 1995.
Hirter, H. *Wahlen 1999: Zusammensetzung und politische Orientierung der Wählerschaft bei den eidgenössischen Wahlen 1995*. Bern, Geneva, Zurich, 2000.
Hirter, H. and W. Linder. *Analyse der eidgenössischen Abstimmungen vom 21. Mai 2000*, VOX no. 70, Bern, 2000.
—— *Analyse der eidgenössischen Abstimmungen vom 24. November 2002*, VOX no. 79, Bern, 2002.
Hobsbawm, E.J. *Nations and Nationalism since 1780: Programme, Myth, Reality*. Cambridge, 1990.
Hoffmann, S. *Le mouvement Poujade*. Paris, 1956.
Hoffmann-Nowotny, H.-J. 'Switzerland', in *European Immigration Policy: A Comparative Study*, ed. T. Hammar. Cambridge, 1985, pp. 206–36.
Hofstadter, R. *The Paranoid Style in American Politics and Other Essays*. New York, 1965.
Holmes, D.R. *Integral Europe: Fast-Capitalism, Multiculturalism, Neofascism*. Princeton, NJ, Oxford, 2000.
Hug, S. and P. Sciarini, eds. *Changements de valeurs et nouveaux clivages politiques en Suisse*. Paris, Budapest, Turin, 2002.
Hunt L., ed. *The New Cultural History*. Berkeley, Los Angeles, London, 1989.
Husbands, C.T. *Racist Political Movements in Western Europe*. London, 1989.
—— 'The Other Face of 1992: The Extreme-right Explosion in Western Europe', *Parliamentary Affairs* vol. 45, no. 3 (1992), 267–84.
—— 'Switzerland: Right-Wing and Xenophobic Parties, from Margin to Mainstream?' *Parliamentary Affairs* vol. 53, no. 3 (2000), 501–16.
Ignazi, P. 'The Silent Counter-Revolution. Hypotheses on the Emergence of Extreme Right-Wing Parties in Europe', *European Journal of Political Research* vol. 22, no. 1/2 (1992), 3–34.
—— 'The Extreme Right in Europe: A Survey', in *The Revival of Right-Wing*

Extremism in the Nineties, eds P.H. Merkl and L. Weinberg. London, Portland, OR, 1997, pp. 47–64.
——— *Extreme Right Parties in Western Europe*. Oxford, New York, 2003.
Igounet, V. '"Révisionnisme" et négationnisme au sein de l'extrême droite française', in *Négationnistes: les chiffonniers de l'histoire*, A. Bihr et al. Villeurbanne, Paris, 1997, pp. 39–81.
——— *Histoire du négationnisme en France*. Paris, 2000.
Imhof, K. 'Wiedergeburt der geistigen Landesverteidigung: Kalter Krieg in der Schweiz', in *Konkordanz und Kalter Krieg: Analyse von Medienereignissen in der Schweiz der Zwischen- und Nachkriegszeit*, eds K. Imhof, H. Kleger and G. Romano. Zurich, 1996, pp. 173–247.
Independent Commission of Experts Switzerland – Second World War, *Switzerland, National Socialism and the Second World War: Final Report*. Zurich, 2002.
Ireland, P.R. *The Policy Challenge of Ethnic Diversity: Immigrant Politics in France and Switzerland*. Cambridge, MA, London, 1994.
Jackman, R.W. and K. Volpert. 'Conditions Favouring Parties of the Extreme Right in Western Europe', *British Journal of Political Science* vol. 26, no. 4 (1996), 501–21.
Jacobs, F. 'Switzerland', in *Western European Political Parties: A Comprehensive Guide*, ed. F. Jacobs. Harlow, 1989, pp. 636–73.
Jahn, T. and P. Wehling. *Ökologie von rechts: Nationalismus und Umweltschutz bei der Neuen Rechten und den "Republikanern"*. Frankfurt, New York, 1991.
Joseph, R. *L'Union nationale, 1932–1939: Un fascisme en Suisse romande*. Neuchâtel, 1975.
Jost, H.U. 'Bedrohung und Enge (1919–1945)', in *Geschichte der Schweiz und Schweizer*, ed. B. Messmer. Basel, Frankfurt, 1986, pp. 731–819.
——— *Die reaktionäre Avantgarde: Die Geburt der Neuen Rechten in der Schweiz um 1900*. Zurich, 1992.
——— *Politik und Wirtschaft im Krieg: Die Schweiz 1938–1948*. Zurich, 1998.
Judt, T. *Past Imperfect: French Intellectuals, 1944–1956*. Berkeley, CA, Los Angeles, Oxford, 1992.
Junker, B. *Die Bauern auf dem Wege zur Politik: Die Entstehung der Bernischen Bauern-, Gewerbe- und Bürgerpartei*. Bern, 1968.
Känel, N. and H. Bigler. *Wenn Extreme Alltag werden: Analyse der asyl- und ausländerpolitischen Argumentationen der nationalen Rechen*. Bern, 2000.
Kaplan, A. *The Collaborator: The Trial and Execution of Robert Brasillach*. Chicago, London, 2001.
Kaplan, J. and T. Bjørgo, eds. *Nation and Race: The Developing Euro-American Racist Subculture*. Boston, MA, 1998.
Kaplan, J. and L. Weinberg. *The Emergence of a Euro-American Radical Right*. New Brunswick, NJ, London, 1998.
Karapin, R. 'Radical-Right and Neo-Fascist Political Parties in Western Europe', *Comparative Politics* vol. 30, no. 2 (1998), 213–34.
——— 'The Politics of Immigration Control in Britain and Germany: Subnational Politicians and Social Movements', *Comparative Politics* vol. 31, no. 4 (1999), 423–44.

Kaspi, A. 'Introduction. Le génocide des Juifs: le négationnisme est-il une entreprise transnationale?' *Relations internationales* no. 65 (1991), 3–7.
Katz, J. *From Prejudice to Destruction: Anti-Semitism, 1700–1933*. Cambridge, MA, 1980.
Katzenstein, P.J. *Corporatism and Change: Austria, Switzerland, and the Politics of Industry*. Ithaca, NY, London, 1984.
Kellershohn, H., ed. *Das Plagiat: Der Völkische Nationalismus der Jungen Freiheit*. Duisburg, 1994.
Kerr, H.H., 'The Swiss Party System: Steadfast and Changing', in *Party Systems in Denmark, Austria, Switzerland, the Netherlands, and Belgium*, ed. H. Daalder. London, 1987, pp. 107–92.
Kitschelt, H. 'Growth and Persistence of the Radical Right in Postindustrial Democracies: Advances and Challenges in Comparative Research', *West European Politics* vol. 30, no. 5 (2007), 1176–206.
Kitschelt, H. (in collaboration with A.J. McGann). *The Radical Right in Western Europe: A Comparative Analysis*. Ann Arbor, MI, 1995.
Kitschelt, H. and A.J. McGann. 'Die Dynamik der schweizerischen Neuen Rechten in komparativer Perspektive: Die Alpenrepubliken', in *Schweizer Wahlen 1999*, eds P. Sciarini, S. Hardmeier and A. Vatter. Bern, Stuttgart, Vienna, 2003, pp. 183–216.
Klandermans, B. and N. Mayer. 'Militer à l'extrême droite', in *Les croisés de la société fermée: L'Europe des extrêmes droites*, ed. P. Perrineau. Paris, 2001, pp. 147–62.
Klöti, U. 'Kantonale Parteiensysteme. Bedeutung des kantonalen Kontexts für die Positionierung der Parteien', in *Schweizer Wahlen 1995*, eds H. Kriesi, W. Linder and U. Klöti. Bern, Stuttgart, Vienna, 1998, pp. 45–72.
——— 'Consensual Government in a Heterogeneous Polity', in *The Swiss Labyrinth: Institutions, Outcomes and Redesign*, Special Issue of *West European Politics*, vol. 24, no. 2, ed. J.-E. Lane. London, 2001, pp. 19–34.
Knigge, P. 'The Ecological Correlates of Right-Wing Extremism in Western Europe', *European Journal of Political Research* vol. 34, no. 2 (1998), 249–79.
Knüsel, R. and J. Hottinger. *Regionalist Movements and Parties in Switzerland: A Study Case on the "Lega dei Ticinesi"*. Lausanne, 1994.
Kobach, K.W. *The Referendum: Direct Democracy in Switzerland*. Aldershot, 1993.
——— 'Spurn Thy Neighbour: Direct Democracy and Swiss Isolationism', *West European Politics* vol. 20, no. 3 (1997), 185–211.
Kobi, S. *Des citoyens suisses contre l'élite politique: Le cas des votations fédérales, 1979–1995*. Paris, Montreal, 2000.
Kohn, H. *Nationalism and Liberty: The Swiss Example*. London, 1956.
König, M. 'Auf dem Weg in die Gegenwart – Der Kanton Zürich seit 1945', in *Geschichte des Kantons Zürich*, 3 vols, eds N. Flüeler and M. Flüeler-Grauwiler. Zurich, 1994, vol. 3, pp. 350–479.
——— 'Rasanter Stillstand und zähe Bewegung. Schweizerische Innenpolitik im Kalten Krieg – und darüber hinaus', in *"Goldene Jahre": Zur Geschichte der Schweiz seit 1945*, eds W. Leimgruber and W. Fischer. Zurich, 1999, pp. 151–72.
König, M. et al., eds. *Dynamisierung und Umbau: Die Schweiz in den 60er und 70er Jahren*. Zurich, 1998.

Koopmans, R. 'Explaining the Rise of Racist and Extreme Right Violence in Western Europe: Grievances or Opportunities?' *European Journal of Political Research* vol. 30, no. 6 (1996), 185–216.

Koopmans, R. and H. Kriesi. 'Citoyenneté, identité nationale et mobilisation de l'extrême droite. Une comparaison entre la France, l'Allemagne, les Pays-Bas et la Suisse', in *Sociologie des nationalismes*, ed. P. Birnbaum. Paris, 1997, pp. 295–324.

Koopmans, R. and D. Rucht. 'Rechtsextremismus als soziale Bewegung?' in *Rechtsextremismus: Ergebnisse und Perspektiven der Forschung*, Special Issue of *Politische Vierteljahresschrift*, vol. 27, eds J.W. Falter, H.-G. Jaschke and J.R. Winkler. Opladen, 1996, pp. 265–87.

Koopmans, R. and P. Statham. 'Ethnic and Civic Conceptions of Nationhood and the Differential Success of the Extreme Right in Germany and Italy', in *How Social Movements Matter*, eds M. Giugni et al. Minneapolis, MN, 1999, pp. 225–51.

—— 'Introduction', in *Challenging Immigration and Ethnic Relations Politics: Comparative European Perspectives*, eds R. Koopmans and P. Statham. Oxford, New York, 2000, pp. 1–9.

Koopmans, R. and P. Statham, eds. *Challenging Immigration and Ethnic Relations Politics: Comparative European Perspectives*. Oxford, New York, 2000.

Koopmans, R. et al. *Contested Citizenship: Immigration and Cultural Diversity in Europe*. Minneapolis, London, 2005.

Kopke, C. and L. Rensmann. 'Die Extremismus-Formel. Zur politischen Karriere einer wissenschaftlichen Ideologie', *Blätter für deutsche und internationale Politik* vol. 44, no. 12 (2000), 1451–62.

Kowalsky, W. *Kulturevolution? Die Neue Rechte im neuen Frankreich und ihre Vorläufer*. Opladen, 1991.

Krauthammer, P. *Das Schächtverbot in der Schweiz 1854–2000: Die Schächtfrage zwischen Tierschutz, Politik und Fremdenfeindlichkeit*. Zurich, 2000.

Kreis, G. 'Philipp Etter – "voll auf eidgenössischem Boden"', in *Intellektuelle von rechts: Ideologie und Politik in der Schweiz 1918–1939*, ed. A. Mattioli. Zurich, 1995, pp. 201–17.

—— 'Introduction: Four Debates and Little Dissent', in *Switzerland and the Second World War*, ed. G. Kreis. London, Portland, OR, 2000, pp. 1–25.

—— 'Antisemitismus in der Schweiz nach 1945', in *Neuer Antisemitismus – alte Vorurteile?* ed. C. Tuor-Kurth. Stuttgart, Berlin, Cologne, 2001, pp. 53–63.

—— 'Zurück in die Zeit des Zweiten Weltkrieges (Teil II). Zur Bedeutung der 1990er Jahre für den Ausbau der schweizerischen Zeitgeschichte', *Schweizerische Zeitschrift für Geschichte* vol. 52, no. 4 (2002), 494–517.

Kreis, G., ed. *Staatsschutz in der Schweiz. Die Entwicklung von 1935-1990: Eine multidisziplinäre Untersuchung im Auftrage des schweizerischen Bundesrates*. Bern, 1993.

Kriesi, H. *Le système politique suisse*. Paris, 1995.

—— 'Movements of the Left, Movements of the Right: Putting the Mobilization of Two New Types of Social Movements into Political Context', in *Continuity and Change in Contemporary Capitalism*, eds H. Kitschelt et al. Cambridge, New York, Melbourne, 1999, pp. 398–423.

——— 'The Federal Parliament: The Limits of Institutional Reform', in *The Swiss Labyrinth: Institutions, Outcomes and Redesign*, Special Issue of *West European Politics*, vol. 24, no. 2, ed. J.-E. Lane. London, 2001, pp. 59–76.

——— 'Wahlentscheide bei Ständeratswahlen', in *Schweizer Wahlen 1999*, eds P. Sciarini, S. Hardmeier and A. Vatter. Bern, Stuttgart, Vienna, 2003, pp. 147–81.

——— 'Zusammenfassung und Schlussfolgerung', in *Der Aufstieg der SVP: Acht Kantone im Vergleich*, eds H. Kriesi et al. Zurich, 2005, pp. 256–70.

Kriesi, H. et al. *Analyse der eidgenössischen Abstimmung vom 6. Dezember 1992*, VOX no. 47, Adliswil, 1993.

——— *New Social Movements in Western Europe: A Comparative Analysis*. Minneapolis, MN, 1995.

Kriesi, H. et al., eds. *Contemporary Switzerland: Revisiting the Special Case*. New York, Basingstoke, 2005.

——— eds. *Der Aufstieg der SVP: Acht Kantone im Vergleich*. Zurich, 2005.

Kröter, T. 'Political Correctness: Vom linken Wahn zur rechten Wirklichkeit', *Blätter für deutsche und internationale Politik* vol. 40, no. 11 (1995), 1367–74.

Küchler, M. 'Xenophobie im internationalen Vergleich', in *Rechtsextremismus: Ergebnisse und Perspektiven der Forschung*, Special Issue of *Politische Vierteljahresschrift*, vol. 27, eds J.W. Falter, H.-G. Jaschke and J.R. Winkler. Opladen, 1996, pp. 248–62.

Kühl, S. *Die Internationale der Rassisten: Aufstieg und Niedergang der internationalen Bewegung für Eugenik und Rassenhygiene im 20. Jahrhundert*. Frankfurt, New York, 1997.

Kury, P. *Über Fremde reden: Überfremdungsdiskurs und Ausgrenzung in der Schweiz 1900–1945*. Zurich, 2003.

Ladner, A. 'Switzerland', *European Journal of Political Research* vol. 30, no. 2 (1996), 469–78.

——— 'Die Basis der Parteien', in *Die Schweizer Parteien im Wandel: Von Mitgliederparteien zu professionalisierten Wählerorganisationen?* A. Ladner and M. Brändle. Zurich, 2001, pp. 73–99.

——— 'Mitgliederzahlen der Kantonalparteien und ihre Entwicklung in den letzten Jahren', in *Die Schweizer Parteien im Wandel: Von Mitgliederparteien zu professionalisierten Wählerorganisationen?* A. Ladner and M. Brändle. Zurich, 2001, pp. 101–47.

——— 'Swiss Political Parties: Between Persistence and Change', in *The Swiss Labyrinth: Institutions, Outcomes and Redesign*, Special Issue of *West European Politics*, vol. 24, no. 2, ed. J.-E. Lane. London, 2001, pp. 123–44.

——— 'The Political Parties and the Party System', in *Handbook of Swiss Politics*, eds U. Klöti et al. Zurich, 2004, pp. 197–242.

Lange, A. *Was die Rechten lesen. Fünfzig Zeitschriften: Ziele, Inhalte, Taktik*. Munich, 1993.

Langmuir, G.I. 'Toward a Definition of Antisemitism', in *Toward a Definition of Antisemitism*, G.I. Langmuir. Berkeley, Los Angeles, London, 1990, pp. 311–52.

Laplace, Y. *L'âge d'homme en Bosnie: Petit guide d'une nausée suisse*. Lausanne, 1997.

Laqueur, W. *Fascism: Past, Present, Future*, paperback edn. New York, Oxford, 1997.
Laske, K. *Ein Leben zwischen Hitler und Carlos: François Genoud*. Zurich, 1996.
Lauretis, M. de, and B. Giussani. *La Lega dei ticinesi: Indagine sul fenomeno che ha sconvolto il Ticino politico*. Locarno, 1992.
Leggewie, C. *Der Geist steht rechts: Ausflüge in die Denkfabriken der Wende*, 2nd edn. Berlin, 1987.
Lenk, K., G. Meuter and H.R. Otten. *Vordenker der Neuen Rechten*. Frankfurt, New York, 1997.
Levitas, R., ed. *The Ideology of the New Right*. Cambridge, 1986.
Liatowitsch, P. 'Holocaust-Leugnung in der Schweiz und Art. 261bis StGB', in *Neuer Antisemitismus – alte Vorurteile?* ed C. Tuor-Kurth. Stuttgart, Berlin, Cologne, 2001, pp. 137–53.
Lijphart, A. *Democracies: Patterns of Majoritarian and Consensual Government in Twenty-One Countries*. New Haven, CT, 1984.
Linder, W. 'Migrationswirkungen, institutionelle Politik und politische Öffentlichkeit', in *Migrationen aus der Dritten Welt: Ursachen und Wirkungen*, eds W. Kälin and R. Moser. Bern, Stuttgart, 1989, pp. 145–57.
––––––– *Swiss Democracy: Possible Solutions to Conflict in Multicultural Societies*, 2nd edn. London, New York, 1998.
Linder, W. and G. Lutz. 'The Parliamentary Elections in Switzerland, October 1999', *Electoral Studies* vol. 21, no. 1 (2002), 128–34.
Lipset, S.M. and E. Raab. *The Politics of Unreason: Right-Wing Extremism in America, 1790–1970*. New York, London, 1970.
Lipstadt, D.E. *Denying the Holocaust: The Growing Assault on Truth and Memory*. New York, 1993.
Longchamp, C. '"Linke und Grüne an die Wand nageln und mit dem Flammenwerfer drüber!" Die Autopartei unter der sozialwissenschaftlichen Lupe', Paper presented at the conference *Rechtspopulismus in Europa: Erscheinungen, Ursachen und Folgen*, Vienna, 5 December 1988.
––––––– 'Den Pelz waschen, ohne ihn nass zu machen. Eine sozialwissenschaftliche Analyse der Entscheidung der Schweiz über den Beitritt zum Europäischen Wirtschaftsraum vom 6. Dezember 1992', in *Europa-Kampagnen: Dynamik öffentlicher Meinungsbildung in Dänemark, Frankreich und der Schweiz*, ed. H. Rust. Vienna, 1993, pp. 9–57.
––––––– 'Die nationalkonservative Revolte in der Gestalt der SVP. Eine Analyse der Nationalratswahlen 1999 in der Schweiz', in *Das österreichische Wahlverhalten*, eds F. Plasser, P.A. Ulram and F. Sommer. Vienna, 2000, 393–423.
Longchamp, C., J. Dumont and P. Leuenberger. *Einstellungen der Schweizer Innen gegenüber Jüdinnen und Juden und dem Holocaust*. Bern, 2000.
Longchamp, C. and S. Hardmeier. *Analyse der Nationalratswahlen 1991*, VOX no. 43, Adliswil, Bern, 1992.
Longchamp, C. et al. *Hin zur Tripolarität im Parteiensystem der Schweiz: Eine Erstanalyse der Nationalratswahlen vom 22. Oktober 1995*. Bern, 1995.
Lorig, W.H. *Neokonservatives Denken in der Bundesrepublik Deutschland und in den Vereinigten Staaten von Amerika: Zum intellektuellen Klima in zwei politischen Kulturen*. Opladen, 1988.

Lowi, T.J. *The End of the Republican Era*. Norman, OK, 1995.
Lüthi, U. *Der Mythos von der Weltverschwörung: Die Hetze der Schweizer Frontisten gegen Juden und Freimaurer – am Beispiel des Berner Prozesses um die "Protokolle der Weisen von Zion"*. Basel, Frankfurt, 1992.
Lutz, G. 'Mobilisierung als Schlüsselfaktor für den Wahlerfolg?', in *Schweizer Wahlen 1999*, eds P. Sciarini, S. Hardmeier and A. Vatter. Bern, Stuttgart, Vienna, 2003, pp. 59–84.
Mahnig, F. and T. Milic. *Analyse der eidgenössischen Abstimmungen vom 22. Sept. 2002*, VOX no. 78, Bern, Zurich, 2002.
Mahnig, H. 'Between Economic Demands and Popular Xenophobia: The Swiss System of Immigration Regulation', in *Regulation of Migration: International Experiences*, eds A. Böcker et al. Amsterdam, 1998, pp. 174–90.
——— 'La politique migratoire de 1970 au milieu des années 1980', in *Histoire de la politique de migration, d'asile et d'intégration en Suisse depuis 1948*, ed. H. Mahnig. Zurich, 2005, pp. 135–159.
Mahnig, H. and E. Piguet. 'Die Immigrationspolitik der Schweiz von 1948 bis 1998: Entwicklung und Auswirkungen', in *Migration und die Schweiz: Ergebnisse des Nationalen Forschungsprogramms "Migration und interkulturelle Beziehungen"*, eds H.-R. Wicker, R. Fibbi and W. Haug. Zurich, 2003, pp. 65–108.
Mair, P. and C. Mudde. 'The Party Family and its Study', *Annual Review of Political Science* vol. 1, no. 1 (1998), 211–29.
Maissen, T. *Verweigerte Erinnerung: Nachrichtenlose Vermögen und die Schweizer Weltkriegsdebatte 1989–2002*. Zurich, 2005.
Marchal, G.P. and A. Mattioli, eds. *Erfundene Schweiz: Konstruktionen nationaler Identität*. Zurich, 1992.
Marin, B. *Antisemitismus ohne Antisemiten: Autoritäre Vorurteile und Feindbilder, unveränderte Neuauflage früherer Analysen 1974–1979 und Umfragen 1946–1991*. Frankfurt, New York, 2000.
Marshall, G. *Spirit of '69: A Skinhead Bible*, 2nd edn. Dunoon, 1994.
Mattioli, A. *Zwischen Demokratie und totalitärer Diktatur: Gonzague de Reynold und die Tradition der autoritären Rechten in der Schweiz*. Zurich, 1994.
Mattioli, A., ed. *Intellektuelle von rechts: Ideologie und Politik in der Schweiz 1918–1939*. Zurich, 1995.
Mazzoleni, O. 'La Lega dei Ticinesi: Vers l'intégration?' *Swiss Political Science Review* vol. 5, no. 3 (1999), 79–95.
——— 'La dimension gauche-droite et le choix partisan. Une perspective comparée', in *Schweizer Wahlen 1999*, eds P. Sciarini, S. Hardmeier and A. Vatter. Bern, Stuttgart, Vienna, 2003, pp. 123–46.
——— *Nationalisme et populisme en Suisse: La radicalisation de la "nouvelle" UDC*. Lausanne, 2003.
——— 'Unité et diversité des "national-populismes" suisses: l'Union démocratique du centre et la Lega dei Ticinesi', in *La tentation populiste au coeur de l'Europe*, eds O. Ihl et al. Paris, 2003, pp. 184–97.
——— 'Multi-Level Populism and Centre-Periphery Cleavage in Switzerland. The Case of the *Lega dei Ticinesi*', in *Challenges to Consensual Politics: Democ-*

racy, Identity, and Populist Protest in the Alpine Region, eds D. Caramani and Y. Mény, Brussels, 2005, pp. 209–227.

——— 'Définir le parti: un enjeu scientifique et politique', in *L'Union démocratique du centre: un parti, son action et ses soutiens,* eds O. Mazzoleni, P. Gottraux, and C. Péchu. Lausanne, 2007, pp. 17–47.

Mazzoleni, O. and D. Skenderovic. 'The Rise and Impact of the Swiss People's Party: Challenging the Rules of Governance in Switzerland', in *Extrême droite et pouvoir en Europe – The extreme right parties and power in Europe,* eds P. Delwit and P. Poirier. Brussels, 2007, pp. 85–116.

Mazzoleni, O. and B. Wernli. *Cittadini e politica. Interesse, partecipazione, istituzioni e partiti in Svizzera: Ginevra, Ticino e Zurigo a confronto.* Bellinzona, 2002.

McClelland, J.S. 'The Reactionary Right: The French Revolution, Charles Maurras and the Action Française', in *The Nature of the Right: American and European Politics and Political Thought since 1789,* eds R. Eatwell and N. O'Sullivan. Boston, MA, 1989, pp. 79–98.

McGann A.J. and H. Kitschelt. 'The Radical Right in the Alps. Evolution of Support for the Swiss SVP and Austrian FPÖ', *Party Politics* vol. 11, no. 2 (2005), 147–71.

Mecklenburg, J., ed. *Handbuch deutscher Rechtsextremismus.* Berlin, 1996.

Meienberg, N. *Die Welt als Wille & Wahn: Elemente zur Naturgeschichte eines Clans.* Zurich, 1987.

Mény, Y. and Y. Surel. *Par le peuple, pour le peuple: Le populisme et les démocraties.* Paris, 2000.

Mény, Y. and Y. Surel, eds *Democracies and the Populist Challenge.* Basingstoke, New York, 2002.

Merkl, P.H. 'Why Are They So Strong Now? Comparative Reflections on the Revival of the Radical Right in Europe', in *The Revival of Right-Wing Extremism in the Nineties,* eds P.H. Merkl and L. Weinberg. London, Portland, OR, 1997, pp. 17–46.

Merkl, P.H. and L. Weinberg, eds. *Right-Wing Extremism in the Twenty-First Century,* 2nd rev. edn. London, Portland, OR, 2003.

Miles, R. *Racism.* London, New York, 1989.

Milza, P. 'Le négationnisme en France', *Relations internationales* no. 65 (1991), 9–22.

——— *Les fascismes.* Paris, 1991.

Minkenberg, M. 'The New Right in France and Germany: *Nouvelle Droite, Neue Rechte,* and the New Right Radical Parties', in *The Revival of Right-Wing Extremism in the Nineties,* eds P.H. Merkl and L. Weinberg. London, Portland, OR, 1997, pp. 65–90.

——— 'Context and Consequence. The Impact of the New Radical Right on the Political Process in France and Germany', *German Politics and Society* vol. 16, no. 3 (1998), 1–23.

——— *Die neue radikale Rechte im Vergleich: USA, Frankreich, Deutschland.* Opladen, 1998.

——— 'The Renewal of the Radical Right: Between Modernity and Antimodernity', *Government and Opposition* vol. 35, no. 2 (2000), 170–88.

——— 'The West European Radical Right as a Collective Actor: Modelling the Impact of Cultural and Structural Variables on Party Formation and Movement Mobilization', *Comparative European Politics* vol. 1, no. 2 (2003), 149–70.

Misteli, R. and A. Gisler. 'Überfremdung. Karriere und Diffusion eines fremdenfeindlichen Deutungsmusters', in *Vom kalten Krieg zur Kulturrevolution: Analyse von Medienereignissen in der Schweiz der 50er und 60er Jahre*, eds K. Imhof, H. Kleger and G. Romano. Zurich, 1999, pp. 95–120.

Monzat, R. *Enquêtes sur la droite extrême*. Paris, 1992.

Moos, C. *Ja zum Völkerbund – Nein zur UNO: Die Volksabstimmungen von 1920 und 1986 in der Schweiz*. Zurich, Lausanne, 2001.

Mooser, J. '"Spiritual National Defence" in the 1930s: Swiss Political Culture between the Wars', in *Switzerland and the Second World War*, ed. G. Kreis. London, Portland, OR, 2000, pp. 236–60.

Moreau, P. *Nationalsozialismus von links: Die "Kampfgemeinschaft Revolutionärer Nationalsozialisten" und die "Schwarze Front" Otto Strassers 1930–1935*. Stuttgart, 1985.

Moreau, P. and U. Backes. 'Federal Republic of Germany', in *Extremism in Europe, 1998 Survey*, ed. J.-Y. Camus. Paris, 1998, pp. 150–76.

Mosse, G.L. *Toward the Final Solution: A History of European Racism*. New York, 1978.

Mudde, C. 'Right-Wing Extremism Analysed. A Comparative Analysis of the Ideologies of Three Alleged Right-Wing Extremist Parties (NPD, NDP, CP'86)', *European Journal of Political Research* vol. 27, no. 2 (1995), 203–24.

——— 'The Single-Issue Party Thesis: Extreme Right Parties and the Immigration Issue', *West European Politics* vol. 22, no. 3 (1999), 182–97.

——— *The Ideology of the Extreme Right*. Manchester, New York, 2000.

——— 'The Populist Zeitgeist', *Government and Opposition* vol. 39, no. 4 (2004), 541–63.

——— *Populist Radical Right Parties in Europe*. Cambridge, 2007.

Müller, J. 'From National Identity to National Interest: The Rise (and Fall) of Germany's New Right', *German Politics* vol. 8, no. 3 (1999), 1–20.

Nabholz, R. 'Das Wählerverhalten in der Schweiz: Stabilität oder Wandel? Eine Trendanalyse von 1971–1995', in *Schweizer Wahlen 1995*, eds H. Kriesi, W. Linder and U. Klöti. Bern, Stuttgart, Vienna, 1998, pp. 17–43.

Neaman, E. 'Ernst Jünger's Millenium: Bad Citizens for the New Century', in *Fascism's Return: Scandal, Revision, and Ideology since 1980*, ed. R.J. Golsan. Lincoln, NK, London, 1998, pp. 218–43.

Neidhart, L. *Plebiszit and pluralitäre Demokratie: Eine Analyse der Funktion des schweizerischen Gesetzesreferendums*. Bern, 1970.

Nevill, A. 'The Good, the Bad, and the Skins. Die Geschichte der Skinhead-Bewegung in England', in *Neue Soundtracks für den Volksempfänger: Nazirock, Jugendkultur und rechter Mainstream*, 2nd edn, eds M. Annas and R. Christoph. Berlin, 1993, pp. 47–64.

Niederberger, J.M. *Ausgrenzen, Assimilieren, Integrieren: Die Entwicklung einer schweizerischen Integrationspolitik*. Zurich, 2004.

Niggli, M.A. *Rassendiskriminierung: Ein Kommentar zu Art. 261bis StGB und Art. 171c MStG*, 2nd rev. edn. Zurich, Basel, Geneva, 2007.

——— 'Diskriminierung durch Plakataushang', in *Rassendiskriminierung: Gerichtspraxis zu Art. 261bis StGB. Analysen, Gutachten und Dokumentation der Gerichtspraxis 1995–1998*, published by the Society of Minorities in Switzerland (GMS) and the Foundation Against Racism and Antisemitism (GRA) in collaboration with the Federal Commission Against Racism (EKR), Zurich, 1999, pp. 265–81.

Niggli, P. and J. Frischknecht. *Rechte Seilschaften: Wie die "unheimlichen Patrioten" den Zusammenbruch des Kommunismus meisterten*. Zurich, 1998.

Niklaus, S. *Wir nicht? Vom Antisemitismus, Fremdenhass, von Rechtsradikalen sowie Neonazisten in der Schweiz*. Basel, 1969.

Nordbruch, G. 'Leugnungen des Holocaust in arabischen Medien. Reaktionen auf "Die Gründungsmythen der israelischen Politik" von Roger Garaudy', in *Jahrbuch für Antisemitismusforschung*, ed. W. Benz, Frankfurt, New York, 2001, pp. 184–203.

Norris, P. *Radical Right: Voters and Parties in the Electoral Market*. Cambridge, 2005.

Olender, M. 'Georges Dumézil et les usages "politiques" de la préhistoire indo-européenne', in *Les Grecs, les Romains et nous: L'Antiquité est-elle moderne?* ed. R.-P. Droit. Paris, 1991, pp. 393–407.

——— 'Indogermanische Urgeschichte und "Nouvelle Droite"', in *Rechtsextremismus: Ideologie und Gewalt*, eds R. Faber, H. Funke and G. Schoenberner. Berlin, 1995, pp. 189–203.

Olsen, J. *Nature and Nationalism: Right-Wing Ecology and the Politics of Identity in Contemporary Germany*. New York, 1999.

Papadopoulos, Y. 'Quel rôle pour les petits partis dans la démocratie directe?' *Schweizerisches Jahrbuch für Politische Wissenschaft* vol. 31 (1991), 131–50.

Parini, L. and M. Gianni. 'Enjeux et modifications de la politique d'asile en Suisse de 1956 à nos jours', in *Histoire de la politique de migration, d'asile et d'intégration en Suisse depuis 1948*, ed. H. Mahnig. Zurich, 2005, pp. 189–252.

Péan, P. *L'extrémiste: François Genoud, de Hitler à Carlos*. Paris, 1996.

Pedahzur, A. and A. Brichta. 'The Institutionalization of Extreme Right-Wing Charismatic Parties: A Paradox?' *Party Politics* vol. 8, no. 1 (2002), 31–49.

Peele, G. *Revival and Reaction: The Right in Contemporary America*, reprinted edn. Oxford, 1987.

Perlmutter, T. 'Bringing Parties Back In: Comments on "Modes of Immigration Politics in Liberal Democratic Societies"', *International Migration Review* vol. 30, no. 1 (1996), 375–88.

Pfahl-Traughber, A. 'Der Extremismusbegriff in der politikwissenschaftlichen Diskussion – Definitionen, Kritik, Alternativen', in *Jahrbuch Extremismus & Demokratie*, eds U. Backes and E. Jesse. Bonn, 1992, pp. 67–86.

——— *"Konservative Revolution" und "Neue Rechte": Rechtsextremistische Intellektuelle gegen den demokratischen Verfassungsstaat*. Opladen, 1998.

——— 'Der organisierte Rechtsextremismus in Deutschland nach 1945. Zur Entwicklung auf den Handlungsfeldern "Aktion" – "Gewalt" – "Kultur" –

"Politik"', in *Rechtsextremismus in der Bundesrepublik Deutschland: Eine Bilanz*, eds W. Schubarth and R. Stöss. Opladen, 2001, pp. 71–100.

Picard, J. *Die Schweiz und die Juden 1933–1945: Schweizerischer Antisemitismus, jüdische Abwehr und internationale Migrations- und Flüchtlingspolitik.* Zurich, 1994.

Piguet, E. *L'immigration en Suisse depuis 1948: Une analyse des flux migratoires.* Zurich, 2005.

Pitterle, K.J. *The Limits of Interdependence: The Development of the Swiss New Right as an Oppositional Force to Switzerland's Regional and Global Interdependence.* Dissertation University of Michigan, Ann Arbor, 1981.

Plasser, F. and P.A. Ulram. 'Rechtspopulistische Resonanzen: Die Wählerschaft der FPÖ', in *Das österreichische Wahlverhalten*, eds F. Plasser, P. A. Ulram and F. Sommer. Vienna, 2000, pp. 225–41.

Poulat, E. *Intégrisme et catholicisme intégral: Un réseau secret international antimoderniste. La Sapinière 1909–1921.* Tournai, 1969.

Prowe, D. '"Classic" Fascism and the New Radical Right in Western Europe: Comparisons and Contrasts', *Contemporary European History* vol. 3, no. 3 (1994), 289–313.

Purtscheller, W., ed. *Die Ordnung, die sie meinen: "Neue Rechte" in Österreich.* Vienna, 1994.

Raboud, I. *Temps nouveaux, vents contraires: Ecône et le Valais.* Sierre, 1992.

Racine, J.-B. and C. Raffestin, eds. *Nouvelle géographie de la Suisse et des Suisses*, 2 vols. Lausanne, 1990.

Reichlin, L. *Kriegsverbrecher Wipf, Eugen: Schweizer in der Waffen-SS, in deutschen Fabriken und an den Schreibtischen des Dritten Reiches.* Zurich, 1994.

Rensmann L. *Demokratie und Judenbild: Antisemitismus in der politischen Kultur der Bundesrepublik Deutschland.* Wiesbaden, 2004.

Rioux, J.-P. 'Des clandestins aux activistes (1945–1965)', in *Histoire de l'extrême droite en France*, ed. M. Winock. Paris, 1993, pp. 215–41.

Roberts, G.K. 'Extremism in Germany: Sparrows or Avalanche?' *European Journal of Political Research* vol. 25, no. 4 (1994), 461–82.

Romano, G. 'Die Überfremdungsbewegung als "Neue soziale Bewegung". Zur Kommerzialisierung, Oralisierung und Personalisierung massenmedialer Kommunikation in den 60er Jahren', in *Dynamisierung und Umbau: Die Schweiz in den 60er und 70er Jahren*, eds M. König et al. Zurich, 1998, pp. 143–59.

——— 'Vom Sonderfall zur Überfremdung. Zur Erfolgsgeschichte gemeinschaftsideologischen Denkens im öffentlichen politischen Diskurs der späten fünfziger und der sechziger Jahre', in *Vom kalten Krieg zur Kulturrevolution: Analyse von Medienereignissen in der Schweiz der 50er und 60er Jahre*, eds K. Imhof, H. Kleger and G. Romano. Zurich, 1999, pp. 55–93.

Rousso, H. *Le syndrome de Vichy.* Paris, 1987.

Rucht, D. *Modernisierung und neue soziale Bewegungen: Deutschland, Frankreich und USA im Vergleich.* Frankfurt, New York, 1994.

Rusconi, G. 'La Lega dei Ticinesi: Gegen die Tessiner "Partitokratie"', in *Rechte und linke Fundamentalopposition: Studien zur Schweizer Politik 1965–1990*, eds U. Altermatt et al. Basel, Frankfurt, 1994, pp. 154–73.

Rydrgen, J. 'The Sociology of the Radical Right', *Annual Review of Sociology* vol. 33, no. 1 (2007), 241–62.
Rydgren, J., ed. *Movements of Exclusion: Radical Right-Wing Populism in the Western World*. New York, 2004.
Sacchi, S. 'Postmaterialismus in der Schweiz von 1972 bis 1990', *Schweizerische Zeitschrift für Soziologie* vol. 18, no. 1 (1992), 87–117.
Saint-Quen, F. 'Vers une remontée du national-populisme en Suisse? Le cas des vigilants genevois', *Schweizerisches Jahrbuch für Politische Wissenschaft* vol. 26 (1986), 211–24.
Salzborn, S. 'Unterwegs in deutscher Mission. Randnotizen zum Wirken eines rechten Emeritus', in *Alte und Neue Rechte an den Hochschulen*, eds C. Butterwegge and G. Hentges. Münster, 1999, pp. 214–17.
Sarkowicz, H. *Rechte Geschäfte: Der unaufhaltsame Aufstieg des deutschen Verlegers Herbert Fleissner*. Frankfurt, 1994.
Schain, M. 'The Comparative Study of Immigration in Britain, France and the United States', Paper presented at *The Association for the Study of Modern and Contemporary France Annual Conference*, University of Portsmouth, 6–8 September 2001.
Schain, M., A. Zolberg and P. Hossay. 'The Development of Radical Right Parties in Western Europe', in *Shadows over Europe: The Development and Impact of the Extreme Right in Western Europe*, eds M. Schain, A. Zolberg and P. Hossay. New York, Basingstoke, 2002, pp. 3–17.
Scheuch, E.K. and H.-D. Klingemann. 'Theorie des Rechtsradikalismus in westlichen Industriegesellschaften', *Hamburger Jahrbuch für Wirtschafts- und Gesellschaftspolitik* vol. 12 (1967), 11–29.
Schiesser, G. 'Die Schweizer Auto-Partei', *Die Neue Gesellschaft/Frankfurter Hefte* vol. 39, no. 4 (1992), 330–35.
Schifferle, A. *Marcel Lefebvre – Ärgernis und Besinnung: Fragen an das Traditionsverständnis der Kirche*. Kevelaer, 1983.
——— *Was will Lefebvre eigentlich? Der Bruch zwischen Ecône und Rom*. Fribourg, 1989.
Schilling, C. *Blocher: Aufstieg und Mission eines Schweizer Politikers und Unternehmers*. Zurich, 1994.
Schloeth, D. *Analyse der eidgenössischen Abstimmungen vom 25. September 1994*, VOX no. 54, Adliswil, Bern, 1994.
——— *Vor die Wahl gestellt: Erklärungen des Wahlverhaltens bei den Eidgenössischen Wahlen 1995*. Bern, Stuttgart, Vienna, 1998.
Schloeth, D. and U. Klöti. *Analyse der eidgenössischen Abstimmungen vom 7. März 1993*, VOX no. 48, Bern, Zurich, 1993.
Schmitter Heisler, B. 'From Conflict to Accommodation: The "Foreigners Question" in Switzerland', *European Journal of Political Research* vol. 16 (1988), 683–700.
Schönekäs, K. 'Bundesrepublik Deutschland', in *Neue Rechte und Rechtsextremismus in Europa*, F. Gress, H.-G. Jaschke and K. Schönekäs. Opladen, 1990, pp. 218–349.
Sciarini, P., S. Hug and C. Dupont. *Example, Exception or Both? Swiss National Identity in Perspective*, EUI Working Paper 32, San Domenico, 1997.

Sciarini, P. and H. Kriesi. 'Stabilité et changement d'opinion durant la campagne électorale', in *Schweizer Wahlen 1999*, eds P. Sciarini, S. Hardmeier and A. Vatter. Bern, Stuttgart, Vienna, 2003, pp. 287–320.

Sciarini, P. and O. Listhaug. *Single Cases or a Unique Pair? The Swiss and Norwegian No to Europe*. EUI Working Paper 25, San Domenico, 1997.

Seidel, G. 'Culture, Nation and "Race" in the British and French New Right', in *The Ideology of the New Right*, ed. R. Levitas. Cambridge, 1986, pp. 107–35.

Seifert, F. 'Das Argument der menschlichen Natur in der Einwanderungsdebatte veranschaulicht am Beispiel Irenäus Eibl-Eibesfeldt', *Österreichische Zeitschrift für Politikwissenschaft* vol. 25, no. 2 (1996), 193–206.

Seiler, D.-L. *Partis et familles politiques*. Paris, 1980.

Seitz, W. *Nationalratswahlen 1995: Der Wandel der Parteienlandschaft seit 1971*. Bern, 1995.

—— *Nationalratswahlen 1999: Der Wandel der Parteienlandschaft seit 1971*. Neuchâtel, 1999.

—— *Les élections au Conseil national de 1999: Aperçu et analyse*. Neuchâtel, 2003.

Serdült, U. *Analyse der eidgenössischen Abstimmungen vom 25. Juni 1995*, VOX no. 57, Adliswil, 1995.

Sheehan, T. 'Myth and Violence: The Fascism of Julius Evola and Alain de Benoist', *Social Research* vol. 48, no. 1 (1981), 45–73.

Shermer, M. and A. Grobman. *Denying History: Who Says the Holocaust Never Happened and Why Do They Say It?* Berkeley, Los Angeles, London, 2000.

Siegrist, C. 'Der zerrissene Jakob Schaffner: überzeugter Nationalsozialist und Schweizer Patriot', in *Intellektuelle von rechts: Ideologie und Politik in der Schweiz 1918–1939*, ed. A. Mattioli. Zurich, 1995, pp. 55–71.

Simmons, H.G. *The French National Front: The Extremist Challenge to Democracy*. Boulder, CO, Oxford, 1996.

Skenderovic, D. 'Die Umweltschutzbewegung im Spannungsfeld der 50er Jahre', in *achtung: die 50er Jahre! Annäherungen an eine widersprüchliche Zeit*, eds J.-D. Blanc and C. Luchsinger. Zurich, 1994, pp. 119–46.

—— 'Die Umweltschutzbewegung im Zeichen des Wertewandels', in *Rechte und linke Fundamentalopposition: Studien zur Schweizer Politik 1965–1990*, U. Altermatt et al. Basel, Frankfurt, 1994, pp. 33–61.

—— 'Nation, Nationalismus und politische Parteien: Die Schweiz – keine Insel in Europa', in *On European Identity: Nationalism, Culture & History*, ed. C. Szaló, Brno, 1998, pp. 131–79.

—— 'The Swiss Radical Right in Perspective: A Reevaluation of Success Conditions in Switzerland', Paper presented at the ECPR Joint Sessions of Workshops, Grenoble, 6–11 April 2001 [Internet version: http://www.extremismus.com/texte/eurex6.pdf, 31 August 2008].

—— 'Constructing Boundaries in a Multicultural Nation: The Discourse of "Overforeignization" in Switzerland', in *European Encounters: Migrants, Migration and European Societies since 1945*, eds R. Ohliger, K. Schönwälder and T. Triadafilopoulos. Aldershot, 2003, pp. 186–209.

—— 'Fremdenfeindlichkeit', in *Historisches Lexikon der Schweiz*. Basel, 2005, vol 4, pp. 796–98.

——— 'Feindbild Muslime – Islamophobie in der radikalen Rechten', in *Der Islam in Europa: Zwischen Weltpolitik und Alltag*, eds U. Altermatt, M. Delgado and G. Vergauwen, Munich, 2006, pp. 79–95.

——— 'Das rechtspopulistische Parteienlager in der Schweiz: Von den Splitterparteien zur Volkspartei', *traverse. Zeitschrift für Geschichte – Revue de l'histoire* vol. 14, no. 1 (2007), 45–63.

——— 'Immigration and the Radical Right in Switzerland: Ideology, Discourse and Opportunities', *Patterns of Prejudice* vol. 41, no. 2 (2007), 155–76.

Skenderovic, D. and G. D'Amato. *Mit dem Fremden politisieren: Rechtspopulismus und Migrationspolitik in der Schweiz seit den 1960er Jahren*. Zurich, 2008.

Skenderovic D. and C. Späti, eds. *1968 – Revolution und Gegenrevolution: Neue Linke und Neue Rechte in Frankreich, BRD und der Schweiz. 1968 – Révolution et contre-révolution: Nouvelle gauche et Nouvelle droite en France, RFA et Suisse*. Basel, 2008.

Skinner, Q. 'Some Problems in the Analysis of Political Thought and Action', in *Meaning and Context: Quentin Skinner and His Critics*, ed. J. Tully, Princeton, 1988, pp. 97–118.

Smith, A. *National Identity*. London, 1991.

Späti, C. 'Kontinuität und Wandel des Antisemitismus und dessen Beurteilung in der Schweiz nach 1945', *Schweizerische Zeitschrift für Geschichte* vol. 55, no. 4 (2005), 419–40.

——— *Die schweizerische Linke und Israel: Israelbegeisterung, Antizionismus und Antisemitismus zwischen 1967 und 1991*. Essen, 2006.

——— 'Enttabuisierung eines Vorurteils: Antisemitismus in der Schweiz', in *Feindbild Judentum: Antisemitismus in Europa*, eds L. Rensmann and J.H. Schoeps. Berlin, 2008, pp. 183–215.

Sprinzak, E. 'Right-wing Terrorism in a Comparative Perspective: The Case of Split Delegitimization', in *Terror from the Extreme Right*, ed T. Bjørgo. London, 1995, pp. 17–43.

Stamm, H. 'Der VPM in der Schweiz. Strammer Marsch an den rechten Flügel', in *VPM – Die Psychosekte*, eds I. Efler and H. Reile. Reinbek, 1995, pp. 147–59.

——— *Im Bann der Apokalypse: Endzeitvorstellungen in Kirchen, Sekten und Kulten*. Zurich, Munich, 1998.

Steinberg, J. *Why Switzerland?* 2nd edn. Cambridge, New York, Melbourne, 1996.

Steinfels, P. *The Neoconservatives: The Men Who Are Changing America's Politics*. New York, 1979.

Stephens J.D. and E. Huber. *Development and Crisis of the Welfare State: Parties and Policies in Global Markets*. Chicago, 2001.

Sternhell, Z. *Ni droite, ni gauche: L'idéologie fasciste en France*, new edn. Brussels, 1987.

Stiftung Dokumentationsarchiv des österreichischen Widerstandes, ed. *Handbuch des österreichischen Rechtsextremismus*, 2nd edn. Vienna, 1993.

Stolcke, V. 'Talking Culture. New Boundaries, New Rhetorics of Exclusion in Europe', *Current Anthropology* vol. 36, no. 1 (1995), 1–24.

Stolz, J. 'Einstellungen zu Ausländern und Ausländerinnen 1969 und 1995: eine

Replikationsstudie', in *Das Fremde in der Schweiz: Ergebnisse soziologischer Forschung*, ed. H.-J. Hoffmann-Nowotny. Zurich, 2001, pp. 33–74.

Strasser, R. *Protestantische Parteien und evangelisch-konservative Christen*, n.d. [1996, 2001], [only Internet version: http://www.efb.ch/Texte/adpp. htm, 31 August 2008].

Studer, B. 'Antikommunismus', in *Historisches Lexikon der Schweiz*, vol. 1. Basel, 2002, pp. 366–67.

Studer B., G. Arlettaz and R. Argast. *Das Schweizer Bürgerrecht: Nationalität und Ordnung des Sozialen in der Schweiz von 1848 bis zur Gegenwart.* Zürich, 2008.

Stutz, H. 'Mäandern im esoterischen Sumpf', *Tangram. Bulletin der Eidgenössischen Kommission gegen Rassismus* no. 6 (1999), 29–33.

—— *Rassistische Vorfälle in der Schweiz. Einschätzungen und Chronologie. Ausgabe 2000.* Zurich, 2000.

—— *Rassistische Vorfälle in der Schweiz. Eine Chronologie und eine Einschätzung. Ausgabe 2002.* Zurich, 2002.

Süess, S. *"Unsere wunde Welt braucht tapfere Herzen": Naturschutz – Lebensschutz – Menschenschutz in der Schweizerischen Liga für biologische Landesverteidigung (1964–1974).* Master's dissertation, University of Bern, 1997.

Sünner, R. *Schwarze Sonne: Entfesselung und Missbrauch der Mythen in Nationalsozialismus und rechter Esoterik.* Freiburg, Basel, Vienna, 1999.

Suter, C., ed. *Sozialbericht 2000.* Zurich, 2000.

Sutton, M. *Nationalism, Positivism and Catholicism: The Politics of Charles Maurras and French Catholics, 1890–1914.* Cambridge, 2002.

Swyngedouw, M. and G. Ivaldi. 'The Extreme Right Utopia in Belgium and France: The Ideology of the Flemish Vlaams Blok and French Front National', in *West European Politics* vol. 24, no. 3 (2001), 1–22.

Syfrig, M. and C. Defaye. *Les nazis parmi nous: Enquête sur les mouvements d'extrême-droite dans le monde.* Lausanne, 1967.

—— *L'extrême-droite en Suisse.* Lausanne, 1967.

Taggart, P. 'New Populist Parties in Western Europe', *West European Politics* vol. 18, no. 1 (1995), 34–51.

—— *The New Populism and the New Politics: New Protest Parties in Sweden in a Comparative Perspective.* Basingstoke, London, 1996.

—— *Populism.* Buckingham, Philadelphia, 2000.

Taguieff, P.-A. 'La stratégie culturelle de la "Nouvelle droite" en France (1968–1983)', in *Vous avez dit fascismes?* ed. R. Badinter. Paris, 1984, 13–152.

—— 'Les droites radicales en France: nationalisme révolutionnaire et national-libéralisme', *Les Temps modernes* no. 465 (1985), 1780–1842.

—— *La force du préjugé: Essai sur le racisme et ses doubles.* Paris, 1988.

—— 'From Race to Culture: The New Right's View of European Identity', in *The French New Right: New Right – New Left – New Paradigms*, Special Double Issue of *Telos* nos. 98/99 (1993/94), 99–125.

—— *Sur la Nouvelle droite: Jalons d'une analyse critique.* Paris, 1994.

—— 'L'abbé Pierre et Roger Garaudy: Négationnisme, antijudaïsme, antisionisme', *Esprit* no. 224 (1996), 205–16.

—— *L'illusion populiste: De l'archaïque au médiatique.* Paris, 2002.

Tarrow, S. *Power in Movement: Social Movements, Collective Action and Politics*. Cambridge, New York, Melbourne, 1994.
Tauber, K.P. *Beyond Eagle and Swastika: German Nationalism since 1945*, 2 vols. Middletown, CT, 1967.
Terkessidis, M. *Kulturkampf: Volk, Nation, der Westen und die Neue Recht*. Cologne, 1995.
Ternisien, X. *L'extrême droite et l'église*. Paris, 1997.
Tobler, R. 'Die Internationale Konvention zur Beseitigung jeder Form von Rassendiskriminierung und die Schweiz', Extended version of a paper presented at the seminar of the Forum Against Racism, 26 February 1994.
Todorov, T. and A. Jacquet. *Guerre et paix sous l'Occupation: Témoignages recueillis au centre de la France*. Paris, 1996.
Tschirren, J. *Negationistische Propaganda in der Schweiz 1946–1994*. Master's dissertation, University of Fribourg, 1999.
Türsan, H. 'Introduction. Ethnoregionalist Parties as Ethnic Entrepreneurs', in *Regionalist Parties in Western Europe*, eds L. De Winter and H. Türsan. London, New York, 1998, pp. 1–16.
Venner, M. *Nationale Identität: Die Neue Rechte und die Grauzone zwischen Konservatismus und Rechtsextremismus*. Cologne, 1994.
Veugelers, J.W.P. 'A Challenge for Political Sociology: The Rise of Far-Right Parties in Contemporary Western Europe', *Current Sociology* vol. 47, no. 4 (1999), 78–107.
Vidal-Naquet, P. *Assassins of Memory: Essays on the Denial of the Holocaust*. New York, 1992.
Vignando, R. and H. Haas. 'Le mouvement skinhead: Une étude empirique', *Crimiscope* no. 15 (2001), 1–9.
Walpen, B. *Die offenen Feinde und ihre Gesellschaf:. Eine hegemonietheoretische Studie zur Mont Pèlerin Society*. Hamburg, 2004.
Walter, F. *Les Suisses et l'environnement: Une histoire du rapport à la nature du XVIIIe siècle à nos jours*. Geneva, 1990.
Watson, J. *The Christian Coalition: Dreams of Restoration, Demands for Recognition*. New York, 1997.
Weber, E. *L'Action française*. Paris, 1985.
Weber, I. *Nation, Staat und Elite: Die Ideologie der Neuen Rechten*. Cologne, 1997.
Weinberg, L. 'Introduction', in *Encounters with the Contemporary Radical Right*, eds P.H. Merkl and L. Weinberg. Boulder, CO, San Francisco, Oxford, 1993, pp. 1–15.
——— 'An Overview of Right-Wing Extremism in the Western World: A Study of Convergence, Linkage, and Identity', in *Nation and Race: The Developing Euro-American Racist Subculture*, eds J. Kaplan and T. Bjørgo. Boston, MA, 1998, pp. 3–33.
Wende, P. 'Radikalismus', in *Geschichtliche Grundbegriffe: Historisches Lexikon zur politisch-sozialen Sprache in Deutschland*, vol. 5, eds O. Brunner, W. Conze and R. Koselleck. Stuttgart, 1984, pp. 113–33.
Wernli, B., P. Sciarini and J. Barranco. *Analyse der eidgenössischen Abstimmungen vom 12. Juni 1994*, VOX no. 53, Adliswil, Bern, 1994.

Wernli, B., S. Wälti and D. Caramani. *Analyse der eidgenössischen Abstimmung vom 26. September 1993*, VOX no. 50, Adliswil, Bern, 1993.
Wicker, H.-R. 'Einleitung: Migration, Migrationspolitik und Migrationsforschung', in *Migration und die Schweiz: Ergebnisse des Nationalen Forschungsprogramms "Migration und interkulturelle Beziehungen"*, eds H.-R. Wicker, R. Fibbi and W. Haug. Zurich, 2003, pp. 12–62.
Widfeldt, A. 'Scandinavia: Mixed Success for the Populist Right', *Parliamentary Affairs* vol. 53, no. 3 (2000), 486–500.
Wiget, M. *Der rasche Aufstieg der rechten Blocker: Die Aktion für eine unabhängige und neutrale Schweiz AUNS*. Master's dissertation, University of Bern, 2002.
Wigger, E. *Krieg und Krise in der politischen Kommunikation: Vom Burgfrieden zum Bürgerblock in der Schweiz 1910–1922*. Zurich, 1997.
Willems, H., et al. *Fremdenfeindliche Gewalt: Einstellungen – Täter – Konflikteskalation*. Opladen, 1993.
Williams, R. *Keywords: A Vocabulary of Culture and Society*. New York, 1976.
Willms, T. *Armin Mohler: Von der CSU zum Neofaschismus*. Cologne, 2004.
Wimmer, A. *Nationalist Exclusion and Ethnic Conflict: Shadows of Modernity*. Cambridge, 2002.
Winock, M. 'L'héritage contre-révolutionnaire', in *Histoire de l'extrême droite en France*, ed. M. Winock. Paris, 1993, pp. 17–49.
Wisler, D., L. Marquis and M. Bergman. *Analyse der eidgenössischen Abstimmungen vom 28. September 1997*, VOX no. 62, Zurich, 1997.
Wistrich, R.S. *Anti-Semitism: The Longest Hatred*. London, 1991.
Wolf, W. *Faschismus in der Schweiz: Die Geschichte der Frontenbewegungen in der deutschen Schweiz, 1930–1945*. Zurich, 1969.
Wolin, R. 'Designer Fascism', in *Fascism's Return: Scandal, Revision, and Ideology since 1980*, ed R.J. Golsan. Lincoln, NK, London, 1998, pp. 48–62.
Wölk, V. *Natur und Mythos: Ökologiekonzepte der 'Neuen' Rechten im Spannungsfeld zwischen Blut und Boden und New Age*. Duisburg, 1992.
Woods, R. 'The Radical Right: The "Conservative Revolutionaries" in Germany', in *The Nature of the Right: American and European Politics and Political Thought since 1789*, eds R. Eatwell and N. O'Sullivan. Boston, MA, 1989, pp. 124–45.
——— *The Conservative Revolution in the Weimar Republic*. Basingstoke, London, 1996.
Zala, S. 'Governmental Malaise with History: From the White Paper to the Bonjour Report', in *Switzerland and the Second World War*, ed. G. Kreis. London, Portland, OR, 2000, pp. 312–32.
Zellhofer, K. and M.A. Gassner. 'SS und Rosenkranz – Völkischer Katholizismus', in *Die Ordnung, die sie meinen: "Neue Rechte" in Österreich*, ed. W. Purtscheller. Vienna, 1994, 100–23.
Zimmer, O. *A Contested Nation: History, Memory and Nationalism in Switzerland, 1761–1891*. Cambridge, 2003.
Zollinger, K. *Frischer Wind oder faschistische Reaktion? Die Haltung der Schweizer Presse zum Frontismus 1933*. Zurich, 1991.
Zollinger, L. *Der Mittelstand am Rande: Christoph Blocher, das Volk und die Vorstädte*. Bern, 2004.

Index

Abellio, Raymond, 271
Abendland, 179–84
Action Française, 232, 243
Age d'Homme, L' (publisher), 227, 239, 261, 263–67
Aktion für eine unabhängige und neutrale Schweiz (CINS – Campaign for an Independent and Neutral Switzerland), 86, 88, 136, 141, 145, 150, 216–20, 221, 223, 242, 249, 281, 322, 392n284
Aktion für freie Meinungsäusserung – Gegen UNO-Bevormundung (AfM – Campaign for Freedom of Speech – Against the Imposition of the UN's Will), 294
Allard, Jean-Paul, 260
Allenspach, Heinz, 195
Almirante, Giorgio, 252
Altermatt, Urs, 59
Amaudruz, Gaston-Armand, 218, 272, 279–83, 285–86, 290, 291, 292, 300, 301, 324, 325, 328, 329, 410–11n92
Andrić, Ivo, 263
Annales d'histoire révisionniste, 262
Anouilh, Jean, 271
Anti-89, L', 251
anti-racism, 20, 27, 180, 236–37
    anti-racist groups, 308, 314, 315, 319
    application of the anti-racism law, 91, 121, 163, 165, 263, 287, 289, 289–91, 296, 297, 298, 310, 366n183, 420n305
    opposition against the anti-racism law, 111, 134, 180, 197, 220, 235–37, 241–42, 248, 251, 281, 294, 295, 324, 325
anti-Semitism, 2, 18, 21–22, 37, 50, 97, 221, 227, 241, 275, 277, 278, 283–84, 293, 297, 327, 329, 339
    anti-Semitic attitudes and statements, 49, 50, 91, 121, 163, 224, 226–27, 230, 232, 233–34, 239, 241, 242, 250, 267–69, 276, 279, 280, 282, 286, 289, 293–99, 302, 311, 323
    negationism, concept of, 283–84
    negationist propaganda, 33, 87, 192, 199, 212, 238, 242, 254, 259, 260, 262, 263, 266, 269, 271, 272, 276, 277, 283–93, 295, 298, 301, 313, 320, 321, 322, 323, 326, 328, 337, 339, 392n284, 404n249, 409n57, 410n86, 410–11n92
Antonio, Robert, 176
Antony, Barnard (alias Romain Marie), 244, 246, 247, 250, 398n96
Arbeitsgemeinschaft zur Enttabuisierung der Zeitgeschichte (AEZ – Working Group for Breaking the Taboo on Contemporary History), 289, 292
Arbeitskreis Gelebte Geschichte (AGG – Living History Working Group), 225–27
Arbora-Verlag, 185
Arfel, Jean, *see* Madiran, Jean
Association des amis de Pierre Gripari (Association of the Friends of Pierre Gripari), 264
Association des amis de Robert Brasillach (ARB – Association of the Friends of Robert Brasillach), 235, 239, 262, 267–72, 301, 403n213, 405n252, 405n266

454 | Index

asylum policy, 62, 67, 70, 74, 78, 79, 80, 83, 84, 89, 101, 103, 104, 105, 107, 110, 119, 121, 129, 131, 135–38, 149–51, 169, 171, 192–93, 195, 197, 219–20, 221, 223, 246, 340, 341
    criticism of, 62, 74, 97–98, 102, 111–12, 136–37, 166, 183, 311–12
    See also refugee policy
asylum seekers, 26, 50, 62, 67, 71, 72, 89, 104, 105, 136, 214, 322, 324
    statements on, 73–74, 84, 88, 100, 110–12, 121, 163, 164, 166–67, 187, 192–93, 195, 197, 219–20, 251, 311–12, 363n50
    violence against, 22, 54, 304, 305, 307, 308, 312
Augier, Marc (alias Saint-Loup), 258, 270, 271
Aula, 198
Aurora, 289, 292
Austria, 3, 4, 54, 58, 123, 156, 179, 222, 275, 334
    extreme right, 54, 207, 275, 282, 287, 290, 297, 299, 319, 327
    New Right, 194, 198, 199, 202, 203, 209–10, 389n199, 389n201
    See also Freiheitliche Partei Österreichs; Haider, Jörg
authoritarianism, 8, 23–24, 40, 78, 92, 125–26, 170, 174–75, 207, 229, 231, 232, 233–35, 243, 244, 246, 251, 271, 311, 332, 339
    authoritarian leadership, 32, 59, 61, 108, 126, 141, 172, 183, 276, 282
    criticism of anti-authoritarian ideas, 24, 176, 190, 200, 339
Auto-Partei der Schweiz (APS – Car Party of Switzerland), 77, 86, 87, 99–114, 146, 147, 324
    See also Freiheits-Partei der Schweiz
Avant-Garde, 301

Bächtold, Jakob, 208–9, 211
Baillet, Philippe, 264, 265
Bandi, Hans-Georg, 225
Banton, Michael, 22
Barbie, Klaus, 282
Bardèche, Maurice, 266, 268, 269, 270, 284, 285, 409n57
Barnes, Ian, 268
Barrès, Maurice, 229, 257
Bärwald, Helmut, 203
Bäschlin, Beat Christoph, 90, 363n60
Bataille, Yves, 301
Bauern-, Gewerbe- und Bürgerpartei (BGB – Farmers, Artisans and Citizens Party), 125–28, 147, 354n37
    See also Schweizerische Volkspartei
Baumgartner, Franz, 188, 326
Belgium, 3, 4, 78, 270, 275, 284, 405n266
    New Right, 254, 255, 258, 260, 261, 262, 268, 269, 302
    See also Vlaams Blok
Bell, Daniel, 14, 177
Berclaz, René-Louis, 272
Bergeron, Francis, 271
Bergier, Jean-François, 224
Berserker, 317
Berset, Elie, 326
Berthod, René (alias Rembarre), 247, 248, 250, 267
Bertinat, Eric, 64–65, 217, 249–51
Betz, Hans-Georg, 15, 26, 111, 113, 123, 322
Bignasca, Giuliano, 116, 117–18, 120–21
Binswanger, Hans Christoph, 212
Bircher, Eugen, 126
Blocher, Christoph
    associates of, 134, 141
    Blocherite wing within the SVP, 129, 134, 135, 141, 147, 149–51, 172, 189
    debate on Second World War, 137–38, 162–63, 169, 374n74
    extreme right and, 322, 325, 328, 423n363
    Federal Council and, 47, 129–30, 134, 139, 160–61, 342

financial resources, 139–40, 142, 171, 217, 374n80
migration policy, 135–36, 137, 164, 166
New Right and, 169, 181, 188, 189, 216, 217, 218, 242, 249, 251
opposition to European integration, 135, 143, 161, 164, 168–69, 188, 217–18, 242, 251
party leadership, 124, 129, 138–41, 154, 159, 160, 172
relationship to other political parties, 83, 99, 107, 161–62
Zurich SVP and, 130–31, 139, 141, 143
Blood & Honour (group), 314, 318, 321
Blood & Honour (skinzine), 318
Bobbio, Norberto, 13
Boimond, Martine, 83, 326, 328
Bonvin, Roger, 247
Borne, Étienne, 243
Borner, Silvio, 203
Borradori, Marco, 115
Bossi, Umberto, 32, 138, 374n76
Bossle, Lothar, 205
Bouchet, Christian, 300
Bourse-Autos, 263
Boutin, Christophe, 265
Brader, Pierre, 260
Brasillach, Robert, 233, 237, 260, 267–68, 269, 270
Brezinka, Wolfgang, 186, 189, 190
Brigneau, François (alias Emanuel Allot), 249–51, 266, 270, 271
British National Front, 314
Brubaker, Rogers, 26
Brunner, Manfred, 188
Buchholz-Kaiser, Annemarie, 200
Bulletin de l'association des amis de Robert Brasillach, 269–72
Bund der Steuerzahler (BdS - Federation of Tax Payers), 144
Bürgeraktion für weniger Staat (Citizens' Action Group for Less State), 100
Burger, Norbert, 327

Bürgerlich-Demokratische Partei (BDP – Bourgeois Democratic Party), 130, 134, 342
Bürger und Christ (Citizen and Christian), 195
Bürki-Flury, Elisabeth, 225
Butikofer, Roland, 234

Cahiers de la Renaissance vaudoise, 234–35, 236
Cahiers des amis de Robert Brasillach, 270
cahiers du journal Controverses, Les, 249
Cahiers européens Hebdo, 301
Camus, Jean-Yves, 124
Canovan, Margaret, 32, 140, 143
Cantini, Claude, 257
Caramani, Daniele, 149
Carnets spirituels, 249
Carter, Elizabeth, 17–18
Carto, Willis, 288, 296
Celtiques, Éditions, 280
Centre d'études sur les nouvelles religions (CESNUR – Study Centre on New Religions), 257
Centre Henri et André Charlier, 244, 250, 264
Centre national de la pensée européenne (National Centre of European Thought), 256)
Cercle Culture et Liberté (Culture and Liberty Circle), 255, 300
Cercle culturel Hagal (Hagal Cultural Circle), 262
Cercle Proudhon (Proudhon Circle), 241, 258–61, 262, 302
Cercle Thulé (Thule Circle), 256–58, 261, 292
Champetier, Charles, 265
Charrière, François, 245
Chenaux, Jean-Philippe, 239, 250
Chevallaz, Georges-André, 235
Chiron, Yves, 250
Christlich-Demokratische Union (CDU – Christian Democratic Union), 177–78, 206
Christlichdemokratische Volkspartei (CVP – Christian-Democratic

People's Party), 63, 123, 142, 145, 354n37
    constituency, 116–17, 136, 153, 156–57, 158–59, 202, 377n156
    elections, 146, 150, 151, 152
    Federal Council and, 46–47, 134
    New Right and, 217–18, 247, 248, 249
    See also Konservativ-Christlichsoziale Volkspartei; Schweizerische Konservative Volkspartei
Church, Clive, 1, 129
Cité catholique (Catholic City), 243
citizenship, 18, 19, 47, 48,
    citizenship policy, 26, 48, 66, 73, 85, 89, 96, 165–66, 222, 321, 351n45
CODE, 295
Collaud, Sylvain, 326
Collegium Humanum, 207
Cologne, Daniel, 300
Combat, 265
Combat païen, 258
Comités Chrétienté-Solidarité (Christendom Solidarity Committees), 244
Commentary, 177
Conservative Revolution, 35–36, 174, 179, 190, 204, 221, 252, 258, 265, 299, 351n132
consociationalism, 2–5, 8, 46–47, 139, 322, 332–33, 342, 343n4
Cornilleau, Claude, 279
Coston, Henry, 249, 266, 271
Countess, Robert H., 291
Courrier du Continent, 239, 272, 280, 281, 282, 285, 286, 292, 300, 324, 325, 328, 329
Courtois, Stéphane, 161–62
Criticón, 178, 181, 189, 194, 205, 266

D'Alessio, Eugenio, 248
Däniker, Gustav, 286
Daudet, Léon, 229
de Beketch, Serge, 250
de Benoist, Alain, 183, 188, 241, 253–54, 255, 257, 260, 261, 264, 265, 266, 267, 270, 271, 280
de Bonald, Louis, 232
Decker, Frank, 13
Défense de l'Occident, 250, 257, 265, 266, 271
Degrelle, Léon, 257, 282
Delacrétaz, Olivier, 181, 235–37, 272
Delamuraz, Jean-Pascal, 224, 226, 374n74
Delcroix, Eric, 242, 262, 271
de Maistre, Joseph, 232
Demokratische Fraktion (Democratic Fraction), 119
Denmark, 4, 140
    See also Progress Party
de Preux, Michel, 239–41, 247, 398n96
de Reynold, Gonzague, 174, 229, 271
Deutsche National-Zeitung, 198, 327
Deutsche Wochen-Zeitung, 328
de Villemarest, Pierre, 250
de Winter, Noël, 271
Diagnosen, 295
Diagnosen-Verlag, 296
Dillen, Karel, 270, 271
Dimitrijević, Vladimir, 263–64, 267
direct democracy, 1, 45, 47, 68, 76, 173, 354n37
    opportunity structure, 4–5, 8, 45, 52, 65, 68, 83, 108, 118–19, 135, 144, 220, 332, 334–35
    statements on direct democracy, 32, 76, 167, 168, 191–92, 203, 222, 234
Diwald, Hellmut, 266
Douguine, Alexandre, 264
Dreher, Michael, 99, 101, 104, 107, 108, 110
Druwe, Ulrich, 17
Dumézil, Georges, 252
Dünnenberger, Ernst, 328, 364n87
Durand, Pierre, 244
Duranton-Crabol, Anne-Marie, 284
Duverger, Maurice, 27–28

Eatwell, Roger, 16, 24–25, 278
Eckartbote, Der, 327

ECOPOP-Bulletin, 212, 213, 214
EDU-Standpunkt, 93, 95, 96, 98, 99
egalitarianism, 8, 13, 14, 20, 23–24, 34, 173, 190, 338
　anti-egalitarianism, 13, 17–18, 19–20, 23–24, 186, 187, 200, 202, 230–31, 232, 233, 237–38, 243–44, 273, 339–40
　criticism of, 8, 23–24, 35, 36, 175–76, 177–78, 190, 191, 194–95, 198, 204–5, 227, 242, 251, 252–53, 313, 339
Ehinger, Paul, 198
Eibl-Eibesfeldt, Irenäus, 35, 74, 186–87, 206, 211, 214
Eidgenoss, 93, 286–87, 323, 328, 410n86
Eidgenössisch-Demokratische Union (EDU – Swiss Democratic Union), 57, 77, 87, 92–99, 136, 146, 147, 197, 202, 286, 323, 328
Eidgenössische Kommission gegen Rassismus (EKR – Federal Commission Against Racism), 310
elections 4–5, 45, 52, 76, 92, 171, 252, 256, 279, 281, 320, 321
　cantonal, 61–62, 64, 78–79, 93, 94, 102, 106, 115–16, 131, 145, 146, 151–52
　campaigns, 29, 62, 79–80, 95, 97, 100–101, 102–4, 107, 110, 117, 127, 131, 133, 147, 149–51, 161, 166, 171–72, 192, 367n150
　constituencies, 3, 50, 59–60, 80–81, 104–6, 116–17, 150, 152–59
　federal, 9, 40, 44, 46, 47, 59–62, 65, 67, 75, 78–80, 82, 93, 94, 100, 101–4, 106, 108, 109, 115–16, 119, 124, 127, 131, 133, 139–40, 145–151, 188, 203, 249, 255, 311, 312, 321, 322, 323, 328, 354n37, 357n7, 357n11, 357n17, 364n87
Elemente, 255, 257
Éléments, 237, 253, 258, 265, 271
Enlightenment, 175, 176, 178, 182, 190, 231, 240, 338, 339

ethnopluralism, 21, 36, 73–74, 89, 98, 164–65, 180, 187, 195–96, 199, 206, 207, 210, 228, 233, 253, 299, 313, 338
Etter, Philipp, 174
Etter, Roger, 328
Études et Recherches, 258
Europäische Arbeitsgemeinschaft 'Mut zur Ethik' (EAME – European Working Group 'Courage to Take a Moral Stance'), 205
Europäischer Arbeitskreis für ökologische Politik (EAföP – European Working Group for Ecological Politics), 209–10, 212
Europa Nazione, 278
Europe-Jeunesse (Europe-Youth), 302
Europe réelle, 261, 280
European, The, 278
European Horizons, 257
European integration, 2, 26, 49, 75–76, 79, 83, 86–87, 88–89, 90–91, 92, 93, 99, 112, 121–22, 129, 135, 149, 151, 156, 161, 168, 203, 215–16, 218, 223, 251, 325, 341, 355n49
　criticism of European Union/ European Community, 87, 88, 99, 112, 122, 150, 164, 168, 183, 192, 203, 219, 250, 368n196
　opposition against European Economic Area membership, 49, 86, 88–89, 90–91, 107, 112, 135, 140, 150, 161, 168, 183, 192, 217, 218, 220, 223, 234, 251, 325, 421n336
　vote on European Economic Area membership, 68, 135, 161
European Social Movement (ESB), 278, 279
Evangelische Volkspartei (EVP – Protestant People's Party), 93, 94, 218
Evola, Julius, 240, 252–53, 257, 259, 261, 264–65, 318
Excalibur (bookstore), 262–63
extremism, concept of, 13–16

fascism, 4, 8, 23, 27, 39–41, 51, 125–26, 162, 174, 229, 234, 240, 252–53, 259, 267–68
    extreme right and, 3, 37, 54–55, 278, 279, 283, 285, 315, 318, 339
Faurisson, Robert, 284, 287–88, 290, 291, 292
Favre, Pierre, 269, 270
Faye, Guillaume, 257, 260
federal initiatives, 45, 62–63, 65, 67–68, 70, 83, 118, 133, 149, 166, 213, 334–35, 354n37, 373n65
    Against Illegal Immigration, 121, 136–37, 138, 142, 193, 219, 324
    Against Mass Immigration of Foreigners and Asylum Seekers, 83, 84
    Against Overforeignization, 71
    Against Overforeignization and Overpopulation, 66, 68
    Against Overforeignization (Schwarzenbach Initiative), 58, 62, 65–67, 70, 128, 183
    Against the Misuse of the Right to Asylum, 121, 137, 138, 151, 219
    Against the Selling-Off of the Homeland, 66, 69, 85
    EC/EU Membership Negotiations: Let the People Decide!, 84, 86–87, 324, 362n40
    Enlargement of the A1 Geneva-Lucerne Highway to Six Lanes, 109
    Enlargement of the Highway A1 Zurich-Berne to Six Lanes, 109
    Exercising Moderation on Immigration, 84–85
    For a Reasonable Asylum Policy, 80, 84, 119
    For the Abolition of the Direct Federal Tax, 109
    For the Abolition of the Right of Associations to File Complaints at the Federal Level, 109
    For the Day Off on the Federal Holiday (1st August Initiative), 84, 85–86
    For the Defence of Switzerland, 67
    For the Limitation of Immigration, 66, 70–71
    For the Limitation of Naturalisations, 66
    For the Limitation of the Reception of Asylum Seekers, 67, 71, 324
    For the Regulation of Migration (18% Initiative), 98, 121, 133, 181, 193
    For the Reorganisation of the Referendum on State Treaties, 66, 68
    Second Gotthard Tunnel Pipe, 109
    Surplus of Gold Reserves to the AHV-Fund - Gold Initiative, 137–38
    Togetherness Initiative, 69–70
    Youth without Drugs, 201–2
federalism, 1, 45–46, 47, 76, 114, 119–120, 167–68, 191–92, 234–35, 259, 309, 327
    party system and, 41, 46, 82, 127, 132
federal referendums, optional, 45, 335, 344n4, 354n37
    anti-racism law, 180, 235–36, 281, 294, 324
    Federal Decree on buying property by people living abroad, 84, 85
    Federal Decree on gas tax increase, 108–9
    Federal Decree on the medical prescription of heroin, 95
    federal legislation on sexual offences, 95
    Federal Statute on Swiss forces for peacekeeping operations, 84, 86, 112, 160, 168–69, 380n223
    Referendum on loan to the IDA, 67, 69
    Referendum on revised alien legislation, 66, 68

Referendum on sectoral
  agreements between
  Switzerland and EU, 84, 87–88
Fehr, Hans, 141, 181
Feldmann, Markus, 125–26
Fellay, Bernard, 245
Fennema, Meindert, 290
Ferraglia, Aldo, 263
Ferraresi, Franco, 264, 265
Figaro Magazine, Le, 253
Filbinger, Hans, 177, 178, 189
Finkelstein, Norman, 227
Fischbacher, Walter, 294, 295, 323
Fischer, Otto, 216, 220
Fischer, Theodor, 286
Fleissner, Herbert, 190
Flückiger, Gottlieb, 211
Forces nouvelles (New Forces),
  254–56, 302
Förster, Gerhard, 289, 289
Fortuyn, Pim, 32
France, 28, 48, 53, 223, 229–30, 232,
  235, 240, 242, 245, 250–52, 268, 270,
  284, 334
    extreme right, 54, 228, 238, 240,
      242, 249–50, 275, 284–85, 287,
      299–303, 304, 315, 317, 319, 336
    New Right, 21, 34–35, 221,
      228, 230–31, 232–33, 236–38,
      241, 243–44, 245–46, 249–50,
      252–273, 299–302, 320, 389n201
    radical right-wing populist
      parties, 57, 59, 78, 239–40, 246,
      302
    See also Front national
Franco, Francisco, 58, 246
Frank, Hans, 256
Fraternité sacerdotale Saint-Pie X
  (SSPX – Priestly Society of Saint
  Pius X), 244–47, 399n129
Freda, Giorgio, 257, 415n196
Frederiksen, Marc, 301
Freiheitliche Partei Österreichs (FPÖ
  – Freedom Party of Austria), 3, 100,
  123, 124, 139, 158
    See also Haider, Jörg
Freiheits-Partei der Schweiz (FPS –
  Freedom Party of Switzerland), 77,
87, 99–114, 119, 136, 146, 150, 151,
  153, 180, 202
    See also Auto-Partei der Schweiz
Freisinnig-Demokratische Partei
  (FDP – Liberal Democratic Party),
  123, 124–25, 133, 134, 142, 145, 224,
  374n74, 354n37
    constituency, 116–17, 136, 153,
      156–57, 202, 377n156
    elections, 146, 150, 151
    extreme right and, 294, 323, 324
    Federal Council and, 46, 74, 127
    New Right and, 180, 181, 189,
      193, 197, 198, 216, 217–18, 227,
      235, 239
    radical right-wing populist
      parties and, 98, 99, 102, 107, 181
Frey, Walter, 143
Friedman, Milton, 169
Friedrich, Rudolf, 185
Frischknecht, Jürg, 201
Fröhlich, Wolfgang, 290
Froidevaux, Didier, 48
Frontenbewegung (Front Movement),
  39–41, 57, 58, 61, 126, 174–75, 184,
  234, 269, 279, 285–86, 300, 310, 311
Front national (FN – National Front),
  63, 64, 78, 239–40, 244, 246, 253,
  260, 264, 302, 398n96
    See also Le Pen, Jean-Marie

Garaudy, Roger, 260, 263, 285, 290,
  292
Genoud, François, 281–82
Genoud, Guy, 247–48
Gentile, Pierre, 305
Gentizon, Paul, 285
Germanier, Paul, 248–9
Germany, 14, 22, 28, 48, 50, 95, 126,
  163, 173, 184, 193, 198, 201, 209,
  221–22, 223, 226, 258, 267–68, 280,
  286, 289, 292, 299–300, 309
    extreme right, 54, 74–75, 90, 198,
      199, 275, 282, 284, 287, 292,
      295, 296–97, 299, 302, 304–5,
      317, 318–20, 327, 328
    New Right, 21, 34, 35, 53, 90,
      176, 177–79, 180–81, 186–87,

188–90, 194, 197–99, 202–5, 206–7, 209–10, 211, 216, 228, 254, 255, 256, 257, 261, 266, 389n199, 389n201
Gesellschaft und Kirche wohin? (Society and Church, Where Now?), 197
Gesellschaft zur Förderung der psychologischen Menschenkenntnis (GFPM – Society for Advancing the Psychological Knowledge of Human Nature), 202
Giezendanner, Ulrich, 108
globalisation, 24, 25, 26, 36, 53, 120, 215, 250, 276, 341
Goebbels, Joseph, 282
Goodwin, Matthew, 5
Gossweiler, Andreas, 320, 321
Grabert-Verlag, 188
Graf, Hans Ulrich, 132
Graf, Jürgen, 192, 197, 288–92, 298, 322, 410n92
Gramsci, Antonio, 34
Grauer Brief, 217, 219
Great Britain, 34, 48, 59, 204, 260, 284, 302, 314, 318, 389n201
Griffin, Des, 296
Griffin, Roger, 19
Gripari, Pierre, 264
Grobman, Alex, 284
Groupement de recherche et d'études pour la civilisation européenne (GRECE – Group for the Research and Study of European Civilization), 236, 253, 255, 256, 257, 259, 260, 261, 262, 264, 266, 300
Gruhl, Herbert, 206–7, 209–10, 211
Grüne Partei Schweiz (GPS – Green Party of Switzerland), 146
Guillaume, Pierre, 287–88
Günther, Hans F. K., 257
Guyot-Jeannin, Arnaud, 265–66

Hagen, Carl I., 138, 374n76
Haider, Jörg, 32, 123, 138, 139
Hainsworth, Paul, 28
Hammer, 317, 318
Hatzenbichler, Jürgen, 198
Haudry, Jean, 260
Haverbeck, Werner Georg, 207, 210
Hayek, Friedrich A. von, 169, 179
Hegg, Jean-Jacques, 63, 74–75, 90, 197, 210–11, 328
Herbert-Gruhl-Gesellschaft (Herbert Gruhl Society), 211
Herbig Verlag, 190
Hess, Rudolf, 256, 319
Himmler, Heinrich, 329
Hitler, Adolf, 49, 98, 246, 282, 295, 319
Hofstetter, Pierre, 285–86
Hohenrain-Verlag, 188
Holey, Jan Udo, *see* van Helsing, Jan
Holmes, Douglas, 20
Horizons et débats, 203
Horizons européens, 257
Hornung, Klaus, 179, 181, 204, 205
Hossay, Patrick, 6
Hottinger, Julian, 116
Huber, Ahmed, 292–93, 323
Huron, Le, 271, 301
Husbands, Christopher, 62
Huyn, Hans Graf, 189

identity politics, 25–27, 30, 31, 37, 52, 83, 114, 121–22, 140, 156, 159, 167–169, 171, 172, 337, 347
Ignazi, Piero, 23–24, 27
Independent Commission of Experts Switzerland – Second World War (ICE), 91, 169, 224, 225, 226, 227
Indlekofer, Ernst, 87, 212, 289, 294, 295, 298, 326–27
Institut des sciences psychosomatiques, biologiques et raciales (Institute of Psychosomatic, Biologic and Racial Sciences), 280
Institut d'études indo-européennes (Institute of Indo-European Studies), 260
Institut zur Förderung der psychologischen

Menschenkenntnis (IPM – Institute for Advancing the Psychological Knowledge of Human Nature), 202
Institute for Historical Review (IHR), 199, 285, 288, 292, 296
Interessengemeinschaft Schweiz – Zweiter Weltkrieg (IG – Interest Group Switzerland - Second World War), 226
International Development Association (IDA), 67, 69
Ireland, Patrick, 65, 70
Irving, David, 257
Islamophobia
    concept of, 23, 96, 97, 193
    statements on Muslim migrants, 90, 98, 164, 187, 195, 197, 220, 237, 246, 312
    statements on Islam, 98, 164, 187, 195, 246, 363n60
Isorni, Jacques, 268, 269, 405n259
Italy, 34, 54, 104, 114, 123, 194, 195, 229, 252, 254, 258, 260, 261, 265, 268, 302, 304, 319, 334, 389n201
Itinéraires, 243

Jacquet, Annick, 26
Jäger-Stamm, Walter, 59
Jenny, Hans R., 184, 185–86, 187
Je suis partout, 268
Jeune Europe (Young Europe), 278
Jeunesses nationalistes révolutionnaires (JNR – Nationalist Revolutionary Youths), 300
Johnson, Carol, 26
Journal Controverses, 249–52
Journal of Historical Review, The, 285, 291, 292
Jungbauernbewegung (Young Farmers' Movement), 126
Junge europäische Schüler- und Studenteninitiative der Schweiz (JES – Young European Pupils and Students Initiative of Switzerland), 194–96, 222, 224
Junge Freiheit, 178, 189–90, 198, 205

Junge Garde (Young Guard), 279
Junge Nationale Aktion (JNA – Young National Action), 326
Jünger, Ernst, 258, 266, 351n132
Junge SVP (JSVP – Young SVP), 130–31
Junod, Pascal, 255, 256, 258, 261, 262, 269, 271, 302

Kaiser, Ralph, 200
Kameradschaft Adlerhorst (Comradeship Eyrie), 282
Kaltenbrunner, Gerd-Klaus, 177, 179, 181, 189
Kaplan, Alice, 267–68, 270
Kaplan, Jeffrey, 14–15
Katholische Volkspartei (KVP – Catholic People's Party), 92–93
Keller, Rudolf, 75, 78, 91, 326, 370n234
Kessler, Erwin, 298
Kind, Reto, 294
Kitschelt, Herbert, 124, 156
Knüsel, René, 116
Knütter, Hans-Helmuth, 198, 205
Kobach, Kris, 69
Komitee für Freiheit im Reden und Denken (KFRD – Committee for Freedom of Speech and Thinking), 180
Kommissionsverlag, 285
Konservativ-Christlichsoziale Volkspartei (KCVP – Conservative Christian-Social People's Party), 63, 127
Kopp, Elisabeth, 74
Kopp, Hans-Ulrich, 189–90
Krebs, Pierre, 256
Krisis, 258
Kristol, Irving, 177
Ku Klux Klan (KKK), 311
Külling, Friedrich, 97
Kunz, Sacha, 321
Künzli, Jürgen, 282

Labin, Suzanne, 250
Ladner, Andreas, 107, 145, 154

Landesring der Unabhängigen (LDU – Alliance of Independents), 146, 208
Langen Müller Verlag, 190
Laqueur, Walter, 36, 315
Leach-Lewis, Peter, 297
Le Chavallier, Jean-Marie, 264
Lectures françaises, 271
Lefebvre, Marcel, 241, 244–46, 247, 248, 249, 250, 399n129
Lega dei Ticinesi, 78, 83, 84, 86–87, 112, 114–22, 136, 146, 147, 168, 324, 362n46
Lega Lombarda (Lombardic League), 114
Lega Nord (LN – Northern League), 104, 114, 123
Leisi, Ernst, 227
Le Pen, Jean-Marie, 32, 63, 64, 239–40, 244, 246, 247–48, 252
Lettre verte, La, 216–17
Lévi-Strauss, Claude, 240
Liberal Party of Switzerland (LPS – Liberale Partei der Schweiz), 146, 272
Libre R (bookstore), 262–63
Liebling, Friedrich, 200
Ligue Vaudoise (Vaud League), 229, 233–38, 239, 272, 281
Lippi, Jean-Paul, 265
Longchamp, Claude, 124
Lorenz, Konrad, 35, 74, 186, 206, 211, 214
Lovey, Roger, 247, 248
Löw, Konrad, 205
Löwenthal, Gerhard, 189, 204, 205
Lübbe, Hermann, 177, 179, 185, 382n18
Lutte du peuple (Struggle of the People), 303

Mabire, Jean, 265, 271
McCarthy, Joseph R., 15
McClelland, John, 232
McGann, Anthony J., 124, 156
Madiran, Jean (alias Jean Arfel), 243, 244, 246, 250, 264, 271

Mahler, Horst, 199
Malliarakis, Jean-Gilles, 257–58, 260, 266, 300
Manz, Heinz, 282, 327
Marie, Romain, *see* Antony, Barnard
Marquard, Odo, 177
Maspoli, Flavio, 115, 116, 117, 118, 119, 362n46
Mathez, James-Albert, 286, 287, 329
Mattino della domenica, Il, 117, 120, 121
Maurer, Ueli, 134, 135, 141, 160, 168, 322, 327
Maurras, Charles, 229, 232, 233, 235, 243, 250, 252, 258, 259, 267
Mayer, Jean-François, 257, 261, 264
Mayor, Claude-Alain, 239, 242
Mazzoleni, Oscar, 114, 118
Meier, Fritz, 58, 63, 71, 83
Meier, Herbert, 179–84, 281, 324
Meier, Pirmin, 181, 182, 183
Meier, Thomas, 190, 193
Meissner, Mary, 83, 250, 326, 328
Memopress, 218, 294–96, 324, 325, 327–28
Menschenkenntnis Verlag, 201
Meves, Christa, 181, 186, 189, 190, 384n70
Meyer, Werner, 285
migration policy, 20, 49, 59, 61, 65, 67–68, 70
    migration agenda of the radical right, 3, 24, 25–26, 48, 51, 62, 64, 70–71, 72-76, 80, 83, 89–90, 92, 96, 97–99, 110–11, 121, 142, 150, 163-67, 171, 183–84, 186–87, 192–93, 195–96, 197, 206–7, 208–9, 213–14, 219–200, 221–23, 237, 246, 266, 311–12, 321, 332, 338, 340
    integration of migrants, 26, 67, 69–70, 73, 89, 164–66, 183–84, 187, 214, 237
    See also asylum policy; citizenship policy
Militant, 250
Minger, Rudolf, 125, 126
Minkenberg, Michael, 25, 28

Minute, 247, 248, 249
Mises, Ludwig von, 169, 179
Mitte, Die, 127
Mitteilungsblatt der Priesterbruderschaft St. Pius für den deutschen Sprachraum, 245
Moeller van den Bruck, Arthur, 258
Mohler, Armin, 179, 266, 351n132
Mois suisse, Le, 280
Molnar, Thomas, 265
Monnier, Pierre, 271
Mont Pèlerin Society, 169, 179
Mörgeli, Christoph, 141, 169, 393n293
Morgenstern, 325
Moser, René, 112
Motta, Giuseppe, 118
Mouvement chrétien-conservateur valaisan (MCCV – Valais Christian Conservative Movement), 248–49
Mouvement conservateur et libéral valaisan (MCLV – Valais Conservative and Liberal Movement), 248
Mouvement nationaliste révolutionnaire (Nationalist Revolutionary Movement), 300
Mouvement patriotique genevois (MPE – Geneva Patriotic Movement), 64
Movimento Sociale Italiano (MSI – Italian Social Movement), 239, 252, 269
Mudde, Cas, 15, 17, 21
Mulas, David, 316
Müller, Hans, 126
Müller, Philipp, 98, 121, 181, 184, 190, 193
multiculturalism, 5, 8, 16, 24, 35, 164, 230, 233, 273, 332
　criticism of, 8, 15–16, 24, 35, 90, 111, 165, 186–87, 193, 198–99, 213–14, 220–23, 339
Musy, Jean-Marie, 329
Mut, 178, 189

Najman, Dragan, 90–91
Nation, La, 234, 235, 237, 239

national elections, *see* elections, federal
Nationaldemokratische Partei (NDP – National-Democratic Party), 327
Nationaldemokratische Partei Deutschlands (NPD – National-Democratic Party of Germany), 319
Nationale Aktion, 58, 82
Nationale Aktion (NA – National Action), 57–76, 77, 78–80, 83, 85, 93, 101, 136, 146, 168, 196, 207–11, 212, 250, 266, 273, 281, 295, 311, 323, 325, 326, 327, 328, 357n7, 357n11, 417n237
Nationale Basis Schweiz (NBS – National Basis of Switzerland), 282, 286, 326
Nationale Blatt, Das, 319–20
Nationale Front (National Front, 1930s), 58, 59, 174, 184, 282,
Nationale Initiative Schweiz (NIS – National Initiative of Switzerland), 319, 321, 324, 325
Nationale Koordination (NK – National Coordination), 281, 323, 324, 326
Nationale Opposition, 313
Nationale Partei Schweiz (NPS – National Party of Switzerland), 319–20
Nation & Europa (Nation Europa), 75, 198, 278, 327, 328
National Hebdo, 249
nationalism, 6, 14, 17, 24, 28, 31, 36, 40, 47, 48, 63, 86, 92, 114, 120, 124, 172, 175, 176, 178, 183, 184, 196, 198, 207, 211, 227, 229, 232, 233–34, 253, 259, 263, 265, 275, 277, 294, 299, 302, 304, 311, 321
　concept of, 18–19, 214–16
　nationalist statements, 75–76, 90–91, 95–96, 104, 112–113, 167–69, 174, 208, 219–20, 221–23, 224–26, 250, 293–94, 313, 321, 322, 332, 337–38
Nationalrevolutionäre Partei der Schweiz (NRP – National-

Revolutionary Party of Switzerland), 313–14, 316, 326, 328
National Socialism, 2, 3, 8, 20, 21–22, 27, 36, 39–41, 50, 64, 91, 125–26, 161–62, 174, 178, 215, 223, 225, 229, 237, 239, 251, 256, 267–68, 329, 378n176
    extreme right and, 37, 275, 278, 282–84, 286–89, 293, 297, 302, 311, 315, 317–18, 320–21
Nationalsozialistische Deutsche Arbeiterpartei (NSDAP – National-Socialist German Workers' Party), 207
Neidhart, Leonard, 133
neoliberalism, 24–25, 34, 52, 77, 100–101, 110–11, 113, 122, 151, 156, 159, 169–70, 172, 179, 191, 248, 336, 340, 381n227
neoracism, 15, 18, 31, 34–35, 76, 192, 231, 253, 299, 338
    concept of, 19–21
        neoracist statements, 74, 89–90, 111–12, 164–65, 183–84, 187, 192–93, 220–23, 236–37, 240–41
    See also ethnopluralism
Netherlands, 4, 275
Neue Anthropologie, 328
Neue Front (New Front, 1930s), 174
Neue Front (NF – New Front, 1980s), 312–13
Neue Nationale Front (NNF – New National Front), 311, 313, 316, 320, 324
Neue Visionen Verlag, 289, 290, 292
New Democracy, 104
Nguyen, Victor, 264
Niekisch, Ernst, 258, 300
Niggli, Peter, 201
1968 movement 8, 23–24, 35, 44, 175, 230
    criticism of 1968, 8, 9, 23–24, 35, 44, 97, 139, 176, 177, 180, 182, 185, 189–90, 200, 204–5, 227, 230, 238, 242, 339–40
Nolte, Ernst, 199, 204, 237
Nordbruch, Claus, 199

Norris, Pippa, 123–24
North Atlantic Treaty Organization (NATO), 80, 99
Norway, 4, 104, 140, 275
    See also Progress Party
Notin, Bernard, 260
Notre Europe, 301
Nouvelle École, 253, 255, 258, 264, 265, 271
Nouvelle résistance (NR – New Resistance), 300, 303, 316
Nouvelles synergies européennes, 265
Nouvel ordre européen (NOE – European New Order), 278, 279–80, 301
Nouvel ordre social (NOS – New Social Order), 257, 282, 300–302
Novalis Verlag, 227

Occident 2000 Viking Jeunesse (Occident 2000 Viking Youth), 302
Odals Rune (Odal Rune), 302
Oehen, Valentin, 63, 75, 82, 209–10, 212, 327–28, 329
Oehler, Hans, 285, 327
Ogi, Adolf, 134, 136
Ökologisch-Demokratische Partei (ÖDP – Ecological Democratic Party), 207
Ökologische Freiheitliche Partei der Schweiz (ÖFP – Ecological Libertarian Party of Switzerland), 210
Oltramare, Georges, 61, 229, 300
Opus Dei, 179
Ordre et Tradition (Order and Tradition), 233
Ordre nouveau (ON – New Order), 301
Orientations, 255, 258, 260
Ortlieb, Heinz-Dietrich, 190
Ostpreussenblatt, 198
'overforeignization'
    discourse of, 8, 49–51, 59, 63, 70, 72–75, 78, 80, 88, 89, 96, 98, 112, 164, 166, 174, 193, 197, 208–11, 220, 325, 338

Movement against, 3, 51, 52, 57–76, 77, 78, 82, 92, 93, 99, 101, 128, 164, 175, 183, 187, 207–11, 213, 227, 327, 329, 333, 335

Pache, Roger, 272, 405n266
Pamphlet, Le, 238–42, 271, 272, 288, 392n284, 398n96
Panorama des idées actuelles, 257
Pardès, Éditions, 261, 265
Partei der Zukunft (Party of the Future), 312
Partei National Orientierter Schweizer (PNOS – Party of National Oriented Swiss), 321, 420n309
Parti nationaliste français et européen (PNFE – French and European Nationalist Party), 278–79, 317
Parti nationaliste suisse et européen (PNSE – Swiss and European Nationalist Party), 317
Partisan, 258
Paschoud, Claude, 238–39, 239, 241, 242, 272, 288
Paschoud (Pache), Mariette, 238–39, 242, 266, 272, 287–88, 392n284, 396n24, 396n29, 410–11n92
Patanè, Giuseppe, 239
Patriotische Front (PF – Patriotic Front), 311–12, 314, 316, 326
Patriotische Volkspartei (PVP – Patriotic People's Party), 326
Paul VI, 247
Pays romande, Le, 143
Permanences, 243
Pétain, Philippe, 251, 252, 268, 405n259
Peters, Reimer, 297
peuple + patrie, 82–83, 250, 326
Pfeifenberger, Walter, 205
Pitterle, Kenneth, 69
Pius X, 243
    See also Fraternité sacerdotale Saint-Pie X
Podhoretz, Norman, 177

Politica Hermetica, 264–65
Poulat, Emile, 264
Powell, Enoch, 59
Présent, 244, 246, 249, 250, 251, 264
Presseclub, 87
Pro Libertate Mitteilungen, 196, 197
Progress Parties (Norway, Denmark) 100, 104, 140
Proudhon, Pierre-Joseph, 259
Prüfen + Handeln, 218, 294, 325
The Public Interest, 177
Pushkin, Aleksandr, 263

Raboud, Isabelle, 248
Race et Nation, 318
racism, 3, 36–37, 53, 55, 78, 111, 167, 174, 198, 210, 230, 236, 240, 253, 275–76, 278–80, 302–3, 310, 314–18, 323, 325, 328, 336, 338
    concept of, 19–21, 22
    racial language, 74, 90, 111–12, 193, 198, 220, 221, 236–37, 240–41, 279, 280, 295, 338–39
    'racial theories', 21, 37, 74, 339
    racist statements, 74–75, 90, 210–11, 279, 280, 295, 302, 311–12
    racist violence, 55, 304–8, 309, 311–12, 315–16, 320–21, 325, 336
    See also neo-racism
radicalism, concept of, 13–16
Rahm, Emil, 218, 281, 294–96, 324, 326, 327–28
Rahn, Otto, 318
Rassinier, Paul, 284
Ratcliffe, Alexander, 284
Rat noir, Le, 301–2
Recht + Freiheit, 289, 295, 298, 326
refugee policy, 70–71, 84, 111
    during Second World War, 49, 91, 126, 223, 226
    issue of refugees, 21, 50, 101, 102, 104–5, 110, 151, 221
    statements on refugees, 21, 71, 72, 73–74, 121, 164–65, 166, 219, 221, 223

466 | Index

See also asylum policy; asylum seekers
Regamey, Marcel, 229, 233–34, 235, 239
regionalism, 52, 78, 114, 119–20, 122, 233–34, 256, 257, 300, 313, 336
Reichenbach, Roland, 240
Renaissance, 271, 301
Renouveau rhodanien (Renewal of the Rhône), 247, 248
Republikaner, Der, 58, 59, 132, 187, 209, 327
Reverdin, Olivier, 271–72
Revue d'histoire du nationalisme révolutionnaire, 303
Revue d'histoire révisionniste, 242, 266
Rhonheimer, Martin, 179
Rothenhäusler-Verlag, 227
Riedweg, Franz, 329
Rigoni, Mario, 321
Rivarol, 232, 240, 249, 250, 251, 269, 271, 287
Roderer, Walter, 192
Roeder, Manfred, 282
Rohrmoser, Günter, 177, 189, 190–91, 202, 205
Romano, Gaetano, 73
Röpke, Wilhelm, 169, 179
Roques, Henri, 260, 284–85, 287, 288
Rosenberg, Alfred, 256, 258, 302
Rouot, Olivier, 249
Rousso, Henry, 284
Rudin, Robert, 195
Rudolf, Germar, 292
Ruf, Markus, 63–64, 74, 82
Russia, 254, 261, 264, 267, 291, 296
Rüst, Peter, 94, 96
Rutz, Edgar A., 134
Rydgren, Jens, 7

Saint-Etienne, Luc, 265
Saint-Loup, *see* Augier, Marc
Salazar, António de Oliveira, 246
Salisbury Review, The, 204
Sanders, Alain, 264, 271
Schaffner, Jakob, 174
Schain, Martin A., 6

Schalcher, Heinrich, 218
Schaub, Bernhard, 288, 292, 321, 410n92, 420n309
Schelsky, Helmut, 177
Schenk, Simon, 197
Scherrer, Christian, 313
Scherrer, Jürg, 102, 111–12
Scherrer, Werner, 94, 96, 98
Schifferli, Pierre, 64–65
Schlomann, Friedrich Wilhelm, 203
Schlüer, Ulrich, 99, 132, 141, 145, 160, 187, 188, 190, 191, 192, 385n108
Schmid, Samuel, 134, 136, 137, 197
Schmidberger, Franz, 245, 246
Schmied, Walter, 197
Schmitt, Carl, 36, 258
Scholl, Heinz, 295
Schrenck-Notzing, Caspar von, 179
Schreyger, Emil, 195
Schriftenreihe Pro Libertate, 196, 197, 198
Schwab, Günter, 207, 209
Schwarzenbach, James, 58–59, 60, 61, 62, 63, 65, 67, 69, 70, 71, 72, 82, 93, 101, 131–32, 172, 175, 183, 187, 188, 191–92, 209, 227, 326, 327, 329, 360n95
Schweizerische Akademiker- und Studenten-Zeitung, 180
Schweizerische Arbeitsgemeinschaft für Bevölkerungsfragen (SAfB – Swiss Working Group for Population Questions), 211–12
Schweizerische Hammerskin-Aufbauorganisation (SHS-AO – Swiss Organisation for the Development of Hammerskins), 317, 319
Schweizerische Hammerskins (SHS – Swiss Hammerskins), 317–19
Schweizerische Katholische Wochenzeitung, 179
Schweizerische Konservative Volkspartei (SKVP – Swiss Conservative People's Party), 127
Schweizerische Liga für Biologische Landesverteidigung (SLfbL – Swiss

League for Biological National Defence), 126, 209, 218
Schweizerischer Bund für Naturschutz (SBN – Swiss Federation for Nature Conservation), 208
Schweizer Demokrat, 82, 83, 87, 90
Schweizer Demokraten (SD – Swiss Democrats), 77, 78–92, 93, 102, 103, 104, 108, 112, 116, 119, 121, 136, 146, 147, 150, 153, 180, 202, 211, 218, 321, 324, 326, 380n223
Schweizerische Republikanische Bewegung (SRB – Swiss Republican Movement), 57, 59–61, 67, 69, 71, 72, 75, 93, 131–32, 141, 179, 181, 183, 187–88, 194, 209, 281, 323, 324, 326, 328, 357n7, 357n11, 364n87
Schweizerischer Gewerkschaftsbund (SGB – Swiss Trade Union Federation), 66
Schweizerisches Aktionskomitee gegen den UNO-Beitritt (SAKU – Swiss Campaign Committee Against UN Membership), 216
Schweizerische Vereinigung für Freiheit, Demokratie und Menschenwürde (Swiss Association for Freedom, Democracy and Human Dignity), 196
Schweizerische Volkspartei (SVP – Swiss People's Party)
 campaigning, 142–44, 147, 149–51, 160, 171–72
 cantonal and local parties 65, 129, 133, 136, 147–50, 151–52, 164–66, 190, 342
 cantonal party of Zurich, 46, 108, 129–36, 139, 141, 143, 147, 149–50, 151, 161, 169, 189, 222, 324
 comparison with European counterparts, 3, 51–52, 123–24, 139, 152, 156, 334
 constituency, 44, 50, 86, 104, 128, 135, 136–37, 152–59, 202, 341, 380n223
 debate on Second World War, 137–38, 162–63, 169
 elections, 42, 101, 102, 103, 127, 128, 131, 145–52, 340
 extreme right and, 294, 322, 323, 324, 325, 326–27, 328
 Federal Council and, 46–47, 134–35, 160–61, 172, 333, 342
 migration agenda and policy, 128, 131, 135–37, 149, 151, 163–67, 171
 New Right and, 86, 88, 141, 144, 172, 178, 180–81, 183, 187–89, 192–94, 197, 201–3, 217, 219, 222, 228, 242, 249, 255, 273, 335
 neoliberalism, 156, 159, 169–70, 172
 old SVP, 52, 124–128, 129, 342
 opposition role, 47, 134, 160, 172
 opposition to European integration, 88, 99, 107, 135, 149–51, 161–62, 164, 168, 171
 other radical right-wing populist parties and, 61, 82, 83, 96, 99, 104, 107, 108, 114, 116, 121, 122, 131–32, 147, 150, 180, 335
 party organisation, 122, 127, 130–31, 132–34, 139, 141–42, 171–72
 party system and, 46, 130, 141–42, 160, 171, 333, 340, 342
 transformation, 3, 9, 46, 52, 123–24, 129–30, 159, 171–72
 See also Bauern-, Gewerbe- und Bürgerpartei; Blocher, Christoph
Schweizerzeit, 132, 141, 143, 181, 187–94, 201, 221, 222, 225
Schweizerzeit Verlag, 188, 189, 227
Swiss exceptionalism, 2, 4, 7, 45, 48–49, 53, 75–76, 78, 83, 99, 168–69, 192, 214–16, 219, 331–32, 337
Scorpion, The, 260
Scruton, Roger, 204
Second World War, 8, 40, 48, 126, 184, 197, 278, 350n37

debate on Switzerland's role during, 2, 49, 50, 91, 112–13, 137–38, 162–63, 169, 171, 183, 192, 216, 223–27, 241, 337–38
Segert, Alexander, 201
Seiler, Hanspeter, 197
Shermer, Michael, 284
Sicherheit für alle (Sifa – Security for All), 145
Skinheads Against Racial Prejudices (SHARP), 314, 315
Skrewdriver, 314
Skuld, 255
Small Springtime of Fronts (1980s–1990s), 281, 303, 305, 308, 311, 312, 316, 324, 326, 408n30
Social Darwinism, 19, 24, 207, 340
Sol Invictus, 258, 265
Soldini, Mario, 61, 217
Sorel, Georges, 258
Sozialdemokratische Partei der Schweiz (SPS – Social-Democratic Party of Switzerland), 46, 136, 142, 146, 149, 150, 151, 153, 156, 157, 202, 293, 323, 376n126
Spain, 58, 195, 246, 268, 302
Spectrum, 194, 195, 224
Spengler, Oswald, 36, 221–22, 258
Spiritual Defence of the Nation, 125, 174, 175, 196
Spörri, Kurt, 98
Springtime of Fronts (1930s), 40, 408n30
STAB-Schriftenreihe, 185
Stadler, Peter, 196, 219, 220–23
Stamm, Luzi, 181, 197, 227
Stäuble, Eduard, 184, 185, 186, 193, 198–99, 225
Steinberg, Jonathan, 1
Steinemann, Walter, 111, 112
Steuckers, Robert, 255, 260, 261
Stiftung für Abendländische Besinnung (STAB – Foundation for Occidental Consciousness), 181, 184–87, 195
Strasser, Otto, 95, 286
Strauss, Botho, 204

Strebel, Marcel, 312, 326
Stuart, Ian, 314, 318
Studentenring (Students' Ring), 139
Studer, Andres J.W., 288, 290, 292, 410n92
Studienzentrum Weikersheim (Weikersheim Study Centre), 178, 190, 202, 204, 205
Sturmtruppen (Storm Troopers), 318
SVPJa (SVP Yes), 142–43
Sweden, 104, 275
Synergies Européennes (European Synergies), 260–61

Tacho, 107–8, 110, 111
Taggart, Paul, 114
Taguieff, Pierre-André, 20, 34, 236, 264, 285
Tarchi, Marco, 260
Tell, William, 48, 168
Th. Gut Verlag, 227
Thibon, Gustave, 241, 264
third way, concept of, 95–96, 299, 313
Thiriart, Jean, 301
Thomas-Verlag, 58
Thule Gesellschaft (Thule Society), 256
Thule Seminar, 256, 257
Tierschutz-Nachrichten, 298
Timor Domini, 179
Tišma, Aleksandar, 263
Tixier-Vignancour, Jean-Louis, 59, 271
Todorov, Tzvetan, 26
Totalité, 258, 265, 271
Totenkopf, 317, 325
Tradiffusion, 249
Troisième voie, 258
Troisième voie (TV – Third Way), 300, 302–3, 316, 421n336
Tschumi, Pierre-André, 209, 211–12
Trois Nornes, Les (publisher), 257
Tuena, Mauro, 190
Turmwart, 285–86

Uhlmann, Hans, 134, 376n120
Union pour la défense des libertés (UDL – Union for the Defence of Liberties), 64

United Nations (UN), 69, 201
  campaign against Swiss
    forces for peacekeeping
    operations, 86, 112, 160,
    168–69, 380n223
  opposition against UN
    membership, 80, 99, 131–32,
    168, 192, 203, 216, 219, 234,
    242, 250, 325, 383n50
  vote on UN membership, 216
United Nations Educational,
  Scientific and Cultural
  Organisation (UNESCO), 237
United States, 14, 28, 34, 91, 92, 113,
  124, 177, 197, 201, 205, 214, 226,
  230, 254, 256, 284, 286, 288, 291,
  296, 297, 299, 302, 317, 389n201,
  414n160
Universale Kirche (UK – Universal
  Church), 296–97
universalism, 24, 176, 177, 236, 338
Universitas Verlag, 190

Valeurs actuelles, 266, 271
Valla, Jean-Claude, 236
Valois, Georges, 259
van Helsing, Jan (alias Jan Udo
  Holey), 293
Varenne, Jean, 260
Venner, Dominique, 237, 271
Verbe, 243
Verein gegen Tierfabriken (VgT –
  Society Against Animal Factories),
  298
Vereinigung Pro Libertate
  (Association Pro Libertate) 196–99,
  225
Vereinigung Umwelt und
  Bevölkerung/Association Ecologie
  et Population (ECOPOP – Ecology
  and Population Association),
  211–14
*Verein zur Förderung der
  psychologischen Menschenkenntnis*
  (VPM – Society for Advancing
  the Psychological Knowledge of
  Human Nature), 87, 199–205

Vérité et Justice – Wahrheit und
  Recht (Truth and Justice), 289,
  292
VgT-Nachrichten, 298
Vial, Pierre, 260, 262, 271
Vigilance, 62
Vigilance, 57, 60, 61–62, 64–65, 69, 71,
  152, 217, 249, 266, 273, 325, 335
Vigilant, Le, 62, 266
Villiger, Kaspar, 225, 310, 320
Vinvenza, Jean-Marc, 258
Visier, 282, 286, 326
Vlaams Blok (VB – Flemish Block), 3,
  78, 270
Vogt, Arthur, 289, 292, 313, 323,
  410–11n92
Volk + Heimat, 58, 63, 64, 70, 74, 197,
  210, 211–12, 295, 323, 328
Volksaktion gegen zu viele
  Ausländer und Asylanten (People's
  Campaign against too Many
  Foreigners and Asylum Seekers),
  417–18n237
Volkssozialistische Partei der
  Schweiz (VSP – People's Socialist
  Party of Switzerland), 282
Volkspartei der Schweiz (VPS –
  People's Party of Switzerland), 279,
  280
Vollenweider, Erwin, 279
Volonté futuriste, 258
von Blomberg, Werner, 329
von Steiger, Eduard, 126
von Wartburg, Wolfgang, 203, 294
von Weizsäcker, Ernst 126
Vouloir, 258, 260
Vrij Historisch Onderzoek (VHO –
  Free Historical Research), 292

Waber, Christian, 94, 97, 99, 197
Waffen SS, 318, 321, 328
Wahl, Max, 93, 286–87, 323, 328,
  410n86
Walker, Michael, 260
Weber, Eric, 311
Wehrwolf, Der, 311
Weinberg, Leonard, 14–15

Weltbund zum Schutze des Lebens (WSL – World Federation for the Protection of Life), 207, 209
Werner, Eric, 237, 239, 250, 251, 262, 266, 272, 397n54
Widmer, Sigmund, 185, 226
Widmer-Schlumpf, Eveline, 129–30, 342
Wiking-Jugend Schweiz (WJS – Viking Youth Switzerland), 320
Wilhelm-Röpke-Gesellschaft (Wilhelm Röpke Society), 179
Wiligut, Karl Maria, 318
Wimmer, Andreas, 72–73
Windisch, Uli, 237
World Anti-Communist League (WACL), 230
World Trade Organisation (WTO), 203
Wüthrich, Roger, 320–21, 323

xenophobia, 2, 3, 15, 18, 24, 31, 35, 72–73, 76, 124, 163, 175, 227, 275, 277, 311, 338
  attitudes, 43, 50, 71, 85
  concept of, 22–23
  statements, 98, 110–11, 121, 166–67, 186–87, 192–93, 195, 197, 208–9, 237, 240–41, 246, 293–94, 308, 312, 404n247

ZeitenSchrift, 297
Zeit-Fragen, 202–4
Zeitgeist, 321
Ziegler, Jean, 260
Zikeli, Gerd, 282
Zitelmann, Rainer, 204
Zofingue (student fraternity), 238
Zolberg, Aristide, 6
Zürcher Bauer, Der, 127, 143, 222
Zürcher Bote, Der, 143, 201